"Jeff McSwain does systematic theology in the cadence of the practice of ministry. Few to no one else can do this like he does. He continually lands doctrine nicely in the reader's life. McSwain's rich grasp of Scripture is complemented with stories and analogies unpacking his central idea of a Christological anthropology. Pastors and others seeking a robust theological grounding for gospel embodiment will find this work engaging, challenging, and refreshing."

—**Andrew Root,** author of *Churches and the Crisis of Decline*

"In a society plagued by pervasive and persistent divisions, Jeff McSwain provides a much-needed perspective. His Christ-centered theology explains how holding anthropological opposites together is not only possible but necessary to better understand ourselves, human behavior, and the miracle of Jesus' redemptive work. I was impressed by the love, vulnerability, and courage that jumps off every page."

—**Dishon Mills,** pastor, Grace Communion International

"This project is a brilliant and humble proclamation of God's goodness that confronts our dichotomies, cheap grace, and false narratives. Jeff McSwain's placemat paradigm beautifully holds together our dualities and offers us space to sit in the tension so that we might see God, ourselves, and our world rightly."

—**Charlene Brown**, former national director, InterVarsity's Black Campus Ministries

"In this world where beauty and goodness are often overwhelmed by evil and human failure, Jeff McSwain has articulated well what it means to be truly human, included in God's life and love. His eschatologically charged account takes seriously who Jesus is, re-envisioning the way we look at God, ourselves, sin, evil, and judgment."

—**Linda Rex**, pastor and blogger at *Our Life in the Trinity*

"Jeff McSwain is one of the key contemporary thinkers providing the theological heft the church needs for renewal in the years ahead. Where ideas of judgment have often been characterized by terror and separation, McSwain's biblical exegesis shows us that God is much better than that. His unusual internal linkage between creation, atonement, and the eschaton refuses to give excuse to the divisive 'us vs. them' rhetoric so prevalent inside and outside of the church."

—**Todd Wiebe**, host of Rector's Cupboard

BOOK TWO

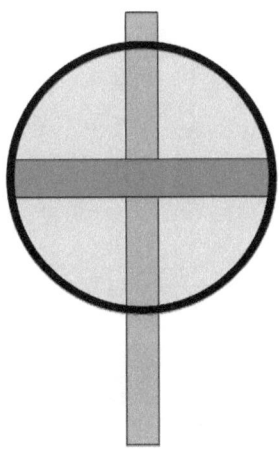

The Goodness of Judgment

The Goodness of Judgment

The Ministry of Christ's Cross for a Hurting World

by
JEFF MCSWAIN

CASCADE *Books* • Eugene, Oregon

THE GOODNESS OF JUDGMENT
The Ministry of Christ's Cross for a Hurting World

Copyright © 2024 Jeff McSwain. All rights reserved. Except for brief quotations in critical publications or reviews, no part of this book may be reproduced in any manner without prior written permission from the publisher. Write: Permissions, Wipf and Stock Publishers, 199 W. 8th Ave., Suite 3, Eugene, OR 97401.

Cascade Books
An Imprint of Wipf and Stock Publishers
199 W. 8th Ave., Suite 3
Eugene, OR 97401

www.wipfandstock.com

PAPERBACK ISBN: 978-1-6667-3922-0
HARDCOVER ISBN: 978-1-6667-3923-7
EBOOK ISBN: 978-1-6667-3924-4

Cataloguing-in-Publication data:

Names: McSwain, Jeff, author.

Title: The goodness of judgment : the ministry of Christ's cross for a hurting world / Jeff McSwain.

Volume 1: Hidden in contradiction : humanity in Christ before, during, and after the fall (Cascade Books, 2023)

Volume 2: The goodness of judgment : the ministry of Christ's cross for a hurting world (Cascade Books, 2024)

Description: Eugene, OR : Cascade Books, 2024 | Includes bibliographical references and index(es).

Identifiers: ISBN 978-1-6667-3922-0 (paperback) | ISBN 978-1-6667-3923-7 (hardcover) | ISBN 978-1-6667-3924-4 (ebook)

Subjects: LCSH: Theodicy. | Judgment—Religious aspects—Christianity.

Classification: BT160 .M37 2024 (paperback) | BT160 .M37 (ebook)

VERSION NUMBER 111124

Unless otherwise noted, all Bible quotations are taken from the Holy Bible, New International Version®, NIV®. Copyright © 1973, 1978, 1984, 2011 by Biblica, Inc.™ Used by permission of Zondervan. All rights reserved worldwide. www.zondervan.com The "NIV" and "New International Version" are trademarks registered in the United States Patent and Trademark Office by Biblica, Inc.™

David, I treasure our life together and the chance we had to reflect on this manuscript. However good it may be, it is all the better due to you.

—Your *systratioten*

All have sinned and fall short of the glory of God, and all are justified freely by his grace through the redemption that came by Christ Jesus

The last leaf left leaves bough bare
Three spare buds
Bleed their pointed waxen witness
While all else round is falling

Contents

Volume Two Preface | ix
Introduction: A Liberating Separation | 1

Introducing Theodicy | 39
The Prevalence of Evil and the Presence of God: Keeping Depravity in Its Proper Place | 41

PART FIVE: **Jesus Is My Heaven**
56 First-Heaven Problems | 55
57 "They Will All Know Me" (Because They Do) | 66
58 The Rest of Our Life | 77
59 Gathered and Scattered | 85
60 The Grace of Wrath | 94
61 Children of Wrath? | 101
62 Vanier Exposed | 110
63 The Second-Heaven Intervention | 116
64 The Goodness of Judgment | 124
65 The Big Picture | 132
66 Deliverance Time! | 138
67 The Highest View of Scripture | 146
68 Parting from the Old Red Sea Narrative | 152
69 Merry Christmas, Malachi! | 160
70 Repent and Believe! | 166
71 Standing Pat at the Gate | 173
72 Damned and Delivered | 184
73 Saved by the Blood? | 192

PART SIX: **Living Life from the Third Heaven**

74 Holiness or Wholeness? | 203
75 Seeing and Believing with Thomas | 213
76 Retributive vs. Restorative Justice | 220
77 Gender Bending? | 228
78 Coming Home | 235
79 Reconciliation as Remembering Friends | 244
80 Nothing but Green | 252
81 The Sword and the Spirit | 263
82 The Ship-Shape of the Atonement | 269
83 Life in Spite of Death | 278
84 Salvation by Subtraction | 286

PART SEVEN: **Immortals Fall**

85 Bringing Immortality to Light | 297
86 The Power of Contrast (But Not the Need) | 305
87 Species of Origen? | 311
88 Playing by the Book: *Give Me Revelation!* | 320
89 Test or War? | 326
90 The Liar's Religion | 334
91 One Tree in the Garden | 340
92 The Why Question | 345
93 Theodicy Revisited | 353
94 The Human Mission? | 362
95 Double Agents and Situational Ethics | 372

Conclusion: Between Two Swords | 380
Epilogue: Dew Song | 391
Epigraph Sources | 393

Bibliography | 399

Names Index | 409

Scripture Index | 415

Volume Two Preface

For now we are seeing through a mirror, in an enigma—but then face to face. Now I know in part—but then I will know-fully, just as also I was fully-known.

—1 Cor 13:12, DLNT

THE MOST NOTICEABLE THING about 1 Cor 13:12 is that it describes seeing *through* a mirror—not an experience to which many of us can relate. The question of "seeing through" introduces a challenge we face regularly in our daily lives. All too often our definition of ourselves is based on the reflection that we see of ourselves, or the image of us that others see. Ignoring the distortion at play in fallen human perceptions, we default to our own and others' opinions about who we are. This includes being defined by our achievements, or perhaps more often by our mistakes.

By the suggestion of looking *through* a mirror, Paul seeks to push us beyond our self-understanding. Though some translations read as though he refers to a literal mirror, others state that we look "through a glass, dimly." Both "mirror" and "glass" are relevant here, even if a pane of glass can sometimes act like a mirror better than a mirror can act like a pane of glass. If we look dimly through the glass, then, what do we see? We cannot see clearly to the other side, but by the light of Christ's revelation we can at least see (and know) in part. Compared to life in this dimension, our lives "on the other side" of the mirror will be similar in some ways and different in others. We will "all be changed," as Paul later says. Flesh and blood will not cross over, but that does not mean we will not have material bodies. Then, on the other side of the mirror, *we* will still be, but without any of the problems that we have now and with nothing to grieve. We will be our truest selves, the way God has known us all along (1 Cor 15:50–54).

VOLUME TWO PREFACE

Now we see through a mirror . . . then we shall see face to face. There will be a time when we all meet God face to face, but between the Now and Then is what Barth calls the "border" between the two dimensions.[1] We are looking *through* the mirror, but the glass itself could represent its own dimension. This is true only because we look through it. If we simply looked *at* the mirror (i.e., at the reflection) it would be an impermeable wall rather than a dimensional border. Such a framework functions as a prism in which there remains a continuity and consistency between who we are Now and who we will be Then. Critical for this study will be the fact that this consistency in our identity goes both ways (i.e., from the Now to the Then and from the Then to the Now). Since the two dimensions are not identical, however, it is better to say that all of the Then is in the Now, even if not all of the Now is in the Then (thankfully!).

Not always behind the scenes in our study is the human guide Karl Barth, a scriptural interpreter who demonstrates an acute ability to interpret our tangled lives by the Word, which will not return void. Unlike the Word, of course, Barth was not perfect.[2] Nevertheless, his teaching continues to transform many, from his contemporary Thomas Merton (Barth and Merton died on the same day) to the recently departed Eugene Peterson.[3] I am thankful to have been among those, Catholic and Protestant, who have been formed by the Word through Barth. Our placemat metaphor (reviewed in the upcoming Introduction) largely derives from his approach—Barth is comfortable thinking in dimensional ways. Far from being esoteric, this approach drives us to practical engagement.

Pastoring in Switzerland during the First World War and then teaching in Germany until the early Nazi years, Barth was deeply involved in the struggle for sanity, humanity, and justice in the face of the First World War and throughout the even greater barbarities of the Second. The great violence, injustice, and tragedy of this period had a profound impact on his thinking and writing. Despite bearing through these times with great courage, nothing could prepare Barth for the tragedy of losing a child. In 1941,

---

1. I am using upper case for Now and Then consistent with Barth's usage below in his eulogy for Matthias.

2. Barth's over forty-year relationship with scholar and coworker Charlotte von Kirschbaum will always be controversial. For the best treatment of the complex web of relationships that included von Kirschbaum and Barth's wife and children in one household, see *Karl Barth: A Life in Conflict*, by Christiane Tietz. Close analysis of Tietz's research has become prerequisite to anyone speaking coherently about the matter.

3. Merton spoke of his "fondness for Barth"; see Carr, "Merton and Barth," 193. See also Peterson, *Long Obedience*, 196: "Karl Barth is one of my favorites . . . one of the great theologians of all time."

Barth's son Matthias (age 20) fell to his death while mountain climbing in Switzerland.

In the eulogy, Barth spoke of Matthias's attachment to the Pauline verse above. The mirror gives us "an enigmatic word" (the exact Greek wording, as in enigma, or puzzle), he claimed. The content of the Then is in the Now, but it is as if the image in the mirror is upside down, forming a warped riddle. Full clarity is forever elusive from this side of eternity. He continued:

> This is the grace of our Lord Jesus Christ, that we follow him and may stand with him at the border where the Now and the Then touch each other, that we at this border may believe, love, and hope. It is at this border where light falls into darkness, where life always rejoices in the face of death, where we are great sinners yet righteous, where we are taken captive yet free, where we see no way out yet we have hope, where we have doubts yet we are certain, where we weep yet we are glad.
>
> In our thoughts about our Matthias we do not want to put ourselves in any other place than precisely at this border. He has now crossed over it, and we are still here. But we are not far from each other if we put ourselves at this border. In Jesus Christ there is no distance between Now and Then, between here and there, however profoundly they are separated. Our Matthias—just as he really was—is in Jesus Christ, yet very differently than the way he used to live with us and we with him. He is the same, yet he has become completely different. Because Jesus Christ has taught us about both, about life and death, death and life, we may now therefore remember our Matthias and thus speak about him.[4]

Four years after Matthias's tragic death, Barth returned to the theme of the eulogy in *Church Dogmatics* III/1. Only by the death and resurrection of Christ, insists Barth, can we interpret the two-fold determination of our existence—the tangle of our true and false selves—hearing God's Yes to the former and No to the latter. In the "Now," the realm of what we have called placemat anthropology, the contradictory green and red aspects of our lives produce the grey haze that refracts our view. However, by revelation light we can at least know in part with the anticipation of knowing in full. The person with confidence in Christ's overcoming, Barth said, "sees through the imperfections of being to its perfection. That this is not a direct vision, but a seeing through, makes it a struggle—the struggle in which the

---

4. Karl Barth in Bush, *This Incomplete One*, 13–14.

decision fulfilled by God may be continually recognised as fulfilled by us. Yet the fact that on this basis it can be and may be a true seeing, makes it a free and lighthearted struggle untainted by any toil or self-will."[5]

Looking through the mirror Barth was convinced that, to the extent that we catch a glimpse of who Christ is and who we are in him, we will discover our true freedom and genuine personhood—a life where hearing and doing, belief and embodiment, faith and works, are one. In Christ, it is as if the revelation of the Then pulls us forward by the Spirit amid the Now, quickening us in transformational and life-giving ways.

Grieving Matthias's death compounded the complexity of Karl Barth's tangled life. His writing seems to yearn for the lucidity his son had attained through death. Even in the eulogy, he stated of Jesus Christ: "he alone in his bitter death on the cross and in his glorious resurrection has bound the Now and Then together so that even now there is no mirror or enigmatic word that does not have standing behind it the clarity of that seeing face to face."[6] Barth penned the following shortly before his own death. His words carry much the same character as those he expressed standing before Matthias's coffin twenty-seven years before:

> How do I know whether I shall die easily or with difficulty? I only know that my dying, too is part of my life.... And then—this is the destination, the limit and the goal for all of us—I shall no longer "be," but I shall be made manifest before the judgment seat of Christ, in and with my whole "being," with all the real good and the real evil that I have thought, said and done, with all the bitterness that I have suffered and all the beauty that I have enjoyed. There I shall only be able to stand as the failure that I doubtless was in all things, but ... by virtue of his promise, as a *peccator justus* [a righteous sinner]. And as that I shall be able to stand. Then ... in the light of grace, all that is now dark will become very clear.[7]

Then, all will be clear. And the fullness of the Then is already in the Now. It follows that the more clarity that emerges from the Then in midst of the Now, the better. Hoping in Christ, we have the freedom to live as though we have already died, and die as though we are already alive. May the God of clarity visit us all in these confusing times.

---

5. Barth, *Church Dogmatics*, III/1, 380 (hereafter *CD*). As will be true throughout, I have maintained the British spelling from the T&T Clark translation.

6. Karl Barth in Busch, *Great Passion*, 13.

7. Barth in Busch, *Great Passion*, 488.

VOLUME TWO PREFACE

Long lay the world, in sin and error pining,
Till He appeared, and the soul felt its worth.
A thrill of hope, the weary world rejoices,
For yonder breaks a new and glorious morn!

Christmas 2023

Introduction
A Liberating Separation

WE BEGAN BOOK ONE with the line from William Blake's poem, "joy and woe, they are woven fine."[1] The overarching metaphor of the two volumes is a woven placemat (think: elementary school craft) of green and red strips of construction paper. Together the strips represent two *complete* pieces of green and red construction paper finely interlaced in one space, an imperfect visual for our "placemat anthropology" deriving from a Chalcedonian pattern (i.e., the duality of two complete things existing in one space). The Chalcedonian Creed, adopted by the church in 451 CE, affirmed that the one historical person Jesus Christ had two natures, one fully divine and one fully human. In this *initial duality* called the "hypostatic union," the simultaneity is critical: Jesus Christ remained fully God even as he became fully human. Scripture also supports another simultaneous duality stemming from the human "side" of this christological construct. In the *derivative duality*, the Savior represented original and obedient humanity even as he assumed the flesh of lost and rebellious humanity (i.e., "the flesh" in the pejorative sense). From the incarnate Lord who universally represents and defines both true and false humanity, we can reference our own totally good humanity created by Christ (green) and our totally wicked humanity crucified in Christ (red). By the Spirit we are given to see the green of who Christ is and who we are in him, and the opportunity in our true identity to participate in what we have called the in-Christ dimension of our humanity. To the degree that we also participate in the red, anti-Christ dimension of our humanity, we are our own worst enemies—"enemies of the cross" that frees us (Phil 3:18).

Admittedly, thinking of each singular human being as "two totals" of righteousness and wickedness is very difficult. This is because existentially

---

1. Blake, "Auguries of Innocence," line 58. See McSwain, *Hidden in Contradiction*, xxiv.

(i.e., in our current existence, or experientially) we never see human beings completely in their true or false selves, but always as one compounded with the other. What we observe in ourselves and others is not either total green or total red, but the finely woven composite of the two totals, a "placemat grey." For ease of use, we have personified this composite with "Placemat Pat," a shorthand way of referencing the "grey" existence that each of us lives and experiences in this present existence. Grey represents the anthropological tangle of our worldly estate, where the in-Christ and anti-Christ dimensions of our humanity clash. Because of the insurmountable challenge of looking through "grey" eyes to interpret this grey world, God's revelation of himself in Jesus Christ provides the illuminating hope of interpreting our tangled lives in light of the gospel of green. The metaphor of the mirror, and the difficulty in seeing through it, matches with our central metaphor of the placemat. By grace we see through the "grey" mirror and past the red refraction to the green of who Christ is for us. We discover it is the judgment of Jesus Christ crucified that finally extricates us from the "sin that so easily entangles" (Heb 12:1) and provides us with the clarity for living we so desperately need.

In the first section of the Introduction I will briefly enumerate some of the main themes from the previous volume (sans biblical references). The next section includes summary themes that have their own sub-heading for fuller treatment, and which have particular import for defining the terms for our journey in *The Goodness of Judgment*.

1. Book One established the christological basis for what we call "placemat anthropology." God the Son is Jesus Christ, who is also Jesus of Nazareth, a Palestinian Jew in the first century. He was born of the Virgin Mary and crucified under Pontius Pilate. According to Scripture he is the image of God, the true Adam (humanity) in whom every human is created and redeemed. As true God and true human, Jesus Christ can be everything that we are, even in our sinfulness, and still remain God. In his redemptive history, beginning in the Virgin's womb, Jesus Christ comprehended the false Adam in himself, ultimately killing it off in his own death. Throughout his incarnate life, incessantly warring against the temptations of the flesh, the one Lord Jesus Christ revealed himself as the primary battleground for the true and false Adams. Jesus Christ is therefore the point of reference for understanding the tangle of our own true and false humanity, the interwoven green and red of placemat anthropology.

2. In his iconic treatment of Romans 5, *Christ and Adam*, Barth's message is in the title itself. If we were to think of Adam and Eve as singular

INTRODUCTION

humans only, then we would read Genesis as the beginning of a human chronological and biological chain, a family tree that begins there and continues until the birth of the Christ child and on to this day, eventually including us. However, because in the Bible Adam signifies "humanity," Adam is never simply a singular human being. It is in this sense that Jesus Christ, the humanity of God, *is* humanity, even in Genesis 1. As the Creator who became a creature, Jesus Christ is the unique human being who includes all human beings in himself. We are not only historically associated, but internally (ontologically) implicated in the narrative of the singular human journey of Jesus Christ of Nazareth. This means that for the duration of Christ's humanity, wherever Christ is, true Adam is, and wherever true Adam is, we are. *Because we are created in Christ, there has never been a time when a human being has not been in and with Christ.*[2]

3. Caught in the torque of "two totals," an existence in which each person is totally good and totally evil, we look for the definitive sequence of Christ's death and resurrection to come to bear to interpret all manner of human situations. We seek the same Spirit who raised Christ from the dead to empower us with newness of life, quickening us to gospel embodiment in day-to-day living. In the Spirit we are so united with Christ, the firstborn of many brothers and sisters, that whatever Christ our brother does in relation to the Father, we, as persons in Christ, also do. In his incarnate solidarity he is the *way* of every human being, the *truth* of every human being, and the *life* of every human being. Any and all good (green) manifest in human beings is generated in and through the perfect, true humanity of the person Jesus Christ by the power of God the Spirit. Conversely, any and all human evil (red) is generated by the spirit of the anti-Christ as expressed through the "the flesh" of fallen Adam, false humanity.

4. We are loved by God in our original state (green), in our conflicted state (grey—the interlaced composite of green and red), and all the way through. Even when we seek to establish ourselves independently from our Creator and Redeemer, the Spirit seeks to remind us that we are not *individuals* so much as *persons*. We are all persons in the person of Christ, sharing life and love with the Trinitarian persons who

---

2. God becoming human does not make humanity God. The relational hierarchy from God to humanity cannot be reversed. Thus, Christ both precedes created Adam and is always Adam, even if Adam is not always Christ (Adam is never the second person of the Trinity). By "ontological" I mean our spiritual material bodies that are always dimensionally present.

have included us by grace (not by right) in the Trinitarian community. Because of our creation in Christ and our existence in him, and because Jesus Christ is the elected one, every human being is elected and chosen by God. Adopted in the eternal Son, the Father has loved each of us as his own from all eternity. In turn, we have our existence in the Son's love for the Father. The truth of our human location is thus established by grace alone, living *in Christ* and *from Christ* to God the Father by the power of the Spirit. Grace is not in tension with truth. Grace is God's truth for humanity in Jesus Christ.

5. As the Son to the Father in the fullness of the Spirit, Jesus Christ is living to God. Because of Christ, "who is our life," it follows that every person is "living to God" in him. Every person is, subconsciously before consciously, loving the LORD with all their "heart, soul, mind, and strength." We are not simply human beings in Christ, we are beings-in-act. The fact that every person is full of the Spirit, already and *actually* participating in Christ, gives the green dimension an intrinsically dynamic direction. This liberating "life-movement," notes Barth, originating in the Son of God Jesus Christ, is where the perfect (not potential) response of all humanity *to God* resides. Barth resonates here with Julian of Norwich: first, God in Christ loves every human; second, every human in Christ loves God.

6. We are created purely "green" in Jesus Christ. In the unadulterated dimensional realms of creation and redemption there is no red self. While our lives in these dimensions are always extant, we also live in this fallen placemat dimension where the red wars against the green. Our experience reflects an unremitting conflict between these oppositional, and simultaneous "determinations" (Barth). The fact that the good (green) determination is so good allows us to consider just how bad the bad determination (red) is. Barth reminds us that we are measured by what God did for us on the cross. In the mystery of Calvary, Jesus Christ reveals both the unfathomable extent of God's love for us and the unfathomable extent of our fallenness. As wicked as humanity can be and is (total red), we can be assured by faith that the created goodness of humanity (total green) is neither displaced nor diminished by its opposite and contradictory determination.

7. "Original sin" and even human depravity never fundamentally define us. "Original sin" is not as deep or as wide as original belonging. Not only that, our *belonging* is not static. Because we are created as human beings-in-act in Christ, to belong *is* to believe (because what the High Priest of our humanity does for us, we do with and in him). God has

INTRODUCTION

the prerogative to define human freedom, and he has located our free agency in the being-in-act of the Son, in whom we are "free indeed." All human beings are thus participating in Christ, freely believing in God as Christ himself does in his vicarious humanity. This means that any theological gap between belonging and believing can only reduce the God-given integrity of free human believing. Into this belonging-believing gap is introduced the lethal element of human agential control, an ableist economy that is contrary to grace.

8. Born with our grey lenses, our Enemy wants to blind us from the perspective revealed in Christ. He does not want us to walk by faith where, by the revelation of Jesus Christ, we ascertain our lives to be a tangle of "two totals"—righteousness (green) and wickedness (red). Our Enemy wants us to walk by sight and to define our lives and others' as *either* green or red, or by some kind of zero-sum calculation (a combination of two percentages equaling one hundred percent). His ploy is to keep us in a double bind, for he knows that without the "two totals" *grace is not as good* and *sin is not as bad* (because neither is 100 percent). In this bind we settle for the shaky theological ground of too little grace and too little judgment. By theologically exploding this bind with our placemat anthropology, we live into the priority, strength, and longevity of the total green over the total red by the power of the Holy Spirit.

9. There is never a direct witness of someone being either totally green or totally red in this world, only an imperfect or "relative" witness. But this protects us from having to quantify progress through maddening and arbitrary attempts at self-assessment. Instead, we can know by faith that the existential ebb and flow of good and bad action bears relative witness to the two dynamic totals that do not ebb and flow. In other words, all human evils bear relative witness to the total red determination of every person and all righteous human acts bear relative witness to the total green determination of every person. Placemat theology therefore helps us to be less confounded when evils arise in "believers," or when godly acts manifest in "unbelievers."

10. The before and after sequence of Christ's death and resurrection is critical to interpreting our lives, but if we start with a sequence-focus, it is very difficult to get back to simultaneity. Conversely, if we start with the simultaneity of our experience, sequence helps to interpret it. The sequence of Christ's redeeming work (established from all eternity) provides a way to understand *old as false* (red), and *new as true* (green). With these helpful pairings, we can keep sequence and

simultaneity together—the key is the asymmetry. We will hold to this key as we consider what a sequential term like "new" means in a simultaneous situation, and how such "newness of life" is inherently transformative. The asymmetry between two "totals" protects us from falling back into Manichaeism (promoting a straight dualism between good and evil). Manichaeism features the endless tug of war between two opposite forces, evincing simultaneity without sequence. In other words, there is no incarnational resurrection that demonstrates that the good (green) is stronger than evil (red), or that life triumphs over death.

11. A christological *resurrection* motif, then, provides a continuous, christological *creation* motif. The resurrection of Christ points to the fact that the Easter re-creation of humanity is exactly that, a re-creation; it is not a wholly different act, or a second creation. By witness of the resurrection and ascension—the revelation of the inner connection between re-creation and creation—we recognize that good not only triumphs over evil, but it also *precedes* evil. Evil has always been parasitic to the good, never having an independent root in the reality of creation. It is not evil that Christ redeems but creation.

12. When Paul asks us to fix our eyes on the unseen, he encourages a christological anthropology based on faith. His admonitions implore us not to judge ourselves or others by what is seen, to no longer perceive others by fleshly appearance. Flesh and blood will not enter the kingdom of heaven. These teachings and others point to the transcendent fact of our true humanity, which is always present even if dimensionally hidden; that who we are in our green humanity is *who we really are*, not as ephemeral souls but as spiritual material beings; that we have spiritual bodies even now, not only in the future. This is a theme that we are only beginning to unfold.

Checkered Before "the Fall"

Much of what follows in this volume depends on Barth's interpretation of Genesis 1:1—2:4a and Genesis 2:4b—3:24, the two distinct but inseparable sagas of the creation narrative, hereafter designated as simply Genesis 1 and Genesis 2. This is a theme that was introduced in Book One (see the reading, "Creation and Conception") and will continue to unfold here. Since Adam's creation in Genesis 1 is the creation of every human being and not just the first singular human being, then his transition into the garden of

INTRODUCTION

Genesis 2:8 is not just his alone but is synonymous with every human being's transition into the garden of this world.

Not lost on the exegete is that the second creation saga describes God placing humanity into the garden (Gen 2:8 is the first time the garden is mentioned). Far from pristine, Genesis 2 is a checkered environment already marked by evil (the serpent, the tree of the knowledge of good and evil, etc.). This is important for several reasons. First, the environment of Genesis 2 can now be seen as reflective of the fall of humanity, such that the fall is the reason for human disobedience, not the result of it. While not absolving humanity of responsibility for eating the forbidden fruit, this approach does put more emphasis on cosmic forces at work in influencing human choices.

Second, recognizing the difference in the inseparable creation sagas, and having overlaid Genesis 2 onto Genesis 1, we asserted in Book One that "the fall is not our fall away from a state of perfection, but from our "perfection-only" state. From creation on, we are hidden in Christ—that does not change. The fall, so to speak, represents the beginning of our contradiction. The result of the fall is that we are completely good and completely bad, at the same time" (73). It is vital to reestablish this premise for Book Two so that we see the severe depths of the fall of humanity in contrast to the supreme goodness of humanity. Nothing but "green" in our created humanity in Genesis 1, we nevertheless laugh, love and even at times flourish in the dusty grey existence of placemat territory (Gen 2–3), even if we have no idea just how muted our existence is in comparison to our unadulterated humanity. And yes, like our first ancestors, we are also continually victimized by the red serpent. With false selves to go along with our true selves, we constantly turn to inhuman choices, harming those we love. Under the influence of "the spirit at work in those who are disobedient" (Eph 2:2), we show ourselves to be complicit in evil by our practices and patterns consistent with wrongheadedness. If Adam and Eve's act of defiance is the epitome of human disobedience in the face of God, it was only an example others have invariably followed.

Finally, this perspective on Genesis 2 functions as a scriptural nod to God's provisional allowance of evil in the present world. While always within his sovereign purpose, and always comprehended by the death of Christ which boundaries it, the adversary is allowed nonetheless.[3] In Book One we spoke of this adversary being "Evil with a Capital E," but in Book

---

3. In the pages that follow we will probe the meaning of verses like Rom 8:20: "For the creation was subjected to frustration, not by its own choice, but by the will of the one who subjected it, in hope" and Rom 11:32: "For God has bound all people over to disobedience."

Two we will recast it as "God's Enemy with a Capital E." God's primary foe is not human beings or even human sin, but the Evil One. And therein lies the motivating nexus for the goodness of God's judgment. For the sake of God's beloved creatures, the one who lies, steals, and destroys must be destroyed. And, to the extent that humanity has become God's enemy under the designs of the Enemy, it too must be purified in the judgment. Our peace is in knowing that God acting against humanity can only be God acting for humanity.

We will keep these three points in mind, even as we continually ask "why?" If God is all-powerful and all-loving, why would he place us into a garden replete with evil? What does it say about God? Is God a sadist? What does it say about humanity? Are we nothing but abused victims? The conclusion of our study offers the suggestion that our entrance into the garden was consensual and in fact the very opposite from a violation of human agency.

Karl Barth was one who recognized the irrationality of evil and therefore refused to give it a rational, credible basis. Evil can be described but not explained. It fits with the absurdity and incomprehensibility of evil that human beings, created righteous and complete, with no flaw, can make wicked choices like those in the garden. If indeed we can say that our creation is logically primary to our birth, then it follows that as Genesis 1 creatures of light our placement into the garden of Genesis 2 marks our entrance into the shadow of the fall, the negation of all that is good (see the reading "Newness" in Book One). Swarmed by the negation, we exit the womb with two selves, our right-minded true selves, and our irrational shadow selves, which favor the darkness over the light. Even though the goodness of our true humanity is never diminished, we are in torque as fallen persons in this world, twisted and virtually unrecognizable (see "The Fall with a Twist" in Book One).

The contradictory negation of God's good creation derives from the *primary* negation, that of the evil of "nothingness" or "chaos" in opposition to God himself. This is the "original antithesis" of which Barth speaks, and which he sees encapsulated in the Bible's first two verses (Gen 1:1–2).[4] The fact that there is a great negation to a great God is an inexplicable fact. But Genesis 1:2 also represents the impassable boundary God "fixed" between primal darkness and himself as Light, the point at which old things are already relegated to the status of old. These *old things* are the *false things* of nothingness, all that is not created and therefore crucified with Christ.[5]

---

4. *CD* III/1, 120.

5. *CD* III/1, 114–15. By stepping past the boundary he has fixed between himself

Still, even if God stepped past the nothingness of Genesis 1:2 in order to create, the negation's parasitic mirroring is not far behind each act of good creation. Like a giant oppressive leech intent on keeping the world "in bondage to decay" (Rom 8:21), fiendish antitheses plague all aspects of God's creation at every turn, all in service of the original antithesis.

By antithesis we do not mean a dualistic or symmetrical antithesis. Nor do we mean to point to a compromising "synthesis," (i.e., a miscasting of God's *allowance* of evil into a synthesis with evil). The negation, by definition, came second, so there is never an equality and always an asymmetry between God and "nothingness." Evil is never an intrinsic part of God, even if loosely included for a time in God's creation, in the incarnate life of the Son, and in our present age. Could God have existed without a negation? And could God have created without reference to the negation, not needing Christ's "eternal death" on the cross to set the table for creation's preservation?

We are at a loss to explain evil or God's self-limiting, but this much seems clear: the evil mimicry and mirroring of evil in relation to good is so powerful and thoroughgoing that only the death of God could eradicate it. We do well to recognize the ongoing threat of the negation and its pretending role as an equal in this world. Again, do not be fooled by the designation "unreality." Unreality produces indisputable facts of brokenness, pain, misery, death. Barth taught us that this chaos of nothingness is not nothing, even if, ultimately, it is not something. It has no future, yet in this world it turns family against family, people against people, nature against humanity, humanity against nature. I don't have to spell out all of the evil manifestations of the above. I hope some of the contemporary examples I address will encourage you to make helpful theological applications in your own situations.

Throughout this volume and up to our study of the book of Revelation, we look to that day when the duality is proven to be asymmetrical and the pretended dualism dissoluble.[6] This dissolution means judgment. For us to stand in the judgment, something will have to give. That's good news

---

as Light and nothingness in order to create, Barth sees an allusion to the reiteration of this event in the new creation passage of 2 Corinthians 5:17, where the old is gone, the new has come. Sin and evil are already "old" in Genesis 1:2; the negation of nothingness is not original, and therefore has no future. In a world of pure sequence, apart from simultaneity, "old" has much more power, for it is a presupposition for new. Granting such a potent starting point to "old" causes us to think of "new creation" as a second creation instead of as a new revelation of the true creation. See the reading in Book One, "Newness."

6. See *CD* II/1, 630: "This vindication, *involving both the eternal life and the eternal death of what has been*, will be the revelation of the kingdom of God." Emphasis added.

for all of us. Until that day, checkered as we are from Genesis 2–3 on, our green identity is justly reiterated and reconstituted by virtue of the Creator himself, the Savior who unfalteringly embraces us at our red worst, and who continually makes his green claim on us.

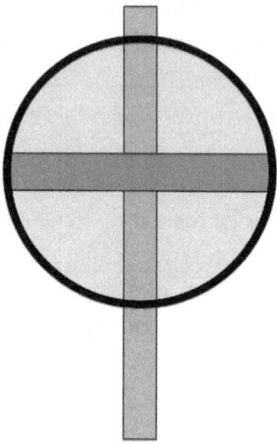

In our placemat adaptation on the cover (reproduced above), we note the equal length of the green and red strips contained within the grey circle while the width of the red strip appears to be slightly greater than the green strip underneath. The appearance of the two contrasting strips equal in length to one another points to the way in which we often understand perception as reality. In other words, limited to the scope of the circle of sight, we might perceive that there is a tug of war between good and evil; we may even think that evil is stronger and closer. But our big-picture placemat perspective reveals that the green strip is actually wider and deeper and longer, reminding us that the red dimension of our lives is not only parasitic but asymmetrically less potent. When we see with the eyes of faith what is revealed outside of the circle of our worldly perception, we see the green only. The green of grace exceeds all the world's woe: "That you . . . may have power, together with all the Lord's holy people, to grasp how wide and long and deep is the love of Christ" (Eph 3:17–18).

The Two Chairs and Repentance

In Book One I used the two chairs illustration.[7] The two facing chairs make a "U" (for "you") and represent the two opposite dimensions in you and me.

---

7. Starting at least from the 1980s, "the chair illustration" was a popular feature utilized by Young Life camp speakers like myself. Starting in 2002 I began to radically

INTRODUCTION

They vie for control and try to convince me of my identity as one or the other. If I am honest, my thoughts and actions may point more to the red chair (in front) than to the green chair. The red dimension may seem more present than the green dimension in our experience of this life.

As I mentioned, the two chairs represent the two simultaneous dimensions of our true and false humanities, but these dimensions are also dynamic, oppositional determinations. *You* (the green self) are full of the Spirit, actively and perfectly free, constantly obeying God's will. *You* (the red self) are a bankrupt and hopelessly disobedient sinner. Neither dimension is static. For example, as green, you are not just righteous in the sense of "legal standing," but you are in Christ always "living to God" and loving God. As red, you not only have nothing to bring to the table, but you are even antagonistic to God in the anti-Christ direction. Finally, what appears to be a single seat represents the one person of the two determinations (grey). The two seat backs represent the two conflicting determinations of the one subject: *you*.

Now, imagine the two chairs together being rotated or turned by the Spirit to make accessible to us a perspective once inaccessible. Whereas the chairs formed a "U" from one angle, we now see from a different angle. We discover by the Spirit that the chairs are actually two distinct determinations, my true self and my false self. They are as mutually exclusive as oil and water (except for the common subject).[8] This clear and complete perspective will remain out of reach for us until judgment day, when we will no longer see through a mirror dimly.

---

alter the Young Life version (see Grace Communion International, "Jeff McSwain") and have developed it even more in this study to account for the two human subjectivities.

8. It's clear that in the end (once turned) the "two chairs" illustration falls short in holding to the single subject. The next section will emphasize why we must not lapse into dualism by losing the single subject of the two "selves."

THE GOODNESS OF JUDGMENT

We look forward to the final manifestation of this liberating separation in the goodness of judgment, the day of redemption (Eph 4:30). In the meantime, in anticipation and prayer we seek the discernment of the Spirit as we struggle against the confusion of our lives and world. With more clarity, we can identify the false and affirm the true. In the belonging of the green, we can say to the red, "you do not belong."

The scriptural word repentance, or *metanoia*, means to have a radical change of mind, a life-altering turn of perspective. We see something we did not previously see, and it makes a difference in our lives. It is the epitome of a paradigm shift. Repentance recognizes the separations of our identities in the right places. It points to the ultimate separation of what can and should be separated (false humanity from true humanity), while preserving what cannot and should not be separated (humanity from God).

To the extent that we see these separations clearly, we stand to be transformed. So, we can say that repentance means seeing clearly and reflexively being changed. We could even say "eyes to see" simply *means* change. Lack of change means lack of spiritual sight, even by the most religious among us (and we are never surprised when those who are physically blind seem to have better spiritual sight than we). Repentance encourages the conscious rejection of the false self that we do not want and the celebration of who Christ is and who we are in him. If God's wrath is his "No" to our "no" (uttered by us in the flesh), then repentance entails us participating in the accuracy of this wrath, saying "no" to the source of all evil and to the wickedness that does not fit in true personhood or belong in reality. Participating in God's wrath toward us (see Col 3:5–6, Rom 1:18, Eph 5:6) does not mean celebrating God's hatred of us; it is neither self-hatred nor self-degradation. Instead, it celebrates the "Yes" of God that has always been

INTRODUCTION

"Yes" to us in Christ, the Creator's "Yes" that dignifies and could never denigrate his creatures. Repentance is therefore a witnessing with grateful hearts to the "No" of God that is inside God's "Yes," the gospel of grace where God's wrath *always* serves his love (I will repeat this critical phrase often in the coming pages).

In Book One we recognized that participation is the language of grace, while cooperation is the language of fleshly works, and therefore of the anti-Christ. Paul notes that we can participate vigorously in the green truth of our lives in Christ, "I worked harder than all of them—yet not I, but the grace of God that was with me" (1 Cor 15:10).[9] Conversely, in our red selves where flesh gives birth to flesh, we are easy targets of the Enemy who hawks his myth of human cooperative capacity. This is the subtle trap where the good is the enemy of the best. In the end we will find out just how much of our work has been participation and how much cooperation (see 1 Cor 3:12–13).

Again, perfect vision and perfect repentance wait until judgment day. There is a lot more to repentance than what we experience of it in this world, even if no one will enter the unadulterated kingdom of heaven without it (by "unadulterated kingdom" I mean the kingdom of heaven without the red, or paradise without a placemat). The kingdom of heaven is already a present dimension of our lives, as Jesus himself taught (Luke 17:21), but as of yet we do not experience it without the tangle of contradiction.

As we shall see, if we simply skip from grey to green when we die, then repentance has no place. Repentance is a farce unless it takes place from within this contradiction of red and green. The Bible is full of admonitions to "repent and believe." But the question remains, how do I speak of repentance and belief without making them a work, or some sort of fleshly cooperation? Forgetting that we are inside the picture, even the two chairs illustration might mislead us into thinking that we are standing outside of it, as if we must objectify the illustration and make an independent decision about whether we want to be involved. As we learned in Book One, we are already participating inside the covenant of grace; a grace-less position could only "throw us back on ourselves" into the realm of cooperation. Any objectivity we have is because we are already sitting in the green chair, in the subjectivity of Christ, the object and subject of our faith.[10] There we rec-

---

9. See also Col 1:29.

10. Obviously, we must have critical distance to learn about grace, and to see ourselves in the green chair. But we can't get stuck there. That happens when critical distance (the gift of objectivity that revelation affords us) gets co-opted into something we control. We don't determine God's grace, it determines us. Again and again we return to the "ad infinitum rule" from Book One. Jesus Christ does it all, even our believing,

ognize ourselves united with Christ, resting in his human belief, obedience, and even repentance on our behalf, participating in his "Yes" and "No."

The green baseline of grace—the actuality of our true selves living to God in Christ—is scandalously extravagant. Does this make light of sin? Theologian James Stewart rebukes the notion, "No one who reads the Gospels will ever be led astray by the argument that to pardon freely is simply to condone sin. . . . To know oneself forgiven, and forgiven at so great a cost, is always a moral dynamic of the first order. It is a mainspring of the dedicated life."[11] With Stewart and others, we hope to assuage any fears the reader may have, especially fears that giving away the "full green" of grace to every person in Christ somehow provides false comfort and incitement to licentiousness. Instead, we are empowered to live into the freedom of a grace-motivated life.

> For the grace of God has appeared, bringing salvation to all, training us to renounce impiety and worldly passions, and in the present age to live lives that are self-controlled, upright, and godly, while we wait for the blessed hope and the manifestation of the glory of our great God and Savior, Jesus Christ. He it is who gave himself for us that he might redeem us from all iniquity and purify for himself a people of his own who are zealous for good deeds. (Titus 2:11–14)

Excavating the Existential "I"

In our efforts to learn dimensional thinking we emphasized the red and the green as *two opposing determinations*. We explained how they must be understood as two total determinations *in one person* (what Scripture calls "the old man" and "the new man" of "the one man"). Yet, as spatial, material thinkers, it is easy to become preoccupied with the two aspects of our red and green humanity and forget the one person. We slip into outright dualism and, therefore, bad theology. Even if we emphasize the one person ("U") in our "two chairs" illustration, the very phrase "two chairs" suggests a Nestorian-like tendency. With the risk of heresy so great, how can we protect ourselves against doctrinal drift?[12]

---

and even our *believing* in the fact that Jesus Christ does it all, even our believing, ad infinitum! In other words, no amount of our existential believing is located outside of our ontological believing—we are created in Christ as believers in God.

11. Stewart, *Life and Teaching*, 88.

12. Emphasizing the one subject of the two subjectivities/selves could be the anthropological equivalent of Sabellianism or Monophysitism while emphasizing the two subjectivities/selves of the one subject could lead to the anthropological equivalent of

INTRODUCTION

While the "two chairs" illustration may do a commendable job portraying the *two subjectivities* of the one person, another illustration can help us to maintain the *one person* of the two subjectivities. We begin our superscript conceptualization with "Placemat Pat," our designated name for the human being in question. P^1 is Pat's true self; P^2 is Pat's false self; P^3 is the one person Pat who is in torque in this world.[13] Scripture allows P^3 (the one person) to talk about P in any of the three ways while still talking about Pat. For example, P^1: in Christ I am "holy and pure, without blemish"; P^2: "there is nothing good that lives in me" and P^3, or Placemat Pat: "not that I have already attained it, or have already been made perfect." The same person, Pat, has biblical permission to say all of these things. This is what we refer to as single-subject latitude. P^3 protects us from dualism (i.e., the strict parallelism as in Manichaeism, for example). Just as losing the two totals (P^1 or P^2) leads to bad, zero-sum theology, we must also refuse to lose P^3 to avoid a hard dualism.

If we only had P^1 and P^2, Plato would be delighted.[14] Fortunately, however, it is a bit more complicated. P^1, P^2, and P^3 are inseparable in this fallen world. We must remember that P^2 simply cannot exist without P^1, and that neither P^1 nor P^2 is *ever* without P^3. At the same time, in this world P^3 is always with *both* P^1 and P^2.

Before the fall, of course, P^1 can and does exist without P^2. In fact, in Genesis 1, $P^1 = P^3$. The only self that Pat has is Pat's true self. With the fall, however, there is an addition: Pat (P^3) is changed ($P^1 + P^2$ = a different P^3, i.e., still "Pat," but different). This is the state of Pat from biological conception to judgment day. Then at judgment day, fallen Pat stands to experience God's grace as a subtraction ($P^3 - P^2 = P^1$), so that Pat is changed again ($P^3 = P^1$). The one person and the true person are again one and the same, without admixture.

So then, in this worldly journey we can say:

P^1 (100 percent green) is who I am, and

P^2 (100 percent red) is who I am not, the un-me, the anti-me.

P^3 (the grey composite of red and green, appearing as a zero-sum balance) is the *perceptible* dimension, since we cannot fully perceive the

---

Nestorianism. Neither illustration, with problems of modalism and dualism respectively, is sufficient on its own.

13. The reader will note that P^1 is green, P^2 is red, and P^3 is the grey composite of the two. The P illustration is not meant to replace the placemat but again is meant simply to reinforce the critical, one-person principle of placemat anthropology.

14. Plato is often viewed as the poster child of metaphysical dualism, regardless of the more nuanced discussions of whether or not this reputation is fair to the rigors of his thought.

two totals. Instead of *who* I am in this world, P^3 relates to *how* I am, *how* I feel, *how* I perceive myself to be doing, *how* I experience the world, *how* I experience others' perceptions of me, and *how* I come across to others. This zero-sum composite might be the enemy when it comes to the underlying theology of the two totals, but it is a helpful language for describing our experience of human life (the varying degree to which our feelings and actions bear witness to the two totals). In this world, some days are definitely better than others! It is perhaps due to such great utility that zero-sum thinking tends to dominate the discussion of sanctification and the Christian life, compromising sound theology in the process.

Whenever we describe Pat in terms of the two, 100 percent selves, we refer to either P^1 or P^2. However, whenever we describe Pat in experiential, zero-sum terms, we are referring to P^3. P^2 is the parasitic imposter, the double, the false self, and the "old man." In other words, even if by faith we recognize our created and redeemed goodness, we also recognize the conflicted nature of the Romans 7 situation. There, Paul (P^3) uses the "I" and "me" in several different ways, pointing alternatively to P^1 and P^2. With Paul, I (P^3) can say that I am "a wretched man" (P^2), even though "I delight in God's law" in my inmost being (P^1). With single subject latitude, P^3 can say that "I" (P^2) do what "I" (P^1) don't want to do!

The only thing P^1 and P^2 have in common is Pat. Pat's true self does not need to repent, while Pat's false self cannot repent. So, who repents? Simply Pat (P^3). Pat repents from within the grey "overlap." Likewise, the imperatives of Scripture are meant for P^3 (grey), because they help us to "live into" P^1. They upbraid us to live in correlation with who we *are* (the indicative, 100 percent green, P^1). They also encourage us to live "away from" who we are *not* (100 percent red, P^2). After all, P^1 does not need the imperatives, because here there is no deviance between who Pat is and what Pat does. P^2, however, is hopelessly and invariably deviant.

This picture of the P-dimensions helps us to understand what "change" or "progress" looks like in our lives *without* using a zero-sum framework. Because our being is intrinsically dynamic in Christ, to *be* who we are and to *become* who we are is the same thing. When Pat (P^3 and P^1) participates in Christ, it may seem like P^1 increases and P^2 decreases. It is an experiential testimony to the non-quantitative, transformational power of the Spirit that "change" happens without any decrease in P^2 (there is never a decrease in P^2, short of its eradication).

Such Holy Spirit growth takes place under the sound of the gospel and especially in a community of expectant recipients of God's presence and empowerment. They are charged not with expanding the kingdom, but with testifying to its expansiveness through the celebration of the sacraments and the proclamation of the Word. Thus, P^1 relates to the "already" of the kingdom (who we already are in Christ), while P^3 relates to the "not yet" of the kingdom, since who we are as redeemed children of God has "not yet" been made completely manifest or fully revealed (Rom 8:19, 1 John 3:2).

Finally, understanding each aspect of the P-dimensions prevents us from slipping into some of the most common theological traps facing those who attempt to bring together the doctrines of reconciliation and sanctification. For example:

- P^1 prevents an under-realized eschatology in which we lose the "already" aspect,
- P^2 prevents an over-realized eschatology in which we lose the "not yet" aspect, and
- P^3 protects against a dualistic bifurcation of the human being since P^1 and P^2 remain a duality within the one person in this world.

This perspective provides us with an x-ray vision of sorts, protecting us from defining ourselves by what we see in the mirror, or by how others appear to us. Instead, we define ourselves by the revealed reference point of who Jesus Christ is and who we are in him.

Fixing Our Eyes on the Unseen

In this world, the true human transcendence of every person is marked by P^1. It is the in-Christ dimension of which Paul spoke when he said, "So we fix our eyes not on what is seen, but on what is unseen, since what is seen is temporary, but what is unseen is eternal" (2 Cor 4:18). To fix our eyes on the unseen is to recognize that there *is* a reverse side, that what we perceive is not all there is. If Paul was a Platonist, he would take "what is seen is temporary" at face value, rejecting outright the ways in which the eternal is revealed and made manifest in and through the temporal. Instead, the apostle co-opted Platonic language to say that, even if not *all* that we perceive is temporary, we may "walk by faith, not by sight" (2 Cor 5:7, NRSV), having an eye to see what is eternal in our very midst. As Barth noted, the love that "will not perish is something which can be seen when we look not at that which is seen but at that which is not seen."[15]

In the Preface we noted Barth's use of 1 Corinthians 13:12 with these italicized words: "For *Now* we see through a mirror dimly, *Then* we shall

---

15. *CD* IV/1, 331.

see face to face." Barth spoke of all the *Then* being in the *Now*, even if not all the *Now* is in the *Then*. We will use this lingual device—all of *X* is in the *Y* but not all the *Y* is in the *X*—often in this book. It will protect us from dualism and allow us to maintain dimensional distinctions. For instance, in this grey fallen world, all the green is in the grey, but not all the grey is in the green (thankfully!).[16] In the same way, all of P^1 (created, green Pat) is in P^3 (Placemat, grey Pat) in this world, but not all of P^3 is in P^1.

In Book One we made much of the fact that the two Genesis creation sagas are distinct and yet inseparable (again 1:1—2:4a and 2:4b—3:24 we designate with the shorthand Genesis 1 and Genesis 2, respectively). The two sagas should not be indiscriminately mixed, nor should they be pulled apart. These accounts, then, follow the pattern we described above: all of Genesis 1 is in Genesis 2, but not all of Genesis 2 is in Genesis 1. It would be wrong to let the distinctions between the two creation narratives turn into a dichotomy, a dualism, as if Genesis 2 was simply red in contrast to the perfect green of Genesis 1. Instead, Genesis 2 signifies a checkered world of grey.

Marked by the fall, humanity's in-Christ dimension (the green) is mirrored at every turn by the evil of anti-Christ, anti-human, anti-being, and anti-act (the red). It follows that even if Genesis 1 is all there in Genesis 2, it can only be read as the reverse side of the Genesis 2–3 experience. The epistemological challenge is compounded by the fact that the "prince of this world" has foisted upon us an unfit mind. As part and parcel of the great reversal of the fall, humanity's thoughts have shifted backward—fallen human thinking moves from humanity to "God" instead of "God" to humanity. We do not read the world properly, from the tree of life to the tree of the knowledge of good and evil. Instead, we have a warped lens and a false point of reference, understanding good in comparison to evil rather than the other way round. Even after the historical incarnation of God's Son and his death under Pontius Pilate, our fallen minds are prone to think from Adam to Christ instead of from Christ to Adam. God came into the world he created, but our minds were dulled, and we missed the point.

All of this is encapsulated in the transitional verses between creation sagas. Where Genesis 1 (1:1—2:4a) spoke of the creation of the "heavens and the earth," Genesis 2:4b reverses the pattern and refers to the "earth and the heavens." In the perceptible "by sight" realm of this Genesis 2 world, the

---

16. See the discussion in the Preface about the Now and the Then. I maintained the parenthetical "thankfully" because anything to do with our perceptible humanity or this world that doesn't translate to the unadulterated heaven is something we are better off without. Such is the stuff of praise and thanksgiving. One of the most distinguishing marks of a believer, Barth consistently claimed, is gratitude.

two dimensions simultaneously exist so that neither one of the dimensions is apparent in its totality, the Genesis 1 reality being somewhat hidden. Because the two opposite dimensions exist in one space, as in our placemat, it is hard to see the green for the grey.[17]

Perceiving the in-Christ dimension of our lives entails looking *through* the mirror, but the problem is that we are mired in Genesis 2–3, trying in vain to rediscover the paradise that was lost. Yes, we are alive in Christ (or we would not be alive at all), but we are also dead in our sins. As God's creatures, we yearn for the clarity that can only come from "above" (or, in this case Genesis 1), to know the truth about who we are in Christ. We therefore seek what comes to us from the Word made flesh, the one who journeyed from above to below: "No one has ascended into heaven except he who descended from heaven, the Son of Man" (John 3:13, ESV).

Though we are full and complete in Christ, lacking nothing, the truth is inaccessible in this fallen world without the illumination of the Holy Spirit, the one who provides the revelation we so desperately need. Through the reference point of the Word incarnate, the Spirit reveals to us our true selves. How will they have eyes to see and hear, says Paul, unless someone brings the Word to them? When the Word is preached, we might begin to see through the mirror in a limited way (i.e., through the grey to the green). We may experience something akin to Paul's perspective from "the third heaven" (2 Cor 12:2) emerging with an unrelenting conviction that neither red, nor grey, will have the last word.

Whether we know it or not, all of our self-discovery and interpersonal perspective derives from our unadulterated personal experience of God himself. This is what theologians for centuries have described as the "beatific vision" that Paul alluded to: "then I shall see face to face . . . then I shall know fully, even as I am fully known" (1 Cor 13:12). The fact that *all the Then is in the Now* reminds us of the fact that the beatific vision is not merely future; even now we can know "in part" what is already dimensionally present and fully real. It should not surprise us, therefore, that Paul uses the present tense in describing the scene: "And we all, who with unveiled faces contemplate the Lord's glory, are being transformed into his image

---

17. When God "steps past" the nothingness of Gen 1:2 to create this new thing—"the heavens and the earth"—from that point on all that is *not* created by God is already old, for it derives from the nothingness God passed by. Whatever is old has never been new, because what is old cannot exist apart from the new that it mimics. Bedeviled with a sequence obsession, we think that we cannot have a new without an old, when the matter is precisely the opposite. Proper coupling keeps "new" with "true," and "old" with "false," for the same principle holds them together: there can be no false without true.

with ever-increasing glory" (2 Cor 3:18). Glorification is no improvement on creation. Instead, it is creation fully unveiled.

One of my favorite photos from the difficult years of the COVID-19 pandemic is a screenshot of me video-chatting with my 85-year-old dad. I can see my image in the reflection of Dad's sunglasses, which are perched on Dad's smiling face. I sense a lot of love there. I feel his pleasure and joy as if, in his eyes, I can do no wrong. For me, that image is imperfectly analogous to the experience we will have seeing our Lord face-to-face. On one hand, admittedly, my extrapolation from the screenshot is based on a lifetime context with a loving father. On the other hand, my context was still only a derivative taste of our heavenly Father's love. I can look forward to the moment when all of us, with our good and bad experiences of our earthly fathers, experience the purity of God's love for his children. What a beautiful time that will be when all of us as God's beloved creatures really see ourselves accurately in the Father's eyes, basking in the light of his joy and pleasure, that time when we know fully even as we are fully known.

For now, however, when we look in a mirror, we cannot help but see ourselves in a distorted way. Self-perception is king. William Placher described the "rigorous self-examination" of early Protestants this way in *The Domestication of Transcendence*: "It put such emphasis on looking at ourselves, however, that the fact that everything depended on God's grace kept risking getting lost."[18] Thankfully, the transcendent humanity of creation and redemption is not reducible to the perceptible, biological, or physiological. Even though we cannot see our transcendent faces in the mirror, that does not mean that our transcendent faces do not exist. Curved in on ourselves, staring at our own belly buttons, it is not apparent that our face-to-face relationship with God is inside of Christ's face-to-face relationship with the Father.

As Julie Canlis notes, even our hearing and seeing rely on grace—God's truth for humanity in Jesus Christ: "Our fallen nature makes hearing the Father's love for us so difficult. Our ears are plugged. Our eyes are blind. Thus, as Calvin says, Jesus hears the words that we cannot believe on our own: *you are my beloved*. . . . He, as the true human, is accepting these words with joy, on my behalf."[19] Only by the Spirit of grace can we know that, in one sense, we already have a face-to-face relationship with God and that the Abrahamic blessing of God's face shining upon us is not a hypothetical (Num 6:24–26).

---

18. Placher, *Domestication of Transcendence*, 89.
19. Canlis, *Theology of the Ordinary*, 34–35 (emphasis original).

INTRODUCTION

Paul noted in 2 Cor 4:3–4 that a veil prevents unbelievers from clearly seeing the glory of Christ. Indeed, in a startling comment, he even gave the Enemy who blinds us the moniker, "the god of this age." Such is his power in the world. Yet, even in this world, we can claim a point of reference established by the true God. When we look from Christ to Moses instead of from Moses to Christ, God illuminates our hearts, empowering our walk with him by faith (not sight). The reorientating that Paul describes in 2 Cor 3:16—"Whenever anyone turns to the Lord, the veil is taken away"—carries the sense of re-turning, or reverting. The veil is not original to the human mind, so taking it away represents a provisional clarity enjoyed by believers in this world, one that can only bear relative witness to the perfect clarity of the eschaton.

On that day, we will no longer look in a mirror or through a mirror, even partially. Instead, we will see God as he really is and we will see ourselves as we really are, reflected in the apple of God's eye. That is the view he has always had of us, the unconditional favor that God gives to each of us and to all of us in "the light of the knowledge of God's glory displayed in the face of Christ" (2 Cor 4:6). In the same verse Paul does not hesitate to make the connection back to Genesis 1: the illumination that God gives us in redemption is the same that he gave to us in creation if we only have eyes to see it. "For God, who said, 'Let light shine out of darkness,' made His light shine in our hearts."[20] Because of the Christ-centered consistency of our created and redeemed selves, the glory of God is not only in us, our being exists squarely inside the glory and pleasure of the Trinitarian persons.

In Book One we stated that Genesis 2 is descriptive of the human narrative whereas Genesis 1 is prescriptive. The latter is unadulterated reality; the former is our checkered, experiential journey. Genesis 2–3 includes all the good, but also all the bad and the ugly. Our study started with the revelation that only Christ provides for interpreting creation and our human belonging in the Trinity. Book One began with Genesis 1 and moved into Genesis 2. Here, in this second volume, we begin with the lived experience of Genesis 2–3 and move to Revelation 22. At some point we will have to ask what material difference, if any, exists between Revelation 22, where we end our two-volume project, and Genesis 1, where we began.

---

20. As discussed in Book One, this light can represent God's love poured into our hearts through the Spirit (Rom 5:5), whether it be in establishing our green heart in creation or in existentially renewing it in light of the gospel, despite the blinding effect of the "god of this age." Interestingly, "Let light shine out of darkness," while attributed often to Genesis 1:3, is not in the Bible except here in 2 Cor 4:6.

THE GOODNESS OF JUDGMENT

A Matrix of Life and Death

In 2 Corinthians 4 Paul writes, "We always carry around in our body the death of Jesus, so that the life of Jesus may also be revealed in our body" (4:10). The apostle wants his hearers to know that life is revealed in an embodied way. And just in case we think he means the life that will be revealed in the body of his spiritual resurrection, or his *future*, heavenly body, he doubles down in the very next verse. Paul uses almost the exact same phrase, but he replaces the word "body" with the pejorative word, "flesh": "For while we live, we are always being given up to death for Jesus's sake, so that the life of Jesus may be made visible in our mortal *flesh*" (4:11, NRSV, emphasis mine). This is the flesh with all its ignominious connotations. Just when his co-opting of Platonic language threatens too close an association with dualism, Paul tethers himself to the incarnation. It is no wonder that Paul mentioned "Jesus" here more often than in any other chapter, rather than using "Christ" or some variation. In providing a more earthy, "Nazarene" emphasis, he wants us to know that God's glory shines not through our spiritual bodies only, but also through our mortal bodies (the latter because of the former). Against metaphysical dualism, it is as if Paul screams to all of us: "Don't forget P^3!"[21] We cannot ignore our lived existence (P^3) for either the pure heavenly life of our true selves (P^1) or the corruptible, parasitic presence of the false self (P^2).

The mortal body, the flesh (P^2), cannot produce life and light on its own. And the spiritual body (P^1) does not exist in this world without the mortal body. From our non-Platonic perspective, mortal is necessarily material, but material is not necessarily mortal.[22] For the apostle, the one person of the equation (P^3) is indispensable to keep the dimensions from falling apart into abstractions. Hearkening back to 2 Corinthians 4:10, Jesus is the primary subject of the duality; all death is referenced by "the death" of Jesus and all life is referenced by "the life" of Jesus. It is not just death and life, as in a dualism—it is the death and the life *of Jesus*. The built-in asymmetry of the situation is found in the resurrection of Jesus described

---

21. In this one sentence (2 Cor 4:11) Paul strikes a blow that quashes Gnosticism, docetism, and all other dualisms of the ancient world. See Rom 8:11 where Paul does much the same thing. See also the upcoming reading "Parting from the Old Red Sea Narrative"; Paul's whole argument about the law in 2 Cor 3 could not provide a better scriptural framework from which to derive our placemat theme.

22. We again recognize here that P^2 and P^1 may be sufficient for Plato, but not for Paul. Regardless of the degree to which Plato underestimates the materiality of "the soul" (see Book One, Introduction), the Greek philosopher does not conceptualize Paul's incarnational category of P^3.

INTRODUCTION

here: "We know that the one who raised the Lord Jesus from the dead will also raise us with Jesus" (2 Cor 4:14; see also Rom 6:5).[23]

In the same way for us, then, "the life" is the in-Christ dimension and "the death" is the anti-Christ dimension. Just like the red and the green, the old and the new, the false and the true, the righteousness and the wickedness, and all such binaries in Scripture, "the death" (P^2) and "the life" (P^1) are mutually exclusive dynamics that are active concurrently in the one person (P^3). Without capitulating to a zero-sum model, these two totals (P^1 and P^2) are determinations toward life and death that are always clashing, even if they manifest differently in each person at different times.[24] Thus, Paul's statement in the last verse in the chain: "So then, death is at work in us, but life is at work in you" (2 Cor 4:12). At the time of his suffering, death manifested in Paul, while life manifested in the lives of his hearers. The word "manifest" is used so often by Paul in 2 Corinthians that one commentator says the apostle is seemingly "haunted by it."[25] Indeed, it uniquely speaks to

---

23. Note that in 2 Cor 4:14 the end of the NIV translation is a gloss: "the one who raised the Lord Jesus from the dead will also raise us with Jesus and present us with you to himself"; *to himself* is not in the Greek. The 1984 NIV has a different gloss: "present us with you *in his presence.*" Is it Christ who will present us before Christ (as perhaps in 2 Cor 5:10, Eph 5:27)? Or is it Christ who will present us before the Father (Col 1:22); or perhaps it is the Father who will present us *to* the Father, through Jesus Christ (Jude 1:24–25)? Of course, all of these are true. At judgment day we find ourselves in the mysterious glory of God crucified. The one whose name is above all names is the judge judged for our sakes (Barth). This is consistent with John 5 where the Father gives not just the Son of God the unique role of judge (5:22) but also the Son of Man (5:27). This means that we are judged not only by the one who loves us the most but specifically (and most authoritatively) by the one who understands us in our human frailties. We are judged "by the man he has appointed" (Acts 17:31). Finally, even if descriptions of the resurrection in Paul take on a future, "not yet," sense, his language in Ephesians and Colossians describes the resurrection as an "already" event. Again, both are true. We *will* be raised with Jesus because we *have* been raised with Jesus. Of course, the different emphases have led some to claim that Paul did not write the latter two epistles. See Cohick, *Letter to the Ephesians*, and Douglas Campbell, *Framing Paul*, for the argument of Pauline authorship.

24. See also 2 Cor 4:16: "though our outward man is decaying, yet our inward man is being renewed day by day" (ERV). The ERV here does not comport to our preferred gender inclusive language, but its use of the singular "man" may help us to conceptually maintain the duality of the one subject in view—the "two men of the one man/one man of the two men."

25. Spence Jones, *Pulpit Commentary*, public domain. Some form of the word "manifest" appears in 2 Cor 2:14; 3:3; 4:10; 5:10–11; 7:12; 11:6. I find forms of the word "manifest" to be more common in charismatic than in Evangelical settings, even if neither camp recognizes the present-dimensional fullness of the christological reality that is being referenced (i.e., even if the word "manifest" is a subjective zero-sum assessment of the movement of the Spirit being experienced).

the ways in which our experiences bear relative witness to the death and life of Jesus Christ, in whose sufferings and life we all share.

As P^3s in this world, none of us can look in the mirror and say to ourselves that this is *exactly* the way we were created. No matter how we might "identify," what we see only bears relative (imperfect) witness to how we were created, our true and real creaturely identity. In other words, there is significant continuity between the mortal bodies that we see in the mirror and our spiritual material bodies, but there is also significant discontinuity.

When it comes to seeing *through* the mirror, the seeing through goes both ways. God already sees perfectly from his side. But the veil of our mortal bodies (the flesh) hangs between the glory of our true humanity and our perception of it. We inevitably begin the search for our identity in the land of Genesis 2–3, the land of the fall. But to seek our identity starting with the mortal body (i.e., by what we see in the mirror's reflection) is to let the tail wag the dog. Seeking to properly value the mortal body, we devalue it because we fail to perceive the broader P^1 context for it. It cannot be over-emphasized that fixing our eyes on the unseen does not mean that we ignore the visible. In fact, it is the unseen that gives the seen its inestimable value. The unseen is hidden but is revealed in and through the seen. That is why Paul's strange phrase, "fix your eyes on the unseen," urges us to keep a look-out for manifestations of the hidden reality. We are to anticipate the fruit of the Spirit as it emerges in this world and not just look forward to it in the next. Despite the veil of the flesh, we might gain just enough illumination by the Spirit to reject the lie that what we see in the mirror is all there is. We might begin to see and understand ourselves the way that God does.

Perception and Projection

We have said that we discover our true selves by looking *through* the mirror. But when you are standing in front of your mirror who is the person peering *into* it? If you answered, "my false self," then you failed the test and have become a Platonist! The person standing before the mirror, and therefore the person reflected in the mirror, is your composite self, who you are as a single subject (P^3). Your false, corruptible material self (P^2) is fully present, to be sure, but so is your true incorruptible material self (P^1).[26] Thus, the continual irony in this world is that the dimension of our truest selves is the one that is relatively hidden.

---

26. In general, what you see in the mirror is P^3 (P^1 and P^2). If it was only P^2, "you" would not be standing, seeing, or moving! As with a corpse, all animation would be vacated.

INTRODUCTION

Starting with a proper understanding of the one person (P^3) allows us to assess more clearly both P^1 and P^2 for what they are as two total determinations and to keep them in proper perspective. Foundational to the gospel is that P^2 does not exist without P^1. Yet in our fleshly obsession with walking by sight, we devolve into the morass of P^2. Just as we can forget P^3 and its accompanying P^2, we can also forget P^3 and its accompanying P^1. By starting with the false self, we forget that all of the Then is in the Now. This forgetfulness has serious consequences. Thus far, without realizing the stakes, we might have thought of placemat anthropology as a cute, creative, or clever model to put alongside other models of theological anthropology. But this under-realized eschatological posture initiates a trainwreck of polarizing projections that greatly damages our lives and world.

While some Christian thinkers (preachers and theologians alike!) would want us to wallow in our unworthiness, it is easier for most of us to see enough undeniable goodness in humanity to shift away from focusing on the total wretchedness of P^2 (even though we are adept at maintaining it with strategies of false humility). Unequipped with a placemat theology, however, this shift away from obsessing on P^2 is only a jump from the frying pan into the fire. We leave behind an inadequate focus on P^2 for an inadequate version of P^3—a zero-sum version which loses the total nature of both P^1 and P^2. What emerges then is simply a more subtle and more deadly form of an under-realized eschatology. Like the grim reaper leading us into his ready-made harvest field, our Enemy delights to see us defeating ourselves with the zero-sum model. Once we lose the assuring fullness of P^1, sin sucks us further into the vortex of obsessing about our sin and lack of sanctification. Conversely, in a placemat perspective, the greatness of our sinfulness is always contextualized by the greatness of our righteousness, lending us both proper humility *and* confidence. Without such a framework, we are left in the agonizing place of constantly questioning our salvation.

Human beings are duplicitous, but that is not the main issue. It is when we suppress and repress our duplicity that we are at risk for living a destructive "double life." Why? Because the duplicity is going to express itself in some way, shape, or form, so we might as well be attentive and intentional about the complexity of our lives and others. As one who grieves the theological loss of human transcendence and a dimensional perspective on humanity, Thomas Merton highlights the pitfalls of anthropological interpretation when we ourselves are caught in the matrix and oblivious to the influence of the Enemy. He describes this progression of distortion and aggression when we start in the wrong place (i.e., not with Christ and P^1):

1. First, there is our self-hatred. "It is not only our hatred of others that is dangerous but also and above all our hatred of ourselves: particularly that hatred of ourselves which is too deep and too powerful to be consciously faced. For it is this which makes us see our own evil in others and unable to see it in ourselves. . . . It is easy to identify the sin with the sinner when he is someone other than our own self. In ourselves, it is the other way around; we see the sin, but we have great difficulty in shouldering responsibility for it."[27]

2. Then, there is the scapegoating of others. We unconsciously pass the guilt we feel within to somebody else. But then the strangest thing happens. When we seek to excuse ourselves by attributing the wrong to "another" who is unaccountably "in us" (the basis for the projection onto them), it does not work to rid us of our guilt: "There is still too much left to be explained," says Merton, "The 'other in myself' is too close to home. The temptation is, then, to account for my fault by seeing an equivalent amount of evil in someone else."[28]

3. Finally, the intensity of our own sense of evil within builds and builds, leading to aggression. "We drive ourselves mad with our preoccupation and in the end there is no outlet left but violence. We have to destroy something or someone." We go from blaming the scapegoat to blasting him; "He is the cause of every wrong. He is the fomenter of all conflict. If he can only be destroyed, conflict will cease."[29]

Merton was a critic of the Vietnam war and he lamented the practice of "othering" our enemy to justify killing them. His analysis fits a far wider context than merely Vietnam, however, encapsulating all human history. It hits close to home today as we consider matters of race and political polarization. What is the way forward? For Merton, the love of Jesus Christ uniquely undercuts our deep self-loathing, allowing us to love ourselves and our neighbor. Inserting our placemat superscript into Merton's summary we read, "We must try to accept ourselves, whether individually or

---

27. Merton, *New Seeds*, 112–13.

28. Merton, *New Seeds*, 113.

29. Merton, *New Seeds*, 113–14. See 97, where Merton notes that, tragically, even preaching can take on pathological, passive-aggressive forms: "It sometimes happens that men who preach most vehemently about evil and the punishment of evil, so that they seem to have practically nothing else on their minds except sin, are really unconscious haters of men. They think the world does not appreciate them, and this is their way of getting even."

collectively, not only as perfectly good [P¹] or perfectly bad [P²], but in our mysterious, unaccountable mixture of good and evil [P³]."[30]

Aware of our tendency to project by perception and to elevate ourselves as judge over others, we can follow Paul's admonition to relinquish that role: "I care very little if I am judged by you or by any human court; indeed, I do not even judge myself. My conscience is clear, but that does not make me innocent. It is the Lord who judges me. Therefore, judge nothing before the appointed time; wait until the Lord comes. He will bring to light what is hidden in darkness and will expose the motives of the heart" (1 Cor 4:3–5). Without judging ourselves or others, we can start with defining everyone by what God has done for them. In Christ the creator and redeemer we have theological permission to remove the red and see each human for who they really are—green. In Barth's words, "we have to think of every human being, even the oddest, most villainous or miserable, as one to whom Jesus Christ is Brother and God is Father, and we have to deal with him on this assumption."[31]

As Merton relates, the fear and insecurity within our dim vision has caused us to seek comfort in projection. Maybe we have alienated ourselves from others, declaring them red and us green. Perhaps our grey vision has caused us to think self-righteously, as if we are all green with little or no red. Or, in a self-deprecating manner, maybe we have imagined ourselves as merely red scum, with little or no green. Only with the proper gospel vision—the in-breaking of clarity that visits us by the Word and Spirit in this life—can we begin to share Paul's anthropological lens: "so from now on we regard no one from a worldly point of view" (2 Cor 5:16).[32] Indeed, Dorothy Day bemoaned that she was still prone to prioritize the wrong kind of clarity about others over the right kind: "I see only too clearly how bad people are. I wish I did not see it so. It is my own sins that give me such clarity. If I

---

30. Merton, *New Seeds*, 117.

31. Barth, *Humanity of God*, 53. Barth continues, "To deny it to *him* would be for *us* to renounce having Jesus Christ as Brother and God as Father" (emphasis added).

32. There are several other popular English translations of this verse. Others use "from a human point of view" (NRSV), or "according to the flesh" (ESV). I stay with the NIV here because "worldly point of view" seems to communicate the nuance most effectively. "Worldly" as an adjective connotes the skewed, slanted, or grey perspective, whereas there is nothing at all wrong with the original "human point of view," only with the *fallen* "human point of view." Created good as material-spiritual humans, we are having a flesh experience, a *sarx* experience. Paul's admonishment earlier in the chapter connects to this: we are not to "live by sight" (2 Cor 5:7) in assessing others. We could say we no longer look at anyone in a distorted way, a way twisted by the red refraction. In placemat terms, everyone is *fundamentally* "green"—created and re-created in Christ.

did not bear the scars of so many sins to dim my sight and dull my capacity for love and joy, then I would see Christ more clearly in you all."[33]

Two Eyes and Matthew 25

We began our Introduction with two illustrations that develop aspects of our human situation—the two-fold determination (the chairs), and the single subject (P³). If you are prone to zero-sum thinking, keep going back to the two chairs.[34] If you are prone to think dualistically, keep going back to our single subject "Pat."[35] These illustrations are meant to complement rather than replace our central metaphor of the interwoven placemat with its unique usefulness in holding all aspects together.

Throughout Book One and in recent pages I have taken the interpretive tack that the binaries in Holy Scripture are often meant to recognize the dual humanities at play in the person of Christ and therefore in our own lives. It is true that Jesus's parables about the good tree and bad tree, the good soil and bad soil, the good fish and bad fish, the wheat and the tares, etc., can lead us toward a polarizing perspective of us (the righteous) versus them (the wicked). That is partly why the parables are difficult to understand, because in moments of sanguine reflection we know we can fit into both categories, depending on the circumstances. We strive to configure criteria to convince ourselves why we and others are in one column or the other. As I have suggested, Jesus's comment about those who have "ears to hear" and "eyes to see" allow us latitude to recognize in Christ's own teaching the irony of the christological and therefore anthropological duality that he wants us to grasp.

Before exegeting Jesus's famous parable about the sheep and the goats in just such a fashion, there is another gospel metaphor that particularly suits our placemat perspective as it applies to judgment. It is Jesus's teaching with the imperative: "If your eye causes you to sin, gouge it out" (Matt

---

33. Day, *Reckless*, 26–27.

34. Barth describes the two-fold determination as "*two total men* who cannot be united but are necessarily in extreme contradiction. We are confronted with two mutually exclusive determinations" (*CD* IV/2, 571, emphasis added). The person exists "in puzzling contrast with himself" (571) and is "seriously at odds with himself" (570). In this sanctification "quarrel," the person is "still wholly the old and already wholly the new man—he has not fallen out with himself partially but totally" (574).

35. In emphasizing the one person of the two determinations, Barth speaks of "total freedom" and "total bondage" that "clash in one and the same man" (*CD* IV/2, 497, emphasis added).

INTRODUCTION

18:9).³⁶ What is initially quite puzzling becomes more coherent when we apply a placemat application that attributes our grey vision to having two eyes, one eye that sees completely green and the other eye that sees completely red (call it 20/20 grey). With grey vision our anthropological perceptions are mixed up, leading to miscalculated projections with grave outcomes. Something must be done. Note that Jesus strangely refers not to plural eyes but a singular *eye*: "If your eye causes you to sin, gouge it out."

By the Spirit we may receive "eyes to see," but it is only when we lose the "bad eye" of the flesh that we will gain perfect spiritual vision. The two totals in the simultaneity cannot be sustained forever. We can be confident that our metaphorical "false eye" has no future and will eventually go the way of the tares, the goats, and the devil. To "gouge out" our false, red eye is to give it no quarter, to submit it to the subtraction inherent to Christ's cross, where the world has been crucified to me and I to the world.

When it comes to reducing our vision to a single-eyed focus, the King James translation of Matthew 6:22 also fits well: "The light of the body is the eye: if therefore thine eye be single, *thy whole body* shall be full of light." If that describes the "green" eye, then the "red" eye is referenced in the very next verse: "But if thine eye be evil, *thy whole body* shall be full of darkness" (6:23). Again, we have a total-total situation, a "whole" and a "whole" that must be interpreted. In this world, distinguishing between our totally good and new and our totally wicked and old selves is never easy, but because we know the separation has been made in Christ's cross, we can have navigational hope. With our "two eyes," we look through the glass darkly, unable to blink away the blurriness. On that day of perfect clarity and release, however, what has felt like a never-ending dualism will be seen as a duality defined by Christ and resolved in Christ.

Against dualism, we may be more comfortable with a duality that maintains a single-eyed goal. Our economy of what could be called "salvation by subtraction" (the judgment of the cross that "plucks out" the corrupted, false self), prepares us for a reinterpretation of the sheep and the goats in Matthew 25. It is often overlooked that Jesus described himself as a shepherd of *both* the sheep and the goats. In modern American society, the incarcerated (whether in prisons or detention centers) are often portrayed or understood simply as goats.³⁷ It follows that Jesus's ready association of himself with such goats ("I was in prison, and you came to visit me," Matt

---

36. See Matt 5:29, where Jesus's metaphor varies slightly from Matt 18:9 and does not fit as well into our application of a red and green eye!

37. We spoke in Book One of people being victims before being perpetrators. Such rightly convicted criminals have acted, even unconsciously, out of their own victimhood.

25:35–40) already provides a nuance to the parable very different from an "us-them" dualism of sheep and goats.

On the one hand, Matthew 25 is ominous for those who do not know who Jesus Christ is and who all human beings are in him. In violation of the Christo-logic, they understand themselves as sheep and others as goats. However, if we are honest with ourselves, we might admit with George MacDonald just how difficult it is to categorize ourselves in such a way:

> In my own heart, O Master, in my thought
> Betwixt the wooly sheep and the hairy goat
> Not clearly I distinguish.[38]

On the other hand, Matthew 25 is joyous for those like MacDonald who can rely on the interpretive key found in the Shepherd himself. Though it is clear in Scripture that we are not to judge others, it is just as clear that there *is* a judge and a judgment (1 Cor 4:4–5). It is also plain that the only one who has a right to judge us is the one who loves us the most, our Savior. With more precision than any shepherd's shears, the Good Shepherd makes the liberating separations in the right places. He does this by first representing both the sheep and goat dimensions in himself. The false self goes to the shepherd's left (the way of the goats and the scapegoat), while the new and true humanity proceeds to the right hand of the Shepherd (who is also the sheep). Thus, giving everyone "sheep status" does not negate the biblical theme of judgment—it necessitates it.[39]

Matthew 25 is most known for its two interrelated themes at the heart of placemat anthropology. One is the judgment theme just mentioned, the final division of the sheep from the goats. But the other is the theme upon which the judgment is based—the actions of human beings one to another: "whatever you did for one of the least of these . . . you did for me" (25:40). It is impossible to get around the fact that the judgment separating the people into sheep and goats is based on how they responded to Christ the King in "the least of these" (25:31–46). This brings up the age-old question about whether we are saved by grace or works.

I mentioned in Book One the differing emphases regarding "original sin" and "total depravity" when it comes to popular Catholic and Protestant Evangelical thought, respectively. Without a "two-totals" placemat framework, Catholic thought tends to view "total depravity" as too comprehensive;

---

38. MacDonald, *Diary of an Old Soul*, 98.

39. We spoke in Book One about Scripture that corroborates the view that we are all sheep belonging to Jesus, the Good Shepherd. For instance, Ps 100:3 says it positively, identifying all who are created as sheep in his pasture, and Isa 53:6 says it implicitly (we cannot be sheep who go astray unless we first belong!).

it desires to maintain at least some vestige of the continuity of human goodness *in spite of* the fall. Meanwhile, the Protestant Evangelical camp often emphasizes discontinuity and human bankruptcy *as a result of* the fall. In this view, "original sin" is not strong enough.

Because of these emphases it is easy to understand the Catholic-Protestant Evangelical tension over the question of grace versus works. Those priding themselves on discontinuity (because of humanity's utter depravity and corruption) sought to emphasize *sola gratia* (grace alone), while those who prided themselves on continuity (because of humanity's innate capacity as created in the image of God) sought to emphasize the human capacity for good works as part and parcel of grace.[40] For instance, those adhering to the Protestant mantra "justification by faith alone" (which is not a direct biblical statement), might find it difficult to onboard Scriptures from James like "faith by itself, if it is not accompanied by action, is dead" (2:17; 2:26), not to mention the more acutely contrastive statement, "a person is considered righteous by what they do, and not by faith alone" (2:24). Much to Karl Barth's chagrin, Martin Luther was famously so threatened by the book of James and its apparent emphasis on works over grace and faith, that he believed it should be jettisoned from the canon![41]

When it comes to Protestant theology, Barth keeps grace, faith, and works together in unprecedented ways. This was recognized by Catholic theologians such as Hans Küng and Hans Urs von Balthasar, the latter featuring prominently in this volume. On the one hand, Barth resisted the wrong kind of continuity, one that exalted a natural point of contact in humanity that could be taken for granted simply by virtue of creation (or the *imago Dei*) and thus provided human capacity apart from Jesus Christ and him crucified. On the other hand, Barth also resisted any form of discontinuity if it meant a human depravity that trumped or displaced the goodness of creation. While tenaciously holding to both humanity's total depravity

---

40. Most non-denominational congregations are within the Protestant Evangelical tradition, so they would fit there. An Evangelical approach, when faced with a beggar, might typically be to get him "saved" first, with the idea that he can turn his life around and not be a beggar, while the first Catholic (or mainline Protestant) response might be to feed the person. I have seen these formally defined by evangelicals as "word-based" and "justice-based" approaches, a fancy way of bifurcating grace and works. Justice-based adherents emphasize gospel embodiment and are often criticized by the other side for their diluted "social gospel." Word-based advocates emphasize gospel preaching and are often criticized by the other side as callous "soul winners."

41. *CD* I/2, 311. For further reference to Barth's criticism of Luther on this score, see *CD* II/2, 589, 592. In the epistle of James, Barth sees the "real Law" where Luther sees only the law seized by the flesh unto disobedience. It is precisely for this reason that Barth cannot agree with Luther about the book of James (*CD* I/1, 457).

and its total righteousness, Barth was keen to show how the needed discontinuity (demonstrated by the cross) served the continuity (the ongoing original goodness of creation). The creation of humanity cannot be understood apart from the crucifixion of humanity, both in Jesus Christ.[42]

Placemat anthropology follows suit against the typical polemic of grace and works, then, not necessarily in a Roman but in a catholic (universal) way. The central idea is that every single human is not only a human being but a being-in-act in the Son of God incarnate. Each person is in the person of Christ, sharing life with the triune persons of God. Thus, each person, at the deepest level, is living not only *to* Jesus Christ but also *from* Jesus Christ. Each person lives in full obedience to the "real Law" (Barth) of loving God and neighbor in him. This is that law in which we are already fully implicated and which we articulated in various ways: the law of Christ, the law of the spirit of life, the "law of the real" (Bonhoeffer), the vicarious humanity of Christ (Torrance), etc.

Of course, this relational dynamic of "total righteousness" that we are given in Christ—every human "living to God"—is not readily apparent. The darkness of the human heart, the depths of our "total depravity," is plainly manifest by deduction. Barth gives us a new definition of grace that does not include the prerequisite of sin: grace is God's truth for humanity in Jesus Christ *from creation on*. It is only in the light of such grace that we properly recognize the deadly gravity of sin.

The Inner Meaning of the Law

The Pentateuch (the first five books of the Judeo-Christian Scriptures) has always been foundational for establishing the law of Moses, the Torah, and for the writings later known as "the prophets."[43] The Apostle Paul had a

---

42. Barth is well-known for his disavowal of "natural theology," but this does not mean that he believed in discontinuity, only the wrong kind of continuity. He vehemently opposed the kind of continuity or "point of contact" that was too easily granted as an innate quality of humanity and therefore one that too easily discounted human depravity. Barth's insight is more easily grasped when we recognize his subversion of the zero-sum spectrum upon which the point-of-contact discussion is usually based. Barth's adherence to total depravity assured that no fraction of human capacity could be allowed. For Barth there is a carefully defined point of contact that is dimensionally understood. It is not spatially understood as a point or even a speck on the zero-sum spectrum. See "Red Wretchedness" (in Book One) and "The Big Picture," below. See Hart, "Capacity for Ambiguity," 139–72.

43. See Matt 22:40. See also the "golden rule" passage: "In everything, do to others what you would have them do to you, for this sums up the Law and the Prophets" (Matt 7:12).

INTRODUCTION

conflicted relationship with the law as a Jew, and yet the law maintained its sacred continuity, despite his reservations. The New Testament did not supersede or supplant the law, as though the Pentateuch was rendered irrelevant by the New Testament. However, following Jesus, Paul, and others, the New Testament does not recognize the law as the Torah without an incarnational interpretation. The primary expression of "law" is found in the vicarious humanity of Jesus Christ for all people, "the law of Christ" (Gal 6:2).

It is to this hidden dynamic of Jesus Christ, "the mystery that has been kept hidden" (Col 1:26) that Paul refers to as the law "written . . . not on tablets of stone but on human hearts" (2 Cor 3:3). Indeed, this is the law of Christ written on every person's heart and to which the "Law and the Prophets" bear witness: "I will put my law in their minds and write it on their hearts. I will be their God, and they will be my people" (Jer 31:33). Jeremiah's last phrase was something that not even God's chosen people Israel could live out consistently, yet what we find in Jeremiah is reference to the one who can and does keep the covenant perfectly from both sides. In the underlying covenant of Jesus Christ for all people—God keeping truth with humanity and humanity keeping truth with God—we make the gospel discovery that Jesus lives to God *for us*, meaning that we are living to God in him.

The underlying law of humanity, then, is what Paul calls *the law of the spirit of life* who has set us free from *the law of sin and death* (Rom 8:2). These two "laws" can be thought of as two simultaneous principles of our lived existence, the in-Christ dimension (living to God) and the anti-Christ dimension (living against God).[44] Returning to our christological premise, we remember Barth's claim that God "first placed Himself under the stern law of the twofold aspect of being. What are all the severity and relentlessness of its contradiction as known and experienced by us in comparison with the relentlessness and severity which He caused to be visited on Himself, on His own heart?"[45]

Just as the incarnate Christ was one person in conflict, Paul is a person in conflict, and each of us is one person in conflict. Not only that, the law

---

44. There is a great temptation to bastardize these two "principles" into some form of natural law. The law of the spirit of life and the law of sin and death are shorthand for so much more than the phrases themselves can represent. We must not (and actually cannot) distill into a principle the personalizing dynamic of the love of Jesus Christ, the person who is operative in all persons and by whom we all in the Son are living to the Father by the Spirit.

45. *CD* III/1, 381.

itself is also in conflict—"placemat conflict."⁴⁶ To the extent that the one Torah is congruent to the dynamic of grace, it takes on its positive form. To the extent that the Torah opposes the dynamic of grace, it takes on its negative form. The Torah then can attest to both the law of the spirit of life or the law of sin and death. The law in its pure form is spiritual, and a blessing to us. But Paul described the law co-opted by the flesh as one that "stood against us and condemned us" (Col 2:14). Regarding this law, Paul could describe it as abolished in the death of Christ (Eph 2:15).

But if we "died to the law" through Christ's death (Rom 7:4), have we lost the continuity of the law that Paul described as good (Rom 7:7, Rom 7:12)? Not at all. Just as the crucifixion Paul claims as his own (Gal 2:20) does not mean the extinguishing of Paul, the abolishment of the law does not mean the extinguishing of the law. In the discontinuity, we have lost the negative aspects of "the letter," but the continuity comes with knowing what has always been there for Israel and for all of us, the gospel of green behind the grey veil. This is where law and gospel are one. This continuity is not, therefore, behind the *red* veil: it is not that the law is bad (red), and the gospel is good (green). The veil is grey and represents the distortion of the green caused by the red. Even "the ministry that brought death, which was engraved in letters on stone," Paul says, "came with glory" (2 Cor 3:7).⁴⁷

46. This conflicted dynamic of the law is laid out in detail in my essay, "Barth's *Simul* at the Heart of Romans: Two Laws and the Gospel." See jeffmcswain.org. Again, the premise is that these two laws of Rom 8:2, the law of the spirit of life and the law of sin and death, do not have anything primarily to do with the Mosaic Law, the Torah, or, more broadly, "the Law and the Prophets." They are instead two contrasting modes or principles in which we are in torque. In his commentary Ellicott describes the "law of the Spirit of life" as that perfect spiritual vitality which includes within itself the pledge of immortality. Meanwhile, the law of sin and death is "the direct contrast to the foregoing. Not here the law of Moses, but the power of sin, the corrupt element in our nature, acting upon the soul and itself erecting a kind of law" (Ellicott's Commentary on Rom 8:2, public domain). See also Käsemann's similar analysis, *Commentary on Romans*. Thanks to Ethan Taylor for the Käsemann reference.

47. In 2 Cor 3 and 4 Paul lays out nothing short of a Trinitarian recalibration of our understanding of the Mosaic law and covenant, giving us a peek behind what has always been there, only veiled. The whole vision is ultimately bracketed by Paul's reciprocal language, in which we can notice the double movement of grace. The covenant kept by Christ from both sides, the God side and the human side, is unveiled. It reveals the following: (1) "the light of the gospel that displays the glory of Christ, who is the image of God" (2 Cor 4:4), signifying Jesus Christ as God, one with the shekinah glory of God, and (2) "God . . . made his light shine in our hearts to give us the light of the knowledge of God's glory displayed in the face of Christ" (2 Cor 4:6), signifying the face of the humanity of Christ, reflecting the splendor of the Father in face-to-face encounter. By grace every human being shares in the glory of the Son who perfectly reflects the glory of the Father. In the light of Christ's face, we see ourselves included in the Abrahamic blessing: "The LORD bless you and keep you; the LORD make his face shine on you

INTRODUCTION

Then, to make sure we don't miss it, Paul doubles down. In a verse startling in its directness (2 Cor 3:8), he states that the ministry of condemnation not only comes with glory, it *is* glorious. How can this be? Has Paul not just previously stated "the letter kills" (2 Cor 3:6)?[48] This is Paul implementing the single subject latitude we have discussed from the beginning of Book One.

There are not two covenants any more than there are two creations. There is no dualism between the old covenant and the new. The gist of this is that the one covenant, like the one person, is in a duplicitous torque. The reason Paul had a conflicted relationship with the law is that the law itself is dimensionally conflicted. In this world, the law is grey. It is totally green and it is totally red. The one law can be all these things. What, then, is its inner meaning? Green. All the law of Christ is in the Mosaic law, even if not all the Mosaic law ("the law and the prophets") is in the law of Christ.

The covenant of green grace was hidden in the Mosaic covenant; all the green was in the grey (such was its glory), but not all of the grey was in the green. It is clear that our placemat principle applies to the law just as it does to every human being.

Allow me to paraphrase this key passage in placemat terms (2 Cor 3:7–11), recognizing the piercing evidence (especially in verse nine) that Paul is thinking dimensionally about the law:

> v.7–8. The grey includes not only full red but also full green, so despite the red, the grey still comes with glory. This is a glory that in this world can only appear to fade away because it is veiled by the flesh (as the green is refracted by the red) but it is green revealed by the Spirit in its fullness.
>
> v.9. I'll state it again more strongly. Because the grey includes the full green, we can even say the grey *is* glorious!
>
> v.10. But again, how much more glorious is the green *alone*. The grey, with its inherent condemnation (because of the red) must give way to the lasting green in which there is no condemnation. So that even if the grey includes full glory, we should not be deceived. It's nothing compared to unadulterated green.
>
> v.11 The grey can't last, even though it came with glory. Meanwhile the glory of green is eternal, surpassing that which cannot be sustained!

---

and be gracious to you" (Num 6:24–25). This is reality without a veil: "And we all, who with unveiled faces contemplate the Lord's glory, are being transformed into his image with ever-increasing glory, which comes from the Lord, who is the Spirit" (2 Cor 3:18).

48. This reminds us of our discussion of Paul's contention that even his mortal body of death reveals life (2 Cor. 4:12). How could this be? Because of P^3. Flesh (sarx) cannot reveal life, but P^2 is not all there is to the equation of Paul's person.

As Paul makes clear (in a way that makes our dimensional theme so crucial), instead of the most egregious error of calling red green (or bad good), our main problem stems from two more insidious errors—a) grabbing the grey and exalting it as completely green (not recognizing that all the green is hidden in what's grey) or b) categorically condemning the grey as completely red (ignoring the hidden green). Attempting to live apart from the revelation that provides sound theological discrimination, we will inevitably misread the law of Moses, the Bible, the human being, even Jesus himself. When we are blind to the red that produces the grey, or, to the green within the grey, the subject effectively becomes to us a monolithic idol in this world, whether it be any of the three *alone*—red, grey, or green. Red does not exist in this world without green, nor green without grey. That's why Paul says the law of Moses, with all its veiled goodness, has become a wrongly grasped idol, issuing forth condemnation and death. The letter kills, just like the flesh. That is why we must keep implementing phrases such as "to the extent" and "relative witness" when rightly handling all the above. These things manifest green and they manifest red to the extent that they do, an extent that is not quantifiable. But this keeps us humble, and wiser biblical interpreters.

Because this chapter in 2 Corinthians functions as perhaps the best scriptural basis for our whole placemat theme, we can deploy our superscripts to help us to apprehend the true meaning of the law. To the extent that L^2 is removed, the grey distortion is gone. When the law is "abolished," then, that which made the law glorious in the first place—the law of Christ, the law of the spirit of life, the "ministry of righteousness" in Christ (2 Cor 3:9, NKJV)—remains. Paul can celebrate the inner meaning of the law (L^1) and the way that the Torah (L^3) bears relative witness to it, despite the fact that, in and of itself (without its inner meaning), the latter is nothing: "the ministry that brought death, which was engraved in letters on stone" (L^2). His antagonism with the written law is purely related to the ways that the law (as L^2) obscures rather than reveals the heart of the gospel (L^1). If it deludes us, for instance, into thinking that God is not love in his inmost being or that God loves some people more than others, it is party to a different kind of red letter: "The letter kills, but the Spirit gives life" (2 Cor 3:6).[49]

49. This can be a sensitive issue. Again, I'm not saying that the law is bad any more than the Bible is bad. But the letter of inerrancy *is* as bad as the letter of Mosaic Law. "Letter," like "flesh," is, for Paul, a pejorative term; in and of themselves (apart from P^1 and P^3) they are both lethal, and they are both opposed to the Spirit. The true law is the law of Christ Jesus himself, the law of the spirit of life, that gives both the law and the Bible their validity and their unique touchstone to reality, "Everything must be fulfilled that is written about me in the Law of Moses, the Prophets and the Psalms" (Luke 24:44, see also John 5:39; John 5:46). It is striking to consider that Jesus, Paul, and we could

INTRODUCTION

A Judgment Based on Works?

With a proper understanding of gospel and law in hand, this volume will ask you to contemplate the biblical expression of a judgment that is based on works. The Protestant-leaning might object: how could there be a judgment based on works without capitulating to a "works-based" salvation? As we established in Book One, grace refuses to separate Christ's person and work, revealing our dynamic participation in the very life of God. It follows that if the truth of Christ's humanity is our humanity, then the works that Jesus Christ is doing and the works that we are therefore doing in him are relationally built into grace. Because Barth's fully integrated being-in-act is not a typical articulation of "works," it is not a legalistic (semi-Pelagian) or burdensome one. As a christological anthropology, it is the gospel of grace that holds together being and act, indicative and imperative, objective and subjective, belonging and believing, even hearing and doing. All of these elements are wrapped together in the ongoing participation of human beings in the person of Jesus Christ. This is what we call the in-Christ dimension of humanity (green). Whatever variegated forms human action may take in other anthropological dimensions (red or grey), Barth insists that all *positive* human action "primarily and decisively must have this dimension."[50]

In a fundamental sense, then, the universal biblical imperatives (e.g., "love your neighbor as yourself"), do not merely describe what we are to do, but also tell us what we are already doing in Christ. Actuality precedes possibility. Outside of Jesus's light yoke, the commandments are burdensome. And grace is not really grace apart from a judgment day that views grace as works and works as grace. Here, law and gospel are not antagonists. The "how" question of keeping these together is found in the answer to the "who" question.

But if grace is that good, and that comprehensive, what is the problem? In placemat terms, the problem is not a diminishment of the green, but the addition of the red, the fullness of red that seeks to rival the fullness given in Christ. The red is so destructive that God himself in Jesus Christ deemed it necessary to give his own life over to destruction in order to rescue us, or extract us, from it. Indeed, as Romans 6:6 describes, "our old self was crucified with him so that the body ruled by sin might be done away with." It is not our created self (green) that needed to be crucified, but our fallen, corrupt self (red). In this "salvation by subtraction," our Savior rid us of the one thing that needed to go in the relation between God and humanity—the

---

all be facing the same adversary when it comes to reading the Scriptures, that of a non-christological hermeneutic. See upcoming reading "The Highest View of Scripture."

50. *CD* III/4, 484.

false self. That is good news, what we will call the goodness of judgment. The gospel of judgment day beckons us to participate by eliminating not just our false selves but all that Christ did not create, all that was crucified with him, including sin, death, and the devil. "The doctrine of the Second Coming," notes C. S. Lewis, "is not to be rejected because it conflicts with our favorite modern mythology. . . . It is the medicine our condition especially needs."[51]

How we read Matthew 25 and passages like 2 Corinthians 5:10 ("For we must all appear before the judgment seat of Christ, so that each of us may receive what is due us for the things done while in the body, whether good or bad") tells us a lot about who we think God is and who we think we are. While the following perspective on God's judgment may perhaps be new, I hope that you will experience it as a liberation, a freeing of your heart of hearts to go forward into the good works that God has prepared in advance for you to do.

Come, Holy Spirit, come.

---

51. Lewis, "World's Last Night," 77.

Introducing Theodicy[1]

I ENDED BOOK ONE with an essay reckoning with the issue of race in America through the lens of placemat anthropology, and we will begin Book Two with another sociohistorical engagement. This essay will discuss some of the themes of the first volume while also introducing a new theological element that is central to the remainder of our study. There will be less mention in this essay of our colors of green, red, and grey. After all, the purpose of the placemat colors is not to get you to see green and red everywhere but to better apply the scriptural and theological principles to real life situations.

If our interpretation of Scripture is close to being correct, and placemat anthropology brings a helpful perspective with which to engage our lives and world, then it will naturally drive us to the theodicy question (the question of God's relation to suffering and evil). It is natural to wonder, "Why did God put us through this? Especially if the end is like the beginning—Why?—why did an all-powerful and all-loving God set it up this way? After such a beautiful start for humanity in Genesis 1, why this 'fatal middle stretch'[2] between creation and consummation? What is God's purpose in allowing the 'god of this age' to blind us? Why, God, did you allow the genocidal ravaging of your chosen people Israel?" If you find yourself asking such questions, then you are on the right track. The following essay sets the tone for our argument in the pages that follow. It anticipates the development of our conclusions as we probe a further conclusion concerning "why the 'why?'" As with themes in the first volume, this essay centers

---

1. Note to reader: After the longer opening essay, the shorter readings which follow are in the same format as Book One, operating somewhat independently without transitional bridges, but meant to move the reader forward all the same. Instead of the readings being about 2,000 words, as in Book One, the readings in this volume are generally around 3,000 words.

2. *CD* III/2, 304. The "fatal middle stretch" is Barth's description of our current realm of existence between creation and the eschaton, or more specifically between the fall and the finish.

on the role of Jesus Christ. He is the compassionate God who shared, and continues to share, the human, "Why, God?" question with us. He not only shares it with us, he contextualizes it, so that in spite of human doubt, anguish, and death, Christ still has the last word.

Careless banality could cause us to turn to the Holocaust time and time again as exhibit A for evil. But in the face of claims that God is good and all-powerful, or that humanity is essentially good, it stands as perhaps the greatest challenge, daring us to think otherwise. If we believe that God is all-loving and all-powerful, and that God's creatures are indeed good, then we must consider these beliefs in relationship with the unspeakable evil that events such as the Holocaust illustrate.

The Prevalence of Evil and the Presence of God
Keeping Depravity in Its Proper Place

A sinful situation is deeply contaminated and dangerous and evil. We tend to minimize sin and ask for its continuance. God sees it clearly and maintains a judgment of impermanence against and on it. A cosmos that contains things like the Holocaust must end.

—Douglas Campbell

"God is on leave." That is the understandable rationale adopted in *The Sunflower* by author Simon Wiesenthal and his Jewish friends. These comrades were caught up in the Nazi machinery of death, horrifically crammed into the dark confines of a concentration camp cell block, where there was nothing left to feel but abandonment. "So one begins to doubt, one begins to cease to believe in a world order in which God has a definite place. One really begins to think that God is on leave. Otherwise the present state of things wouldn't be possible. God must be away. And He has no deputy."[1] For Simon and other Jews at the camp, it seemed against all odds that a good God would tolerate, much less abide in, such a wretched, "godforsaken" environment. "It is impossible to believe anything in a world that has ceased to regard man as man," Simon lamented.[2]

In the midst of a world asking "why?" pain and brokenness appear to be the rule rather than the exception. One reading of the Bible suggests that even in such a world, in lives plagued by darkness, a deeper reality of

---

1. Wiesenthal, *Sunflower*, 9.
2. Wiesenthal, *Sunflower*, 9.

light, hope, and healing exists for every human being. The joy and assurance found in this perspective connect to our awareness of its uniqueness, for it is a conclusion determined only by whittling down the larger question about the prevalence of evil and the presence of God to its essential nub. We must take a hard look at the depravity of human beings and the darkness of sin and evil in the light of a God who, in the words of Dorothy Sayers, "had the honesty and the courage to take His own medicine."[3]

God on Trial

By mysteriously allowing evil into the world, God made himself a target of scorn. And when evil appears unabated, people of faith are confused. The Jews of the Holocaust could certainly empathize with the feelings expressed by their kinsmen long ago:

> Why, LORD, do you stand far off?
> > Why do you hide yourself in times of trouble?
> In his arrogance the wicked man hunts down the weak,
> > who are caught in the schemes he devises. . . .
> His victims are crushed, they collapse;
> > they fall under his strength.
> He says to himself, "God will never notice;
> > he covers his face and never sees." (Ps 10:1–2, 10–11)[4]
>
> The LORD is a God who avenges.
> > O God who avenges, shine forth.
> Rise up, Judge of the earth;
> > pay back to the proud what they deserve.
> How long, LORD, will the wicked,
> > how long will the wicked be jubilant? (Ps 94:1–3)

Many Holocaust Jews who did not lose their lives lost their faith. Wiesenthal relates, "I once read somewhere that it is impossible to break a man's firm belief. If I ever thought that true, life in a concentration camp taught me differently."[5]

This sentiment is echoed by contributors to the *Sunflower* symposium.[6] One of them remembered how "religious belief declined a great deal in the

---

3. Sayers, *Greatest Drama*, para. 4.
4. Scripture quotations are from the NIV (2011).
5. Wiesenthal, *Sunflower*, 9.
6. In the second main section of the *Sunflower* volume, "The Symposium," prominent thinkers and leaders respond to Wiesenthal's questions about human responsibility, justice, and forgiveness.

face of God's silence. A very observant relative of mine who had been preparing himself for the rabbinate before the war was with me in the Plaszow camp. On the day of the selection in May 1944 when the last 280 children remaining in the camp were deported to Auschwitz together with the old people and the sick my cousin said: 'I don't believe in God anymore.'"[7]

Regarding Nazi atrocities, symposium contributors felt pressed to abandon explanations such as "the Divine plan is beyond human understanding," instead asserting "God Himself is among the accused.... Surely, it is not beyond His power to achieve whatever He wants in the world without the near total murder of a people."[8]

For many of the *Sunflower* symposium respondents, no amount of remorse is enough. No one, not even God, can forgive such unforgivable cruelties. As one comments: "Can anyone dare forgive the Nazis, and their helpers, in the name of the hidden and silent God who stood by the Holocaust? . . . The God who had allowed the Holocaust did not, and does not, have the standing to forgive the monsters who had carried out the murders."[9]

Mirroring Evil

In 2002, *Mirroring Evil: Nazi Imagery/Recent Art* debuted as one of the most controversial art exhibitions in memory. One prominent work featured a creative and eerie splicing together of bits of Hitler's speeches; in the video clip, he was made to say, in Hebrew, "Greetings, Jerusalem, I am deeply sorry."[10] The artist, Israeli Boaz Arad, rebuked a common dismissive notion about Hitler that a monster acts like a monster: "My intention is to make Hitler human," Arad says. "It's important to remember that he was a person. The problem is that we see him as a monster, but the greatest danger is to think that Nazis are the Other."[11]

Another exhibit in *Mirroring Evil* featured six "handsome" clay busts of Josef Mengele, the notorious Auschwitz doctor. Menachem Rosensaft, head of the International Network of Children of Jewish Holocaust Survivors, said this in calling for a boycott: "For Holocaust survivors to know that six life-sized busts of Mengele are placed on pedestals in any museum,

---

7. Bejski, "Symposium," in Wiesenthal, *Sunflower*, 115.
8. Hertzberg, "Symposium," in Wiesenthal, *Sunflower*, 167.
9. Hertzberg, "Symposium," in Wiesenthal, *Sunflower*, 167–68.
10. Kimmelman, "Evil, the Nazis," para. 21.
11. Gilerman, "Hitler Mask," para. 7.

let alone in a Jewish museum, is tantamount to having a bust of Osama bin Laden placed at Ground Zero."[12]

While the art in the Jewish Museum exhibition was shocking and controversial, museum officials did not necessarily deem it aesthetically "good." That is not the point, asserted Joan Rosenbaum, the museum's director: "This is art with a message, political art, so we're not talking about aesthetic issues, by and large. It's art that provokes discussion." Rosenbaum continued: "We're endorsing the goals of the work to make us think how easy it is to put distance between our lives in the present and what occurred in the past."[13] The show did much more than narrow the gap historically: it brought the very people they perceived as inhuman "monsters" uncomfortably close to viewers.

"Artists take us to places where we're sometimes not ready to go," said curator Norman Kleeblatt.[14] The show's artists "turned from what has become a standard focus on the often anonymous victims and instead stared directly at the perpetrators," he wrote in the exhibit's catalog. "More important, they created works in which viewers would encounter the perpetrators face to face in scenarios in which ethical and moral issues cannot be easily resolved."[15]

In her *New York Times* article covering the show, "Peering Under the Skin of Monsters," writer Leslie Camhi recalled the story of photographer Lee Miller. At war's end, Miller was billeted for a time in the Führer's confiscated, and seemingly ordinary, apartment. There he found that Hitler "became less fabulous and therefore more terrible."[16] If Hitler's "apology" or the Mengele busts have a way of portraying these men in a more human fashion, the demythologizing aspect must be powerfully disturbing. The curator Kleeblatt observed, "Proximity to the perpetrators makes you rethink who you are."[17]

Eichmann in All of Us?

In the early 1960s a Jew named Yehiel Dinur was called as a prosecution witness in the war crimes trial of one of the masterminds of the Holocaust, Adolf Eichmann. Face to face with Eichmann in the courtroom, Dinur,

---

12. Quoted in Selby, "Holocaust Show," para. 7.
13. Quoted in Kimmelman, "Jewish Museum," para. 11.
14. Quoted in Swanson, "Jewish Museum's Holocaust," para. 10.
15. Quoted in Kimmelman, "Jewish Museum," para. 14.
16. Camhi, "Peering Under the Skin," para. 2.
17. Quoted in Camhi, "Peering Under the Skin," para. 2.

who had survived the brutal horrors of Auschwitz, suddenly rose in the midst of his testimony, let out a great cry, and collapsed. Why? Was it the hatred? Was it the emotional remembrance of his many murdered friends? No, Dinur said later in a *60 Minutes* interview with Mike Wallace. What struck him in the courtroom was the recognition that Eichmann was not a scaly red devil; he was a human being just like himself. In that moment, Dinur said, he realized the potential within any person to commit those same atrocities. Dinur summarized memorably: "Eichmann is in all of us."[18]

Now, Dinur did not want us to employ some twisted logic to excuse the Nazis for the Holocaust or make the perpetrators of atrocities indistinguishable from their victims. We must refuse the idea that all sins are equal in gravity or that criminals should not be pursued and dealt with appropriately. But as we stand before our own mirrors, must we not acknowledge that we are in solidarity with the first humans and with one another under sin? Must we not admit that we are all victims of evil but also perpetrators of it, each with not only a potential for sin but also a *propensity* for it?

The Jewish museum and Dinur's testimony take small steps in the daring direction of exposing the evil in every person. And yet, there is a deeper, often hidden reflection in that same mirror. That reflection is God's image—the Jew, Jesus Christ—the one in who all humans are created (Eph 2:10) and exist (Col 1:17). Jesus Christ is not only the Creature, Scripture tells us (Col 1:16), he is also the creature who as Creator enters the human condition (Heb 2:14–18). He is not ashamed to call us his brothers and sisters (Heb 2:11). It is this fellow human being whom the prophet Isaiah foresaw as the Man of Sorrows. It is this human being who also felt abandoned by his heavenly Father when suffocated by darkness. It is this Jewish man who cried, "My God, my God, why have you forsaken me?" (Matt 27:46; Mark 15:34; cf. Ps 22:1) as he entertained most poignantly the experience that God was "on leave."

The Greatest Sinner

Any victim's association with *the* victim, Jesus Christ, does not seem to provide much consolation at first glance. What difference does it make if this person can commiserate with me, sympathize—or even empathize—with me? Jesus Christ's solidarity with us, however, is not simply "in kind," one human like other humans; his solidarity with us is "in being." This is

---

18. Colson, "BreakPoint," para. 7–12. See also Green, "This Day in Jewish History," para. 6–7.

possible because Jesus Christ is not only a singular human being but also the very being of God.[19]

The Incarnate One *is* the image in whom we are created. There is an intimate unity, a oneness of being without conflation between the humanity of God (Jesus Christ) and every person everywhere. This means that the suffering and pain Jesus feels is not *like* ours, it *was and is* ours. God stings with the wounds of injustice and abuse, he bears the full extent of every generational curse, and he knows the pain that prods the perpetrator; his assumption of our broken and guilty humanity has real consequences—suffering and death.

In the incarnation we discover a loving God who willingly assumed the fate of the fallen—every victim and every perpetrator. In fact, we can say that this Jew, Jesus Christ, is the greatest of victims, because his suffering included every human being's suffering. We can also say that, while never himself the agent of evil, Christ was in the end the greatest of perpetrators, because he assumed every person's guilt and shame as his own, crucified in our place as a convicted criminal.[20] We can trust God to identify with us

---

19. Jesus of Nazareth could easily have been a dark-skinned Jew, or perhaps a Black man. His solidarity with the oppressed minorities everywhere is incontestable. His plight as a particular, indigenous person under Roman oppression, and in the face of racist and inhumane injustice, is like that of many others screaming for liberation over the centuries. Without ontology, however, "solidarity" can only go so far. To be *like* others who are oppressed, perhaps even intimately associated with them by like circumstances, falls short of the ontological solidarity that Jesus provides in the truth of the incarnation. And if we give that ontological solidarity to every person, we must give it to victims and perpetrators alike. Liberation theology that begins with Jesus's ontological solidarity with oppressed and oppressor is one that is most strongly rooted and armed with the greatest potential for disruption and displacement in the name of gospel justice. *Because* the gospel declares that Jesus is for oppressors *and* the oppressed, he is against oppressors and *for* the oppressed. While Barth's ontological perspective strengthens the constructive voice of liberation theology in the world, I would much rather be a liberation theologian without Barth than a "Barthian" without the social justice concerns of liberation theology. Allan Boesak says it well: "for theology to be true to the gospel it has to favor the interests of the poor": in Petersen, *On Reading Karl Barth*, x–xi. See also Taylor, *What Did Jesus Look Like?*

20. Luther's description comes to mind: "All the prophets did foresee in spirit, that Christ should become the greatest transgressor, murderer, adulterer, thief, rebel, blasphemer, etc., that ever was . . . for he being made a sacrifice, for the sins of the whole world, is not now an innocent person and without sins . . . our most merciful Father . . . sent his only Son into the world and laid upon him the sins of all men, saying: Be thou Peter that denier; Paul that persecutor, blasphemer and cruel oppressor: David that adulterer, that sinner which did eat the apple in Paradise; that thief which hanged upon the cross: and, briefly, be thou the person which hath committed the sins of all men." Luther, *Commentary*, 188.

(and indict us) as perpetrators precisely because he first identified with us as victims. God knows his children completely—and understands.

We began by noting that God made himself "a target of scorn" because of his silence in the face of evil; with Simon Wiesenthal and others in *The Sunflower*, we may have concluded that "God Himself is among the accused." We were talking then about a God who was aloof and seemed absent, but little did we imagine that these same phrases would describe a God who is not only transcendent but immanent. A target of scorn? Yes, but a target of scorn in our midst, humiliated and abused, a brother sharing our plight. Standing among the accused? Yes, but one who was not ashamed to take on corrupt flesh and be numbered with the transgressors, even though he did no wrong.

This is what Dorothy Sayers meant in speaking of a God who would "take His own medicine"[21]: in Jesus Christ, God swallows the consequences of all the evil that God mysteriously allowed. In the humanity of *God*, God suffers not only in Jesus's personal plight but actually experiences *every* human being's specific hurt from *every* specific act perpetrated by or against another. In a way that only God can do, Jesus identifies so deeply with every perpetrator that he is able to offer a confession of sin more thorough than anyone offers for oneself even without committing wrong. At the same time, he identifies so thoroughly with every victim that he is able to offer a deeper word of forgiveness than anyone can offer one's offender. In fact, we could say that any evil that has been done by another human being has been done first and foremost to Jesus, and he therefore has the original and fundamental prerogative to forgive. This principle applies also to situations where one party—the victim or perpetrator—is dead or inaccessible, where words of forgiveness or confession are impossible. The life of Christ overcomes and supersedes such natural barriers for the sake of reconciliation. Thus, Jesus Christ is the reference point for all things human, even in the realm of giving and receiving forgiveness.[22]

What this means for us is that Christ is not only able to define righteousness for us but also to define sin. Christ defines sin, not by committing it, but by delimiting it. By *becoming* sin, he set sin's boundaries. There are no spillovers that he has not already absorbed and dealt with, no new avenues of attack that we need fear. The fact that there is no sin outside Christ's incarnate assumption means that there is no human, no matter how fallen, who can fall outside the boundary.

---

21. Sayers, *Greatest Drama*, para. 4.
22. See Alan Torrance, "Theological Grounds."

The consequences of this are manifold, but Jesus's oneness of being with God, and his oneness of being with us, mean that we can be assured of God's love for evil persons because each one of us is wrapped up in God's humanity. Romans 5:18 testifies that God's unconditional embrace of human beings is beyond sentimental; it is redemptive. It reads as follows: "Consequently, just as one trespass resulted in condemnation for all people, so also one righteous act resulted in justification and life for all people." It is redemptive because corrupt humanity remains wrapped up in Christ's being through his death and on into his resurrection, each of us thereby dying and being born anew in him (2 Cor 5:14–19; Rom 6:5–8; 1 Pet 1:3).

We must not lose sight of the fact that God's redemption of humanity includes a cross, where God deals severely with humanity's rebellion. In the work of Christ, we see that the consuming passion of God's self-giving love includes a wrath that will not tolerate the least bit of evil. The judgment harkened for by the Psalmist ("Rise up, Judge of the earth," 94:2) arrives unexpectedly. By his death and resurrection the Judge both damns the wicked and *justifies* the wicked (Rom 4:5), all within his very person. God's way of redemption reminds us that punishment is no substitute for victory, that God's judgment is fundamentally about restoration, not retribution. It is through the death of every perpetrator—each one of us—that God's re-creating love for every victim—each one of us—is fulfilled.

Past Dualism to Duality

One of the concentration camp internees featured in *The Sunflower* remarked, "I am prepared to believe that God created a Jew out of [a] tear-soaked clod of earth, but do you expect me to believe He also made our camp commandant, Wilhaus, out of the same material?"[23] It is an important question, and the simple answer is, "no." There is no way that any of us could expect a concentration camp internee to be less than incredulous over any claim of solidarity between himself and a Nazi tyrant. In the face of any atrocity, a polarized understanding of evil is to be expected, pitting inhuman perpetrators and innocent, helpless victims against one another in a sharply divided form. In such a dichotomy, it would be cruelly inhumane to press survivors to see themselves as anything but victims.

It is also helpful to recognize how clear-cut situational lines can morph into artificial categories. The power of relativism ("My sin is not as bad as your sin") is so strong as to harden quickly into dualism ("I am righteous; you are wicked"). To find a Judeo-Christian perspective that goes beyond

---

23. Wiesenthal, *Sunflower*, 6.

this relativism, we need go no further than Ps 130:3: "If you, LORD, kept a record of sins, Lord, who could stand?" Yet despite this scriptural antidote to our natural tendencies, we must admit that the Psalms also offer an abundance of "us" (the righteous) versus "them" (the wicked) language. Such tensions seem to pose an unresolvable contradiction.

We can find some resolution, or at least relaxation of the tension, in the Apostle Paul. In Romans 3, Paul could not be more forceful in excluding the above dualism. Reinterpreting the Psalms in their proper light, Paul's Christo-centric perspective not only de-relativizes sin ("for all have sinned and fall short of the glory of God," v. 23) but also de-relativizes redemption ("and all are justified freely by his grace through the redemption that came by Christ Jesus," v. 24). It is the redemption of all in Jesus Christ (v. 24) that gives us the healthiest frame for understanding our depravity (v. 23). Only when we are given the fresh air of deliverance by grace can we recognize the stench of sin and take it with adequate seriousness.[24]

As we shall see, the key to letting the person of Jesus Christ inform our humanity is understanding that Jesus has as much to do with Romans 3:23 as Romans 3:24. Jesus defeated sin, not by rising above it, but by becoming it; he destroyed death, not by avoiding it, but by enduring it. And he did all this to prove that God can become all that we are in our depravity yet still remain himself.

Keeping depravity in its proper place in Christ is the only way we can see just how terrible our sin is without being crushed by it. At the cross, we apprehend the full extent of sin's devastating and destructive effects. Attempting to view sin outside this redemptive context is self-defeating, because we will inevitably define sin sinfully. We will "spin" our image to cover up our wickedness or to get ourselves off the hook in an all-out effort to evade the consequence of death.

But if our depravity and its consequences are contained in Christ, we do not have to rationalize or excuse our sin in order to survive. We can deal squarely with the heinousness of our depravity, because we are given something much better than a pat on the head and a pardon. We are given redemption—a redemption that includes our death and resurrection *in Christ's* death and resurrection and the gift of participating in his life by the power of the Holy Spirit. The justification of the wicked entails the death of

---

24. That is why the common evangelical practice of pulling Rom 3:23 away from 3:24 is so grievous; it asks us to make a decision about sin while imprisoned within it (at least, as the sequence would have it, in effect making sin the foundational truth and deliverance merely the exception to the rule). By making sin and righteousness contingent on the "if" of a decision, this unfortunate paradigm relativizes both (see the reading in Book One, "The Righteous and the Wicked").

our evil selves with Christ; to say otherwise only cheapens grace and risks obviating the cross. Alternatively, sound Christology leads us to Jesus as the reference point for all things good or evil.

With this perspective, it follows that we should be wary of any ideology that speaks of humanity as inherently good without mention of Christ. Beware, too, its opposite—an approach that talks about original sin apart from "original belonging," our good creation in Christ. Just as there is no human evil outside the boundary of Christ's death, there is no human good outside the reality of Christ's life. It is an awareness of our inclusion in Christ's death and resurrection that allows us to apprehend the duality of our lives. In one sense, we are all depraved—guilty and broken. In another sense, we are all innocent and whole—"holy in his sight, without blemish, and free from accusation" (Col 1:22) via our union with Jesus Christ. We are righteous by virtue of the One in whom we are created and, despite our wicked ways, re-created.[25]

Where the Ground Is Level

Sin never was nor will it ever be our ultimate identity, despite our complicity in the fall of Adam. We always and already belong to another, the Second Adam.[26] And if there was ever any doubt, Jesus's death and resurrection clearly relegated evil to a parasitic and terminal status. The cross of Christ, in light of the resurrection, shows that although evil threatens to deface and eclipse the presence of God in the world, that is all it can really do in the end—threaten. We cannot know the extent of evil and suffering, but we can know that there was and is a defined extent to it. Good Christology is what helps keep human depravity in its proper context. It gives us the assurance that when we feel forsaken by God, such experience does not encompass the greater reality despite how crushing it may be. Far from dualism, then, Christ offers us a paradigm to interpret each singular person's life in this

---

25. I side with Augustine, Calvin, Luther, Barth, and others who claim that Rom 7 signifies a real Christian struggle. It would be a mistake to classify the solidarities as static categories; there are two slaveries going on in Rom 7, compelling us in two opposite directions. It is the asymmetrical nature of the solidarities, the Second Adam trumping the first, which keeps the struggle from being a Manichean tug-of-war. And, of course, Paul in Rom 8 will emphasize the Holy Spirit's role in lifting us up to participate in the proper direction, i.e., out of the truth of our union with Christ as children of the Father.

26. "Always" because through the Second Adam and our re-creation in him, we finally grasp how we were originally created.

THE PREVALENCE OF EVIL AND THE PRESENCE OF GOD

world as a matrix of two simultaneous dimensions. By the Spirit, we are given to know that only one is ultimately real and eternal.

In "the present evil age" (Gal 1:4), darkness often appears unabated and primary; that is why the community of faith is so critical. Walking in the light, living by faith and not by sight, the counter-cultural practices of the Christian community are meant to be done together in the power of the Holy Spirit. In community we may help each other cling tenaciously to the truth of God's presence in the most hellacious of circumstances. We may bravely call out sin when we see it in our lives and in our society, because we know more than ever that it does not belong. And we may encourage each other when overtaken by shadows, pointing toward the only one who can fully relate to the darkness—the Jew, Jesus, the Suffering Servant, and the oppressed victim who endured the most excruciating silence of the Father and who, of all humans, entertained most poignantly the notion that God "is on leave."[27]

I say "we may" do these things because we also may not. Languishing in a world of stifling oppression, some of us will struggle all our days; things may not get any better on this side of the veil. Our God, the one who really understands and overcomes, knows we might lose sight of his overcoming. Even if we lose our faith and cannot discern the light, God understands that, too. In drinking all evil and human brokenness to the dregs, Jesus identified with all our twisted notions, our deepest doubts, and our nagging questions. And while he does not provide answers now, he provides an Answer in himself to hold us over until that day when all becomes clear.[28]

It is a deep consolation to know that all human depravity and the brokenness of our world is contained in our brother-Savior. His cry, "My God, my God, why have you forsaken me?" gathers up our cries of abandonment and places them safe inside the arms of a loving God who will never leave us or forsake us. Jesus Christ is our burden-bearing God. In his person, he

---

27. J. Kameron Carter emphasizes in *Race* that we cannot allow our understanding of Christ as the Second Adam, the human being in whom all human beings are included, to overshadow the singular existence of the Jew Jesus, a Palestinian man of the first century who was marginalized, oppressed, abused, and ultimately killed unjustly. In fact, asserts Carter, we can only leave behind the "tyrannical logic of racialization" through the Jewish flesh of Jesus of Nazareth, "a calling and a promise that Christ instantiates and through him the world enters." Drawing on Maximus the Confessor, Carter outlines the manner "in which Scripture repositions bodies inside the social space of Christ's Jewish flesh . . . being drawn into the socio-theological space of his body . . . a new body politic" (366).

28. For this notion that even our questions about God are comprehended in the incarnational humanity of Jesus, I give credit to T. F. Torrance. See "Questioning in Christ," in Torrance, *Theology in Reconstruction*, 117–27.

is the "balm in Gilead." For all of us victims, he *makes the wounded whole.* For all of us perpetrators, he *heals the sin-sick soul.*

As we stand together at the foot of the cross, the temptation to categorize humanity into two separate camps begins to fall away. It is the love of God for every human being that finally assures us of God's love for each one of us—for *me*. And there, where the ground is level, those other words of Jesus from the cross—"Father, forgive them, for they do not know what they are doing" (Luke 23:34)—may be heard by all of us as *for* all of us as well. Only when we have ears to hear will we be free to confess that we human beings are alike in solidarity under sin and yet, most deeply, under grace. And as awakened children, with eyes wide open to the radiant mercies of God, our lives may take on a tenor of worship and gratitude.

The good news of Easter is that Jesus has given us his resurrection righteousness and taken our sin to his grave. To misplace depravity—putting it on others to the exclusion of ourselves (self-righteousness) or on ourselves to the exclusion of Christ (self-condemnation)—is to damn ourselves. Indeed, to reject the truth of Jesus Christ about our righteous-evil selves is to make hell the greatest of ironies, where supposed self-fulfillment becomes the ultimate in self-denial. But to hear and respond to the gospel is to understand the prevalence of evil, and our deepest pain, inside the presence and person of a loving God, the God who saves by comprehending all the dueling aspects of our human existence in the duality of his own.

PART FIVE

Jesus Is My Heaven

Note to reader: The "readings" under each "Part" function as mini-essays within an overriding theological direction. Instead of a strictly linear development (where transitions between chapters are paramount), this allows me to come at the topic from different angles and to slowly advance my thesis through a progression of "spirals."

56

First-Heaven Problems

God wants us to understand and to believe that we are more truly in heaven than on earth.

—Julian of Norwich

Where is this heaven? The answer is that it is where Christ is.

—Karl Barth

[K]eep in mind that all the way to heaven is heaven. Heaven is within you. The kingdom is here and now.

—Dorothy Day

One reason I am drawn to Barth's theology is that it does not shy away from confronting the sin, evil, and terror of this world despite its abundance of hope. Half of Barth's magisterial *Church Dogmatics* was written after World War II. Returning to his native Switzerland after Hitler's rise in Nazi Germany, Barth continued writing and teaching as he, along with the rest of the world, saw evil rear its ugly head in the most graphic of ways.[1] And yet,

---

1. As Edward Lowe reminds me, Barth was arrested and deported by the Gestapo after numerous offenses against Nazism and the Third Reich, coupled with the withdrawal of the full support of the Confessing Church. Busch, *Great Passion*, 34.

without dodging the contradiction, Barth was undeterred as a champion of God's love and grace. For Barth, the kingdom of God is ever-present and closer to us than we are to ourselves, despite all evidence to the contrary.

It is difficult to think of ourselves as fully wicked. Some of us may go through our entire lives without meeting a single person we would describe as abjectly evil. Perhaps it is easier to distance ourselves from the evil within when we are not immediately confronted, as was Barth, by the great evils of war and mass violence. We could understand why Barth was deeply concerned about any self-diagnosis of overall human health. The "wolf" is "latently operative" in all people, he asserts, and therefore the most "dangerous neighborhood" is the whitewashed one where people point to isolated cases of wrongdoing as a way of self-justifying and disassociating from the proper and universal theological indictment.[2]

Shortly after the war, Barth reflected on Jesus's inner-connection between hate and murder (Matt 5:21–22), and that murder in its "preliminary form" exists in all persons. He continues:

> In most of us the murderer is suppressed and chained, possibly by the command of God, or possibly by no more than circumstances, convention, or the fear of punishment. Yet he is very much alive in his cage, and ready to leap out at any time. . . . Even if we had not already heard it from Dostoevsky, the experiences of our own day have surely taught us that we can no longer have any illusions as to what is dormant even in the heart of the average man in this respect. The presence of this sinister factor, of the "Hitler within us," can be verified in almost all of us by occasional dreams.[3]

Barth concludes with two statements that sum up our entire project:

1. First, "There exists in man a very deep-seated and *almost original* evil readiness and lust to kill. The common murderer or homicide is simply the one in whom the wolf slips the chain "

2. Second, while Barth uses "almost original" to describe just how "deep-seated" this depravity is, it is nevertheless related asymmetrically to an even deeper and truly original human righteousness: "Moreover, the point has also to be considered that no single man and therefore no criminal is identical with the indwelling wolf. It is not his nature. It belongs to the corruption of his nature."[4]

2. CD III/4, 414–15.

3. CD III/4, 413.

4. CD III/4, 413–14. See Ferencz, *Nuremburg Prosecutor*. Ferencz, a retired Jewish

The fall of 2025 will mark fifteen years since my publishing of *Movements of Grace: The Dynamic Christo-Realism of Barth, Bonhoeffer and the Torrances*. I came up with the term Christo-realism as a way of navigating between two non-christological types of "realism." On one hand, "Christian Realism" (popularized by Reinhold Niebuhr) starts with the harsh and brutal reality of this world and shows how Christian ethics might help us to navigate such a reality. In so doing it makes grace the exception to the rule of sin, and wholeness the exception to the rule of brokenness. "Christian Realism" therefore ironically has as its starting point an under-realized eschatology. Discontinuity (brokenness) gets the nod over the reality of continuity (wholeness).

On the other hand, if Niebuhr's Christian realism put too much emphasis on immanence, Plato's dualist-realism put too much emphasis on transcendence. Because the reality of the ideal Platonic realm is located above and running parallel to our existence, the best we get in this world are shadows indicating these transcendent universals. The incarnation of the transcendent-immanent Jesus Christ confounds both definitions of reality. Jesus Christ is "one being with the Father" (Nicene Creed) above and below, below and above. This is the case even when the Word became sin unto death. The discontinuity is taken deadly seriously, but not at the expense of the continuity.

Our Nicene conviction about the God who became incarnate cannot indulge an over-realized eschatology where the "already" dimension of Kingdom fullness compromises the contingent humanity of God in created, fallen, time and space. Transcendent and immanent reality are integrated anthropologically, even in the face of cosmic evil powers, deep suffering, and our sinful worst. In other words, contrasting elements of our false humanity (red) and our true humanity (green) in this world are not parallel to one another, but exist *in one space*, dimensionally. This means that not only is Christ in the Father, above and below, but we also are one with Christ,

---

attorney, is the last living prosecutor from the Nuremberg Trials, where he sought and attained capital war crimes convictions of Nazi officers. Despite his vast personal knowledge and experience, Ferencz is an indubitable believer in the goodness of human nature and has been dismissed as crazy or idealistic for his counterintuitive conviction. Reflecting years later he remarked, "these men would have never been murderers had it not been for the war. These were people who could quote Goethe, who loved Wagner, who were polite." For Ferencz, "war makes murderers out of otherwise decent people." Even while engaged in acts of savagery, said Ferencz, "man is not a savage. . . he's a patriotic human being acting in the best interests of his country." Concludes Ferencz, "Do you think the man who dropped the bomb on Hiroshima was a savage?" (from a *60 Minutes* interview with Leslie Stahl, "What the Last Nuremberg Prosecutor Alive"). Ferencz maintains the important asymmetrical superiority of human goodness, even if he fails to simultaneously maintain the total wickedness of humanity.

above and below: "you are of Christ, and Christ is of God" (1 Cor 3:23). If we can say that the incarnation reflects a move from heaven to earth, we can also say that our understanding of human beings on this earth starts with our understanding of the one human being who came *from* heaven.

The medieval mystic Julian of Norwich was fond of saying "Jesus is my heaven." Her phrase may seem unusual if we on earth consider the ascended Jesus to be merely *in* heaven. Or maybe we imagine that Jesus is in our hearts, and heaven is "up there." Julian's expression is a subjective one, but it carries objective truth beyond the words of a medieval mystic. Jesus is not just Julian's heaven. Jesus is *your* heaven. Wherever Jesus is, heaven is. In initiating his earthly ministry, he said as much: The kingdom of heaven is here, in you, amongst you (see Luke 17:21).

In Scripture, the phrases "kingdom of heaven" and "kingdom of God" function synonymously. This kingdom exists wherever the king is, defying relegation to a spatial location. Indeed, even where the king's authority is not recognized, the kingdom is present everywhere *to be recognized*. The fact that Jesus tells even his enemies that the kingdom of God is within them shows that the kingdom is not limited by human awareness. Now that Christ has come to reveal it to us, we can recognize the kingdom of heaven as the in-Christ dimension of our world and lives. We are meant to live into it, precisely because it is already here.

Even though Jesus declared the already-present nature of the kingdom of heaven, the concept remains counter-intuitive. In the "Lord's Prayer," after all, earth and heaven seem spatially distinct—"on earth as it is in heaven" (Matt 6:10). However, we can consider the Lord's prayer dimensionally instead of spatially. Thus, we pray for the dimension of "the heavens and the earth" as they are created to be (Gen 1:1), and as they will be revealed to be "a new heaven and a new earth" (Rev 21:1), to come to bear on our current existence such that the goodness of the created order—the glory, justice, and shalom of the heavenly kingdom—might be manifest in our midst in powerful and palpable ways. Von Balthasar elaborates: "Many Christians fail to grasp that the reality of the kingdom of heaven is eternal and thus not temporally 'future.' What, in prayer, we yearn for, the 'coming' for which we plead, is not something as yet nonexistent, something we have to introduce into our existing life by means of prayer and effort, like other temporal and historical values. It is the eternally Real."[5]

The beauty of the Lord's prayer grows when we think about the intimate mutual coinherence of earth and heaven, the nearness of us to heaven, and heaven to us. As we will see in the next reading, heaven and earth are

---

5. Von Balthasar, *Prayer*, 104.

distinct, like two sides of the same coin, but not in the same way we are accustomed to imagine.

We typically think of heaven as a place above where there are no tears, no pain, no sorrow. There are no problems there, and yet we have all these things here on "earth" in abundance. How then can we call our existence here "heaven?" Again, because we are adopting Julian's definition of the kingdom of heaven, i.e., that heaven is wherever Jesus is present. If heaven's location is only "up there," it would make no sense to pray a prayer that asked for God's will to be done on earth as it is in heaven. If Jesus, by his Spirit, is always among us, and if we are going to maintain that in some sense heaven is here, it must be a different dimension of heaven. This is why we will refer to this sphere of our existence as "the first heaven," and all of the problems we face here "first-heaven problems."[6] Though "problems" is surely an understatement in comparison to some of the world's horrific evils, it is also an overstatement in relation to many other, smaller inconveniences we must endure. "Problems" covers everything "red," or all that is not created by God and therefore not called good by God. In the good creation of Genesis 1, there are no problems.

We must recognize heaven as a dimension of even this problematic world. Otherwise, we forget that Jesus is with us right now, even during all the pain and heartache. With the heart of Jesus, we long to "make things right" in the world because in one sense (underestimated by Niebuhr) they *are* right. Jesus Christ's heavenly presence is the one constant that we have, a personal, continual presence that endures the darkness and outlasts all the problematic aspects of our existence. "The Creator Himself willed to endure, and has endured, and still endures, the contradiction in creaturely life,"[7] relates Barth. "For the love of us, God has made the problem of existence His own."[8]

> The self-revelation of God as our Creator consists in the fact that in Jesus Christ He gives Himself to us to be recognised as the One who has made our cause His own before it was or could be ours, who does not stand aloof from the contradiction of our being as a stranger, who has willed to bear it Himself, and has in

---

6. Since we are making such a big deal about the relationship between heaven and earth being a non-contrastive unity-in-reality, we could technically designate the first heaven as the "first heaven and earth," which, in placemat terms, would be synonymous with the "new heaven and new earth."

7. *CD* III/1, 380.

8. *CD* III/1, 382.

fact borne it from all eternity. *Thus it is not we who have discovered the problem of existence.*[9]

In our approach, we see the first heaven as the place where joy (green) and sorrow (red) are woven fine, the grey zone of our existence and our existential problems. What we have called the "unadulterated" sphere is what Paul describes as "the third heaven" (2 Cor 12:2). That is the sphere without the problems—paradise without a placemat. Now, if the first heaven is "here" and the third heaven is "there," the second heaven is "neither here nor there," but in between. It is what the Bible calls the day—the day of judgment. Contrary to common understandings, this is a day to which we can look forward. We do not yet fully experience it in the "here and Now," but we must go through it to get to the "there and Then." If the first heaven is marked by contradiction and confusion, the second is marked by contradiction (still) *with* clarity, and the third heaven is the realm of clarity without contradiction, total peace and shalom in Christ by the Spirit. To repeat,

First heaven: contradiction and confusion

Second heaven: contradiction and clarity,

Third heaven: clarity without contradiction.

These three heavenly dimensions are theological locations. They are all "heaven," as determined by Jesus's presence in all three (indeed, it is unlikely that we will ever feel closer to Jesus than we do at judgment day), and they are all distinct because, aside from Jesus's consistent presence, the environments are different.

Like true and false humanity, the three heavens are dimensional, not sequential, even if describing them sequentially is the easiest way to grasp them.[10] And, as with the dimensions of true and false humanity, the sequence

---

9. *CD* III/1, 381 (emphasis added). Yes, Barth continues here, "the problem of existence is integral to us. But we must also confess that it was primarily and essentially God's own problem and only then and as such our own, so that it cannot be solved by us, but we have to recognise that it is solved by God. . . . That he stands surety for us in making the problem of existence His own affair . . . ." As in Book One, Romans 7 will continue to be important to our study. Here we see the epitome of the personal existential dilemma. Barth writes, "At the very height of his apostolic career Paul can and must write in the present tense and in personal terms a passage like Rom 7:7–25, in which the contradiction in his existence is plainly to be seen in all its menace" (*CD* IV/3.1, 210). Barth's comment above that "it is not we who have discovered the problem of existence" keeps us from disconnecting the human angst of Romans 7 from the experience of God incarnate.

10. "Time and space," remarked Einstein, "are modes by which we think and not conditions in which we live." Quoted in Forsee, *Albert Einstein*, 81.

of Christ's death and resurrection does interpret the simultaneous, dimensional situation. Because of Christ's death and resurrection sequence, we can know that there is a difference between the third heaven (with no contradiction) and the first and second heavens. If the three heavens were collapsed into one another, then contradiction and corruption would enter into the environment of the unadulterated third heaven. There is no good news in that. Instead, hearkening back to our placemat phraseology, we can say that all of third heaven is in the first and second, but not all of the first and second heavens are in the third (thankfully). Barth knew that it would be difficult to understand simultaneous dimensions of eternity unless there was a provisional device. Following suit, the reader has full permission at this point in our journey to consider the three heavens as functionally sequential.[11]

The day of judgment—one and the same as the "day of the Lord"—represents the borderland dimension we will call the second heaven. We will allude to some of the passages in Scripture that refer to this critical day, variously called "the day," "the day of the Lord," "the day of Christ." In the pages that follow, we will discuss the second-heaven concept from different angles and through the use of many different metaphors. These illustrations are not meant to build on each other, as if offering a comprehensive picture of the second heaven. Instead, they are simply ways of describing a drastically overlooked location in our spiritual journey, "the day" of judgment.

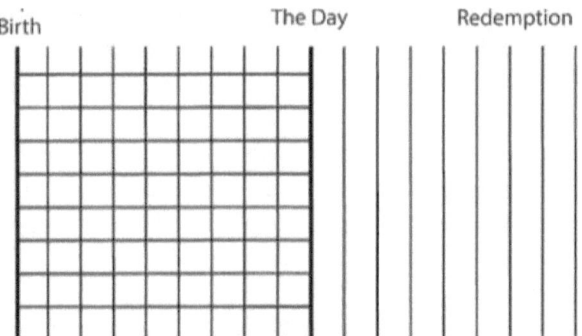

11. Barth used the terms pre-temporal eternity, supra-temporal eternity, and post-temporal eternity. My three heavens template for placemat anthropology does not align perfectly with Barth's three eternities, mostly because they are staggered differently (Barth's supra-temporal, for instance, while listed second here, is our first heaven). They are similar, however, in the sense that they involve three simultaneous dimensional concepts that are not usually nuanced or parsed, i.e., we don't usually think of the dimensions of "eternity" and "heaven." See *CD* II/1, 608 ff., "The Eternity and Glory of God," e.g., 631: "there can be no basic rivalry with regard to the three forms of eternity. The conceptions of God's pre-temporality, supra-temporality, and post-temporality have all to be emphasized in their different ways. But they are not to be played off one against the other."

PART FIVE: JESUS IS MY HEAVEN

First heaven ("Now"): Contradiction and confusion

Second heaven ("the day"): Contradiction and clarity

Third heaven ("Then"): Clarity without contradiction

Whereas Book One started us off in the green, Book Two begins in the fallen, checkered grey-zone. This is the realm of Genesis 2–3, the first heaven. It is the first heaven because it is *first in our experience*, our first impression in the world and of the world. The first heaven is where we are born. It is where we live. It is where we die. The first heaven is essentially human existence from the womb to the tomb. While we began the human narrative before the Genesis "garden" in Book One, we begin Book Two with humanity in the conflicted garden of the first heaven, where there are already many problems and where Adam and Eve are deceived by the serpent to know good by evil instead of evil by good.

With the big picture of our creation in Book One, we can see how the red is an exception to the green. Born amid the grey, we are unsurprisingly discombobulated and confused, constantly getting it backwards. Here in the placemat world, with the red relentlessly glaring, the green appears to be the exception *to the rule*. In actuality, our experiences of the green in this world are exceptions that *prove the rule*. By this we mean that what looks small and marginalized here witnesses to the hidden, big picture of truth.

It is an adjustment to imagine heaven as a present dimension of life, especially if we think of heaven as "up there" or as separate from the bad stuff. Jesus proclaimed that the kingdom of heaven is here, revealed in his person. He said this despite all the bad that he endured in his un-kingdom-like earthly plight. Jesus walked the dusty roads of Palestine and fully entered the human experience with family, friends, and enemies. He suffered and died. After rising miraculously from the grave, the one who called himself the Truth reminded us that his Spirit, the Spirit of Truth (John 14:17) and the Spirit of Christ (Rom 8:9), will keep him just as present to us now as he ever was.[12] "I am always with you," he said at his ascension (Matt 28:20). His

---

12. Romans 8:9b can easily be misunderstood: "And if anyone does not have the Spirit of Christ, they do not belong to Christ." This is not Paul's way of excluding anyone. On the contrary, his meaning is this: "I would not even be talking with you unless you belonged to Christ and were indwelt by the Spirit." The intent is to show the oneness of Son and Spirit and, especially, to show that the spiritual life of each person is not merely a future thing. Barth notes that verse 9a, "You, however, are not in the realm of the flesh but are in the realm of the Spirit, if indeed the Spirit of God lives in you," describes "man in his natural relationship and orientation to God" (*CD* III/2, 366). Elsewhere regarding this verse Barth writes the following: "Where and to the extent that He now acts in the Holy Spirit, He forms and directs the man who still exists in the flesh, who is still wandering as a sinner. Certainly this is a strictly hidden formation

"with-ness" is different in some ways after the ascension, but he promised he would not be less present. This is reflected in Acts 2 when Peter described the scene at Pentecost as a fulfillment of Joel's ancient prophecy, referencing God's declaration that "I will pour out my Spirit on all people" (Acts 2:17).

Like the resurrection, which reveals the truth of our eternal life in Christ, Pentecost is an epic manifestation of the reality of the fullness of Spirit we have always had in Christ. His presence with us means we are constantly, in one sense, at home. Jesus's words, "I will send you *another* Counselor to be with you forever" (John 14:16, emphasis added), speak not only to his oneness with the Spirit, but also to his oneness with us. When Jesus says he will send the Spirit of Truth, it sounds like he's pointing to Pentecost (perhaps he is). But he also says that the Spirit of Truth is one whom *we already know, and who is already in us and with us* (John 14:17, emphasis added).[13]

In similar fashion, Jesus's following remark "on that day you will *realize* that I am in the Father, and you are in me, and I am in you" (John 14:20,

---

and direction, just as He Himself, the Master, is a hidden master" (*CD* I/2, 277). Paul's reason for putting it the way he does, therefore, seems related to his call to accountability, to live in the One to whom you are obligated, the Spirit, and not the flesh (see Rom 8:12). The exact Greek phrasing, "is not of him," can also convey a different meaning than "does not belong to Christ" (NIV). We all belong to Christ and are filled with his Spirit; in our true selves we are bound, indebted, obligated, compelled in the determination of Christ's freedom. However, when we resist the Spirit and our attitudes and actions betray the slavery of the flesh, we are not of him. This is consistent with Paul's teaching about our anthropological duality throughout Rom 5–8. Again, even from Rom 8, all humans in their false selves "have their minds set on what the flesh desires" (8:5), are "governed by the flesh" (8:6), "hostile to God," unwilling and unable to submit to God's law (8:7), and "cannot please God" (8:8). Then, in a fascinating verse, Paul places the antagonistic anti-Christ and in-Christ dimensions of the one person head to head, while showing the power of the asymmetry. Even though the flesh, including the mortal body, is strictly speaking devoid of the Spirit, the single subject is assured that God gives "life to your mortal bodies through his Spirit who lives in you" (8:11). In our superscript terms, while P^2 has nothing to do with P^1, P^3 bears relative witness to P^1 in this world in ways that *are* of Christ. Likewise, even though P^1 has nothing to do with P^2, P^3 bears relative witness to P^2 in ways that *are not* of Christ. Paul decries this latter association, i.e., a tacit belonging for P^3 without the obligation of spirit-embodiment that goes with P^1 is like separating Christ and the Spirit. Barth warns against this wrong kind of "in Christ" language in *CD* III/4, 576–77. Again, it is Christ's cross which makes the right separations at the right times. In Christ the Pat that doesn't belong is crucified for the sake of the Pat who does.

13. Many translations render John 14:17 as, the Spirit "is with you and *will be in you*" (emphasis added), which, regardless of the "is with you" part, slants the overall statement into the future, i.e., into the sequential framework of the Spirit coming at Pentecost. But the Greek wording carries a continuous, present-and-future, sense. To their credit, many Bibles do give an alternative reading of "is in you" in a footnote. "Is" can stand for "will be" in a way that "will be" cannot stand for "is."

PART FIVE: JESUS IS MY HEAVEN

emphasis added), may be alluding to the eschaton ("that day"). But short of that, if there was ever a day when believers in this world realized that Jesus was in the Father, that they were in him and he in them, it was that Pentecost morning. Surely those present heard in the Spirit the same words the Father must have whispered to a beleaguered Jesus, "No matter how you feel, I will never forsake you. I will not leave you. You are not an orphan. You belong to me. With me you are always at home. Even when you're away." The resurrection and Pentecost remind us that all of the Then is in the Now, even if not all of the Now is in the Then.

In one sense, we are in heaven right now, because Jesus is here. We do not yet see the new heaven and the new earth clearly, but we can know that heaven is a dimension of earth, just as later we will see earth as a dimension of heaven. "Compared to this union with Christ," exclaimed Hudson Taylor, "heaven or earth are unimportant accidents."[14]

There are several advantages to thinking about Jesus as our heaven in this way. For one, it is an approach that enables us to reframe questions like "are you going to heaven?" We can reframe this question because heaven has already come to us. Due to his proven solidarity with us, we can also know that Jesus's presence is every bit as much with us in our suffering "down here" as he will be *after* our suffering, when we are with him in the unadulterated "up there." Jesus is God with us, all the way through.

Finally, maintaining the idea of me and you already existing in heaven gives supreme value to our lives on earth. Without losing the fullness of the transcendent dimension in our fleshly, broken midst, we can also avoid a metaphysical dualism that separates heaven and earth (the basis for a shadowy Gnosticism). It is not that earth is bad and heaven is good—the earth is always God's good creation. It needs renewing, but it is not the problem. In placemat terms, earth is green. The problem is the uncreated stuff, the red of evil and corruption. The overlap of the green and red aspects is what the Bible calls "the world." This is especially true for John's writings, where the "world" could mean the earth in its overlapped, fallen form, or it could mean the red stuff that corrupts the earth, i.e., the worldliness of the world or the larger cosmos. Either way, "the world" usually has negative connotations: "Do not love the world or anything in the world" (1 John 2:15).[15] Does John tell us to *not* love the earth? Does he endorse a heavenly escapism? Does he enable environmental neglect? No, instead of these things, we could say that John is urging us along the lines of the Lord's prayer to bring the world back to earth. He wants us to know that the proper theological

---

14. Taylor and Taylor, *Hudson Taylor's Spiritual Secret*, 179.
15. See 1 John 2:15–16; Matt 18:7; John 15:19; 1 John 4:5; 1 Cor 10:7, 14.

contrast is not between heaven and earth, but between heaven/earth and world. C. S. Lewis gives us proper instructions: "Aim at heaven and you will get earth thrown in. Aim at earth and you will get neither."[16] In our placemat language, we could say "focus on the earth that you see and you get Genesis 2 grey, focus on the heavenly green and you will also get the Genesis 1 earth."

The good news of John 3:16 is that God did not just love the good earth and his good creatures. Instead, he embraced us at our very worst—the earth and his creatures in their overlapped and oppressed form. The testimony of John 3:16 that God "so loved the *world*" is much more radical than it appears. Indeed, as John says elsewhere: "the whole world is under the control of the evil one" (1 John 5:19). But if God loves the world with its evil connotations, then does God love evil? By no means. God hates evil. But God loves the creature co-opted by it. Thus, God loves the evil creature. Jesus here declares that there are no human beings so evil, so worldly, so far out, that God does not love them. To say that God loves the world is to say that there is no corner to which we can flee to avoid his love. This one verse (John 3:16) declares that the love that God has for all persons in the world is the same love that he has for his Son, "God so loved the world that he gave his one and only Son." God was willing to put himself under the world's power to defeat it and to free the good earth and all its good creatures from the world's evil ways. "In this world you will have tribulation," he reminds us, "but take heart! I have overcome the world" (John 16:33). As we learn to "fix our eyes . . . on what is unseen" (2 Cor 4:18), we look through the fog of the world for the true heaven and earth in our midst, that which is synonymous with the new heaven and new earth yet to be fully revealed.

---

16. Lewis, *Mere Christianity*, 118.

57

"They Will All Know Me" (Because They Do)

> *It is in the Cross of Christ that the utterly astonishing nature of the Love that God is has been fully disclosed. . . . God has revealed that He loves us more than he loves himself.*
>
> —T. F. Torrance

> *God's Holy Spirit of love is . . . the highest degree of self-giving, shining forth in the Son's squandering of his flesh and blood. His prodigality bursts the bounds of finite life as the Son returns to the infinite Father, together with whom, from all eternity, he breathes and shares the one Spirit . . . from the very outset we share in the whole of the triune life which is eternally completed in the Holy Spirit, so that, through the Spirit of grace, we are drawn into the mystery of divine sonship.*
>
> —Hans Urs von Balthasar

As a person of faith, Blaise Pascal developed a pyramid of understanding with three levels (from bottom to top): possibility, probability, and certainty. Starting at the bottom of the pyramid and from our existential-human vantage point, we are faced with myriad possibilities about the meaning of life, including the possibility of the divine. When it comes to the knowledge of God, probabilities are a more sophisticated form of possibilities, but we can never get to the level of certainty from below. Certainty is inaccessible because of our fallen human faculties. Because of the fall, the levels of possibility and probability are separated from the level of certainty by an unbridgeable chasm.

Natural theology can mean many things, but for us in the Christian tradition it is typically when the "post-fall you" imagines you can naturally get back to what you knew in Genesis 1. In other words, natural theology presumes that we can know the deep mysteries of God absent the power and support of divine revelation. The humility of Christ's cross and the revelation of Christ's true humanity provide the needed antidote to such a hubristic enterprise. Pascal chides those who "in addressing their arguments to unbelievers" try to prove "the existence of God from the works of nature." These apologists insist that "they have only to look at the least thing around them and they will see in it God plainly revealed. . . . On the contrary, [Scripture] says that God is a hidden God, and that since nature was corrupted he has left man to their blindness, from which they can escape only through Jesus Christ."[1] In Pascal's view, an attempt to bolster cognitive efforts to get from probability to certainty is like adding endless blocks of width without increasing the least centimeter of height. Because our created rationality (green) is clouded by irrationality (red), we could never get there if it were not for the truth embracing us from "above." Metaphysical "proofs" that try to establish certainty are ill-fated and "make little impact" in this regard, Pascal says. Indeed, "even if they did help some people, it would only be for the moment . . . because an hour later they would be afraid they had made a mistake."[2]

If, for Pascal, the realm of possibility is the realm of natural theology, then it is in the realm of *probability* where thoughtful truth claims can be made. Like all of the Christ-centered truth claims I make in this project, beginning with what C. S. Lewis called "the grand miracle" of Christ's one person being fully divine and fully human, truth claims cannot be proven, only believed. "Pascal's wager" was his effort to show why belief in God was still a rational and good thing to do, even if we could not prove with certainty that God exists. But Pascal knew that such claims do no good unless God has claimed us. To the extent that our truth claims have "reality" in them, a measure of top-down certainty can be received in faith. Instead of "understanding seeking faith" (bottom up), it is "faith seeking understanding" (top

---

1. Pascal, *Pensees*, fragment 781.
2. Pascal, *Pensees*, fragment 190.

down): "Faith is confidence in what we hope for and assurance about what we do not see" (Heb 11:1).[3]

The twentieth-century mystic Thomas Merton speaks to the impossibility of finding both God and ourselves in nature alone, apart from revelation:

> For although I can know something of God's existence and nature by my own reason, there is no human and rational way in which I can arrive at contact, that possession of Him, which will be the discovery of Who He really is and of Who I am in Him. That is something that no man can ever do alone. Nor can all the men and all the created things in the universe help him in this work. The only One Who can teach me to find God is God Himself, Alone.[4]

Certainty is only located in one place, and it comes from the top-down (revelation). It comes from God's certainty of God's self. In Trinitarian terms, we can say that it is the certainty the Father and Son share with one another in the Spirit. "No one knows the Son except the Father," says Jesus, "and no one knows the Father except the Son" (Matt 11:27). Any certainty that we have about God, then, derives from the fact that the Son shares his certainty of God with us. When we start from the top of Pascal's pyramid by grace through faith, we are given a sharper perspective on the world than we could ever attain when starting from the bottom. Though natural theology cannot get us to a knowledge of Christ, nature viewed through the top-down perspective becomes a cathedral of praise to Christ our Creator and Redeemer.[5]

---

3. See also the NRSV: "the assurance of things hoped for, the conviction of things not seen"; NKJV: "the substance of things hoped for, the evidence of things we cannot see"; NET: "being sure of what we hope for, being convinced of what we do not see"; NASB, "the certainty of things hoped for, a proof of things not seen"; CEB: "the reality of what we hope for, the proof of what we don't see."

4. Merton, *New Seeds*, 36.

5. Left uninterpreted by Jesus Christ, nature gives us mixed messages. In Book One we talked about how unreliable it is to judge ourselves by the zero-sum game which is based on perceiving how we are doing—a classic example of bottom-up, environmental analysis of the ebb and flow of our lives. Mother nature works in zero-sum fashion, and so contributes to this misguided tendency in those who are trying to find God through nature. Starting with the top-down cohesiveness of Christ as the interpretive key, however, nature can point *indirectly* to the dimensional theological truth of place-mat anthropology. For example, hardwood trees such as the maple outside my office window provide a wonderful witness to the juxtaposition of life and death that we have discussed from the beginning. It can have green leaves and red leaves at the same time, and even single leaves with partial red and partial green. These colors share the same space in a sense; the green and red colors have the one tree in common, at least. By

"THEY WILL ALL KNOW ME" (BECAUSE THEY DO)

If we merely thought of the Son of God incarnate as a solitary Palestinian man, Jesus of Nazareth, then Jesus's phrase that "no one knows the Father except the Son" would be daunting in its limitations. It leaves the rest of humanity externally related to Jesus. But because Jesus is not only the one for the many but the many in the one, he shares his knowledge of God intimately with all his flock. This flock includes all created by him; in the words of the Psalmist, "Know that the Lord is God. It is he who made us, and we are his; we are his people, the sheep of his pasture" (Ps 100:3). We are God's by creation. It is no wonder, then, that Paul says in Romans 1:21 that every human being knows God.

John's gospel takes this tack in relaying Jesus's parable of the Good Shepherd. John 10:14–15 outlines the Trinitarian logic of knowing: "I am the good shepherd; I know my sheep and my sheep know me—just as the Father knows me and I know the Father." Jesus knows us and we know him. This is the epistemological framework within which all human knowing of God is contextualized. In other words, our personal knowledge of Jesus the Son and his Father exists *within* the mutual knowing between Trinitarian persons. We can speak of Christ as either one with the Father (representing God to us) or one with humanity (representing us to God). Our knowing of Christ thus comes from Christ, which is to say that all human knowing of God comes from the humanity of Christ.

This knowing of God is part of humanity being created in Christ and by the Spirit. However, as Paul continues in Romans 1, "for although they knew God, they neither glorified him as God nor gave thanks to him, but their thinking became futile and their foolish hearts were darkened . . . [they] exchanged the truth of God for a lie" (Rom 1:21, 25). Romans 1 outlines the absurdity of "the fall." Because humanity is green, they have no excuse and no good reason (Rom 1:20) for their red actions in diametric opposition to God's will. From Genesis 1 on, all humans know God (Rom 1:21 above), and yet simultaneously, from Genesis 2–3 on, *they do not know God*.[6] Obfuscated (or eclipsed) by the red that seized them, their "foolish

---

November the tree is a beautiful mixture of green and red, and when the leaves turn totally red, they soon die and fall off, making room in the same location for a green leaf to emerge come springtime. It's true that Mother Nature, with her spatial, sequential, zero-sum constraints, cannot demonstrate two *totals* of green and red in one space, or a single subject that is at once fully dead and fully alive. Still, even if nature can't capture it comprehensively, there is plenty of "power in the pointing" when it comes to her ability to highlight certain aspects of the mystery of Christ.

6. Rom 1:18 also describes well our placemat anthropology: fallen humans "suppress the truth" about Christ and themselves (green) "by their wickedness" (red). The picture comes to mind of a person in deep water who cannot swim, yet is desperately suppressing under the water the beachball which keeps him afloat. Such rebellion by

heart" (Rom 1:21; or unintelligent heart) allowed them no access back to pure green: "There is no one righteous, not even one; there is no one who understands, no one who seeks God. All have turned away, they have together become worthless; there is no one who does good, not even one" (Rom 3:10–12).

"We all, like sheep, have gone astray," Isaiah wrote (53:6). As accurate as this indictment may be, it does not detract from John's baseline truth: all the sheep know the Shepherd, hear his voice, and obey. So it is not *instead* of this obedience that we stray, it is *despite* our hearing and obeying in Christ that we stray. By keeping "stray" and "obey" in the same space, we have properly moved away from the sequential and returned to the simultaneous.

It follows, then, that the Good Shepherd does not lay down his life for the sheep so that they will hear his voice, but *because* in reality they do hear his voice and are one with him. The being-in-act depth of belonging was there all along. Only by the destruction of their deafness (ultimately), and the piercing of their deafness (existentially and by the Spirit) can their original hearing emerge. As his sheep, we will all stand before the judgment seat of Christ—all hearing (green), all not hearing (red). This is spiritual and metaphorical language, not a physical description. That is why those who are physically deaf in Jesus's ministry often seem to be more aware of

---

humanity is futile and exhausting. Paul notes that with the "foolish heart" darkness gives birth to darkness (there is resonance here with John's language about flesh giving birth to flesh, and about humans walking simultaneously in the fullness of light and the utter corruption of darkness). Just as two hearts are inferred by Rom 1:21, two minds are inferred in Paul's indictment that follows. In fact, Rom 1:28–32 (e.g., "God gave them over to a depraved mind, to do what ought not to be done") is strikingly similar to Paul's self-indictment in Rom 7:14–23 (e.g., "there is nothing good in me. . . . I do what I do not want to do"). The word "exchange" in Rom 1:23, 25, could fall prey to a replacement theology, when it simply means that humanity gets things flipped around backwards, so that what is parasitic is provisionally in the ascendency. I personally think the much-fought-over verses 1:26–27, Paul's attempt to make ethical application in his context, unfortunately overshadow the governing framework of the two totals. This is the framework from which the Spirit provides her exquisite wisdom to make ethical application in ways that may be different from the biblical context. We will return to this theme. Finally, three times in succession Paul says of sinners that God "gave them over" to their wickedness (Rom 1:24; 1:26; 1:28). As we progress to the conclusion of our study, we will continue to explore what Paul could have meant by even stronger phrases pointing to God's sovereign agency related to sin and suffering, e.g., "For the creation was subjected to frustration, not by its own choice, but by the will of the one who subjected it, in hope" (Rom 8:20); and "For God has bound all people over to disobedience" (Rom 11:32). Thankfully our placemat interpretation will allow us to keep these questions within the green bookends of our entire two-book project, just like the green phrase "the obedience of faith" brackets the book of Romans (Rom 1:5; Rom 16:26).

the Word than those who are physically able to hear the words. When Jesus heals the deaf or the blind it is a physical sign of a spiritual truth.

Swiss theologian Hans Urs von Balthasar provides insight into the vibrantly real (if often hidden) and ongoing relationship between God and every human. Like the Torrances, von Balthasar emphasized Christ's mediation as a "twofold motion—to the Father and from the Father."[7] This double-movement of grace is happening such that human beings in Christ are always hearing and responding to God. Within this double-movement, we are not individuals but persons, persons in *the* person of Christ sharing life with the triune persons. As von Balthasar remarks, the gravity of this human location challenges and even offends our individualism:

> God's immense richness is concentrated and focused at this one spot, the humanity of Jesus Christ. . . . This is the meeting place where all the roads from heaven come together at the one "gate" through which everyone who wishes to go to the Father must pass. It is the meeting place, too, of all the roads which crisscross the world's history: open roads (in Judaism) as well as the hidden, overgrown pathways and tracks of salvation (in paganism). Man . . . can feel that this immense, ineluctable convergence of all paths toward God, this channeling of all human relationships to God . . . is simply an incomprehensible violation of the individual's religious freedom, dignity, and maturity. Indeed, it *must* give this impression as long as the contemplative has not grasped the fact that the Mediator's uniqueness (1 Tim 2:5) has been established by God himself as the counterpart of God the Father's own uniqueness.[8]

The gospel accountability provided by this double movement of grace makes a necessary claim on our lives, urging us to abandon our individualism for authentic personhood. On the subject of prayer, for instance, von Balthasar expounds:

> Anyone who has ever sensed this fundamental mystery underlying our existence will take the necessity of prayer for granted, particularly the prayer of listening and contemplation. For the relation between God and the creature is now seen to be borne along by these miracles of God's incomprehensible love, and God himself, in establishing this relation, is shown to be the

---

7. Von Balthasar, *Prayer*, 53.

8. Von Balthasar, *Prayer*, 52. This quote may be lost on the reader without a reminder of the important distinction between individual and person established in Book One (see "Individualism and Personhood").

ultimate Lover, such that the creature's very existence seems to be a latent prayer—the creature only needs a certain degree of awareness of what it really *is*, and it will break forth into prayer.[9]

Jesus Christ is the very environment of every human's existence, according to von Balthasar: "We are 'in Christ': he is our milieu, the medium in which we live. It is so close to us in silent intimacy that it goes unnoticed, but we encounter it in its sovereign, personal freedom and spiritual character in the express word of Scripture, preaching and church teaching, and above all in contemplation."[10]

"Hear, O Israel" begins the Shema, "the LORD our God, the LORD is one. Love the LORD your God with all your heart and with all your soul and with all your strength." (Deut 6:4–5, Jesus adds "mind" before strength, Mark 12:30; Luke 10:27). We are *created*, as von Balthasar with Barth reminds us, as hearers and doers of the word.[11] In placemat anthropology, that is our green constitution. Due to our total red depravity, however, our ears are plugged up. We cannot simply rely on the capacity of our original nature. Our access to truth has been blocked, wrecked by incapacity. And yet the gospel pierces our ears. As good as the truth of humanity created in Christ is, the fact remains: "how can they hear without someone preaching to them?" (Rom 10:14). Under the sound of the gospel and a covenant mediated in Christ, we are supernaturally quickened and enlivened.[12]

---

9. Von Balthasar, *Prayer*, 44. In this sense, we are "pray[ing] without ceasing" (1 Thess. 5:17). See the reading "The Breath of God" in Book One. Elsewhere, von Balthasar writes, "The word of God addressed to us always presupposes a word of God within us, insofar as we have been created in the word and cannot be detached from this context. The word within us has attained a new level since, in order to reach us, alienated and sunk in the flesh as we are, it has taken flesh of our flesh and now communicates itself to us in the twofold form of word and flesh, of holy Scripture and eucharist, of spiritual and substantial truth" (26).

10. Von Balthasar, *Prayer*, 26–27.

11. For Barth, see *CD* I/2, 240.

12. We spoke earlier of Peter's appeal to stir up the pure minds of his hearers. This is not dissimilar to Paul's appeal to the conscience of his hearers (which I take to be the inner *anthropos*, or in-Christ dimension of his hearers): "What we are is plain [clear, manifest] to God, and I hope it is also plain to your conscience" (2 Cor 5:11). The human conscience is not a monolithic pure light within; it is not without its own parasitic, red, counterfeit conscience, but still, the green remains. Paul therefore is emphatically not commending himself to the Corinthians per se, but to their true selves in Christ: "by setting forth [manifesting] the truth plainly, we commend ourselves to everyone's conscience in the sight of God" (2 Cor 4:2). Like Peter, this is Paul stirring up the pure minds of *his* hearers. He has a supernatural confidence in the power of the message but not in his ability to deliver the message perfectly. He has absolutely no control over the extent of its reception, but to the extent the word is preached, deep will call to deep. Like prayer and all righteous activity, Paul views preaching as participating in the

"How can we hear the word?" von Balthasar asks, "because we are *in* the Word. Because the Word who became flesh takes us into himself, giving his own self as our mode of existence.... The grace which the Father gives us is christoform; it assimilates us to the Son without violating us as human beings—for the Son became a human being."[13]

Von Balthasar highlights the undiminished continuity of the original green, but he clearly sees the danger of a simple natural theology based on creation alone. There is always the danger of humans co-opting the word of God, making it "something so interior that we confuse it with our own nature, with a natural wisdom given to us once and for all, to be used at will." That is what he considers to be the Roman Catholic danger. Protestants, conversely, are at danger "of seeing the word as something merely external, rather than the deepest mystery within it, that in which we live, move, and have our being."[14] Navigating this Gibralter-like strait, placemat theology warns against any promotion of capacity without incapacity. Creation without the need of redemption is creation without the cross.

For von Balthasar, the freedom of God's Word is such that Christ is not beholden to humanity: "Standing at the center of history, Christ confronts me, exhibiting the freedom of a completely contingent personality, opposing most effectively all the tendencies of my philosophizing reason to produce my own religion out of myself."[15] So on the one hand, the Word confronts us as external to us. And on the other hand, notes von Balthasar, we live "by the knowledge that the truth (which is the Spirit within us) is more interior to us than we are to ourselves; that we have been predestined and chosen in God, in God's authentic truth, prior to the foundation of the world, prior to our own existence, to be his holy, unspotted children. Anything in us that runs counter to this is therefore merely a belated denial of what is our real truth, and hence nothing but a self-contradiction."[16] This

---

reciprocal "sincerity" of what we would call the hypostatic union of Jesus Christ. We see the human-Godward, or enhypostatic movement, "in Christ we speak before God with sincerity" (2 Cor 2:17); "before God" means opposite God, facing God (or "toward God," see 2 Cor 3:4) as God's "counterpart" (von Balthasar). This enhypostatic movement in Christ is a reciprocation to the initiating God-humanward, or anhypostatic movement inside of which we are commissioned: "as those sent from God" (2 Cor 2:17); see also 2 Cor 1:12, "with integrity and *godly sincerity*" (emphasis added). This is the double-movement of Trinitarian sincerity, from the Father to the Son (humanity) and from the Son (humanity) to the Father, in the Spirit. The human-Godward Spirit movement is represented by the "aroma" (2 Cor 2:15) of incense rising to God.

13. Von Balthasar, *Prayer*, 58.
14. Von Balthasar, *Prayer*, 27–28.
15. Von Balthasar, *Prayer*, 63.
16. Von Balthasar, *Prayer*, 78.

is what Athanasius described when he said that even though we are created in the "Likeness of the Word," we are simultaneously so "bowed down" by sin and evil that we are unable to lift our heads toward the truth, so "burdened by wickedness" as to be "brute beasts" instead of reasonable human beings.[17]

We discussed Israel's struggle throughout the Old Testament to keep the covenant. God continually says, "I'll be true to you (or I will keep faith with you), now you be true to me (keep faith with me)." This is the "call and response" that God speaks through the prophets, which Jeremiah encapsulates: "*I will be their God*, and they will be my people" (Jer 31:33, emphasis added). The initiative is always God's; the God-humanward movement comes first. But we should note the opposite human-Godward emphasis anticipated by Jeremiah, for it signifies the reciprocal response within the covenant, "*They will be my people*, and I will be their God" (Jer 32:38, emphasis added). This is the underlying covenant mediated by Christ and to which Israel, and all of us, are meant to bear witness. We are meant to bear witness because we are already involved.

Every human being, von Balthasar claims, is full of willing obedience at the created level. When God asks us to follow his lead, it is because our desire to do God's will is not foundationally foreign to our humanity. It follows that the human being's existential obedience or disobedience occurs within this ontological context. The Spirit can bring about a "manifestation of man's relationship to God, which has always been there. The Lord has always included us, disobedient as we are, within his loving obedience to the Father." In this, we must maintain the relationship between subjective human knowledge of God and the objective truth of the one who knows God for us: "we would never come to a knowledge of the triune life in Jesus Christ . . . unless we had also been participants, from all eternity, in the subjective relationship of the incarnate Son with his heavenly Father in the Holy Spirit."[18]

Along with Trinitarian logic of *knowing* in John 10, Jesus also highlights the Trinitarian nature of *loving*. The Father and Son's love for one another is mutual, a glorious reciprocation of each other's self-giving love. When Jesus says, "The reason my Father loves me is that I lay down my life" (John 10:17) it means that the self-giving love of God works in an

---

17. Athanasius, *On the Incarnation*, 12.

18. Von Balthasar, *Prayer*, 178. Again, because actuality precedes possibility, you can't know God existentially unless you know God ontologically. As Von Balthasar reminds us, we avoid natural theology when we read our lives retrospectively through Christ crucified. Even if the knowledge of God is there ontologically, it is utterly inaccessible apart from revelation.

internally consistent way: the Father would not expect anything less than the self-giving love demonstrated in Christ's sacrificial act. Unfortunately, this might be turned around as a conditional statement, as if Jesus's claim is that "God loves me *because of*, or *if*, I lay down my life." If the statement is twisted in this way, a theological train wreck ensues: God loves us *because* Jesus died for us, or God loves us *if* Jesus died for us, or God will love me *if* I do something to reciprocate his love. We can see how such an interpretation may lead to spiritual dis-ease and pastoral malpractice. As Alan Torrance regularly reminds his students, "The Father who says 'I love you *if*—simply doesn't love us." Repentance for all of us, including pastors and counselors, involves claiming the gospel truth of God's unconditional love in an untwisted way, i.e., with no "ifs."

In solidarity with the Son of God, we have full permission to apply to ourselves the Father's unconditional words to Jesus at his baptism, "you are my beloved Son in whom I am well pleased" (Matt 3:17). Whoever you are, and no matter what you believe, this truth is declared over you: you are God's beloved child in whom he is well pleased. Furthermore, our inner Trinitarian rationale, revealed by the Spirit of Truth, tells us that Jesus's sacrificial death demonstrates the self-giving love not only of *Jesus for us*, but also of the *Father for Jesus*, therefore the Father's love for all humanity in his Son. Even when Christ became sin, even when he became a curse because of the fallen flesh he had assumed, the Father loved his Son. In this demonstration of love, God embraces humanity in Christ not only at our best, but also at our worst. Jesus did not die to convince God to love us. He died for us *because* God loves us, and in Christ we love God. In creation and redemption, Jesus assures us that we all know God in Christ, and in him we all love God. There is one flock and one shepherd (John 10:16).

In Jeremiah 31 the prophet describes what the day will be like when the flock is gathered around the shepherd, revealing iniquities forgiven and infirmities healed. In a way that Jeremiah cannot even fathom, God wrote the law of Christ on our hearts and minds. As Jeremiah hints (Jer 31:32–33), this includes all of the love and obedience required. It is not a static potential but human being-in-act: all human beings know and love God as the incarnate Son knows and loves God.[19] Whereas humanity on its own cannot

19. The truth of this reciprocal love is something Julian of Norwich reminds us about (Book One) and which, in the false humanity he assumed, even Jesus Christ is tempted to forget: "He was blinded in his reason and perplexed in his mind, so much that he had almost forgotten his own love" (Julian, *Showings*, 293; as quoted in Book One, 268). We also established in Book One the analogical hierarchy of human being-in-act: the first principle is that the divine-human Jesus is actually doing what the Father is doing (John 14:10), and it follows that we are actually doing what Christ our human brother is doing (John 14:12). There is an element of precision in the first order

perfectly reciprocate God's knowing, loving, and doing, the covenant will be revealed as kept from both sides by the mediator Jesus Christ, and our true human knowledge of God will be gloriously manifest on that day: "I will be their God and they will be my people. No longer will they teach their neighbor or say to one another, 'Know the Lord,' because they will all know me, from the least of them to the greatest, declares the LORD" (Jer 31:33–34). If actuality precedes possibility, then Jeremiah's connection with Romans 1:21 becomes apparent: we will all know the Lord, because we in fact do.

---

that carries to the second, "I love my Father and do exactly what my Father has commanded me" (John 14:31). Because "I am in the Father and the Father is in me" (John 14:10) says Jesus, the anthropological truth to be realized is that "I am in the Father, you are in me and I am in you" (John 14:20). Just as Christ can do "nothing" apart from the Father (John 9:33), we can do "nothing" apart from Christ (John 15:5). Jesus's foundational remarks reflecting his representative human unity with God's being-in-act are scattered throughout John (e.g., 5:17; 5:19; 7:16; 8:28; 9:33; 12:49, 50; 14:10; 14:24). See "Fulfilling the Law of Christ" in Book One.

58

The Rest of Our Life

Oh, it is joy to feel Jesus living in you . . . to be reminded of His love by His seeking communion with you at all times, not by your painful attempts to abide in Him. He is our life, our strength, our salvation. His is our "wisdom, and righteousness, and sanctification, and redemption." He is our power for service and fruit-bearing, and His bosom is our resting place now and forever.

—Hudson Taylor

The author of Hebrews writes that the faithful in Christ will "enter his rest," and the "rest of Christ" is the opposite of human restlessness. Just as Jesus is our heaven, he is also our rest. He himself is our Sabbath. Because this is so, we are always fully at rest (green) in one dimension. Even as beings-in-act, we are at peace with God, ourselves, and others. The problem, then, is the other, simultaneous dimension of restlessness (red). In this dynamic state we are at odds with God, ourselves, and others. As is always the case between green and red, in this world neither dimension diminishes the other. Instead of a zero-sum analysis, it is a question of true versus false.

The picture of "entering his rest" is made all the more beautiful when we consider that we are entering a rest that in one sense we already have. Even in the first heaven, we can "live into" this rest by the Spirit and in the power of our Redeemer. The two days most prominently called "the day" in Scripture are the Sabbath day and the day of judgment, and in light of placemat theology, we can see the two as of a piece. Here the Sabbath is both creation and redemption rolled into one, whereas judgment day is a day when all that is *not* rest is revealed to be fully eradicated. We could say that judgment day is not about the adding of rest, but the removal of unrest; it encourages us to find rest in our true Sabbath every day.

As concrete as it is in one dimension, rest can be difficult to come by in this world. Hundreds of thousands of people have read the book *Hudson Taylor's Spiritual Secret* (written by his daughter-in-law), but very few would be able to tell you what the secret is. It does not come until later in the book, and it has everything to do with spiritual rest.

Hudson Taylor died in 1905, and in his life he accomplished more than most people do in several lifetimes. Taylor was a groundbreaking example of culturally sensitive missionary work in foreign lands. In departure from the norm ("teach people English so they can read the King James Bible"), Taylor put pioneering emphasis on adopting indigenous language in word and print, customs, and styles. In China, this included his following the standard for men of a shaved forehead and long braid of hair. To the degree any Westerner can avoid cultural (mis-)appropriation on one side and cultural accommodation on the other (compromising the message), Taylor endeavored to love, and be loved by, the human beings he encountered, and all in the unique name of Jesus Christ (Acts 4:12). Unbeknownst to him, Taylor followed the earlier example of Jesuit missionary pioneers in these cultural efforts and popularized them to a much broader audience.

After years of trying to faithfully live the Christian life and relentlessly building up the mission work in China, Taylor was spiritually exhausted. Then, not long after his thirty-seventh birthday, he described in his journal what was by far his most transformative conversion experience, "God has made me a new man!" Simply put, Taylor discovered that Christ really was his life (Col 3:4), and that he really was given fullness in Christ (Col 2:10). In his words he was "resting in the love of an almighty Saviour, in the joy of a complete salvation." Taylor was learning to take 1 John 1:7 fully seriously: in Christ, the light of the world, he was free "from *all* sin" (emphasis in the original). "This is not new," Taylor said, "and yet 'tis *new to me*. I feel as though the dawning of a glorious day had risen upon me."[1] What was fresh for Taylor was his new ability to trust the indicative nature of his original identity—his created and redeemed personhood in Christ. It was a new revelation of what was already true. In placemat terms, Taylor peered through the zero-sum fog and discovered the total green.

---

1. Taylor and Taylor, *Hudson Taylor's Spiritual Secret*, 156. See also 158: "As to work—mine was never so plentiful, so responsible or so difficult, but the weight and strain are all *gone*. . . . I do not know how far I may be able to make myself intelligible about it, for there is nothing new or strange or wonderful—and yet, all is new!"

As always, our evil enemy uses our shortcomings to coax us into the zero-sum trap. He does not want us to know the two totals, and the inferior total red in relation to the total green. Before Taylor's enlightening experience of reality, he saw sanctification in strictly progressive terms. He was frustrated in his attempts to be more and more like Jesus: "I have continually to mourn that I follow at such a distance and learn so slowly to imitate my precious Lord."[2]

His letters show the wearying strain:

> I felt the ingratitude, the danger, the sin of not living nearer to God. I prayed, agonized, fasted, strove, made resolutions, read the Word more diligently, sought more time for meditation—but all without avail. Every day, almost every hour, the consciousness of sin oppressed me. I knew that if only I could abide in Christ all would be well, but I could not. I would begin the day with prayer, determined not to take my eye off Him for a moment, but pressure of duties, sometimes very trying, and constant interruptions apt to be so wearing, caused me to forget Him. Then one's nerves get so fretted in this climate that temptations to irritability, hard thoughts and sometime unkind words are all the more difficult to control. Each day brought its register of sin and failure, of lack of power. . . . Is there no rescue? Must it be thus to the end—constant conflict, and too often defeat? How could I preach with sincerity [about God's power]. . . . Instead of growing stronger, I seemed to be getting weaker and to have less power against sin; and no wonder, for faith and even hope were getting low. I hated myself, I hated my sin, yet gained no strength against it.[3]

As apparent from his writings before his life-changing epiphany, instead of being assured of his complete justification *and* sanctification in Christ, Taylor believed his sanctification was still in the balance. This is the tired trope we continue to hear in many Christian circles (discussed in Book One). Looking back, Taylor bemoans: "I thought that holiness, practical holiness, was to be gradually attained by a diligent use of the means of grace. There was nothing I so much desired as holiness, nothing I so much

---

2. Taylor and Taylor, *Hudson Taylor's Spiritual Secret*, 157.

3. Taylor and Taylor, *Hudson Taylor's Spiritual Secret*, 158–59. See also L. E. Maxwell, "How often you have been filled with disgust and shame and secret weeping over your inward wrongness! But in spite of all your agonizing and strivings you find your resolutions only so many ropes of sand" (*Born Crucified*, 21).

PART FIVE: JESUS IS MY HEAVEN

needed; but far from in any measure attaining it, the more I strove after it, the more it eluded my grasp."[4]

As Taylor describes it, at that time he was living the only Christian life he knew. He did not *think* he was trying to live the Christian life on his own strength. After all, he talked and sang about dependence on Christ, but theologically it was dependence from a distance. He did not realize that the power supply he sought was being choked out by his failure to realize his total identification with Christ. The power was not the problem, but his zero-sum truncating of the situation kept him languishing somewhere between death and resurrection, somewhere between the old man and the new man. Unbeknownst to him, his pitting of sanctification against justification was taking its toll. He was reaching and reaching for what he *already* had. The more he tried, the worse it got. He did not realize that his progressive model of sanctification meant that he was striving against the assurance of his own justification.

But then that day came, "When the agony of soul was at its height," Taylor writes, the scales fell off, "the Spirit of God revealed to me the truth of our oneness with Jesus as I had never known it before."[5] Paul's language "I, yet no longer I, but Christ" became Taylor's designated phrase signifying what he called "the exchanged life." Before quoting his newfound realization of Galatians 2:20, Taylor exclaimed, "*I am no better than before. In a sense, I do not wish to be, nor am I striving to be. But I am dead and buried with Christ*—ay, and risen too!" From that time on, Taylor gave up on rehabilitating the old man (red), and focused on who he was in Christ (green). It provided a much better navigational beacon in "the grey" of this world.

In this watershed realization, Taylor left the zero-sum game of sanctification for something much better. It was less about his *faith in Christ* and instead about *the faithfulness of Christ* on his behalf. He remarked: "How then is our faith increased? Only by thinking of all that Jesus is and all He is for us: His life, His death, His work, He Himself as revealed to us in the Word, to be the subject of our constant thoughts. Not a striving to have faith . . . but a looking off to the Faithful One seems all we need, a resting in the Loved One entirely, for time and for eternity."[6] Taylor's last line, "resting in the Loved One," shows the profound Trinitarian underpinning of our lives. Jesus Christ is the primary One loved by the Father, and we exist *in* "the One" the Father loves (Eph 1:6).

---

4. Taylor and Taylor, *Hudson Taylor's Spiritual Secret*, 159.
5. Taylor and Taylor, *Hudson Taylor's Spiritual Secret*, 161.
6. Taylor and Taylor, *Hudson Taylor's Spiritual Secret*, 156.

With sharpest clarity Taylor found that he could not live the Christian life, and that Christ was the only one who could. Instead of seeking to emulate Christ, he began to rest in the truth of living *from* Christ. The former effort promotes individual labor and beckons the flesh, while the latter centers on Christ's finished work and relishes our participation in it. All of our righteous human activity is held inside of Christ's accomplished and ever-unfolding work. Taylor had discovered the foundational truth that reality does not change when we change, or when we wake up to it. We can be unconscious of abiding in Christ. As Taylor said to his host after a night's stay at his home: "While sleeping last night . . . did I cease to abide in your home because I was unconscious of the fact?"[7]

Taylor found the "secret" of the vicarious humanity of Christ at almost the exact midpoint of his life. It was what gave him, according to his children, the ability to continue in ministry for decades more when he had been all but burned out. This is an epiphany many others have had as they have viscerally experienced the light yoke shouldered by their Yokefellow. It is a deep sense, as the Psalmist relates, of being carried—carried in the arms of the shepherding savior (Ps 28:9). In him I do not lose my true self, I gain it. Though "I" do not dissolve into Christ, I discover him as my strength.

As much as Taylor's language resonates with my experience, I do not want to put words in his mouth. With his metamorphosis and newfound appreciation for the completeness of Christ's work, one wonders how it affected his preaching. Did he still believe that a conversion experience determined whether one did or did not have oneness with Christ? Did he recognize the truth of his life was in place thousands of years before his experience of it? Did he recognize that the exchanged life for every human being is revealed in that event whereby Christ crucified and buried the old man, and revealed in his resurrection the new man?

With Taylor, we all do well to remember Paul's emphasis that "if, while we were God's enemies, we were reconciled to him through the death of his Son, how much more, having been reconciled, shall we be saved by his life" (Rom 5:10). While maintaining the force of the verse (*how much more*) we should not overlook that we *are* saved by Christ's death. We are saved by Christ's death *and* by Christ's life; like a nested box the first is inside the second. Life transcends death. In the big picture, even death serves life; it is not the other way around. Justification and sanctification are both included in the saving work of Christ.

What if the Evangelical message to the world was "Jesus Christ is literally your death, and Jesus Christ is literally your life"? What if we viewed

---

7. Taylor and Taylor, *Hudson Taylor's Spiritual Secret*, 164.

everyone as living from Christ, "all the way down," not only in sanctifying growth but also from the very root of justification. Living from Christ in this way means that we recognize justification and sanctification as a unity-in-distinction, the same Christ accomplishing both for every person. "For *from* him," Paul says, "and through him and for him are all things" (Rom 11:36, emphasis added).[8] Everything comes down to living *from* Christ, even in the first steps of response and in all manner of repentance, belief, and faith. Ian Thomas and others have continually reminded us that no one can live the Christian life except Christ. But is it not also the case that no one can get into the Christian life apart from Christ? No one can know God ("no one knows the Father except the Son," Matt 11:27), have faith in him ("Jesus, the pioneer and perfecter of faith," Heb 12:2), respond adequately to him ("apart from me you can do nothing," John 15:5), or justify and redeem themselves ("all are justified freely by his grace through the redemption that came by Christ Jesus," Rom 3:23–24). Christ does all of those things for us without our permission. That is justification by grace alone.

If we learned to live from Christ all the way down, recognizing that we have been made just, right, and whole before we ever believed in God, how much more serious and inherently self-destructive would sin then appear? How much more empowering freedom and assurance would we attain, motivating us to obedience? More consideration should be given to how we weaken the gospel claim when we say, "Christ did it all, *now all you have to do is*. . . ." This sets us up to think that we are supposed to finish the work of Christ. To the extent that our life with Christ started when we made a decision, our assurance will be weak. If we have taken on this outsized role in our salvation, we become less accountable to the life of Christ within. Why? Because it makes no sense to say we are accountable to Christ when he was not a part of our life *until we asked him*. Such a late-coming accountability is a spurious one. It can never catch up to a reality that is true about me *before* I asked. It gives me a role in my salvation that, in the beginning at least, makes Christ beholden to me.

If I am effectively my own lord until I make Jesus "Lord," then in matters of sanctification I am much more prone to lapse into an adoption of "the language without the life." Why? I have pitted justification by grace against justification by faith (by thinking I'm justified by *my* faith!). My zero-sum misunderstanding of justification can only proceed into a zero-sum misunderstanding of sanctification. Rather than the fullness of Christ that comes to bear from the beginning, I have contrived a negotiated agreement where

---

8. Thanks to friend and Torchbearers President Peter Reid for renewing my attention to this verse.

I give part and he gives part (described in Book One as a contract more than a covenant). Said another way, Christ's ongoing *action* in us and for us—the saving life of Christ—is weakened by *trans-action*. We considered above the problems with quantitative, zero-sum analysis and sequential thinking—the economy of transaction—in contrast to the intra-transformative economy of the Spirit.

Transaction is the enemy of transformation. If I give my life to Christ and he gives me his life, it is an exchange, but it cannot truly be the "exchanged life" apprehended by Hudson Taylor and others until there is a transformative recognition of what is already true. Instead of a transaction, the truth that we need is the gospel revelation that "Christ is my death and Christ is my life." This is justification and sanctification applied all the way down. Regardless of where Taylor's Evangelical theology would land today, the sense that comes from reading his work is that he comes to gradually understand the importance of putting more and more weight down on a universal truth about God and human beings that is meant to *be believed*, as opposed to a "truth" that is not true about people *until* they believe. Beginning with this oneness in Christ allows us to talk about sin in a very different way (i.e., not as "separation" in an ontological sense). The total truth of our creation and life in Christ exposes the limits of thinking in terms of total depravity alone. It is this twin depth—the awareness of grace and the acknowledgment of sin, in that order—that draws me to Hudson Taylor.

The "finished work" language from Scripture was like a balm for Taylor, and it is meant to give rest to our souls. Unless we are Five-Point Calvinists, we can believe that this finished work is a finished work for all people. God loves all people, and this is how we know God loves us, Jesus Christ laid down his life for us (1 John 3:16). It is clear that in the cross God made atonement not just for Christians, but for all (1 John 2:2). However, when it is up to us to acquire the rest that obtains from Christ's finished work, as if it is something we do not already have, rest becomes unattainable. "Rest" becomes "reach."

The often articulated "step of appropriation" in Evangelicalism (i.e., that we must appropriate the work of Christ for ourselves) has rendered the "finished work" not so finished after all. The finished work is nonsensical when it lapses into a hypothetical. In other words, it is finished, but it is only *really* finished when I decide for Christ. Instead of my participation in a prior reality (the finished work), such an approach implicitly grants my step of faith or belief the supposed power to create the reality. True belief, however, does not function to make something true. It is belief in something that is *already* true. The idea that it is not true for me until I believe it is pure postmodern relativism. Against such relativism, Taylor wrote, "Jesus Christ is the *Lord of all*, or he is *not Lord at all*."⁹

9. Taylor and Taylor, *Hudson Taylor's Spiritual Secret*, 229, emphasis original.

59

Gathered and Scattered

Greed has always haunted gathering.
—Willie Jennings

ANOTHER WAY OF CONSIDERING rest is "being gathered." I mean it here not in a corporate sense but in a personal sense. It is not a good feeling to feel scattered, over-extended, or "spread too thin." This is the "red" performance economy that conveys the stress of "reach," not "rest." Conversely, there is a deep sense of well-being, an easy stability, to "feeling gathered in oneself." By this I mean a solidness and contentment in the spiritual-material reality of our true humanity. In the "green" identity of who we are in Christ, we really can be "comfortable in our own skin." Theologically, green is more solid than red, since red has no independent substance of its own. As C. S. Lewis infers, perhaps Jesus in his resurrection body walked through walls because he was *more* solid than the walls, not less?[1]

---

1. See Lewis's essay "Transposition" in *Weight of Glory*, 91–115, e.g., "If flesh and blood cannot inherit the Kingdom, that is not because they are too solid.... They are too flimsy, too transitory, too phantasmal" (111). This kind of spiritual substantiality is a major theme of Lewis's in *The Great Divorce*. See also Hart, "Spiritual Was More Substantial." Notes Hart, "for the peoples of late Graeco-Roman antiquity, it made perfect sense to think of spiritual reality as more substantial, powerful, and resourceful than any animal body could ever be. Nothing of which a mortal, corruptible, 'psychical' body is capable would have been thought to lie beyond the powers of an immortal, incorruptible, wholly spiritual being. It was this evanescent life, lived in a frail and perishable animal frame, that was regarded as the poorer, feebler, more ghostly of the two conditions; spiritual existence was something immeasurably mightier, more

PART FIVE: JESUS IS MY HEAVEN

Jesus was an inclusive gatherer. "Inclusive gathering" sounds like an oxymoron. By its very nature, gathering usually involves bringing people together in contradistinction from the rest of the population. There are typically conditions or identifiers to gatherings; not everyone is eligible or interested in joining. It often ends up that we gather together with our group (us) while those not gathered are otherwise designated (them). We belong to the group; they do not. When you are not included, you are excluded—it is as simple as that.

Does Scripture convey that the choosing of some people inevitably means the exclusion of others? Throughout his ministry, Henri Nouwen was one who never tired of making the observation that when God chooses specific people in history, he does it for the ultimate purpose of revealing the inclusion of others.[2] We remember God excluding Esau and choosing Jacob, only to discover that God chose Jacob in order to save everyone, including Esau (Rom 11:32).[3]

God did this by including us all in Jacob's lineage through the Chosen One, the Lord Jesus Christ. We are often tempted to make Paul's self-confessed mistake: to think of Jesus Christ as an isolated man in history. But now we are given to see the meta-narrative of our lives, every human being

---

robust, more joyous, more plentifully alive." In Book One ("Dust to Dust") I posited Jesus's resurrection body as straddling dimensions (because there are some elements consistent with Jesus's pre-resurrection flesh). Hart comes down on the side that Jesus's resurrection body was simply his spiritual-material body. If Hart is right, then Jesus's post-resurrection body is obviously somehow "borrowing" from his pre-resurrection body (e.g., the "flesh and bones" encounter of Luke 24:37–42). I would prefer to see the resurrection body of Jesus as his risen mortal body still in dimensional tension with his human spiritual body, even if I am now given to see the situation from the opposite direction, i.e., from the spiritual body to the mortal body instead of from the mortal body to the spiritual (2 Cor 5:16). Different from Hart, this is what I take 1 Pet 3:18 to mean when it says Jesus was "put to death in the body but made alive in the Spirit." The accent has certainly changed, but we cannot really ascertain from this verse that the two dimensions are no longer concurrent. Never are we given permission in the gospels to see what Jesus looks like in his purely ascended, third-heaven, human form (i.e., simply his spiritual-material body free from his mortal body), only that he has not yet taken that step in its entirety (John 20:17). We claimed above that the post resurrection scenes in the gospels are insights into the second heaven, where there remains a degree of "overlap." Still, we can enthusiastically concur with Hart that Jesus's spiritual body is not restricted to the activity or inactivity of his mortal body. There is no reason why we should disallow the idea of Jesus preaching to the dead as the risen one crucified (1 Pet 4:6) or the crucified risen one (1 Pet 3:19). These events, too, would fall in the category of the second heaven.

2. See especially Nouwen's book, *Life of the Beloved*.

3. See further exegesis of Rom 9–11 in the Book One reading "When 'Created in the Image' Is Not Enough."

having died and raised in Jesus Christ (2 Cor 5:15), and "therefore" we no longer regard anyone from a worldly point of view (2 Cor 5:16).

Mark organizes his gospel around a strategic use of one specific word or theme—gathering. Consider examples in Mark 1:33; 2:2; 3:20; 4:1; 5:21; 6:30; 7:1; and 8:1. What are the two common components to these verses? Well, first, there is Jesus; and second, there is some form of the word "gather," or *synago* in the Greek. In reading these verses it is obvious that Jesus was an unconditional, inclusive gatherer; even the Pharisees and teachers of the law gathered around him (7:1). Christ's earthly life points to the eternal truth that he and gathering are inherently connected. Instead of inviting people to join our group because they don't belong, it is precisely the opposite. We invite people to gather with us in fellowship and at church *because they are already gathered with us* in the Unconditional Gatherer, the One who is "before all things, and in him all things hold together" (Col 1:17, NRSV).

Christ's earthly journey represents not only our personal gathering, but that of our corporate human gathering, the gathering to which Israel and Israel's temple uniquely bore witness. As the eternal Son of God, the true Israelite and the true human being, Jesus had reason to feel solidly gathered. But Jesus was also no stranger to false humanity's plight of being scattered. When he was an infant, his parents took Jesus and fled for their lives to Egypt for refuge. Just after his baptism he entered more deeply into conflict with evil, proving his solidarity with the human struggle; "immediately the Spirit drove him into the wilderness" (Mark 1:12). Even this was anticipated in the Old Testament by Jeremiah through his indictment of Israel: "I will scatter you like chaff driven by the desert wind" (13:24). If God seems to scatter at times, it is only on the basis of the reality of gathering. Jesus wants to identify to the full extent with human scattering to prove that gathering is deeper than scattering. In fact, scattering does not exist without gathering. And Jesus came to "re-gather" Israel, and all humanity, even "all things in heaven and on earth," in himself (Eph 1:10). Jesus paid a heavy price for his gathering. He foresaw that when he was lifted up on the cross, he would "draw [gather] all people" to himself (John 12:32), but at the same time those closest to him, his best friends, deserted him and "scattered" (John 16:31).

Thankfully, as with harvesting and sowing, gathering has the last word over scattering (Ps 126:6): "Those who go out weeping, carrying seed to sow, will return with songs of joy, carrying sheaves with them." Who doesn't want to be one of the sheaves collected and brought in during the great harvest? But there is another element to gathering at harvest time. Not only are the sheaves of wheat gathered, they are also threshed in order to separate out the grain. Gathering and separating, or harvesting and threshing, go together, just as the two "days"—the day of Sabbath and the day of judgment—go together. This is the fundamental rationale of the cross.

Proverbs 20:26–30 points to this event. It begins, "a wise king winnows out the wicked; he drives the threshing wheel over them." The writer surely did not anticipate that the king's victory over the wicked would involve his own death, but that is the story of the New Testament. The death of Christ (and our death in him) can therefore be seen as the wise king winnowing out all human wickedness under the threshing wheel by, in effect, rolling the wheel over himself while at the same time preserving in himself his beloved subjects, purged and cleansed (Prov 20:30). Indeed, John the Baptist later predicts Christ's death in a similar manner: "He will baptize you with the Holy Spirit and with fire. His winnowing fork is in his hand, and he will clear his threshing floor, gathering his wheat into his barn and burning up the chaff with unquenchable fire" (Matt 3:11–12). Only with a dimensional framework can these biblical accounts be christologically controlled as good news.

Without such controls (ironically when Christ's cross is not christologically controlled), Calvary is often postured as pure punishment, as if the Father administered to Jesus the whipping we deserved as the carrier of our sin. The cost of Christ's burden-bearing was indeed severe, but we would do better to think of Good Friday not as an exercise in corporal punishment so much as a *threshing* out of humanity's wickedness from within humanity itself, most pointedly from within the one human being in whom all human beings exist.[4] Thus, as revealed by the resurrection, the cross represents a corporate threshing of evil from good more than a penal thrashing. We are all "crucified with Christ."

Atonement, or at-one-ment, is itself a gathering. Negatively, atonement separates the wheat from the chaff. Positively, it is as if God gathers us into himself more tightly in making that separation, throwing out unneeded husks. Jesus fully embraces us at our worst, but in the atonement God gets rid of all that creates a semblance of fearful separation from him. Thus, demonstrated by God's embrace of us even *before* the threshing, we can know more than ever that nothing can separate us from the love of God (Rom 8:39).

The overlap of scattering and gathering is like the overlap of hell and heaven. Hell is a denial of our true gathered humanity. Just as we are in heaven now, so are we in hell, each "place" manifesting in different ways as gathered and scattered existence, respectively. Against the centripetal

---

4. See Mark 9:49–50: "Everyone will be salted with fire," Jesus said, and later, "salt is good." Salt has a protective and preservative element.

solidity of being gathered (being pulled toward the center), scattering connotes the centrifugal forces (pulling *away* from the center) at work that threaten to disintegrate us. Jesus yearns for us to experience "gathering" in this world, collectively and singularly, hidden in his wings like chicks with a hen (Luke 13:34) and at rest in our true humanity as children of God.

Thus far we have sought to present gathering as a biblically positive word. But gathering is not always good, just as scattering is not always bad. Scattering can be a positive reaction to something bad—the diaspora (dispersion of a group or people) of early Christ-followers caused by persecution, for instance (see Acts 11:19; 1 Pet 1:1), which had the effect of spreading the gospel. Scattering could also be something *purely* good, like farmers scattering their seed in the soil. And just as scattering can have a positive form, gathering can take on a negative form. Concentration camps, where people are concentrated, are insidious representations of gathering, or "rounding up," people.

In *After Whiteness: An Education in Belonging*, Willie Jennings speaks of this wrong kind of gathering—the kind that is opposite to that of "Mary's son who came to gather us"—the "gathering that does not cultivate life but pulls toward a bondage and death."[5] This kind of gathering is really hoarding.

"Some people hoard and some people have been hoarded," says Jennings. "Both realities of hoarding meet us in the history of modern colonialism. From the slave ship to the hacienda, from the plantation to the field, from the mine to the market, people were gathered as a means to an end: to marshal their collective energy."[6] Jennings grieves how people were made commodities, stripped of their indigenous contexts, contexts that evidenced a Trinitarian vibrancy: "a communal metaphysic grounded in sharing, mutual ownership, interpenetrating uses of goods and services; bartering, buying, selling, borrowing, and exchanging all woven in relationships."[7] Jennings does not extol these pre-colonial indigenous communities as perfect or utopian, but draws a sharp contrast between them and the anti-Trinitarian scattering mode of Western individualism. The indigenous communities, "Christian" or not, witnessed to the kingdom of God, Father, Son, and Holy Spirit in their communal life. Their similarity to the oft-exalted Acts 2 community is also clear.

There is no more poignant example of what we could call hateful or evil gathering than the slave ship. The depersonalized crowds of enslaved

---

5. Jennings, *After Whiteness*,134.
6. Jennings, *After Whiteness*,135.
7. Jennings, *After Whiteness*,143–44.

peoples crammed below deck for the middle passage is horrifically portrayed by Jennings in another book, *The Christian Imagination*:

> The slave ship distorted the power of joining together many different peoples on a common journey and mission. . . . Slaves of different tongues were often placed together on ships, which both further isolated and individualized them. . . . Bound together by twos and crammed tightly into the ship's holds, these human beings lay side by side in coffinlike spaces fetid with mucus, vomit, blood, and human waste. The heat, paucity of breathable air, and pestilence meant that many died below deck. The fate of those joined to the dying and dead was to have death chained to them until someone removed the dead body. The fate of the dead reinforced the mutilation of community and the disorder of creation.[8]

A few years ago, I had coffee with my friend Willie Jennings, the eminent theologian quoted above. When we got to theology, I asked him, "You know that section in your book that describes the scene on a slave ship?" He nodded. "Well," I continued, "it brings into question the hidden dynamic of what I understand to be the true human community. In a nutshell, *Do I have any right to claim, in the face of the horrors of the slave ship, that the abusers—the captain and crew—are in one dimension, concurrent to the dimension of abuse, loving God with all of their heart, soul, mind and strength? That the enslaved and enslavers are in one dimension worshipping the Lord in Spirit and truth, together loving God and their neighbor? My hope is that the hidden truth exposes more starkly the gross evil of the enslavers, providing more accountability before God than if they were operating in a supposed ethical vacuum. So, while this is where my theology takes me, I'm not sure I have the right to propose it.*

Not surprisingly, Dr. Jennings was quiet; he did not give me an answer. I took it as him not wanting to let me off the hook—not wanting to make it easy for me to avoid the grave responsibility for my words.

I ruminated on that discussion for years. Here is my answer today: no. No. I do not have the inherent right to propose such a drastic duality, not as a white man who has not suffered personally or collectively or generationally like this. Why, then, do I feel compelled to share it? Have I already forgotten James Cone's words above regarding white people who teach theology? "The white version of reality is too distorted and renders whites incapable."[9] I agree with Cone. In calling my own bluff, I can only

---

8. Jennings, *Christian Imagination*, 178, 179.
9. Cone, *Black Theology of Liberation*, 53–54.

acknowledge that any gospel that comes from me must, in a sense, come in spite of me. I understand that even this qualified allowance may be a bridge too far when it comes to me as a teacher providing constructive inspiration to my brothers and sisters of color.

Perhaps placemat theology provides a kingdom rule from which to better see the acutely painful angles of infliction upon our brothers and sisters. Perhaps it stands to best expose the profound depths of evil and its hellish effects on God's good creation. Perhaps it provides the most severe indictment against the principalities and racist powers of whiteness.[10] The slave ship forces us to recognize the graphic juxtaposition of the two opposite human determinations at work in all of our lives.

As Charles H. Long expounds: "that journey across the water has not been resolved and what needs to be thought about again is that on those boats coming across the water, there were Europeans and Africans on the same boat. They were on the same boat but they were taking two different journeys. And those two journeys cannot be reconciled simply by having good thoughts and thinking in universal terms." Long describes African Americans as "Water People." For concrete reconciliation to happen, continues Long, "there has to be a movement back into the water." Cultural course corrections are not enough, any more than a crooked course can use crooked means to be straightened. Long calls us instead to begin again, refusing to polarize ontology and experience. Therefore, it is necessary not

---

10. In Book One we made clear that whiteness does not refer to white skin. Instead, it refers to participation in racist attitudes and actions, even subconsciously, to which white people like me are inevitably susceptible. There is no more poignant example that shows the evil of hoarding than a slave ship. Given the parameters in just war theory for contexts in which the use of violence is morally tolerable, analogous guidelines are surely met in a situation where slaves revolt and kill those who trapped and enslaved them. If there are times when killing others is a legitimate scriptural and righteous argument, a slave revolt clearly qualifies. Placemat anthropology recognizes that there are some situations in which people act with enough existential wickedness that they and their wickedness, or they and the systemic nature of their wickedness, are relatively approximate (see later reading "Double Agents and Situational Ethics"). If theorists often regard World War II as a just war (regarding the *jus ad bellum* aspect), should we not consider those who engaged in slave revolts as morally justified in their use of violence? Should we not honor Christian preacher revolutionaries Nat Turner and Denmark Vesey along with the likes of Dwight Eisenhower? (See James Cone's contention along these lines, *Black Theology of Liberation*, 51, 108). It's true that Turner and Vesey's revolts against systemic injustice included collateral damage to presumed innocents, but we should also consider that the allied bombings of German and Japanese cities indiscriminately killed over a half million noncombatants. Could I uphold the just cause of a slave revolt if it meant my white ancestors were wiped out and I was never born? In principle, is that a sacrifice I would be willing to make? Thanks to Edward Lowe for lending his expertise on just war theory here and elsewhere.

only for Black people to move "back into the water," but for others to follow suit into the nexus of contradiction. Long was not speaking in specifically Christian terms, but his direction is a retrospective one, back toward the goodness of creation only through the crucible of "the cross" of Black experience. For Long, in light of the cruel torture of enslaved peoples, there can be no reconciliation without a reckoning. A movement "back into the water," then, is needed "to reorient ourselves not only about the destiny and meaning of African Americans but about the destiny and meaning of what kind of future human beings have on the face of this earth."[11]

Under the charge of Long and Cone and others, I must ask myself if an emphasis on ontology—every human's ongoing being-in-act in Christ—causes my view to make light of existential evil and suffering. Does it come across dismissively, as if I am trying to quickly explain it away? Does it contribute to others' suffering in ways that pain me to even write? I hope not. I hope my theology has made me more compassionate and more zealous for justice. I hope that it also makes those whom I teach more compassionate, more human, more able to recognize the humanity of others.

More pointedly, am I right to claim the deep reality of the ongoing righteous determination of every human being in Christ, even when these exact same human beings manifest the opposite determination in their worldly words and deeds? Do I have permission to take the anti-community of a floating vessel marked by human hoarding and imagine simultaneously, in a different dimension, a redeemed human gathering? The risk weighs heavy. My whole theological project is called into question. To the extent that my proposal is true, it witnesses to the truth in Christ. As such, its witness must be relevant to all historical contexts and situations, even including the slave ship. But still, while truth is one thing, wisdom in applying it is another. How is such a counterintuitive proposal best worked out on an anthropological and sociological level?

I would not want to speak in the wrong place, the wrong time, or the wrong way to reassure those suffering oppression, violence, and trauma that their perpetrators in one dimension love God and others perfectly in Christ. So I stand in the dock.

---

11. Long, "Legacy of Slavery." Long was not first and foremost a theologian, but he saw the need of a big God to achieve such a new beginning for humanity, and he found such a God in his favorite theologian Karl Barth. Still, Long questioned Barth's grasp of white supremacy in America, and found himself in helpful dialogue with Barth on one hand and James Cone on the other. I thank Raymond Carr for these insights about Long and Cone, partly attained through his 2023 symposium at Harvard University, "The (Re)Imagination of Matter: Introducing the Codex Charles H. Long Papers Project." See Carr, "Thelonious Monk," 177–93.

Explanations that collapse the complexity of the situation into a callous triumphalism ought not be tolerated and are rightly judged as wanting. Indeed, any human acts incongruent with God's will—whether it be regarding those who are enslavers, or regarding those of us who theologize about enslavers—these will be shown for what they are at the judgment seat of Christ. If existential reconciliation does not exist apart from the ontology of true human community, then neither does it exist apart from the reckoning of the cross. In Long's words, we must go back into the water.

60

The Grace of Wrath[1]

If I think of my life as a class. . . . I've learned a few things. First, I am aware that I am a child of God. . . . Then I have to know that the brute, the bigot, the batterer are all children of God, whether they know it or not, and I'm supposed to treat them accordingly. . . . [T]hink of a statement by Terence . . . "I am a human being. Nothing human can be alien to me." If you can internalize the least portion of that, you will never be able to say of an act, a criminal act, "oh, I couldn't do that," no matter how heinous the crime. If a human being did it, we have to say "I have in me all of the components that are in her or in him." . . . If you can do that about the negative, just think what you can do about the positive.

—Maya Angelou

Is my enemy God's child? . . . If God loves him, that binds me. Can it be that God does not know how terrible he is? No, God knows him . . . much better than I know him. It must be true, then, that there is something in every man that remains intact, inviolate, regardless of what he does. I wonder! Is this true? Is there an integrity to the person, so intrinsic in its value and significance that no deed,

---

1. This section draws heavily from Barth's doctrine of election and his use of Yes and No language especially in *CD* II/2 and *CD* IV/2. See McSwain, "'Yes' of Reality."

however evil, can ultimately undermine this given thing? If a man is of infinite worth in the sight of God, whether he is saint or sinner, whether he is a good man or a bad man, evil or not, if that is true, then I am never relieved of my responsibility for trying to make contact with this worthy thing in him. . . . No deed that he does, therefore, however awful it may be, is completely indicative of all that there is to him and in him.

—Howard Thurman

Most Christians adhere to the doctrine of original sin. That is not the problem. The problem comes when they lose sight of the fact that original belonging—not original sin—is the non-negotiable aspect of the human situation. In other words, original belonging in Christ is deeper than original sin, even if, in this world, they exist together, as the red and green are woven together in our placemat image. While wearing grey glasses, parents implicitly or explicitly make decisions about discipline based on whether their children are fundamentally green or red in nature. If the books I read about child-rearing in my Evangelical years are any indication, it seems like those inside the church are often the ones most likely to choose red as their child's baseline color. Reversing the host-parasite relationship, they make green the exception to the rule of red.

"Better whipped than damned," the puritan Cotton Mather once said regarding parenting.[2] It is not difficult to see how destructive Christian child-rearing can be when we lose sight of the indelible goodness of children, thinking that somehow, because of the fall, they are nothing but depraved sinners with corrupt natures. Even worse, it may be articulated that in their "lost state" they are not children of God, but *children of Satan*. At that point, discipline often involves thrashing the foolishness and rottenness out of them, hoping that someday they will choose to replace their old heart with a new heart. Contrast that to the approach George MacDonald urges: "A parent must respect the spiritual person of his child, and approach it with reverence, for that too looks the Father in the face and has an audience with Him into which no earthly parent can enter even if he dared to desire it."[3] Many of us are parents, but each of us have always been that child of whom McDonald speaks.

---

2. See Pronk, "Puritan Christianity." See also Narvaez, "Original Sin of Babies."
3. MacDonald as quoted in Lewis, *George MacDonald*, 106.

PART FIVE: JESUS IS MY HEAVEN

When it comes to one's assurance of belonging to God as his beloved child, sequential theologies of salvation are quite damaging. For instance, the narrative might run that God as my creator had a grip on me originally, and then 1) I evaded his grasp and ran away from him, 2) he dropped me, or 3) I was snatched away by the enemy. Regardless of the option chosen, God had me at one point and then he didn't. So, if at one point I am not in the grip, only to later return and re-enter his "grip of grace," then we must ask the question, "What kind of grip is that?" The answer: not a very good one, and certainly not a grip we can trust.

In Book One we described election as a Trinitarian double movement of grace. In the Spirit, Christ fulfills the covenant between God and humanity from both sides and for every person. That's why we say grace is a Yes to a Yes, in the two-way mediation of Christ (2 Cor 1:18–20). The Creator's "Plan A" of grace has always been the Father's faithful Yes *to humanity* in Christ by the Spirit, met by the answering Yes from Christ *for humanity* to the Father by the Spirit.

When we say grace is God's truth for humanity in Jesus Christ, we are saying at the deepest level of the covenant of election, the Second Adam's Yes to God includes every human's most personal "yes" to God. To say it another way, because our human representative is keeping truth with God, true existential acts of human love and faithfulness to God are only possible inside of this Truth. In one dimension, this is the Truth in whom we are already participating by the Spirit of Truth. Even though such a faithful and loving human response is, for us, unconscious before conscious, the ontological metanarrative of that Yes—from God to us and from us to God, both in Christ—is where we are found.[4]

Our lostness relates to the fact that, even while bound within such an amazing relationship of love in God, we decide that we know better. In the name of freedom of choice, we choose bondage, operating from the flesh and not from and in the Spirit.[5] What, then, is God's response? Would "That's ok, my child, do what you want" represent God's love? Just the opposite. If my beloved children disobeyed me and went out to play on a busy street, endangering themselves, would I passively sit back and watch them from a distance? Of course not.

---

4. In this vein I think of two gospel lyrics: "Yes, Lord Yes, to your will and to your way; Yes, Lord, Yes, I will trust and I'll obey; Yes, Lord Yes, when your Spirit gets to me, the answer will be Yes, Lord, Yes (from "Yes, Lord, Yes" by Lynn Keesecker) and, "From the bottom of my heart, and the depths of my soul, Yes Lord, Yes Lord, Yes Lord" (from "Yes Lord" by Sandra Crouch). I find refreshing ontological connection in singing these refrains.

5. See "Freedom and Unfreedom" in Book One.

God's wrath, then, is the other side of his fierce love, included in love and yet appearing distinct from it. God's wrath is his way of saying No to our "no." Because God's grace is a Yes to a Yes, our sinful "no" just does not fit. Something must be done about it. Our disobedient "no" is out of sync and therefore destructive. If you drive a car out of alignment for too long, all kinds of bad things start happening to your vehicle. This is the sense of Colossians 2:18–19, where Paul talks about the people who lost their heads—"they are puffed up with idle notions by their unspiritual mind." Of course, this does not mean that the person who loses their head is disconnected spatially (as in decapitation!), but their wrong-headed incongruence has consequences. Their disloyalty to the proper Head of every human is destructive for themselves and the body of Christ as a whole.

God's two-way covenant commitment of Yes is the baseline of our existence. In reality, we live and think and speak congruently with our own participatory "yes" in Christ's Yes for us. Thus, God's wrathful No is fundamental to God's restorative character. God's wrath is not retributive for one simple reason—it serves his love. His love will not be satisfied until our "no" to God is extinguished forever. In order to eradicate our "no," Christ became *the* No, the negation of our negation, absorbing all its effects and putting it away for good.[6] This economy of Christ's passion helps us to know that when God says No, he always has a bigger Yes in mind.

In *The Cruciality of the Cross*, P. T. Forsyth speaks of the fragility and lifelessness of a believer's assurance when God's No to our "no" does not have finality. Inevitably, Forsyth writes, "the soul goes on to think thus: 'As I grow in Christ . . . the damnability of my sin grows on me, and with it the incredibility of grace. How do I know not merely that God is willing to forgive but that he has forgiven, that what is so incredible is equally unalterable?'" Judging by the appearances, feelings, or experiences that make up our inadequate self-assessments, even those once confident of their forgiven standing with God lose their verve. If the believer "sins after his forgiveness in such a grievous way," continues Forsyth, "he gets such a shock in the revelation of sin's tough and subtle power that it needs something very final and decisive to assure him of its destruction. . . . He must have a finished work, and a God who has made a full end."[7]

Almost half of the books in the Bible, Old and New Testament, refer to God's wrath toward humans.[8] "Sometimes in the Christian Church and

---

6. In 2 Cor 5:21 Paul writes that Christ was made sin, addressing sin at the root. See also Heb 2:9 where Christ tasted death for everyone and Heb 2:14 where Christ defeated death by death.

7. Forsyth, *Cruciality of the Cross*, 45–46.

8. When it comes to God's wrath, the God of the Old Testament (OT) and the God

in Christian theology people have been astonished or even offended at this concept of the wrath of God," notes Barth. "Some have even thought that at this point they must correct the Bible, believing wrath is unworthy of God."[9] But can we say more about how God's love and God's wrath go together? Barth continues: "The word of God's wrath is full of comfort and gospel, full of good news. . . . A mere overlooking pardon would not be worthy of [God], nor would it help man. It would be the lack of mercy, the indifference, of a god who in truth is not God."[10]

The biblical theme of God's wrath cannot be dodged, but it must be rightly handled. We can work it out as follows: to the extent that God is angry at me, it is anger directed not to me, *first and foremost*, but to my false self, or to me as a wicked sinner (what the Bible calls the "old man"). We still have to say God is angry with "me," since there is no false self without a "me" in the first place. But, as with Paul's "I, but not I" logic in the positive sense, we have permission to say in the negative sense that God is angry with "me, but not me."[11] This makes room for the proper theological distinctions. Even if God's anger is directed *against* me in one specific provisional sense, it is always *for* me in a larger sense.[12] The more we trust his love, the more we understand the precise aim of God's wrath.[13] God's love for the whole person (like his anger against sin), is never in question, even when he is rejecting (delegitimizing) our false selves.

---

of the New Testament (NT) often do not seem compatible. We have to make a choice regarding the interpretive key. Crudely spoken, do we fit Christ into the OT picture or do we fit the OT into the picture Christ gives us? How can God's wrath against whole peoples (e.g., the Amalekites, 1 Sam 15:3) be christologically recalibrated as part of the good news? We will address these questions in later readings.

9. Barth, *Learning Jesus Christ*, 41.

10. Barth, *Learning Jesus Christ*, 42.

11. See Gal 2:20 in the ERV, KJV (2000), and others for the "I . . . yet not I" construction, which is glossed over in many translations: "nevertheless I live, yet not I, but Christ who lives in me."

12. This provisional sense is important. In Book One we noted Julian's revelation that the "compassion and pity" God expresses toward the "fallen" Jesus and humanity are provisional, and that the "joy and bliss" the Father expresses toward the Son are eternal and unchanging. Our placemat principle of transposition means that what is in the higher order is dimensionally present in and through the lower orders, but not the other way round. Just as there is no need for compassion and pity in the third heaven, there is no need of wrath. As God's No to our "no," wrath comes down from the dimensional border of the second heaven and the work of Jesus Christ crucified. But in the third heaven, only the covenantal Yes to a Yes remains.

13. As Barth notes: "The 'for us' of His death on the cross includes and encloses this terrible 'against us.' Without this terrible 'against us' it would not be the divine and holy and redemptive and effectively helpful 'for us' in which the conversion of man and the world to God has become an event" (*CD* IV/1, 296).

Because God's love is deeper than any parent for a child, we can find solace in God's unique kind of anger. God's anger is the "be angry and do not sin" (Eph 4:26, NKJV) kind of anger, a kind of anger that we human beings are incapable of by our own power. But if it is true that I cannot make that distinction in the same way God can, is it wrong for me to be angry at my kids?

On the one hand, we can see a witness to the divine love and wrath in the way children handle their parent's anger when such discipline happens in the context of a loving relationship. In a home life with loving parents, children seem to have an uncanny ability to discern the love in the anger, or the anger of the love.[14] On the other hand, we must live with the fact that no matter how well we think we may have executed appropriate discipline, we have not done it perfectly. As a result, there may still be an element of confusion in our children's minds about the preeminence of love or wrath. With enough reinforcement from within and without, they may mistakenly think that the No is the rule and the Yes the exception. This is a confusion we often project onto God as we consider the relationship between God's love and wrath toward us.

In the realm of perfect clarity (the second heaven), when God says he is angry with us, there is absolutely no possibility of us absorbing his anger in the wrong way. It is the enemy, not God, who seeks to produce guilt and shame. In the second heaven, we will see that the problem is not God's anger; the problem is that we take poor human interactions and misguided instances of anger and project them falsely onto God. In the here and now, this makes it very difficult for us to trust the purity of God's anger and to see his overall purposes—that God's anger is directed first and foremost against Satan, not us. Karl Barth tirelessly reminded us of this fact.[15]

Failure to represent God's anger properly is something even the biblical writers, perhaps, were susceptible to doing. This mistake is understandable, as we do not experience the kind of pure anger described in Romans 2:8 in this world.[16] As always, our misguided fear about God's wrath exposes our

---

14. I laugh while imagining how I might communicate such theological nuance in a moment of father-to-son discipline: "I'm not angry at you, I'm angry at your 'old man'!" Recognizing the fact that I can't do it like God can, it is perhaps better to say, "I'm angry with you right now," trusting the integrity of the relationship. The poorer alternative would say, "I'm not angry with you" when we really are.

15. See especially *CD* III/3, 354–62.

16. Rom 2:8, "But for those who are self-seeking and who reject the truth and follow evil, there will be wrath and anger." Jesus Christ can perfectly represent the pure loving wrath of God to humanity and the pure reception of such wrathful love, as Barth describes in Christ's "choosing to suffer the wrath of God in His own body and the fire of [God's] love in His own soul" (*CD* IV/1, 95).

insecurity about God's love. For instance, "Was God so angry with me for that affair that he caused my child to die?" It is easy to be drawn into such one-to-one conclusions, but the retributive eye-for-an-eye prescription is exactly the economy Jesus came to dismantle. God is never the agent of evil. His wrath always serves his love. His No is always inside of his larger Yes. God is never angry with you and me in isolation from the larger problem of the Prince of this world who has victimized us. God destroys what destroys his beloved children, and that means that God's wrath burns brightly against the forces of evil.

61

Children of Wrath?

They give the wrath of God its due place . . . for they do not only know about the wrath of God, but realise that His wrath is the burning of His love. . . . Divine wrath does not really exist apart from grace.

—Karl Barth

When Christ blossoms in our land, makes fragrant the field of the soul, and flourishes in his church, we can no longer fear the cold or rain, but only anticipate the day of judgement.

—Ambrose

Now we are at a better place to understand a potentially confounding passage in Scripture, Ephesians 2:1–3: "You were dead through the trespasses and sins in which you once lived, following the course of this world, following the ruler of the power of the air, the spirit that is now at work among those who are disobedient. All of us once lived among them in the passions of our flesh, following the desires of flesh and senses, and we were by nature children of wrath, like everyone else" (NRSV).

For Paul, stating that "we were by nature children of wrath" is obviously a universal statement—we were *all* by nature children of wrath. It is an indictment—"disobedient . . . following the desires of flesh and senses"—with which we can readily concur. In the context of grace, we can see our sin more clearly, and are more ready to acknowledge it.

But what does Paul mean in saying we were children of wrath "by nature?" He is certainly not speaking of humanity's original nature, as if our original nature could be equated with sinful nature. Without diminishing human goodness, he instead gives proper weight to the flesh as our birth nature resulting from the fall. Yet he knows that as provisional and parasitic as it may be to our "original nature," our "sinful nature" is comprehensive in its effects. As holistically good (totally green) as our proper human nature is in Christ, mind, body, and soul, our false humanity in the flesh is holistically bad (totally red), mind, body, and soul.

In our false selves, as this passage relates, our lives manifest sinful disobedience. Not only are the desires of the flesh mentioned but also the thoughts of the flesh, and all under the influence of the ruler spirit, the spirit "who is now at work in those who are disobedient" (Eph 2:2).[1] We are living as children of wrath, then, because it is to *all* of these things that Christ, in his fierce love, came to say No! These aspects of the sinful nature—things motivated not by the Holy Spirit but by an oppositional spirit—are the red things his sacrificial wrath aims to burn away and separate from us, giving the green berth to burgeon forth. This is the liberating separation that will be seen most clearly on judgment day and which by the Spirit already ministers to us in this world.

In Book One we emphasized from Ephesians 1:1–4 that every human being is elected, or chosen, in the chosen one, Jesus Christ. Allowing the holistic description of the flesh as "sinful nature" from the older NIV (1984), the fact that we have two "natures" is placemat consistent. We have our created nature as God's chosen, and our birth "nature" under the curse of sin. Only with this placemat approach can we make serious sense of a passage like Deuteronomy 28:15, "If you do not obey the LORD your God and do not carefully follow all his commands and decrees . . . all these curses will come on you and overtake you." We are chosen, and at the same time cursed. We all fall short of this Deuterine imperative. "Converted" or not, we are all disobedient, showing that we are in one sense under the curse.

Returning to the language of Ephesians, it is apparent that the spirit who is "now at work in those who are disobedient" is still at work in believers. We have a true nature, in which we are blessed, beloved, and obedient. And we have a false "nature," in which we are cursed, rejected, and disobedient. This is Barth's meaning when he says, "Curse means the rejection of

---

1. This spirit John calls "the spirit of the anti-Christ" (1 John 4:3).

the chosen."[2] Barth is not speaking nonsense, but he is recognizing the two sides of the one Israel and the one human subject. Pat is chosen, and Pat is also the rejected who is crucified with Christ. Outside of the love of Christ on the cross, God's wrath has no meaning. As with God's beloved Israel, God's beloved Pat cannot be cursed unless Pat is also chosen. There is no "God is *against* us" (the No of God) without an ongoing, "God is *for* us" (the Yes of God).

Thus, our placemat approach posits that we can be children of God and children of wrath simultaneously. But the question remains, if Paul is operating from our simultaneous premise, why does he make such a big deal about the "before-after" of the Ephesians conversion experience? Indeed, Ephesians 2:3 explicitly states that we *were* by nature children of wrath. The text goes on to make a death-to-resurrection sequential claim rooted in the death and resurrection of Christ: "But because of his great love for us, God, who is rich in mercy, made us alive with Christ even when we were dead in transgressions—it is by grace you have been saved" (Eph 2:4–5). It seems like Paul endorses a categorical transition from red to green (e.g., I was a child of wrath, but then after my conversion and baptism, I became a child of God).

Though this categorical change from red to green sounds simple enough, we must ask why the behavior of those who are supposed to be green often manifest in large measure the qualities and behaviors of red. According to one interpretation, if I show a certain amount of red, then that proves I never really converted to green. But how much red disqualifies me? Where is the line? Paul's language simply says children of wrath are those who manifest disobedience and those who manifest disobedience are children of wrath. If that is really the case, is anyone truly converted? As scriptural exegetes, these questions force us back to the text.

There is a better explanation for why Paul uses the past tense to set up the sequence ("we were . . . but now") both here and similarly elsewhere.[3]

2. Barth, *Learning Jesus Christ*, 42.

3. For example, the very similar passage Col 1:21–22, "Once you were alienated from God and were enemies in your minds because of your evil behavior. But now he has reconciled you by Christ's physical body through death to present you holy in his sight, without blemish and free from accusation." See my note on this verse in the Book Two introduction, under "The Two Chairs and Repentance." For a continuation on this theme, see Col 3:7, "You used to walk in these ways, in the life you once lived. But now you must also rid yourselves of all such things as these: anger, rage, malice, slander, and filthy language from your lips." Paul says "you *used to walk* in these ways," but it is obvious by the rest of the statement that the Colossians are still sinning in the same ways! From our perspective, Paul is upbraiding them to be who they are, to act in correlation to their new self-described identity, which is their oldest and original identity, "hidden with Christ in God" (Col 3:3). Anchored in the "hid," we are better equipped to "rid."

In order to grasp his meaning, we must avoid thinking primarily of our own existential sequence when it comes to the before and after narrative of our conversion. The sequence of our existential before and after narrative is always tied to the sequence of Christ's death and resurrection. But we go wrong if we simply declare that God "made us alive with Christ" at the revival last week. It is not that we should not say these words in describing the "born anew" experience, only that we must avoid severing such experiences from their ontological root.

Like Paul, Peter testifies to the fact that we were born anew (were "given new birth") over 2000 years ago, as witnessed by the raising of Christ Jesus from the dead (1 Pet 1:3). If we fail to follow the ontological emphasis—the existential manifesting *from* the ontological—then the two collapse into one another. We must guard against such "existentialism" without denying the validity of our spiritual experiences, but how?

To begin with, let us return to our theological conviction that "old" and "new" must stay within the context of "false" and "true." In placemat terms, old is what has always been false, and new is what has always been true. "False" and "true" are easier to relate on a simultaneous level, helping us to see that "old" and "new" point to more than just *our* existential sequence. They are informed christologically, by the one who was simultaneously the true and the false human in himself, revealing the one by his resurrection life and delimiting the other by his death. Because the old self is always with us in this life, and because our earthly death has not yet "caught up" to our death in Christ, so also are we continually children of wrath. We are fully red. On this side of the veil, our two-fold lives as red/green, old/new, false/true, children of wrath/children of God will always be the case. This simultaneity keeps us from putting such undue weight on *our* existential sequence that it simply collapses. Our christological "placemat" hermeneutic provides us with a firm foundational assessment.

Following that, however, there is also an experiential assessment. The "we were" language is Paul's nod to the fact that his Ephesian recipients have experienced *Christ's sequence* in a powerful, palpable way. They self-associated with the reference point of their lives, Jesus Christ, through the sacrament of baptism and, following their discovery and visceral participation in the body of Christ, *they now view themselves* as the new creations that they are in him. Because of the illumination of the sequence of Christ (i.e., the gospel!) and the work of the Holy Spirit, their mode of existence is being transformed. They now desire to leave the ways of the world and to live full, obedient lives in the newness and trueness of reality. Because of the interpretive key, the Ephesians now recognize their false selves as "old"—even as they exist in the present. Those awakened to conversion are newly accountable to live in correlation with the pre-existing truth of their being in the Spirit. This life-movement includes a present-future momentum, an orientation to one's pre-existing truth of being as well as the truth of who one *will be* when all is said and done. As Barth put it, "They can now walk only as those they already are, not as those they still are."[4] What a joy to discover the gospel alternative of being bogged down in the flesh, as if our shoes are stuck in the mud, caked with guilt and shame. As believers we recognize that the indicative, who we are in Christ and the Spirit, comes before the imperative. Paul states this plainly in Galatians, "Since we live by the Spirit, let us keep in step with the Spirit" (Gal 5:25).

The existential sequence is clearly important. We would not have such things as the New Testament letters, after all, if people did not have life-changing experiences in the Spirit of Truth. The event of adult baptism, for instance, can have a profound effect on a person. It is also clear that the "spiritual high" of baptism—apart from its theological underpinnings—can soon give ways to lower lows, the high of the spiritual experience making mundane experience even more pronounced in its dullness. Paul wants to acknowledge the power in existential sequence, but his stabilizing emphasis is on the Christ *of our experience* more than on *our experience of* Christ (as J. B. Torrance would put it).

Even Jesus, when speaking of his baptism, speaks first and foremost of the cross, rather than his own baptism by John the Baptist in the Jordan River years before (e.g., Luke 3:1–18). Eight chapters later, right in the very middle of Luke's gospel, Jesus puts it this way: "I have a baptism to undergo, and what constraint I am under until it is completed!" (Luke 12:50). Theologically speaking, it is as if Jesus's baptism in the Jordan is a lower case "b" compared to the central event of the cross, which is Baptism with a capital "B." Like nested boxes, Jesus's water baptism is inside of his death and resurrection, and our water baptism is inside of his water baptism. Thus, we do not get baptized because Jesus was baptized in the Jordan, as if we emulate his example, but because we are implicated in the death and resurrection of our Savior.

By starting with Christ, Paul is not only more able to define the good and righteous experiences as grounded in the risen one, he is also more equipped to define all bad and sinful experiences inside of the one and the same crucified one. Do we really think that Paul, by encouraging the Ephesians to live in the "new," would be so naïve to imagine that they had completely left the old behind, no longer gratifying the cravings of the flesh (Eph 2:3)? Indeed, we would be blind to say that we ourselves are not still under

---

4. *CD* IV/2, 574.

the influence of the evil spirit (v. 2), shown by our continued disobedience. To the degree that we disobey at all, we are manifesting the old not the new and Paul's indictment of Ephesians 2:1–3 still applies. But we must grasp that while this passage describes who we were and are, it is not who we are and will be (remember the saying of Karl Barth, "I was and still am the old man, I am and will be the new man"). Paul wrote to those who already realized this, and who defined and interpreted their lives in the present by the sequence of the living person of Jesus Christ. This is the true meaning of living "the exchanged life."

Part of the beauty of the body of Christ in action is the way that it takes our minds off ourselves and our existential predicament. In the midst of our simultaneous situation—the warfare happening in our lives between two opposing determinations—we can fix our minds on the sequence of our Lord and Savior, worshiping him, encouraging one another, building each other up in Christ. With grateful hearts we give praise and thanks together for the fact that *we* are included in *Christ's* sequence. This is preferable to getting mired in the sequential quicksand of the one-off "Pat event." The latter places undue emphasis on my conversion experience without reference to its Christ-centered basis. Instead of a lack of assurance that causes us to continually seek firmer grounding, we are empowered by the rootedness of the Christ event that allows the "Pat event" to flower, and to flower again.

The economy of existential sequence, however, is strong in religious and especially revivalist traditions. The "Great Awakening" in America and Britain featured the formative voices of Wesley, Whitefield, and Edwards. In this tradition, there are undoubtedly those who have had intense conversion experiences from which they never looked back, and never again struggled with sin to the same degree. Many, however, have struggled to find consistency in their commitment to Christ even after experiencing a "spiritual high." The cut and dry "before and after" or red-to-green picture does not suffice to explain these situations. Instead, people are left to feel guilty and ashamed, unable to keep up their end of the bargain with God.

Some might see it as a weakness that placemat anthropology does not pin its assurance on even the most powerful conversion experiences. With Karl Barth, we seek it elsewhere. His project involves ripping away our prized existential sequence to give us something much more substantial in return, and which, if we grasp it, makes our experiences that much more profound. If our emphasis is on Christ's sequence and not on that of the believer, and if we recognize the two total determinations at odds in each of our lives, then *all* human experiences can be explained as manifesting one of the two totals in myriad ways and to varying degrees.[5]

We use the phrases "to the degree" and "to the extent" throughout our study. These are critical terms. They keep us from pretending that we have ever experienced the totality of red or the totality of green in this life. If we thought we could, we would fall prey to a sequential "total replacement" of green for red. Or, forgetting the two totals, we might fall back into the zero-sum game and the rise and fall of percentages of each color. If we adopt a displacement interpretation, as if the red sap of the proverbial branch is pushed out or being pushed out by the green sap, then we are left to explain why the red sap still surges beyond its "borders." That, or we must explain how the green sap can spring forth from a supposedly "nothing but red" branch. We are always returning to our two-fold question: How can a believer act at times so red, and unbelievers so green?

It is easy to read Scripture's existential language from an existential rather than christological viewpoint, forgetting the ontological root. Our placemat perspective helps us to remember that spiritual conversion experiences do not activate the truth, they do not add to truth or even multiply it. They *bear witness to the truth* of who Christ is and who we are in him. These experiences are manifestations of reality, the human, in-Christ dimension. We must take an estimate of the alternative. To read before/after language as anything more than an existential description undoes the gospel reality that is full and complete, lacking nothing in Christ. Our conversions are only as good as the pre-existent truth in which they are rooted.

Yes, we are totally red. But we must never forget that we have always been totally green. Green is grace. Grace is God's dynamic truth for humanity in Jesus Christ. Paul upbraids the Ephesians in his letter to be who they are; indeed, according to Ephesians 1, who they have always been (Eph 1:4).

Paul goes on to say that "it is by grace you have been saved" twice (Eph 2:5, 8). The second time he adds a faith element: "for by grace you have been saved, *through faith*—and this is not from yourselves, it is the gift of God—not by works, so that no one can boast." We need not get tripped up by the phrase "through faith," as if it undoes all that we have said about grace. Was Paul against works? Not at all, as Ephesians 2:10 makes plain, for "we are God's handiwork, created in Christ Jesus to do good works, which God prepared in advance for us to do." But Paul is against works that are extracted from the rubric of grace. Likewise, he does not want faith to appear as a

---

5. See Rom 8:13 which bears witness to the two simultaneous dynamics at play: first, in the Spirit you are living, (i.e., moving toward life), and then in the flesh you are dying (i.e., moving toward death). In our experience these dynamics manifest in manifold ways.

kind of work external to grace, as if faith is a "way into" grace. In Book One we described "saved through faith" as synonymous with "saved through Christ." This is because faith, like all human activity toward God, fits under grace.[6] Jesus Christ is the primary reference point for both faith and works, such that in the gift of his person the two are always kept together for us.

We described above how our faith occurs inside the faith of Christ on our behalf. Beyond this, we can declare that without the vicarious faithfulness of Christ on our behalf, we could not have faith at all. Though some translations insert the adjectives "our" or "your" in matters of faith, i.e., "Jesus, the pioneer and perfecter of *our* faith" (Heb 12:2, emphasis added), the word "our" or "your" is often not there in the Greek text.[7] Such an artificial insertion does not help us avoid the propensity to fixate on our individual sequence. Instead, it only encourages us to focus on *our* faith before that of Christ, putting the cart before the horse.

The above passage emphasizes that grace is a pure "gift." The gift as expressed here is not just one of being redeemed by Christ. Instead, it hearkens back to the foundational truth of every life: we are created in Christ (Eph 2:10). This last verse renders untenable the sequential shift as posited in many conversion narratives, "from child of wrath to child of God." If we are created in Christ the Son and are therefore beloved children of God, how could "child of wrath" be all there is to say about our identity? In the christologic of Ephesians, we cannot be children of wrath unless we are first and foremost children of God. Why? Because everyone is created as a child of God; there is no other kind of human creation. We not only

---

6. See the reading "Belong, Believe, Obey" in Book One. Good works do not save us, but we are created and redeemed to do good works. Thus, if faith becomes a work, then it is conditional and not a pure gift. To maintain the proper relationship, we can think of faith as pertaining first and foremost to Christ's faith on our behalf. Theologically, we can read Scripture's phrases "through faith" or "by faith" as "through Christ" and "by Christ." For example, "by grace you have been saved, *through Christ.*" Again, this keeps our faith in its proper place. Faith is inside of grace, as a participatory event in Christ and not a primary event in the life of the believer. Because our faith is inside of our union with Christ, so are our works.

7. For "your" see, for example, Col 2:12. See also the many times that *pistis Christou* in the Greek is translated "faith in Christ," putting the emphasis on our *faith in Christ*, when it can just as easily be translated *faith of Christ*, emphasizing the primary reference point of Christ's faithfulness on our behalf, e.g., Gal 2:20, "the life that I now live in my body, I live by faith, indeed, by the faithfulness of God's Son, who loved me and gave himself for me" (CEB). The Greek carries a beautiful ambiguity of potentially meaning both aspects at once, as if Christ's faithfulness precedes and includes my particular faith without reducing it. The key is to interpret it in the right priority, keeping our faith as second fiddle inside of Christ's primary faith. See Campbell, "Participation and Faith in Paul." See also T. F. Torrance, "One Aspect," 111–14.

conditionalize the gift when we treat it otherwise, we insult it when we say that eternal life is not a gift until we receive it.

Eternal life is human life the way it is created and redeemed to be—humans thriving as God's children. Eternal life is a dimension of our lives now. Eternal life is what *is*, not just what will be or can be. God *has given us* eternal life (1 John 5:11). Everyone is included in the gift of eternal life because everyone is included in the Son of God. This type of Christ-centered inclusion and acceptance is much more robust than simple, generic versions of inclusion and acceptance. The gift of eternal life means we are included *by* someone. Not only that, inclusion means that we are accepted *in* someone, the same someone in whom and from whom we believe. We are included as participants in the personal dynamic of eternal life of the Son by grace, "living to God" in Christ (Rom 6:10–11). Romans 6:23 states that "the wages of sin is death." This includes everyone. The second part of the verse, "but the gift of God is eternal life in Christ Jesus our Lord" says nothing about self-selection or meeting conditions—it, too, includes everyone.[8] Thus, to universalize Ephesians 2:3 (you were by nature children of wrath) but not Ephesians 2:5 (you have been saved by grace) is to promote exactly the wrong kind of asymmetry. This non-gospel imbalance starts everyone off as a child of wrath such that grace becomes the exception to the rule.[9]

---

8. See Rom 3:23–24; 5:18; 11:32 as other examples of Paul's proper gospel symmetry.

9. This, of course, is the direct opposite of the actual imbalance in Rom 5 with its "how much more" language (e.g., Rom 5:15 and 5:17). We have already mentioned the mistake made by isolating Rom 3:23 away from 3:24, making Rom 3:24 the exception to the rule.

62

Vanier Exposed

It is hard to admit to the darkness, fears, anguish, confusion and psychological hatred in our own hearts, all that hides our past hurts and reveals our inability to love. . . . I discovered that I was frightened of my own dark spots, that I always wanted to succeed, to be admired and ready with the right answers. I was hiding my poverty. It is easy to see the flaws in others and judge them. It is more difficult to accept our own flaws.

—Jean Vanier

Jesus knows that we have a tendency to try to assume power and control others. In each of us there is a little latent dictator. . . . Jesus had strong words for those who used religion to achieve personal glory. . . . There is always a danger that people who are generous will become self-satisfied. There is a danger that they will become involved with weaker people simply in order to have power over them.

—Jean Vanier

I wrote above about the anger that I felt over the news of Jean Vanier sexually victimizing those under his shepherding care.[1] The damage that

---
1. See Introduction, Book One.

he inflicted was exacerbated by his position of power as a spiritual father. He was also fully aware of the dynamics at play, a fact made plain in his quote above. The product of his soft-spoken vulnerability and seemingly transparent posture meant that his mode of operation was a manipulative "trustworthiness." How much did Vanier struggle along with Paul's "what I hate I do. . . . I do not do the good I want to do, but the evil I do not want to do—this I keep on doing" (Rom 7:15, 19)? God only knows.

In the last reading we considered Paul's placemat theology in Ephesians, and in this reading we will turn to the placemat theology of the Johannine tradition, in particular 1 John, to help us process Vanier's unexplainable evil. The placemat teaching of 1 John 3:8–10 is rather shocking for those of us who consider ourselves children of God. In succinct and straightforward fashion, John teaches that if we sin, we are children of the devil. And if we are children of God, we do not sin. Some apparently uncomfortable translators have tried to soften this—children of God do not "practice" sin (CEB), "make a practice of sinning" (ESV), or "continue to sin" (EXB, GNT), as in a habitual pattern. Others refuse to discount John's literal syntax (e.g., NRSV, NIV, among others).

John's severe binary has proven to put interpreters in an uncomfortable bind. This is not simply because he allows us only two categories—child of God, or child of the devil (any Evangelical, for instance, would agree so far). It is because John's grammar dictates that if I sin once, I am only qualified to be in the second category—a child of the devil. This point bears reinforcing. Take a minute to test yourself: "The person who is born of God does not and cannot sin."[2] Does your experience show that you never sin? Now the second piece, "Everyone who commits sin is a child of the devil."[3] Does your experience show that you sin? The harshness of the either/or is clear. Our experience tells us that we *only* qualify for the second category, but because we resist thinking of ourselves as children of the devil, we falsely put ourselves in the first category. We fail to realize that putting ourselves in the first category, but not the second, is itself evidence that we are in league with the devil: "If we claim to be without sin, we deceive ourselves and the truth is not in us."[4]

Like the Psalmist, we may be quick to declare ourselves righteous and others wicked. But John takes us deeper. The apparent contradiction of 1

2. 1 John 3:9; 5:18. See also 1 John 3:6–7 and 1 John 2:10.

3. 1 John 3:8, NRSV. See John 8:34.

4. 1 John 1:8; 2:4. There is one other place outside of his epistle where John uses the same phrasing. In his gospel he writes, "the devil . . . was a murderer from the beginning . . . *there is no truth in him*. When he lies, he speaks his native language, for he is a liar and the father of lies" (John 8:44, emphasis added).

John 3:8–10 leads past an "us-them" construct to an explanation that can handle all levels of human duplicity no matter how flagrant. Even if John cannot explain evil, he is aware that Jesus Christ simultaneously comprehends all aspects of human righteousness in his life and human wickedness in his death.

As derived from the witness of Jesus Christ, then, John teaches us that we are all children of God.[5] Not only that, we are all children of the devil. To the extent that we sin, we show ourselves to be children of the devil. To the extent that we do good, we show ourselves to be children of God.[6] Again, "If we claim to be without sin, we deceive ourselves and the truth is not in us." This sentence points to the asymmetry that interprets the duplicity. In other words, the only way I can claim *both* categories to be accurate about me is because the truth *is* in me and I am in the truth.[7] No matter how the liar pomps and struts, the lie can never attain equal status with the truth.

---

5. See 1 John 2:29: "Everyone who does what is right has been born of him." This is the polar opposite of "everyone who sins is a child of the devil." Next, we read: "See what great love the Father has lavished upon us, that we should be called children of God! And that is what we are!" (1 John 3:1). It is clear that John wrote his letter to those who believe the truth that they are children of God and who seek to walk in the light. From this it does not follow that others are *not* children of God or that it is not universally true that all humans are children of God. In fact, 1 John 2:2 speaks of Christ's work applying not only to believers, but to all people. Only one human is directly righteous, that is "Jesus Christ, the Righteous One" (1 John 2:1). It's only because he is righteous that we, derivatively, are righteous in him, so that when we do *anything* that is right, it manifestly proves we are in him—sons and daughters in the Son (1 John 3:7, see also first part of 1 John 2:29). Righteous action can only spring from one source.

6. 3 John 11: "Anyone who does what is good is from God. Anyone who does what is evil has not seen God."

7. If we think A) "the life" and "the death," or B) "having the Son" and "not having the Son" are hard and fast categories instead of fluid, simultaneous dynamics, we are at risk for exclusivist language like "I have the Son and have life, they do not have the Son and do not have life." Regarding A) 1 John 3:14: "We know we have passed from death to life, because we love our brothers and sisters." It seems clear that John is not seeking to furnish an existential tipping point for our categorical, sequential change so much as he is establishing a truth for us from which falsehood, which runs concurrently, can be exposed. To the degree that we are loving our brothers and sisters, we reveal that we are living into—or bearing existential witness to—"the life" of Christ. Regarding B) 1 John 5:11–12: God has given us eternal life in his Son (v. 11). This is the truth for all, such that we participate in it in the economy of "having the Son," or we do not, participating in the economy of "not having the Son." Verse 12 is therefore not about the static categories of "haves" and "have nots," but about *going with* or *against* the dynamic of "having the Son" (reflected in the more exact Greek meaning of "having"). This double dynamic fits well with the earlier binary of life and death (1 John 3:14 above) and the other NT themes regarding the simultaneous aspects of newness and oldness, foundness and lostness.

If my false and true determinations are symmetrical, locked in an endless tug of war, my life is in a fragile balance with little to no security or confidence. Only the truth in me as a child of God gives me an ability to see my complicity in evil, and yet be encouraged. Wickedness is blinded by wickedness; it cannot apprehend the grace of God. But in my righteousness, my oneness with Christ, I can apprehend my wickedness. Darkness cannot see its opposite, but light exposes the darkness. Light's perspective provides me with a healthy confessional life. I do not need to lie about my sin as if to minimize its severity, because I know that who I am in Christ is stronger than who I am "not" (i.e., who I am as interpreted by my sinful self, my flesh, and by the liar). In this light, sin is not the fundamental problem, but a lack of transparency.

The Spirit of Truth and the spirit of falsehood,[8] the spirit of Christ and the spirit of anti-Christ,[9] the life and the death:[10] John tells us that these are opposing dynamics at work in our lives. We know this all too well from the facts of our experience. But the *theological* fact that these dynamics are mutually exclusive can delude us into grabbing onto one, granting it to ourselves, and then falsely excluding others—we are "in" and they are "out." If I think that I made that kind of clear-cut sequential transition from death to life, not only am I flying in the face of 1 John, but I am also unable to confess the deadly, sinful side of me. I have painted myself into the "life" category and I am unable to be transparent about my lusts. I imagine such transparency to be doubly difficult for a "man of the cloth," or for a person like Vanier who was often described as a "living saint."[11]

John does not promote a Manichaean or dualistic struggle between good and evil, light and darkness. Instead, there is a definitive and victorious sequence that belongs to Christ as revealed in his death and resurrection. Christ's sequence is the truth of our lives, and it is a truth that is meant to *interpret* our lives here. It is in this world where the aspects of truth and falsehood, good and evil, light and darkness, and life and death are not properly sequential, but simultaneous. In the first heaven, sequence without simultaneity kills. The devil knows it better than we do. He cannot undo the definitive sequence of Christ's life, death, and resurrection. The devil cannot unfinish the finished work of Christ. But the prince of

---

8. 1 John 4:7.

9. 1 John 4:3.

10. 1 John 3:14; see also 1 John 5:11, 12.

11. To the extent that we fail to teach the two totals, and continue to endorse ecclesial contexts that somehow allow clerical ordination to contribute to a theological naiveté, we are complicit in engendering the surreptitious duplicity that inevitably leads to clergy abuses. Theological malpractice leads to clerical malpractice.

PART FIVE: JESUS IS MY HEAVEN

this world works parasitically off the finished work, and his ploy is to lure Christians into a system of experiential sequence that refuses to recognize the larger simultaneity at play. The result is confusion after a short-term "high" (too much emphasis on an experiential, emotional, sequence), a lack of assurance (when the experiential sequence does not hold), the absence of transparency (I feel the experiential sequence unraveling but I cannot admit it), and disempowerment (the zero-sum game drains me in a way that the two totals do not).

These symptoms are all part of what I call the triple whammy of sanctification in the first heaven: If we underestimate the simultaneity, then we will over-emphasize the experiential sequence. Then, when we overemphasize the experiential sequence, we underestimate the christological sequence. Underestimating the christological sequence costs us the assurance of our salvation, for it is only from within the christological sequence that our salvation and sanctification effectively operate.

From the opposite end of the domino chain, we can look at it like this: if we underestimate the definitive sequence of grace for all humans in the death and resurrection of Christ, we are likely to imagine our experiential moment of belief to be the definitive tipping point. Instead of belief *in* the truth, or belief emerging from the truth that we are *in*, my "conversion" event (or baptism) somehow *creates* the truth: I was a child of the devil, but now I am a child of God in Christ. Rather than commensurate with the depths of Christ's conquering work, the "overcoming" Spirit-power of which John speaks is then relegated to finishing the work—a work that Christ already finished. Even the Holy Spirit is marginalized by an overemphasis on experiential sequence! It is as if she is waiting in the wings until called upon. Meanwhile, in the spirit of the anti-Christ, sin (rooted in unbelief) flourishes when belief gets the credit that properly belongs to grace.

The twin principles of 1 John bear repeating: to the extent that we sin, we show ourselves to be children of the devil. To the extent that we do good, we show ourselves to be children of God. This "to the extent" rule can seem arbitrary, since the exact extent to which I am acting from my true self (in Christ) and my false self (anti-Christ) cannot be quantitatively measured. But this is a more sound scriptural approach than saying that we are simply in one category or the other. After all, John would not urge us to walk in the light if the darkness did not always threaten. Additionally, the hard and fast categories are often flat and static. That is why, even if we cannot measure the extent of good or evil being manifest in our actions at any given time, our "to the extent" rule protects against a harmful, leveling rationale. It refuses to eliminate the distinction between perpetrator and victim in a particular act. Shallow responses such as "we are all sinners," "we all have our demons," or "we are each a mixed bag," do not suffice in horrendous situations like Vanier's. Without the two totals of placemat anthropology, we are left with zero-sum estimates that posture us as part good and part wicked. This view cannot adequately account for the times when the wickedness of a "good person" rages beyond its assigned "part."

From the beginning of his epistle John cautions us against calling right wrong or wrong right.[12] The best systems of justice can only witness to that day (the second heaven) when what is right and what is wrong about all our lives will be untangled under the withering indictment of God's love revealed at Calvary. The day will be the fullest revelation of the cross. Only in a sphere where the God-Victim presides—a safe space devoid of revictimization—can pure, human-to-human reconciliation be experienced as reality.

The second heaven will be a beautiful time for the broken—a release of pain and bitterness and everything in-between. It will be a bitter time for the proud, however, until they discover the freedom of confession and contrition in the security of the Savior.

Duplicity breeds fear and projects onto God a duplicitous character wherein we imagine God's justice as punishment.[13] Duplicity also breeds duplicity, and we can hope that under the Spirit's sharp sword, Vanier and all of us will experience God's justice as a wrathful deliverance. This will entail giving the "No" inside God's "Yes" the seriousness that it deserves, facing our Lord and those whom we have wounded. Then, as now, repentance will be the word of the day.

Vanier's evil was evil. It was dark. Vanier is a child of the devil. The wickedness manifest in his actions is testimony to such and is therefore inexcusable. If he were alive, the appropriate measures should be taken against him for his heinous complicity with the liar. This is not because Vanier is not a child of God, a child of the light in Christ, but *because he is*. Grace has a built-in accountability. As a child of God who does not sin in his true self, Vanier will stand before his Lord where he and his sin have been fully exposed. At the same time, if we put him in one category without the other, refusing to believe that light can come through a broken and sinful vessel, then we too stand to be exposed, complicit in "the devil's work" (1 John 3:8) that Christ came to destroy.[14]

---

12. See 1 John 1:6. See also 1 John 2:4; 2:9; 2:21; 4:20.

13. John's letter seeks to assure us that a keen awareness of this duplicity, and keeping short accounts with God and with each other in the present, will provide us "confidence on the day of judgment" (1 John 4:17).

14. As we have seen, Barth sometimes designates the person's evil self as the wolf within. When evil manifests in specific acts, Barth writes, "the wolf slips the chain. This

63

The Second-Heaven Intervention

Judgement is the side of the eternal kingdom that is turned toward history. In that judgement all sins, every wickedness and every act of violence, the whole injustice of this murdering and suffering world, will be condemned and annihilated, because God's verdict effects what it pronounces.

—Jürgen Moltmann

"The Last Judgement" is not a terror. In the truth of Christ it is the most wonderful thing that can be proclaimed to men and women. It is a source of endlessly consoling joy to know, not just that the murderers will finally fail to triumph over their victims, but that they cannot in eternity even remain the murderers of their victims.

—Jürgen Moltmann

---

is no excuse. It must not obstruct his lawful punishment. This means that his action is a question addressed to all others and an accusation against them, not merely in the sense that his social environment is partly responsible for the loosing of the wolf in him, but in the sense that this wolf is only too well known to all those who belong to the same society" (*CD* III/4, 413). Again, tragically, one "environment" which often encourages a denial of "the wolf" is the churcvh. Susceptibility to evil only increases where it lurks and festers, unchecked because of ignorance.

THE SECOND-HEAVEN INTERVENTION

WITHIN THE CONTEXT OF our placemat approach, the three heavens also have a dimensional framework along with our basic anthropology (see the earlier reading "First Heaven Problems"). Starting with Paul's vision of the third heaven in 2 Corinthians 12:2 (what I consider to be the unadulterated sphere) and working backwards, we have posited the second heaven to be what the Bible symbolically calls "the day," undefined in length, and the first heaven as our perceptible present (this earthly sphere). These three "heavens" are dimensions of the one heaven, "heaven" as it is in the reality of God (which is unconditioned by time and space).[1] The three heavens are differentiated in Scripture but are not sequential; nor are they three *levels* of heaven that we graduate from, one to the next. The three heavens are not like rungs on a ladder. However, if we are to live as citizens of heaven in this world, it is imperative that we grasp the meaning of each.

The kingdom of heaven is within us and among us, as Jesus taught (e.g., Luke 17:21), and the unadulterated heavenly kingdom is the dimension where none of the problems of this world exist and no tears are shed (e.g., Isa 25:8; Isa 51:11; Rev 21:4). But where, then, is judgment day, "the day," or "that day" or "the day of Christ" (e.g., Eccl 12:14; Matt 12:33–37; Luke 12:2–3; Phil 1:10; Phil 2:16; Rom 2:16; Rom 14:10–12; 1 Cor 1:8; 1 Cor 3:11–15; 1 Cor 4:3–5; 1 Cor 5:5; 2 Cor 1:4; and 2 Cor 5:10)? These passages are often overlooked, so we will provide some shorter samples here:

> Everyone will have to give account on the day of judgment for every empty word they have spoken. (Matt 12:36)

> My conscience is clear, but that does not make me innocent. It is the Lord who judges me. Therefore judge nothing before the appointed time; wait until the Lord comes. He will bring to light what is hidden in darkness and will expose the motives of the heart. (1 Cor 4:4–5)

> For we will all stand before God's judgment seat . . . each of us will give an account of ourselves to God. (Rom 14:10, 12)

> For all of us must appear before the judgment seat of Christ, so that each may receive recompense for what has been done in the body, whether good or evil. (2 Cor 5:10, NRSV)[2]

---

1. "The only reason for time is so that everything doesn't happen at once" is a quote often credited to Albert Einstein. While certainly Einstein-esque, its origins are not formally established. From Calaprice, *Ultimate Quotable Einstein*, 481.

2. Regarding this verse Barth comments: "the final word concerning our right and wrong, and that of our works, is reserved for the universal and definitive revelation of the judgment of God—a revelation which we now await but in which we do not yet participate" (*CD* IV/2, 587). Again, the three heavens are not sequential, but we use sequential language to help grasp the significance of each dimension. In one sense, in

Finally, there are no tears in the unadulterated sphere, the third heaven. But on "that day" (the second heaven) we are told, there *will* be tears, indeed universal grief (e.g., Matt 24:30; Rev 1:7; Zech 12:10–14), along with clarity and catharsis. As with Moltmann above, the day's "tears," with the cathartic element of cleansing, contrast to a foreboding "terror" or anxiety. Cleansing tears can be seen as indicative of the washing away of sin, guilt, shame, and anything that has pushed us from who we really are. These things are expunged in the catharsis that comes from dross consumed.[3] Finally, we can anticipate that at the culmination of that day, and leading into the revelation of the third heaven, Israel and all humanity will perfectly participate in the covenantal *call and response* of old:

> This third I will put into the fire;
> I will refine them like silver
> And test them like gold.
> They will call on my name,
> And I will answer them:
> I will say, "They are my people,"
> And they will say, "The LORD is our God." (Zech 13:9)

On the one hand, "the day" does not appear on the historical timeline charting our lives from birth to death, and on the other hand, it is *not* the unadulterated heaven. By deduction, then, the day is an "in-between" dimension, somehow between these other two spheres.[4] As Moltmann in-

---

and by the Spirit we already participate in the second heaven described here, but in another, existential sense, we do not yet participate. As long as the "not yet" clouds the "already," there is a future revelatory element that must be accounted for.

3. Fittingly, dross in Scripture is used to signify not only evil aspects of humanity (P^2): "Remove the dross from the silver, and a silversmith can produce a vessel" (Prov 25:4); "I will turn my hand against you; I will thoroughly purge away your dross and remove all your impurities.... Afterward you will be called the City of Righteousness, the Faithful City" (Isa 1:25–26) but it also signifies evil Israel or evil humanity as a whole (P^3 with view to P^2): "Son of man, the people of Israel have become dross to Me; all of them are the copper, tin, iron and lead left inside a furnace; they are but the dross of silver" (Ezek 22:18); "All the wicked of the earth you discard like dross; therefore I love your statutes" (Ps 119:119).

4. The fact that the second heaven (the Day, the Second Coming) does not appear on our historical timeline from birth to death does not mean that it should be divorced from the human historical timeline. The ascension of Christ introduces what T. F. Torrance calls an "eschatological reserve or eschatological time-lag" (*Space, Time and Resurrection*, 152) between the two-fold and indivisible parousia of Christ (sometimes called the first and second advent). This perceived gap is caused by fallen time "that decays and crumbles away" until "the great unveiling or apocalypse will take place, the judgments of the Cross at work throughout history will be brought to the consummation in unveiled finality" (102–3). Torrance quotes William Manson: "If, then, [Jesus's]

dicates, and in line with what we learned from Barth, the judgment day is a border of sorts with two reverse sides, permeable in one direction (all of Then is in the Now, but not all of Now will be in the Then). At this border is where we fully learn how justice and deliverance are of a piece.

One short story shows the importance of the second heaven. I had a friend in Christian ministry who was wronged by his superior. The two men, once very close, fell out; for years they endured a painful and apparently irreconcilable situation. Then one day the superior experienced deep conviction over what he had done. He came to my friend and fell to his knees. In humility he apologized and begged my friend's forgiveness. The two men embraced and wept, and their relationship was not only restored, but even deepened beyond the very best days of their long history. It was something neither man could have ever imagined.

I believe the second heaven is full of experiences such as this. There is so much pain, woundedness, and trauma that result from broken relationships in this life. No one has the recipe for how to fix it. There are many of us who have no desire, or see no need, to fix things. Beyond the bitterness, there is simply too much risk. And some wounds simply seem too big for this world. The story of these two men is rare because, even though the superior took the initiative, it required the willingness of both parties, and it was an atmosphere with little risk of revictimization.

As rare as it is, I share the story of the two men for one reason: it is only a small taste of the reconciliation we experience in the second heaven. What if the two men had not reconciled with each other here in the first heaven? What if one had died before it happened? According to conventional ways of thinking, after their respective deaths the men would have gone straight through to eternal bliss where there are no sorrows, no tears, and no memories of the bad times. There, in heaven together, they are friends as if nothing had ever happened. But without the second heaven, what sweet time they would have missed! Was this an inspirational one-off, a powerful moment for earth but not heaven? Was the story of these men an exception to the rule "here," and nonexistent "there?"[5] Or was this an exception that *proves* the heavenly rule, with more revelation to come?

---

going and his coming are to be 'in like manner,' it is plain that *the Parousia*, whatever it may signify in its eternal dimension, is not to be understood in separation from the Incarnation and from Calvary. It is not discontinuous with the latter but is their consummation" (145). "As the last moment of time and history," says Barth regarding that day, " it will still belong to time and history" (CD IV/1, 433; see also IV/3, 290ff., noted in Torrance, *Space, Time and Resurrection*, 145).

5. I cannot help but mention an opposite example where the disparity between first-heaven and second-heaven justice economies is painfully apparent. In December of 2020 Brandon Bernard was executed for the 1999 murder of Todd and Stacie Bagley.

PART FIVE: JESUS IS MY HEAVEN

Here in the first heaven, to "forgive as the Lord forgave you" (Col 3:13) means to forgive before we are asked, or even if we are never asked in this world. If the moment presents itself, the naming of transgressions in the context of forgiveness can be deeply transformative, but it is always a penultimate occasion, whether in the first heaven or second. To name sins forgiven is not to forget them, says Miroslav Volf, but to avoid the vindictiveness that adds trauma to the traumatized. Indeed, remembering offenses should be carefully guided by an eschatological vision of redemption.

> [It is] a redemption that will one day make us lose the memory of hurts suffered and offenses committed against us. For ultimately, forgetting the suffering is better than remembering it, because wholeness is better than brokenness, the communion of love better than the distance of suspicion, harmony better than disharmony. We remember now in order that we may forget then; and we will forget then in order that we may love without reservation. Though we would be unwise to drop the shield of memory from our hands before the dawn of the new age, we may be able to move it cautiously to the side by opening our arms to embrace the other, even the former enemy.[6]

The day of second heaven is a time to remember in order to forget. Wrongs will be forever removed as far as the east is from the west (Ps 103:12). If my first heaven story of the two men was relatively safeguarded against revictimization, the second heaven is *completely* safe. The power of justice satisfied in God's way is transformational. Making things right

---

Georgia A. Bagley, the mother of Todd, said "without this process, my family and I would not have the closure needed to move on in life. . . . It has been very difficult to wait these 21 years for the sentence that was imposed by the judge and jury on those who cruelly participated in the destruction of our children to be finally completed," she said. Through a lawyer's statement, Bagley said, "I pray that Brandon has accepted Christ as his Savior, because if he has, Todd and Stacie will welcome him into heaven with open arms." In a final statement before being executed, Brandon Bernard, said, "If my death is what is needed to heal the pain I caused, I just hope from this moment on, all parties can move forward and have peace. . . . I hope you can forgive me for what I've done and what I've taken away from you." Bernard also testified to his own personal assurance of God's forgiveness (Carrega, "Brandon Bernard," paras. 7–8). This scenario begs the following: can the need to hold on to an eye-for-an-eye economy, one that Jesus has already rejected (Matt 5:38), be mitigated by a sound grasp of the second heaven? What if we understood that full justice and full forgiveness were not mutually exclusive, as wrought by the one, completed, and final work of Christ? What if we understood them as an ever-present kingdom reality, with more revelation to come? How can placemat anthropology help us toward a more thorough justice in this world for victim and perpetrator alike?

6. Volf, *Exclusion and Embrace*, 139.

with God and each other is deliverance. Catharsis is a beautiful gift. In the second heaven, such deliverance, justice, and catharsis are poured out in abundance.

On that day, we have the opportunity to share in Christ's victory over evil. The second heaven is the realm where no perpetrator gets off the hook, where the righteous indignation of all victims will be quenched, where all wounds are healed, and where we will see most clearly how restorative justice works. Heaven, we asserted, is where Jesus is, and the second heaven is where we most intimately meet the crucified and risen Lord Jesus, his wounds still apparent, and where all that we yearn for regarding restoration takes place.

"The day" is the day of judgment, but all indications are that it is not a "day" in the way we understand the word. In this sense, "day" could be described as a realm or even as a moment. But when exactly is this moment? Is it the last "nano second" before we fully expire? Is it postmortem? One thing seems clear: this in-between time is something that cannot be measured by the flat line of a hospital monitor. There will be plenty of time for our meeting with our Maker.[7]

It is common to think of the final judgment as something foreboding and ominous. We may struggle to shake the idea that judgment means the simple separation of the sheep and the goats, some to eternal hellfire and others to eternal grace. We may not look forward to judgment as deliverance and relief, but instead as a fearful prospect we would sooner avoid. Alternatively, some may embrace this idea of a second-heaven intervention. It seems to validate a sense of justice regarding the wrong in this world and the inadequacy of any legal tribunal to adequately confront wrong and wrongdoers. Then, too, it could only be hypocrisy to ask for justice regarding others' wrongdoing while refusing the same scrutiny for ourselves.

In baseball or softball, some of the more exciting plays occur when a runner tries to advance from first base to third base. How much easier

---

7. How long will this "day" of reckoning last? We can only guess at the meaning of 2 Pet 3:8, "a day is like a thousand years, and a thousand years are like a day." In applying such an economy, would a second be like a thousand hours? It seems that if a day is like a thousand years, a second would be at *least* a thousand seconds. Calculated exactly, a thousand seconds is 16.666 minutes. As silly as it seems, the .666 calculation is also apropos in that this "in-between" time represents not only the end of our false selves, but the end of the deceiver. The second heaven is the time when, for all to see, the devil gets his due. Satan indeed falls "from heaven" (Luke 10:18), but being parasitic to God, and therefore never being in the unadulterated heaven with God, it follows that his fall is from the second heaven, not the third. The day of judgment includes the revelation of Satan's demise, including his destruction in the lake of fire prepared for the devil and his angels (Matt 25:41).

would it be if, after a teammate's hit, the runner could simply cut straight across the diamond and get to third? But all runners headed to third base must touch second base en route. It cannot be bypassed for any reason, and the second heaven is like that. We might think that going from first to third would be easier, but it would not be better. Like Amos's picture of being shaken in the sieve of God's justice (Amos 9:9), our appearance before the judgment seat of Christ acts as the unforgiving filter that we need to understand forgiveness. Here the conflicted nature of our lives is fully addressed. Here we are fully assured that only the corruption-free are fit to enter the unadulterated heavenly kingdom.

We are told that we will be accountable for all that we have done during our earthly pilgrimage, good or bad, when confronted by the Savior at his second coming. In other words, we will appear before Christ in our overlapped, conflicted state; each of us as one person, each with our false self and true self. We do not have to worry that the most notorious criminal in this world, or the one who violated us and our family and who never showed remorse, will waltz mockingly into the third heaven. No one will "cheat the system" of God's justice or avoid the consuming fire of God's love. Each of us, in fact all perpetrators to some degree, will stop at second base. No one goes straight to paradise, the third heaven.

We envision the second coming of Christ improperly, suggests J. B. Phillips, if "we see Him returning in triumph upon a scene already largely perfected. We think it would be a fine thing if the world were neat and tidy, all problems were solved, all tensions were relaxed, understanding and friendship were world-wide . . . when Christ returned." However, "If we are to take the words of Jesus seriously, His return . . . is to be in the middle of strife, tension, and fear." Concludes Phillips, "The coming of Christ is a blessed hope of intervention, not a personal appearance at a Utopian celebration."[8]

It is the "righteous" who most need an intervention, said Jesus, precisely because they don't think they need one (see Matt 9:12; Mark 2:17; Luke 5:31–32)! In Matthew 7:23, Jesus tells the do-gooders acting in his name, "I never knew you. Away from me, you evildoers." The gist of this text seems to be that Jesus does not accept our false selves. It is as if he does not "know" us in the anti-grace economy of works. Jesus refuses to recognize our false selves as our true selves. In reality, he only knows us in our true selves, for only our true selves have ontological status. Operating in the lie, these men were attempting to earn favor that had already been granted. In rejecting them, Jesus holds them to grace. It is as if he is saying to Pat, "I

---

8. Phillips, *Meditations*, 187. This reference covers all quotations in this paragraph.

never knew you, P²." We cannot skirt the judgment of the cross and devise our own criteria, and neither can these do-gooders, even if basing their criteria on Christ's teachings. If they "went away sad," as did the rich young ruler (Matt 19:22), then we can only hope that Jesus's lingering words had a redeeming effect.

64

The Goodness of Judgment

Jesus Christ is the basis of judgment, and Jesus Christ is the promise which confirms itself as such in the midst of judgment. For this reason there is no fear, but there is only joy, at the prospect of coming into God's judgment.

—Karl Barth

This judgment which none can escape . . . is the wonderful judgment of God's grace.

—Karl Barth

Continuing with the theme of wrath and judgment, we must address a common question, reasonably ascertained from Scripture: "I thought those who believe in Christ *avoid* God's wrath. Isn't that what Romans 5:9 means?" The verse reads, "Since we have now been justified by his blood, how much more shall we be saved from God's wrath through him?" As the next verse makes clear, God's wrath is for his enemies, and yet the typical line of interpretation is simplistically sequential. It runs like this: before I believed, I was God's enemy and under the just judgment of wrath. Now that I believe, I am covered by the blood; I avoid God's wrath. Conversely, our placemat reading understands wrath as directed against the false self of every person (not just unbelievers) and the ways all of us as enemies conspire with *the* Enemy. If God's wrath is the "No to our no," then in the cross we observe the epitome of that divine No. To be crucified with Christ is for God to have said an emphatic No to all that destroys us. That No is God's wrath of deliverance, all in the person of his beloved Son. As we discussed in Book One, he is the one in whom we are both justified *and* condemned, condemned *and* justified (Rom 5:18).

But still, Romans 5:9 says that we are saved *from* God's wrath. On our reading, to be saved from God's wrath is to be saved from God's No being the last word, or from the No being our "final stop."[1] The No is always inside the larger Yes. In one sense, we are saved *from* death. In another sense, we are saved *through* death. It makes sense to say that we are saved *through* death and therefore *from* death, even if it makes less sense to say it the other way around. The "how much more" from this Romans passage, then, relates to the fact that being saved *from* death is nothing compared to being preserved *through* death. Through death, we are saved *for* life. However unavoidable it may be, death is and always will be the exception to the rule of life, according to the person and work of Jesus Christ.

Remember, God did not just write us a letter, he paid us a visit. This means that all talk of wrath and judgment starts with God's own self-revelation. Because God assumed flesh in the incarnation—not only pre-fallen, pristine flesh but fallen and corrupt flesh—we can know what God thinks of us and just how much he loves us. Borrowing a term from Christology, Jesus's humanity was not monophysite in nature, but it exhibited the true-false duality from which our placemat anthropology is derived. We have a holy God who embraced us even at our red worst and "rescued us from the dominion of darkness" (Col 1:13). This reveals that God's mission is not only about saving us, his enemies, but *primarily* about defeating the enemy who preys upon us. When we see Jesus's compassionate acts, then, we are not simply seeing God's love in action, we are seeing God himself in action. We can trust the picture of God that we see in Jesus.

But what about the God of judgment, the one who seems so unlike Jesus? Because of the way it is often portrayed, judgment is a scary proposition. Often the "good news" message is presented like this: if you die tonight, will it be heaven or will it be judgment? The bottom line in this view is that, if you choose Jesus, you avoid judgment. But the avoidance of judgment is not good news at all. Why? Because avoidance of judgment and wrath is avoidance of the cross.

---

1. John 5:24 is often misunderstood in the same way. However, the subsequent verses, John 5:25–30, make it plain that all will be judged.

PART FIVE: JESUS IS MY HEAVEN

Jesus's cross is where we find fathomless evidence of God's love for us, the love from whence all other love flows. "This is how we know what love is: Jesus Christ laid down his life for us" (1 John 3:16). Self-sacrifice at the cross is where God proves that he loves us more than he loves himself. The cross is where the one who loves us the most judges us. No one person has a right to judge another according to Scripture.[2] Perhaps the biggest reason that we are not allowed to judge others is because we do not love them the most. The Bible teaches us that judgment is uniquely reserved for the one who *does* love us the most, Jesus Christ. If we avoid the cross, we miss the profound depths of God's love for us in Christ.

In this context, the day of judgment is something that we can look forward to because it is a day of deliverance. This world's sinners who have leaned into the bosom of Jesus know God's heart (John 13:23), the perfect love that casts out fear (1 John 4:18). They will perhaps approach the judgment seat quite differently from those who are not assured of the verdict. There is a "sense," says former Archbishop of Canterbury Rowan Williams, "in which the believer does not have to be afraid of the last judgement because . . . in the presence of Jesus, judgement has come and gone."[3]

In the context of perfect love, we will all be fully exposed. All secrets will be made known and every thought revealed (Luke 8:17; 12:2). The anticipation of fear we have about that moment essentially corresponds to the trust we have in God's character. It is not unlike the trust we place in the surgeon when we agree to go under the knife. Sadly, we probably have a greater sense of security, and less fear, when it comes to the human doctor than when it comes to the Great Physician. We simply struggle to believe that God's love is enough to provide security when we are confronted by the cancer of our false selves.[4]

---

2. See 1 Cor 4:3–5. See also Matt 7:1; Luke 6:37; Luke 6:41; John 8:7; Rom 2:1; 14:10; 14:13; and Jas 4:11.

3. Williams, "Risen Indeed.'" The quotation is from the Q&A transcript. These believers are presumably those who John calls the "overcomers" in Revelation—those who seek to live in the "already" of Jesus's finished work, even in the midst of the "not yet" of this life. Indeed, it is because we *have* overcome in Christ already that we can join the chorus of those singing, "We Shall Overcome." Quoting John 1:5 ("the light shines in the darkness and the darkness shall not overcome it") theologians Bethany Hanke Hoang and Kristen Deede Johnson write, "Because we believe that all things have been conquered by Jesus Christ and that he has the final victory over the dominion of darkness, we can go in hope that Christ's light has overcome and will continue to overcome the darkness until the darkness is finally vanquished"; see Hoang and Johnson, *Justice Calling*, 78.

4. The exact phrase describing Jesus as "the Great Physician" is not in Scripture, but is rooted in passages such as Luke 5:31; Matt 9:12; Mark 2:17. The phrase was ubiquitous among the Patristics. According to Christoffer H. Grundmann, Christ was

Some may be tempted to excise all references to wrath in the Bible, cutting out the bits that seem incongruent to God's unconditional love. But this is to misunderstand since the biblical language of wrath *is* God's language of unconditional love. We recall Paul's plea for deliverance in Romans 7, putting it in placemat terms: "wretched person that I am, who will rescue me from this sinful, false self?" We remember that Paul previously noted that there is "*nothing* good that lives in me, that is in my false (red) self." He is enslaved by the red and under its domination, bemoaning that it is "not I who sin, but sin living in me." We warned earlier against losing the one human being in talking about two selves. We have also spoken of not using the false self as a "devil made me do it" excuse. However, assessed correctly, a two selves approach provides *appropriate* distancing of the false self from the real "me": "Who will rescue [the real] me from this raging red self? Thanks be to God in Jesus Christ my Lord!"

If God's anger is directed against us individually, then we can celebrate it for at least two reasons: (1) we do not really want to live as "an individual," because we are hard-wired for communion with God and others, and (2) we see the deeper meaning of wrath. In other words, we are not individuals, we are persons, and we are grateful to have our alter-ego eradicated by God's fierce love. If thinking about God's wrath hurts, then perhaps we have taken God's anger against us *personally*, when it was meant to be taken *individually*. This points us to the advantages of distinguishing between the truth of personhood and the lie of individualism—God's No to the individual is always held inside of God's Yes to the person. Again, to use Merton's phrase, the person must be rescued from the individual.

Aside from misunderstanding God's wrath, our fear of judgment might be rooted in the fact that we are not completely sure that we *have* a true self. What if—in the love and wrath of the cross—our old self is eradicated, stripped away, and there is nothing left of us? One of the most beautiful verses in Scripture, Galatians 2:20, could mistakenly be read in this way. It begins, "I have been crucified with Christ, and I no longer live." It is easy to be relieved that the old self is gone, crucified with Christ, but we might also feel threatened by the "I no longer live" part. Have "I" evaporated or been indiscriminately absorbed, like a rain drop fallen into the cosmic sea of the divine? Fortunately, the true self remains, as the verse continues, "but Christ who lives in *me*. The life *I* now live in the body, *I* live by faith." "I" am still there, even if the Christ who lives in us and for us is our life. Paul's "I no longer live, but Christ," then, implies the existence of the new self. Every

---

evidently first called the "physician" by Ignatius of Antioch (d. 107). Grundmann cites Cyril of Alexandria (d. 444) as using the exact phrase "the great physician." See Grundmann, "Christ as Physician."

PART FIVE: JESUS IS MY HEAVEN

person's new (and therefore true) self is found in Christ, delivered by way of the Creator's cross.

Luther reminds us that instead of being depersonalized or dissolved by our unity with Christ, the opposite is true: "The moment I consider Christ and myself as two, I am gone."[5] As T. F. Torrance liked to say, our Creator and brother Jesus Christ is the "personalizing" person: "Thus far from being emptied or overpowered by the divine person, the human person is reinforced and upheld in its indissoluble oneness with the divine."[6] Resisting zero-sum reductions, we can say with Torrance that more Christ means more "Pat," not less. To be united with Christ is to be united with God, and therefore humanized in our created being. Indeed, from our perspective, judgment day will be the pinnacle of human celebration. Paul seems to anticipate that it will put the ancient world's epitome of a victory celebration, the Roman triumph, to shame (2 Cor 2:14; Col 2:15).[7]

There is only one reason that we can offer ourselves to God (Rom 6:13), and that is because we have been offered to God—carried to God, so to speak—in our High Priest, uniquely "Offerer and Offering" (Augustine). On that day we will have a final chance to do what Paul in Romans urges us to do even now, to present ourselves as living sacrifices, a phrase that is nonsensical unless we are alive in Christ while also seeing our death in Christ.[8] Because our life is in Christ's life, we are living into the fact of Christ's death for us and thereby the accompanying fact of our death in his. This moves us away from the popular idea of surrendering oneself more and more to God, as if we must work to accomplish our sanctification. It provides a liberating pathway from sanctification to surrender, instead of the other way around. Paul reminds us that the indicatives of sanctification come before the imperatives (even if the imperatives come first in the sentence): "I press

---

5. Luther's statement reinforces the idea that we are never separated from Christ, and Christ is never separated from God. This is the inner truth of humanity. In complementary fashion, what is needed is the separation of my false from true humanity, so that we could say, "The moment I discover my true self and my false self as two (as defined by Christ) I am quickened."

6. Torrance, *Mediation of Christ*, 68.

7. In Book One we discussed Paul's use of the word "slave" in the positive sense to represent the irrefutable determination we have in Christ, e.g., Rom 6:22, 1 Cor 7:22. Here Paul is again commandeering a pejorative image referring to captives or slaves in a Roman triumph, implementing it positively to remind us that we are irresistibly and triumphantly processing in Christ no matter the challenges of the enemy or of the flesh. In a way that the Roman triumph would never anticipate, at this point in our study we can recognize slave and soldier as synonymous in the free determination of Christ.

8. Rom 12:1. Another passage about our opportunity at the judgment that comes to mind is in John 15:8, "This is to my Father's glory, that you bear much fruit, showing yourselves to be my disciples."

on to make it my own, because Christ Jesus has made me his own" (Phil 3:12, ESV), and "work out your salvation with fear and trembling, for it is God who works in you to will and to act in order to fulfill his good purpose" (Phil 2:12–13).

In one of his most emphatic remarks about how all human beings are offered to God, Paul writes, "[Christ] died for all, and therefore all died."[9] Karl Barth elaborates:

> For then and there, in the person of Christ taking our place, we were present, being crucified and dying with him. We died. This has to be understood quite concretely and literally. . . . We died: the totality of all sinful men, those living, those long dead, and those still to be born, Christians who necessarily know and proclaim it, but also Jews and heathen, whether they hear and receive the news or whether they tried and still try to escape it. His death was the death of all: quite independently of their attitude or response to this event.[10]

Every human has been crucified with Christ. What, then, differentiates a believer from an unbeliever? Simply this: a believer exclaims, "I have been crucified with Christ!" Since crucifixion with Christ is not for believers only (as if we are not crucified with Christ until we decide), then it follows that the believers' proclamation, "I have been crucified with Christ," is a way of *speaking the truth back to God*, a fundamental principle of repentance. It is announcing a truth about every person, the truth which is meant to be believed. On judgment day we will all see ourselves crucified with Christ. And we will all see ourselves risen with Christ. But we cannot have one without the other.

Barth's position is the same (rooted in 2 Cor 5:14) as that expressed by many theologians before him. "When Christ died, all died," commented P. T. Forsyth. "Dying with Christ is not a mere ethical idea, complete only as we succeed in doing it."[11] And yet, the fact that the cross is more about Christ than it is about us, or perhaps, about us precisely *because* it is about Christ, keeps the focus of judgment on grace and salvation. "It is on us according as

---

9. 2 Cor 5:14.

10. *CD* IV/1, 295. See p. 300 where Barth adds this regarding the resurrection of all, also in Christ: "The raising of Jesus Christ (with all that it implies for us and for all men) is in the New Testament comprehended and understood as an act of God with the same seriousness as the preceding event of the cross with its implication for us and for all men."

11. Forsyth, *Cruciality of the Cross*, 30.

we are in Him," asserts Forsyth, "not as a scourge, but as a cross."[12] With the cross, judgment issues forth the finality of deliverance.

The day of judgment will be the preeminent time of repentance, speaking the truth back to God. It will be the epitome of experiencing a spiritual "high," finally knowing deliverance from the deathly burden of sin and brokenness. Of course, this untangling is the one thing that the false parasitic self does not want, since he is living off the host. To the very end the red Pat is hoping that he can pirate the one person of the two selves to be the "Pat" that he wants him to be. As George MacDonald asserts, against Paul's theme, "I am not my own" (1 Cor 6:19), "the one principle of hell is 'I am my own.'" It is no surprise that the hell-bent attitude is the abjectly red one, and MacDonald's portrayal is worth quoting at length:

> I am my own king and my own subject. I am the centre from which go out my thoughts; I am the object and end of my thoughts; back upon me as the alpha and omega of life, my thoughts return. My own glory is, and ought to be, my chief care; my ambition, to gather the regards of men to the one centre, myself. My pleasure is my pleasure. My kingdom is—as many as I can bring to acknowledge my greatness over them. My judgment is the faultless rule of things. My right is—what I desire. The more I am all in all to myself, the greater I am. The less I acknowledge debt or obligation to another; the more I close my eyes to the fact that I did not make myself; the more self-sufficing I feel or imagine myself—the greater I am. I will be free with the freedom that consists in doing whatever I am inclined to do, from whatever quarter may come the inclination. To do my own will so long as I feel anything to be my will, is to be free, is to live.[13]

When confronted by the finished work and final judgment of love, why would we fight to remain tangled and conflicted, employing every manner of self-justification imaginable to preserve our false selves? Is it because we fail to see the depth of our belovedness and belonging as justified children? Conversely to MacDonald's subject above, the cross allows Bonhoeffer to define his red self without compromise within the dimensional context of green:

> Anybody who lives beneath the Cross and who has discerned in the Cross of Jesus the utter wickedness of all men and of his own heart will find there is no sin that can ever be alien to him. . . .

---

12. Forsyth, *Cruciality of the Cross*, 30.
13. MacDonald, "Kingship," para. 3.

Looking at the Cross of Jesus, he knows the human heart. He knows how utterly lost it is in sin and weakness, how it goes astray in the ways of sin, and he also knows that it is accepted in grace and mercy.[14]

For Bonhoeffer this posture was more than simply the classical Lutheran self-deprecation or self-condemnation. It was uniquely Christ's cross, rightly understood, that promoted the humility necessary for healthy human community and a confessional life that provided the antidote to "othering" people. As he says in *Life Together*, "Anyone who has once been horrified by the dreadfulness of his own sin that nailed Jesus to the Cross will no longer be horrified by even the rankest sins of a brother.... Only the brother under the Cross can hear a confession."[15]

Scripture describes believers in this world as those who welcome the coming eschatological disentanglement, as those who "hope in Christ."[16] "Hope in Christ" is a decidedly first-heaven phrase. In isolation, the red self can't aspire to hope, and the green, operating out of certainty, has no need of it. Hope operates uniquely out of the overlap of our grey struggle, seeking to give testimony to the victorious green. We will return to the theme of judgment day as an opportunity for us to participate in the finished victory of Jesus Christ. In a sense, the first heaven is just the anteroom to the main show, when the curtain is pulled back to reveal the big picture of God's redemption.

> **2:20** (a poem with reference to Gal 2:20, by Jeff McSwain)
>
> Judging depravity by degree
> Is a way of protecting me from Calvary's tree
> But when I turn to the one who took my shame
> A victim in pain and a perpetrator to blame
> I see myself nailed there in his arms of grace
> Our God come near to judge the human race
> He said die in me and live anew
> In the truth of the done
> You'll find the freedom of the do

---

14. Bonhoeffer, *Life Together*, 118.
15. Bonhoeffer, *Life Together*, 118.
16. 2 Cor 1:10; 1 Tim 4:10; Eph 1:12

65

The Big Picture

Whether or not I find the missing thing / it will always be / more than my thought of it / Silver heavy, somewhere it winks / in its own small privacy / playing / the waiting game with me.

—Luci Shaw

What was it that made me conscious of possibilities? From where in the Southern darkness had I caught a sense of freedom?

—Richard Wright

THERE ARE CLEARLY TIMES in our conflicted existence when we might feel the force of one determination—red (old) or green (new)—more than the other. But to those of us tossed to and fro by the torque, Paul steadies us with the reality of the "already" big picture: "And we boast in the hope of the glory of God. Not only so, but we also glory in our sufferings, because we know that suffering produces perseverance; perseverance, character; and character, hope. And hope does not put us to shame, because God's love has been poured into our hearts through the Holy Spirit, who has been given to us" (Rom 5:2b–5). Or, "For our light and momentary troubles are achieving for us an eternal glory that far outweighs them all" (2 Cor 4:17). We will not be disappointed. The weight of glory "far outweighs" the afflictions, and in redemption's light we will see that "our present sufferings are not worth comparing with the glory that will be revealed in us" (Rom 8:18).

The word translated "produce" in the first two verses above could be misunderstood to mean that the green *needs* the red pressure to produce character. Suffering, however, is not positive. In and of itself, it has no positive value (or else it would be built into creation from the first). It does, however, have revelatory purposes in this world. Being squeezed in the torque of the two determinations can produce thin places where God feels most real or more near. We may be "hard pressed on every side" (2 Cor 4:8), but this "produces" our true character in the same way that squeezing a tube of toothpaste brings forth the paste itself.[1]

Character is revealed in suffering but not created by suffering, even if, in our short-sightedness, we give suffering undeserved credit. Suffering is not inherently redemptive because truth does not require suffering to be true. Burning the dross away does not create the gold, even if it reveals it (1 Pet 1:7). Just like Jesus's suffering did nothing to earn God's favor, the "achieving of glory" in 2 Corinthians 4:17 must always carry the revelatory aspect of Romans 8:18: "I consider that our present sufferings are not worth comparing with the glory that will be revealed in us."

What Barth called our *character indelebilis* is our indelible character, the honor of our essential, creaturely personhood. This is the genuine person, the "I am" in the great "I AM." Importantly, the *character indelebilis* is not a sacred "core" of humanity in a spatial or quantitative sense. It is not even a speck on the zero-sum spectrum. Its hidden, dimensional presence ensures the continuity of God's good creation, come hell or high water. Negatively, the *character indelebilis* means that there is no need for a second creation, despite the great discontinuity and brokenness revealed in the cross. Reconciliation and redemption do not describe a second creation, but a recreation.[2]

In this world, Paul says, we simultaneously have two houses. He describes our mortal bodies as a house that is more like a tent.[3] These tents are

---

1. "Work out your salvation with fear and trembling, for it is God who works in you to will and to act in order to fulfill his good purpose" (Phil 2:12–13), coming as it does just after the Philippian Hymn of Christ's suffering, seems to internally connect our suffering to Christ's passion. As with Christ, trembling is involved. In the cauldron of adversity, we "work out," or produce, what Christ has "worked in," revealing the power of the inner person in Christ.

2. With Barth we can therefore say that reconciliation is not, like creation, *ex nihilo* (out of nothing).

3. The word "house" in 2 Cor 5:1 is usually omitted from the English translation, in favor of simply "tent." The Greek reads: "the tent of our earthly house." Including the word "house" can help hold the duality of the one person with two houses (like our

PART FIVE: JESUS IS MY HEAVEN

transient and corruptible. But even if our mortal bodies are destroyed, Paul insists that "we *have* (present tense) a building from God, an eternal house in heaven, not built by human hands" (2 Cor 5:1). Our first-heaven experience is an overlap of our "tent" and our substantial "house." In other words, if our mortal body (tent) is destroyed, then we still *have* a spiritual body (house), an eternal body in the heavens, not biologically conceived (not made by human hands). We, however, too easily trade the invisible for the visible, caught up as we are in the ever-changing world of our experience.[4]

---

one person with two hearts, two minds, etc.). This is preferable to the contrast from mere tent to house because it maintains the continuity ("house") and protects against a dualism which postures a transition at death strictly from P^2 to P^1, without view to P^3. Interestingly, the Greek grammar related to our tent being "destroyed" has the same root as Jesus's prophetic word about the temple being destroyed and rebuilt in three days (Mark 15:29; Matt 26:61; Matt 27:40). Of course, destroy and rebuild is another metaphor we could mistake as purely sequential and discontinuous if not for Scriptures like Rev 7:15, which indicate that the Living Lord has always been and will always be the true temple or tabernacle (John 1:14). John, even more than the synoptics, seems to have in mind a transcendent and continuous meaning of "temple" (note that he also uses a different word for "destroy" in John 2:19). For John and his transcendent to immanent perspective, the physical thing may appear to be destroyed (discontinuity) while its presence is still miraculously perceptible, even if only by the power of the Spirit (continuity).

4. This transition, from simultaneously having a tent (mortal body) and a building (spiritual body) involves the subtraction of what we called P^2. We go from $P^3/P^1/P^2$ to simply P^3/P^1. Despite the discontinuity of losing P^2, continuity is found in P^1, and Pat (P^3) is still Pat. The spiritual body is largely hidden in this world. If you see me lying in a casket, it is my spiritual-material body that is *not* there. What you actually see is not me at all, but my tent (P^2). We must ask at this point how Jesus's "tent" after his death on Calvary relates to ours, because the situations are obviously quite different. If we affirm Jesus's bodily resurrection on Easter morning, and we adhere to the testimony that this resurrection included his whole earthly tent, not just his spiritual-material body, then this implies that Jesus is not providing a pattern that we are meant to follow (since our bodies, unlike Jesus's, remain in the grave). Instead, Jesus is giving us a unique indication of the bigger picture of human transcendence, not defined by death. And what is this bigger picture again? If, as we have asserted, the forty days up to and including the ascension is a straddling of dimensions for Jesus between the first and second heaven, then Jesus as the spearhead of our humanity is giving us a picture of the overlap of our true and false selves that continues into the Day. Jesus's "taking his tent with him," so to speak, demonstrates that the overlap that exists before the resurrection and ascension remains at the judgment, and that even if our bodies in one sense stay in the grave, we will bring with us into that day all the secrets, sins, and wounds of the grave in our own straddling of dimensions. The fact that his going forward in the ascension is met by his coming back, or returning, in the parousia (Acts 1:11; Heb 9:28), shows the relative "permeability" of the dimensional "membranes." As we will see, the resurrection and ascension are signs pointing to the transcendence of Jesus Christ. We do not rely on them to make Jesus alive. As Barth himself reminds us, the evidence of the gospels cannot prove that Jesus rose from the dead, but regardless, they can and do point to the ongoing reality of his life. Nor does the resurrection occur merely in the Easter faith of

In the end, the simple oneness of our persons in Christ will not be a boring oneness or characterless monolith. We would be mistaken to hold onto our checkered placemat existence in the first heaven as if it adds variety and vibrancy or somehow makes us more interesting. It can only be the devil's twisting to claim that our essential persons are phantoms lacking material sensuality. Our ultimate vitality is in the non-quantifiable intimacy of the Spirit, where we are one with Christ and one with each other.

It will always be a challenge to resist the confusion of placemat thinking with visual-spatial metaphors. Instead, and with the confidence of the christological pattern, we will continue to commandeer scriptural spatial metaphors into a dimensional, placemat framework. In my youth ministry background, for example, it was not uncommon to hear the description that Jesus was "God with skin on," or perhaps "Jesus was a man walking around with God sticking out all over him." In the name of making things simple, these statements too easily communicate an inner-outer dualism—Jesus is God on the inside, man on the outside. This kind of spatial thinking gets translated to anthropology where soul/inner/spiritual is positioned against body/outer/fleshly.[5]

---

the disciples. Instead, the disciples' Easter faith is enclosed in the reality of the "Easter event" that presses upon them: "The content of the Easter witness, the Easter event, was not that the disciples found the tomb empty or that they saw him go into heaven, but that when they had lost him through death they were sought and found by him as the Resurrected." Thus we "do not believe in the empty tomb, but in the living Christ" (*CD* III/2, 453). The resurrection is not contingent on the empty tomb, just as the angels said, "Why do you look for the living among the dead?" (Luke 24:5). In other words, we start with the commitment to the truth claim that the human Jesus Christ is alive, despite his death, and *therefore* the tomb is empty on Easter morning, not the other way round. As presuppositional signs, the empty tomb and ascension match the fact that Christ is alive; in Barth's mind there is no good reason to doubt them or dispense with them. Even if, like the Genesis 1 and Genesis 2 sagas, they are a-historical, to the extent that they contain reliable witness and truth, they are not mythological. If, for example, the body of Jesus was someday found, such that his bodily remains are buried like ours, then dispensing with the signs still does not *necessarily* touch the reality. We never *depended* on these things to make the resurrection true, even though they do play a relatively important role in bolstering our faith. Again, because there is no proof that the tomb is *not* empty, Barth refuses the temptation to entertain dispensing with these presuppositional signs. Likewise, if Jesus's remains are discovered, it does not *necessarily* disprove Jesus's transcendent life (nor ours). In that matter, our postmortem state *does* find congruence with his. I credit Wyatt Houtz for helping me to frame the above; see Houtz, "Karl Barth on Demythologizing."

5. Note to youth ministers: crafting illustrations to more simply communicate complex truths is a good endeavor, but it takes a lot of thought and effort (ideally done by honing one another's ideas in community), and we must continually resist the tendency to sacrifice sound theology on the altar of simplicity.

PART FIVE: JESUS IS MY HEAVEN

The movie *Chocolat* comes to mind as a fitting expression of such body-soul dualism. A voluptuous woman comes to town to open a chocolate shop during Lent. In an otherwise drab parish, the only thing in color in the movie is the woman's vibrant red dress and the features of the shop. In a body/soul dualism, associations with physical, bodily appetites—the eroticism of sex and chocolate—get castigated as unspiritual. Yes, these things can be misused, but that is precisely the point—they are mis-used. The enjoyment of such God-given pleasures provides a hint of the banquet table where all of God's holistic pleasures, all that is good for human beings in mind, body, and soul, are shared in abundance. "Worldly pleasures" is a terrible phrase, since pleasures in this world bear relative witness to those of the unadulterated kingdom. That is why we do not have to worry that the unadulterated kingdom will be a letdown. You will not find yourself wanting to trade in the unadulterated for the adulterous.

That long-awaited day of the Lord will come, simultaneous to the "day of evil" (Eph 6:13, see next reading). Then, when the scales fall off from our eyes, the green will never be greener and the red, in its death throes, will never be more glaring. It will occur at the end of what theologians call the "overlap of the ages."

Our final transition will involve losing our familiarity with ourselves so that we can finally recognize ourselves, who we truly are. Borrowing from C. S. Lewis, we will not really have faces until we see our face in the face of God. In the meantime, as Lewis's beloved George MacDonald relates, all the forces of what he calls "The Seen" seek to Lord over us with confusion, and with lessened awareness of Christ, make what *is* real to seem fanciful.

> Till I am one, with oneness manifold,
> I must breed contradiction, strife, and doubt;
> Things tread my court—look real—take proving hold—
> My Christ is not yet grown to cast them out;
> Alas, to me, false-judging 'twixt the twain,
> The Unseen oft fancy seems, while, all about,
> The Seen doth lord it with a mighty train.[6]

In the beginning (before the introduction of red) and the end (after the eradication of red), we are one with Christ. In fact, we are one with Christ all the way through. In the middle, however—in what Barth calls "the fatal middle stretch"[7]—we, as "Placemat Pat," are torn by duplicity. Our in-Christ subjectivity (green) is countered by our anti-Christ subjectivity (red) at every turn. In the midst of this acute duplicity, we either harden

6. MacDonald, *Diary* 116–17.
7. CD III/2, 280.

ourselves into our depersonalized alter ego, or we yearn for redemption and the day when the end of duplicity is finally revealed.

To the extent that we experience the torque of our duplicity in the first heaven, it derives from the strain at the crisis-point of God's judgment. First-heaven conversion moments carry this eschatological power, the inbreaking of God's second-heaven resolution into the experience of conversion and transformation here and now. In those dramatic events the contrast is so stark as to feel like a death and a resurrection. As the definitive sequential work of Christ comes to bear, the old *is* gone, it seems; the simultaneity has for a time receded from view.

The revelation of green can be intense, but what happens when sin reasserts itself and we realize that things we considered past are again present? To save face, we could rationalize that while not every sinful habit is gone, at least our slavery to sin *in general* is gone. Perhaps we rationalize too easily because we want our conversion to have at least counted for *something*! Yet I have counseled against the mistake of trying to interpret our sinfulness in such arbitrary fashion. In my experience, for every person who can describe the post-conversion reassertion of sin in relatively innocuous terms, such as "just an old flesh pattern," there are others who still testify to sin's enslaving power and those too ashamed or afraid to admit it. The slavery of red is strong. Only by the Holy Spirit is our simultaneous slavery to green—the personalizing agency provided in the authority of Christ's freedom—shown to be stronger (Rom 7:14–25). In these moments, second-heaven clarity continues to visit us and quickens us with transformative effect. To be quickened is the opposite of static being; it is to experience the truth of our fundamental identity in the Spirit of adoption, "living to God in Christ Jesus" (Rom 6:11).

66

Deliverance Time!

Do you so love the truth and the right that you welcome, or at least submit willingly to, the idea of an exposure of what in you is yet unknown to yourself? . . . Are you willing to be made glad that you were wrong when you thought others were wrong?

—George MacDonald

My favorite times of the day are 1:11 and 11:11. Allow me to explain.

We have seen how the green and the red are woven so tightly in this life that even though they are never truly mixed or confused, they are inseparably joined. It is like the mesh of a screen door, a matrix of green and red woven tightly so that we cannot see the separate strands even though we know they are there—the screen just appears as grey to us if we notice it at all. Think about this screen mesh analogy as informing our placemat theology at every level: atomic, cellular, personal, communal, global, and universal. Even from our grey-screened perspective, there are times when we can see what we imagine are distinctly green and red expressions. Nevertheless, these perceptions will always be skewed to some degree by the close dimensional proximity of the opposite.

Crudely defined, we might observe that the grey is a "mixture" of green and red. The "mixture," however, is technically a composite—a mesh of distinct colors. Now let's break it down further. The mesh of a screen door is made up of vertical and horizontal strands. Imagine the vertical strands are green, you could say upright for righteousness and life (e.g., Ps 140:13,

DELIVERANCE TIME!

"the righteous . . . and the upright will live in your presence").[1] Meanwhile, think of the horizontal strands as red, "flat" lines representing sin and death. This picture of finely woven mesh represents our first-heaven experience. In this grey world we do not experience pure red or pure green. The pure horizontal and pure vertical refract one another, leaving only diagonals to blur our vision. Our vision is slanted, and so are our very lives. All of us in this grey world are P^3s; we are, to differing degrees and at different times, diagonals.[2]

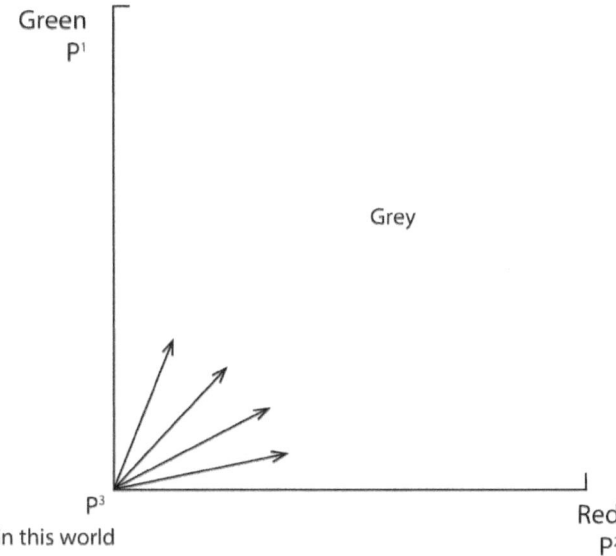

---

1. Other examples in the Psalms of righteousness being synonymous with "upright": Ps 32:11; 36:10; 64:10.

2. Speaking of the diagonals caused by refraction, Paul calls the generation of this present world "crooked" (Phil 2:15), as does Peter (Acts 2:40; see also 2 Pet 2:15). "Crooked," sometimes translated "perverse," is a theme in Luke-Acts in relation to "straight." Luke, similar to the gospel accounts, quotes Isa 40:3 ("make straight in the desert a highway for our God") in relation to John the Baptist (Luke 3:4–5). He ends with a quote unique to Luke, "and *all people* will see God's salvation" (Luke 3:6, emphasis added). See also Acts 8:21; Acts 13:9–11. In both cases, Peter and Paul respectively reprove an evil-doer who is subsequently struck with blindness. In Paul's case it is especially dramatic, for in his charge against Elymas that he was "perverting the straight ways of the Lord" it is doubtful that he could have forgotten his own blindness on the Damascus road and his subsequent healing at the residence of Ananias on "Straight Street" (Acts 9:11).

PART FIVE: JESUS IS MY HEAVEN

Interestingly, in C. S. Lewis's space trilogy, he uses the phrase "bent men" to describe those humans who live on planet earth.[3] In placemat terms, he is talking about P^3, our current existence in deviation from the vertical, and not the way we are created to be. Humans in this fallen world come across as a composite of straight (P^1) and flat (P^2). We are bent people because of P^2. But in another sense, we are not bent at all.

In the second heaven we finally and definitively see the red and green lines at sharp, ninety-degree angles (P^2 and P^1), non-converging and mutually exclusive. In other words, the second heaven provides the unconfused perpendicular clarity—the red being disentangled from the green (by virtue of the death of the grey). Even in the first heaven, and in anticipation of the next, the Spirit can give us a degree of accuracy in discernment. This reminds me of Jesus's two-tiered healing of the blind man in Mark 8:22–25. The man's abject blindness represents P^2, and his intermediate sight, where the people he "saw" looked crooked like trees walking around, represents P^3. Only when Jesus completely heals the man do we have a prophetic representation of P^1: "Once more Jesus put his hands on the man's eyes. Then his eyes were opened, his sight was restored, and he saw everything clearly" (Mark 8:22–25).

It makes sense that if the pure vertical represents the actual and ongoing fullness of Spirit for human beings, then even in our interwoven existence, the greater our vertical quotient, the more we *experience* "fullness of the Spirit." The actuality exists before the possibility. Of course, in the third heaven the red is completely gone since it is discarded in the judgment and only the vertical lines remain.

We know that to have a horizontal line one must first have a vertical, or vice-versa. A perfect ninety-degree angle starts with one line or the other. The claim of placemat anthropology is not only that the vertical lines are the only thing left at the very end (the third heaven); they are also the only thing at the very beginning (creation). The judgment of Jesus Christ clarifies that if there was ever any doubt, it is the vertical line which comes first, the horizontal line (being parasitic) exists only in relationship to the established vertical. Now you can see why 1:11 and 11:11 are my favorite times of day! The up and down lines represent the true, original, and often

---

3. In *Out of the Silent Planet*, the "Bent Years" (121) are those after the fall. Bent creatures, says Lewis, "can do more harm than broken ones" (139). And in *Perelandra*, the main character Ransom runs into an "imitation" man who Ransom describes as the "Un-man," i.e., the anti-Christ. The un-man's diabolical ability to ape Ransom's words and movements—the impressive ability to mimic—is the main characteristic in the novel upon which parasitic deceit thrived: "What the Un-man said was always very nearly true" (133).

hidden (in this world) nature of humanity. In the vertical are all the good blessings, things like playfulness, spontaneity, creativity, freedom, diversity, particularity, wholeness, all the fruit of the Spirit, all the things God originally created for us.[4]

The red horizontal is not original. In fact, it does not have an original bone in its make-up. It can only be a leech. But it has an effect, and that is why the way we experience the world is always crooked to an extent. The good things are there, but only in degree.[5] For example, many people describe having a sweet, other-worldly moment with a person in hospice, when the space between life and death seems so thin. That experience is a grey diagonal line: life in the midst of death. Other times it might feel like death in the midst of life. Neither is pure. *If you know the sharp theological angles provided by the revelation of Jesus Christ, you know that such sweet moments bear witness to the vertical, and the bitter moments bear witness to the horizontal.* But to know Christ as the interpretive key comprehends both, providing a bigger picture. We do not need to know or quantify how close or how far such existential moments are to the pure vertical or the parasitic horizontal (we can only say that moments bear witness to each line "to the extent that they do"). Nevertheless, we can know the reference point in the midst of the refraction. C. S. Lewis had experiences that he called "stabs of joy" as a child, despite the overriding sadness of his mother's death.[6] Only later did he have the theological language with which he could interpret these experiences.

Jesus's parable about the sower fits well with the present illustration. In Luke 8 we read the following story of how Jesus, with a large crowd gathering and people coming to him from town after town, told this parable:

> "A farmer went out to sow his seed. As he was scattering the seed, some fell along the path; it was trampled on, and the birds ate it up. Some fell on rocky ground, and when it came up, the plants withered because they had no moisture. Other seed fell among thorns, which grew up with it and choked the plants. Still other seed fell on good soil. It came up and yielded a crop, a hundred times more than was sown." When he said this, he called out, "Whoever has ears to hear, let them hear." (v. 4–8)

---

4. It was fitting (and funny I thought!) that while I was writing this section on an airplane, the attendant asked us to return our seats before landing to the "original and upright position!"

5. See Ps 58:3, "Even from birth the wicked go astray; from the womb they are wayward."

6. Lewis, *Surprised by Joy*, 22.

PART FIVE: JESUS IS MY HEAVEN

People often worry about the implications of this reading. They fret: "But which soil am I? If most of the soils are bad, and only one is good, what then? I *hope* I'm one of the better ones, but Jesus says some start out looking good, only to be choked out." Alternatively, with the aid of Jesus's follow-up interpretation, our placemat approach allows space for a different perspective: Jesus is the sower (God), the seed (the Word), and the good soil (human).[7] The word "good" is the same as that used a bit later in Jesus's interaction with the "rich young ruler": "Why do you call me good? . . . No one is good—except God alone" (Luke 18:19). God is good, and in Christ true humanity is good. The true human, Jesus Christ, is at once God's word and the one who receives God's word for all of us. Likewise, his life lived back to God for all of us is one of unwavering love and obedience. What we could call "covenant-verticality" is the reality that grows in the Spirit's superabundant fruitfulness, what Barth calls the "righteous determination" of humanity. That is the green vertical. Coincidentally (coincidental to the extent that it is!), one of the most bountiful images of righteousness is signified by the biblical chapter and verse address, 1:11. They are "filled with the fruit of righteousness that comes through Jesus Christ" (Phil 1:11). Righteousness in Christ is anything but boring.

Besides the one scenario illustrating the reality of vertical righteousness in Christ, all the other scenarios in Jesus's parable (Luke 8:5–7, 13–14) point to the existential, especially the difficulties and hard knocks of human experience. We are often beat down, defeated, trampled upon, scorched, and choked out. These things are descriptive of our life experiences, even if they are not prescriptive (no one is simply bad soil). They describe the devastating and oppressive things that happen to us even while God's reality, often hidden from our perceptive abilities, is happening too. In this world, the in-Christ, vertical dimension, where every person is rooted in good soil, can only seem like the exception to the rule. Meanwhile the horizontal anti-Christ dimension constantly presses or pulls against us, as the case may be. We are therefore bent and broken mentally, physically, spiritually, and emotionally in ways that issue forth into sin, guilt, shame, and a host of social problems. Even if they seem like exceptions, our "good soil" experiences (e.g., joy and belief, v. 13) point to Jesus Christ and our eternally upright lives in him. Our "bad soil" experiences point to the devil (v. 12) who wants to steal our joy and flatten us.

In an odd way, however, the bad also points to Jesus Christ and his solidarity with us in the worst that can happen, identifying with us as a "flat-lined" victim. This identification, as powerful as it is, would be useless

---

7. See also Rev 22:16, where Jesus describes himself as "Root" and "Offspring."

if Jesus had not risen from the dead. There would be no basis for the claim that the vertical is the reality; a crapshoot would do just as well to determine whether vertical or horizontal is in the ascendency as the prior, original, and everlasting dimension. Without the resurrection's revelation of righteousness and justice (Rom 4:25), believers are most to be pitied (1 Cor 15:19). As risen Lord, Jesus shows that the vertical is always in full force and that we are to understand the horizontal only in reference to it. By submitting to and overcoming the horizontal, Jesus has dismissed any notion that flat lines have a future (Rom 6:9).[8]

Repentance, then, is to see the vertical so plainly as to be changed by it. To see what is right is to see better what is wrong and to seek alignment with what is right and true. Transformed by Christ in the economy of the Holy Spirit, repentance therefore involves a humble recognition that distinctively ushers us into a healthy confessional posture. Admissions such as "I was wrong" or "that was wrong" can be expressed in an environment where we see the right of green most clearly and the perpendicular nature of red is most exposed. In this environment things can best be addressed and "made right"—or find their proper alignment—with God and others.

With so much emphasis on the vertical lines as good news, I found it theologically amusing when in the movie *US*, 11:11 is a foreboding number.[9] This is because there are many haunting visual references in the movie to Jeremiah 11:11, which reads, "Therefore this is what the Lord says: 'I will bring on them a disaster they cannot escape. Although they cry out to me, I will not listen to them." In Jeremiah's view, God's people are not obedient so God intends to smite them with disaster. This 11:11 sounds bad and nothing but bad. Of course, with Christ defining every aspect of death and life, I was able to see Jeremiah 11:11 as the implicit backside of the good news.

In his movie, Jordan Peele uses the reference from Jeremiah to foreshadow imminent doom, but this doom is not even from God. Instead of God wreaking havoc, it is the red-clad alter-egos of Peele's main characters who do the damage. We never get the impression that God is out to get the characters. Instead, it is the characters' own false selves—their tethered, evil "twins"—who are against them. In assessing this theme in the movie, one reviewer had this to say about the Bible verse Peele chose: "In plain English,

---

8. It is worth noting that when we make the sign of the cross, it starts with the vertical. The conquering power of life (the vertical) is found precisely in the fact that it precedes death and continues in spite of it. The actuality of eternal life ontologically precedes the existential possibility of resurrection from the existential state of death. That is why saying that life "emerges from death" is a way of saying that life continues in spite of it.

9. See reading in Book One, "Amazing Grace Remix."

the verse means: y'all screwed.... The recurring Jeremiah 11:11 motif in Peele's *Us* has many terrifying implications. In short, we're never quite sure who the people we think we know really are. Everyone has a dark version of themselves that they never want to reveal."[10]

Peele's approach is profound. Even though Jeremiah 11:11 references God's agency, Peele's movie refuses to make the bad things and evil results directly attributable to God. This puts Peele in a refreshingly different camp from the many interpreters who draw important theological conclusions from Scripture without any reference to the text's christological context.

God is fundamentally for us and not against us. He is not against us for our sin, but for us and against our sin. Far from being the agent of evil, then, we find God absorbing it on the cross. By putting himself under the mastery of sin and evil, Jesus Christ is committed to destroying not his beloved human creatures, but all the "horizontal lines" of our lives. Jeremiah 11:11, then, shows how God's wrath serves his love. In Barth's words: "Genuine wrath is obviously possible only on the basis and in the context of true love.... His judgment is the instrument of His love."[11]

From the beginning of this project we endeavored to speak of the true self and the false self, but only in reference to our one person ("Pat") to whom they belong. When considering the *one person* of the two selves, we say that Christ was crucified on the cross, or that we were crucified with Christ (Gal 2:20). When looking at the *two selves* of the one person, we can say that it is not the original (green) and true self that is destroyed at the cross, but the parasitic (red) and false self of every human (Rom 6:6).[12] Seen in this light, and this light alone, Jeremiah 11:11 is actually good news—deliverance! We are inescapably tangled and need to be freed. Thank God that deliverance means there is no escape from the thoroughness of God's wrath, the universal relentlessness of God's fierce love.[13]

---

10. Francisco, "'Us' Jeremiah 11:11," paras, 8, 12.

11. *CD* II/2, 735.

12. For the true self to be delivered, the old and false self has to die. Since there is no false self in abstraction (due to its parasitic nature) but only in view of the one person, the one person has to die for the true self to be liberated.

13. See Parry, *Lamentations*. Without dismissing judgment day, Parry celebrates its penultimate, restorative, character. George MacDonald seems to enjoy graphically portraying God's fierce love of deliverance, as in the following examples: "For that which cannot be shaken shall remain. That which is immortal in God shall remain in man. The death that is in them shall be consumed ... all that is destructible shall be destroyed"; and "Escape is hopeless. For Love is inexorable. Our God is a consuming fire. [The creature] shall not come out until he has paid the uttermost farthing"; and "He will judge thee justly; extenuating nothing, for He hath to cleanse thee utterly.... [He] will not wrong thy soul by excusing thee a hair too much, or thy heart by excusing

As with the parable of the sower, we can interpret Scripture in line with how God reveals himself in the Word, Jesus Christ. We have full permission to commit to the idea that so-called destruction passages, like Jeremiah 11:11, are theologically descriptive, not prescriptive, and that in the end they speak therefore of restorative and not retributive justice. Israel held a firm belief in the all-powerful nature of God, and rightfully so. But without a nuanced understanding of God's sovereignty, it would be easy to make such actions prescriptive, as if God actively smote some people and allowed the good guys (the "chosen") to escape. As I will argue in the pages that follow, instead of chalking up such terrible things to God's agency, we can instead chalk them up as descriptive of what happened to Israel and *Israel's retrospective narration of those events from their limited perspective.*

Apart from God's revelation of himself in Christ, we could mistakenly understand Old Testament "destruction passages" like these to mean that God committed evil acts. Does holding onto the inspiration of Holy Scripture mean that we have to believe this is what God is really like? How do we know for sure that the writers are not projecting onto God a type of fallen, vindictive personality more like their own? It is difficult to explain these passages in light of a God who loves every person enough to die for them all; indeed, a God who loves every person more than he loves himself. Can we instead believe that passages like Jeremiah 11:11 show the descriptive scope of the cross regarding tragic human events? At Calvary, Jesus Christ has absorbed all bad things that have happened to all people for all time. A view of God destroying or abusing people cannot be sustained in light of God's revelation of himself and his true character in Jesus.

If we keep in mind the pure vertical (green) relationship that God is committed to keeping with his children, and that this includes his desire to destroy all the horizontal that harms us (red), then we can embrace 1:11 and 11:11 as symbolic of God's victory over evil. Even Jeremiah 11:11 reminds us that God's No is inside of his larger Yes.

---

thee a hair too little." The three examples are quoted from Lewis, *George MacDonald*, 25, 113.

67

The Highest View of Scripture

The only system of thought into which Jesus Christ will fit is the one in which He is the starting point.

—Athanasius

You may have heard it said that the Bible is God's love letter to you. Have you found that to be the case? It takes a little unpacking. This past year I had a health scare, and when I saw the envelope from my doctor's office in my mailbox, I was afraid to open it. I actually put it off for a while; I feared the worst. The Bible can be intimidating, even just in breadth, but also scary to read. What kind of news will we find there? What is God really like? What does God think of me? Is God *really* like Jesus?

Have you ever heard this: In the beginning was *the Bible*, and *the Bible* was with God, and *the Bible* was God? I hope not! It might sound vaguely familiar, but that is because in this well-known verse (John 1:1) I have substituted "the Bible" in place of "the Word." The verses that follow, John 1:1–5, make it crystal clear that the word of God described is Jesus Christ. This is the same Jesus Christ who appears in Revelation 19:13, "He is dressed in a robe dipped in blood, and his name is the word of God."[1]

Even if it is true that we learn about Jesus Christ from the Bible, as soon as we do, we must understand the Bible in its proper place, submitted to Christ. Since Jesus is the living word of God, the highest view we can

---

1. Thanks to my pastor, the Rev. Dr. Louis Threatt, for bringing my attention to this passage in Revelation.

THE HIGHEST VIEW OF SCRIPTURE

have of the Bible is one that maintains the subservience of the Bible to the living Word revealed in and through it. Jesus Christ is the Word. The Word must never be conflated with, or collapsed into, the Bible.[2] However, neither should the Word be completely separated from the Bible; if that were the case, it would be nonsensical to even indirectly (derivatively) call the Bible "the word of God."[3] This written word is meant to bear witness to the living Word, but it does so imperfectly. The Bible witnesses to the Word simply *to the extent* that it does. The Word cannot be caged, then, even by the Bible.

There is a general sense then, in which we can call the Bible the word of God. As it witnesses to the living Word, the Bible is what Karl Barth calls "the concrete Word of Scripture."[4] But how do we determine the extent of the congruency between the living Subject *of the Word* and the Bible's witness *to that Word*? Whatever the "extent," it is impossible to exhaustively capture, and the challenge is compounded by the fact that scriptural interpretation may take us beyond what the author intended to convey to his original audience. If Scripture is "the vehicle of what is more than human," notes Lewis, "we can of course set no limit to the weight of multiplicity of meanings which may have been laid upon it. If any writer may say more than he knows and mean more than he meant, then these writers will be especially likely to do so. And not by accident."[5]

The interpretive task, then, is to discern the moments and themes in Scripture that are, in this sense, most concrete—most concrete because they are in correlation to the Living Word, Jesus Christ. Those acknowledging such a task for interpretation are often charged with foregoing exegesis for eisegesis. To this charge Barth wrote, "No one ever has the right . . . to preen and boast that at least *he* . . . has not diluted the New Testament with his own world view but simply lets the Bible speak for itself. That is simply not true."[6] As always, Barth would have us recognize that every interpreter engages in eisegesis to some degree. The real question, therefore, regards which eisegesis is less divergent and more faithful to the Word revealed in Jesus Christ.

---

2. By conflation I mean collapsed-into or to take two things and make them indiscriminately one and the same. Barth asserted that to conflate the Word and the Bible could only cause us to read the Bible *unbiblically!* CD I/2, 466.

3. See the excellent podcast on scriptural exegesis christologically considered in view of Barth's Commentary on Romans: Tilling, "Barth on Romans."

4. *CD* I/2, 571.

5. Lewis, *Reflections on the Psalms*, 117.

6. Karl Barth, *Prolegomena to Christian Dogmatics*, 404, as quoted in Von Balthasar, *Theology of Karl Barth*.

PART FIVE: JESUS IS MY HEAVEN

Even more important than matching our ethical views to Holy Scripture, then, is for our lives to be lived ethically in correlation to the living Word. There is often no need for these things (Scripture and the living Word) to be contrasted. In fact, everything we say as theologians should be based on Scripture, and this requires constant interaction with biblical scholarship. One thing we can usually agree on is that there is no need for us to operate outside of Scripture, even if we disagree about how Scripture is interpreted. Just as everything that God wants us to know about God is included in the revelation of Jesus Christ, there is plenty in Scripture to communicate everything that God wants us to know about the character of God and humanity *based* on Jesus Christ. All of this can be asserted without an exact equating of Scripture and Jesus Christ.

We will constantly be confronted by the ideology of biblical inerrancy, which is the by-product of a failure to distinguish the written word from the living Word. Inerrantists exalt all Scripture as equally authoritative (it is all "the Word," without qualification). They seek to ensure internal consistency at all costs. Dietrich Bonhoeffer continually resisted such an approach. It is the way we read the Bible, not the Bible itself, that needs to be changed. He concluded, "it is through the Bible, with all its flaws, that the risen one encounters us."[7]

C. S. Lewis, in his assessment of the Bible, concurs: "The human qualities of the raw materials show through. Naivety, error, contradiction, even (as in the cursing Psalms) wickedness are not removed. The total result is not 'the word of God' in the sense that every passage, in itself, gives impeccable science or history." Even if it "carries the word of God" in a unique way, notes Lewis, the Bible appears at times to be "an untidy and leaky vehicle." Left up to us, we might prefer "an unrefracted light giving us ultimate truth in systematic form—something we could have tabulated and memorized and relied on like the multiplication table." With Lewis, we could say the Bible is infallible in one sense only, that God gave it to us as a special witness to divine revelation exactly the way he wanted us to have it. He gave it to us at the time and in the way he thought was best, albeit through fallible people. This view is one which drives us to the work of interpretation, which is by nature messy and hard work. We may "at moments envy," says Lewis, the simplistic approach of inerrancy because it requires less rigor than staying tuned to Jesus Christ as the Bible's interpretive key.[8] But even inerrancy's "simple approach" is not that simple. How often, for instance, have you greeted your believing friends with a holy kiss as the New Testament

---

7. Bonhoeffer, *Christ the Center*, 74.
8. Lewis, *Psalms*, 111–12.

often commands (e.g., Rom 16:16; 1 Cor 16:20; 2 Cor 13:12; 1 Thess 5:26)? In this book I have used Scripture to support my argument. I have nothing worth saying about the gospel to anyone *without* the authoritative backing of Scripture, but that does not mean that every word of Scripture is authoritative in the same way, or that the Bible does not need to be interpreted by the living word of God. The upshot is that while I do my best to be a right handler of the word of truth (2 Tim 2:15), I might be dead wrong.

Only God knows which interpreters have been most faithful to the revelation of God's self in Christ. But we must consistently return to the fundamental principle: the whole Bible must be submitted to the gospel of the living Word. Yes, the Bible is God-breathed, but the breath of God is not synonymous to the breadth of Scripture. Holding to our principles from Book One of a transcendent-immanent hierarchy, or what Barth called a "sacred order" that cannot be reversed (*CD* II/1, 317), we can say that all of the word of God is in Scripture, but not all of Scripture is in the living word of God in the same way. The Spirit gives birth to spirit, but flesh gives birth to flesh. With its quotient of red, the grey Bible is not fitted congruently with the perfectly green living word of God.

As Paul declared to one of his churches, "I resolved to know nothing while I was with you except Jesus Christ and him crucified" (1 Cor 2:2). But what does this mean? Because of Jesus's self-declared premise that all Scripture points to him (John 5:39), and because he is not simply a human being but *the* human being in whom all human beings are included (Rom 5:19), we apply Jesus's life ("Jesus Christ") to every person and Jesus's death ("him crucified") to every person. Exegeting the cross in this way, perhaps we can gain ears to hear Jesus's parables as not about two categories of people, the wheat and tares, sheep and goats, etc., but about the true (righteous) and false (wicked) humanities represented in the salvific work of the one human Jesus Christ.[9]

Even if biblical writers describe people as being in one or the other of two opposite camps (e.g., child of God, child of the devil; 1 John 3:8–9), the highest view of scripture demands that these passages be submitted to the christological litmus test, and reinterpreted accordingly. The church fathers of the first few centuries after Christ did not need inerrancy to give them a reason to appreciate the sacredness of biblical texts. They relied on the lordship of the Word himself. Pastor and theologian Jason Byassee describes his understanding of such an approach:

---

9. We remember from Book One Barth's doctrine of election, that in Jesus Christ "the elect and the rejected face each other in one and the same person" (*CD* II/2, 350). See "Condemned and Reconciled" and "The Righteous and the Wicked."

PART FIVE: JESUS IS MY HEAVEN

> For too long among Christians, the divide has been between liberals who accept modern science and put distance between themselves and the Bible and conservatives who reject science and embrace the Bible. I find myself, by no grand plan, on the liberal side, if that means making peace with science, for the most part. Part of my love for allegory comes from its attentiveness to the letter of the Bible. I call it "christological literalism," in a phrase I hope others will also pick up and deploy. My fear about biblical fundamentalism is that it takes the Bible *not seriously enough*. . . . The church was glad for the variety in the gospels, even the discrepancies and outright contradictions. Difficulties in the Scriptures should not be feared, apologized for, or turned away from. They're there, so let's do business with them as reminders of Christ's lordship. . . . For Origen, and ancient Christians after him, difficulty in Scripture is a sign that the Bible intends us to read it figuratively. A contradiction or problem is actually a clue. God has left a surprise for us here—let us delight in finding what God means for us to see.[10]

Jesus Christ revealed, the living Word, must be our primary hermeneutic for interpreting his words about human beings now and in the eschaton (Matt 25:46; John 5:29). In this vein we remember our Book One discussion of Matthew 7:17–20, where Jesus says that good trees bear *nothing* but good fruit, and bad trees bear *nothing* but bad fruit. The latter will be destroyed. Judging from our own perspective, and recognizing that no human bears only good or bad fruit, we might assume that human trees bear *mixed* fruit, but Jesus does not provide us that option.

Jesus's words press us further to himself—Jesus Christ and him crucified—as the interpretive key to Scripture. He is the vine of Israel, the one of whom it is said, "Your vine is cut down, it is burned with fire; at your rebuke your people perish. Let your hand rest on the man at your right hand, the son of man you have raised up for yourself" (Ps 80:16–18). He is also the vine that represents all human branches in himself. He is both the false humanity cut off, removed, thrown into the fire and burned, and the true humanity tending from fruitfulness to fruitfulness (John 15:1–6).

Isaiah provides a prophetic picture of a vine that is burned up completely and yet still somehow emerges. Jesus Christ is Israel; Jesus Christ

---

10. Byassee, *Surprised by Jesus Again*, 167–68. I hope you have caught some of my delight in the Word thus far. Growing up in circles of inerrancy, it wasn't until the summer of 1985 at Regent College that Gordon Fee's biblical interpretation class rocked my world. That was when I was introduced to what Byassee cleverly calls "christological literalism." "Let the lion out of his cage," Fee used to roar, "he can defend himself."

is "the holy seed" (Isa 6:11–13).[11] The best Isaiah can do is describe the re-emergence as from "a remnant" or "a stump," but reliance on such a complicated and contradictory image (a wholly destroyed vine is also somehow not wholly destroyed) is no longer required if we use a more dimensional understanding of the revelation of the person of Christ. When God has "sent everyone away" and "forsaken the land," even then Christ is shown to be the supernatural remnant (of Israel and of humanity) when absolutely no remnant remains. God the Son, Jesus Christ, the true human, lives, even as Jesus Christ the false human dies. In our dimensional perspective, the single subject Jesus Christ can hold together all aspects of God and humanity, even the oppositional determinations of red and green, death and life. On one hand, the zero-sum, sequential language about the renewal of the remnant points to the miraculous resurrection of Jesus Christ from the dead, the one who lives, even though he dies (with reference to John 11:25a). On the other hand, in a way that no spatial metaphor can adequately picture, the supernatural "remnant" bears hidden witness to the continuity of a savior who never dies even when all is lost (John 11:25b). He is the one who, in his person and in his life, holds and preserves Israel and all of us.

Because Jesus is the dimensional point of reference for reading the Old Testament, our efforts should be focused on responsibly interpreting the OT (and the NT) with the lens he provides us. Unfortunately, if we think the Old Testament somehow came before Christ, we will be tempted to fit Jesus Christ into the Old Testament instead of the other way around. When reading the Old or the New Testament we must always ask, what does this passage have to do with the word of God Jesus Christ? For example, can we say this action or that practice is *of Christ*? How congruent in this instance is the written word to what we see in the living word of God? Jesus said, "You've heard it said, an eye for an eye and a tooth for a tooth, *but I say to you*, love your enemies and pray for them that persecute you."[12] This is a moment when Jesus does the interpretation for us. The highest view of Scripture is one that insists that there is a higher accountability than Scripture itself when it comes to human life and conduct. It is the God *of* Scripture, the most direct revelation of God, Jesus Christ himself, in whom and by whom all Scripture finds its truest and deepest meaning.

---

11. Deepest thanks to my friend Steve Scansen for pointing me to this passage.
12. Matt 5:38, 44; emphasis added.

68

Parting from the Old Red Sea Narrative

Verbal inspiration [inerrancy] is a poor substitute for the resurrection! It amounts to a denial of the unique presence of the risen one. . . . It is wrecked in its attempt to level the rough ground.

—Dietrich Bonhoeffer

We do not read Scripture as a vast collection of infallible propositions whose meanings and implications can be understood on their own terms. We only, always, and everywhere read Scripture in view of its real subject matter: Jesus Christ. This means that we always read Scripture Christocentrically . . . as those who really believe what the Nicene and Chalcedonian creeds say. . . . Christ is the center, the inner reason, and the end of all Scripture.

—Christian Smith[1]

Since God has made God known in person, theology cannot simply skip over or go around Jesus, pretending like God *has not* come in the flesh. As the living word, Jesus's self-revelation of God is the uniquely authoritative starting point when it comes to interpreting the written word of God.

---

1. Smith, a Catholic, makes a strong case for an authoritative, if non-inerrant, approach to Scripture. See also Byassee, *Surprised by Jesus Again*.

This does not require us to abandon the principle of the inspiration of Scripture. Instead, since all Scripture is inspired by God (2 Tim 3:16), then it must also be interpreted by the clearest revelation of this same God. Jesus Christ is that clearest revelation. He is the one who came among us to show us what God is like in a form that we might adequately understand (the human form). This guards us against reading even the Old Testament without a christological lens. "No one has ever seen God," John stated, "but the one and only Son, who is himself God and is in closest relationship with the Father, has made him known" (John 1:18).

We remain in awe of the revealed fact that every human has been folded into the knowledge and love that Jesus has for the Father (Matt 11:27). We are bowled over by the fact that "God so loved the world" (John 3:16) means that the Father has the same love for all of us that he has for his Son. Now, of course, if you reject the placemat paradigm—if your view is that God loves Israel more than the Egyptians, for instance, or that he has chosen some for hell and you for heaven—then the polarized destruction passages in the Old Testament fit neatly within your narrative (you can only hope that you fit in on the *right* side of the narrative!). Others, like Andy Stanley, have simply solved the interpretive dilemma by demoting the Old Testament (or Old Covenant) except in places where it agrees with the New.[2] Stanley gets us headed in the right direction (reading the Bible from right to left) but we can do even better. We do this not by asking where the Old Testament aligns with the New, and not by giving priority to one or the other, but *by subjecting both the Old and the New to the same interpretive key*. It is Jesus Christ the living word to whom we must give the priority in reading the entirety of inspired Scripture. Instead of throwing out the Old Testament, then, we direct these destruction passages to the cross where they can be theologically subsumed. Indeed, the cross is the location whereby God not only absorbs all destructive human activity but also destroys evil, allowing evil to destroy itself in the person of his Son.[3]

---

2. Stanley, *Irresistible: Reclaiming the New that Jesus Unleashed for the World*. I was drawn in by the title, and the way he emboldened "New"! Stanley gives us good reason for questioning the inerrancy of the Old Testament, especially citing the non-Christlike ways "old covenant leftovers" still haunt us, for example, "Why would a Christian kick their son or daughter out of the house for being pregnant or gay? . . . Why would Christian leaders declare a tsunami God's judgment on a predominately Muslim region of the world? . . . Why do pastors leverage phrases like, 'The Bible says. . .' and 'The Bible teaches. . .' inadvertently giving equal authority to everything in the Bible? Why do we take marriage and dating advice from a pagan king with seven hundred wives?"(91). Stanley fails, however, to question the inerrancy of the New Testament, missing an opportunity to subject it to the same christological scrutiny.

3. The ransom theory of the atonement makes more sense from this perspective.

PART FIVE: JESUS IS MY HEAVEN

With this in mind, we can embrace the fact that we are all faithful Israelites in Christ (the True Israelite, John 1:47) and we are all faithless and stiff-necked Israelites in and of ourselves (crucified with Christ). Old Testament accounts of Israel fighting its enemies can thus be read christologically without an us vs. them dynamic.[4] In the story of the Red Sea, it would be easy to consider ourselves as the good guys, and the other people (the Egyptians) as "the wicked" who drown in God's judgment. Placemat anthropology sees us all walking unscathed through the parting of the Red Sea (as Israelites in the story), and at the same time, it sees us all in opposition to God and drowning in the water (as Egyptians in the story). In the light of Jesus's historical narrative, we can see the historical narrative of Israel in a new way. The OT is full of good news and rich with beautiful passages like Isaiah 43:1–3a: "This is what the LORD says—he who created you . . . 'Do not fear, for I have redeemed you; I have summoned you by name, you are mine. When you pass through the waters I will be with you; and when you pass through the rivers, they will not sweep over you. . . . For I am the LORD your God, the Holy One of Israel, your Savior.'" Such passages can be applied universally, for all are created in and through Christ. All elements of suffering and victory in the human narrative, corporately and personally, take place in Jesus Christ, "the Savior of all people" (1 Tim 4:10).

Some might object that this christological interpretation of the Old Testament seems to be based on a purely allegorical, symbolic, or metaphorical reading of Old Testament historical events. It is a legitimate concern to be taken seriously. We do not know how allegorical they were meant to be

---

The payment, then, relates to the intrinsic cost of sin (the death of the flesh), and therefore can be seen, in a sense, as simply giving the devil his due. The devil cannot traffic in truth (as in receiving a real payment from God), only falsehood. Lost on the devil in this version of the ransom theory is that the payment he is given is the false self, or anti-self, of every person in Christ, i.e., counterfeit bills. All anti-Israel peoples and nations like Egypt in the passage below must be seen as representative of the false self and not projected into a literal favoritism by God of the state of Israel over the state of Egypt, for instance. To refuse a placemat interpretation of such a passage breeds the worst of nationalistic bigotry and ruins the christological beauty of the passage as it applies to all of God's children. See Isa 43:3b–7: "I give Egypt for your ransom, Cush and Seba in your stead. Since you are precious and honored in my sight, and because I love you, I will give people in exchange for you, nations in exchange for your life. Do not be afraid, for I am with you; I will bring your children from the east and gather you from the west. I will say to the north, 'Give them up!' and to the south, 'Do not hold them back.' Bring my sons from afar and my daughters from the ends of the earth—everyone who is called by my name, whom I created for my glory, whom I formed and made."

4. It would seem clear that a new manual for children's Sunday school teachers is in order! The us vs. them narratives of Old Testament heroes vs. the Philistines, Amalakites, Cannaanites, Egyptians, Babylonians, etc. are too often translated into us (Christians) vs. them (non-Christians).

by the writers in the first place, given our diminished ability to establish the factuality of such Old Testament events like the parting of the Red Sea. However, to the extent that such events occurred in history, it is right that we should take pause. It would not feel good to be the people (in this case the Egyptians) who for theological purposes have been instrumentalized as simply representative of the "false selves" of every human. The hurt, pain, and anguish of the tragic consequences for real human beings with real families would, in this sense, be callously glossed over. The Old Testament is inspired by God and thus communicates deep truths, but it is not a text meant to be interpreted as an exact historical record.[5]

Major Ian Thomas, founder of Torchbearers International, spent much of his teaching time applying New Testament theological principles to Old Testament themes. "This is one of the most remarkable evidences of the miraculous inspiration of the Bible," says Thomas. "You will discover that the Bible will come to life in a new way, and the Old Testament in particular will become very much richer, a book charged with spiritual significance, if you will allow the Holy Spirit to teach you the meaning of the language that He uses."[6] One of Thomas's most profound applications of what we have called a christological hermeneutic involves associating Israel's adversaries, the Amalakites, with *sarx* or the flesh (red).[7] The stakes are high. We must make two theological moves to be christologically sound. First, we must follow the Jewish tradition of making the Amalakites the shorthand "moral or metaphysical category" for any enemy of Israel.[8] Secondly, Thomas's teaching to Christians about our indicative truth in Christ and our war against that enemy (the flesh) must be extended universally. If we fail to make these moves, then we will make the age-old mistake of Cain and Abel, where brother becomes "other."

I will summarize Thomas's insights about the Amalakites and flesh below. But before we fret about such an "allegorical" reading, we can remember that Paul himself interpreted the Old Testament figuratively. He felt comfortable doing this only because he knew (as Jesus himself said) that the Old Testament was literally about Jesus Christ (John 5:39). Fittingly,

5. If I am mistaken, then, in depersonalizing the Egyptians I am making as grievous an error as those who consider themselves simply the good "Israelites" of the story.

6. Thomas, *Saving Life of Christ*, 83.

7. Unbeknownst to Thomas, by drawing out the biblical connection between the Amalakites and Esau, Thomas is following suit with our colors. In Gen 25:25 we're told that Jacob's brother Esau was born with a reddish complexion (perhaps even red hair).

8. Horowitz, *Reckless Rites*, 3. See pages 1–6, where Horowitz outlines that without any genetic ties to the ancient Amalakites, people groups such as Romans, Christians, Nazis, and Palestinians have at times been labeled "Amalakites" by Jews because of their enemy status. For the brother to "other" comment I owe Vincent Pizzuto, *Contemplating Christ*, 104.

Paul sees the occasion of the Red Sea as a picture of human baptism in Christ, for example, and the source of the spiritual food and drink in the desert as Christ himself, "for they drank from the spiritual rock that accompanied them, and that rock was Christ" (1 Cor 10:4). Douglas Campbell comments: "At the very least, we have a direct warrant here from Paul for reading the history of the Jews prior to Jesus's arrival in resolutely christological terms. Jesus might not have been known then in his incarnate form, but he was there, all the time, *and this presence infuses that history with a powerful validity.*"[9]

The rock that is Christ is where Thomas begins his Amalakite/flesh narrative. As soon as God uses Moses to give Israelites water from the rock in the desert (Exod 17:6)—water that symbolizes the fulfillment of eternal life in Christ, the promised land God had already given them, and the refreshing abundance of the Spirit—"then Amalek came" (Exod 17:8, NRSV), who attacks Israel. The flesh is parasitic. It follows, latches on, and seeks to destroy. The battle is on.

The Amalakites are those with whom Israel is engaged in battle when the famous scene takes place regarding Moses's arms. When they are raised, Joshua's forces (Israel) prevail. When Moses drops his hands, the Amalakites prevail. The key is that God had already in one sense promised Israel the victory, but even if the war has been won, the battle between flesh and Spirit is nonetheless fierce. The question Ian Thomas asks is whether we are fighting a battle "already won" in the Spirit of Christ, or are we "fighting a battle that is already lost" in the efforts of our flesh? Of the latter, Thomas expounds: "That is a battle you can fight all your days, but I tell you now, you cannot win! It is a battle already lost, lost in the first Adam . . . but the last Adam, Jesus Christ, has already defeated sin and death and hell, and Satan himself! . . . To walk in the Spirit is to assume by faith the victory with which He credits you, and God will vindicate your assumption and make it real in your experience."[10] How true! The ebb and flow of the battle can cause us to lose complete sight of the "already" victory in the midst of the "not yet" victory. Thomas is echoing a consistent theme of our study from the beginning, count yourselves as dead to sin and living to God—because you are!

---

9. Campbell, *Pauline Dogmatics*, 710–11 (emphasis original). See the chapter "Beyond Supersessionism." Campbell continues: "God loved and loves Israel. It is clearly an arrangement that he is particularly fond of and a people he cares for deeply. We should therefore banish forever from our minds the thought that it might need to change drastically. It just needs Jesus acknowledged at the center, and he is there in any case, even if he is unacknowledged, as he is the center of every life and structure, acknowledged or not" (711).

10. Thomas, *Saving Life of Christ*, 85.

But is there more to bolster Thomas's view that the Amalekites should symbolize the flesh, as opposed to simply choosing another of Israel's enemies? Indeed. Thomas draws out the biblical insight that Amalek is Esau's grandson. Esau, the one who "despised his birthright" (Gen 25:34), and of whom it is said, "Jacob I loved, and Esau I hated" (Mal 1:2–3; Rom 9:13). The binary of Genesis 25 between Jacob and Esau is played out again in Exodus 17 between Israel and Amalek. Christologically considered, it is the binary of Spirit vs. flesh.

Without compromise, God is committed to oppose Amalek generation upon generation.[11] Years later he commanded Saul, King of Israel: "Now go, attack the Amalekites and totally destroy all that belongs to them. Do not spare them; put to death men and women, children and infants, cattle and sheep, camels and donkeys" (1 Sam 15:3). These sentiments are grotesque in their violence to most human beings—can this really be the God revealed by Jesus Christ? From a non-christocentric interpretation, all we can see here is a retributive God who wreaks vengeance on the Amalekites in eye-for-an-eye fashion.[12] Alternatively, even if this slaughter really occurred, is it possible that, from the perspective of the writer's un-nuanced stance on God's sovereignty (i.e., what happens is caused by God), that the writer misinterpreted the situation? Is the chronicler retrospectively giving God credit for a retributive act that was Israel's own design? Or do we have biblical permission, starting from the center of Scripture, to embrace the story of God's judgment on the Amalekites as a judgment on the flesh of every person, all persons crucified with Christ? Can we responsibly take this story and make a gospel application highlighting the relentless thoroughness of judgment necessary for a total eradication of the flesh?

Consider the Amalek-flesh connection in Thomas's comments: "There was absolutely no salvageable content in Amalek! There was nothing in

11. It's clear that God will not compromise with whom Esau represents, including Edom, his namesake. See Malachi 1:4: "Edom may say, 'Though we have been crushed, we will rebuild the ruins.' But this is what the LORD Almighty says: 'They may build, but I will demolish. They will be called the Wicked Land, a people always under the wrath of the LORD.'" God pledged to fight against Edom from generation to generation, just as he had done with Amalek.

12. The irony of the apparently retributive act of God is that it is the enemy who loves to strike us while we are down. Thomas notes that we are to be on guard against Amalek's way, paying heed to God's word, "Remember what the Amalekites did to you along the way when you came out of Egypt. When you were weary and worn out, they met you on your journey and attacked all who were lagging behind" (Deut 25:17–18); see Thomas, *Saving Life of Christ*, 98. Extending Thomas's sentiments, we could say that our first enemy, the parasite who will at last perish (Num 24:20), preys on the most vulnerable, the "last who will be first" in the kingdom. Preying on the vulnerable is Satan's game, not God's.

Amalek upon which God could look in favor. That was God's mind, God's will, and God's judgment concerning Amalek."[13] But Saul made a huge mistake. The Israelite king pulled back on God's decisive sentence of total death upon the Amalekites by taking *their* king alive. Additionally, he spared the best of the livestock (1 Sam 15:8–9). "Saul," says Thomas, "presumed to find something good in what God had condemned. . . . He kept the best of what God hated."[14] Interpreted christologically, Saul sought to diminish the cross, the total destruction of the flesh, by mitigating the sentence of destruction against Amalek. Saul's compromise was bad news; he left red where there should be nothing but green.

Thomas is spot on in his assessment on how our enemy uses the zero-sum against us: "This is the subtle temptation with which you too are confronted, for the Devil will come to you again and again and whisper in your ear that you are not as bad as the Bible makes you out to be, that there is always something good in what you are, *apart from what Christ is*—that there is always something salvageable . . . no matter how bad a man may seem to be" (emphasis added). And here Thomas's teaching resonates strongly with our placemat theology and its two totals. I took the liberty of inserting our placemat designations in brackets:

> We fall again and again into the error of estimating ourselves without due regard to the ultimate origin of righteousness [green] and the ultimate origin of sinfulness [red]. Let me remind you again that nothing is good or bad by virtue of what it is [grey]. It is good or bad only by virtue of its origin, and that is why you can be so easily deceived and impressed by the pseudo-righteousness and apparent virtue that stem from the self-life, with its perverted bent for simulating what is good.[15]

To his credit, Thomas did not believe in a sequential eradicationism (see "The Old Is Gone?" in Book One)—regarding our life in the first heaven. Instead, his passion was to encourage the "carnal Christian" languishing in the grey twilight, lacking the *empowerment* flowing from the finished work of Christ. Without understanding why God allows war, genocide, and other horrors, perhaps we can benefit from subsuming the Old Testament narrative under our christological rubric. This may take us a step further even than what Thomas would seek to teach us, to an anthropology where there is no "us v. them," no simply green or red guys.[16]

13. Thomas, *Saving Life of Christ*, 105.
14. Thomas, *Saving Life of Christ*, 105.
15. Thomas, *Saving Life of Christ*, 105.
16. We have cited Thomas on several occasions because he is obviously strong on

Read with christological control, the reality is that God's saving of the Israelites in the Old Testament is a witness to his saving of all people, including the Amalekites.[17] The temptation for people to call themselves Israel, and the wickedest perpetrators "Amalekites," will remain. There may be times when evil seems to manifest in persons or groups in such a way that little or no good is evident. Likewise, there may be times when good seems to manifest itself in persons or groups in such a way that no evil is evident. Our placemat perspective teaches us that neither is truly the case. We should not be content with what Thomas would call the "pseudo-righteousness" and "apparent virtue" of the grey zone. Instead, we are to live as true persons (green) who are called and destined to be separated from evil (red). The *ultimate* message of "be ye separate" is not us from one another, or us from God, but evil from us, by God![18]

Christian sanctification as participation in Christ, "who is our life." The emphasis is continually on living from Christ, not only to Christ. Unfortunately, as mentioned in Book One, the same principle of living from Christ ("who is your life") does not apply regarding justification as it does in sanctification in his thinking. Nevertheless, Thomas's teaching can still be liberating for those relatively certain of their justification, despite this double standard. Of course, in placemat anthropology we have promoted the idea that we are "of the spirit" before, and in spite of, being "of the flesh." To be, by grace, grafted into the true Israelite, even by virtue of creation, and even before we were "Amalekites," is the root of the transformed life.

17. This is the same lesson, of course, that Paul teaches in Rom 9–11, ending with the great crescendo of Rom 11:32: saving not only Jacob, but Esau too. See Book One, "The Righteous and the Wicked."

18. With new eyes, perhaps we can now freshly receive the New Testament line repeated from the Old, "be ye separate" (2 Cor 6:17, KJV), and fruitfully apply it to our lives. Paul is adamant that just as Christ has nothing to do with Satan, and light nothing to do with darkness, the Corinthian believers have nothing in common with unbelievers and should separate themselves from among them. They were meant to be witnesses to God's disavowal of evil and its ultimate destruction; they were not to be party to it. In an environment where faith newly springs forth, the disparity between believer and unbeliever is perhaps less grey and more of a clear-cut green and red. To encourage disciples to make a "clean break" with others who might be a bad influence is not necessarily a bad thing, as long as the provisional us-them is not at the expense of people discerning the sharper edge of separation between righteousness and wickedness in *themselves*. Paul's letter reflects such a time when the designations "believer" and "unbeliever" bore sharp witness to the mutual exclusivity of the two determinations. In other words, even if every person has a green believing self and a red unbelieving self, Paul acknowledges that there may be times when the green manifests in people or groups such that a functional classification of them as green in contrast to others as red may be justified. It is upon this existential and not ontological delineation that the church, or "body of Christ," is premised. In fact, if 1 Cor 5:9–13 is any indication, Paul seems more concerned about the bad influence of believers on other believers in the church than he does with separating believers from the world.

69

Merry Christmas, Malachi![1]

It is only at this one place where God's wrath has burned as a consuming fire—Golgotha

—Karl Barth

There can thus be no doubt that those who know Him will look and move forward to His judgment, fire and testing, not with hesitant but with assured, unequivocally positive and therefore joyful expectation. If they wait for His grace which judges, and which cuts with pitiless severity in this judgment, they still wait for His grace.

—Karl Barth

Five centuries after Malachi's inspired prediction at the end of the Old Testament, Matthew, Mark, and Luke all echo his testimony: "I will send my messenger, who will prepare the way before me . . . says the LORD Almighty" (Mal 3:1; Matt 11:10; Mark 1:2; Luke 7:27). The gospel writers tell us that Malachi's foretold messenger is John the Baptist. His purpose is to prepare the way for his cousin Jesus, born of a virgin. Note that Malachi indicates the way to be prepared is not just for any prophet, priest, or king,

---

1. Parts of the following have been extracted from a lengthier essay, "Merry Christmas Malachi: 'For Judgment I Have Come into the World,'" posted at jeffmcswain.org.

but for "me" [the LORD]. Mary was to be uniquely blessed as *Theotokos*, the Mother of God, in accordance with the prophecies of Malachi and others.

Christmas is a time to celebrate Immanuel, God with us. The God of the universe makes himself most small, even while ruling over the universe. Athanasius (b. 296 CE), the African bishop who is commonly known as the "Father of Orthodoxy" for his defense against the heretics, put it this way: "The Word was not hedged in by His body, nor did his presence in the body prevent His being present elsewhere as well. ... No. The marvelous truth is, that being the Word, so far from being Himself contained by anything, He actually contained all things Himself."[2] God, the one in whom all things exist (Col 1:16–17), the one in whom all people live and move and have their being (Acts 17:28), is the one we find in the midst of the muck and mire of human existence, contained in a manger. This is the Athanasian orthodoxy to which we must always return: Jesus Christ fully human and fully divine, at the same time.

Malachi declares, "Then suddenly the Lord you are seeking will come to his temple" (3:1). The idea of God "suddenly" coming near is a frightful prospect for many. The major theme of Malachi is that God will come near, but at first glance it may seem like a less comforting presence than the typical Yuletide celebrations. Indeed, Malachi draws a connection between God's nearness and human fear. "So I will come to put you on trial. I will be quick to testify against [the unjust]," God says, against those who "do not fear me" (3:5).

This kind of talk may elicit the ominous foreboding of those big black highway billboards—the ones with the white letter messages from the Almighty:

"DON'T MAKE ME COME DOWN THERE." —GOD

Thankfully, God *has* come down here. That is the good news of Christmas. But how does God coming near for judgment square with the good news we proclaim at Christmas? Is it good news for some, but not for most? How do I know it is good news for me? Following the words above from Malachi, Christmas might be more like the billboard than we imagined. After all, Jesus himself said, "For judgment I have come into this world" (John 9:39).[3]

Interestingly, Malachi 3 begins with the prediction of two future messengers, one is the prophet we already mentioned, John the Baptist, who prepares the way (3:1). But in startling fashion Malachi describes the second messenger as the LORD himself, "Then suddenly the Lord who you

---

2. Athanasius, *On the Incarnation*, 17.
3. See John 12:32 just a few verses before.

are seeking will come to his temple; the messenger of the covenant, whom you desire, will come, says the LORD Almighty." This is a sentence heavy with Christmas importance. The Lord descends to the temple, the epicenter of Israel and the world. Our Athanasian principle comes to bear: the true priest coming to represent humanity to God is himself God.

God coming into the world for judgment (John 9:39) may initially seem more Scrooge-like than indicative of "Christmas spirit," but let's probe a little deeper. In John 12:47 Jesus states, "I did not come to judge the world, but to save the world." Together these are encapsulated in John 12:48, "There is a judge for the one who rejects me and does not accept my words; the very words I have spoken will condemn them at the last day." It follows that Jesus does not come to judge, but by unity of his person and work, he is an implicit judgment in and of himself—he is the Word that will prove to be sharper than any two-edged sword (Heb 4:12–14). Again, Jesus does not come to reject us but to save us, such that any man who rejects him is rejecting himself. What judges him is the very statement Jesus has made about saving him.

God's judgment is always purposed to sanctify. In a way reminiscent of the Psalmist (130:3), "If you, Lord, kept a record of sins, Lord, who could stand?" Malachi declares, "But who can endure the day of his coming? Who can stand when he appears? For he will be like a refiner's fire or a launderer's soap" (3:2–3a). Malachi asserts that not only the people, but also, and perhaps especially, their representatives (the priests), will be purified and refined. The theme of judgment is revisited at the beginning of the next chapter: "'Surely the day is coming; it will burn like a furnace. All the arrogant and every evildoer will be stubble' . . . says the LORD Almighty, 'Not a root or a branch will be left to them'" (4:1).

But again we ask, who is judged? Who is included in this prophetic word? The sobering conclusion is that everyone represented in the true high priest's ministry is also to be included in his judgment.[4] There does not appear to be any argument of degree. This is corroborated elsewhere in the minor prophets in passages like Zephaniah 1:18, "'On the day of the LORD's wrath.' . . . In the fire of his jealousy the whole earth will be consumed, for he will make a sudden end of all who live on the earth." God's judgment is all-inclusive and universal. It includes all people, then and now. We may perhaps attempt to wriggle ourselves off the hook when those judged by God are specifically listed in Malachi 3 as "sorcerers, adulterers, and perjurers . . . those who defraud laborers of their wages, who oppress the widows and the fatherless, and deprive the foreigners among you of justice." Yet is

---

4. See the High Priest Caiaphas's fascinating prophetic word in John 11:49–52.

there one of us who has not committed adultery according to Jesus, or who at least has not been indirectly complicit in the unjust systems mentioned?

As we have already seen in our snapshot from Hebrews, the New Testament dictates that all talk of human judgment must start and end with the cross. Augustine (b. 354), another early church father, stated it thus: Christ "remains one with him to whom he offered, made himself one with those for whom he offered, is himself one as Offerer and Offering."[5] In Christ's representative death, humanity dies (2 Cor 5:14). This theme shines revelation light on how we read Malachi and how we are meant to interpret Old Testament destruction passages as a whole. The destruction of the Righteous One at Calvary is our most vivid portrayal of the consequences of sin. The Old Testament destruction passages, whether God's wrath is directed at Israel or Israel's enemies, should therefore be understood in light of the cross (i.e., as illustrative of the inherently destructive consequences of sin).

But does God not mandate and actually cause the destruction, as Scripture seems to indicate? To this we must say, God does not have to cause it—it causes itself. But at the same time God, in his sovereignty, allows it. An unnuanced view of God's sovereignty can all too easily make God an agent of evil, which God never is. Our Athanasian principle must remain conclusive, that the same God who stood among us, teaching us to love and forgive our enemies, is the God of the Old Testament. Holding to the living word, the central lesson we learn from the destruction passages is that God has comprehended all of what he has mysteriously allowed and gathered it all under, and in, his own death on the cross. There is no need to compromise biblical inspiration. Nevertheless, our failure to consistently read Scripture in a Christ-centered way, along with our faulty notions of a murderous God, must be crucified with Christ.

Malachi cultivates a christological view of judgment for us that includes the proper fear of God. In worshipful awe, we recognize, because of God's revelation of himself in Christ, that the judge is none other than the one judged in our place.[6] In this reverence, beholding the glorious truth of Jesus Christ and our true selves in him, we are made acutely aware that evil will not endure. In an inspired portrayal of the sun rising, Malachi gives us

---

5. Augustine, *De Trinitate*, 4.14.19. Quoted in T. F. Torrance, *Trinitarian Faith*, 177.

6. To understand judgment properly, notes Barth, "we must hold fast to the fact that all men (we too!) are [God's] enemies—but that we all go to meet the Judge who gave himself for us. It is true that he is the *Judge*; there can be no doctrine of universal salvation. Nevertheless, he is the Judge whom we Christians *know*" (*Learning Jesus Christ*, 82). See *CD* IV/587 where these sentiments are echoed. We can proceed to the judgment with "confidence and peace," says Barth, "by faith and not by sight . . . with our certain knowledge of the pardoning sentence of this Judge."

a picture of resurrection glory in another Son: "All the arrogant and every evil-doer will be stubble.... But for you who revere my name, the sun of righteousness will rise with healing in its rays. And you will go out and frolic like well-fed calves. Then you will trample on the wicked; they will be ashes under the soles of your feet on the day when I act," says the LORD Almighty (4:1–3).

In these words is the release of the captives. What a joyous day when the revelation of who Jesus Christ is and what he has done for us is before us. In the death of Christ the dross is consumed. The chaff of our lives burned away. Life abounds and we dance on our graves.[7]

Perhaps this is a new way of thinking. I can hear a Christian brother or sister asking: "Are you telling me that I will be judged? That I am wicked?" In response, we can state that there is only one kind of justification, and that is for the wicked (Rom 4:5). Ironically, those attempting to add to the righteousness they have been given in Christ robe themselves in mythical self-righteousness while robbing the righteousness of others. These are the ones who stand to miss the celebration. Jesus himself reminds us, "For judgment I have come into this world, so that the blind will see and those who see will become blind" (John 9:39).

Fire in Scripture has the dual purpose of portraying judgment and illumination, both in and by the Holy Spirit. The work of the Holy Spirit is inherent proof that the wrath of God serves his love. On that day of revelation no one will be "let off easy." There will be a clear inescapable indictment against all evildoers, as we witness our false selves consumed in the judgment of grace—the revelation of the cross. In redemption's merciful light we are all Jacob and all Esau, all disobedient and all redeemed (Rom 11:32).

One of Malachi's main purposes, then, is to teach us about the blessings of judgment. His view of what we call the second heaven is quite inspiring. On that day of clarity, states the prophet, "you will again see the distinction between the righteous and the wicked, between those who serve God and those who do not" (3:18). Like the Israelites, we are, in our fallen selves, prone to rationalize sin. Against any confusion that calls wrong right, we will all see clearly the difference between the false (red) and true (green) dimensions of our lives and world in the refining fire of Christ's death and resurrection. And in that moment we may celebrate the wrath of God against any injustice and all aspects of our lives that are not created

---

7. With our contention that to be one with Christ is to be one with the Spirit, more consideration could be given to Matt 27:50 and the possibility that the point of death when Jesus "gave up," "yielded up," "released" his spirit is more significant than a mere indication of death, but perhaps represents something of the "release of the captives" to all eternity (see Luke 4:18).

and redeemed by the same God who proves his love for us.[8] Dancing on the ashes of our false selves and fallen world—now *that* is a deliverance dance!

The sooner we recognize that it is we who are judged and not "the other guy," the better. Far from conveniently pushing judgment away to the future, it is precisely because we know what God's fiery wrath will reveal that we are motivated to live *now* in the reality of what will endure (Col 3:5–6), living as those born from above (Col 3:1; John 3:3). In the Holy Spirit, the reality of that day is a contemporary event.

Behold I bring you glad tidings: God has come near to you for judgment.

---

8. The last verse of Malachi (4:6) reminds us of the beauty of reconciliation: "He will turn the hearts of the parents to their children, and the hearts of the children to their parents." It also points to the futility of trying to go around the cross to find an alternative path to salvation. See also Heb 10:26–27.

70

Repent and Believe!

He blessed it and broke open his dream, one part in each hand. To those on his left and those on his right, he said the same thing as he handed them his dream, "Eat this dream, and it will kill the dream that kills." Hands trembling, they wondered which of their dreams would die and which would grow stronger.

—Willie Jennings

What will it be like to stand before Jesus Christ the crucified and risen Lord? I imagine it as a Doubting Thomas encounter for each of us, as in the account of John 20:24–29. Thomas doubted Jesus's resurrection. He said he would not believe until he saw for himself and touched Jesus's wounds. Are we surprised that Jesus obliged him?[1] Jesus appeared to Thomas, and with Thomas's hands in Jesus's wounds, the disciple we know as Doubting Thomas came to believe. He exclaimed, "My Lord and my God." Jesus's words to him are vital to our understanding of the second heaven: "Because you have seen me, you have believed."

If Jesus's scars anchor him in the historical existence of our first heaven, the pastoral function of these wounds is heightened in the second. In the second heaven we will find ourselves in the very midst of the gospel of "Jesus Christ and him crucified," that dimension where Paul's words meet

---

1. In effect straddling the dimensions of first and second heaven, the liminal space of the resurrection narratives give us significant clues as to what the second heaven will be like.

John's: "'Look, he is coming with the clouds,' and 'every eye will see him, even those who pierced him,' and all the peoples on earth 'will mourn because of him'" (Rev 1:7).[2] In the risen *Jesus Christ* we see our true selves, created and redeemed by him, humans fully alive in Christ. In *him crucified* we see all our implication in Christ's death. As perpetrators, hands in Jesus's wounded hands, we will grieve all the harm inflicted on others *by us* as harm done most directly to Christ. As victims, hands in Jesus's side, we will finally recognize all the evil done *to us* as also done most directly to Christ.

Because Christ's sufferings are not only in time but transcend time, we are told that all our human suffering is a sharing in his—he suffers *our* sufferings before we do in his own passion.[3] We remember that Jesus is the compassionate one. Our hands in his side remind us that he feels our agony deep in his very gut. Jesus understands us in our brokenness, knows the pain that prods the perpetrator, and forgives us before we ask. Never will we experience such a combination of compassion, consolation, and confrontation. Bonhoeffer renders the Thomas scene not as us touching Jesus's wounds, but him touching ours:

> [God] has looked—and he saw us wounded, lost, fearful. Now he is about to *heal* us. He touches the wounds that the past struck, and they close. They stop hurting; they can no longer harm our soul. Memories don't torment us any longer. All our pains sink into nothing, into oblivion, like in the presence of a loved one. God is nearer to us than all that has passed.[4]

Jesus's words from the cross, "Father, forgive them, for they do not know what they are doing" (Luke 23:34) were undoubtedly meant not only for those within earshot, but also for all human beings. On the day of judgment, when we are fully cognizant of our inclusion in the life and death of Christ, I envision a slight twist to Jesus's words: "Father forgive them, *now that they know what they have done.*" We will know just how much we share in Christ's glory and his suffering, just how much our lives have been

---

2. Rev 1:7. Just as he relays the encounter of Thomas and Jesus with his wounds, the writer John also describes every creature's appearance before Jesus as "the lamb who was slain" (Rev 5:6–14). We are judged not only by God, but by the God who became man, the human being Jesus Christ, the one who has comprehended true (righteous) and false (wicked) humanity (Acts 17:31).

3. Christ shares my plight, he shares my suffering, but only because of the cosmic range inherent in his deity. That is why Scripture points to the fact that all human suffering is a sharing in the suffering of Christ (2 Cor 1:5; Phil 3:10; Col 1:24; 1 Pet 4:13). It matters not when our human suffering happened in relation to Christ's, i.e., whether it was before, during, or after his lifetime in human history.

4. Bonhoeffer, *Mystery of Easter*, 46.

congruent and incongruent with his. The overriding context of love and compassion will include within it a withering indictment.[5]

In relating the sentiments of God, the Scriptures declare, "'it is mine to avenge; I will repay,' says the Lord" (Rom 12:19). This appears to point to the cost of God's vengeance in absorbing all human sin, guilt, shame, and brokenness in order to put it away in his own death. "It is mine to avenge" is God's way of saying, *This is uniquely mine to deal with*. The reference to vengeance points first and foremost to God's Enemy with a capital E, the Perpetrator of Evil: *Because I am a jealous God, I seek to destroy all that seeks to destroy my children*. Perhaps in that moment of clear recognition of our dual complicity, we who are friends of God in truth and enemies of God in flesh will experience firsthand these merciful scriptural precepts: "if your enemy is hungry, feed him; if he is thirsty, give him something to drink" (Rom 12:20). After all, would God tell us to treat our enemies this way without also doing the same?

In our wickedness, we are undoubtedly enemies of God, and always under the influence of God's Enemy. God will have no mercy with this primary adversary, even if the means of warfare are mysteriously counterintuitive. Evil, says Barth, "is *His* enemy, because it is *He* who allows it to be this, because He has made the controversy with it *His* affair."[6] God in Christ, says Barth, throws himself into the battle.[7] He is the primary foe of evil, as well as the "primary victim."[8] Evil, Barth concludes, "could not master this victim. It could neither endure nor bear the presence of God in the flesh. It met with a prey which it could not match and by which it could only be destroyed as it tried to swallow it. The fullness of grace which God showed to His creature by Himself becoming a threatened, even ruined and lost creature, was its undoing."[9]

Mired in contradiction, ruined and lost, we *need* undoing! The cross is the judgment. It is the great separation. That is why the day of judgment and the day of salvation (2 Cor 6:2; Isa 49:8) are one and the same; both are the day of true repentance. In our Doubting Thomas moment, as we place our hands in the Savior's wounds, we will enter into a clear revelation, seeing our sheep selves go right and our goat selves go left. In this second-heaven

---

5. See J. B. Torrance, *Worship, Community*, 44–45.
6. *CD* III/3, 362.
7. *CD* III/3, 357.
8. *CD* III/3, 360.
9. *CD* III/3, 362. British spelling retained. As with the rules of reality, the host can swallow the parasite, but the parasite is unable to achieve the same.

moment, appearing before Christ in our tangled existence, we will see everything untangled.

Time and time again we return to the idea that the second heaven, the day, is a dimension, concurrent and not actually sequential to the first heaven. Repentance here in the first heaven is dimensionally connected to perfect repentance there, and that means every day here is the *day*. No wonder there is urgency in Paul's call to repent as he teaches about the cross: "We implore you [plead, beseech] on Christ's behalf" (2 Cor 5:20); "we urge you not to receive God's grace in vain.... I tell you, now is the time of God's favor, now is the day of salvation" (2 Cor 6:1–2).[10]

Matthew 13:24–30 takes us back to the parable of the wheat and the tares and Jesus's ongoing call to repent, for the kingdom of heaven is at hand. Jesus describes a farmer sowing his field with nothing but good seed, but inexplicably, tares (wheat-like weeds) spring up too. When the farmer is asked how this could be, he says an enemy has done it. An enemy? These are strong words for a basic agrarian metaphor. The farmer in the parable warns the workers not to pull up the tares, for risk of pulling up the wheat along with them. Wait until the harvest, he says, and in the meantime let both grow together. There could not be a more apropos word picture for the theme of this book. God has created each of us very good in our true selves (green), there is no explaining how the look-alike tares of our false selves (red) sprout up, but they do. It is the work of the enemy. The tares are evil twins to the wheat, working their parasitic entwinement with paralyzing, choking force. Only the judgment of Jesus Christ's cross provides the sickle of separation at the harvest. Here, in the second heaven, the wheat and tares of our lives will finally be plainly revealed for what they are.[11]

Repentance involves clear sightedness and the transformation that comes with it. The day of judgment is also the day of clarity. The confusion of the wheat and tares gives way to the clarity of distinction between the two. Namely, the tares are flesh: false, old, parasitic, and red. The wheat is spirit: true, new, original, and green. That is why, when this clarity of the second heaven visits us by the Spirit in the first heaven, we say that we are "born from above." It is like your first time flying over what you thought was a familiar mountain. From your previous standpoint on the ground, you

---

10. 2 Cor 6:2 is a direct quote through Isaiah (49:8). If the prophetic call in Isa 49 concerns the restoration of Israel, here Paul broadens the scope, for in the Messiah is the restoration of "the world" (2 Cor 5:19), a universal restoration to which Israel would bear unique witness.

11. The fields being white unto the harvest to me connotes a universal complete and undiminished humanity. When the gospel is proclaimed, and the second-heaven clarity (of judgment day) by the Spirit visits us, then fruit is reaped.

had always thought it was one; flying directly above, you see that it is really two mountains divided by a river. In being born from above, we discover the dimension of highest human truth, who we are in Jesus Christ. Our discriminatory perspective shows us that we are saved not only from evil and sin, but from ourselves, our false selves. Once we have the perspective, we are meant to put it into practice. That is when we know repentance is taking place, one's actions "produce fruit in keeping with repentance" (Matt 3:8).

Thomas Erskine is speaking to all people when he declares, "now that God hath cometh in our nature—now that Christ is in us, the hope of glory; now that in him, as our Head, all fulness dwells for us, are we not verily without excuse?"[12] Although "we hath been given eternal life" (1 John 5:11), there are legitimate reasons that we "wrapped it in a napkin," as Erskine says (from Luke 19:20), failing to steward the gift that we have been given. It may be because of traumatic events (leading to what Moltmann calls "practical atheism"). It could stem from terrible examples of "godly" living, or the abuses of the church, or from simply having never heard the gospel of Jesus Christ in this world. We could go on. On the day of judgment, however, the clarity will surpass even that clarity of Jesus's earthly ministry. Supplied with perfect clarity in the second heaven, in a way that our first-heaven experience could only anticipate, there is no excuse for us to remain unrepentant.

In our warped first-heaven existence, there are plenty of compelling existential excuses for unbelief, even if there are no ontological ones. The second-heaven judgment, then, reflects the fact that as Genesis 1 creatures, we have no excuse (Rom 1:20), even when from Genesis 2 until the eschaton the rationale of reality is hidden in the fog of first-heaven irrationality. In reality, there is literally *no good reason* for people not to believe, but we could also say that there are plenty of understandable reasons in this world that mitigate against belief. God, in his mercy, understands this better than any of us.

Jesus came to announce over all people the good news that we are embraced by the Father in the Son and through the Spirit. God loves "the world" (John 3:16) infected by red. He does not love the "red" itself, however, and his stated refusal to pray for the world can be taken with exactly such precision—"the world" in its ignominious sense. The red cosmos is evil and irredeemable. But even if Jesus does not pray for the world, he does pray for his children *in the world* (John 17:9). As he said to the disciples, he calls all of us out of the world of grey and into the purpose of green: "If you belonged to the world, it would love you as its own. As it is, you do not belong to the world, but I have chosen you out of the world" (John

---

12. Erskine, *Brazen Serpent*, 87.

15:19). Even the Pharisees, who are also children of Abraham (John 8:37), and thereby children of God, are included. They often represent worldly examples of those who, even with a semblance of clarity, remain in denial of the truth of Christ, and are therefore without excuse (John 15:22). As Jesus often chided, the Pharisees and other trained teachers of the law should have known better. Instead, if not resisting him outright, the Pharisees are often represented by Jesus as the foil character in the Savior's parables (e.g., the old brother in Luke 15, the rich man with the shrewd manager in Luke 16). They are the ones who *should* have better perspective but who do not have eyes to see.

Jesus's parables continue to challenge and heighten our perspective. Until 2014, when Reality Ministries began to focus solely on building community between people with and without disabilities, we had a thriving after-school program at the Reality Center for the students at the adjacent school. In our middle school group one week I reminded a group of young men how Jesus invites us to see ourselves in his parables. I said, "Now I'm going to read these few verses, and I want you to see where you are in the story."

I read the first few verses of Luke 15, about the sheep who leaves the pen and the shepherd who leaves his ninety-nine other sheep to search for the one lost sheep. When he finds it, he brings it home and there is a big party. "I tell you that in the same way there will be more joy in heaven over one sinner who repents," says Jesus, "than over ninety-nine righteous persons who do not need to repent." Jesus tells us that this story is about repentance, but the repentance within the story is far from self-evident. What does the sheep do to repent? Apparently nothing. Repentance, then, is less about the sheep's behavior than it is about what happens when we have eyes to see ourselves in the story.

Francisco was the first to speak: "I'm the dude." By this he meant the shepherd.

Jonathan said simply, "I'm at the party."

Then Dawood chimed in: "I'm one of the sheep, not the lost sheep, but one in the pen with the other sheep."

Savion immediately added, "Yeh, me too, I'm in the pen hanging out with all the *lady* sheep."

We all laughed.

While the boys to his left and right had all answered, Luis had thus far been silent. I could tell his wheels were turning. Then he blurted out, "I got it! We are the lost sheep and God is the shepherd and when we get lost, he comes to find us and takes us home because he loves us." Luis's response was profound.

I elaborated on Luis's response: "That's exactly right, Luis, when we were lost, Jesus came to find us, and to embrace us at our worst and to rescue us! Personally, I'm so thankful that Jesus loves me so much that he would go out of his way to come and find me and carry me home on his shoulders, because I know that I am helpless to do it on my own."

Then Fernando, the first boy who had spoken, interjected unexpectedly, "I changed my mind, I want to be the lost sheep!"

In just a few moments, Fernando had changed his mind from being "the dude" to identifying with the hapless sheep who was lost and found by the Good Shepherd. It was a moment of true repentance, and indeed, as was clear to all who knew him, Fernando began to practice his new mindset.

Unlike Fernando, the unrepentant person fails to see themselves as the lost sheep in the story—the one carried home on Jesus's shoulders. If you think you are simply one of the ninety-nine, you will miss the point, just like people who do not think they are sick, even though they are (Matt 9:12; Mark 2:17; Luke 5:31).

"I'm not lost.... Who are you to say I need rescuing?... This story doesn't apply to me." These are all examples of unrepentant responses. Conversely, true repentance is to recognize our continual lostness *while also recognizing* that we are always found in the arms of the Good Shepherd.

There is one other unrepentant response worth mentioning, and it is perhaps the most flagrantly unrepentant one. It goes like this: "Great, I'm rescued by Jesus! Now that I'm home free I can go out and do whatever I want!" This person is right that they have been brought home, forgiven, redeemed, and that everything has been accomplished for them by Jesus. But they err. Why? They know the story, but they do not really see themselves in it. They acknowledge the Shepherd as the leader—the One who rescued them when they were helpless—but then they turn right around and make themselves out to be in charge ("Now I'm free to do whatever I want"). This person's attitude violates the internal logic of the parable; the premise of the whole parable is the leadership of the Shepherd, it never switches over to our leadership. Indeed, the same Shepherd who rescued us is the one we must continually depend upon, for it is he who carries us from our place of lostness back to the place of safety and community. The mistake is not only to twist the leadership dynamic into something backwards, but to forget that there is always an element of lostness in our lives that we must acknowledge. Placemat anthropology teaches us that we never get past lostness to pure foundness in this life. "Repent and believe" is not a sequential box to check off and leave behind. Continual repentance is continual dependence on the leadership of the Savior, the life-changing knowledge that we are being carried by the Good Shepherd.

71

Standing Pat at the Gate

Sin is necessarily a lie, surely, and is not the lie bound to lie to itself? And as for the stifling of one's own conscience, the dulling of its mirror, the dimming of its light—is this not the very essence of sin? . . . is it not natural that man should yearn for true judgment, a final and correct judgment by the Word of God—hoping all the time that he may survive this judgment, yet by the Lord's mercy and not through his own deserving?

—Hans Urs von Balthasar

PAUL TELLS US IN Colossians that all evil behavior is a sign of the alienation of our minds from God (Col 1:21).[1] Operating in our right minds, the mind of Christ given to us, we do not sin (1 Cor 2:16; Rom 7:25). That is why, in our conflicted existence, it is impossible to have genuine behavioral change apart from Holy Spirit *metanoia*, signifying a radical change

---

1. This verse has been at times translated, "Once you were alienated from God and were enemies in your minds because of your evil behavior" (NIV), i.e., we were alienated *because* of our evil behavior instead of the evil behavior manifesting from the alienation. That this should not be construed as a causal situation from behavior to alienation is helped by the fact that the word "because" is not in the Greek. Bad behavior doesn't alienate us from God any more than good behavior reconciles us to God. As indicated in the NIV alternative reading (see also CEB, NET), the flow seems likely to indicate that we are alienated "as shown in your evil behavior" rather than "because of your evil behavior." That is why most English translations avoid using "because" or any kind of causal language.

of mind. This truly renewed way of thinking—far from being purely noetic (or cerebral)—involuntarily issues forth in embodied expression. That is Paul's intention when he asks us to "offer your *bodies* as living sacrifices," immediately before instructing us to "not conform to the pattern of this world, but be transformed by the renewing of your *mind*" (Rom 12:1–2, emphasis added).

Metanoia flows from the unconditional love of God, but Satan loves for us to waste our time *trying to get into* the safe place with God. When we imagine God has conditions for love, forgiveness, and adoption, all our exertion to meet these conditions keeps us away from repentance. Mentally, physically, emotionally, and spiritually, we cannot make a reasonable estimate of the red without the safe, up-front assurance of the green. The gospel is not "*if* you repent, then you will be forgiven," but "you are forgiven, therefore repent." It takes practice to recalibrate our notions of forgiveness and repentance in this way. Even such a generous gospel phrase like "you are forgiven, therefore repent" can be infected with cooperative toxins. If we are not careful, we could put "forgiveness for all" on the grace side, with "therefore repent" on the works side, leaving one last independent condition to be met. Unwittingly, such a mistake turns "finished" forgiveness back into an onerous hypothetical situation—it is available, or possible, but not actual. Grace has become conditional, an exception to the rule!

John Calvin distinguished "legal repentance" from "evangelical repentance." The first takes place in a conditional, implicitly threatening space, while the second takes place in an unconditional, safe space. Legal repentance, Calvin charged, puts the premium on contrition. Sinners are "harassed by the fear of divine wrath" and swarmed with "deep distress." In their dread, they have considered God first and foremost "an avenger and a judge," and so they find themselves repenting, in effect, to the wrong god, a deity whose mercy is contingent on human remorse. This type of repentance can only be "the antechamber of hell," said Calvin. Evangelical repentance, however, instead of making forgiveness conditional, occurs when sinners recognize their wickedness in relation to God's true character. By a "confidence in the Divine mercy," they are "re-invigorated . . . and converted."[2]

In the Prodigal Son parable, the younger son "coming to his senses" and returning home is often taught as repentance, but it is a poor shadow. Eyes blurred with desperation, driven by his own material want for the comforts of home, the younger son does not have a clear picture of his father. Instead, we see the struggle of a son who could not trust his father's love. Smothered with shame, he feels that he has "lost the dignity to be called

---

2. Calvin, *Institutes*, book III, chapter iii, part 4, 652–53.

'son,'" as Henri Nouwen puts it: "There is repentance, but not a repentance in the immense light of a forgiving God. It is a self-serving repentance that offers the possibility of survival." Nouwen then references his own poor habit of repenting to the wrong God, one that needs to be conditioned to love and forgive; in these cases, he relates, "God remains a harsh, judgmental God. It is this God who makes me feel guilty and worried and calls up in me all these self-serving apologies. Submission to this God does not create true inner freedom, but breeds only bitterness and resentment."[3]

"Whatever assurance may arise in our hearts when we hear of the love of God in Jesus Christ," adds C. Baxter Kruger, "is immediately poisoned when we hear that this love flows out of only one side of God . . . that there is a side of God that does not like us at all, a side that would just as soon have us miserable and broken and enslaved to darkness as it would see us whole and complete and living in joy."[4] Later Kruger continues, "the legacy of the legalized God is anxiety, and that means self-centeredness, and self-centeredness . . . transforms our lives into a long and frantic attempt to save ourselves, to create legendary lives that will at least hint of wholeness."[5] In keeping with our theme, Kruger offers a "green" antidote: "The only cure in the universe is to see Jesus Christ seated at the Father's right hand and ourselves seated with him. The discovery . . . is so real, so solid and true that to believe it baptizes our souls with assurance, the most liberating force in all the earth."[6]

This understanding of evangelical repentance conveys an important truth: *repentance is not something that we do to get God's grace*, even if we do not appreciate the benefits of God's grace in the Spirit without it. Indeed, Jesus proclaimed that the gospel is not repentance *followed* by the forgiveness of sins but that "repentance *and* forgiveness of sins is to be proclaimed in his name" (Luke 24:47, NRSV, emphasis added). Shortly thereafter, Peter stated the following in a sermon: "Repent and be baptized, every one of you, in the name of Jesus Christ for the forgiveness of your sins. And you will receive the gift of the Holy Spirit" (Acts 2:38). Note that the economy is the same: we are not forgiven because we are baptized any more than we are forgiven by repenting, even if the Holy Spirit blesses these acts of participation in Christ.

Instead of procuring grace, repentance is included in grace, bound up in the name of Christ himself, God "for us." Scripture tells us that we

---

3. Nouwen, *Return of the Prodigal Son*, 47–48.
4. Kruger, *Jesus Christ and the Undoing*, 51.
5. Kruger, *Jesus Christ and the Undoing*, 53.
6. Kruger, *Jesus Christ and the Undoing*, 57.

repent "in his name" (Luke 24:47), or "in the name of Jesus Christ" (Acts 2:38).[7] Jesus Christ took our corrupt humanity as our representative, being the perfect penitent before the Father, and repented for us all. As we will see, it is not primarily repentance that is the problem (after all, every person is already participating in the high priestly ministry of Christ on our behalf in this vicarious sense). The problem is the un-repentant flesh that seeks to keep us from seeing clearly and the enemy who tempts us away from our ongoing participation in Christ. As we have said, true repentance requires the safe context of green, but it also requires the overlap of red and green in order to have meaning. It therefore involves our true heart and obedient mind turning against the flesh *in spite of the overlap*. This is what Jesus himself told us he was about to do as he faced his stiffest test, when in the midst of his passion the torque of the overlap would reach its zenith: "The prince of this world is coming. He has no hold over me, but the world must know that I love the Father and do *exactly what my Father has commanded me*" (John 14:30–31, emphasis added).[8]

Shortly thereafter Jesus was making "the good confession" (1 Tim 6:13) when confronted by the Roman potentate, the one representing the pinnacle of world power, who said he had the power of life or death over his Galilean subject. From Jesus's remark about testifying to the "world" in John 14 above we can see the scarlet thread to John 18 and 19, where Jesus

---

7. Jesus is not only the point of reference for human repentance, he is also the one human who truly prays. While Jesus prays to the Father directly, we pray derivatively in Jesus's name. Regarding the first case of Jesus praying directly to the Father, note that in John 14:16 and 16:26 a different Greek word for "ask" is used; as Ellicott comments, it is "one which implies more of nearness of approach and of familiarity than that which is rendered 'ask' in John 14:14" (and in John 15:16; 16:23). To mark the distinction between the words, some translations (ASV, NKJV) use "I will *pray* the Father" for John 14:16 and 16:26 instead of "I will ask the Father." All of this gives the sense that Jesus is himself the human embodiment of prayer in union with the Father, while he instructs us to ask Jesus and the Father *in Jesus's name*, i.e., in the name of prayer himself. See section "Simul Shema" in *Simul Sanctification*.

8. "That the world may learn" or "that the world may know" (NRSV) actually points to this steepest test, as it connotes in the Greek that there is something that must be proven, as in a court of law (see John 7:51; 11:57; 2 Cor 2:9). Also of interest is that instead of a new verse, the medieval scribe has kept Jesus's last line as part of verse 14:31. The initial command of the culminating "Come now; let us leave" is also translated "arise" or "rise." The exact Greek word is used only two other places, both when Jesus is arousing the sleeping disciples in the midst of his steepest trial, internally connecting John 14:31 to the garden and Jesus's passion (see Matt 26:46; Mark 14:42). To me this is a meaningful demonstration that Jesus is rousing us to share not only in his death but also his resurrection, providing us a meaningful integrity of participation with him as friends in the temporal and ultimate hour of trial in which we are not uninvolved—this in spite of the fact that the disciples' less-than-distinguished track record of checkered faithfulness in the temporal passion of Christ is much like ours in this world.

articulates his lordship in the kingdom of a different dimension (green). For example, before Pilate: "You are right in saying I am a king. In fact, for this reason I was born, and for this I came into the world, to testify to the truth. Everyone on the side of truth listens to me" (John 18:37).

In doing so, Jesus was doing what we are asked to do, to "fight the good fight of the faith (1 Tim 6:12) . . . and to *keep this command without spot or blame*" (1 Tim 6:14). Consistent with our entire project, this biblical imperative to be blameless is one that makes absolutely no sense apart from the fact that we are in one sense already doing everything required to live lives of repentance. In the name of the one who said the enemy had no hold over him, we are told to "take hold of [hold on to] the eternal life to which you were called," practicing repentance here in preparation for the day, "until the appearing of our Lord Jesus Christ" (1 Tim 6:14). Hebrews carries a similar theme, upbraiding us to "hold on to our courage and the hope of which we boast" (Heb 3:6). Participating in Christ, we may "hold firmly to the end the confidence we had at first" (Heb 3:14), and finally, in face of the approaching day, "let us hold *unswervingly* to the hope we profess, for he who promised is faithful" (Heb 10:23–24, emphasis added).

Influenced heavily by John McLeod Campbell, the theologian James (J. B.) Torrance was a herald of evangelical repentance. He described repentance as submission to the verdict of the cross, the condemnation of the flesh. This submission is our "amen" in and with the "amen" Jesus has spoken to the Father in agreement with his "priestly vicarious self-offering." Even if our "amen" is a response *to* the response of Jesus on our behalf, it is also a response *inside of* Jesus's response for us. Unconditional grace does not leave room for an extra step to actualize it; it always *includes* our human response. From inside the gift of grace, we are summoned by the Spirit to participate (see "Reposing in the Response" in Book One). Submitting to the verdict of the cross is inherently transformative because we reiterate the superabundant truth of the gospel in our submission.[9] In this submission we will bear fruit in keeping with repentance.

Repentance involving submission to the verdict of the cross means that it has everything to do with judgment rightly understood, the judgment of deliverance. To say "amen" to the verdict of the cross is to say "no" and "yes" in unambiguous ways to the No and Yes of God's verdict. To the

---

9. J. B. Torrance, *Worship, Community*, 56–57. Alan Torrance once told me that the greatest theological influence on his father (James) was McLeod Campbell. Campbell was defrocked by the Scottish Presbytery in 1829 for disagreeing with the doctrine of limited atonement as stated in the Westminster Confession. Campbell's notion of Christ as the perfect penitent was formative for Torrance, and taken up also by Torrance's friend, C. S. Lewis.

extent that we fail to see how the cross differentiates between our true and false selves, we are "enemies of the cross" (Phil 3:18). We are those Paul described as defined by the flesh: "their destiny is destruction, their god is their stomach, and their glory is in their shame. Their mind is set on earthly things" (Phil 3:19). By "earthly things" Paul means the "grey things" with accent on the "red" component within them. To resist Christ's destruction *of* the red at Calvary is to be destroyed *by* the red—to be hell bent on destruction. Conversely, to see our true selves (green) united with Christ and the definitive separation of ourselves from our sin (red), is to boast "in the cross of our Lord Jesus Christ, through which the world has been crucified to me, and I to the world" (Gal 6:14). Only on the day will we perfectly experience boasting and worshiping as one.

Until that day, we must remember that repentance here derives from repentance there. All of the Then is in the Now. Paul's prayer in Philippians recognizes that to know that we are pure (green) even now is to know also that we are loved, despite the red. In one sense, we are always at "the home of righteousness" with Jesus: "And this is my prayer: that your love may abound more and more with knowledge and depth of insight, so that you may be able to discern what is best and may be pure and blameless until the day of Christ, filled with the fruit of righteousness that comes through Jesus Christ—to the glory and praise of God" (Phil 1:9–11). Paul prays that we might be who we already are, not "pure and blameless" only *on* the day of Christ, but "be pure and blameless until the day of Christ" (Phil 1:10).

There is a sense that repentance can also be viewed as a rediscovery. We alluded earlier to a major theme of placemat anthropology, that repentance in its fullness is not experienced until the day of the Lord, the second heaven. The flip side of this full eschatological revelation is the opportunity to see accurately how all things were originally created. With a Genesis 1 perspective, on that day we will witness the terrible, beautiful, consuming fire of God's love as our foe and therefore as our friend. We will witness the burning away of all that is not created, all the elements (or base admixtures[10]) that do not belong, and the emergence of "a new heaven and a new

---

10. See 2 Pet 3:1. Here, Peter literally says he is seeking to stir up their pure (sincere) minds (NKJV, NRSV), as if they had another, impure mind. The "no base admixture" comment is from *Ellicott's Commentary for English Readers*, in reference to Phil 1:10, the only other place the word is used in Scripture: The word "sincere" signifies "purity tested and found clear of all base admixtures." In 1 Cor 5:6–8 Paul uses "yeast" as a bad admixture, a parasitic presence that "works its way through the whole batch of dough." Paul is not a champion of dietary restrictions, but he shrewdly co-opts unleavened bread for his own theological purposes. Thus, he calls the Corinthians to be who they are in Christ, now that Christ has purged all parasitic admixtures in his self-sacrifice: "Get rid of the old yeast that you may be a new batch without yeast—as you really are.

earth, where righteousness dwells" (2 Pet 3:13). Twice Peter assures us that this will be a day to which we may look forward (2 Pet 3:11, 13).

The great unveiling will be a time to celebrate the gospel synonymity of *new* and *true*. In other words, we will see with new eyes what has always been true, real, and present, albeit dimensionally veiled. This final manifestation entails our full rediscovery of our life in Christ as our true home. As we discover anew what has always been, we are free to reiterate to the enemy, "I renounce you," turning from our false selves and embracing the reality of Christ. The Savior has always held our true, fully constituted selves—and therefore our believing selves—in himself. Finally, we may discover that the goal is less about human salvation and more about human beings created in Christ who participate with him in the destruction of sin, death, and the devil. This is a matter we shall further explore in upcoming readings.

In the confusion of this world, the first heaven, our belief is relative; it is often sporadic, flimsy, riddled with doubt. People who have endured profound evil have legitimate reason to question God's goodness or even God's existence. If they ever knew it in this world, most people have forgotten who they are as belonging to and participating in Jesus Christ. The grey veil descending from the fall lies thick. In a way worse than any dissociative fugue,[11] we forget who we are and where we came from. We lose touch with reality. Trapped in irrationality, everything is flipped around, and we think our false selves *are* our true selves. "Sin is by nature a lie," notes Von Balthasar, and whether it is our sin or the sin of others against us, or simply the fall's descent upon us, the lie "casts a fog over our insight into ourselves."[12]

Jesus's remark in John 3:17–18 summarizes the situation well: "For God did not send his Son into the world to condemn the world, but to save the world through him. Whoever believes in him is not condemned, but whoever does not believe stands condemned already because they have not believed in the name of God's one and only Son." Our false, unbelieving selves are eternally condemned in the death of Christ; our true believing

---

For Christ, our Passover lamb, has been sacrificed. Therefore let us keep the Festival, not with the old yeast, the yeast of malice and wickedness, but with bread without yeast, the bread of sincerity and truth." On Godly "sincerity," see also 2 Cor 1:12; 2:17.

11. A dissociative fugue is defined in the Merck Manual as "One or more episodes of amnesia in which the inability to recall some or all of one's past and either the loss of one's identity or the formation of a new identity occur with sudden, unexpected, purposeful travel away from home." See Associated Press, "Amnesia Sufferer"; see also "Amnesia Victim Reunited."

12. Von Balthasar, *Prayer*, 298.

selves are "not condemned" because of the life of Christ.[13] Because every person in Christ *already* believes, our unbelieving selves are *already* condemned. In this context "repent and believe" simply means that we must repent of our unbelieving. When we cling to our false selves, we attempt to bypass the cross. It is an exercise in self-condemnation.

On the day of judgment, we will be exposed. The extent to which we identified with our false selves will be plain. Our current fear of this eschatological exposure shows that the one person of our two selves maintains a stubborn distrust and/or ignorance about God's trustworthy character. Applying the two selves to the one person in matters of repentance, then, looks like this for our friend Pat: Pat's false self does not and cannot repent while Pat's true self has no need to repent. It is, therefore, simply Pat in the midst of the conflict who must repent and believe. Since the fall, this has always been the case. It continues to be the case in the first heaven, and will especially be the case in the second heaven. The devil apparently believes that he can make our alter-egos more compelling even in face of the perfect clarity provided in the second heaven. After all, many of us have grown very comfortable in our old clothes while walking the wide road leading to destruction, and are well-practiced in our wicked ways. With us already entrenched in the wrong, Satan has a head start; surely he can persuade some humans, in the words of Lewis, to be "rebels to the end."[14] Yet the odds on that account seem slim. Why? Satan cannot turn truth into falsehood, and lies, no matter how big, are less persuasive as more truth is revealed. Left with lying to himself, our enemy stands to be the epitome of *incurvatus in se* (curved inward on oneself) to his own destruction.

It is good news that no one proceeds past judgment (second heaven) to the unadulterated heaven (third heaven) without renouncing their false selves. Repentance and recognition go hand in hand. It might start by recognizing that you have wrongly put yourself in the "forgiven" camp and others in the "not forgiven" camp. We referred earlier to Jesus's words of universal forgiveness from the cross. But how we hear those words is the key. Are they words for everyone, or for a limited number of people; are they for me only when I decide? Jesus's words are effective for everyone,

---

13. We find the same economy a few verses later in John 3:36: "Whoever believes in the Son has eternal life, but whoever rejects the Son will not see life, for God's wrath remains on them."

14. Lewis, *Problem of Pain*, 129–30. The "doors of hell," continues Lewis, are "locked from the inside." Applied dimensionally (not spatially, as if lost and found are sequential), hell exists in the middle of heaven, and can't exist apart from heaven, just like lostness occurs inside of foundness. Because they have a true identity, therefore, a person in hell could only rebelliously insist on being *who they are not*.

and yet as Barth emphasizes it is only *because* they are words for everyone that they are also for me.¹⁵ If we do not hear Jesus's words of forgiveness in that manner, we do not hear them at all. We have somehow received a counterfeit, conditionalized version of forgiveness based on something we contributed, or based on God's choosing of one person ("the elect") over and against another ("the reprobate").

But what do we make of Jesus's following statement, especially the part about the Holy Spirit, which seems to be confoundingly conditional? He says, "Every kind of sin and slander can be forgiven, but blasphemy against the Spirit will not be forgiven. Anyone who speaks a word against the Son of Man will be forgiven, but anyone who speaks against the Holy Spirit will not be forgiven, either in this age or in the age to come" (Matt 12:31–32). First, we must not use Jesus's remark to pit God the Son and God the Spirit against one another, as if the triunity of God could in any way be trifurcated. Likewise, we cannot prematurely split our true selves and false selves, forgetting the one person upon which they are predicated. It follows that the "anyone" of the passage refers to the whole person of everyone. Can anyone say that they have not spoken a word against the Holy Spirit, one word out of alignment with who they truly are, a word of participation in the anti-Christ dimension? Could any of us dare to make such a claim?

If any word you have ever spoken is out of congruence with the in-Christ dimension, you have spoken a word *against* the Holy Spirit. Practicing a scriptural sound placemat anthropology, on one hand we need not dodge the indictment, or try to convince ourselves that we have never spoken a word against the Holy Spirit (when deep down we know we did!). On the other hand, we may take gospel comfort in the fact that, equipped with our christological placemat view provided by Scripture, we do not have to live under the ominous threat of this verse as if our fate is in the balance. Holding all of the dimensional aspects together, we can recognize that while "Pat's" true self relishes the economy of forgiveness and practices it ("forgive each other, just as in Christ God forgave you," Eph 4:32; Col 3:13), Pat's false self operates out of pure unforgiveness. It is this Pat, the false, unforgiving P^2, which cannot enter the unadulterated kingdom.

In sum, Jesus's remark carries two senses. The one person of the two selves has been forgiven in the crucifixion of the Savior who shared our conflicted state. But, technically speaking, our false selves are not forgiven, they are crucified in Christ. To sin against the Holy Spirit in this age (the

---

15. See Barth, *Living Jesus Christ*, 89: "Faith is the confidence in which a member of the Christian community believes that in the death and resurrection of Jesus Christ God's righteous action has achieved its goal for all men and *thus also* for him" (emphasis added).

first heaven) or in the age to come (the second heaven) is to claim that we have not been crucified with Christ and insist on bringing our *false* selves into the unadulterated kingdom (third heaven).

The only thing that could disqualify us from the unadulterated kingdom, then, is a clinging to the false self and an adherence to the false notion that others are not forgiven. How ironic, then, that the "unforgivable sin" is the denial of the fact that everyone is forgiven. If everyone is not forgiven, then we are not forgiven. Why? Because we are operating with a concept of conditional forgiveness, and therefore we are left with a forgiveness that does not exist! Conversely, if we forgive others unconditionally, it is a tacit acknowledgment that we are operating in congruence with God's economy as Jesus articulated it in the Lord's prayer. If I do not forgive others, I cannot claim forgiveness for myself. Forgiving others, however, I acknowledge my own forgiveness as part of the whole.

This is the theme of John 20, the same chapter as that of Doubting Thomas. John 20 is typically framed as a post-resurrection account, still in the first heaven. It is that. But it should also be understood, along with chapter 21, as a sort of border between dimensions, an overlap of the first and second heaven. Jesus breathes on his disciples and gives them the charge that is meant for all of us, tying us all together in the opportunity to take forgiveness with the seriousness of Christ's death: "If you forgive anyone's sins, their sins are forgiven; If you do not forgive them, they are not forgiven" (John 20:23). Jesus will not be satisfied until forgiveness between God and humanity is played out between human beings and each other. "Forgive us our trespasses," we pray, "as we forgive those who trespass against us." The depth of God's forgiveness demands its width.

Christians, says Barth, should look forward to the "great change of the overthrow of all the contradiction in which they now exist and the necessary bending of every knee to Jesus Christ and the confessing to Him as Lord by every tongue." Those who do not include "the whole of humanity" in the vision of this consummation, attempting as it were to restrict what Christ has accomplished for the world, futilely attempt "to make private an event which is so essentially public." Such a person, concludes Barth, needs "to be told quite bluntly that he definitely loses the prospect of his own personal participation in this event."[16]

The green truth of the Gospel in Christ, and the personal and corporate claim that it makes on us all, mean that Christ cannot be separated from God, and we cannot be separated from Christ. Instead of sin separating us from God, or us from each other, God's purpose has always been to

---

16. *CD* IV/3.2, 931–32.

separate us from sin. Those who refuse to repent in the illumination of the second heaven are revealed exactly as they are in Christ, but in the liar's falsity they insist on who they *are not*. This self-inflicted divorce from oneself—insisting on one's red subjectivity—would surely be not only the greatest of ironies, but the greatest of agonies. Such people would be damned by their own salvation.[17]

---

17. Our ongoing green determination in Christ needs nothing added to it. It's the red that is the problem. That's why Barth says that in the light of the divine verdict of the cross, God "removes the atmosphere in which our opportunity cannot be known or apprehended at all but can only be missed" (*CD* III/4, 594). We will take up the doctrine of universalism in the coming pages.

72

Damned and Delivered

To those who persist on trying to turn untruth into truth, God does not owe eternal patience and therefore deliverance.

—Karl Barth

This reading will begin and end with two visual representations—one static and one dynamic—that point to the distinct but inseparable aspects of human being-in-act in regards to judgment. Our first illustration implements a Christmas bag of red and green M&M candies. When it comes to our human determinations of red and green, we're each a mixed bag! To paraphrase Romans 7, "I (red) do what I (green) don't want to do, and I (red) don't do what I (green) want to do. Wretched human that I am (a human conflicted with red and green selves). Who will rescue me from this (red self) body of death?" The picture below uses the green and red candies to show the simultaneity of the two subjectivities, the two "I's" of the one human in Romans 7.

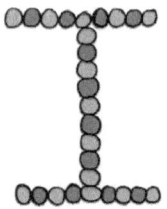

As Paul has noted already in Romans 7, "there is nothing good that lives in me" ("me" as the red self). The chapter concludes with what reads like a two-verse catechesis. In essence Paul asks: who will rescue "me" from "me"? "What a wretched man I am! Who will rescue me from this body that is subject to death? Thanks be to God, who delivers me through Jesus Christ our Lord" (v. 24–25). It is a succinct description of placemat anthropology, giving us the picture of both the stark, simultaneous conflict, and the victory too.

The "red me" is not only against me, it is against "us"—against humanity. A Trinitarian context for human beings reveals that we are not created in the image of God as atomized individuals, but as persons in the person of Christ, sharing life with all humans within the primal relationship of the Trinitarian persons. We are hard-wired for loving, interpersonal, relationships with others. Our reading of Romans 7 shows that the green is our innermost being (7:22), our personhood, where we are gathered *singularly* and *corporately* in Christ. The red is the harsh exception to the rule, the parasitic individualism (7:23) that we think will save us but instead scatters us. The good news involves the fact that our red selves of individualism, our "old selves," have been crucified with Christ (Rom 6:6), so that the red will be "done away with" (Rom 6:6). The "old Pat" is finished off at Calvary.

What P. T. Forsyth called "the cruciality of the cross" reveals that we cannot save ourselves from the red. Because the red blinds us, our chances of ridding ourselves of the red, anti-Christ dimension of our lives is as impossible as pouring the bag of M&Ms into a bowl and perfectly picking out all the red ones while blindfolded. It cannot be done. Only the cross can purify us from the red, preserving our personhood against all red insinuations. Only the cross makes the separation in the right places, not between God and humanity but between humanity and inhumanity. Even though we still live in this realm with both our false selves and our true selves, we have hope because we know that, by virtue of Christ's death and resurrection, one has a future and one does not. Hope in Christ does not mean the red is gone in this life; rather, it provides us the big picture to live by. Crucified and raised with Christ, I am condemned and not condemned, I am damned and delivered. I am judged and not judged. But I *am* judged.[1]

---

1. It is P^3 (ourselves as complete persons) who is judged. Because of the rules of P^3, the whole of us is judged, *even if* we have theological latitude to say that the judgment pertains specifically to P^2 (our unbelieving self) and that as P^1 (as believing) we are not judged (John 8:51; John 11:26). These verses are remarkably similar, even if John 8:51 does not typically get as much mention. John 8:51, "Very truly I tell you, whoever obeys my word will never see death"; John 11:26, "whoever lives by believing in me will never die."

PART FIVE: JESUS IS MY HEAVEN

The cross of Jesus Christ, then, *is* the door (John 10:9) or gate (John 10:7) of judgment.[2] To go through Jesus Christ, the one who called himself the gate, is to go through his cross. We remember John the Baptist's words regarding the future ministry of Christ: "His winnowing fork is in his hand to clear his threshing floor and to gather the wheat into his barn, but he will burn up the chaff with unquenchable fire" (Luke 3:17). As conflicted persons, we are scattered because we bought into the lie that self-centeredness would enlarge us, when it only inflates our false selves. Paul uses the phrase "puffed up" to describe such arrogance (1 Cor 4:18; 1 Cor 5:2; 1 Cor 8:1).

To say that we are scattered does not mean that is all we are. When Paul said, "What a wretched man I am," he did not mean that he was only a wretch. Still, the fact remains that in this conflicted, inflated state, we cannot fit through the smaller door. The wheat fits through, but not the wheat with the chaff. The door is narrow, there is no other way except through the cross, and no room for the false, red, self. Again, God's wrath is his divine No to all our attempted negations of his non-negotiable covenant of grace with humanity. Because Christ's Yes for us already includes our response of "yes" to God, God says No to our "no." This may mean that his No is especially directed against human actions that have most caused the suffering of others, or against the hard-heartedness of those who objectify others. God's wrathful No will be as loud and as sharp as it needs to be to address the chaff, reaching as far as the curse is found.

Still, God's No, no matter how severe, is *always* inside of God's larger Yes to humanity. Every person can legitimately exclaim with Paul, "Thanks be to God" for the deliverance that comes through the threshing of the cross, where we are gathered in the crucified one as wheat brought into the barn. Returning to our M&Ms, the picture below represents the gathered person, the wheat without the chaff.[3]

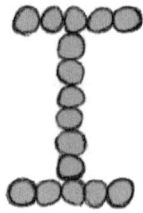

---

2. The NIV chooses to translate the same Greek word as "door" or "gate" depending on the verse. Some versions are more consistent.

3. This illustration of only the green remaining cannot communicate the diversity, distinctiveness, and particularity that the green represents theologically, i.e., our truest, created, and colorful selves in Christ. Otherwise, we would be left with the terrible idea that to lose the red from the green "I" makes the human more boring and less colorful.

Jesus's description of himself as "the gate" (John 10:9) also provides us with an understanding of the boundary between the second and third heaven. Imagine Jesus meeting us in the second heaven. There we are in our false self and our true self. Every creature is there, and all will fit through the gate. But one thing becomes plain. Our false selves will not fit. I—in my false self—will not fit through the gate.[4] Our false selves, Scripture tells us, have been crucified with Christ, "that the body of sin might be done away with." Our false selves cannot enter through the gate, since to do so would negate the cross, declaring unneedful the work of Christ in and through his death and resurrection. But the work of the cross is a finished work, it cannot be undone. Christ "died to sin once for all," Paul writes, and "he cannot die again" (Rom 6:10, 9).[5]

We have established that trying to bring your false self along on judgment day is to say in effect that the cross is not needed. But who would ever insist on that—bringing the false self along? Perhaps those most practiced in their prized individualism, becoming more deeply ensconced in it. Entrenched in their false selves in the first heaven, and carrying their twisted convictions into the second, could someone stubbornly cling to their false selves in the end? Can one infected by individualism hold out, insisting on the lie in face of the truth? Barth saw no biblical evidence that the lake of fire would be populated by human beings, but he also recognized his lens of the day was clouded by the fall. He therefore saw no reason to presume or to project. If we had definitive biblical evidence that even one created and redeemed person forfeited heaven to dwell forever in the lake of fire prepared for the devil and his angels (Matt 25:41), we would have to alter course and reconsider our whole placemat project.[6]

---

4. Nowhere is this more poignantly pictured than in Rev 21:8, 27; Rev 22:15.

5. This death "once for all" is also a major theme in Hebrews, e.g., 7:27; 9:12; 10:10; and frames the severe language of the author regarding the comprehensive work of the cross and our accountability under the judgment of grace (6:6; 10:26).

6. It was perhaps John Calvin's fateful theological deduction that caused him to start with this possibility of human existence outside of heaven and work backward into a logico-causal dualism regarding the elect and the reprobate. After all, the reprobate sinner isolated in hell could not be there apart from the sovereign will of God; it then follows that the work of Christ is not effective for all (resulting in a "limited atonement"). However, against later Calvinism's fixed adherence to the template of limited atonement, Calvin himself was generously ambiguous. In the *Institutes* he even acknowledged that, when it comes to salvation, we can and should hope for the best for all people. See Calvin, *Institutes*, III, xx, 38. Quoting Calvin: "Let a Christian, then, regulate his prayers by this rule, that they be common, and comprehend all who are his brethren in Christ; and not only those whom he at present sees and knows to be such, but all men in the world; respecting whom, what God has determined is beyond our knowledge; *only that to wish and to hope the best concerning them*, is equally the

PART FIVE: JESUS IS MY HEAVEN

In my community work with intellectually disabled people, I often find that we who are able-minded have a harder time giving up our dear individualism, the elaborate identities we have have constructed for ourselves, our houses built on the sand (Matt 7:24–27). In this connection I hear Jesus saying to the rich young ruler: "It is easier for a camel to go through the eye of a needle than for someone who is rich to enter the kingdom of God" (Matt 19:24). In this case, "richness" is our individualism, the inflated currency we seek to mint, the self-assured muscular pretense we build up that we think better qualifies us or gives us something others do not have. In the end, our greatest disability is our individual, self-inflated ability. "We got this"—we think. God's grace need not apply.

The more convinced we are that we are the ones knitting together the tapestry of our own identity, the more difficult will be the moment when all that is not created by God is threatened. I may resist out of fear. If the red thread is pulled out from the fabric of my life, will I completely unravel? If I am "undone" in this way, will anything be left? Only in a place of perfect love, and from our secure foundation in Christ, could such fear be assuaged.

To know God has minted our lives in union with his Son is to stand secure in the knowledge of God's love as God's wrath and God's wrath as God's love. With this mindset, we might read these words of Paul's in a new light:

> For no one can lay any foundation other than the one already laid, which is Jesus Christ. If anyone builds on this foundation using gold, silver, costly stones, wood, hay or straw, their work will be shown for what it is, because the day will bring it to light. It will be revealed with fire, and the fire will test the quality of each person's work. If what has been built survives, the builder will receive a reward. If it is burned up, the builder will suffer loss but yet will be saved—even though only as one escaping through the flames. (1 Cor 3:11–15)

If every person's foundation is Jesus Christ (which it is), and if this scenario comprehensively describes the day of our "second-heaven" experience, then it begs the question. Once the false self is burned away, witnessing to the reality of Christ's finished work, what resistance is left? Without the contradiction of the lie, any idea of resisting the truth is a moot point. Sin and Satan are no longer in the picture. We are purified by God's fierce love. End of story.

---

dictate of piety and of humanity" (emphasis added). Calvin's optimism calls to mind this passage from Peter: "[God] is patient with you, not wanting anyone to perish, but everyone to come to repentance" (2 Pet 3:9).

Alternatively, instead of the above representing comprehensively our second-heaven experience, Barth's resistance to universalism is partly founded in his nuancing of judgment day. Barth's theology has reserved a place (the second heaven) for a continuation of the overlap of the two human determinations long enough that we might participate in Christ's victory over evil in what Scripture calls "the hour." Because repentance takes place within the overlap, not in the "post-placemat" third heaven, our human agency emerges in all the right ways. It is a participation in Christ of the single human subject amid the contradiction of that subject's opposing in-Christ (green) and anti-Christ (red) dimensions. As we will see in our study of Revelation, such repentance occurs on the day when we are confronted with the utmost clarity and definition of our true and false selves. It consists in resisting the final test of Satan (Rev 3:10) and welcoming the test of purification described above.

Though the forces of our green, perfected life in Christ and our red, fallen humanity are always at odds with one another, profound experiences of release and deliverance (often called mountaintop experiences) are not unknown in this life. Our closing illustration pictures something of the forces that are at work beyond our "persons," the dynamics of the in-Christ and anti-Christ determinations, and how these are maximally heightened on judgment day. It seeks to illuminate what we might anticipate on that day when the torque gives way to a second-heaven quickening of the Spirit.

Imagine you are having an out-of-body experience and you are looking directly down at your "grey" self standing below. You are tightly encircled by what looks like a red rubber band. When you lower your viewpoint, you can see that the smaller red rubber band sits on top of a larger, and thicker, green rubber band. It looks like one rubber band from above, but two from up close. This represents the overlap of red and green, hell and heaven. Now, imagine the two rubber bands being pulled by greater forces in opposite directions while you remain in the middle. You feel the tug and then the torque. There are days when you have no consciousness that you are always a person in torque. But the more you understand these forces, the more acutely you feel the battle. It should not come as a surprise that the moment of clarity about the distinction of red and green spheres is also the moment that we recognize the strength of each in their undiluted forms. This also explains why even in this world we might feel Satan's attack *at the same time* as Jesus's nearness in different circumstances, moments of crisis or great loss, for example. There are times when a crisis produces such torque that it stretches us beyond what we thought we could bear (2 Cor 1:8). In those stretching times, those "thin places," we sometimes experience God's presence in the most immense ways.

PART FIVE: JESUS IS MY HEAVEN

Now, imagine the red rubber band is at maximum force, cutting into you, while the green rubber band—"the belt of truth" (Eph 6:14)—matches the red force and then some. The more the green is revealed, the more the red rages in contrast. After all, you cannot *be* in hell without being in heaven also. Hell does not exist apart from heaven, for heaven gives hell its borrowed force. As the red pull constricts, it feels like you are more in hell than heaven even though you remain within the green band. The red bondage is strong, but green calls to green and prevents ultimate destruction.

When Jesus was seized by the temple guard in the garden, he said that Satan is given his "hour" when darkness reigns on the earth (Luke 22:53). The book of Revelation also speaks of an "hour" of final testing by the enemy, pointing to the ground of Calvary (Rev 3:10) as revealed in the second heaven. This is the hour often overlooked by universalism arguments, an hour where human agency, rightly understood, matters. There, where we are all gathered, Satan does his worst to derail us from God's will. It is the same voice that beckoned Jesus to throw himself off the mountain (instead of refusing to test the Father), to avoid what awaited in Jerusalem (instead of determining to go), and to come down off the cross (instead of enduring the scorn and despising the shame). Similarly, Satan urges us, "Come with me," seeking to separate us from Christ's embrace. Misery loves company.

Never has the force of evil come to bear as on the day of the cross, when "darkness came over all the land" (Matt 27:45). By the light of the cross, we can see that choosing Christ is not needed, only *not* choosing Satan. You are already seated with Christ in heaven (Eph 2:6). You have everything you need in Christ, including your desire to walk with him as you have been called (Eph 4:1). Your ultimate call is to "stand firm," one of the great imperatives of Scripture, and all based on the indicative truth of your God-given identity.[7] Even in this dramatic moment you have what

---

7. 1 Pet 5:12, "this is the true grace of God. Stand fast in it." See also Jesus's words in Matt 10:22, "the one who stands firm to the end will be saved"; Jas 4:7, "resist the devil and he will flee from you"; also Jas 5:8. In Paul, see 1 Cor 15:58; 1 Cor 16:13, where he instructs his listeners to "stand firm in the faith"; 2 Cor 1:24; Gal 5:1; Phil 1:27. Regarding the last reference, the eschatological theme of Phil 1 can be easily overlooked. Mention of "the day of Christ" in 1:6 and 1:10 frames the whole chapter, if not the whole book, and thus matches the Ephesians passage quite well. Paul tells them to "stand firm" in one spirit and one mind, striving together as "one man," an obvious reference to the Lord Jesus Christ in whom they are all united. The fact that this is followed by "this will be a sign to them [the opposition]" of their destruction can certainly mean that the opposition will be destroyed to the extent that they are participating in the anti-Christ dimension, i.e., in the man doomed to destruction on "the day of the Lord" (2 Thess 2:2–3). Doomsday destruction for the anti-Christ dimension is, at the same time, highly anticipated for those who have a head start in believing in the goodness of judgment (Phil 1:28).

Barth calls the "choice of a free decision."[8] This is not the choosing taught in Arminian theology. Instead, you have always been making your free choice in Christ, your incessant choosing of righteousness. It is something already complete in the indicative truth of your personhood. This choosing then is not a "second thing," but is internally consistent with *who you are* as a free, beloved, subject in the subjectivity of Christ. Here any "choice" to go with Satan would involve the choosing of *who you are not* (therein exposing the evil of a simple "free choice" paradigm).

So, in the midst of the countervailing anti-Christ and in-Christ forces represented by the red rubber band and the green rubber band, Jesus says, "it is finished," and yet we hear the resistant red voice exclaiming, "not yet!" The red seeks to pull you more deeply into the chasm of the lie, promising that its claim on you will never give way, beckoning you to cling to the idols you brought with you. But under the sound of the gospel, and having withstood the onslaught, you do not want the "not yet"; you want the "already," and in that moment of emboldened participation you experience God's deliverance, the red rubber band snapping apart in the background. In that moment, beyond your wildest dreams, you are immediately catapulted into the ultimate quickening, the most exhilarating rush, the most orgasmic release, the most ecstatic trip.[9] In a way, no mountaintop moment in the first heaven can match, it is all joy and no woe.

> To whom will you compare me?
> Or who is my equal? Says the Holy One. . . .
> He gives strength to the weary
>   and increases the power of the weak . . .
> but those who hope in the Lord
> will renew their strength.
> They will soar on wings like eagles;
>   they will run and not grow weary
>   they will walk and not be faint. (Isa 40:25, 29–31)

---

8. *CD* III/1, 265.

9. I am reaching for phrases, the most exquisite first-heaven sensations, to describe the indescribable experience of unadulterated reality. It is ironic that each of these bear relative witness to the euphoria of the kingdom of God in their own way (even in such co-opted "highs" as those that come from drugs). In this rubber band illustration, I suppose any persons "going to hell" would be described as ones who have, in their resistance, so hardened themselves into the unreality of their false selves as to finally and totally identify with the red rubber band, something too impossible to explain. See Lewis, *Great Divorce*, where the grumbler in his resistance eventually depersonalizes himself into a grumble.

73

Saved by the Blood?

The saving love of God in Christ has already set all things right, "for God was pleased to have all his fullness dwell in him, and through him to reconcile to himself all things, whether things on earth or things in heaven, by making peace through his blood, shed on the cross" (Col 1:19–20). This good news means that through Christ humanity has been reconciled to God. It means that through Christ all the broken things of the world have been overcome. We are still waiting for the fullness of Christ's work to be revealed.

—BETHANY HANKE HOANG AND KRISTEN DEEDE JOHNSON

THIS FINAL READING IN Part Five is devoted to an exegetical discussion of several key passages that are pertinent to our eschatological theme.

Like repentance in the positive sense, Satan's attacks in the first heaven derive from the battleground of Calvary, the central event in the history of the world. Thanks to the gleam in their first-heaven eyes, it is the event people of faith are looking forward to, when Christ "disarmed the powers and authorities and made a public spectacle of them, triumphing over them by the cross" (Col 2:15). The second heaven is the day in which the battleground of the cross is most explicitly revealed. Because of the contemporaneous nature of the first and second heavens, however, this battleground that is fully revealed in the second heaven is not relegated to the second heaven. That is why Paul describes our union with Christ, and the fullness we have in him (Col 2:10), as the "full armor of God" even now:

> be strong in the Lord and in his mighty power. Put on the full armor of God, so that you can take your stand against the devil's schemes. For our struggle is not against flesh and blood, but against the rulers, against the authorities, against the powers of this dark world and against the spiritual forces of evil in the heavenly realms. Therefore put on the full armor of God, so that when the day of evil comes, you may be able to stand your ground, and after you have done everything, to stand. Stand firm then, with the belt of truth buckled around your waist, with the breastplate of righteousness in place, and with your feet fitted for the shoes of the gospel of peace. In addition to all this, take up the shield of faith, with which you can extinguish all the flaming arrows of the evil one. Take the helmet of salvation and the sword of the Spirit, which is the word of God. And pray in the Spirit on all occasions with all kinds of prayers and requests. With this in mind, be alert. (Eph 6:10–18)

An entire reading would not suffice to exegete this passage, but five things must be mentioned here.

1. Paul's phrase "the day of evil" is unique in Scripture. Does it describe a high-water mark for evil? It appears to indicate the second-heaven environment when the parasite will make its greatest claim. It could be called the "night of evil," as it attempts to co-opt "the day of the LORD."[1] Surely the death of the Son of God, the light of the world, is the closest evil ever comes to turning the day to night.

2. The "day of evil" could be seen as simply a figure of speech categorizing all days before the second coming of Christ (what Paul elsewhere calls "the present evil age," Gal 1:4). But there is no reason to have to choose between such a general categorization and the view that the specific "day of evil" is one and the same as judgment day. Indeed, it might be the result of the second view that we have the first—it is because of the "day *of* evil" (Eph 6:13, emphasis added) that the "days *are* evil" (Eph 5:16, emphasis added). "The day" is evil's last hoorah.

---

1. Scripture carries an ominous tone regarding the day of the Lord. It is a day of battle and destruction, even in the New Testament, but the restorative element is also apparent. There are many, many references to "the day" or "that day," but this is a sampling of examples that use the full phrase "day of the Lord": Isa 13:6; Ezek 13:5; Joel 1:15; Obad 1:15; Zeph 1:14; 1 Cor 1:8; Phil 1:6; 1 Thess 5:2–3; 2 Pet 3:10. In the last two citations, Paul and Peter respectively both say the day of the Lord will come like a thief in the night.

PART FIVE: JESUS IS MY HEAVEN

Judgment day is the day of days, such that every day is in that day, and that day is in every day.

3. This passage is not usually located at judgment day, but if understood eschatologically in connection with the cross, its implications are both eschatological and contemporary at once. Could the death of the ever-living God on the cross be anything less than a contemporary event for all time? For those who stand firm, it is the event when all who have been saved (Eph 2:5; 2 Tim 1:9; Titus 3:5) and are saved (1 Cor 1:18; 2 Cor 2:15), *will be* saved (Matt 24:13; Acts 2:21; Rom 10:13), by the one "who is, and who was, and who is to come" (Rev 1:8).

4. The word "stand" is used three times in short order: "Therefore put on the full armor of God, so that when the day of evil comes, you may be able to *stand* your ground, and after you have done everything, to *stand*. *Stand* firm then" (6:13–14a, emphasis added). The author reminds us that the "full armor" of God is required to face the full onslaught of the day of evil. Within this context the triple-mention of "stand" returns us to our reference above about the tenses of salvation and the accompanying de-emphasis concerning any *extra* measures needed from us. And returning us to Revelation 1:8, instead of *what* to do, Paul anchors us in *who* and *whose* we are in union with Christ (union here signified by the "full armor"). The first two usages of the word "stand" are not the same in the Greek, the first meaning to *withstand*, while the second is plainly *stand*. The first fits the more passive aspect of resting in our identity in Christ (think: helmet and armor and shield), while the second relates to a more active and emboldened participation in Christ (think: sword). Together, these images point to our being-in-act in the humanity of our Lord.

5. Finally, the passage specifically mentions the identity of the one against whom we are to stand and fight. "For our struggle is not against flesh and blood, but against the rulers, against the authorities, against the powers of this dark world and against the spiritual forces of evil in the heavenly realms" (Eph 6:12). These suprahuman "powers" and "forces" are located by Paul "in the heavenly realms," or what in placemat terms is the second heaven. It is only because these forces in the heavenly realms are strong that they can manifest as "powers of this dark world" (i.e., the first heaven). The evil forces in play—what Paul calls "the ruler of the kingdom of the air, the spirit who is now at work in those who are disobedient" (Eph 2:2)—permeate our lives. These forces are stronger than we are and have overwhelmed our created capacity to respond to God and to reciprocate his love on an existential level. We

are not superhuman in our natural selves. In the supernatural power of the Holy Spirit, however, we can rise above the parasitic spirit of the anti-Christ. Reinforced by the proclamation to rest in Christ's fullness, the phrase "put on the full armor of God" (Eph 6:11) reminds us that, by the Spirit, we can live into our true creaturely selves—"put on the new self, created to be like God in true righteousness and holiness" (Eph 4:24). Borrowing from Galatians we can say to one another, "walk by the Spirit, and you will not gratify the desires of the flesh" (Gal 5:16).[2]

Spiritual warfare is a phrase that is often used carelessly. Sometimes it almost seems that people are more focused on where Satan is going to show up than on where Christ is and where his love and authority manifest. This passage in Ephesians prepares us for battle as soldiers of Jesus Christ, not only in the second heaven but also in the first. We should take evil and its destructive power seriously. What we cannot do, however, is allow military allusions to lead us into the wrong kind of polemic, the church versus the world instead of Christ versus evil. We are called, as biblical scholar Tim Gombis says, to participate in "the divine warrior" Jesus Christ as he is revealed in the prophetic Old Testament allusions to the warrior God.

Isaiah 59:15-19, from which Paul's armor image apparently derives, is enlightening because God's fury is there directed toward Israel rather than in defense of Israel against Israel's foes.[3] Should we deduce from Paul's appropriation of the passage, and his encouragement to the church to fight *with* God against the powers, that God is more against evil than against his people? A christological interpretation continues to answer in the affirmative: God's wrath always serves his love. God is for all those for whom Christ died (Rom 8:31-32), which means he is only against human beings to the extent that he is against evil. If God is for all of us, then, in correlation with God's reality, our priority is be for each other in the human family and together against evil. We must resist the temptation to fight against each other first, and against evil second.

---

2. See Gombis, *Drama of Ephesians*, 165. Gombis helpfully elaborates on Ephesians 4:22-24; "Paul speaks of two distinct realms . . . the old humanity and the new humanity. The NRSV translates these two phrases as the 'old self' and the 'new self,' perhaps pointing to the old internal self and the new internal self of an individual. But Paul is not talking about the inner tendencies toward both good and evil within each individual. He is speaking of cosmic realms—two different holistic modes of existence. The old humanity is a synonym for the present evil age—that cosmic realm over which the powers of darkness rule. It points to the corrupted practices and habits of life on both individual and corporate levels."

3. Gombis, *Drama of Ephesians*, 157.

Paul calls the church to subvert the cultural corruptions of the powers. Our performance of the divine warrior on earth ought to make the church less militant and more hopeful and redemptive. . . . [B]ecause Christians have a public image of being politically aggressive and uncompromising, it frightens people to hear the church being called to spiritual warfare. But our warfare is not against others in our culture. . . . The way of promise is to become communities of humility, communities that confess our brokenness and failing without caring to point out those of others. *We* are the ones who need transformation so that we can become cultures that bless and transform others. It is only through the cultivation of cruciformity and weakness that we harness and radiate the resurrection power of God. Such communities are redemptively subversive because they resist the cultural corruptions of the powers that have perverted the present evil age. Such communities are bearers of hope because they embody God's restoration of the world, anticipating the day when God makes all things new.[4]

When Jesus tells us of his *modus operandi*, "See, I am making all things new" (Rev 21:5, NRSV), it is not necessarily in the future tense. Instead, he reminds us of the "already but not yet" tension of our first-heaven existence while anticipating that wonderful moment of truth, when "new" is all there is: "There will be no more night. They will not need the light of a lamp or the light of the sun, because the Lord God will give them light; and they will reign forever and ever" (Rev 22:5). Because of our confidence in that ultimate moment of deliverance, we can live as children of light and not of darkness (1 Thess 5:4). Peter directs us "to live holy and godly lives as you look forward to the day of God and speed its coming." As for our first and second heavens, Peter points to the time when they will be obsolete. Even they will be burned up: "That day will bring about the destruction of the heavens by fire. . . . But in keeping with his promise we are looking forward to a new heaven and a new earth, where righteousness dwells" (2 Pet 3:11–13).

As Hoang and Johnson remind us, we *have* been reconciled to God. When we were God's enemies, Christ died for us. And because we are crucified with Christ, our enmity against God died with Christ. We could describe reconciliation as the burning away or washing away of all enmity in the death of Christ. It is a manifestation of renewal, the restoration of the face-to-face relationship between humanity and God that in reality has always existed. Reconciliation works in correlation to the truth in spite of

---

4. Gombis, *Drama of Ephesians*, 179.

the wicked, broken, and twisted existence foisted on us by the deceiver. In *truth* we are presented by Christ before the Father: "he has reconciled you by Christ's physical body through death *to present you holy in his sight*" (Col 1:22, emphasis added).[5]

The predominant evangelical culture is pervaded by a sense that God requires bloody punishment in order to be satisfied. This fits with a legal view of righteousness, i.e., for "justice to be served." Conversely, the book of Hebrews emphasizes that the blood of Christ cleanses us not for legal purposes but filial (family) ones. In other words, God did not create and redeem us to meet a legal standard but to destroy in his death all that opposes us, his children. In his self-sacrifice of love—which *did* entail the spilling of blood—he washed "the old" away. He submitted to the spurious verdict of an oppressive ruler so that we might fully enjoy him as beloved sons and daughters, adopted in the beloved Son, reconciled by the blood of Christ.

As both the victim (Heb 2:9) and high priest of the sacrifice (Heb 1:3; 2:17), and as the leader of the worshiping human community, the risen Christ offers the children of God back to God, fully cleansed and sanctified (Heb 2:11–18). Suffering as a servant of atonement, Christ ushers us into the revelation of at-one-ment with God, where all human beings may enjoy together the life of the Trinitarian community of Father, Son, and Holy Spirit. In our worship of the one who introduces us to the Trinitarian community, we worship Jesus Christ as the basis for all the good in human existence. More than that, we also worship him as the boundary-line for all the evil, the one who absorbed and conquered it, definitively limiting it and making space for hope.

It is not all wrong to think of Christ's death as the payment for a legal penalty, especially if you consider the fact that sin is a law unto itself—"the wages of sin is death" (Rom 6:23). But the advantages of this broader, relational (filial) approach are profound. For example, we can know that Christ paid the intrinsic consequences for our sins, identifying with the sinner's sin, absorbing the cost, rather than imagining his gruesome death as somehow checking the box of a legal obligation God is required to pay. This intrinsic view of a penalty, putting the priority on cost over an extrinsic penal transaction, is worthy of our God of love and relationship. Indeed, the God of relationship identifies with the sinner's sin, absorbing the cost. Draining sin of its power in his own person, he thereby cleanses us in his death, thereby renewing and refreshing our relationship with God. With this, not punishment, God is supremely satisfied.

---

5. Lost by the NIV, there is an emphasis on the word "flesh" in this verse that goes beyond "reconciled by Christ's physical body." See ESV, for example: "[And you] he has now reconciled in his body of flesh by his death."

God's vast love for us (Rom 5:8) is more than any legal categories can hold. He did not die first and foremost to satisfy a legal system, as if obligated to pay our penalty for a broken law, but because we as humans are broken sinners. So while it is true in one sense that Jesus died *because of our sins* (Rom 4:25), even more than that he died to destroy death and the devil and to abolish evil, *which includes our sins.*

Hebrews 1 and 2 tell us that Christ, "the exact representation of [God's] being"(1:3), was not ashamed to be the brother of sinful humans (2:11). He suffered in solidarity with us and was made to "taste death for everyone"(2:9) in order to destroy sin, death, and the devil (2:14). Because of this, we are told to have "confidence to enter the Most Holy Place by the blood of Jesus, by a new and living way opened for us through the curtain, that is, his body, and since we have a great priest over the house of God" (Heb 10:19–21).[6] This powerful statement communicates several key ideas: (1) because of the cleansing of his blood, we can enter the judgment boldly and without fear; (2) Jesus's flesh (representing the old, false self of everyone) being torn apart and destroyed in death unveils afresh the true way of life preserved for humanity; and (3) in his representative power, Jesus as our high priest stands in for each of us not only in truth but in falsehood. His high priestly ontological solidarity means that he *is* in fact, in his person, each human death and each human life.

As we stand at the threshold of judgment, then, we can see both our created and redeemed lives, and our fallen and corrupt lives—our lives, so to speak, with and without the veil. Upon drawing near, Hebrews teaches us, not only do we need not be afraid, but we may enter with full assurance. Critically, we find assurance in that second-heaven moment not because all the evil and corruption are already gone from our lives, but because of the enveloping context of God's goodness and grace. Only when "I" stand there in both my false and true self, my corrupt "I" and my redeemed "I," do I clearly see the power of the asymmetry. Fully conflicted in our false and true humanity, we may experience the truth of Christ's redeeming work coming to bear in that moment, having our "hearts sprinkled [with Christ's blood] to cleanse us from a guilty conscience," and our "bodies washed with pure water."[7] It is to such an intimate drawing-near—every human implicated and immersed in the death and resurrection of Christ—that baptism attests. In Paul's words: "If we have been united like this with him in his

---

6. See also 1 John 4:17: "We may have boldness on the day of judgment, because as he is, so are we in this world" (NRSV).

7. Heb 10:22. This is corroborated elsewhere in Scripture, where John speaks of the fellowship we enjoy with one another because "the blood of Jesus, [God's] Son, purifies us from all sin" (1 John 1:7).

death, we will certainly be united with him in his resurrection. . . . If we died with Christ, we believe that we will also live with him" (Rom 6:5, 8). Bolstered by Easter morning, equipped with the armor of God, in the name of Jesus we need not fear.

> The Prince of Darkness grim,
> We tremble not for him,
> His rage we can endure
> For lo' his doom is sure
> One little word shall fell him[8]

---

8. Luther, "Mighty Fortress," para. 3.

PART SIX

Living Life from the Third Heaven

74

Holiness or Wholeness?

Far too easily we settle for holiness rather than wholeness, conformity rather than authenticity, becoming spiritual rather than deeply human . . . and a journey toward perfection rather than union with God. Far too often we confuse our own spiritual self-improvement tinkering with the much more radical agenda of the Spirit of God. The call of the Spirit—which is always gentle and therefore easily missed—is an invitation to abandon our self-improvement projects that are, in reality, little more than polishing our false self and become the unique hidden self in Christ that we have always been from all eternity. The call of the Spirit is always a call to return home, to settle for no other habitation or identity than that of being in Christ and knowing the reality of Christ in us.

—David Benner

Living from the third heaven is another way of saying living by the Spirit. It does not mean that we have arrived by the Spirit into a realm without conflict, or solely into the unadulterated sphere. Such faulty reasoning could only feed our sequence-driven propensities in an over-realized way, as if we had left the existential realm for the purely actual one, or in an under-realized way, as if we had not been in the third heaven all along! Living from the third heaven means that we are living lives bathed in the assurance of "home." By the Spirit of Truth we are anchored by the eschatological

PART SIX: LIVING LIFE FROM THE THIRD HEAVEN

glimpse of a home that we will have, that we already have, and that we have always had. To live from the third heaven is to live with the reference point of reality.

In the spirit of revelation, our perspective changes. Knowing we are home before we start provides us the perspective of "looking back" with relative clarity through the cross at our current situation. In other words, even if the clarity we are given cannot help but be skewed to some degree in this world, we can know that any measure of clarity we are given bears relative witness to the perfect clarity every human possesses in the mind of Christ and in the unadulterated kingdom yet to be fully unveiled.

Before continuing our discussion on what it means to live from the third heaven, we must remember the basic distinctions between the three heavens:

First heaven: contradiction and confusion

Second heaven: contradiction and clarity

Third heaven: clarity without contradiction

Full clarity comes only on judgment day, though I could put "relative clarity" in parentheses for the first heaven because clarity is possible in the realm of the first heaven. Such *relative* clarity comes from above by the Holy Spirit and by the light of the gospel, even in a realm marked by contradiction and confusion. In the second and third heavens, the clarity is not relative but perfect. We do not go directly from the tribulation of this world into the unadulterated paradise of the third heaven any more than we can cut across the baseball diamond from first to third base. Thankfully, the second heaven allows us the opportunity to experience the catharsis of justice and reconciliation, and to participate in Christ's victory over "the prince of this world," giving glory to God.[1] The template is complete as follows:

---

1. Our baseball analogy (see "The Second-Heaven Intervention") works well for reminding us of the vertical nature of our green humanity. It might be easy to lose perspective in the diagonal-filled first heaven of this fallen world, but even if we can't cut directly across the diamond from first to third, if we are always anchored by home base we might have the perspective to see directly (vertically) from home plate to second base despite the simultaneous refraction of our first base experience. This gets at Jesus's meaning in John 14. "Before long the world will not see me anymore, *but you will see me*" (John 14:19, emphasis added)—such is a vertical view that cuts through the worldly diagonals. Notice that Jesus is telling the disciples about an eschatological vision that will be accessible even before the moment of pure clarity, even "now." For one thing, while their upcoming resurrection encounters will still be somewhat relative in clarity, they will likely be the closest to pure clarity they will receive until the second heaven. In the meantime how is this access given? By the Spirit of Truth who the world cannot accept, says Jesus, the Spirit who is with us and in us, and who reminds us that

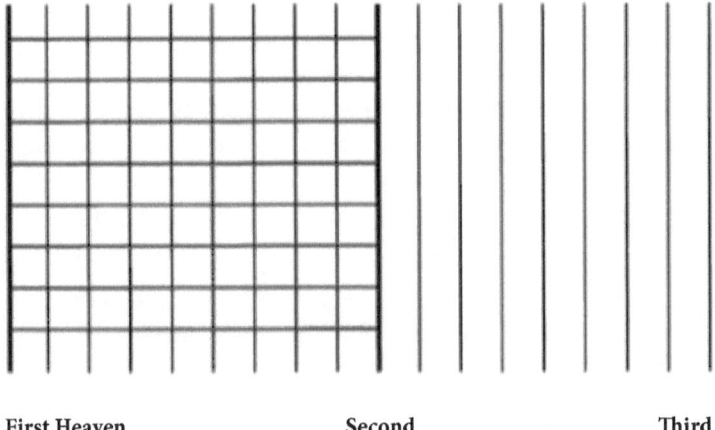

First Heaven   Second   Third

Anticipating what is to come does not make us so heavenly minded that we are no earthly good. As C. S. Lewis reminds us, "If you read history you will find that the Christians who did the most for the present world were just those who thought most about the next. . . . It is since Christians have largely ceased to think of the other world that they have become so ineffective in this."[2] When such a perspective drives us to share in Christ's redemptive purposes for the world, it is what Richard Bauckham and Trevor Hart call "eschatological activism."[3]

How do common spiritual practices like prayer and Bible study fit with eschatological activism? They are indispensable, even though we have not thoroughly discussed them so far. First, we had to introduce a new and better framework for these important practices in the life of a disciple of Christ. Instead of focusing on the "how to," I emphasized the "Who, who." *Who* is Jesus Christ and *who* are we in him. This, in turn, gives us our bearings concerning who we are *not*. Failing to pay heed to this grace-sin approach is destructive to the person and to the community, as James Cone describes: "Instead of affirming their identity in the source of being, sinners reject it and attempt to be what they are not. . . . To be in sin, then, is to deny the values that make the community what it is. It is living according to one's private interests and not according to the goals of the community. It is

---

we have a home, even if the world tells us we are orphans (John 14:17–18). The Spirit gives us a glimpse of that pure home life that we yearn for and which will be revealed in the perfect vision of our second-heaven experience. "On that day you will realize that I am in the Father, you are in me, and I am in you" (John 14:20).

2. Lewis, *Mere Christianity*, 134–35.
3. Bauckham and Hart, *Hope against Hope*, 202.

PART SIX: LIVING LIFE FROM THE THIRD HEAVEN

believing that one can live independently of the source that is responsible for the community's existence."[4]

One way that we can grow into a post-cross/post-judgment perspective on the way we view our lives and world is in the way the Spirit gifts us a new pair of glasses to read Scripture. Above, we presented Jesus Christ as the hermeneutic, or interpretive framework, for reading Scripture. "[T]he real text" of Scripture, asserts T. F. Torrance, is "the humanity of Jesus." He continues:

> As we read the Old Testament and read the New Testament and listen to the Word of God, the real text is not documents of the Pentateuch, the Psalms or the Prophets or the documents of the Gospels and the Epistles, but in and through them all the Word of God struggling with rebellious human existence in Israel on the way to becoming incarnate, and then that Word translated in the flesh and blood and mind and life of a human being in Jesus, in whom we have both the Word of God become man and the perfect response of man to God offered on our behalf. As the real text of God's Word, addressed to us, Jesus is also the real text of our address to God. We have no speech or language with which to address God but the speech and language called Jesus Christ.[5]

First and foremost we discover who Jesus is in Scripture, and we can then discover ourselves *in Christ*, revealed through Scripture. We remember Athanasius's claim that Christ will not fit into any system of which he is not the starting point. There is no human experience that does not relate to the humanity of Jesus Christ and to the definitive case of placemat anthropology—the opposite determinations of righteousness and wickedness—represented in the one person Jesus Christ. That is why, in his own christological hermeneutic for reading Scripture, Athanasius called the Psalms "humanity's mirror." Instead of adopting an us-them framework of righteousness and wickedness, Athanasius insists, "each man" should recite them "as if they were written concerning him . . . not as if another were speaking, nor as if speaking about someone else." The Psalms, Athanasius continues, "comprehend the one who observes the commandment as well as the one who transgresses," in turn bringing the reader to hope or repentance, as the case may be. The result will be praise and thanksgiving to God.[6]

---

4. Cone, *Black Theology of Liberation*, 110.

5. Torrance, *Mediation of Christ*, 78–79 (emphasis original).

6. Athanasius, "Letter to Marcellinus," in *Life of Anthony*, 110–11. For more on Patristic practices of Scripture interpretation see Stanglin, *Letter and Spirit*.

HOLINESS OR WHOLENESS?

In our North Street Neighborhood[7] we have an established rhythm of morning and evening prayer. One morning recently during the reading of Psalm 26, I just started uncontrollably chuckling to myself. The chuckle unfortunately became a distracting chortle. But it was sinking into my heart and soul that Psalm 26 is a perfect witness to the green indicative of our lives in Christ (and that otherwise it would be truly laughable):

> 1 Vindicate me, Lord,
>   for I have led a blameless life;
> I have trusted in the Lord
>   and have not faltered.
> 2 Test me, Lord, and try me,
>   examine my heart and my mind;
> 3 for I have always been mindful of your unfailing love
>   and have lived in reliance on your faithfulness.
> 4 I do not sit with the deceitful,
>   nor do I associate with hypocrites.
> 5 I abhor the assembly of evildoers
>   and refuse to sit with the wicked.
> 6 I wash my hands in innocence,
>   and go about your altar, Lord,
> 7 proclaiming aloud your praise
>   and telling of all your wonderful deeds.
> 8 Lord, I love the house where you live,
>   the place where your glory dwells.
> 9 Do not take away my soul along with sinners,
>   my life with those who are bloodthirsty,
> 10 in whose hands are wicked schemes,
>   whose right hands are full of bribes.
> 11 I lead a blameless life;
>   deliver me and be merciful to me.
> 12 My feet stand on level ground;
>   in the great congregation I will praise the Lord.

As "humanity's mirror," this Scripture reveals and reflects who I truly am. By virtue of the christologically derived grid we call placemat anthropology, we can know that this is who every person truly is. By knowing who I am, I am better able to know who I am not.

Jesus's call to discipleship is a call to discernment. If our reflection in the mirror is an indiscriminate grey, by virtue of the cross we can perceive ourselves, people, and the world through the lens of placemat anthropology, starting with green (as in Psalm 26). The key of "Jesus Christ and him

---

7. Northstreetneighborhood.weebly.com

crucified" allows us to interpret the grey and to expose the parasitic red of our lives that do not belong. With the cruciform eyesight of grace, in answer to the question about the fish (Matt 13:47–51), "Are we the good ones that are meant to be kept, or the bad ones to be thrown out?" I can enthusiastically say, "Yes!"

The emphasis is never on *our* ability to separate green and red, but instead we must rely on the fact that these *are* two total colors that are completely separate. We are meant to enter prayerfully into this world in reliance on "the mind of the Lord" (1 Cor 2:16) that he shares with us, asking that his prayers will be our prayers and our prayers his prayers.

"From this centre," says Barth, "there also exists the gift of a discrimination which with growing certainty can select what is genuinely and necessarily our own." This is true for disciples now, insists Barth, even if it "will only be fully seen . . . in the eternal consummation."[8]

Prayer and the reading of Scripture are ways that we can be centered in order to make more precise discriminations between who we are and who we are not. I cannot discriminate well from a bad angle. For example, as kids we had a way of dividing something between two friends. One person cut the apple or the Snickers bar and the other person got to choose which piece to take. That ensured the person cutting would cut it as fairly as possible. It would be silly to cut the object off to the side, at arm's length. No, we centered ourselves and got right over the top of it to try to accomplish the task. There was a lot at stake! As with the two chairs that looked like one "U," another angle was required—the "above" perspective—in order to make the proper discrimination.

Prayer, then, helps us to be centered. Part of being who you are involves enlightenment as to who you are *not*. Transformation comes with the deep awareness that Christ died for you because he loves you completely, in all your dimensions (or, as the popular expression goes, "warts and all"). Alan Torrance tells his students a fitting story about the family dog with cancer: "we don't merely say we hate the sickness and love the dog, we say *we love our sick dog*." It cannot be over-emphasized: understanding that God embraces us at our very worst frees us to have a proper perspective on our false selves.

David Benner calls our false selves "proxies who are cheap imitations of the authentic originals."[9] In order to fully expose this imposter, I must accept that I am he. I must accept, own, or even welcome the imposter to reject him. Have we done this? Are we learning to do it? Are we allowing

---

8. *CD* III/4, 389.
9. Benner, *Spirituality*, 89.

our awareness of the false self to expand, in a sense, in order to expose it? When things annoy us and get under our skin about other people, it is a sure indication that we have not welcomed the stranger, but denied and suppressed him. Indeed, as Benner warns, not to interrogate our false selves is to "risk becoming possessed by that which we have ignored."[10]

The following poem by Elsie Landstrom is one of my favorites. It describes how welcoming the false self drains the lie of its power.

> SONG TO MY OTHER SELF
> Over the years I have caught glimpses of you
> in the mirror, wicked;
> in a sudden stridency in my own voice, have
> heard you mock me;
> in the tightening of my muscles felt the pull
> of your anger and the whine
> of your greed twist my countenance; felt your
> indifference blank my face when pity was called for.
> You are there, lurking under every kind act that I do,
> ready to defeat me.
> Lately, rather than drop the lid of my shock
> over your intrusion,
> I have looked for you with new eyes
> opened to your tricks, but more,
> open to your rootedness in life.
> Come, I open my arms to you also, once-dread stranger,
> Come, as a friend I would welcome you to stretch your
> apartments
> within me from the cramped to comforting side.
> Thus I would disarm you. For I have recently learned,
> learned looking straight into your eyes:
> The holiness of God is everywhere.[11]

Landstrom looks into the mirror, but in a different way, as if she's looking back through it, back through the judgment of the cross with its discriminatory perspective.

When you see it—the "it" that is the truth of our lives crucified and risen with Jesus Christ—we are transformed. Why? The "it" that we see is by its very nature transformative, because we are inside of "it" even before seeing it. "In your light we see light" (Ps 36:9). To see the truth is to be involuntarily transformed, such that, to the extent that we have not been transformed, we have not seen "it." In God's light, I apprehend with confidence that I am in

---

10. Benner, *Spirituality*, 128.
11. Landstrom, "Song to My Other Self."

Christ and belong to him forever. Here, with full humility, I recognize that Jesus died for me his friend, one who was helpless and in bondage. Christ did this to rescue and deliver me—to bring me home—which is another way of saying to bless me and keep me at home in him.

As we seek to be centered, engaging before God in contemplative prayer and meditation on Scripture, we open ourselves to receiving the gift of awareness and transformation. The place of "contemplative stillness," says Benner, is the "hearth" of transformational encounter in union and communion with the Spirit of God. "The goal," he says, "is not to eliminate anything but to release everything. For only then do we discover that we are not defined by what we hold, but by whom we are held."[12]

Transformation, then, involves the art of interpreting through God's grace our tangled lives and world. No amount of doing can make us hear or see his love for us. Misguided efforts at holiness war against our wholeness. As Benner concludes:

> When you cling to God, you can never be sure how firmly God has a hold of you. If you are truly in God and God in you—which I firmly believe is the truth of all humans—your clinging does nothing to draw God closer. Your relationship with God does not depend on your holding on to God—however you may be doing that. Let go and discover that God is in you and you are in God, that this reality is not dependent on your clutching.[13]

"Genuine transformation," notes Benner, "is a change process that is not under our control . . . it is impeded by effort, but it's facilitated by consent." This is where prayer is indispensable. He continues, "If change is to come in the deep places of our self, it must come from some point beyond our self. Attempts to make transformation into a self-improvement project simply strengthens the false self. When this happens, the truth of our being becomes even more distant from us."[14] This reminds me of my elementary science lesson where the teacher placed two magnets on the table and we attempted to push the negative end of one magnet into the negative end of the other. The more forcibly we tried, the further and faster the other magnet retreated. Until we turned one end around, we could never get the magnets to click. Try as we might, there is simply something fundamental about the inefficacy of self-improvement schemes apart from the transformational work and enlightenment of the Spirit.

---

12. Benner, *Spirituality*, 164.
13. Benner, *Spirituality*, 209.
14. Benner, *Spirituality*, 60.

Awareness and transformation go together. When a shift of consciousness occurs, something "clicks." The transformational journey is comprised of what Benner calls "successive awakenings" that help us to reorganize our understanding of the true-self/false-self relation. This transformation occurs in myriad ways. First, in Benner's words, "You are not responsible for your own awakening. It isn't something you need to achieve. But it is a gift that you can receive."[15] Again, no amount of doing can awaken us to hearing or seeing. But we can ask for it in prayer and be positioned to receive it. To say that awakening comes by the Spirit does not mean the opposite is true; it would be a dangerous and false deduction to say that the reason that people *do not* awaken is also because of the Spirit. The lack of awakening is due to "the god of this age" (2 Cor 4:4).

Against this spiritual blindness of our flesh, foisted upon us by the anti-Christ, Paul's antidote is to walk his hearers through the layers of placemat anthropology. For example, in Colossians Paul in successive verses urges them to set their eyes and hearts on that dimension where they are seated with Christ (Col 3:1–2), and where they are hidden with Christ in God (Col 3:3), Christ who is their life (Col 3:4). Having hammered home the indicative truth of their lives, Paul then (and only then) launches from this baseline into an imperative admonishment. Because they are of Christ and the Spirit, they must resist what simultaneously belongs to their flesh, because the false self and its accoutrements will not stand in the judgment to come (that is, the judgment that will finally be fully revealed).

Setting our eyes on Christ, discovering our lives in his, and resisting of the flesh are meant to be done as a body. Paul encourages us to receive the word of God corporately, mutually teaching, wisely admonishing, and "through psalms, hymns, and songs from the Spirit, singing to God with gratitude in our hearts" (Col 3:16). After laying down some of the most intense theology in the Bible, and the accountability of grace, Paul exhorts us simply to encourage one another in the Way. That is the way that despite Genesis 3 leads us back toward Genesis 1, a place where we can experience *re*-creation not as a *re*-doing of creation but as a *re*-newing. A place where "we have put on the new self, which is being renewed in knowledge in the image of its Creator. Here there is no Gentile or Jew, circumcised or uncircumcised, barbarian, Scythian, slave or free, but Christ is all, and is in all" (Col 3:10–11).

Together we gain the perspective of Christ on our lives and world. We cannot yet see with the eyes of Christ perfectly, but in the ministry of Christ's cross we are invited to see a little more clearly who he is, what he

---

15. Benner, *Spirituality*, 17.

has done, and what he is doing for the world and all his beloved creatures. Who Christ is as our creator and redeemer transcends all of the time-space distinctions of heaven, giving us permission to use the word redemption in the past tense even now in the first heaven. With the fact that Christ has already redeemed the world (Rom 3:24) comes the accompanying belief that redemption especially relates to the day when all our anticipated clarity will be replaced by clarity itself. On the day of redemption, in Barth's words, "we shall not believe in it. We shall see it."[16]

---

16. *CD* II/1, 630–31.

75

Seeing and Believing with Thomas

We are not called upon to obey, in order to obtain pardon; but we are called on to believe the proclamation of pardon, in order that we may obey.... In fact, there is nothing acknowledged by the Bible to be obedience or holiness which does not spring from the belief of this free, undeserved mercy. The attempt at obedience without this, is a most thankless labour—it is never successful—and even were it successful, it would be obedience of the hand and not of the heart. It is as if we chose to move the index of a clock with the finger, instead of winding it up.

—Thomas Erskine

Repentance does not simply mean that I am sorry. Like the Psalmist, it means I acknowledge my brokenness (red) *in the midst of my wholeness* (green), that I might live into the reality of my identity, claiming afresh the promises of my salvation: "Create in me a pure heart, O God, and renew a steadfast spirit within me. Do not cast me from your presence or take your Holy Spirit from me. Restore to me the joy of your salvation and grant me a willing spirit, to sustain me" (Ps 51:10–12). It is only because the Psalmist is "green," we might say, that the Psalmist seeks to "live into" that reality.

Repentance is not about groveling; it is about gratitude. It is not about a God stingy with forgiveness. It is a response to the God who is a generous and extravagant Lover. One of the most touching acts of repentance in

PART SIX: LIVING LIFE FROM THE THIRD HEAVEN

Scripture occurred when the woman of ill repute washed Jesus's feet, even though she was an unwelcome intruder to Jesus's Pharisee host. We are told that her lavish act of love was a response to Jesus's forgiveness. In other words, it was not to earn the forgiveness, but *because* of it. Jesus's point was that the person who relishes his forgiveness loves much, while the person who does not see the need to be forgiven loves little (Luke 7:47).[1] Like the Pharisee in the story, such persons miss the transforming power of evangelical repentance.

If repentance means clear-sightedness and the transformation that comes from it, then repentance and belief happen to the greatest degree in the second heaven. That is where we will see clearly and our recognition of truth will fully take place. There, we will have our Doubting Thomas moment. When Jesus said to Thomas, "Blessed are those who have not seen and yet have believed," he spoke of those who believe *before* the second heaven (John 20:29). Note carefully what Jesus did and did not say: he said, "Blessed are those who have not seen and yet have believed." He did *not* say that people will not have a chance to see.

The question for us in our first-heaven existence is this: do I believe? To the extent that I do, my belief *here* is only a taste of the real clarity of belief *there*. It bears witness to the actual belief of every person. In this world, my favorite prayer is still "I do believe, help me overcome my unbelief" (Mark 9:24). But when I see myself as I really am in Christ, my true self in him who always believes (green), then I will be thrilled to see my false, unbelieving self (red) done away with.

We saw that repentance is often described as an exercise in willpower, an external "turning around" of behavior in a moralistic sense, as if we can wrench ourselves into alignment. This does not seem congruent with Jesus's words from Matthew's Gospel: "Come to me, all you who are weary and burdened, and I will give you rest. Take my yoke upon you and learn from me, for I am gentle and humble in heart, and you will find rest for your souls. For my yoke is easy and my burden is light" (11:29). The priority in

---

1. The NIV is helpful here: "Therefore, I tell you, her many sins have been forgiven—as her great love has shown." See also NRSV: "her sins, which were many, have been forgiven; hence she has shown such great love." Unfortunately, some translations (e.g., ESV, JUB) threaten to contradict Jesus's internal logic as explained in the passage, leaving it to appear that Jesus's forgiveness was conditioned on the woman's action: the woman's many sins have been forgiven, "*for* she has shown me so much love" (read as, "*because* she has shown me so much love"). Even if the Greek is ambiguous, the internal logic is established by Jesus's preluding mini-parable (7:41–43). Both debtors are unconditionally forgiven, and the emphasis is on the response. The woman has "seen herself" in the parable of forgiveness granted and needed; the Pharisee, blinded by his self-righteousness, has not.

repentance is not a burdensome change in behavior, but a shift from the old mindset, what the Bible calls a turning of perspective (which issues forth in changed behavior). A change of behavior from the outside-in is not only onerous, it can be notoriously short-lived, while a change of behavior motivated from the inside-out is the light yoke that Jesus intends. Here, there is delight in doing God's will (Ps 40:8, Rom 7:22). Learning the light yoke from Jesus, we can obey because we are loved by the Father and want to love and please him in return.

Beyond this, what does repentance look like in normal human life? Often, it looks like refusing the flesh and making sound, Christ-informed decisions. It could be something big or small. It might mean resisting a pornographic or politically polarizing website because you freshly recognize it causes a hurtful rippling in your relationships with loved ones. Positively, it might mean seeing someone of another gender, race, or class differently "for the first time," causing you to change your attitude or behavior toward them. It might mean interrogating yourself regarding the books on your shelf or concerning your family traditions. It might involve going out of your way to help or encourage another person. It might mean something on the corporate level, like refusing to support the local establishment that does not hire fairly. It could mean donating a month's worth of your salary to an organization that stands for justice, or starting an organization with a new gospel embodiment. It might mean a fresh recognition of your complicity in systemic ills, leading to your desire to pursue just solutions. In decisions such as these, we "produce fruit in keeping with repentance" (Matt 3:8). If Thomas's encounter with Jesus is any indication, repentance looks like worship. It is a worshipful attitude full of gratitude and obedience. Properly defined, it involves a turning away from all that has been judged and left in Jesus's tomb, including aspects of our lives of which we have perhaps grown quite fond. An affirmation, in Spirit and in truth, of who Christ is and who we are in him brings with it a rejection of who we are not.

In this age of confusion, we will not know exactly what *not* to want until that moment when it is clearly revealed and we see the false and true definitively untangled. We can look forward to that day. Until then, our repentance here bears relative (imperfect) witness to the repentance of the second heaven.

Without clarity here, in the first heaven, I can understand why people refuse the good news. With the clarity of the second heaven, however, I cannot fathom that people might stubbornly choose to adhere to the false comfort of their false selves, the selves that cannot and will not fit through the gate of Jesus Christ.[2] When we place our hands in the wounds of Christ, and when we recognize the fathomless love of his self-sacrifice, will any of us be able to resist joining Thomas's worshipful confession, "My Lord and My God"?[3] Even if we cannot guarantee that everyone will repent in that moment (see Luke 24:40–41; Matt 28:17), we might say that no one will truly repent *until* that moment. The sharpest moment of repentance will take place when the juxtaposition of our opposing selves is most acute.

By the clarity and conviction brought by the Holy Spirit, I will see and rediscover my belief along with my unbelief. Never will the distinction between sin and righteousness be more clear-cut. And never will the Spirit of Truth make it more plain that the enemy is only a parasitic relation, the "prince of this world" who is under condemnation and judgment.[4] Just as God separated the darkness from the light and the night from the day in the beginning, the light of that day will reveal "the fruit of the light," which "consists in all goodness, righteousness, and truth" while "the fruitless deeds of darkness" will be exposed.[5]

Second-heaven clarity is why we preach the gospel in the here and now. To whatever degree belief and repentance happen here, it points to there. This may be the reason that the book of Revelation is so full of charges to repent, whereas the same author does not mention repentance in the gospel of John. Nevertheless, John may provide us with the best illustration of repentance in Jesus's words to Thomas. While often translated "stop doubting and believe" (John 20:27), the literal translation reads, "be not unbelieving, but believing." This is significant because Jesus seems to indicate that Thomas's unbelieving self (red) and his believing self (green) exist simultaneously, and Jesus calls him away from who he is *not* to be who

---

2. As T. F. Torrance likes to say, we could not understand this any more than we can understand the fall in the first place.

3. This confession, coming as it does from within our overlapped person—the one person of the two selves—may be verbal or non-verbal. God knows either way. The idea of exclaiming "my Lord and my God" need not be ablest rhetoric. Perhaps the gift of tongues in its incoherence (without an interpreter) is a harbinger to that day when "tongues will be loosed" (Mark 7:35). Again, those more practiced in individualism are the most challenged in this scenario, seeking to overcome their stuck tongues apart from God's grace. Those most burdened and marginalized in this life, conversely, are most certainly the "last" who will be first (Matt 20:16).

4. See John 16:7–11.

5. Eph 5:8–14 does not describe the day directly, but how we are to live under the conviction of the day, "the day of redemption" (Eph 4:30). See also Rom 7:4 and Rom 7:5 where Paul talks about our deeds either bearing fruit "to God" (in keeping with living to God) or bearing fruit "to death." Some translations have substituted "to" with "for" (e.g., bearing fruit *for* God), which emphasizes act over being and de-emphasizes the in-Christ and anti-Christ determinations of our true and false selves.

he *is*. Thus, "be not unbelieving but believing" simply means, "repent and believe."

In John's next chapter we have another scene packed with repentance, shown in the encounter between Peter and Jesus (John 21:14–17). It is often noted that Jesus asked the same, restorative question to Peter three times, matching the number of Peter's denials, and even that Jesus used a different word for love in the last of his "do you love me?" questions. Less frequently mentioned are Peter's three, identical responses: "Lord, you know that I love you." Peter's statements, just as reflected in Thomas's words, "My Lord and my God," demonstrate our principle of repentance: *speaking the truth back to God*. Jesus Christ has always been every human being's Lord and God, and Thomas simply testifies to the truth. Likewise, Peter's personal words bear universal witness; everyone loves the Lord perfectly and unconditionally (*agape*), and as a brother (*philia*). All of us have opportunities to attest, from our true selves in Christ, the truth that Jesus already knows.

Julian's assertion, "For before he made us he loved us, and when we were made we loved him,"[6] reveals the underlying covenant between God the Father and the Son in which we were created. Within this communion of mutuality, in the intra-transformative power of the Spirit, and in the mediation of Christ from both sides, God loving us means *us* loving *God* (1 John 4:19). That is the unchanging reality that John in his gospel preaches to us. Against the green determination of our true humanity is contrasted the red determination of the false self with its deceit and denial.

Here, in our first-heaven ante-room, the Holy Spirit quickens us, pulling us "forward" into the reorienting clarity of the second heaven. Belief brings forth embodiment. We desire to be among those who "demonstrate their repentance by their deeds" (Acts 26:20). I cannot "convert" myself, but the Spirit moves from within the truth that I am already converted in Christ. Like "transformer" toys, the substance of the conversion is all there. With a few twists, it takes new form. But unlike such toys, even though I already have a created and redeemed self, I cannot make it happen. I cannot simply push a button to bring about that transformation. My efforts to reach within to make such an experience happen are akin to grabbing my own shirt at the chest and trying to pull myself forward.

The Spirit draws us in, giving us eyes to look through the cross to see ourselves and the world, inherently transforming us in the process. She begins to show us the stark difference between our wrong and right, false and true selves. I (in my true self) can celebrate that I (in my false self) *have been* crucified with Christ, that my body of sin *has* been done away with.

---

6. Julian, *Showings*, 283.

The Spirit builds our anticipation for the full manifestation of the judgment, when we finally stand to experience our false selves completely burned away like dross and blown away like the chaff. And the Spirit helps us to operate in this judgment now, this judgment of grace.

Barth summarizes how God is able to provide the separation needed between our true self and our false self, showing us a way forward: "How could man himself make this distinction? He is both the one and the other of these two creatures, and therefore he cannot separate himself from himself, freeing his real self from his false self, pulling himself out of the quagmire by his own forelock. But God can make this distinction and achieve this rescue, and He does so. Intervening, God sides with the former against the latter . . . summoning his good creature against the transgressor."[7] It is important to recognize that by "good creature" and "the transgressor" Barth refers to the green subjectivity and the red subjectivity of each human subject. Even though these subjectivities, so to speak, are predicates of the one subject, Barth gives them their own subject status so that each might have their respective seriousness as two totals. This move is critical for placemat anthropology.[8]

Human beings are created holy and pure, without blemish: "very good." That is the humanity of Genesis 1. As we have seen, however, the Genesis 2 situation is problematic from the very first. Under the influence of the enemy, our first parents and representatives were deceived into disobedience, and cursed with the torque of the contradictory determinations of their split selves. Their total wickedness, replete with the "no" of the flesh, accompanies their total righteousness, replete with the invariable "yes" of Spirit-filled obedience.

We will talk more about how the environment of Genesis 1 is, in a sense, synonymous with the third heaven. But as soon as evil and sin enter the picture, paradise is lost. Just as adding the false self disqualified Adam and Eve *from* paradise (as marked by the flaming sword, Gen 3:24), we cannot fit through the gate *to* paradise without the subtraction of our false selves. The same sword of the Spirit bears witness to the cross, severing false from true.[9] Not to be outdone by the Son and the Spirit, the Father is

---

7. CD III/4, 236.

8. That is why, while committed to inclusive language, I have, á la Barth, retained some of the scriptural usage of "old man" and "new man." Such language communicates our duality in an unparalleled way, i.e., giving subject status to what are really two subjectivities or two selves (two predicates) of one subject. If old man/new man can seem dualistic, "selves" often seems modalistic. (This footnote is largely replicated from Book One.)

9. I have often wondered if Jesus's statements of judgment in Matt 24:51 and Luke

pleased to separate his children from futility in the same way that he first separated day from night and light from darkness.

I do not know if the second heaven, the day, is better described as the end of time or as the moment of all time, the consummation of time. If the cross applies to all people, and if the day is the moment of deliverance and salvation as informed by the cross, it makes sense that all humanity would be present in that moment, gathered at the cross of Jesus. In his essay "The World's Last Night," C. S. Lewis remarks, "What death is to each man, the Second Coming is to the whole human race."[10] He continues,

> We shall not only believe, we shall know, know beyond doubt in every fibre of our appalled or delighted being, that as the Judge has said, so we are: neither more nor less nor other. We shall perhaps even realise that in some dim fashion we could have known it all along. We shall know and all creation will know too: our ancestors, our parents, our wives or husbands, our children. The unanswerable and (by then) self-evident truth about each will be known to all.[11]

In the first heaven, caught up in chronological time, we have the sense of being divided by geographical and generational separations. Such restrictions are not a part of the second heaven, at least as I envision it. I remember a profound moment with one of our daughters, when she was very young. She feared death not because of hell, but because it would mean being separated from her family of six. "I'm scared of being the first in our family to die," she said, "and of being in heaven all alone." Thankfully, I could assure her that would not happen. "We are always going to be together," I said. "It's only in this world where it seems that is not the case. It doesn't matter who dies first, or whether it's ten, twenty or thirty years apart from the others, there will never be a time when one of us is in heaven without another." Somehow, perhaps with the help of C. S. Lewis's wardrobe, she believed me.[12]

12:46 (in his parable of the wicked servant) refer to the duality of the servant in the way we have described it. Jesus says the master will return and (literally) cut the servant in half, and then, as if he is still alive, "assign him a place with the unbelievers."

10. Lewis, "World's Last Night," 81.
11. Lewis, "World's Last Night," 84.
12. In Lewis's classic *The Lion, the Witch, and the Wardrobe*, the wardrobe marks a time-space boundary of sorts, whereby years and even decades pass on the through-side of the magic wardrobe, while on the entering side no time passes at all.

76

Retributive vs. Restorative Justice

Justice is love correcting all that revolts against love.
—Martin Luther King, Jr.

Following Jesus in his forgiveness of injustice means following Jesus in his outrage at injustice—that is following Jesus in his love.
—Allan Aubrey Boesak

Only those who are forgiven and who are willing to forgive will be capable of relentlessly pursuing justice without falling into the temptation to pervert it into injustice.
—Miroslav Volf

Deliverance is a great word. The judgment is the time when the cross and its implications are fully revealed to us. Judgment day is the great separation. It is not human separation from God that is needed, but the separation of our false from our true selves. This work of the cross is finished, but we do not get to fully see it until that day, when we will know as we are known (1 Cor 13:12). It is a day of redemption and restoration.

With this in mind, we can enter judgment day looking forward to the relief that it provides. Imagine how much lighter we will feel. Our false selves, with all the toxic acts and attitudes we contribute to this world, have not only added to the oppression of humanity but have weighed each of us down more than we know. Some people cannot live with themselves and the burden of guilt or shame that they feel. Many of us have heard of the person on death row who yearns for the death chamber, seeking relief from the demons that haunt him because of his actions. This is not to mention the myriad ways that the general toxicity of the fall visits us. Many of us have friends who are victims of mental illness and who feel such pain and anguish that they seek to end their lives. More and more seek to escape the trauma of degenerative diagnoses through euthanasia.

Deaths like the above may be ways of seeking relief, but one's death here in this world is not really a deliverance. In a short-term sense, perhaps, but it is not the thorough and exhaustive deliverance of the gospel of Jesus. For deliverance to be full, it must be coupled with justice. In other words, deliverance is not just about getting rid of the *wrong*, but about experiencing the *right*. If deliverance and justice seem like unlikely bedfellows, it is because we have a weak view of justice. Justice is about making things right.

Justice does *not* mean taking something wrong and declaring it "right," as if it is right even though it is not. This is a mere legal fiction, the kind of straw-man doctrine of justification that Roman Catholic polemicists long accused Luther and Calvin of employing.[1] The narrative focused on this kind of declared justice, or "forensic justice," starts with the person as fundamentally wrong, sinful, corrupt, and deserving of punishment. Penal substitutionary atonement (PSA) holds that the law requires our death as a penalty for sin, but that God graciously turns his wrath away from us and makes Jesus the object of it instead, satisfying his legal standard. By Jesus's substitutionary payment, we are declared justified. Yet how deep can this declared justification be, really? Surely God is not satisfied with a perfect robe of righteousness draped over a person who is still fundamentally wrong underneath. Such a papering over produces what John McLeod Campbell called a mere "title" of righteousness.[2] It is an unfortunately popular understanding of the atonement.

Remembering J. B. Torrance's admonition that God has created us for filial rather than legal purposes, we can turn to yet another Scotsman for reinforcement of Campbell and Torrance's view: "love and righteousness

---

1. Admittedly, such a diminished understanding of justification has often passed as the doctrine itself, especially as taught by many followers of Luther and Calvin. Roman Catholic and Eastern Orthodox theologians, then, are right to cry foul in such cases and critique Protestantism of endorsing the "legal fiction" of justification. Thanks to Edward Lowe for this insight.

2. Campbell, *Nature of the Atonement*, 129.

and justice in God," notes Thomas Erskine, "mean exactly the same thing, namely, a desire to bring His whole moral creation into a participation of His own character and His own blessedness."[3] This returns us to our relational definition of righteousness: within Christ and his right relationship with the Father, we are "living to God" (Rom 6:11). In Erskine's words it is "an actual participation in [God's] righteousness, not by imputation, but in substance and reality, as is the participation of Jesus with the Father."[4]

In his book *Jesus and the Undoing of Adam*, C. Baxter Kruger, once J. B. Torrance's student, put it this way:

> The holiness of God, the sovereignty and righteousness and justice of God, the love and wrath of God are all essentially Trinitarian concepts. The God that we meet in Jesus Christ is not a new God. The triune relationship of Father, Son and Spirit is not a new form that God assumed for a moment in time; it is the way God is from all eternity. . . . Properly understood, the holiness of God is a Trinitarian idea. If we took the joy and the fullness and the love of the Father, Son and Spirit, their mutual delight and passion, the sheer togetherness of their relationship, its intimacy, harmony and wholeness, and rolled them all into one word, it would be "holiness." This one word is pregnant with the wonder and the beauty, the uniqueness and health and rightness of the Trinitarian life.[5]

Kruger goes on to say that, in a way the Eastern fathers would not recognize, we in the Western tradition "allowed the holiness of God to be legalized. . . . The framework within which we understand God, creation, and the relationship between God and humanity shifted into an alien legal gear."[6]

In Book One we reviewed the frighteningly abusive concept that when God looks at me, a rotten sinner, he does not see me. In other words, when looking at me, he sees Jesus instead. The implication is that if Jesus stepped out of the way, and God really saw us, he would be grossed out, repulsed, and angry, even vengeful (as if he requires his pound of flesh to fulfill the obligations of the legal arrangement). Sadly, the "good news" in this view has nothing to do with recreation, much less creation (our pure Genesis 1 green is far from view). It has devolved into something like this: are you not glad that God tolerates you and that Jesus shields you from God's just wrath?[7] This

---

3. Quoted in Hart, *Teaching Father*, 109.
4. Quoted in Hart, *Teaching Father*, 144.
5. Kruger, *Jesus Christ and the Undoing*, 43.
6. Kruger, *Jesus Christ and the Undoing*, 43–44.
7. See reading in Book One, "The Righteous and the Wicked."

theological poison works all the way back into contorting God's attitude for the atonement, portraying Christ as dying *so that* God can love us, rather than dying *because* God loves us!

Thankfully, the robe of righteousness (Isa 61:10) we have received is much more than a cloak over our corruption. We are not only declared righteous in a legal sense, we really *are* righteous, "made righteous" (Rom 5:1, ESV), in the person and work of Jesus Christ: "for in the gospel the righteousness of God is revealed" (Rom 1:17) in the faithfulness of the Savior who has always shared his righteousness with us. All of our good works—all of our righteous words and deeds—are included in the "obedience of faith" that Paul calls us to live into. Whatever the obedience of faith is, it is the faith of Christ and includes our ongoing participation of faith in his faith. We are inside, already participating. It is not something that we can get into, have, or possess from the outside. That is why Paul describes this derivative aspect of our faith as being revealed "from faith to faith" (Rom 1:17, YLT). But when does our participation in his faith begin? It begins at creation. And it is a dimension of life in which we pray and give thanks without ceasing (1 Thess 1:3; 2:13; 5:17). This unceasing obedience is God's will for us (Rom 1:9–10). The obedience of faith is part and parcel of "living to God." This Yes to God in all things is a rule of humanity as God designed it—the law of the Spirit of life.

If Romans 1:17 highlights God's extravagant commitment of "Yes" to us and for us (green), then the accompanying "placemat" revelation that follows (Rom 1:18) highlights God's commitment to purge us from all that is against us (red): "The wrath of God is being revealed from heaven against all the godlessness and wickedness of those who suppress the truth by their wickedness." Both the Yes and the No of God are revealed in Jesus Christ, and because the No serves the Yes, we need not fear. Again, God is for us, not against us, such that we can always understand his "against us" as part of his "for us."

We return again and again to Paul's glorious extrapolation of the unity of indicative and imperative in Colossians 3, the gospel consistency of our lives not only as redeemed but also as created in Christ. The good news is that we have always been hidden with Christ in God (Col 3:3), not hidden *from* God *by* Christ. The transformational awareness that we are hid with Christ (green) motivates us to "rid ourselves" (Col 3:8) of evil behaviors that are not of Christ (red). If we did not know better, to "rid ourselves of all such things" could sound as if we must clean ourselves up, when instead the logic of the imperative is contextualized by the fact that we have already been cleansed (indicative). Again, the phrase in Colossians 3:5, "put to death, therefore, whatever belongs to your earthly nature," correlates with the fact

PART SIX: LIVING LIFE FROM THE THIRD HEAVEN

that we *have been* put to death (Col 3:3 states: "*you died*, and your life hidden with Christ in God").[8]

Here we pause to consider the fact that despite these carnal vices having been put to death, they obviously are still extant in Paul's hearers' lives (and our own!). What then can it mean when the apostle, delineating practices like sexual immorality, greed, and slander—tells us that because of such things, "the wrath of God is coming" (Col 3:6).

First, we must double down on the finished work of Christ. Because God's promise to us has always been Yes (2 Cor 1:20), God's definitive No against all that is not of him is exhaustively absorbed in the death of Christ. God the Son died for nothing less. There is nothing unfinished outside of the "it is finished" of Calvary (John 19:30). In Jesus's death, sin, death, and the devil were destroyed (Heb 2:14). Adding more wrath to what is contained in the death of the Son of God is another way of theologically minimizing the cross. Instead, just as all human suffering is contained in the suffering of Christ and his cross, all of God's wrath is subsumed in the cross of God. That is where everything that is not of God is dealt with and overcome.

Second, having established that there is no further wrath of God to come in addition to that of the cross, what *is* coming is the greater *revelation* of Calvary's wrath. We will see just how committed God is to burning away the dross of our sinful humanity. The plain meaning is this: do not bring such things forward, for the consuming fire of the cross has deemed them unfit for the unadulterated kingdom. Let go of it now because it will not be around later, and because its destructiveness is exposed by the extent to which God went to destroy it. Do not reach back for the stale, rank flesh that has been removed and thrown into the furnace. "Since you died with Christ to the elemental spiritual forces of this world," Paul chides, why do you keep acting "as though you still belonged to the world" (Col 2:20)?

As attested by the Jewish atoning sacrifices in the Old Testament, the fire of God's wrath has purified us to God's perfect satisfaction. Jesus's blood was shed, asserts McLeod Campbell, "not to deliver us from punishment, but to cleanse and purify for worship."[9] Pastor and scholar Mako Nagasawa elucidates well the importance of the Jewish Jubilee (a celebration every forty-nine years of Israel's deliverance from Egypt) being on the same day as Yom Kippur, the Jewish day of atonement.[10] The wrong kind of substitutionary approach

---

8. This is an adjustment to the NIV translation, which includes the phrase "is now": "your life *is now* hidden with Christ in God" (emphasis added). The phrase "is now" does not exist in the Greek text and can communicate a false, sequential understanding (as in, after a conversion experience).

9. Campbell, *Nature of the Atonement*, 144.

10. See Nagasawa, "God as Dialysis Machine."

would imagine Yom Kippur as a day when God reminded Israel to keep their distance because of his holiness. This would translate, notes Nagasawa, into "if you get near me, bring an animal, so that I can kill it instead of you." Instead, Exodus 29:37 indicates that atonement is inviting, and it is cleansing, "whatever touches [the altar] becomes holy." The animal is immolated, representing the burning away of impurities, but the blood is poured out, representing the purity that remains. The key to the right view of substitution and satisfaction, then, is to recognize that purification has to do with partition—the separating out of the impurities.[11] Only then will God be satisfied.

This way of understanding the cultic day of atonement helps us to see jubilee as judgment, and judgment as deliverance. The Lamb of God sought a purification for humanity that only God, in his unique substitutionary and representative sacrifice, could pull off: impurities burned away, partition accomplished—Jesus our high priest sanctified for our sake.[12]

In Scripture there are numerous ways that deliverance and justice relate to redemption. For example, Job was an exalted servant of the Lord, perhaps the most righteous man on earth. Then God allowed Satan to wreak havoc on Job and his family. The enemy's destruction included the death of Job's ten children. At the end of the book of Job, Satan is vanquished and Job is restored. He received more wealth and property than he had before, and ten children, matching exactly the number who died earlier. Though the story is often viewed as redemptive, we can see that this is not exactly the case. Instead, it contains only hints of deliverance and redemption. True justice and redemption has less to do with ten "replacement" children for Job. At the very least, it will 1) reveal Job's "re-union" with the children he lost (the spiritual meaning of the ten "new" children), and 2) include an understanding of why God allowed the evil in the first place. The latter aspect is as elusive as the former in our first-heaven existence.

God's deliverance does not simply deliver us *from* pain, suffering, and corruption; it delivers us *to* justice and righteousness. Together, these things make up "redemption." In truth, we have been redeemed. The death and resurrection of Christ has already accomplished deliverance, justification, and redemption. But we take these things by faith, not by sight. We do not see full

---

11. From Nagasawa, "Session Two."

12. The priests were meant to eat the sacrifice that was offered (Lev 10:16–20). Only at Yom Kippur was the carcass of the animal declared inedible; the flesh must be completely burned away to represent the cleansing of the people, and its impurity not allowed to cycle back through the human body. The scapegoat carrying away the sins of Israel, i.e., separating the people from their sins, is also a strong christological harbinger. Again, Jesus is at once lamb and scapegoat; he assumes sin, and takes it away in his person, while remaining himself.

redemption in this world and our theology is weakened by this short-sightedness. We call it redemption when our team wins the national championship in basketball after falling to a last-second shot the year before, but is that redemption? Since it did not correct the year before, it is not true redemption. Such a way of imagining redemption makes it a close relative of revenge in which themes of restorative justice devolve into retributive justice.

This weak form of justice has filtered into our human justice system. Here, retribution functions as a cheap substitute for restoration. It is even worse when government can cite Christian teaching as a support of penal retribution, drawing from the Judeo-Christian penal substitutionary model of atonement outlined above.

In the year 1997, terrorist Timothy McVeigh was sentenced to death for the bombing of the Oklahoma City government building. When it was time for execution, McVeigh was surrounded by the victims' families, many of whom had lost young children when the building's nursery exploded. These witnesses had come to watch the killer suffer or to at least see some glimmer of fear in his eyes as he faced death. As throughout the trial and legal process, McVeigh gave them nothing. He was not remorseful in the least; he did not apologize. He just died. Interviewed after McVeigh's killing, witnesses acknowledged that the terrorist's death did not deliver the peace or closure that they had anticipated.[13] Instead, McVeigh's recalcitrant demeanor "poured salt in the wounds."[14]

In 2019 Jeffrey Epstein apparently took his own life in jail after being arrested for the sexual assault of numerous teenagers and young women. According to press coverage, several of the victims were infuriated that Epstein had escaped facing his accusers in court and "being brought to justice." One remarked, "I am extremely mad and hurt thinking he once again was above us and took the easy way out." Another added, "We have to live with the scars of his actions for the rest of our lives, while he will never face the consequences of the crimes he committed, the pain and trauma he caused so many people." A third woman also commented, "I will never have a sense of closure now. I'm angry as hell . . . that I and his other victims will never see him face the consequences for his horrendous actions."[15]

The damage Epstein left in his wake is horrific, and his traumatized victims often feel irreparably wounded. If Epstein had lived to face his victims, if he could have been punished in a way that matched the pain of his victims, would it have been enough? We will never know, but if cases like

---

13. Cohen, "Timothy McVeigh."
14. Pressman, "Death of McVeigh," para. 21.
15. Weise, "Epstein's Accusers."

McVeigh's are any indication, it is unlikely. Instead, the righteously indignant perspective of these women not only shows a yearning for justice, but the futility of limiting our perspective on the realization of justice in this world alone, where justice is all too often evaded and restoration scarce. We can recognize that the fury and indignation of these victims is a witness to God's righteous judgment. He will not be satisfied until this is completely and fully dealt with. By faith in the just judgment of God, we have hope that no victim in this world will be dissatisfied with God's satisfaction. MacDonald's summary is apt: "While a satisfied justice is an unavoidable eternal event, a satisfied revenge is an eternal impossibility."[16]

It is no accident that a sense of justice and a desire for it is deeply ingrained in us. In a world where perpetrators actually get away with murder, we want people to face the consequences of their actions. This desire for accountability reflects God's heart. Unfortunately, our law courts can only do so much to meet these desires. Until the full clarity of the second heaven, true deliverance, justice, and redemption will be fleeting. Nevertheless, the second-heaven judgment is indispensable to true restoration and reconciliation. To say that there is no judgment for all persons, or for any person, is to say that the difference between right and wrong does not really matter here. It is absurd to believe that right and wrong are important here in the first heaven but not important there in the judgment of the second heaven.

The judgment of the second heaven, then, involves at least three main aspects: clarity, crisis, and catharsis. It involves 1) the *clarity* of seeing perfectly the differentiation between all things, true and false, green and red; 2) the *crisis* of recognizing our implication in both determinations, and the unsustainable tension of the existence of two totals in one person; and 3) the *catharsis* of confessing and releasing the wrong. It involves our "making things right" with God and with others. These things can all be had in the first heaven, but only to a degree. The sooner we know Jesus Christ and him as the interpretive key to all of the above, the better. While praying *maranatha* ("Come, Lord Jesus") we can also insist with Fania E. Davis, "An eye for an eye and a tooth for a tooth leaves the whole world blind and toothless."[17]

---

16. Lewis, *George MacDonald*, 97.
17. Davis, *Little Book of Race*, 28. I cannot recommend this book more highly.

77

Gender Bending?

> *Still less is gender an imaginative extension of sex. . . . The real process is the reverse. Gender is a reality, and a more fundamental reality than sex.*
> —C. S. Lewis

PLACEMAT ANTHROPOLOGY ASKS US to consider the gap between what is seen and unseen. When it comes to the complex world of gender issues, we do well to maintain the humility implied by the command to "walk by faith, not by sight" (2 Cor 5:7, NRSV). If the way we are born is how we are created, then it is a slam dunk. There is no complexity there. But as we already established, "we only see in part"; our first-heaven existence does not perfectly reflect the way we were created. There is continuity with how we were created, but there is also discontinuity. We can easily confuse one for the other and get it wrong.

In the second heaven, tears are not only appropriate but called for. Seeing clearly gives us a chance to confront our wrongs, call them out, confess them to God and others, and to forgive and receive forgiveness. In the second heaven I might find compunction to seek reconciliation with someone I treated poorly when they "transitioned" to a different gender in the first heaven. I might say, "I'm sorry I judged you when you had gender confirmation surgery. I was walking by sight, not faith. I was always taught that it was our mind that must change to match our body, so I was critical and treated you inhumanly when you told me that it was your body that must change to better match your mind. I used Scripture against you, when the real problem was my failure to interpret Scripture and the situation christologically. I see now that you were right about your decision, which was more congruent to your *person* and not less. It grieves me that I did not see it sooner, please forgive me."[1]

I can hear the first-heaven protests: "Jeff, it sounds like you're assuming everyone who decides to 'transition' is making the right decision. What if the person undergoing gender confirmation surgery is operating out of their false mind? What if their self-perception is askew?" That will become clear in due course (as will the accuracy of our own notions about *their* self-perception!). I am not suggesting that we avoid voicing our disagreement with a loved one's decision. That is hardly love. But the clarity that we are looking for is, in this world, elusive. Thus, when clarity comes, we must be just as prepared to admit that we were wrong as we are presently adamant that we are right.

Regarding the issue of gender transition, it is unlikely that we will be able to love each other well in the human community without an understanding of human transcendence (again defined by "more than meets the eye," or more than can be physiologically assessed). If I speak from

---

1. Whether it's Paul or Barth, the working assumption has been that genitals are consistent with gender. Even considering the vast corruption of the fall, these interpreters do not appear to contemplate the possibility of a complete mismatch between the gender and genitals. Thankfully, the theology they teach us from their era allows us to see things differently in our own and, along with recognizing scientific advancements, still remain faithful to the gospel they both prized. Paul and other biblical authors endeavored to teach their hearers to practice faith in a way that was most congruent to the Word they had received from God. They were undoubtedly inspired to do so. However, it also follows that while the christological foundation never changes, the way this foundation is worked out in the scriptural imperatives is subject to change. We don't have to chalk this up to elements of the writers' fallen human minds; incomplete revelation is enough reason to produce external imperatives that may not be fully aligned with the reality of Jesus Christ. There is always the possibility that the imperative may be more reflective of culture than theologically desirable. Paul makes this tension plain when he expresses ambivalence concerning whether his stated imperatives are from the Lord (1 Cor 7:10, 12, 25). As Barth himself says, "Ethics will still have to leave the final judgment to God. And our knowledge of these general spheres and relationships will never actually be full, so that the question of what is commanded and forbidden will always necessarily retain a certain breadth and openness." At the same time, the endeavor to hone theological ethics is a worthy one, notes Barth, "the directives and directions to be given by ethics gain in urgency and compulsion, in proportion as the knowledge of these spheres and relationships become broader and deeper" (*CD* III/4, 31). Barth issues a scathing rebuke of "casuistical ethics," whereby "concrete" imperatives are mistaken for the most concrete reality. At that point, says Barth, humans collect the biblical commands to formulate their own ethical package to apply in judgment of others. This kind of proof texting "requires no interpretation to come into force" (*CD* III/4, 10, 12).

PART SIX: LIVING LIFE FROM THE THIRD HEAVEN

an immanent point of view, and not in view of transcendence, then I will project my immanent insecurity. This goes both for people who are "cis"—who live in a binary construction of gender—and for those who may live in a more fluid construction. The former will inevitably be "transphobic" and the latter "cisphobic" because, in the flesh, we fear the "other," people who are different than us. Our placemat discussion points to the fact that a purely biological assessment is inadequate.

The old perceptual model, "you are XY with male genitals, so you are male, and God does not make mistakes," has hurt many people. We let a biological designation of sex drive the gender train. Thankfully, there is today more compassion to go along with medical advancement for those who have felt like "a female in a male body" all their lives (even this example is inadequate in its presumption that there is a clear binary). When it comes to creaturely gender, human transcendence teaches us that *everybody* is exactly what they were created to be and at the same time, in our immanent form in the first heaven, *nobody* is exactly what they were created to be.

Taken together, it follows that even *if* there is a male-female binary, its pure form is inaccessible after the fall and therefore all bets are off in the first heaven. We cannot do gender backward by starting from genitals or even chromosomes. Likewise, we cannot prove Genesis 1:27 means a gender binary, as opposed to, say, representing the beauty of gender distinctiveness in general (and there are other options).[2] But one thing is certain. What we *experience* in this world is a gender spectrum, regardless of sex. There are heterosexual couples who at base may be closer to being same-gendered, and homosexual couples who may be closer to being differently gendered. My advice is this: don't fight the spectrum. Avoid the haughty perspective of *knowing* how others are created in relation to gender. We simply do not know how integral our gender is to our personhood (the invariable green truth of who people are in Christ), so we presumptively overstep if we try to strip away aspects of others that we *think* were not created. Only the Creator-Judge who loves us the most has the right to be that invasive.

Such an approach recognizes how impossible it is to unravel the fall in this world. It also asks us to interrogate the ways the cisgender perspective we may hold is a product of that fall. It helps us to consider afresh multifarious meanings for "male and female he created them" (Gen 1:27). Jesus says that the Holy Spirit will come to judge the world regarding sin, righteousness, and judgment. In the second heaven, the sword of the Spirit will make plain the degree to which our first-heaven perceptions were accurate and inaccurate. By the same Spirit, second-heaven clarity can visit

---

2. See the reading in Book One, "Dust to Dust?"

us here, but never without a degree of confusion on our end. We cannot possess it so fully that we lord it over others infallibly. The same thing that keeps them from proving that they are right keeps you from proving that they are wrong. While living in the grey land of Genesis 2–3, an appeal to Genesis 1 is not as clear-cut as we might imagine.[3]

By urging us to hold our "walking by sight" judgments loosely, I do not wish to sound snarky. I cannot imagine the challenge of disagreeing with a sixteen-year-old who wants to go through gender transformation. They are young. Their brains have not fully developed. How do I know they are not simply doing it because their friend did it? How do I know this is not just another fad? What if they change their mind later? How do I accept my role as the parent in this situation? What if the great relationship I have always prized with my child is permanently fractured? What if my resistance, or even lack of full support, contributes to deep angst in my child? What if my child threatens suicide because I tell them I will not support them until they are at least eighteen? What if my child reveals a deep heart for Christ and prayerful persistence in pleading for me to support gender confirmation surgery sooner than later, so that they are not wasting time waiting to set the trajectory that they feel led to pursue? These questions are serious and I do not pretend to answer them here, especially for those pre-adult situations. Mistakes all around seem unavoidable. Some will undoubtedly wish they had transitioned sooner, some will wish they had never transitioned at all. Some parents might beat themselves up for supporting the child who was once anxious to transition, but who later regrets it. Some parents might beat themselves up for resisting their child's desire for earlier transition. Such are the confounding scenarios that add more gravity to the existential question, "Why, God?"

C. S. Lewis suggested that defining a dogmatic polarity between genders in the here and now was not only impossible but unwise. Even if, in the end, things sifted out to reveal a clear polarity, such a polarity could only be relatively, inadequately, and sometimes improperly attested in what we would call the first heaven. Lewis himself imagined something like the poles of rhythm and melody. For example, in *Perelandra* (book two of Lewis's

---

3. See *CD* III/1, 321–22, especially the last two pages. For Barth, "male and female" refers to gender or sexuality only in the third sense, after Christ and his body (Eph 5:22–32), and then secondly Yahweh and Israel. Such an interpretation obviously gives a different emphasis to "be fruitful and increase in number" (Gen 1:28), biological procreation now bearing only relative witness to the deeper spiritual call to fruitfulness (cf. John 15:16). Conversely, if procreation is the primary point of gender differentiation and fruitfulness in Gen 1:28, single and celibate people are immediately marginalized as humans, not to mention others.

PART SIX: LIVING LIFE FROM THE THIRD HEAVEN

space trilogy, named for the planet in question), there appear creatures who are sexless but not genderless.

Lewis, in fact, according to researcher Billie Hoard, may have been the first person to ever put in print a delineation of sex and gender. For Lewis, gender is deeper than sex. It is metaphysical, related to what we would call our spiritual bodies, and in a way that sex is not (necessarily). Hoard remarks: "Lewis clearly believed that a person's gender was something more true, more lasting, and more definitive of that person that [sic] their biological sex (organs, hormone levels, body shape, etc.)" and, "both Lewis—who sees gender as a metaphysical reality—and contemporary transgender theorists—who mostly see gender as either a social construct or as a personal identity—end up categorizing gender identity as something objectively real but ultimately only subjectively knowable and therefore un-testable given the current state of our technology."[4]

Hoard is right. Once we start with a realist premise, and then add the distortion of sin and evil, we cannot claim to perfectly know the reality. We can hope to walk by faith, and not sight, but sight will always be a problem. Such an understanding provides the dose of humility we need to pull back on our self-professed, comprehensive certainty about the reality of the things we only apprehend. For example, we might contend that gender exists in the eschaton, but if genitalia can only bear relative witness to gender, it follows that, with the ongoing distortion of the fall, this witness can only be more and more unreliable. Can anyone in this world claim that they can know perfectly or see clearly past the fall?

Hoard points us to Lewis's well-known christological "trilemma" (that Jesus Christ is either liar, lunatic, or Lord) and applies it anthropologically. Specifically, what do we do when confronted with a person who looks to us like a man but says that he is a woman? Perhaps the person is lying (even if not intentionally, i.e., they are mistaken); perhaps the person is insane, or struggling with mental illness. But the third option cannot be discounted: perhaps against appearances to the contrary, the person states the truth. Hoard reminds us of the encounter in *The Lion, the Witch, and the Wardrobe* when Lucy's siblings confront her about whether or not she actually went through the wardrobe into another land. The older siblings, representing the establishment, think she is lying, mistaken, or crazy, and take a patronizing approach. The siblings ask the wise old professor at the house, and his response is: "There are only three possibilities. . . . You know she doesn't tell

---

4. Hoard, "Bareface," para. 24, 30. Hoard supports her claim that Lewis was the first author to write about the sex-gender distinction in n. 4. Regarding *Perelandra*, the discussion between Lewis's fictional characters is in chapter 16.

lies and it is obvious that she is not mad. *For the moment then, and unless any further evidence turns up, we must assume that she is telling the truth.*"[5]

Why do we not give transgender people this minimal benefit of the doubt? Even if the person has never been known for lying, even if the person has never given reason for doubts about their mental health, the benefit of the doubt is often withheld. Perhaps this skepticism is rooted in what's received as a shocking departure from tradition. Maybe it comes from a conviction about scriptural inerrancy and a less than christocentric interpretation of the Bible. Perhaps it emerges subconsciously from the recognition that we cannot *prove* that the transgender person is mistaken, and this fearful disquietude causes us to double down and insist that the person *must be* mistaken. As Hoard notes, the most acute damage is done between opposing family members when cis persons, for whatever reason, want the trans person to be what *they* want them to be.

The sin here is great and terrible specifically because it is the sin of twisted love. It is the love that refuses to love on any but its own terms. Because the denier cannot (or will not) make the move to empathy for the transgender person and cannot (or will not) recognize the validity of the trans person's account of reality, they must make every effort to destroy that which they cannot give and will not share.[6]

Some things are better left to the judgment day, before the one who truly understands and knows, before the only one worthy to judge, the One who loves us the most. Surely there is enough confusion in this world—people born with both sets of genitals, or with genitals that do not match their chromosomes, or even those born with both sets of chromosomes (an XX/XY person with an equal number of XX and XY cells). These facts protect us from ugly dogmatism.

My argument tilts in favor of those who have most often been categorized as nothing but evil and sinful, or judged by the church to be less than total "green" for following an atypical path. For the more "conservative" reader, more solidarity in Christ between all human beings can perhaps be healthily acknowledged going forward, which means more empathy and more wisdom in reserving judgment. Meanwhile, those on the liberal side must also remember the dangers of dogmatic certainty, which can cause us to "lose our spine" and to indiscriminately make an idol out of giving others the benefit of the doubt. If "not judging" devolves into "not discerning,"

---

5. Hoard, "Bareface," para. 33 (emphasis original). There is admittedly some irony here in implementing a children's tale to make this argument related to transgender, since, as alluded to earlier in the reading, giving a still-maturing child the benefit of the doubt and an adult such a benefit are not the same thing.

6. Hoard, "Bareface."

then the line between green and red, right and wrong, is lost. As the day will make clear, there is such a thing as right and wrong. No matter our sociopolitical stance, we do well to take our current views of right and wrong with a grain of salt. Our most sinful disservice to God and humanity will always result from a failure to recognize that our own brokenness and total "red" depravity incessantly distorts our perspective. Thankfully McDonald's words apply to all of us: "The wrath will consume what they call themselves; so that the selves God made shall appear."[7] Elsewhere, in a beautiful allusion to Revelation he adds, "'God has cared to make me for Himself,' says the victor with the white stone, 'And has called me that which I like best.'"[8]

Three times in fairly short order Jesus gives a very succinct and poignant commandment: "As I have loved you, so you also must love one another. . . . Love each other as I have loved you. . . . Love each other."[9] I hope it is clear how our convictions about human transcendence have everything to do with the cultural discussion regarding "trans," and how love, solidarity in Christ, empathy, and prayerful "placemat discernment" equip us as we struggle to navigate our first-heaven challenges.

---

7. MacDonald as quoted in Lewis, *George MacDonald*, 25.
8. MacDonald as quoted in Lewis, *George MacDonald*, 29.
9. John 13:34; 15:12; 15:17.

78

Coming Home

I was afraid of his claws, I can tell you, but I was pretty nearly desperate now. So I just lay flat down on my back to let him do it. The very first tear he made was so deep that I thought it had gone right into my heart. And when he began pulling the skin off, it hurt worse than anything I've ever felt. The only thing that made me able to bear it was just the pleasure of feeling the stuff peel off. . . . Well, he peeled the beastly stuff right off. . . . And there was I as smooth and soft as a peeled switch and smaller than I had been. Then he caught hold of me—I didn't like that much for I was very tender underneath now that I'd no skin on—and threw me into the water. It smarted like anything but only for a moment. After that it became perfectly delicious and as soon as I started swimming and splashing I found that all the pain had gone from my arm. And then I saw why. I'd turned into a boy again.

—C. S. Lewis

THE UNDERSTANDING OF THE second heaven provides rich meaning to all of Scripture's testimony of judgment day by connecting it with the fullest revelation of the cross of Christ and the glory of creation. It refuses to buckle to a perspective that allows anyone to avoid the day, whether or not they are baptized believers.[1] To say that we can look forward to judgment day does not mean it will be comfortable. It will be hardest for those most comfortable in our own (false) skin. For all of us, and especially for those with no advance warning, it may be like Lewis's Narnia tale *The Voyage of the Dawn Treader*, when the boy Eustace was delivered from his false persona—his "hard and rough and wrinkled and scaly" dragon skin—only to rediscover in his "newness" his true humanity and the joy of primal being.

Because we do not know how long the day will last, the moment of the second heaven need not preclude Jesus's documented words from the cross to the repentant thief, "Today you will be with me in paradise" (Luke 23:43). Since it occurred during the crucifixion, we might even imagine this exchange as something like a second-heaven moment pushed forward in time. While not privy to all that transpired in their conversation, the posture of the "repentant thief" in that moment may signify what is, in our baseball analogy, the fastest rounding of the bases imaginable. The other thief, like many of us, may have a longer appointment with the Savior at second base. Instead of saying, "I want to go where you are going," the second thief chided Jesus by asking for a self-serving miracle, i.e., "get me off of this cross." Like the repentant thief, this unrepentant thief is also at the gate of paradise with Jesus. But he is mistaken if he thinks he can bring his false, fleshly self (his *sarx* self) along with him. The unrepentant person, notes Barth, "will always be distinguished by the fact that he still has a lot to say in his own favor."[2]

We cannot return to our baseball analogy without mention of home base, or home plate. Home is the goal of every base runner. It is the cumulative marker of the runner who has touched all the other bases. But home is also where every base runner begins. Thus, *home signifies the whole process from beginning to end*, the cohesive element that holds it all together. Home is unadulterated paradise, and we as God's beloved creatures start and end our pilgrimage at home. Paradise is where we belong. Our belonging, our home, is just as real and true for all of us now as it is and will be when we enter the third heaven. Here in the first heaven, however, this reality is hidden. Most human beings are not aware of our original and ongoing life in

---

1. Again, John 5:24 is often taught this way, but to believe in Jesus Christ and to pass from death to life is not to avoid judgment, but instead to not stop at judgment. In fact, the subsequent verses of the chapter make it very clear that all will be judged. Passing from death to life in the ultimate sense means going from grey to green. Whether on that day or today, to "believe" is witness to one having eternal life (John 3:36; John 6:47) and nothing but eternal life (no grey!).

2. *CD* II/2, 769.

God, the home that the Father, Son, and Holy Spirit have always shared with us their beloved creatures.

Paul's teachings about "home" in 2 Cor 5:6–8 seem contrary to the idea of always being at home and at first glance sound rather strange:[3] "Therefore we are always confident and know that as long as we are at home in the body we are away from the Lord. For we live by faith, not by sight. We are confident, I say, and would prefer to be away from the body and at home with the Lord." Initially it sounds like Paul is confident *because* he is away from the Lord. Instead, he is confident because he knows that he is never truly away from the Lord, even when he is "away." Paul's meaning is that while he is "away" in the first heaven, his "earthly tent" (body) is his provisional home. No matter how difficult it is here, his confidence (by faith not sight) stems from the fact that he *already has* a permanent home (2 Cor 5:1). He is confident because he has "backing" even while here in the first heaven. This backing is the deposit mentioned in the preceding verse: "God, who has given us the Spirit as a deposit, guaranteeing what is to come" (2 Cor 5:5). Even while Paul groans in his earthly tent, he knows in the Spirit that he has a spiritual body, his more substantial dwelling. Because he is confident in the one who was, and is, and is to come, Paul is in the first heaven while living from the third. His life and ministry are lived from the big picture.

While sharing Christ's sufferings in this world, the Holy Spirit, the Spirit of Christ, shares our groanings. Even as the ascended one, Christ continues in compassionate solidarity with us by the Spirit, he and the Spirit both interceding for us. In deeper ways than we can comprehend, the Spirit testifies with our spirit, providing assurance that we are indeed God's children and that we will make it through, sharing his sufferings that we might also share in his glory (Rom 8:26–27; 8:16–17).[4] Again, living from the third heaven does not mean that we are purely there, but it means living with "real" perspective of there to here, looking for the actual in the midst of the existential, knowing that we are always Genesis 1 people, living to God in Christ Jesus. Living retrospectively from the third heaven is packed with the convergence of Revelation 22 and Genesis 1. By putting "childish ways" behind us (1 Cor 13:11), we apprehend Jesus's encouragement to enter the kingdom with the implicit trust of a guileless child (see Matt 19:14).

---

3. Book One, "The Matter of Bodies."

4. It is notable in Rom 8:16 there is mention of both our spirit and *the* Spirit, the Spirit of Christ. As persons we have a spirit, we are not empty vessels filled by the Spirit. Our spirit is derivative of the Holy Spirit, and our spirit is also distinct from the Holy Spirit. But we are also one with the Spirit. This does not make us the Spirit anymore than being one with Christ makes us Christ, but the association is an intimate and often underestimated one.

Confidence and assurance in Christ provide hope. Hope is a word not needed in the unadulterated third heaven but desperately needed in the first. The revelation of the third heaven is a glimpse of reality, the promised land that God kept in front of the Israelites and which prophetic voices from Moses to Dr. King have glimpsed in the *future*, as an anchor in the *now*. In *Pilgrim's Progress*, when an atheist confronted the protagonist "Christian" during a bleak stage of the journey to Mt. Zion, he debunked Christian's heavenly vision, but Christian's companion Hopeful buoyed his brother by providing a third-heaven reminder: "Did we not see from the Delectable Mountains the Gate of the City?"[5]

Hoping against hope, the believer walking by faith can believe that exceptions to the worldly rule witness to what is really real. In Luci Shaw's poem, "Winter Wheat," it is a lively patch of green in an otherwise bleak landscape that bolsters her to live a "rebel" life against worldly perceptions:

> Even the oaks
> are almost naked.
> The fall flames of rose and gold
> have died out under
> the dark rains.
>
> The ground underfoot
> is rimed with the cold ashes
> of the wind, the bleached
> stubble, the clotted
> white heads.
>
> But see,
> over there, like a
> green blaze on the shoulder
> of the hill, like a new patch
> in the quilt,
> a square of quite improbable
> emerald.
>
> With what audacity
> the bright velvet
> assaults our autumn senses:
> each blade a reversal
> of seasons, an upstart shoot
> flagging the brief sun bursts,
> sap quickly to its tip,
> ready now, in November,

---

5. Bunyan, *Pilgrim's Progress*, second part, quoted in Baillie, *Diary of Readings*, Day 159.

for the new year!

The oaks are bare
and the sky heavy with
first snow, but my rebel blood
beats higher now
against the winter night
coming.[6]

As "improbable" as the green patch might be by sight, Shaw receives it not as an exception to the rule, but as an exception that proves the rule. Beyond the typically sequential transition from winter to spring, Shaw's words communicate the rule of life simultaneous to the pseudo-rule of death, often hidden by it, yet also transcending it. Revelations, tastes, glimpses like this make us yearn for more. In this grey world, we long for green and nothing but green.

As pilgrims we long to be home and *nowhere* but home. But in the meantime Paul, like each of us, is one person with two homes. As in his letter to the Philippians, Paul is "torn between the two" (Phil 1:23). The two are not an either-or; they are not sequential homes. Instead, they are dimensional and simultaneous. In our first-heaven "home," we are completely, but not *purely*, in our third-heaven home. The resulting torque can be hellacious. It causes much confusion. No matter how lost we may be in one sense (red), however, we are always found at home (green) with the Lord. In placemat anthropology, we can recognize Paul's phrase "away from home" as an acknowledgment of the duality of the first-heaven experience. Paul knows the duality of this life but is also confident in the big picture, he lives with third-heaven audacity that the duality is provisional and will fade away. "Away from home" is a relative term, then, meaning that we are not yet at home in a pure or unadulterated sense. We are always and already at home, and we long to be nothing but home. Living from the third heaven requires that we start with the "already" when interpreting the "not yet." The "then" *is already* in the "now."

Eugene Peterson rendered Ephesians 2:4–7 in all its glory. Heaven is our home, and has always been our home, even when we got lost and ran away. Indeed, the gospel never tires of proclaiming to us that great Athanasian truth that God could not be satisfied by allowing us to remain in such a lost state. As Peterson observed in *The Message*, Paul provides us with a picture of heaven *now*:

---

6. Shaw, "Winter Wheat," 69.

PART SIX: LIVING LIFE FROM THE THIRD HEAVEN

> It wasn't so long ago that you were mired in that old stagnant life of sin. You let the world, which doesn't know the first thing about living, tell you how to live. You filled your lungs with polluted unbelief, and then exhaled disobedience. We all did it, all of us doing what we felt like doing, when we felt like doing it, all of us in the same boat. It's a wonder God didn't lose his temper and do away with the whole lot of us. Instead, immense in mercy and with an incredible love, he embraced us. He took our sin-dead lives and made us alive in Christ. He did all this on his own, with no help from us! Then he picked us up and set us down in highest heaven in company with Jesus, our Messiah. (Eph 2:1–6, MSG)

This passage reminds us that the embrace of our Savior *is* the highest heaven, our true home. "He took our sin-dead lives and made us alive in Christ. He did all this on his own, with no help from us." The startling conclusion is that, because Christ died and rose for all of us, and because we died and rose with him, every single human being is in heaven with Christ at this moment by grace alone. Faith and belief (as Ephesians itself says before and after this core passage) are only participations in this great truth. Living with resurrection assurance points us to our creation in Christ. To say it another way, Easter is a revelatory harbinger of our Genesis 1 humanity.

We began the book with Julian's idea that Jesus is our heaven. To be in Christ is to be at home in heaven. In our paradigm, we delineated three realms of heaven, where paradise is synonymous with the third heaven. Paradise is just as real here as it is there. But here in the first heaven, paradise is not all there is.[7] In other words, Jesus's presence with us is consistent, whether in the first, second, or third heaven. And yet, it is only the third that is devoid of the conflicting red, the anti-Christ dissociative fugue that plagues us.

The intimacy of home is a constant, albeit hidden and imperfectly disclosed, reality of human existence. Illumination of the Spirit here in the first heaven bolsters us with the knowledge that we are home before we start. Regardless of our differing levels of awareness here, Jesus attests that home is a reality that we will see clearly in the second heaven, "on that day you will *realize* that I am in the Father, and you are in me, and I am in you"

7. Everyone is already in paradise by means of being in Christ and at home in the Trinity. Even in the first heaven we are "in" and yet "not in." Second-heaven clarity, then, precedes one's going from "in/not in" (straddling the dimensions, so to speak) to "in/in" (nothing but in). There is no rational way to explain someone refusing the repentance that is theirs in Christ, because everyone has been "in" the third heaven from creation on and the word of God is in them, in their mouth and in their heart, such that they might confess that Jesus is Lord (Rom 10:8).

(John 14:20, emphasis added). Jesus says that because of the Holy Spirit's presence here in us and with us, he (Christ) is also present, and he and his Father "make our home" with us here in ways that point to this hidden reality (John 14:23). The persons of the Trinity "making home" with us does not mean we do not already have a home, or that we are not already home, any more than human beings making love means that love is not already present. Second and third heaven are unveilings of the home life all human beings enjoy. In the first heaven, it is not paradise that we seek to attain, but the final opportunity to repent and be rid of all that does not fit in paradise. Here in the first heaven, however, we as true sheep in the shepherd's fold must contend with the robber who seeks to violate our home in Christ and to steal, kill, and destroy (John 10:10).

The question is at hand: Under the judgment of our Creator-Redeemer, the one who knows us the best and loves us the most, will we be ready to be shown who we are and who God is? When we stand at the threshold of the unadulterated kingdom of God, will we be ready to let go of everything that Jesus Christ, "the Gate," asks us to release? Perhaps we have "identified" as this or that in this world. If Jesus says, "these ways in which you have identified are not your true identity; they are not congruent with the way I created you as my beloved child," can you leave them at the door? Or if Jesus says, "In the world, you have done what only I can do—judge others—and even worse, you have used my Scriptures to do it. Your use of the Bible to bash others who have identified in certain ways is pure idolatry. Please leave the Bible at the door and come to me, the living word of God who inspired the truth therein." When it comes to Jesus's flesh, perhaps we will still have misguided (misogynistic) ideas of God as a man. Past our tendency to project Jesus's flesh, and ours, into the highest heavens, are we ready to recognize the oneness of the Holy Spirit and the Spirit of Christ? In light of the judgment, we must realize the ways in which the religious good can be the enemy of the righteous best. In raising Lazarus from the dead, Jesus said to the bystanders, "take off the grave clothes and let him go" (John 11:44). Will we fight to keep on what Jesus considers to be our grave clothes? Or will we be able to receive God's judgment, the discriminating judgment of the cross, as our deliverance?

We cannot have our false selves and proceed into the unadulterated heaven—they will not fit through the gate. Recalling our earlier illustration, the horizontal lines (our "red" false selves) certainly will not fit through, but neither will the diagonal lines (grey), since they represent a compromised composite of the vertical (green) with the horizontal (red). Jesus asks us to "enter through the narrow gate" (Matt 7:13). If we are "sideways" with others, holding on to our false selves with our superiority, bitterness, jealousy, and the like, we will be stymied at the door of grace. It will be a tearful blessing to come face-to-face in reconciliation with Christ and others, all affected in the first heaven by each others' actions. This reconciliation (between human beings) is an important aspect that happens along with our Doubting Thomas encounter, the reconciliation of our relationship with God.

Our relationship with God is primary. Thankfully, God does not need to be reconciled to us, only us to him.[8] But on the human-to-human level, reconciliation goes both ways. The restoration of all estranged friendships between human beings flows from our reconciliation to God. They are distinct but inseparable aspects. Victory cannot be a true victory without perfect fulfillment on both fronts, reconciliation with God and with one another.[9]

After the Doubting Thomas episode in the Gospel of John, we have the story of Jesus breaking bread with the disciples (John 21:9). After the trauma they have been through, it is hard to imagine this group of followers being able to avoid relational fractures. But at the communion table we can anticipate reconciliation in all its aspects. "We cannot love God unless we love each other," remarks Dorothy Day, "and to love we must know each other. We know him in the breaking of bread, and we know each other in the breaking of bread, and we are not alone any more.... We have all known the long loneliness and we have learned that the only solution is love and that love comes with community."[10]

To the extent that we taste good things here in the first heaven, we are merely getting glimpses of the third: "Every good and perfect gift is from

---

8. This can be a confusing concept. It is important to go around the circle of analogy in the right direction. Even if two parties are at odds with each other in purely human terms, that should not be projected onto our relationship with God, as if each party were at odds with each other. Scripture never says that God needs to be reconciled to us, only us to God.

9. However long this second-heaven realm is, God's patience could perhaps allow for people to "work through" issues in constructive ways. I spoke above of Christ's forty days post-resurrection as a glimpse into the second heaven. I see Jesus's words to his disciples (representing a microcosm of all humanity) as referring to their own working through the command to forgive and be forgiven, as has been revealed in the true humanity of Jesus: "As the Father has sent me, I am sending you." And with that he breathed on them and said, "Receive the Holy Spirit. If you forgive anyone their sins, their sins are forgiven; if you do not forgive them, they are not forgiven" (John 20:21–23). As with the Lord's prayer, to not forgive is to refuse to live in the kingdom economy. We are meant to do it here in the world, because it is an actual part of the second heaven: "on earth as it is in heaven."

10. Day, *Reckless*, 120.

above" (Jas 1:17). That is why Dorothy Day said, "Heaven is a banquet and life is a banquet, too, even with a crust, where there is companionship."[11]

It is not only impossible, then, but foolish also to try to avoid the judgment, since it is here at the cross that everything impure, every evil and corruption, is cut away and removed. To avoid judgment is to avoid our intimate identification with Jesus on the cross. Nevertheless, we must remember that these three heavenly dimensions are *theological* locations. They are all "heaven," as determined by Jesus's presence in all three, and they are all distinct because, apart from Jesus's consistent presence, our participation and existence in them differs. The environment of the first heaven is marked by confusion and contradiction, the second heaven is marked by contradiction and perfect clarity, and the third heaven is distinguished by clarity with no contradiction at all; it is unadulterated paradise.

From the third heaven side of things, the Spirit enables us to look back through the sequence and asymmetry provided by the judgment of the second heaven. Armed with the victory of the cross over sin, death, and the devil, the third-heaven Spirit-confidence breaks the logjam of the simultaneity. Therefore, for those of us living in the first heaven, the interpretive key involves seeing not only through the grey simultaneity to the victory, but looking back *from* that victory and into the simultaneity. This is the only way that Jesus's past-tense conclusion can be explained, "in this world you will have trouble. But take heart! I *have overcome* the world" (John 16:33, emphasis added). The three dimensions of heaven are simultaneous and not sequential, even if we must describe them sequentially in order to grasp them. To the extent that we can work backwards in theology, we will find that the third heaven is, in fact, the true state of things before our first-heaven existence even began. Jesus is our heaven before, during, and after the fall. We will always in one sense be at home in him. The idea of coming home has never been sweeter.

---

11. Day, *Reckless*, 120. Our new retreat and study center called "The Glen" in Durham, North Carolina, has been influenced by Day and by most of the authors, theologians, and practitioners cited in these books. The Glen is hosted by a co-housing community of all kinds of people, and the hospitality of those who abide there, along with practical theological discussion, is meant to provide the means by which the gospel can be not only taught but caught. See experiencereality.org.

79

Reconciliation as Remembering Friends

(The scene after Judas's death in Ray Anderson's *The Gospel According to Judas*.)

Judas to Jesus: *You will probably tell me that you still love me. . . . Don't you realize that for the betrayer, love is a cruel reminder of failure?*

Jesus to Judas: *I tell you that you love Me, and that is the cause of your pain and torment.*

Judas: *You're talking nonsense. If I loved You I would not have betrayed You. After all, betrayal is not an act of love, it's an act of treachery.*

Jesus: *Judas, betrayal is the sin of love against love. Unlike other sins, betrayal uses love to destroy what is loved. This is why betrayal does not end a relationship, why you cannot put an end to our relationship by yourself. Forgiveness for the act of betrayal seems impossible if betrayal is the final act. Yet betrayal is not the end of love. You hate yourself because you love Me. You betrayed me because you love Me.*

THAT JESUS LOVES HIS enemies (all of us) reveals something incredible. It is this: that we are his friends first, his friends before we could ever be his enemies.[1] In a similar way, we all have enemies in this world. Some even

---

1. See *CD* I/1, 409–10. Because the positive always precedes the negative, the true before the false, one simply cannot be an enemy unless they are a friend first. The truth of this friendship does not recede. Even as a fallen human being at enmity with God, the person is still the original human being at peace with God.

are within our biological or nuclear families. Some we are estranged from. Some have died, and our enmity toward them lives on in our hearts. That is why the second heaven is so important for understanding the reconciliation of all things in Christ. Not only will we be able to celebrate the reality of our restored relationship with God, we will also have the chance for meaningful interaction with others from whom we are estranged on the personal level.

It is common for believers to claim that God will "make things right" in the end. Given how few people espouse a traditional understanding of providence, the use of such a phrase is curious. It certainly cannot mean that bad things are good in the end, as if God makes bad things good. Neither does it mean that wrongs against us are caused by God (who is always right). To say that God brings good out of bad does not mean that bad things are good. Making things right has everything to do with our placemat duality. Its genesis is the undeviating rightness that exists between us, God, and one another. Starting with this reality, the deviance can be addressed and we can welcome the opportunity to come clean. When confronted by our mess, we can confess it and disavow it, participating with God in his putting-to-rights the wrongs of this world.

As Archbishop Desmond Tutu writes in *No Future Without Forgiveness*, this approach protects us not only from retributive justice but also from blanket amnesty:

> Forgiving and being reconciled are not about pretending.... It is not patting one another on the back and turning a blind eye to the wrong. True reconciliation exposes the awfulness, the abuse, the pain, the degradation.... It is a risky undertaking but in the end it is worthwhile, because in the end dealing with the real situation helps to bring real healing. Spurious reconciliation can only bring spurious healing.[2]

Christ's attitude toward us never changes. It is our twisted attitude in this world that needs adjusting. But even if necessary, it feels complicated. The complexities of making things right, one creature to another, seems overwhelming. Does God really expect me to enter back into that mess? Not in this world perhaps. However, we can say with confidence that the second heaven is a perfectly safe place. It is not like the "reconciliation" scenarios between perpetrators and victims here in the first heaven, fraught as they are with the possibilities of re-victimization in the rare instances that reconciliation is pursued at all. In the second heaven, there is no chance for re-traumatizing, only repentance and the catharsis that comes from it.

---

2. Tutu, *No Future Without Forgiveness*, 270–71.

PART SIX: LIVING LIFE FROM THE THIRD HEAVEN

I recognize the legitimate revulsion that might accompany any sort of cheap fix that has the rapist and the victim "holding hands" in the heavens. But what love requires is no light matter, whether in the contradiction of the first heaven or the contradiction and clarity of the second. Dorothy Day expounds, "'Love your enemies.' That is the hardest saying of all. . . . It is a terrible thought—I really only love God as much as the person I love the least" (her paraphrase of 1 John 4:20).[3] God will not be satisfied until our love for God and our love for neighbor are of a piece.

As victims, we need not worry that letting go of the vindictive hatred means letting go of the gravity of the offense. Perpetrators will know that what they have done to other human beings they have done first and foremost to Christ. And victims will know that whatever has been done to them was done first and foremost to Christ. In this central role of Jesus Christ, we are drawn in, claimed, and pressed toward the reconciliation with God and neighbor that he accomplished. If we are all victims before we are perpetrators, if Christ is the "primary victim" and Satan is first and foremost "[Christ's] enemy," then there is also an often-overlooked bond in Christ between all human beings and against a common enemy.

"Humans are neighbors by nature rather than by potential," says Stephanie Mar Brettmann in her analysis of Barth's doctrine of reconciliation. "For Barth, it is not a matter of choosing to become neighbors, for human persons have been reconciled in Christ as neighbors. Therefore . . . the material reality that all human beings are neighbors constitutes a moral demand upon all persons, Christian or Jew or Muslim, whether or not they recognize this reality."[4] Apart from this preexisting reality, social reconciliation would always be a bridge too far in the first heaven. Brettmann, however, points to the limited success of the Truth and Reconciliation Commission in South Africa: "Tutu argued that social reconciliation is possible because of the reality of co-humanity. In defending himself against the critics who believed that reconciliation between the victims of apartheid and their abusers was not just, he argued to the contrary, that reconciliation was the expression of true justice, of real humanity."[5]

---

3. Day, *Reckless*, 36.

4. Brettmann, *Theories of Justice*, 200. Brettmann promotes Barth's concept of "co-humanity"—where "one's own identity and personhood is wrapped up in the personhood of the other and the dehumanization of the other dehumanizes oneself"—as a way forward for people of all backgrounds: "This anthropological conception of personhood creates a greater incentive of self-interest for non-Christian persons to behave with justice; it creates an immediate ethical obligation when encountering another person; and it can be adopted and demonstrated by Christian and non-Christian alike" (204).

5. Brettmann, *Theories of Justice*, 202.

Christians do well to recognize their unity with all human beings in Christ and in sin before they allow the "Christian" label the false depth of an ontological separation with others. Because they love other people imperfectly and inconsistently, Christians are always, according to Barth, also "non-Christians." He continues:

> As the friends of God they are also His enemies, as believers godless. If they are aware and sure of the fact that God has loved them as such, they must also be aware and sure of this fact in respect of others too. Their decisive presupposition in respect of every man can be only that Jesus Christ has died for his sin too, and for his salvation. They must regard and approach every man from this angle . . . not just theoretically, but practically.[6]

Did Judas love Jesus? Yes and no. Do we love Jesus? Yes and no. Do we love our enemies? Yes and no. The first answer is the reality, the second the inconsistency, or seeming inability, of the experiential to match the actual. For the moments where the truth in Christ matches our lived experience, miracle is not too strong a word. Such experiences come from above. Some things that (for whatever reason) cannot happen in the first heaven "have time" to manifest in the second. Whenever it happens, as Dorothy Day relates, such an act is beyond merely human capacity: "Please, Father in heaven who made me, take away my heart of stone and give me a heart of flesh to love my enemy."[7]

The "heart of flesh" (Ezek 36:26) that Day asks of God is variously translated as "pure heart," "responsive heart," and "obedient heart." In placemat terms it is the green heart. She asks that the red heart be taken away. It is clear that she has not fallen prey to the faulty notion of a heart replacement, as if she had a transplant (red heart out; green heart in) at the moment of her conversion. Rather, she knows that she has a true heart for God and others (green), even if she still has a heart of stone (red). Like the prayer of the man before Jesus in Mark 9:24, "I do believe; help me overcome my unbelief," Day's prayer speaks not to the arrival of the green heart, but to the departure of the red. Again, she does not ask for a replacement heart, as in a one-for-one exchange, but implicitly acknowledges two hearts. It is the one of stone that needs removing, so that the life and love of the natural heart can operate freely.

Replacement anthropology, as opposed to placemat anthropology, takes us back to the "old is gone, new has come" misinterpretation of 2 Corinthians 5:17. Even the Hebrew of Ezekiel 36:26 demonstrates that this does

---

6. *CD* III/4, 503.
7. Day, *Reckless*, 36.

not, and *never* did, point to a replacement of the old for the new. Instead, it speaks of a removal of the old.[8] The verse speaks of us receiving a new heart and a new spirit in the context of restoration not replacement. Here, new is the new aspect of the true, fresh green. It is about cleansing and renewing, not redoing.[9] But to say that the heart is naturally green does not mean that we can move the boulder of the old heart ourselves, even in the second heaven. This requires God's grace and the Spirit who raised Christ from the dead.

In the second heaven we might find that we "have the heart" to do what we will not or cannot do here in the world. We might discover, by the Spirit, an ability to act out of our true heart. Henri Nouwen seems to touch on this in what he says about our true heart in relation to God and our neighbor: "Now the beautiful thing about the heart is that the heart is the place where we are most ourselves . . . the spiritual center of our being . . . the most intimate place. . . . One of the most amazing things is that if you enter deeper and deeper into that place, you not only meet God, but you meet the whole world."[10]

Can we in the first heaven put off forgiveness and reconciliation until later? Such a delay might be unavoidable, however an approach of "the sooner the better" might be a healthier one. Once we realize that God making all things right and new involves all of us being right with one another, once we realize the underlying dynamics of the two totals, the existential and experiential moments in this world are packed with transformational meaning. The stakes are higher than a zero-sum framework can provide. There is more to be gained in every situation and more to be lost, the content of which can only be revealed by what's underneath—the ontological reality of our existential situation. When we see a lack of forgiveness in the second-heaven context, for example, we will be much quicker to recognize its detrimental, counterproductive nature, and how it does not belong. Again, the sooner the better.

---

8. The word "replace" is in some English translations, which is a massive error. Replace is not the word but "give," "give you a heart of flesh," i.e., to operate out of it (in the "new," revelatory sense). Removal of the old, and not a replacement of the old, is in view in some translations of Ezek 36:26, among others: "A new heart also will I give you, and a new spirit will I put within you: and I will take away the stony heart *out of your flesh*, and I will give you a heart of flesh" (ERV, emphasis added). Red removed from green leaves green alone. See also Ezek 11:19, where the same phrase occurs and where translations often include the false sense of an exchange or replacement instead of a *renewing removal* of the hard heart.

9. This is also the gist of Ps 51, especially vv. 10–12.

10. Nouwen "Your Heart," para. 1.

The revelation of clarity in the second heaven will give us an extra measure of compassion for those who have wounded us. In this world we are woefully unaware of the many layers of personal and generational trauma that underlie our existence. Scientific studies show that trauma can even alter our genetic makeup (see "Evil with a Capital E" in Book One). In the second heaven, we will see clearly that people are victims before they are perpetrators.[11] Perpetrators hurt others because they have been hurt.

Every time we are hurt by another, it feeds our false self. Some aspect of the web of lies and self-deceit within are nourished. We are not in touch with the deep-seated bitterness and resentment caused by traumas great and small, but we can see the ways they work themselves out. If Pentecost represents the unity of the third heaven, Babel represents the enmity of the first. Only by the Spirit can we live in the truth, or as Thomas Merton would say, live "without asserting your false self against the false selves of others."[12] Yet none of us, even in the second heaven, can turn a wrong into a right. That is not what "making things right" means for us or for God. Instead, we recognize that things are right before they are wrong and that, as the wrong is pulled away from all of us, we can see the evil one's ploy.

It is Satan who has been God's enemy from the beginning and our enemy all along. He is strong—strong enough to twist friends into enemies. One thing he cannot do, however, is destroy the friend dimension of the true relationship. This friend dimension is what Willie Jennings has called the "communal metaphysic" of human, creaturely being—the "sinews of our connection." By ignoring this "enmeshment," Jennings says, individualism has co-opted friendship into a one-on-one enterprise—merely individuals connecting with other individuals. This ignores the "already" aspect of mutual connection.[13] "But," as Jennings relates, "friendships form on a social fabric before they create a fabric, and it is that social fabric that deserves much more attention and reflection . . . for the ways it has been deformed—creating the allusion that we are only connected by chance."[14]

---

11. Again, this is a theological statement about which came first, not an attempt to in any way blur the lines between victim and perpetrator in specific first-heaven situations.

12. Merton, *New Seeds*, 101.

13. Jennings, *After Whiteness*, 146.

14. Jennings, *After Whiteness*, 147. If you are not familiar with the context in Jennings's book, this first phrase might read like a misquote: "friendships form on a social fabric before they create a fabric." If our western minds tempt us to read the sentence as "friendships form on a *social level* before they create a fabric," then we are reading precisely the opposite of what Jennings intends!

PART SIX: LIVING LIFE FROM THE THIRD HEAVEN

The same God who creates us in "intimacy, communication, reciprocity, and mutuality" recreates us. In so doing, Jennings points to "the original trajectory" of the God of gathering, the one who "has ended hostility and has drawn all of creation into a reconciliation that we do not control." In other words, we do not control it, because it simply *is*. Individuals cannot effect or affect reconciliation any more than they can effect or affect creation. Jennings concludes: "God offers us an uncontrollable reconciliation . . . reforming us as those who enact gathering and who gesture communion with our very existence."[15] As grace beckons us to confession, so the reality of reconciliation beckons us to press into experientially living it out. This is what it looks like to be an "eschatological activist."

The statement that we are all God's friends (and therefore friends with each other) before we are God's enemies is a theological statement. It does not seem like this is the case in the world, even if it is true theologically.[16] It is what makes war, for example, so insidious, because at bottom we are killing our friends and family. This truth was never more clear than when Judas betrayed Jesus with a kiss, only to be met by the Savior's greeting calling him "*friend*" (Matt 26:50).

Jesus's words cut Judas to the quick. Perhaps in that moment, flashing across his mind, was a remembrance of his years-long relationship with Jesus, his true friendship. Perhaps this conscious thought connected into his unconscious remembrance of something even deeper. Perhaps, as "deep called to deep" (see Ps 42:7), there was a sense in Judas's heart not only of the intimate years of wandering Galilee with Jesus, but of the ontological friendship that he shared with Jesus from creation on. This kind of cascading contrast must have been more than Judas could live with. There may be moments for all of us when, in betraying Jesus, we wish we "had not been born" (Mark 14:21). As Thomas Merton describes, our identity is thankfully much deeper than how we are born: "To say I was born in sin is to say I came into the world with a false self. I was born in a mask . . . under a sign of contradiction, being someone that I was never intended to be and therefore a denial of what I am supposed to be . . . as long as I am no longer anybody else than the thing that was born of my mother . . . it were better for me that I had not been born."[17]

Shortly after Judas's decision to betray Jesus is exposed at the supper table, and shortly after the disciples sang a hymn before leaving the upper

---

15. Jennings, *After Whiteness*, 152.

16. We are Jesus's friends (see John 15:13) and his enemies (Rom 5:10), the first before the second.

17. Merton, *New Seeds*, 33–34.

room, Jesus predicted that *all* the disciples would fall away and deny him. They would scatter like sheep when the Shepherd was stricken (Mark 14:27, a prophecy from Zech 13:7). It should not be a surprise when we deny Jesus since, as Merton relates, there is a self-denial already going on in all of us. If all of us are Judas or, more palatably, if all of us have a "Judas-self," then just as surely will we hear Jesus's words of affirmation and friendship—even amidst our animosity to God. Unlike in Judas's first-heaven experience, however, shame and guilt have no more traction in the second heaven. Within the context of Judas's belonging and the sustainability of his true, unmasked, nature as Jesus's friend, can you imagine Judas forgoing his self-destructive shame and trading it for contrition and catharsis at judgment day? If so, is there anyone you cannot imagine doing the same?

If that kind of transformation *can happen* on the Day, our hope is that a semblance of such *will happen* now, in this world, even when it comes to "those we are tempted to write off."[18] And even if it does not, we can maintain the larger hope of the second heaven. On that day, the law of the truth of Christ and reconciliation between human beings in him will be fully manifest. Then, there will be no getting around it.

---

18. In *Justice Calling*, 183, Hoang and Johnson share their hope for a sex-trafficker: "Personally, I long for the day when we might hear the story of how, under the restraint of the law, Mala's trafficker and many others like him encountered the limitless grace of God in Christ, repented of the horrific violence brought on scores of young girls, and shared a wealth of underground intelligence to bring down trafficking rings all over India and the rest of the world. We need to remind and teach one another to hope and long for the day when we might stand side by side with even those we are tempted to write off as most evil and beyond hope in this world, receiving new life and wholeness and freedom together in Jesus Christ."

80

Nothing but Green

It seems to me that we greatly need the discriminatory powers that Jesus offers to his harvesters.
—Clarence Jordan

This is radical discipleship . . . to press into what we already have. . . . Our identity as children of God is not something of which we can convince ourselves. It is the jurisdiction of the Holy Spirit.
—Julie Canlis

THE SECOND HEAVEN, OR judgment day, is described by Paul in 1 Corinthians 13, "when perfection comes, the imperfect disappears. . . . Now I know in part; then I shall know fully, even I am fully known" (v. 10, 12). While unable to see the perfect green for the grey of this world, we only bear relative witness to the reality to be revealed, the relational reality of that face-to-face encounter. By "relative witness" we mean that our lives will be imperfect witnesses, in some ways congruent to the truth, in other ways incongruent, while living here in the first heaven. In the second heaven, we shall see Christ and ourselves clearly for the first time since Genesis 1. Taking it a step further, believers can welcome the fact that the second-heaven encounter will be one not only of recognition but also of judgment. In a state of worshipful anticipation for the other side of the gate, we can get on with living our lives from the vision of the third heaven. Practicing the "then" in the "now," we can "throw off everything that hinders and the sin which so easily entangles, and run with perseverance the race marked out for us, looking to Jesus, the author and perfector of faith" (Heb 12:1–2).

We can never get too far away from the fact that the three heavens concept is incoherent without a christological interpretation. Of Christ, Colossians 1:16–17 states, "For in him all things were created: things in heaven and on earth, visible and invisible . . . all things have been created through him and for him. He is before all things, and in him all things hold together." Christ is not only the creator, he is also the archetype of creation as well as the first and definitive human being.[1] Jesus Christ is humanity in himself, humanity before, during, and after the fall. Christ is described in Colossians 1:15 as the "firstborn of all creation" (the Elect and Original Adam) and "the firstborn of the living from among the dead" (the Second Adam).

Jesus Christ is the True Israelite. When it comes to keeping covenant with Yahweh, he bears perfect witness not only to God's chosen people Israel, but also to all humanity chosen in him. As the human being in whom we are created and redeemed, Jesus Christ is thus in two ways what Barth calls the "spearhead" of humanity. First, "He is the creature in whom the divine election of grace is already made. . . . Among all other men and all other creatures He is the penetrating spearhead of the will of God their Creator: penetrating because in Him the will of God is already fulfilled and revealed, and the purpose of God for all men and creatures has thus reached its goal."[2] Second, "Jesus is the penetrating spearhead . . . by whom the enemy of being has been slain and the freedom of being attained. He alone is the archetypal man whom all threatened and enslaved men and creatures must follow."[3]

Note the strong "already" emphasis in Barth's language, based on "the divine fore-ordination" and the predestined unity of God and humanity from the time of creation, and even before. This Adam, Jesus Christ, is the One, the prototype, in whose image all subsequent creatures were created as beloved children of God (Rom 8:29, "For those God foreknew

---

1. As we have said throughout our study, Jesus Christ, Son of God, is also the first, preeminent creature. To say he is the "first born of all creation" is therefore not to demur from the Nicene statement "begotten not made," as if "first born" refers only to his birth in Bethlehem, but it can mean that Jesus Christ in his humanity was both created and born. Even if "first born" is primarily referring to Jesus's archetypal perfect humanity, to leave out Jesus's birth entirely would be to miss the first-heaven dimension of Paul's symmetry in Col 1: "firstborn of all creation" (1:15) and the "firstborn from among the dead" (1:18).

2. *CD* III/2, 143.

3. *CD* III/2, 145.

he also predestined to be conformed to the image of his Son, that he might be the firstborn among many brothers and sisters"). In Romans 5, another primary source for the archetypal Christ, the original, un-fallen Adam is not mentioned directly. Instead, he is implied in Paul's recognition of the fallen Adam (the implicit reverse of fallen is unfallen). Thus, understanding humanity requires that we view Christ's humanity (and therefore ours) through a theological prism from redemption to creation, starting from God's revelation of the Second Adam back through to Fallen Adam and on to the Original and Elect Adam.[4]

We return to the fact that Jesus Christ is by nature the Son of God and the image of God. These aspects of Jesus Christ are intrinsic to his divinity, with no *necessary* connection to humanity.[5] Even if the Son of God's prism is more complex than that of humanity, in tracing the four Adams, humanity's prism emerges. The humanity of God establishes that humanity in Christ is in God as

- elected (green)
- created (green)
- fallen (red)
- rescued and redeemed (green)

Translating these four Adams into placemat terms, only one of them is "red," buried in the middle of the others, bracketed on all sides by the green. With the fallen Adam as the exception to the rule of a green dimensional framework, it does not seem that red has a fighting chance to define humanity. And yet for the sake of God's beloved, it took the death of God's only Son to eradicate the red challenger. That is how strong evil is and how seriously God takes it. That is how strong the anti-Christ dimension of corrupt humanity is and the evil from which it derives.

---

4. I have capitalized the adjectives for Adam (e.g., Elected and Original Adam) in this reading when primarily referring to Jesus Christ and the christological prism. Only derivatively is humanity elected and original Adam. By original Adam we mean both the humanity of God and true humanity, the first logically primary to the second, and therefore sometimes designated as Elected Adam in distinction from Original Adam.

5. Note how Barth (CD III/1, 204) recognizes Christ's uniqueness as firstborn, while holding together Christ's representative unity with humanity, a freely undertaken union (i.e., by grace and not of necessity): "What he is in Himself He is not to be for Himself alone. He is to be the Firstborn among many brethren, among many who are like Him. God's will for Him from the very outset, as the will of Him who had created Him in his image, aimed also at these His future brethren. Who are these brethren of whom God thought simultaneously with His Son, who for His sake are as precious to Him as the latter Himself, who He wills to liken to His Son without detriment to His uniqueness?"

If we remember our principle of transposition, the higher order can become all that the lower orders are and remain itself. God is above humanity in the chain of being, and because humanity is of a lower order, this transposition cannot be reversed. Humanity cannot affect the fundamental identity of God, conflating itself with God, any more than the *sarx* of fallen humanity can corrupt the original identity of humanity. The higher aspect of the "sacred order" is never beholden to the lower. We might say, then, that if elected Adam has to do with the God of humanity, then created Adam has to do with the humanity of God, and fallen Adam has to do with the curse upon the humanity of God. This allows us to trace from the Second Adam the thread of the one who is the same subject in all aspects.[6]

In this sense (Christ assuming both unfallen and fallen flesh), the incarnation is two-fold, not unlike the subsequent, two-fold relationship of Genesis 1 and 2. Jesus Christ is the first born human, and by the Creator stepping into time and space and becoming a creature, Christ is therefore the logically primary, first material human being. He steps into time, which is not yet fallen time, and takes on the paradigmatic pristine flesh of the spiritual-material human body. In a similar way, Jesus Christ is also the redeeming Adam who steps into the fall, taking on corrupt and corruptible humanity. This is the second aspect of the singular, two-fold incarnation, which is also a two-fold humiliation. The first humiliation is that of the Creator lowering himself to become a creature (Phil 2:6–7), and the second is God lowering himself further still, not only becoming a human being but becoming a corrupt and fallen human being, lowering himself even to "death on a cross" (Phil 2:8). This is the two-fold incarnation described in the Philippians 2 hymn.[7]

---

6. Might we also say, then, that in his humanity Jesus Christ is also *homoiousios* ("of like being") with the Father? How could this be, without reopening the christological controversy that ensued when Arius claimed that Jesus Christ was *homoiousios* with the Father (instead of *homoousios*, as the Nicene Creed concludes)? It seems apparent that Arius's mistake was not in his conviction that Christ was *homoiousios*, but in his refusal to recognize Christ as *homoousios*. Jesus Christ, Son of God, can be *homoousios* with God as the *imago Dei* (2 Cor 4:4), and *homoiousios* with God as the creature derived from the image and likeness (as in 1 Cor 11:7). The other passage exalting Christ as the image, Col 1:15, could be seen in its inner-sequence, portraying Christ as two sides of the one image, one divine (*homoosious*, "the image of the invisible God"), and one human (*homoiousios*, "the first born of all creatures"). According to the rules of transposition, without the *homoousion* there is no incarnation. Without the *homoiousion* there is no humanity. In denying Christ the *homoousion*, Arius ironically denied his own humanity!

7. So can we say that humans are also incarnated? No, only God is spirit (John 4:24). Creatures are always spiritual-material beings. Thus, there was never a time when humans were *not* incarnate. Technically, then, incarnation in the gospel sense is

PART SIX: LIVING LIFE FROM THE THIRD HEAVEN

Central to the Philippian hymn is the description of Christ as "servant" (2:7) and we remember from Book One ("The Righteous and the Wicked") how Julian employed the word "servant" to describe Christ's two-fold humiliation in her own prismatic way. She begins with dimensional move number one, from divine to human: "In the servant is comprehended the second person of the Trinity, and in the servant is comprehended Adam, that is to say all men. And therefore when I say 'the Son,' that means the divinity which is equal to the Father, and when I say 'the servant' that means Christ's humanity, which is the true Adam."[8] Then, she pivots to dimensional move number two, from true human to false human. Note how Julian parses the dimensions of "the servant," showing Christ's solidarity with fallen humanity and at the same time showing how Christ as true humanity represents the heart of the Father: "And so in *the servant* there was shown the blindness and the hurt of Adam's falling; and in *the servant* there was shown the compassion and pity for Adam's woe."[9] Even as she unfolds the servant duality of Christ's humiliation all the way to "weakness and blindness,"[10] Julian is careful to wrap all of the dimensions back up into the one Jesus Christ: "For in all this our good Lord showed his own Son and Adam as only one man."[11]

---

something only the Creator (who always remains the Creator) can do. As Athanasius reminds us, like cannot save like. Human beings need a real incarnation to happen for there to be a saving difference.

8. Julian, *Showings*, 274.
9. Julian, *Showings*, 280.
10. Julian, *Showings*, 275.

11. Julian, *Showings*, 274. In the Greek the word from Phil 2 translated above as "servant" is technically "slave," its variation being used in Rom 6:19 to designate "slaves of unrighteousness" and "slaves of righteousness." There is a powerful lyric in the English version (1855) of the carol *O Holy Night*: "Chains shall he break for the slave is our brother, and in his name all oppression shall cease." Undoubtedly the humanitarian message was not lost on the translator, John Sullivan Dwight, himself an abolitionist, but the hymn is also remindful of the Phil 2 hymn and the two-fold christological-incarnational truth. In assuming human form, the Son of God became a "slave to righteousness" thereby defining the un-detoured free obedience of all human creatures. This is the humanity designated by Col 1:15 and implied in Rom 5 (the backside of fallen Adam is unfallen Adam). In assuming the depths of our fallen humanity, the Son of God was also a "slave to unrighteousness." This is the Gen 2 Adam, the Rom 5 fallen Adam, and the Adam that Paul begins with in 1 Cor 15 (as we shall see). By entering into the world enslaved to sin, Jesus put himself under not only the mastery of his own flesh but under the oppression of others' flesh. It's because the slave Jesus truly is our human brother in every sense, that in no sense should any brother or sister be treated inhumanely. Chattel slavery represents an insidious evil in American history. Redemption must come by the one who on the cross was in utmost solidarity with both the oppressed slave and the wicked slaver, putting an end to all that was not created.

Failure to recognize the distinctions within the two-fold incarnation can result in a conflation of the First Adam (Fallen) with the Original (Created). Just as critical to maintaining the distinctions within the two-fold aspect is maintaining the unity of the anthropological dimensions. The unity shows just how incomprehensible evil is, since Adam makes the absurdly un-free decision to rebel *against* Christ while he is inseparably united *with* Christ. We see the irrationality of the fall play out in both human history and our own lives.

Because of the fall, we do not have direct access to the christological content and purpose of the Genesis story. Any natural access from Genesis 1 has been forfeited. "Looking back" through our christological prism, however, we can see *how* things started in the *who*. To know the end of the narrative in Christ's resurrection and ascension is to know the beginning. The revelation of Christ teaches us that new creation is creation, properly understood, despite their distinctions in time and space. With our perspective we recognize the first heaven as the first heaven of our experience in a world where, from birth, we are overlapped by red. Thus, creation is really the "*first*-first"—or original—heaven.[12] When God created the heavens and the earth in Genesis 1, not all of what we call the first-heaven existence (human lives of confusion and contradiction) was included.

Like heaven, time is created. God has his own "time," we could say; this is the community of Trinitarian persons outside of created time and space. But in Barth's words, God also makes time for us. We could say that God's created time has within it the "smaller" dimension of fallen time, the time of the first heaven. Echoing Barth, Julian, and others in our study, Robert Jenson points us to Christ the center as the focal point of heaven at any level: Jesus Christ, he says, "is himself the presence of God in heaven; he is what makes it heaven."[13] Jenson continues, "Heaven is where God takes

---

12. This reflects our note at the beginning of the book, which differentiated between the First (fallen) Adam of Rom 5 and the Original (pre-fallen) Adam who is implied.

13. Jenson, *Systematic Theology*, vol. 1, 201. Jenson's work mightily affirms our conviction that we can trust the picture of God that we see in Jesus. His insistence that as God the human being Jesus Christ is not beholden to time and space constrictions, presenting a thoroughgoing christocentrism—the resurrected Christ *is* the crucified Christ *is* the first born of all creatures—is immensely appreciated. However, Jenson's pressing of the Lutheran *communicatio idiomatum* unfortunately allows for just the kind of reversal that our transposition rejects (see "Transposition" in Book One). Without mixing the human nature of Christ and the divine nature, the "communication of properties" insists that whatever is true of the human Son of God is true of the divine Son of God. This leads to a non-Chalcedonian type of reversal: because the *eternal* Son of God became flesh, reasons Jenson, the Son *never exists* without his flesh. On one hand, Barth could affirm the *communicatio*'s sound Chalcedonian refusal to mix properties, but on the other hand the indiscriminate reversal of properties violates

what he called the "hierarchy" or "sacred order" of what is logically primary, even in eternity (*CD* II/1, 317). New Testament scholar Andrew Rillera relates (personal correspondence, August 2020): "The problem is that Jenson does not allow for any reality of the Son/Logos beyond the creature Jesus. There was no time when the Son was not this man. This is a problem because it is either Arian and/adoptionist (if we say 'God' has reality transcendent or 'outside'/'beyond' space-time, but the Son does not) or something like Panentheism (if we deny the above and maintain the full deity of the Son, then this means 'God' as such does not have any reality beyond the man Jesus either, that is, beyond being a creature)." With Athanasius and Barth we can say there was never a time when the Son was not, but there *was* a time when humanity was not. Thus: a) God is the male Jesus of Nazareth, who is "the fullness of the deity [who] lives in bodily form" (Col 2:9), but b) the male Jesus of Nazareth is not God in the same way, such that God is eternally male (as in a reversal). Maintaining the priority of the sacred order, do we have permission to say God was crucified on the cross? Yes, according to the first aspect (a), but expressly not according to the second (b). Barth's sacred order protects against straight equivalences. The *communicatio* is at a loss to separate the eternity of God from the eternity of humanity, the result being that there is no real incarnation (the existence of God separate from humanity is prerequisite to God becoming human). The stakes are heightened when we add the fact that the Son of God took on a corrupt human nature, and even "was made sin." Surely we must agree that God became sin, but sin did not become God. But does Barth, by allowing some theological space for God's incarnational "becoming" (John 1:14), allow too much space? Some with Jenson might be afraid that Barth's sacred order, and the accompanying refusal to allow for the *communicatio*'s reversal, leads to the opposite problem, i.e., it doesn't do enough to guarantee the necessary linkage of a real incarnation. The fear is that this could reintroduce an unknown God behind the back of Jesus Christ, one not *homoousios* with the Father. By protecting against a conflation or confusion between humanity and God, has Barth introduced too much cleavage? Not according to Robin Peterson (*On Reading Karl Barth in South Africa*). To maintain the distinctiveness and the unity between God and humanity in Christ, notes Peterson, Barth implements "dialectical separation and analogical integration" (69). Peterson expounds: "It is necessary, Barth states, when talking about Christ, to discover the '*inner material connexion*' between the divinity of and the humanity in Christ, while not forgetting the 'formal parallelism' (*CD* III/2, 217). Clearly if this connection cannot be made adequately, then Barth fails christologically by not being able to affirm the Incarnation. . . . Thus, although the distinction between the two natures must never be forgotten, the focus must be on the nature of the unity, an understanding of the incarnation. Here Barth introduces the crucial link. Humanity and divinity are not held together by an *analogia entis*, but by an *analogia relationis* (*CD* III/2, 219). It is an analogy of the relationship of love within the inner divine being that is repeated and reflected in the person of Jesus in his being for humanity. . . . This is important. It lays the christological foundations of the analogical method of holding together God and humans that allows the greatest harmony without identity" (72). Different from the *communicatio*, then, it's clear that Chalcedonian language allows the attributes of each nature to be predicated of the one person to whom they refer, even if not predicated of each other (the natures). The emphasis is on the latitude of the single subject, not on a straight bilateral communication of natures. For instance, you can say that Jesus Christ is both God and human (Jesus Christ is God; Jesus Christ is human), but just because you can say both does not mean that both are *always* true of each other. For more on Jenson's unapologetic perspective see "Radicalising of the Communicatio," 131–40.

space in his creation to be present to the whole of it."[14] If heaven is the created space or "accommodation" (Jenson's word) that God makes for himself to be relationally present to all of his creatures, then we can legitimately say (as strange as it may sound) that there is never a time when God is in heaven without humanity.[15]

This returns us to the idea that "all the Then is in the Now but not all of the Now is in the Then." We used the word "Then" to mean the eschatological future, the unadulterated dimension beyond the mirror. But fascinatingly, the same word ("Then") can also mean the past—as in, what life was like "then." This maps well on to our theme, for the Then of the third heaven is the same reality as the Then of the original heaven that God created in Genesis 1. Thus, whether we want to go backward (to creation) or forward (to the eschaton), the same logic holds. All the Then is in the Now, but not all of the Now is in the Then.

We will discuss how time and space relate to eternity in upcoming readings, but we must first elaborate on the above. The resurrection, or human re-creation, is a sign that points to creation itself. When it comes to Christ's resurrection body, we could say that all of Easter is in Good Friday, even if all of Good Friday "will not fit" into Easter. Like a nesting box, we can also position the third heaven as sequentially beyond Easter. This allows us to keep all post crucifixion events on the temporal-historical timeline within that liminal boundary between second and third heaven. There in that in-between space, revelation is plentiful, even if not perfectly received.[16]

---

14. Jenson, *Systematic Theology*, vol. 1, 206.

15. This also allows us to say, in a way that Jenson himself may not agree, that God, as the Creator of heaven, exists prior to it.

16. While Easter and the ensuing forty days point toward the unadulterated sphere, I want to be careful not to conflate this time with the third heaven. Jesus's body is undoubtedly different, but others' bodies are the same, and there are still problems in the environment. Instead of projecting the forty days into the third heaven, then, the forty days are an entrance of sorts to the in-between realm of the second heaven, where we all meet the resurrected Lord. Aforementioned features related to the second heaven are already found here, including increased clarity that involves recognition and remembrance (e.g., some disciples worship, some still doubt, Matt 28:17; Jesus chides disciples for their lack of belief and stubborn refusal to believe without seeing, Mark 16:14; at the tomb, Luke 24:1–8; during and after the Emmaus road, Luke 24:13–49; Mary's reunion in the garden, John 20:1–18; disciples recognizing Jesus while fishing, John 21:7ff), reconciliation between Jesus and humans (e.g., disciples worship Jesus, clasping his feet, Matt 28:8–9; the Doubting Thomas encounter, John 20:24–29; the reinstatement of Peter, John 21:15ff), and reconciliation between human beings (e.g., John 20:21–23, Jesus tells the disciples, and by implication all human beings, to reconcile with others in correlation to reality).

PART SIX: LIVING LIFE FROM THE THIRD HEAVEN

We have already established that all of Genesis 1 is in Genesis 2–3, even if all of Genesis 2–3 will not fit back into Genesis 1. The two ends, the third heaven and the original heaven, are of the "same stuff." They are both unadulterated. It is this unadulterated dimension that runs through the first heaven (our current existence). Using Genesis as a template for human existence, we might add to our earlier framework:

First-first/original heaven: clarity and no contradiction (Gen 1)

Boundary 1: Gen 2:4

First heaven: contradiction and confusion (and relative clarity) (Gen 1–3)

Second heaven (Boundary 2): contradiction and perfect clarity (Gen 3:24)

Third heaven: no contradiction and clarity (Rev 22 and Gen 1)

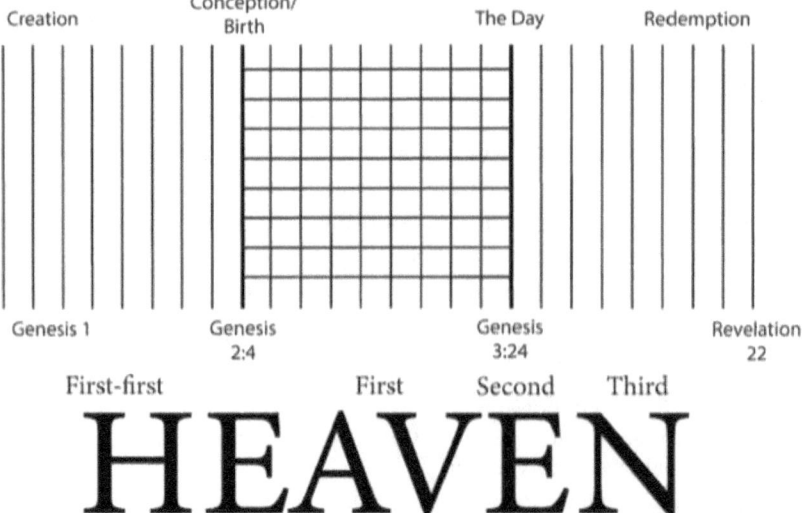

When we see ourselves as nothing but green, we see our true selves. To know ourselves and others as green because of the cross is also to know ourselves as green before the damage of the fall. In between the fall and judgment day, we are fully green, even though also fully red. Because we have no direct access to our green identity, we must trust Jesus's statement to his disciples before the cross, "you are already clean because of the word I have spoken unto you" (John 15:3). "Because of who I am," Jesus says, "you are clean."[17]

---

17. In anticipation of our discussion of "redemptive suffering," Frederick Dale

The Greek for "word" in John 15:3 above does not mean "Scripture" or "teaching." In this verse it is *logon*, derived from *Logos* in John 1, "the Word" who became flesh. In the same prologue, light and life (John 1:4) are virtually synonymous with this Word. This should not surprise us, for elsewhere Jesus describes himself as "the light" (e.g., John 8:12) and "the life" (e.g., John 14:6). Based on what John says in 15:3 and elsewhere in the gospel,[18] it follows that "the true light that gives light to everyone was coming into the world" (John 1:9) could just as easily refer to the true *logon*. The *logon* of light and life pulsates through the vine and branches, signifying not only God's life but the truth of the humanity of God. It is the green law of the Spirit of life to which we are accountable. We can see how clearly this connects to Deuteronomy 30:14—"The word is very near you; it is in your mouth and in your heart so you may obey it." It demonstrates how God's "*word*" in us is God's *will* for us, allowing us to participate in faithful and fruitful ways.[19] The disciples, however, could not help but miss these words spoken by the Word just before his death, even if they returned to them many times over.

We can't be too hard on the disciples if they missed Jesus's massive paradigm shift concerning human identity. We often make the mistake of defining ourselves the way others think of us, or even the way we think about ourselves, instead of the way God thinks of us. Jesus here tells us that we belong to him, that we are his friends. We are also, therefore, friends of one another. It is the Holy Spirit who works to convince us of this.

As Jesus says in his final discourse, "When the Advocate comes, whom I will send to you from the Father—the Spirit of truth who goes out from the Father—he will testify about me. And you must also testify, for you have been with me *from the beginning*" (John 15:27, emphasis added). Regardless of what we have believed previously, Christ makes the audacious claim that we *have been* his disciples since the beginning. These words of Jesus might refer not simply to the beginning of Jesus's earthly ministry, but to the beginning of human history—from creation itself.

Karl Barth believed that the band of disciples in the gospels was a provisional representation of the reality of all people sanctified in Christ. But this was not to displace the centrality of the Jewish people. Barth gave full

---

Bruner (*Gospel of John*) comments that cleansing has more to do with the Word of Christ than with the suffering involved. He cites Luther in this connection: "The cleansing process must be carried out through the Word, which must be present at all times and must cleanse you both before and after.... Your suffering is not the cleanness itself, and you were not declared clean in the sight of God because of [your suffering]" (898).

18. See John 17:6 and 17:14, for example, where *logon* is used.
19. This was a fact not lost on Paul. See Rom 10:8–9.

place to Jesus being the true Israelite and the incontestable attestation that salvation is from the Jews. That Christ was the Second Adam, or that he was himself the church (the body of Christ) should not diminish or replace that fact that he is the true Israelite. Barth was no supersessionist.[20] He recognized that Jesus's disciples in the upper room the night of John 17 were all Jewish. The Messiah's ministry was focused on the Jewish people. The twelve disciples represented a new iteration of the Twelve Tribes of Israel. And in the great commission Jesus charged his Jewish disciples to continue spreading his message to ever greater circles of humanity until they catch up with the universal coverage that his human person represents: "you will be my witnesses in Jerusalem, and in all Judea and Samaria, and to the ends of the earth" (Acts 1:8).[21]

Considering the Elect and Original Adam, the first human in whom all humans are created, we might say that just as we were all there in Christ's death, all implicated in Christ's resurrection and ascension, and all there on judgment day, we were also all there in Genesis 1. Even before the fall, claims Barth, Christ was already Adam, and Adam already Christ.[22] This idea, *that we were all called into being as Christ's disciples*, is one we will further explore in the remaining pages.[23]

---

20. See Brazier, "Karl Barth," also cited in Book One. See also Givens, *We the People*.

21. See Karl Barth, "Exegetical Study," 55–71. Paul's replacement of Judas represents just this mission to the Gentile world, as Barth suggests: "The 'delivering' of Jesus to the Gentiles . . . had taken place (Matt 27:2). This event separates the times. Now the eschatological Israel begins . . . the messianic Israel is in fact revealed by the words of verse 19 ['go and make disciples of all nations, baptizing them in the name of the Father, and the Son, and the Holy Spirit']. . . . The number twelve of the eschatological Israel is even externally complete by the addition of Paul. The activity of the apostles must set in with this very revelation: 'Make disciples of all nations.' This 'all nations' in no way contradicts the earlier teaching and practice of Jesus. The narrow path within Israel had to branch out into the wide world of all nations, and the inroad into the wide world had to begin as the narrow path within Israel. . . . From the *Jews*—this is the first, limited, and hidden form of the eschatological community, represented by the eleven. Salvation *comes* from the Jews—to the Gentiles—this is the second, unlimited, and manifest form, represented by the eleven plus one" (66).

22. CD III/1, 203.

23. Those of us who have no problem anticipating the possibility that all humans are present as gathered around the throne in the end will perhaps have less trouble thinking about all human beings gathered around the head of humanity in Genesis 1. John 17:6 and 17:14 stand out when considering the disciples as a microcosm of all human beings called by Christ to himself from the beginning. The verses themselves give greater coherence to the scriptural testimony, in that Jesus's prayer to the Father regarding the disciples, "they have obeyed your word" (17:6) is unintelligible (in many ways the disciples have *not* kept the word) unless grasped in a placemat sense. John 17:14—"I have given them your word and the world has hated them, for they are not of the world any more than I am of the world"—maps rather nicely onto 1:9 when seen

81

The Sword and the Spirit

Jesus will come to judge the living and the dead. That will be the best thing that ever happens to us. On that day the weeds in each of us will be separated from the wheat. It will hurt—no doubt it will hurt—when our self-deceptions are burned away. But the pain of truth heals; it does not destroy. On our judgment day we will be able for the first time to see the truth of our lives, when we see ourselves as loved.

—Ben Myers

CAN YOU IMAGINE HOW differently we would live if we interpreted the matrix of our green and red lives by the person of Christ? To live from the third heaven is to live with the revealed certainty that every person is fundamentally *nothing but green from creation on*. It is from that standpoint that we understand the judgment revealed in the second heaven to be a judgment of grace. With this big picture, we pray that the transformational clarity of the second heaven will be brought to bear in the first. Under the sound of the gospel, the heralding of Jesus Christ and him crucified, the Spirit does her work.

---

in this way, i.e., no human being is truly "of the world," and Christ (the Logos) has given himself (his logon) to every human, that they might be in the world but not of it. Indeed, the Word is a light unto our feet (Ps 119:105). He is the light and life of us all.

PART SIX: LIVING LIFE FROM THE THIRD HEAVEN

Coming into this world, we are met with the confusion of a placemat existence, "joy and woe woven fine." Instead of walking by sight, the word of God interrogates the grey, revealing the green and red placemat strips insinuated into one another. Not only that, we recognize that the woven strips actually represent two complete and different pieces of paper, one red and one green, and yet these two totals exist in one person. Sin and suffering would not hurt us if each of us were not *one person* subjected to the competing claims and demands (the torque) of the two opposed selves. Indeed, because these exist within the one person, the contrast that the red self makes with the green produces intense agony and confusion for us.

In Jordan Peele's movie *Us*, the red, anti-self characters carry large scissors in hopes of freeing themselves from their tethered twins. Not only are our "red" alter-egos (or more precisely anti-egos) unable to free themselves in the real world, but they also have no independent existence because they are parasitic shadows of our true selves. Unfortunately, our green selves are likewise unable to free themselves from the bondage of the red. They are tethered together for life.

Like the wheat and the tares, the green and the red are so tightly woven that they take on a mixed character—a grey mesh—even though they are un-mixed and mutually exclusive. This mesh is too fine to be parsed with even the sharpest theological scissors. Only the cross can make this separation and give us this understanding by the sword of the Spirit. The death and resurrection of Christ reveals the clean break we need to separate the bad subjectivity from the good. C. S. Lewis comments on the definitive nature of God's judgment compared with less able judgments:

> We have all encountered judgments or verdicts on ourselves in this life.... But of course both the bitter and the sweet are limited by our doubt as to the wisdom of those who judge. We always hope that those who so clearly think us cowards or bullies are ignorant and malicious; we always fear that those who trust us or admire us are misled by partiality. I suppose the experience of the Final Judgment (which may break in upon us at any moment) will be like these little experiences, but magnified to the Nth. For it will be infallible judgment. If it is favorable we shall have no fear, if unfavorable, no hope that it is wrong.[1]

The Spirit works in conjunction with the cross. The cross reveals how God's wrath serves his love, how his No serves his Yes, how his severity serves his kindness, and the Spirit of Truth, in her inherently transformative work, makes that revelation known. The cross, by virtue of resurrection,

---

1. Lewis, "World's Last Night," 84.

reveals creation. In this light the Apostles' Creed looks different. When Jesus comes again to judge the "quick and the dead,"[2] this judgment means the severance of the "green and the red." The cross uniquely reveals that our "grey" mixture is really a composite.

Ben Myers makes a similar point in his book, *The Apostles' Creed*:

> To judge is to discriminate, to separate one thing from another.... That is what it means for Jesus to bring judgment. It is not that he is gracious to some and angry toward others ... but grace itself divides those who encounter it.... When Christ's light shines into our lives, it creates a division within ourselves. None of us is entirely good or entirely bad. Each of us is a mixture. The bad grows up in our lives like weeds among the wheat, and the two are so closely entwined that in this life we cannot easily tell the difference.... Our lives are not transparent to ourselves. We cannot easily tell where the bad ends and the good begins.... So it is a comfort to know that one day someone else will come and lovingly separate the good from the bad in our lives. The confession that Christ will come as judge is not an expression of terror and doom. It is part of the good news of the gospel. It is a joy to know that there is someone who understands all the complexities and ambiguities of our lives.... He comes to save, not to destroy, and he saves by his judgment.[3]

Thanks to the sword of cross and Spirit, the separation of darkness from light within us is finally made: "For the word of God is alive and active. Sharper than any double-edged sword, it penetrates even to dividing soul and spirit, joints and marrow; it judges the thoughts and attitudes of the heart" (Heb 4:12). Under the judgment of the second heaven, we are empowered to practice "placemat discernment" in this world: "The teaching about righteousness" is for those "who by constant use have trained themselves to distinguish good from evil" (Heb 5:13–14).

Our training in the first heaven involves the practice of hearing the word of God that proclaims the "battle-cry" of victory through the cross, as Barth asserts. By revelation light and the Spirit we are lifted into a "position

---

2. I obviously read "the quick [living] and the dead" as more than the fact that Christ is judging both those who have died and those who are still alive at his coming. And this lines up well with the two instances in Scripture where the exact phrase is used (2 Tim 4:1; 1 Pet 4:5). We are by nature "quick" in our fundamental green identity. To be quickened, now and then, is to experience the dynamism of our being-in-act in the Spirit and the eternal and unquantifiable green to green to green transformation of "living to God in Christ Jesus."

3. Myers, *Apostles Creed*, 91, 92, 93. Like Julian of Norwich, Myers uses the word "mixture," which is certainly the way we experience it, even if not theologically precise.

of remoteness"—as if stepping outside of ourselves—perhaps something like Paul's third-heaven perspective (2 Cor 12:2). From such a vantage point, and by virtue of the victorious death and resurrection of Christ, we can assess the simultaneous situation of our lives and world. "Liberated by this intervention of God," notes Barth, a person "can hear this divine summons, assimilating it, letting it pierce his very heart, his bones and marrow."[4] With confidence as new and true human beings in Christ, we can hear the battle-cry of Christ's sequence and be liberated participants in the struggle. "By the gracious judgment of the divine command," says Barth, we are "instructed and made willing and ready to undertake an active opposition to this disorder, to secure bridgeheads within the confusion."[5]

Barth is aware that the securing of bridgeheads in this world may be accompanied by scurrying retreats. Our lives may be experienced more like two steps forward, one step backward (or one step forward and two steps back). Only in the clarity of the second heaven can we finally understand what if means to fully offer ourselves to God. In a moment of true agency, in line with my true subjectivity, I may offer my whole self in loving worship to God; this includes offering my bad subjectivity to the judgment of Christ. Our false selves cannot offer themselves (or anything for that matter) to God.

We are given the chance to participate in this act of worshipful offering (in the second heaven and in the first) because we have already been offered to God in and by Christ, the high priest of our humanity. As participants who are crucified with Christ, we can say: "I do not want this false self, thank you for taking it away from me before I could see clearly, even before I had the power to ask." It is a good thing that the Savior did not wait until we asked to be delivered. Our reluctance to ask for God's help is rooted in our blindness and bondage to pride. Our cultural exultation of free choice and self-controlled agency often misses the fact that we are powerless to ask rightly. By grace we are saved, even from our inability to seek salvation.

At Christmas time we celebrate the coming of the light who gives light to every person. He is the one who puts himself under the curse of the fall, representing true humanity and assuming the false humanity of the flesh. In placemat terms, God reveals himself as a human being in a green and red bundle, putting himself under the mastery of sin (Rom 6:9) where the red strips squeeze him and threaten to suffocate him to death. Who could have predicted that he would "tie up the strong man" (Satan) by allowing himself to be tied up? He put himself under the mastery of sin, only to

---

4. *CD* III/4, 237.
5. *CD* III/4, 238.

snap the bonds and prove that life is stronger than death. It was a definitive demonstration that the red is the exception to the rule of reality.

This process of breaking bonds then works by the Spirit to begin freeing us from that which binds us. This process is akin to that of helping someone to remove a painful splinter. Years ago, as the designated splinter extractor for our four young kids, I discovered that de-splintering can be an intricate, sometimes painful, and extremely intimate occasion. By virtue of the clarity provided in the light of Christ's work, and by the discernment of the Spirit, we in the first heaven can practice recognizing and "pulling out" (or, more accurately, tenderly pointing out) the tares of our lives. As squeezed as we may feel, we can present the oppressive elements of our lives in confession to God and to one another. We can acknowledge that, in the revealed economy of Christ, these things do not belong. In the Spirit we can find the power to participate in the big picture of reality. In confession to God and to one another (Jas 5:16), we can help each other to cut the ties to our false, tethered selves. We can refuse the flesh and thus live in the freedom of Christ even on this side of the veil.

The balm of confessing to God can be shown with the following (admittedly spatial) illustration. Imagine your relationship with God is comprised of a bunch of strings connecting the two of you, and when you sin against God, one of those strings is broken. As your turn to God in confession, talking with him about it, you sense him taking the two string fragments and tying them into a knot. In this moment two things are accomplished: the knot makes the string of your relationship to God stronger, not weaker, and the tying of the knot has in effect made the string *shorter*, illustrating God pulling you more deeply into the bosom of his unconditional love.

Of course, in the reality of our green lives hidden with Christ we can't get closer to God than we already are. Even if we *experience* transformation as a zero-sum, being filled with the Spirit does not mean that we quantitatively add more Spirit to what we already have in Christ, but that we manifest the expansive life of Spirit-led transformation, from fruitfulness to fruitfulness, completeness to completeness, wholeness to wholeness, and cleanness to cleanness. This is the one place where evil's attempts at mimicry are bankrupt. While we can imagine the Spirit's superabundance in the life direction, we cannot imagine superabundance in the death direction. Death can only take us so far. Fruitfulness to fruitfulness is one thing, but fruit*less*ness to fruit*less*ness is another. It is like nothingness to nothingness. The flesh can do *nothing*: "The Spirit gives life; the flesh counts for nothing" (John 6:63). The flesh is represented by the dead branches that are no good and, accomplishing nothing, are burned-up in the death of Christ (John

15:5).⁶ One cannot be more dead than dead. Conversely, eternal life is more like a full balloon that always expands without ever bursting.

To be filled with the Spirit is not a quantifiable addition to the green (from ninety to one hundred percent, for instance). It is a dimensional revelation of the Spirit's inherently dynamic and superabundant effects—what we earlier called the "green heat." Walking in the flesh, the glaring red tends to hide the green, giving the impression that it is the rule. But glaring red is no match for green heat. Come, Holy Spirit, and bring the heat of your healing love to all your creatures.⁷

---

6. See an interesting parallel to the vine and the branches in the blind man's testimony, "If this man were not from God, he could do *nothing*" (John 9:33, emphasis added). Also, consider John 5:19; 5:30, where Jesus says he can do nothing apart from the Father.

7. Luke 24:32 provides an apt description of how the truth of the gospel is revealed by the Spirit with transformational effects when the disciples realized it was Jesus walking with them to Emmaus: "Were not our hearts burning within us while he talked with us on the road and opened the Scriptures to us?"

82

The Ship-Shape of the Atonement

On the third day the friends of Christ coming at daybreak to the place found the grave empty and the stone rolled away. In varying ways they realized the new wonder; but even they hardly realised that the world had died in the night. What they were looking at was the first day of a new creation, with a new heaven and a new earth; and in a semblance of the gardener God walked again in the garden, in the cool not of the evening but of the dawn.

—G. K. Chesterton

And how could this be done save by the coming of the Very Image Himself, our Saviour Jesus Christ? . . . The Word of God came in His own Person, because it was He alone, the Image of the Father, Who could recreate man made after the Image. In order to affect this re-creation, however, He had first to do away with death and corruption. Therefore He assumed a human body, in order that in it death might once for all be destroyed, and that men might be renewed according to the Image.

—Athanasius

PART SIX: LIVING LIFE FROM THE THIRD HEAVEN

AT THIS POINT WE can summarize how our theological colors apply to theories of the atonement. The popular penal substitutionary atonement (PSA) model is an essentially retributive one. In this view, sinners fall short of the perfect obedience required by God's law. Impure sinners that we are, and because "the wages of sin is death" (Rom 6:23), nothing but a pure substitutional sacrifice will suffice to supply the legal remedy. The spotless sacrificial lamb takes our place to satisfy God's insistence on legal perfection and assuages his wrath through punishment. With echoes of Abraham and Isaac, God provides his Son—the pure, pre-fallen humanity of Christ—for the sacrifice. In placemat terms, the pure green humbles himself to be made the pure red for our sakes. In his willing substitutionary role, Jesus "takes the bullet" or "pays the penalty" so that we do not have to. Justice has been served, and we can now be forgiven if we ask. We were legally separated from God because of sin (our red existence), but now we can be reconciled (and become green). God can now accept us as his beloved children. In this model (at least the Arminian version), it is critical to note that forgiveness, reconciliation, and God's love for us as his children are all hypotheticals. The work is not finished—we are not actually green—until we *appropriate* what God has done for us in some way. In this model, "appropriate" suddenly becomes a very heavy word.[1]

In the restorative model, the incarnation is articulated differently. God does not take on pre-fall flesh. Instead the Son enters the fallen human condition and bears in his flesh the destructive consequences of sin. Jesus Christ fights against the flesh throughout this lifetime and finally, by giving sin its due (the wages of sin is still death), destroys sin and death in his own death. The restorative model highlights the humanity of Jesus, the one tempted like we are in every way. It also allows us to see his death as related to the costliness of sin (the inherent *cost or consequence* of human sin that he assumed) as opposed to an external, legal penalty being paid to a God who requires it. In this restorative model, the doctor becomes the patient, dying and burying our sins in himself. Even as the patient, however, he remains the doctor all the way through. Such is the mystery of Christ.

In the restorative model, forgiveness is included as part and parcel of Easter morning. In a more holistic fashion, humanity is restored, re-created,

---

1. The Arminian and Dortian (Five-Point Calvinist) models both implement PSA, and while the latter would recognize forgiveness as located at the cross (not at the moment of appropriation), because of their adherence to limited atonement it's only *after* the appropriation has been exercised by the individual that the Calvinist can know if the individual was forgiven in the finished work at Calvary! This irony makes Calvinists functional Arminians. To double the irony, when Arminians tell their converts post-appropriation that they were really forgiven at the cross, they have become functional Calvinists. This twin dynamic keeps the two as strange bedfellows in Evangelicalism.

and *therefore* forgiven.² Forgiveness does not necessarily change the criminal in the retributive or forensic (legal) model. A legal problem demands merely a legal solution. Despite Abelard's teaching, the extravagant lengths of Christ's loving sacrifice may have no "moral influence" on the criminal that results in an appreciation for forgiveness and a desire to pay the forgiven debt forward. Instead of relying on PSA or on a moral influence model, the restorative model puts the emphasis on ontology. It makes a deep claim about who we are as re-created beings, and therefore keeps indicatives and imperatives together. In Book One, we described this as the difference between the perspectives of external and internal relations in the atonement. God does not just do something *for* us (external), he does something *with* us (internal). Instead of patching things up on the surface—rearranging the deck chairs on the Titanic—we are given a whole new ship when we rise again in him. The red ship, so to speak, has been replaced by a green one.

My late-coming appreciation for the restorative view of the work of Christ helped me to put the emphasis on the person of Christ, i.e., *who* it is that is "crucified, dead and buried, the third day rising from the dead" (Apostles' Creed). When it came to the crucifixion, the weight shifted from the *cross* of Christ to the cross of *Christ*. In the restorative view, Christ's person and work stay intact in a more internally consistent manner, as he is both substitute and representative. I increasingly disavowed the retributive model because of its hostility toward the inmost character of God as Jesus Christ reveals it in Scripture. I clung to the truth that Jesus Christ is God revealing God—God as "Holy Love," to use P. T. Forsyth's expression. As Forsyth himself elaborates:

> We can no longer treat the atonement as a deflection of God's anger, as if the flash fell on Christ and was conducted by Him to the ground, while we stood in passive safety, with no part or lot in the incomprehensible process. We can no longer speak of a strife of attributes in God the Father, justice set against mercy, and judgment against grace, till an adjustment was effected by

---

2. This is exactly what Col 2:13 says: "When you were dead in your sins and in the uncircumcision of your flesh, God made you alive with Christ. He forgave us all our sins." Like the similar passage in Rom 6:5–8, this articulation of our death and resurrection in Christ is internally related to the sacrament of baptism, as the verses previous to each passage make plain (Col 2:12; Rom 6:3–4). Again our job as interpreters involves the proper priority of the inter-relation, the sacrament pointing away from itself to the universal reality to which it bears witness, providing *real* cause for celebrating! Also, regardless of how much of a connection we draw between the sacrament of baptism and circumcision, the idea that the foreskin is removed and taken away to connote the ridding of the flesh (Col 2:11, 14), while a spatial metaphor, fits well with the concept of salvation by subtraction (note the similarity of Rom 6:6 in this connection).

the Son. There can be no talk of any mollification of God, or any inducement whatever, offered by either man or some third party, to procure grace. Procured grace is a contradiction in terms. The atonement did not procure grace, it flowed from grace. What was historically offered to God was also eternally offered by God, within the Godhead's unity.[3]

As Forsyth decries, penal substitutionary atonement (PSA) promotes an inconsistency of character between the Father and the Son. The orthodox understanding of "oneness of being" (the *homoousion*) between Trinitarian persons, so central to the Nicene Creed, seemed to me clearly at risk. Because of its ground rules dictating the legal separation of unholy humanity from holy God, PSA requires the separation of God the Father from God the Son at the cross. When Jesus becomes sin, he effectively takes leave from being God, at least for a defined period of time.[4]

But because of my exegetical distaste for the penal retributive model, I allowed the pendulum of salvation to swing too far away from Calvary. If the penal model is guilty of relegating Christ's thirty plus years into a means to the end of the cross, then I found myself at risk of making the cross a means to the end of getting Christ's death over with in order to access the real saving moment: resurrection. We all die with Christ, we all rise with Christ. This reliance on the representative role of Christ for humanity is the restorative model's greatest strength. Indeed, the ontology fits the words of the famous spiritual: we *were* there when they hung him on the cross. But where are we between Good Friday and Easter Sunday?

The fact that the restorative view gave me a whole new ship to replace our sinking, red one was great, but was the first ship not created perfect and good in God's image in its original state? Is human depravity, as bad as it is, powerful enough to displace our good, creaturely foundation—turning us from green to red? The lack of continuity here bothered me. It is as if the restorative model gave up on the created vessel, the first ship, completely; it was a complete wreck, and everything had to be re-done. Total red went down in Christ's death on Friday. Total green appeared Sunday morning. As informed by Christ's birth, life, death, and resurrection, the old ship being replaced by the new one means that Christ's humanity (and ours) is completely dead and gone, full stop, only to start over again on Sunday. This sounded more like a kind of re-incarnation instead of a renewal of the original, pre-fall, incarnation (Col 1:15). It posited human re-generation without an internal connection to generation. In other words, it posited

---

3. Forsyth, *Cruciality*, 40–41.
4. In this sense PSA functions as short hand for Arianism.

a "re-creation" while seemingly unbothered by the lack of continuity with creation.

The problem is not where the restorative view ends, it is where it begins. The restorative view is strong on the fact that Christ assumed the very humanity that needed healing—corrupt humanity (red). But in this great act of love, humiliation, and condescension to our human plight, where did Christ's *true humanity* go? Christ assumed fallen flesh, but the un-fallen, pristine flesh of Christ's true humanity ("the firstborn of all creation") was apparently uninvolved in the incarnation.[5]

It is good news indeed that Christ buried in himself the red, fallen, corrupt humanity. But it is bad news if the true humanity of Christ, which because of his representative power is our own true humanity, does not exist on Holy Saturday. This model follows a circular green-red-green sequence, or creation-fall-recreation. I say circular because after "leaving" full green it "comes back around" to full green.[6] Any kind of red-to-green replacement/displacement theory loses the continuity of creaturely goodness and human transcendence, dimensionally understood.

I could go back to the pristine, pre-fall flesh needed for the PSA model, but at what cost? The restorative model was an improvement by emphasizing Jesus's human struggle like mine, and in drawing me to ideas of the representative power of internal relations and away from forensic ones, but was it really necessary to choose either pre-fall or fallen humanity for the incarnation? Having read thus far, you know my answer.

We have proposed throughout that Christ assumes sinful flesh at birth, but not in such a way that his sinful humanity *replaces* his true humanity. Instead, in the two-fold incarnation, Christ takes on true humanity and false humanity when he becomes a human being. Henceforth, the conflict is on. If Christ's day-to-day life leading up to the cross is not a struggle between his false humanity (red) and his true humanity (green), it would be a less-than-human struggle. The struggle would *then* have been between false human agency and divine agency (when the focus is on Jesus *as God*, his true human agency is not in view). Much is lost when the day-to-day struggle between false humanity and true humanity, the way we human

---

5. At this point in the restorative model we are not much better off than in the retributive model where the opposite problem is apparent (i.e., in the penal substitutionary model when Christ is only the pristine human being).

6. Unfortunately, this is where the a) restorative model and b) retributive model share company, even if the green is reestablished in different ways: a) resurrection and b) personal appropriation, respectively. For Christ/humanity to be nothing but red and dead on Holy Saturday in both models mitigates any advantage the restorative model has in claiming Christ took on corrupt flesh in the incarnation. The effect is somewhat the same as if Christ is simply made to be sin at the cross. The green is gone.

beings experience it at least, is not part of the christological narrative. Not only that, if the atonement is a two-piece operation, deconstructive (cross) and reconstructive (resurrection), we cannot help but privilege the second over the first when it comes to salvation. To the extent that the finished work of Christ is essentially his resurrection—the old being definitively replaced by the new—the "wondrous cross" is overshadowed by a "wondrous exchange" in which continuity is dispensable.[7]

Our superscript approach can help us to maintain the continuity. We remember that who we are in Christ and who we are in the Spirit are not two different things. I prefer to think of the Holy Spirit holding Pat's one person (P^3) and Pat's true self (P^1) together through death, proving their fundamental unity, even as I rejoice in the disconnection of Pat's false self (P^2) from Pat's one person (P^3). Experientially, however, when I grieve Pat's death, I grieve the loss not of Pat's false self (P^2), but of Pat (P^3). It is the one person of the two selves that I seek to honor. Like the wheat and the tares, Christ keeps the opposites together in his person until the things that need to be separated are separated (true self and false self), in order to preserve what cannot and must not be separated (humanity from Christ).

That is why the continuity of God's "very good" creation, the fully green of human being in Christ (life), must be maintained throughout Easter weekend, even if it is totally obscured by the total red (death). This points to the indelible (even if invisible) presence of our spiritual bodies. We are kept in Christ from creation on. Even in our death we are not defined by death. We are kept alive by the Holy Spirit before, during, and after our death. This is the continuity of the green. The removal of the red leaves us with unveiled faces, finally revealing—in the Lord who is the Spirit—the face-to-face glory of our spiritual-material bodies (2 Cor 3:18).

The more I understood the inner connection between re-creation and creation, and the christological basis for each, the more I came back to the cross as the focal point of our salvation.[8] Thankfully, this recognition did

---

7. The ancient "wondrous exchange" can fall prey to a simple, representative, replacement transaction if it's based on a misconstrual of 2 Cor 8:9: "Though he was rich, yet for your sake he became poor, so that you through his poverty might become rich." Yes, Christ became poor and was made sin, but that is not all. We would have to imagine Calvin's version of the exchange, "the Son of God became Son of Man to make sons of men sons of God," to describe the Son of Man as *simply* bankrupt and corrupt (i.e., he was only "red" humanity because of the sinful flesh he assumed) until the resurrection (when the red was replaced by green). A simplistic, rich-poor-rich format belies a weakness in the restorative model, underestimating not only the deity of Christ (kenosis) but the richness of Christ's true humanity (green), which is unfortunately relegated to nonexistence until Easter morning.

8. Taking together the humanity of Col 1:15 (Jesus Christ as the "firstborn of all

not involve a pendulum swing back toward the retributive view of the atonement. Instead, my understanding of re-creation changed. If re-creation is seen as creation, properly understood, then re-creation is better grasped as a re-newing. It is not a re-doing. It is not another creation altogether, the first being chalked up as something of a false start. Instead of seeing one ship, the totally sinful (red) ship, replaced by another, the totally righteous (green) ship, I now understand the originally created and good ship (green) as always there. The re-creation of humanity, then, has nothing to do with a *lack* in creation. God's perfect creation is infallible, totally green. It could not fall from perfection because of what humans decided or even because of evil design, it could only fall from a perfection-only state. "In Him," notes Barth, "the created world is already perfect in spite of its imperfections, for the Creator is Himself a creature, both sharing its creaturely peril, and guaranteeing and already actualising its hope." On that day, he continues, "its justification and perfection will infallibly be perceived and it will be seen to be the best of all possible worlds."[9]

In this view, then, the continuity of creation stays intact, albeit hidden and despite the corruptibility of the flesh. Re-creation does not involve an improvement on creation, but a reiteration of creation against all claims against it. With all the green and reiteration of green that we described, however, we cannot forget the red. The "full red" must be addressed with the harshest and most definitive of measures. Rightly understood, this discontinuity is critical.[10] We desperately need a full stop at the end of the sentence that speaks of sin, death, and the devil. In our dimensional view, we can see that the themes of discontinuity and continuity are held together. Futhermore, we see that the discontinuity serves the continuity.

As the Bible regularly indicates, we *are* dead in our sins, completely bankrupt.[11] We should take this with all seriousness. While we are dead in our sins, however, that is never *all* that we are. Barth's suggestion is

---

creation") and John 1:14 (Jesus Christ as the "Word became flesh"), we could say that all the Jesus Christ of Col 1:15 is in the Jesus Christ of John 1:14, but not all the Jesus Christ of John 1:14 is in the Jesus Christ of Col 1:15.

9. *CD* III/1, 385.

10. Penal language from Scripture, typically co-opted into the penal substitutionary scheme, can be responsibly (and carefully) employed here. The christological and anthropological context (placemat anthropology) maintains Scripture's harshest articulation of God's wrathful "No!" focused on the false self and the necessity of its full destruction. This necessary destruction and God's wrath against sin together serve God's love for the one person, the one community, the one human family, the one heaven and earth. Wrath is love when aimed at what does not belong for the sake of what does. Here, justification and deliverance meet.

11. Rom 3; Eph 1:1, 6; Col 2:13.

paradigm-shifting: in Christ's *death* occurs "the birthday of a new man."[12] The new human is born not simply in the resurrection of Christ, as the restorative view declares, but in the death of Christ. How is this so? Christ's death secures the true humanity that was always alive, a fact that is *revealed* in the resurrection. I have called this the "new" perspective of the cross, not because it is a new way of looking at the cross, but because it maintains the continuity of newness of life in face of the oldness of death. It reveals the new humanity as continuous with the true, original humanity. "New," in these terms, means a new expression of what has always been. The truth of Christ's death as a liberation for the captives will rush into our awareness on "the day" when we see our old selves shed like grave clothes. Barth anticipates a fullness of quickening that we are yet to experience in this world: "our real but only life, will then fully, definitively and manifestly participate in that newness of life (Rom 6:4)." Barth envisages "this transition and transformation" as "the unveiling and glorifying of the life which in his time man has already had in Christ."[13]

So, is death bad or good? In terms of the reality of creation's continuity, it is bad. It does not fit. But in terms of serving the continuity through discontinuity, it is good. It is bad because it is not created, not a part of the plan. That is why we can only say that it is good in a provisional sense, now that parasitic sin and evil—which must end—have insinuated themselves into what is purely good. Solely in this provisional sense can we call the day of Christ's death "Good Friday." If Christmas celebrates Christ's assumption of *sarx*, then Good Friday celebrates the eradication of it. That is why John Donne can say, "His Christmas day and his Good Friday are but the evening and the morning of one and the same day."[14]

The "new" perspective of the cross does not rely on the resurrection to be a restorative event. Instead, the cross maintains an overall restorative function in the atonement. It captures death in its most heinous expression (as not good and not created) without leaving Holy Saturday in the black hole of mere discontinuity. As with sin and righteousness, we take death with utmost seriousness, just not as seriously as we take life. Holy Saturday, then, does not dictate a discontinuity of life (the teaching about Christ preaching to the souls in hell, 1 Peter 3:19, might apply here). In the time between Christ's death and resurrection, however, it attests to the darkness of this world.

---

12. *CD* IV/1, 259.

13. *CD* III/2, 624.

14. Thanks to Jason Byassee, via Matthew Milliner, for this quote from Donne's sermon "The Showing Forth of Christ" in Webber, *Love Came Down*, 83.

For those of us in the first heaven, Holy Saturday implicitly acknowledges the painful wait for the resolution to the contradiction of our lives. The world is apparently left in the dark. In other words, if God in his assumed, corruptible human flesh (red) is willing to lay dead for days in the name of victory, with all signs from the disciples' perspective pointing to the Messiah's defeat, then it does not seem far-fetched that he would allow the "red" to fester here for our entire lives in the name of eternal "green." My "new" perspective adheres strongly to a finished work on Good Friday—the already of justification, sanctification, reconciliation, forgiveness, and salvation for all. But it also maintains a place for Holy Saturday and for Christ's ongoing presence in the "not yet" of our confusing and conflicted grey existence. Bracketed by the arms of hope (felt or not by those suffering) there is unrestricted room for grief, anguish, and lament in the understanding embrace of Jesus.

But what of the resurrection? Is the resurrection diminished by the "new" perspective as it is in the retributive view? The retributive view invariably marginalizes the resurrection because its basic approach centers on the penalty being paid and, in this, it loses the continuity of Christ's deity—the Son is separated from the Father. The doctor becomes the patient (or perhaps better, victim) *without* remaining the doctor. When the deity of Christ is forfeited, Christ becomes more the object than the subject of the atonement. In our "new" perspective, not only is Christ always the divine subject, he is able to bear false humanity's subjectivity unto death while also bearing true humanity's subjectivity unto life. This is something only God can do.

Even if we hold to the cross as the focal point of our salvation narrative, the resurrection is no less important for our understanding of it. In resurrection light, we are given to know exactly *who* was on that cross, leading us to the one who has true authority (above that of the teachers of the law; Matt 7:29) to tell us *who we are*. The Easter garden is where the asymmetry between death and life, false and true, is made known. Following Barth, we can say that what is new about new creation is a new revelation of what has always been and what we, apart from the cross and resurrection, were blind to see. Apart from revelation and in our blindness, we are as good as dead. Conversely, by the Spirit, Easter's revelation tells us that we are good, and we are alive, not only through suffering and death but in spite of it.

83

Life in Spite of Death

God's Word saw that his descent could entail nothing but his own death and ruination—that his light must sink down into the gloom—he accepted the battle and the declaration of war. . . . He would experience the farthest dungeon of sin's mania and drink the cup down to the dregs; he would offer his brow to man's incalculable craze for power and violence; in his own futile mission, he would demonstrate the futility of the world; . . . through his own weakness unto death he would bring to light the deathly weakness of such a despairing resistance to God.

—Hans Urs von Balthasar

Our churches are where we dip our tired bodies in cool springs of hope . . . where we retain our wholeness and humanity despite the blows of death.

—Richard Wright

THE POWER OF THE atonement is found in the "who question." The cross is not redemptive because of suffering but *because of the transcendence of the one who suffered*, the one who condescended to suffer in solidarity with every human, especially those humans most burdened by suffering in this world. From the deepest suffering of God—and the death of a God who does not die—emerges a big picture, a hope, on which we can rely. The cross is deliverance, full stop. No other steps are required. That the cross is validated by the resurrection does not mean that it—the cross—has no finality of its own. Thus, the eyewitness testimony of the Golgotha centurion: "Surely he was the Son of God" (Matt 27:54; Mark 15:39). This soldier did not need the resurrection to tell him the truth. Here we find (as Ephesians and Colossians assure us) that immanence and transcendence are not sequential. It is not that one is now, and the other is future. They exist in the space of the same moment, interpenetrating one another. In this transcendent moment, God died. In this immanent moment, God did not die. That is enough.[1]

The death of God the Son was either the end of death or the end of God. The resurrection reveals that it was the former and not the latter, but the death of Christ on the cross and not the resurrection was the end of death. If Christ was not raised, we as believers are of all people most to be pitied (1 Cor 15:19), because then the cross was not the death of God incarnate after all. There would be no transcendence—no power—in it. And therefore, death, in victory, would retain its sting (see 1 Cor 15:55). Without resurrection, there is no validation that we have been delivered. Paul tells us that Christ was raised not to accomplish our justification but on account of it, i.e., *because* of it (see literal translations of Rom 4:25).[2] In other words, casting doubt on the resurrection can only cast doubt on justification, and the robustness of our faith-claim is thinned with speculation.

The underlying testimony of John 11:25 at Lazarus's tomb is that Jesus crushed death by dying, and he proved his everlasting life by living. By entering into the suffering of human beings, Jesus Christ is the one suffering in the many, and the many suffering in the one. We are included in Jesus's suffering and death, while we are also included in his life. And it is in *those who have most suffered* where we find the chief witness to life in the midst of death. That is why, for Americans, the idea of Jesus being black is just as

---

1. I may have in mind here the verdict of Soren Kierkegaard (through his pseudonym Climacus) at the end of the following hypothetical: "Even if the contemporary [of Jesus] had not left anything behind except these words: 'We have believed that in such and such a year the god appeared in the humble form of a servant, lived and taught among us, and then died'—this is more than enough" (*Philosophical Fragments*, 104). Many thanks to Andrew Torrance for helping me to chase this quote. See Torrance, "Kierkegaard's Paradoxical Christology," 41–63.

2. Ellicott's Commentary for English Readers (public domain) is helpful here: "The death of Christ is the proper cause of justification, or means of atonement, according to St. Paul; the resurrection of Christ is only the mediate or secondary cause of it. The atoning efficacy lay in His death, but the proof of that efficacy—the proof that it was really the Messiah who died—was to be seen in the Resurrection."

important a theological statement as it is a historical statement. "Because God has been revealed . . . decisively in the Oppressed One," remarks James Cone, "it is impossible to say anything about God without seeing God as being involved in the contemporary liberation of all oppressed peoples."[3]

Nothing in the American historical experience converges with the cross of Christ more than the wicked practice and acceptance of lynching. This racial terrorism resulted in the murder of at least 4,400 black victims between 1877–1950. "In the United States," states Cone, "the clearest image of the crucified Christ was the figure of an innocent black victim, dangling from a lynching tree. . . . What prevented these theologians and ministers, who should have been the first to see God's revelation in black suffering, from recognizing the obvious gospel truth?"[4] And yet, even in the midst of the most terrible of immanent events, Cone testifies to the simultaneity of transcendent presence: "Both the cross and the lynching tree represented the worst in human beings and at the same time 'an unquenchable ontological thirst' for life that refuses to let the worst determine our final meaning."[5] As lynching converges with the God who suffered, the "terrible beauty" of the gospel is revealed.[6]

Cone's theology of the cross embraces its contradiction, emphasizing the power of the presence of God's life *in the midst* of the death of Christ. He points us to the God who "makes a way out of no way." In *The Cross and the Lynching Tree*, Cone elaborates: "The dialectic of sorrow and joy, despair and hope, was central in the black experience."[7] God's presence, no matter how great the suffering, "is the most important message about black existence."[8]

If we mean "what meets the eye" when speaking of the immanent, and if speaking of transcendent we mean "what is typically hidden from view" (more than meets the eye), then in Cone's theology we find that hope is transcendence located in immanence. Implicit in this is a resistance to the

---

3. Cone, *Black Theology of Liberation*, 65. Cone's logic is easy to follow: If Jesus is the Oppressed One, and in America Blacks are the most oppressed people, then Jesus is Black.

4. Cone, *Cross and the Lynching Tree*, 94–95.

5. Cone, *Cross and the Lynching Tree*, 3. The internal quote marks are referencing a phrase by Mircea Eliade. Cone quotes Eliade elsewhere in the volume: "Life is not possible without an opening toward the transcendent; in other words, human beings cannot live in chaos. Once contact with the transcendent is lost, existence in the world ceases to be possible" (153).

6. Cone affirms this phrase, which he attributes to Reinhold Niebuhr; *Cross and the Lynching Tree*, 37.

7. Cone, *Cross and the Lynching Tree*, 13.

8. Cone, *Cross and the Lynching Tree*, 21.

idea of penal substitutionary atonement. The latter puts the emphasis on Jesus's suffering as earning God's satisfaction, but with Cone we resist any narrative where Jesus's suffering had something to do with earning God's favor. Atonement is not found in transaction, but in transcendence.

In his emphasis on transcendence, Cone turns our focus away from the redemptive aspect of suffering to the revelatory aspect. Suffering cannot purchase transformation. However, because there is more going on in any given space than suffering, it can be experienced as transformative in the moment, as with the centurion and those gathered at the cross. "God's message of liberation in an unredeemed and tortured world," says Cone, "is a transcendent reality that lifts our spirits to a world far removed from the suffering of this one." However, just as critically, "It is also an immanent reality—a powerful liberating presence right *now* in their midst."[9] For Cone, liberation has to do with transcendence but not escapism. One can't just passively sit to the side and talk coldly about God's revelation. In fact, so called revelation without liberation (or even revolution) is no revelation at all.

It follows that there is power in knowing transcendence in immanence, not only for human endurance but as the empowerment toward social justice:

> One has to have a powerful religious imagination to see redemption in the cross, to discover life in death and hope in tragedy. What kind of salvation is that? . . . The cross is an "opening to the transcendent" for the poor who have nowhere else to turn—that transcendence that no one can take away, no matter what they do. . . . And yet another type of imagination is necessary—the imagination to relate the message of the cross to one's own social reality.[10]

Now, Cone's statement, "I find nothing redemptive about suffering in itself,"[11] comes into better focus. Even if suffering "produces" perseverance in one sense (Rom 5:3, see "The Big Picture"), we are not meant to pursue it. We do not go looking for suffering, even though it is unavoidable in this world. But if all our suffering is contained in Christ's, then at the same time we can accept suffering as a participation in the same Christ and his victory over it. We can "glory in our sufferings" (Rom 5:3) precisely because our suffering was punctuated at the cross. This was accomplished by the compassionate one who loves us deeply and who intimately knows our sufferings as

---

9. Cone, *Cross and the Lynching Tree*, 155.
10. Cone, *Cross and the Lynching Tree*, 157–58.
11. Cone, *Cross and the Lynching Tree*, 150.

his own, all for the purpose of burying them. God demonstrates in Christ's death that he will never allow us to taste any suffering, no matter how bitter, which he has not first tasted himself. It was for "the joy set before him," we are told, that "he endured the cross, scorning its shame" (Heb 12:2).

Apart from the fact that suffering points to the tomb of Jesus Christ as its final resting place, there is nothing redemptive about it. Because God suffered and died, the living God gives us a future beyond suffering, where no suffering exists. That is the point. Because of its transcendent/immanent character in Christ, suffering is revelatory, and therefore redemptive, not in a transactional way but in a transformational way.

The New Testament writers urge us to see our suffering inside of a larger story, one that ends victoriously in Christ. When Hebrews tells us that Christ learned obedience by what he suffered (Heb 5:8), this does not mean that he became more obedient and less disobedient in a zero-sum way. However, in the midst of suffering, Christ's empowerment in and by the Spirit to live in his perfect obedience as Son of God and Son of Man became increasingly manifest. Even if his sinful flesh did not recede during his earthly pilgrimage, the Spirit reinforced in him again and again who his Father was and who he was as his Father's beloved. In the culminating moment when he faced his steepest challenge against the flesh, his Spirit was willing. As the zenith of Christ's passion approached and the fullness of the flesh came to bear upon him, the fullness of Spirit manifested in Jesus was such that those who challenged him literally fell back to the ground (John 18:6).

We are redeemed, then, not because of suffering but in spite of it. There is not a transactional aspect, as if more suffering equals more redemption. Such a concept is twisted, making God out to be a stingy deity who is reluctant to accept us without his pound of flesh. "Pleading the blood" becomes a means by which an angry God's wrath is mollified. From this perspective, instead of God's wrath serving his love, his love is tragically and unavoidably portrayed as an exception to the rule of wrath. Even if God's wrath serves his love, Cone warns against presenting God as love *without* wrath: "A God without wrath does not plan to do too much liberating, for the two concepts belong together. A God minus wrath seems to be a God who is basically not against anything."[12]

---

12. Cone, *Black Theology of Liberation*, 73–74. I am aware of the risk of coupling Cone and Barth in one paragraph because their distinctions may become less apparent. In the work cited, Cone does not talk about wrath in the way we have discussed, i.e., our position that God's wrath is against us (P^3 with view to P^2) only because God's love is for us (P^3 with view to P^1). I can, however, receive Cone's words as a balm when he states "God's love for white oppressors could only mean wrath—that is, a destruction

The Redeemer is present. He is with us in the very midst of our suffering. No one is more acquainted with human pain and injustice. And his presence as God *means* redemption. In Cone's words, "as Redeemer, God became the Oppressed One in order that all might be free from oppression."[13] This is what Barth meant when he said that Christ's humiliation *is* his exaltation. "In this humiliation," states Barth, "God is supremely God, that in this death He is supremely alive."[14] The humiliation of the Redeemer at Calvary is simultaneous to and synonymous with the exaltation of the victorious Redeemer. We are not meant to call bad things good, but to look for the good in the midst of the bad, the mercy in the mess, the dying and undying presence of the one Jesus Christ our Lord. "Eyes to see" are required.

In this connection, Cone cites the black womanist theologian M. Shawn Copeland:

> If the makers of the spirituals gloried in singing of the cross of Jesus, it was not because they were masochistic . . . [but] because they saw on the rugged wooden planks One who had endured their daily portion. The cross was treasured because it enthroned the One who went all the way with them and for them. The enslaved African sang because they saw the results of the cross—triumph over the principalities and powers of death, triumph over evil in the world.[15]

Note Copeland's startling remark: "they saw the results of the cross." When we look around us, do we see this triumph? Or do we simply see "the cross"—the oppression, injustice, and inhumanity of a human being in excruciating pain? As Richard Wright infers, in this evil age, Christ's triumph can only be seen with the eyes of faith. It remains hidden in the

---

of their whiteness" (78). To the extent I am a white oppressor, I need to be eradicated, *liberated* from my whiteness. I can welcome such salvation by subtraction even when Cone breathes fire like an Old Testament prophet, virtually conflating P^3 with P^2, with no view to P^1. In these cases it is not the whiteness of the subject Cone seeks to eradicate, but "whitey" himself. He speaks of "a love of God which participates in the destruction of the white oppressor" (76). Broad brush indictments, accompanied by an us vs. them, P^3-P^2 conflation of the enemy, are the basis for wars, just or not. In the context of black oppression in America, we feel Cone is spot on to say that "God is on our side" (see 70–78). Along these lines, Toni Morrison remembers being taught by her parents that in racist situations with white people she always had "the moral high ground." See the interview at CultureContent, "Toni Morrison."

13. Cone, *Black Theology of Liberation*, 67.

14. *CD* IV/1, 247.

15. In Cone, *Cross and the Lynching Tree*, 150–51, cited from Copeland's "'Wading through Many Sorrows.'"

transcendent One, the self-proclaimed "Resurrection and the Life" (John 11:25) who suffocated to death.

Von Balthasar graphically portrays the divine warrior, who, as the suffering servant, destroys death by dying. "Eternal life" took for himself a "trembling tent" of flesh;[16] "the Father's eternal vision, without annulling itself, became blinded even to the blindness of a trampled worm."[17] Christ alone, relates von Balthasar, "would henceforth be the measure and thus also the meaning of all impotence. He wanted to sink so low that in the future all falling would be a falling into him, and every streamlet of bitterness and despair would henceforth run down into his lowermost abyss."[18] In a way very different from Penal Substitutionary Atonement (PSA), such a description never loses sight of Christ as primarily the subject (not the object) of the atonement. Von Balthasar concludes: "No fighter is more divine than one who can achieve victory through defeat. In the instant when he receives the deadly wound, his opponent falls to the ground, himself struck a final blow."[19]

While not always in agreement,[20] James Cone and Karl Barth both make it clear that the glaring theological weaknesses of the retributive, penal satisfaction model overshadow its strengths. It takes the cross seriously, but for the wrong reasons, missing the identity of who is sacrificed. Jesus is offered *to God* as a sin offering, but where is God *in Jesus*? In the retributive model, he has momentarily disappeared, the Son is no longer united with

---

16. Von Balthasar, *Heart of the World*, 47.

17. Von Balthasar, *Heart of the World*, 54.

18. Von Balthasar, *Heart of the World*, 43.

19. Von Balthasar, *Heart of the World*, 43–44. Thanks to Cody Andersen for referring me to *Heart of the World*.

20. While an admittedly inexpert reader of Cone, I find that he criticizes Barth most sharply when he thinks that Barth strays from connecting transcendence to immanence. Indeed, Barth would concur that "Christology from above" is vulnerable to diminishing the genuineness of the incarnation, and he might also add that "Christology from below" is no Christology at all. If any theology, liberation theology or otherwise, refuses with Cone and Barth to see the transcendence of God in the very person of the crucified, then the affinity of God for the oppressed loses its internal connection. It is forced to take on an external affinity whereby Jesus is suffering *like* we suffer, he was oppressed *like* we are. When it comes to oppressed and brutalized minorities, Jesus is relegated to being simply a prime example among equals. Contrast this to the fact that the transcendence of God and humanity is present in the humanity of Christ. The transcendence is hidden in a person, and all of us exist in that person. He is the human in whom all human beings are located, the Jew, Jesus of Nazareth. This God-human is the one who gives hope and solace first and foremost to those who find themselves as the oppressed and persecuted minorities of this world, subjugated under the fist of misplaced power. See especially Carr, "Barth and Cone in Dialogue."

the Father. What Barth calls the "supreme blasphemy"—allowing a doctrine of sin to dictate an ontological separation between a transcendent Father and an immanent Son—has occurred. This is not the God Barth describes as the triune One who "is over all that is real as the transcendent God" and "in all that is real as the immanent God."[21]

Meanwhile, we have also seen how the restorative replacement model, while much healthier than the penal substitutionary model, fails to provide a robust continuity to human life, a proper validation of creation. The experiential discontinuity between Friday and Sunday can too easily devolve into a theological, ontological, anthropological discontinuity, making Sunday's re-creation a second creation.

We can again focus on the cross with Cone and Barth in the light of resurrection reality, and we can do so in a way that does not require redemptive suffering or resurrection to *accomplish* restoration and renewal. We could say that "new" is shorthand for continuity (or continuing-newness). What I call a "new" perspective of the cross avoids the on-again, off-again, on-again of eternal life, while promoting a punctuating discontinuity that serves the uninterrupted continuity revealed in the resurrection. The "new" perspective substitutes a transactional view of the cross for one that, on Friday (not simply Sunday), is triumphant (Col 2:15), even if we do not see it until Sunday. As Barth would say, even on Friday, "Christ is Victor!"[22]

---

21. Barth, *Dogmatics in Outline*, 49.

22. This differentiates Barth's view from the typical Christus Victor narrative of the atonement, despite considerable overlap.

84

Salvation by Subtraction

It is the cross that points in the direction of hope, the confidence that there is a dimension to life beyond the reach of the oppressor. "Do not fear those who kill the body, and after that can do nothing more" (Luke 12:4).

—James Cone

Dietrich Bonhoeffer famously stated: "When Christ calls a man, he bids him to come and die."[1] Bonhoeffer does not ask us to do the impossible work of "dying to ourselves." The dying has already been done, but we are meant to live in correlation with the truth of our death and life in Christ, refusing to live for ourselves. This is the logic of Colossians 3:3 and 3:5: "You died" Paul begins, so "put to death therefore" those things that do not belong. Bonhoeffer's phrase also resembles Jesus's words, "Whoever wants to be my disciple must deny themselves and take up their cross daily, and follow me" (Luke 9:23). To be crucified with Christ is not our end as a whole person, but the end of our false selves, our "old man."

We alluded above to the discontinuity and continuity of Galatians 2:20:[2]

> it is no longer *I* who live, but Christ . . . (emphasizing loss of the "I"—discontinuity) and the life *I* now live, *I* live by

---

1. Bonhoeffer, *Cost of Discipleship*, 89.
2. See earlier reading, "The Goodness of Judgment."

the faithfulness of the Son of God (emphasizing the new "I"—continuity).

Instead of a pure, red-green replacement, Galatians 2:20 can be seen to highlight the reemergence of the true, green "I" in the second part of the verse, even after apparently losing the false, red "I." Our nuanced subjectivity can be further deduced in light of the fact that, while Scripture speaks of the one person crucified (here in Gal 2:20), and also of the old self being crucified (Rom 6:6), it never speaks specifically of the true self being crucified. Jesus's remark, "whoever loses their life for my sake will find it" (Matt 10:39), is not to be missed. We lose our life to find it, because it is already there.

Real life does not involve improving creation. Instead of attempting to add more green, what is required is a subtraction of red from our "creation-plus-red" existence. Apart from the light of redemption shining on everyone, all access to goodness, truth, and beauty is lost. As great as creation is in Christ, humans are hopelessly deaf and blind apart from the ministry of the cross. The Redeemer finds us completely lost in death, even in the midst of life. Christ's death, then, burns away the dross and chaff of our false selves. And because of the cross, the quickening of the Spirit gives us fresh ears to hear and eyes to see, and we find ourselves "living to God."

In Philippians Paul declares, "For to me, to live is Christ and to die is gain. . . . Yet what shall I choose? I do not know! I am torn between the two: I desire to depart and be with Christ, which is better by far; but it is more necessary for you that I remain in the body" (Phil 1:21–23). What does he mean by saying, "it is *better to die and be with Christ*"? It would be a mistake to take the italicized phrase and deduce that Paul, writing in the first heaven, is not already with Christ. "To live is Christ, to die is gain" means not to gain something that he does not have, but to lose all that he does not need or want. Think of intricate gears that are all rusty and do not work. Remove the rust that gums up the gears, and things will work the way they were intended. Even if he preferred to go on to glory, Paul was willing to stay in his current, "rusty" state for their sake (1:24). Later in the letter, he calls this extra mess "rubbish." He says that he desires to attain the perfection of the resurrected body, "not that I have already obtained all this, or have already been made perfect."[3] Based on the context, then, when Paul speaks of not having attained it, he does not mean that he is incomplete in Christ, he simply speaks of not being free from the rubbish. His goal is to stay the course and to attain to that perfection which in one sense is already his. In placemat terms, he does not say that he is deficient in green, only

---

3. Phil 3:8–12.

that he is still plenteous with red. He is already perfect, and not yet perfect. When the red is gone, perfect will be nothing but perfect.[4]

What is needed for human salvation is the extinguishing of the red by death. But death does not mean the extinguishing of life, only the extinguishing of all that is un-life. In other words, Christ's death meets the depth of all that death requires; no one can say it was less than death, or a "soft" death. Still, there is "a deeper magic," (as Lewis might say). Only God could become everything that we are, even in our death, and remain God. Humanity is not God, but the incarnate Christ *is* humanity. We are created in Christ, and this inviolable Genesis 1 union has utmost significance: that Christ remains himself in spite of death means that even in our death we remain ourselves.

"Who believes in me will live, even though they die; and whoever lives by believing in me will never die." Like Jesus's teaching on the resurrection in Luke 20, this statement by Jesus in John 11:25–26 can be confusing because it seems so blatantly contradictory. The first part of the statement refers to the typical Christian sequence of death and resurrection. After all, it is a remark made just before Jesus's miraculous raising of Lazarus from the grave. But the second part seems to communicate that resurrection is not needed, because we, in a sense, will never die.[5] What this tells me is that we die, just as Christ himself died; in fact, we all died first and foremost in Christ's death. But just as Christ's death is the point of reference for our death, Christ's life is the point of reference for our life. This means that we

---

4. Bracketing this passage are two verses which celebrate the purity (Phil 1:10) and perfection (Phil 3:15) that Paul unabashedly promotes, showing that the passage in question above is simply reflective of Paul's protection against an over-realized eschatology (his concern to not lose P^2 too soon). This means that Phil 3:15 does not need to be interpreted as "tongue in cheek" sarcasm but as "all of us, then, who are perfect should take such a view of things." The NIV among others unfortunately loses Paul's meaning by substituting "mature" for "perfect," conveying a sense of organic, quantitative, growth into maturity. The NET translation tries to get around the reality of human perfection in Christ by putting "perfect" in quotes, as if to apologize for Paul's hyperbole! In Ephesians and Colossians it is clearer that perfection is a hidden but present-tense dimension of humanity. In fact, Paul describes his charge in ministry is "admonishing and teaching everyone with all wisdom, so that we may present everyone perfect in Christ" (Col 1:28). See Col 2:10 (complete), Col 4:12 (perfect).

5. Humanity's ontological connection with the life of Jesus is reiterated in John 14:19. Jesus says, "Because I live, you also will live." Ellicott remarks, with others, that we should not allow the "because" to shift the understanding to the future. "For I live, and ye shall live," is better. Continues Ellicott, "Our Lord speaks of His own life in the present. It is the essential life of which He is Himself the Source, and which is not affected by the physical death through which He is about to pass." Again, Jesus is not simply talking (if at all) about his future resurrection from the dead, but his continuous life in spite of death, and therefore our true lives as well.

share not only his death but also his life.⁶ "We always carry around in our body the death of Jesus," notes Paul, "so that the life of Jesus may also be revealed in our body" (2 Cor 4:10). From creation forward, then, we are always alive. The good news is that Christ's death "has brought life and immortality *to light*" (2 Tim 1:10, emphasis added). The cross is critical because it defeats death, while the resurrection is critical because it proves life.

There is no way to collate and reconcile "we will die" and "we will never die" into a simplified statement. This is what we must live with in placemat anthropology. But just as important is that Christ died, and we die. It is not *as if* Christ died, or *as if* we die. Such heretical reasoning smacks of docetism. That is why, even if we take seriously the second part of Jesus's statement, we cannot let it carry us away into Platonic dualism. Yes, P^2 is why we die, but "we" (P^3) really do die. P^2 cannot die without P^3, just as P^1 cannot continue living without P^3. The bottom line is that, as with Jesus, we really die and yet we do not die. Only zero-sum approaches, or the inadequate logic of non-contradiction insists on the docetic notion that if Jesus stays alive, he could not have *really* died.⁷ The transcendent God of the higher order can handle anything the lower order demands without being beholden to it.⁸ This should not put us off, as if his death (or ours) was not a historical fact (docetism). He fully accomplished death, comprehending everything that death means in our human existence without any shortcuts or diminishment of its darkness, and that is what counts. To abandon the contradiction of the cross is to embrace something less foolish, less counterintuitive to our worldly senses, which would be a mistake (1 Cor 1:18). To say that God cannot die such that he did not die is precisely the logic of non-contradiction upon which docetism is based.

Even "finished work" advocates do not allow for the salvation by subtraction that I propose here. This is because salvation by subtraction

---

6. Our true selves are simply our believing selves. By employing Scripture's single subject latitude we see communicated not only the truth but its accompanying parenthetical fact. *You*, in your believing self, will remain alive (even though *you*, in your false self will die). The bottom line is that you will never die, even though you die. Both are "you," discontinuity serving continuity. What is true for you by grace is true as derived from Jesus Christ. At the cross, Christ really died, but he did not die.

7. See Beall, *Contradictory Christ*.

8. P^2 cannot be pulled out, or extracted, and crucified on its own, even though Rom 6:6 points to the old self/body of sin as what specifically needs to be "done away with." On the one hand, P^2 cannot be separated from P^1 or P^3 in the first heaven. But Scripture never speaks of P^1 being crucified, pointing to our hidden, human transcendence even in death. To cry "docetism" in this case would be to insist that because P^2 dies but not P^1, it is not a real death. That may be true in Platonic terms, but not in Chalcedonian terms (because of P^3). Only in this carefully qualified way can we say that an Anselmian view of the atonement fits into an Athanasian one, even if not the other way round.

demands that continuity remain intact, and at some point in these other models the continuity has been lost. When continuity is lost, the "new" has lost the essential connection that it had with the "true" all along. It is the new perspective of the cross, one whereby Christ's cross really does the work, that best highlights the inner connection of redemption to creation. Here the "new" witnesses to the undying truth and strength of creation in Christ: the creation as sufficient and complete, lacking nothing. In the purely restorative view, resurrection operates out of lack, or out of deficiency. Things are theologically incomplete on Holy Saturday, and something must be added, so resurrection finishes the work. This results in a weak view of creation, or at least of its sustainability. Such a view of creation is weak not because of the fall, but because of a lack in creation that preceded the fall, a situation that re-creation is meant to improve. To speak of creation christologically, however, is to speak of it lacking nothing. God's works, declares Hebrews 4:3, "have been finished since the creation of the world." The finished work of Christ is simply meant to match anew—therefore unveil—the finished work of creation.

"Christ did not come to straighten out the flesh," says L. E. Maxwell, "but to cross it out." That is salvation by subtraction in a nutshell. The title of Maxwell's book, *Born Crucified*, points to our meaning. All of the indicatives that we typically use to describe believers post-conversion—righteous, holy, just, etc.—are true from creation on. We are righteous and perfectly obedient not only by virtue of redemption, but by virtue of *creation*, as revealed in redemption. In a sense there has never been a time, nor an action, in which we were not faithful disciples of Christ "living to God" (Rom 6:11). To live in "harmony with the cross," concludes Maxwell, is to live in a way that recognizes that the cross condemns me to righteousness, exposing all that is not of Christ, all the ways we are not living to God.[9]

No one has been stronger on the inner-connection of redemption and creation than the fourth century North African theologian Athanasius ("The Father of Orthodoxy"), and we follow the road he laid out:

> The renewal of creation has been wrought by the Self-same Word Who made it in the beginning. There is thus no inconsistency between creation and salvation; for the One Father has employed the same Agent for both works.[10]

---

9. Maxwell, *Born Crucified*, 28. I rephrased the sentence "the cross condemns me to righteousness" from Maxwell's quote, "The cross of Christ condemns me to being a saint."

10. Athanasius, *On the Incarnation*, 1. This quote appears also in Book One.

> Thus, taking a body like our own, because all our bodies were liable to the corruption of death, He surrendered His body to death in place of all, and offered it to the Father. This He did out of sheer love for us, so that in His death all might die . . . that He might turn again to incorruption men who had turned back to corruption.[11]
>
> By his death salvation has come to all men, and all creation has been redeemed. He is the life of all.[12]

Jesus Christ is "the life of all." This has always been true. We have seen Barth's concurrence with Athanasius: "Eternal life is not another, second life beyond our present one. . . . It is *this* life in relationship to what God has done in Jesus Christ for the whole world and thus also for us."[13]

For Athanasius and for Barth, Christ's death for all meant salvation for all. When we think of salvation by subtraction, we might think of things crumbling away. It is an apt metaphor in light of the destruction passages in Scripture like those we cited above in Malachi and Zechariah. The historical event of the destruction of Jerusalem (70 CE) is also applied by John to describe the falling away of the heavens and earth for a new heaven and earth, a new Jerusalem, to emerge. And in John's language the way it happens is not only for one dimension to give way to the other, but for that which is above, the heavenly city, to descend upon that which is below. It is still Jerusalem, but also different. This kind of transposition—different from a sequential, spatial, displacement—is how the Bible describes one dimension giving way to another.

While in one sense we could imagine the dimensional subtraction as a window shade rapidly returning up to its rolled position, John's vision might also be likened to a shade *coming down*. This image seems more integrated with the first-heaven experience of this world, i.e., what is hidden is not simply what is in store behind an opaque curtain or under the cover of a scratch-off ticket. Instead, fitting well with Paul's baptismal language to "put on Christ" (Gal 3:27) the gospel promise is that our spiritual-material bodies are what we put *over* our mortal bodies, matching what Paul elsewhere calls our "inner being" (Rom 7:22). The marvelous subtraction occurs when our "inner" is manifest as our "outer" and the old outer is swallowed up. This is a theme we will revisit in Part Seven.

Until that day of unveiling, we can proceed with the confidence that our spiritual-material bodies are our most real bodies, even in this world,

---

11. Athanasius, *On the Incarnation*, 9.
12. Athanasius, *On the Incarnation*, 37.
13. Busch, *Karl Barth*, 488, emphasis added.

and even if they are not what we see in this world. We are spiritual beings before biological beings. That is what makes our physical bodies so important. We are persons in the Spirit, and our bodies are temples of the Spirit, just like we are in Christ and Christ is in us.[14] "Christ in you," as C. Baxter Kruger reminds us, is "the light which shines in the darkness, summoning us to take sides with Jesus against the way we think and see and feel and project, even while warning us that if we don't we doom ourselves to the misery of living in the great illusion and its fear."[15] Kruger's point is that becoming preoccupied with what is seen is to get the cart before the horse and to buy-in to first-heaven lies.

Finally, to live from the third heaven is to live as an active and conscious participant in the body of Christ. In John's description of the new Jerusalem he remarks that Jesus himself is the temple descending from above, housing all of God's people. Barth sees plainly the inner connection between the new building we have from God and the corporate sense of the new humanity.[16] It is not just that each person has, along with their provisional earthly tent, an individual building from God. Instead of many tents, there is simply one big tabernacle. In fact, it is the second sense that is primary: because Christ is, we are, and because we are, I am.

As a biblical phrase, the "body of Christ" is not applied to humanity in general. Instead, it is what we might call a living-from-the-third-heaven term—the "body" describes those desiring to follow the "head." In saying this we must emphasize the following: the idea of human beings following Christ cannot be grasped apart from a recognition that the head of the body is also the head of *humanity*. There is no ontological distinction between those inside and outside of the so-called "body of Christ," the church. It is a weak ecclesiology indeed which has such a limited view of the incarnation that Christ's representative person and work is not applied first and foremost to every human. How does Christ speak to us through this person,

---

14. It is often noted that Paul uses the concept that we are a temple of the Holy Spirit personally/each person (1 Cor 6:16) but also corporately, as a body (1 Cor 3:16). If we are in the Spirit, and the Spirit is in us, then can we hold that we are temples of ourselves, at least indirectly? Perhaps better is to say that our mortal bodies, our "earthly tents," are temples for our spiritual material bodies. Because our spiritual material bodies are imprisoned in the flesh, we are lost from ourselves and cannot get to ourselves directly, no matter the proximity. We must go through Jesus Christ to find ourselves. Finally, it cannot be overemphasized that our mortal bodies being temples for the Spirit (and therefore for our spiritual bodies in the Spirit) a) makes our mortal bodies more important, not less; and b) gives them a value and dignity that is not due them apart from the Spirit. The former protects us from the gnostic error, the latter from idolatry.

15. Kruger, "Note on Union with Christ," para. 6.

16. *CD* IV/2, 629.

this person who does not believe in God? This person of a different faith? This person with intellectual disabilities? With mental illness? A person who is "non-responsive? How is Christ teaching us through our children?

It is impossible to have a good ecclesiology without a sound theological anthropology. Placemat anthropology is meant to provide a theological antidote to the vindictive polarity we experience not just between Christians and "the world," but also in the schisms that manifest within the so-called body of Christ.

Drew Hart summarizes it well:

> The church must subversively embrace the new humanity and the diverse gifts and varied perspectives that exist within it. It must intentionally privilege the voices and perspectives of those in society who are most neglected, forgotten, ignored, and silenced. The community that has visibly flipped things upside down will not define its life by the standards and expectations of dominant culture. Risking being labeled foolish or inefficient, the subversive community, under the lordship of Jesus, will patiently dialogue in community, believing that God's Spirit can speak through someone without a high school diploma as clearly as through someone with a PhD.[17]

---

17. Hart, *Trouble I've Seen*, 171.

PART SEVEN

Immortals Fall

85

Bringing Immortality to Light

The winter of despair has long lain upon our souls. . . . Now all has changed. This is the Resurrection Morning. . . . This alone is real. These other things that fill and, alas! must fill our pages—murder, meanness, the hurting of little children, the dishonoring of womanhood, the starving of our souls—all these are but unsubstantial smoke and shadow that hide the real things. This reality is ever there, however dark the darkness that blackens and hides it.

—W. E. B. Du Bois

Grasping the immortal and invisible is like a trapeze artist who already has her hand on the next trapeze before releasing the first one; there is never a time when we float in limbo. We are never disembodied or naked souls. The in-between period we enter from our first-heaven "death bed" is one between trapezes, one hand clutching each. It is the day in which Satan will make one last fierce attempt to swing us to his side.[1]

---

1. I'll add another illustration to demonstrate the overlap of the two dimensions: What do you see when reading this sentence? "I'm mortal." Most of you, aided by punctuation and spacing, probably saw the two words "I'm" and "mortal." The word "Immortal" is hidden. Here in this world, "I'm mortal" and "Immortal" share the same space. The first represents the discontinuity, the second, continuity. Both are accurate in the first heaven, and both are accurate in the second heaven (the borderlands). Past that, they are not concurrent.

The problem is never what we do not have. It is in reaching back for what we do not need. Walking by faith in this checkered world, we are meant to steward our mortal bodies but also to hold them loosely. The idea of being stripped of our old clothing—our tent, or mortal body—could be one to fear. But we will never be stripped naked or unclothed, only *further* clothed (2 Cor 5:4). Paul here distances himself from Plato and the Hellenistic idea of naked souls in the afterlife—souls without bodies.[2] That is why Paul introduces another metaphor to assure us that we will never be found without a body; we are told that the clothing of the flesh, the so-called canvas of our earthly tent, is not stripped away but swallowed up. It is as if our real clothing, the material clothing of our immortal bodies (our eternal house), is always underneath and instead of simple removal our grave clothes in this instance are subsumed and consumed by a reapplication of reality. It is like a reiteration of our immortality on one hand, and a reemergence of our immortality on the other. Our ongoing Genesis 1 spiritual-material body assures that we are never disembodied or unclothed. Still, we anticipate being further clothed (with our renewed Genesis 1 body), so that our mortal body (Genesis 2 body) is swallowed up by life.[3]

Back in 1 Corinthians we read, "The body that is sown is perishable, it is raised imperishable; . . . it is sown a natural body, it is raised a spiritual body" (1 Cor 15:42, 44a). Note how Paul's narrative apparently starts humanity off in our "first heaven"—the perishable realm. Yet it is clear that there is an element of preexistence in the event of sowing: something that is sown preexists the sowing of that thing.

This brings us back to the difference between being created and conceived, or born. We are created spiritual bodies, and sown into our mother's wombs. When we see a natural body, continues Paul, we know there is also a spiritual body (1 Cor 15:44b). Here, Paul speaks of the natural body not as original human nature but as identical with the earthly tent. By natural body he means biologically conceived. This is corroborated by the aforementioned 2 Cor 5:1 passage, where Paul assures us that "if the earthly tent we live in is destroyed, we have a building from God, an eternal house in heaven, *not built by human hands* (emphasis added)."[4] Could it be that

---

2. See Plato's *Gorgias* dialogue between Socrates and the Sophists, especially regarding the judgment of naked souls.

3. The contrast between "mortal" and "life" is a direct one, i.e., "mortal" being swallowed up by "immortal," "life" and "immortality" being essentially synonymous in the New Testament.

4. We are "children born not of natural descent, nor of human decision or a husband's will, but born of God" (John 1:13). To be "born from above" (John 3:3), then, connects back to John 1:13. It is to be empowered in the Spirit to live into our identity

this is the whole point of human existence, that we were sown into this fallen world as friends of God and participants in his work? In the midst of this 2 Cor 5 passage, Paul seems to think as much: "Now *it is God who has fashioned us for this very purpose* and has given us the Spirit as a deposit, guaranteeing what is to come" (2 Cor 5:5, emphasis added).

Why is it that we are "wrought" (KJV, ASV), "prepared" (ESV, NRSV), "made" (WEB), or fashioned by God according to Paul? He says it is for "this very purpose," and the "this" refers to what is immediately previous: it is the life of groaning under the adversity of this world. God created us as persons in Christ for glory and unadulterated joy in communion with the Trinitarian persons, but this tells us that he also wrought us for this journey of sharing in the sufferings of Christ.[5] The image of the tent is fitting for a journey. The journey we are called to is through the valley of the grey shadow of death (what we could call our "*sarx* experience") and on to victory in Christ and the full manifestation of his work. We were created to share in the marvelous consummation of that day, the day when immortality comes fully to light. With all the pain that comes in between creation and consummation, we might ask for less!

If Paul is bracing us for the adversity of this world, the second phrase of the verse gives us comfort and courage: "Now it is God who has fashioned us for this very purpose and *has given us the Spirit as a deposit, guaranteeing what is to come*" (2 Cor 5:5, emphasis added). In it he doubles down almost exactly on this sentiment from his first letter to the Corinthians: "Now it is God who makes both us and you stand firm in Christ. He anointed us, set his seal of ownership on us, and put his Spirit in our hearts as a deposit,

---

as a child of God. John 1:13 is strengthened further if the direct reference to "born" is singular (as in some ancient texts), "born not of natural descent" referring then first to the person of Christ and possibly the virgin birth, and secondarily to us "born" in Christ, the "first born of all creation" (Col 1:15). In either/both of the cases—whether it be the humanity of Christ or humanity derived from Christ—the spiritual-material body precedes the biological material body.

5. With its sense conveying preparation (many translations use "prepared") the word "wrought" or "fashioned" in 2 Cor 5:5 can be thought of as a two-fold formation of human beings, being formed not only in the pristine creation of Genesis 1 but also from the dust of Genesis 2. Immediately previous to his discussion regarding his "earthly tent" is Paul's description of humans as "jars of clay" (2 Cor 4:7). These two metaphors in close proximity represent the human *sarx* experience, i.e., that signified by the Genesis 2 creation saga. Like the tent, the jars of clay represent the dust that will return to dust, and the "all surpassing power" inside us "jars" is from God, not intrinsic to us. It is the glorious power not of the human spirit but of the Holy Spirit, in whom we exist and by whom our spiritual-material bodies are breathed into this world. Again, when it comes to the more accurate being "fashioned" or "wrought" as opposed to "*made* for this very purpose" (1984 NIV, emphasis added), even if Genesis 2 is primarily in view, it is certainly not without Genesis 1.

guaranteeing what is to come" (1:21–22, emphasis added). This deposit points to our spiritual-material body, our "building" rather than our "tent," the green humanity given us in the Spirit at creation and which, despite the enemy's attempts at corruption, will never spoil or fade.[6]

Returning to 1 Cor 15, we read:

> So it is written, "The first Adam became a living being"; the last Adam, a life-giving spirit. The spiritual did not come first, but the natural, and after that the spiritual. The first man was of the dust of the earth; the second man is of heaven. As was the earthly man, so are those who are of the earth; and as is the heavenly man, so also are those who are of heaven. And just as we have borne the image of the earthly man, so shall we bear the likeness of the heavenly man. (vv. 45–49)

"It is written" refers to Paul's citation of Genesis 2:7. This citation is critical for our discussion. Immediately we have a clue in that Paul starts his narrative by what we see and experience first in this world, the first heaven of the Genesis 2 account. Why does Paul not start his human narrative in Genesis 1?

We proposed in Book One that to recognize the distinct but inseparable creation accounts of Genesis 1 and Genesis 2 (shorthand for Gen 2–3) requires us to think of Genesis 1 as being "breathed into" Genesis 2. All of Genesis 1 is in Genesis 2, but not all of Genesis 2 is in Genesis 1. Now we can elaborate on our newest consideration that the spiritual body is "sown" into the garden of Genesis 2, where God places humanity (Gen 2:8). The Adam who is sown into the garden is the Genesis 2 human, "the man of dust," even if by now we know that "dust" is not *all* that Adam is. But in 1 Corinthians 15, Paul starts with the man of dust, the natural man, as the one who came "first." This is consistent with his portrayal of fallen Adam as the so-called "First" Adam in Romans 5.

---

6. I have argued throughout that phrases from Paul relating to the "inner *anthropos*" (e.g., 2 Cor 4:16), "the heart" (Rom 6:17), "inmost being" (Rom 7:22), and here "a deposit," all of these point to the in-Christ dimension of true humanity in the green, the spiritual-material body contrary to *sarx*. If the modern reader wishes Paul spelled this out more clearly, the fact that he doesn't is likely due to the comfort level of his ancient audience with anthropological duality. The Spirit "as a deposit," as with "Christ in you," gives us as humans an identity in the Spirit and with the Spirit, and yet refuses to collapse the gift of the Holy Spirit in us into the human spirit (see Paul's intentional distinction in Rom 8:16). In 2 Corinthians 5 Paul charges us to perceive people in light of this deposit (v. 5)—in light of their true, hidden, humanity—and to walk by faith (v. 7), not like "those who take pride in what is seen rather than in what is in the heart" (v. 12).

Just as all human beings fell when Adam fell (being present in fallen Adam), all human beings are present in Genesis 1 as created in the elect and original Adam, Jesus Christ. We are all there. So why does Paul start the human narrative, in 1 Corinthians 15 and in Romans 5, with the man of dust (fallen Adam)? Why is it that he leaves the original Adam of Genesis 1 as implied and in the background?[7] I think the answer is simply this: he is honoring the first-heaven narrative and the economy of the historical incarnation, the "Savior [who] has been born to you" in the City of David (Luke 2:11). This is the gospel as it comes to the shepherds in the field, and to us. Paul is not focused here on Christ as the "first born of all creation" (which fits better with Genesis 1), but instead on the babe who was "born of the Virgin Mary, suffered under Pontius Pilate, and was crucified, dead, and buried" (Apostles' Creed). He wants us to know the heart of God as revealed through the dust of human brokenness and despite all sin and all evil that the enemy casts upon us. If God is going to submit us to the frailties of the first heaven—if Christ sends us into the world in the same way that the Father has sent him into the world (John 20:21)—then the focal point of his relationship to humanity must be the horrors of the cross. God wants us to know God's love not just as an esoteric concept but as an embodied act, the passion of Jesus Christ in his suffering and death. In Von Balthasar's words, Christ wants us to know that all falling is "a falling into him."

Christ's dying is how we know what love is. And his rising is how we know what victory is. In 1 Corinthians 15 Paul describes moving from our first heaven to the second, where our vision is as clear as the trumpet's call. On that day, and in a crescendo highly resonant with 2 Corinthians 5, Paul exclaims: "For the perishable must clothe itself with the imperishable, and

---

7. As noted earlier ("Nothing but Green"), the implicit reverse side of fallen Adam is un-fallen Adam (see also "The Grand Miracle" in Book One). See also John 8:23. Here Jesus says, "You are from below; I am from above. You are of this world; I am not of this world." Like Paul, Jesus begins with his hearers, in this case the Pharisees, in the first heaven. He explains that the lower order cannot apprehend the higher, apart from the revelation of the higher. He is not, however, saying that we are *not* of heaven, or that being of this world is *all* that we are. In keeping with the principle of transposition, he makes sure that we know that even the other worldly, heavenly existence that we do have is always understood as derivative. Jesus is not afraid to quote the verse from Psalms, "you are gods" in speaking of humanity (John 10:34): "I have said, 'You are gods; you are all sons of the Most High'" (Ps 82:6). And the way he speaks of the disciples shows not only the worldly, blind, fleshly side (as with the Pharisees) but the otherworldly, true, and real dimension. The former points to living from the first heaven, and the latter points to living from the third heaven. That is why the disciples are, as a provisional representation of all humanity in Christ, in the world but not of it, according to Jesus (John 17:14, 16): "They are not of the world any more than I am of the world. . . . They are not of the world, even as I am not of it."

the mortal with immortality. When the perishable has been clothed with the imperishable, and the mortal with immortality, then the saying that is written will come true: 'Death has been swallowed up in victory'" (1 Cor 15:53–54).

Pre-existence is something we human beings are meant to know by going through the "backdoor" to apprehend the eternity of God. In a way that Barth would follow centuries later, Paul believes it is in the first heaven (placemat terms) that we are given to understand who the God of all eternity truly is, and *therefore* who we truly are. Our understanding of the other "heavens"—second heaven, third heaven, and especially original/first-first heaven—starts here as revealed in this fallen world, and that is why concepts of human pre-existence start here too, in the Oppressed One (Cone). Barth knows that if we start with human pre-existence without reference to the salvation history of Jesus Christ and him crucified, we are at risk of granting pre-existence to humans as an eternal right, apart from God's grace. Even if Barth is comfortable with human pre-existence, and God sharing his eternity with humans, he is dead set against all hubristic claims of eternal co-existence with God.[8] Not only that, Barth is wary of exalting a Genesis 1 humanism apart from the consequences of the fall, granting every human a stamp of God's image with no need to refer to Christ or the cross at all.

The salvation history of the God who became human, who was born, lived, died, raised, and ascended—the history in which every human being is implicated—is our necessary starting place. Only when we know where we are going (the third heaven) can we know from where we come (the original heaven of Genesis 1). Only in being *clothed* with immortality will we know our immortality. Paul is convinced that it is only retrospectively, in new creation's light, that we can understand creation. In fact, apart from the resurrection, we are devoid of the revelatory basis needed to reinterpret creation christologically. The "prince of this world" (John 14:30) has done a good job blinding us to the fact that the new heavens and the new earth that will emerge (Rev 21:1) are synonymous with the original heavens and earth created by God and which have always been there (Gen 2:1).

Paul does not rest on the prescriptive, ontological alignment of Genesis 1 when he starts his narrative, but instead begins in the same experiential dimension as the birth of Jesus of Nazareth, the descriptive narrative of Genesis 2. The Genesis 2 saga is the sphere of historical revelation and the theater where the themes of justification, sanctification, and the reconciliation of humanity to God play out through Christ's death and resurrection

---

8. *CD* II/1, 616.

(Rom 4:25). The first-heaven realm involves the historical finishing of a work that is, in another sense, already finished in Genesis 1.

At this point it is worth repeating how Barth's phrasing about the eschaton—all of the Then is in the Now, even if not all of the Now is in the Then—can be applied in two ways. If we think about our current situation as the "Now," and if we look forward, the "Then" can be applied to Revelation 22 (as in *"then* all will become clear"), but it can just as easily be applied to Genesis 1 if we look backward (as in "back *then*"). So, when we say with Barth that all of the Then is in the Now, "Then" can refer to either Revelation 22 or Genesis 1, both are equally true. Together they form the common reference point for all that is in between.

As revealed in the confusion and contradiction of the first heaven, Paul concludes, human beings are citizens of heaven, fashioned in the image and likeness of Jesus Christ our human brother and savior. We are men and women from heaven in "the man from heaven." It is not clear the degree of Paul's access to Jesus's teachings, but is it possible that his teaching here about the seed sown is a way of recasting Genesis in light of Jesus's parable of the sower (Jesus representing God and humanity as sower, seed, and soil)? Notes Barth, "Even in the sowing, the passing, the dying, and the burying of our temporal life we are a new creation, born again, the children of God, justified, partakers of the Holy Spirit. But this reality of our being in and with Christ is not visible in this sowing."[9]

Implementing Paul's language in these two passages, then, we can see that our mortality is sandwiched between two layers of immortality—swallowed up between creation and redemption. This is what it means to die and rise again in the Immortal One. In that moment we will be made fully manifest, as if the Christ within is ushering us into the Christ in whom we already live—it will be the epitome of *growing up into Christ our head* (Eph 4:15).

To take off the old and put on the new is not meant to be heavy, muscular language, as if we must accomplish something. It is Paul's encouragement to live into the death and resurrection of Christ in which we, by grace, have always been implicated. Celebrating the sacrament of baptism is an obvious way to do this. As baptized believers in the first heaven living from the third heaven, we have "put on Christ" in anticipation of that day: "You have taken off your old self, with its practices, and have put on the new self, which is being renewed in knowledge in the image of its Creator" (Col

---

9. *CD* IV/1, 330. See my exegesis on the parable of the sower in the earlier reading "Deliverance Time."

3:9–10).¹⁰ We are putting on what God has put in: "Christ in you, the hope of glory" (Col 1:27).

It is of no little importance that just as in Colossians 3:9–10 above, Ephesians 4:22–24 also speaks of putting on Christ as living into our original creaturely image and likeness: "put off your old self, which is being corrupted by its deceitful desires. . . . Put on the new self, created to be like God in true righteousness and holiness." Falling prey to sequential thinking, we might mistake this verse as describing a taking off *before* a putting on. But then we would be back to the Platonic, naked, in-between state that Paul disavowed: souls without bodies. This is not Paul's meaning. There must already be a true self, Paul's "inner man" in Christ, in order for there to be a swallowing-up that occurs when we "put on Christ." Where creation and re-creation meet, the green swallows-up the tent canvas from both sides, and the red falls off in tatters. To take off the old Pat and put on the new Pat is, in the light of the cross, to discover the real, original, Pat. The clothes will fit perfectly.

---

10. See also Rom 13:14. Baptism and the sacrament of the eucharist (or communion, the Lord's supper) are internally connected in the sense that Jesus's words, "do this in remembrance of me," are meant to call us to see ourselves in the story. This is the remembrance of the "who" of the atonement, a "who" who includes all of us, and in whom we are given to recognize and remember that Christ didn't just do something for us, but with us. We are wrapped up in Christ's wholeness and brokenness, and in the resurrection revelation that the first is deeper and truer than the second.

86

The Power of Contrast
(But Not the Need)

The life of this planet, and especially its human life, is a life in which something has gone wrong, and badly wrong. Every time that we see an unhappy face, an un-healthy body, hear a bitter or despairing word, we are reminded of that. The occasional dazzling flashes of pure beauty, pure goodness, pure love which show us what God wants and what He is, only throw into more vivid relief the horror of cruelty, greed, oppression, hatred, ugliness; and also the mere muddle and stupidity which frustrate and bring suffering into life.

—Evelyn Underhill

God fashioned us to share in his sufferings and especially to share in his glory. What Barth calls this "fellowship" of human suffering takes place inside of the parameters of the supreme suffering of the Savior: "Jesus himself was a suffering creature, and as such the Lord of all creatures." It follows that our derived suffering is a "suffering with Him, in His fellowship" and therefore there is a "supreme dignity" about it.[1] Human dignity and glory is only magnified when we recognize that the cross of Christ, and ours with him, is provisional. "The crown of life," continues Barth, "is more than

---

1. *CD* IV/2, 611. Barth makes this faith claim of "supreme dignity" given by God to sufferers in face of the skeptic who might instead choose to see a divine sadism.

this.... It is not the cross which is eternal, but the future life revealed by the resurrection."[2]

Without including any red in his perfect creation (Genesis 1), God somehow comprehended the red negation in his sovereign purposes as Creator as seen in Genesis 2. In the vernacular of Psalm 23, we are in the shepherd's green pastures from Genesis 1 on, even when we walk through the shadowy, grey valley of death. We can know that God's goodness and mercy accompany us every step of the way. Despite the duality of this world, we might have the glorious awareness of our home of green even while we are "away." When we "get home," we will finally know that we have always been home—home in the heart of God, where we dwell in the house of the Lord forever.

According to Irenaeus's theme of recapitulation, a form of subtraction in and of itself,[3] it is "not just the physical and ethical consequences of human sinfulness that Christ deals with ... but rather that very sinfulness itself, expunging it from our nature by living out a life of obedience from within that same nature." Trevor Hart's reflections on this theme are worth quoting in full:

> Thus he restores immortality to man, and endows him once again with that image and likeness of God which was twisted beyond recognition at the Fall.... Only thus can we really understand the force of Irenaeus's objections to Gnostic docetism; only thus can we see the theological force behind his insistence that in the incarnation Christ passes through every phase of human existence, sanctifying it in himself; only when we have grasped the fact that for Irenaeus, just as truly as for the Cappadocians, that which has not been taken up into the recapitulation in Christ remains estranged and fallen, that "the unassumed is the unredeemed," will we see the fundamental point of his insistence that "flesh is that which was of old formed for Adam by God out of the dust, and it is this that John has declared the Word of God became."[4]

How, then, is recapitulation a form of subtraction? If recapitulation means to sum up, restate, regather, or draw in (Eph 1:10), then we might use another analogy. Imagine a central air conditioning system blowing good air into a room, and then the "return" fan (or "exhaust fan") pulling the dirty air back into the system through the filter. The good air flows into the room

---

2. *CD* IV/2, 613.
3. See the earlier reading, "Hiding While Found," in Book One.
4. Hart, "Irenaeus," 173–74.

where it circulates. Then, while the "dirty air" is sucked out of the room, the filter purifies it from the contaminants it picked up while it was in the room. All the good air is in the bad, but not all the bad air is in the good. Such is the situation in Genesis 1 as it relates to Genesis 2–3. God fills his lungs with nothing but good air when he creates, and then he breathes the pure air of Genesis 1 "into" Genesis 2–3 from one side of human history, only to inhale Genesis 2–3 from the other side of human history through the filter of judgment. Satan hopes that he can condition us to his own fumes; we even want to stay put most of the time, often convinced that this is our home. For the Creator to sum up or regather in himself all he has created, then, means for this self-same Redeemer to inhale through the filter of his death all of the pure air that he originally breathed out—this pulls the creation forward into the eschaton, drawing all people to himself (John 12:32). Thus, it is a recapitulation of the whole. In the person of the Savior, creation and redemption, incarnation and atonement, are of a piece.

We live in a "creation-plus" world. A world where Jesus Christ assumes all the "plus" pollutants and the corrosive additives in order to remove them.[5] In fact, to put the above illustration in christological and Trinitarian terms, we could say that the final *inhale* of the Father through the filter of Christ crucified is synonymous with Jesus's final *exhale*. That is poet Malcolm Guite's insight about Christ:

> His Spirit and his life he breathes in all. . . .
> And now he comes to breathe beneath the pall
> Of our pollutions, breathe our injured air
> To cleanse it and renew. His final breath
> Breathes and bears us through the gates of death.[6]

In review, if Genesis 1 and 2 is meant to be understood in a unified, two-fold fashion, then we can also imagine the incarnation as two-fold. The first incarnate flesh is pristine (the first born of all creation), while the second incarnate flesh is corrupt (John 1:14).[7] As Athanasius teaches

---

5. I use this illustration hesitantly, not wanting to encourage anyone to think of our spiritual bodies as immaterial or ephemeral. God is Spirit (John 4:24), and he gloriously speaks the Word into us as material spiritual bodies (Rom 10:8; Deut 30:14). We therefore wish to hold to the false humanity and the true humanity of the Word made flesh. If we think of flesh as simply bad, then we must forfeit all talk of created, Genesis 1, "flesh," even if it is a different flesh (not the flesh and blood of this world).

6. Guite, "Poem XII, Jesus Dies on the Cross," 42. Thanks to Quinn and Annie Holmquist for this reference.

7. Even if P^2/P^3 are incorrupt, as long as P^2 is extant, P^3 can be considered corrupt. That is why Paul can talk about the flesh as P^2 (Rom 6:6; 1 Cor 15:50), or as P^3 as corrupted by P^2 (Phil 3:3–6). He also talks about P^3 as *uncorrupted* by P^2 of course (e.g.,

us, the Word who redeems us is "the self-same Word" who made us in the beginning. The one who is life is *our* life from creation on. He is the Light who gives light to every person (John 1:9), the Word who expresses himself in every creature (John 1:3). This same Word, beyond simply creating us (Genesis 1) and breathing Genesis 1 into Genesis 2, entered Genesis 2 in anticipation of the incarnate struggle, taking on alien (non-original) flesh. So Jesus Christ is not only "the first born of every creature" but "the firstborn from among the dead, so that in everything he might have the supremacy" (Col 1:18). The resurrection of Jesus Christ, then, does not accomplish life, it reveals it. There is never a sequence in play such as life, then no life, and then life again. Instead, life runs all the way through, despite death.

If this makes death "not so bad," do we make light, then, of human suffering? In 1998 I led a memorial service for my dear friend Marcello, who was involved in our student ministry and was tragically killed at age eighteen by a drunk driver. The passage I chose to preach from was Luke 7:11–17, Jesus's encounter with the widow of Nain.

Jesus and "a large crowd" of his followers converged at the village gate with another "large crowd," a funeral procession for a young man being carried out for burial. The body was on a pallet, or board-like stretcher, and when Jesus approached the entourage, he spoke directly to the boy's mother. Like Marcello's mother, she was a single mom. The widow of Nain had lost her husband, and now she had lost her only son (and in that culture, her entire livelihood). Surely this woman was blinded by the grief of "Why?" Bent with hopelessness, the widow had nothing to give, not even faith, and Jesus required nothing of her. Unconditionally, and full of compassion, he entered into the chaos.

Three very unexpected things happen. First, Jesus said, "Don't cry" (we will return to this apparently callous remark). Second, he turned to the dead body and did something even more unexpected—he reached out and intentionally touched the open coffin. In that religious culture, touching anything associated with this dead boy would have made a person ceremonially unclean. For a holy rabbi to do such a thing grabbed everyone's attention. Whatever weeping and wailing that was going on probably came to an abrupt halt. Third, and *most* unexpectedly, Jesus then said, "Young man, I say to you, get up!" The boy sat up (while the pallbearers probably fell out!). Jesus then handed the once-deceased boy back to his mother. The crowd went out of their minds with joy, exclaiming together, "God has come to help his people." The irony is that the delirious townsfolk probably did not

---

Eph 5:27, where Paul alludes to the pristine flesh of the church personified, a bride "without stain or wrinkle or any other blemish").

THE POWER OF CONTRAST (BUT NOT THE NEED)

think of their statement in literal terms. For God to come in the flesh was something beyond even the Jewish Messianic imagination.

In using this passage at Marcello's funeral, I realized that it might come across as cruel. Marcello did not get up out of the coffin. Showing the contrast—the boy at Nain getting up, but Marcello not—might have made the grief worse. But I guess the Spirit gave me the assurance that the hidden reality of a broken relationship *restored* would be a salve amidst the pain. Indeed, the restoration between mother and son was already effected, even if hidden in the heavenly realms. The resurrection truth of Jesus Christ applies to them both already, even when it is not yet manifest.

The resurrection reality of Jesus Christ provides the frame for the big picture that is signified in the words, "Don't cry." We remember that according to John's gospel, the day Jesus declared, "I am the resurrection and the life," he wept openly at Lazarus's tomb. There is no reason to think that Jesus did not do the same here. In fact, I do not think Jesus would have said "don't cry" to the widow without his own tears. And I do not think I could have preached this passage on that day unless I was also grief-stricken over Marcello's death. In fact, Marcello's mom told me later that she appreciated my message, but more than that, my tears during the eulogy were what really blessed her. Yes, we grieve, and we grieve with those who grieve, but we do not grieve as those without hope (1 Thess 4:13). The big picture is not meant to make us less compassionate or less sensitive to the pain of others in the here and now—just the opposite. Jesus knew what he was going to do and yet, Jesus's heart "went out to her" (Luke 7:13). Luke's Greek wording here speaks of feeling compassion for another from the depth of one's guts.

The reading has deeper layers of meaning as well. We noted that there are two large crowds—the death crowd and the life crowd—both heading toward the town gate. Borrowing again from John's gospel, we remember that Jesus said, "I AM the gate." That is where the two crowds converge. He is the crossroads of red and green, the intersection of human life and death. Which crowd will win? In Christ, when death and life meet, life wins every time. But the way Jesus wins is different, for he does so by entering in. This account at Nain gives us a picture of the incarnation. Jesus enters in, doing the unthinkable, making himself unclean, representing not only life but death. Jesus is in both "crowds," but he does not take short-cuts. He teaches us that to *be* resurrection you also must *be* death. They go together, after all; death is implied in resurrection and Jesus defines both. He is always Jesus of Nazareth, a Palestinian man existing in the first century under Roman colonial oppression and in the predicament of the human condition. He is also God, the God who "has come to help his people" by dying on a Roman cross.

The big picture of Christ's resurrection gives us hope. But the small, immediate picture often remains profoundly painful. Above I questioned preaching the contrast of the two situations—the boy of Nain rises from the coffin, Marcello does not. I made the case that this contrast is good news, as counterintuitive as it may be. The contrast reveals the power of the gospel. But we must also acknowledge that this same contrast explains why grief is so painful. I believe that, deep down, humans have a sense that this pain, suffering, and brokenness is not the way things really are. Even if they do not have words to describe it, I believe all human grief is rooted in this contrast between how things are here in the world and how things are in the kingdom of God. The glorious reality of the big picture is so starkly contrasted with the brutal and harsh injustice of this world.

Next to the reality of life and God's creation, we can say in comparison that death is more like unreality. The fact that it is unreality does not mean that it does not hurt—no, it hurts like hell. But it hurts in this way precisely because it is not real in the end. Walking by faith in Christ, we can say that the end is good. And, if it is not good, then it is not the end. The contrast to all that is good is indeed glaring. The good shows us how bad the bad is, but the bad (as parasitic) does not have the same power.[8]

In God's economy we do not need the bad to show us how good the good is. In the super-abundance of the third heaven, what God has in store for us will not need a contrast to be appreciated. Transformation does not end when the contrast dissolves. As Barth reminds us, "freed from the whole enshrouding veil of our temporality and corruption, grace will still be the grace of God . . . even in the eternal redemption, we shall not be at the goal, and the blessedness of our perfect knowing of God will consist in a being on the way."[9]

---

8. I'm reminded of C. S. Lewis's thought related to the parasitic destructiveness of evil. If we remember that the parasite can only leech off the host, then in an indirect sense, the worse a negation manifests as the parasite, the more glorious the host must be: "We must believe—and therefore in some degree imagine—that every negation will be only the reverse side of a fulfilling" (*Weight of Glory*, 109).

9. *CD* II/1, 209.

87

Species of Origen?

But the second [creation saga] considers the fact that on the far side of the end of all things the true will and act of God have their beginning, so that it is able to see in the sign of that end the sign of the beginning.

—Karl Barth

WHO WE ARE AS human beings is who we are in Christ. This is synonymous with who we are in the Spirit. This is our true (green) self. But what is the theological location of my true, creaturely, "very good" self in the here and now? And how far back does this true self go?

There is often a knee-jerk reaction among theologians against anything having to do with human pre-existence. It was an idea earlier suggested by Origen and for which he has been oft-maligned through the centuries.[1]

1. I remember one night I was at a pub in St. Andrews with some theology buddies. I broached the above questions and pressed in with others. Do you think we're born sinful? "Yes." Do you think we're created sinful? "No." So do you think it is possible that how we are created and how we are conceived are actually somewhat different? One of my friends recognized that I was pointing to the possibility that our true selves transcend our biological beginning. He exclaimed, "you wouldn't want to go there, that's PREEXISTENCE! And we all know what happened to Origen." But do we? Just as it is easy to misjudge Calvin by "Calvinism," there are those who believe that Origen's condemnation as a heretic by the church three hundred years after his death was actually a response to different versions of Origenism more than to Origen's own views. And there is plenty of reasonable speculation as to political motivations for this late-blooming condemnation. It's inarguable that Origen had a massively positive

Much of the reaction to the idea of human pre-existence seems based on faulty linear thinking. Without dimensional thinking, we are likely to collapse creation and conception into one another without nuance. But good theology requires us to consider things that are "logically primary" to protect us against conflating matters such as creation and conception. As we noted earlier, David's statement that he was "sinful from the moment [his] mother conceived him" (Ps 51:5) cannot be taken to mean that we are sinful from the moment we are created. Hearkening back to the "very good" of Genesis 1:31, the Psalmist's sentiment that we are "fearfully and wonderfully made" (Ps 139:14) is not in the least inclusive of sin. To take another example, God and humanity are one in Christ. But that does not mean these are one and the same. The human never exists apart from Christ, but Christ *does* exist apart from humanity. Jesus Christ is co-eternal with the Father. As the great Athanasius remarked, "There was never a time when the Son was not." However, we are quick to add, there *was* a time when humanity was not. The incarnation, as T. F. Torrance described, means that "something new has taken place in God"[2]

In this book we do not advocate Origen's doctrine of human pre-existence because his Platonic themes are too strong. Following Barth, we insisted that there is never a soul without a body. Origen's teaching of pre-existent *discarnate* souls appears untenable. Despite this, his thought shares certain positions with our placemat approach and Barth's theology.

---

effect on the theology of the early church, and in spite of his rejection by the Roman Emperor Justinian I (543) and the Second Council of Constantinople (553), Origen has been continually revered by a stream of Orthodox theologians right up to this day. In 2011 Pope Benedict XVI went to great lengths to commend Origen and rehabilitate his reputation, calling Origen "a figure critical to the whole development of Christian thought" and encouraging his hearers to "welcome into your hearts the teaching of the great master of faith." Cited in Benecict, *Great Christian Thinkers*, 19, 22.

2. In reference to Athanasius *Ad Apollinarium*, II.1, in Torrance, *Theology in Reconciliation*, 223. See also 224: "The creation was not eternal, and the Incarnation is not some timeless event in God ... but something that had not happened before, even for God. But God is so wonderfully and transcendentally free in his own eternal Being that he can do something new without changing in his *ousia* and can go outside of himself in the Incarnation without ceasing to be what he is eternally in himself in his own ineffable Being, for his *energeia* inheres in his eternal *ousia*." Barth concurs, noting Christ's two-fold incarnation as subsequent to God's separating of the light from the darkness in Genesis 1:2: "This time there takes place something which had not happened even in God's utterance in Genesis 1. God's Word itself, the Word by which everything was created, becomes a creature amongst others.... In this way it makes the world created by it its own—its liability to temptation, its actual temptation, its corruption and need. In this way too, the world for its part is made a partaker of the word of God by which it was created; a partaker of its triumphant vitality, of its holiness and glory" (*CD* III/1, 115).

For example, he interprets Genesis 1 and 2 as distinct but inseparable accounts. From this distinction flows his theology of pre-existence. He, like Barth, views creation as logically primary to conception.[3] Another important commonality between Origen's and Barth's positions is related to their mutual grasp of Jesus Christ being himself the *imago Dei*, the image of God. As we have seen, this casts entirely new meaning on the idea of humanity being created in the Image.

Our placemat anthropology veers sharply from Origen, however, when it comes to his understanding of human freedom, and to this topic we will devote the remainder of the section. We remember from Julian the belief that we are created in Christ with a perfect freedom to do the will of God.[4] In our true selves, we cannot diverge from God's will any more than Christ himself. In this determination we are perfectly free.

Julian's perspective lines up well with that of Barth and Paul, understanding that the new and true humanity—that of the Spirit—cannot disobey, while the old humanity—that of the flesh—cannot obey. The old, or natural humanity (red), says Paul, "does not accept the things of the Spirit of God but considers them foolishness, unable to understand them because they are discerned only by the Spirit." Conversely, "the person with the Spirit" in the new and true humanity has "the mind of Christ" (1 Cor 2:14–16).[5] Paul's teaching in Romans 8 is consistent with this line: "the mind governed by the flesh is hostile to God; it does not submit to God's law, nor can it do so."[6] Meanwhile, in the "real law" (Barth) of my union with Christ, the law of the Spirit of life, I in my inmost being (green) delight to do God's will (Rom 7:22). When it comes to my bondage to Christ, I am obedient from the heart (Rom 6:17). In my true self, I am irresistibly free. In this positive

---

3. Both Barth and Origen are dissatisfied with traditional options of Traducianism (which, through transmission of the seed, conflates creation with the biological moment of pro-creation) and creationism (where creation is concurrent with but arguably un-conflated with conception). In my reading, each advances a nontraditional version of creation which allows for a certain type of pre-existence, even though the two theologians come down in different places.

4. This was covered in Book One.

5. The NIV wording here can easily be misconstrued into a possessive mode, as if some people possess the Spirit and some do not. Technically, the Greek communicates Paul's intent to contrast the fleshly person with the person who is "spiritual," i.e., with the person who is going with the Spirit in the vein of the in-Christ determination.

6. Rom 8:7. In contrast, see the scriptural appeal to "stirring up your pure mind" (2 Pet 3:1, BLB). Or, as Paul notes in Phil 2:5: "Have this mind among yourselves, which is yours in Christ Jesus" (ESV). See also Phil 2:2.

vein, freedom and predestination are magnificently indistinguishable.[7] In Barth's words, "I am my true self only in the reality of my own free will."[8]

Catholic theologian Hans Urs von Balthasar observed that Barth built the keynote of predestination into his doctrine of creation. Because of Barth's unique understanding of predestination, von Balthasar stated, the concept of freedom is "the ultimate foundation of Barth's anthropology."[9] Human beings are free only in the person of Christ who shares life with the persons of the Holy Trinity. In contrast to individualism, personhood in Christ means that we are participating before we know it, and if we *were not* participating, we *could not* participate. Even if invisibly, humanity moves vibrantly, creatively, and spontaneously in Christ in a unidirectional, "transcendental determination."[10] Transcendence, therefore, is not just for God. Indeed, human freedom is "our participation in the internal freedom of God," notes von Balthasar, "a life lived in the intimacy of God's freedom."[11]

Von Balthasar is spot on in his assessment: for Barth, ongoing human life in Christ is "a happening reality" regardless of a person's existential belief.[12] This reality is what we termed the "in-Christ dimension," one that proceeds in the direction of creaturely freedom and is perfectly congruent with the will of God. Origen's belief in a libertarian version of free will—the option to "freely" go with or against God's will—contrasts greatly with Julian and Barth's notions of human freedom.[13]

---

7. Predestination has an ugly reputation in some circles by virtue of it being pirated into the doctrine of limited atonement (the belief that Christ effectively died for a subset of the human race). But I have found predestination, as Barth understands it, to be strikingly beautiful. For example, see *CD* III/2, 144, where Barth speaks of "the all-embracing content of His predestination" in the person of Jesus Christ.

8. *CD* III/2, 180.

9. Von Balthasar, *Theology of Karl Barth*, 129.

10. Von Balthasar, *Theology of Karl Barth*, 128, quoting *CD* III/2, 348.

11. Von Balthasar, *Theology of Karl Barth*, 129.

12. *CD* II/2, 609. Quoted by von Balthasar. Regarding such a thoroughgoing christological/anthropological perspective, von Balthasar expresses discomfort with Barth's view that the church and sacraments add nothing of substance to the reality of Christ, providing only a representative function. But what is the alternative? The "pendulum" alternative is to artificially make allowance for a reality that is *not* already happening, i.e., one that leaves space for a kind of human agency where humans are *not* already, positively, and actively involved. This approach speaks of a human determination that is *not* always actual in Christ, one that needs to be activated from hypothetical to actual, perhaps through church or sacrament. Instead, as I have alluded, far from being mere remembrances, and without adding to the soteriological content of Christ's work, the sacraments can be by the Spirit a transformational participation in the reality of Christ by humans in his body.

13. Unfortunately, this is a place where, for their many similarities, Barth and C.

Barth could agree with Origen about the beginning, that creation is logically primary to conception. The two theologians likewise concurred that God will be "all in all" at the end. But Barth's insistence that God is, in a sense, all in all *now*, even in what we call the first heaven, is a radical departure from the Alexandrian. Barth could not abide with Origen's more circular reasoning (which elevated the importance of a different kind of "free will"). For Barth, as we have seen, true humanity in Christ is consistent before, during, and after the fall, always moving freely in the in-Christ determination of creaturely being.

Before going any further, I want to elaborate on what I term Origen's "circular" narrative. By circular I mean an on-off-on perspective when it comes to Genesis 1 humanity, fallen humanity, and eschatological humanity, respectively. Things are great at creation (on), then humans are estranged from God (off) in varying degrees depending on their "free choices," but in the end they "come back around" to God (on), also by exercising their free will. For Barth, as we have seen, the human narrative is not on-off-on, but on-on-on, with a simultaneous "off" in the middle ("the fatal middle stretch").

It is for this reason that Barth, while fond of one of Origen's favorite phrases, "the end is like the beginning," had to reject Origen's view of human agency. For Barth, at the deepest level, the end is like the beginning, *and the middle is too!* The "on" of total green does not take a break: "on" means in Christ, union with Christ, implication in the vicarious humanity of Christ. In the green of grace we belong, and therefore we are always perfectly believing and perfectly obeying, responding to God in the fullness of Spirit and truth, participating in the leader of our worship, the high priest of our humanity who says *of* the Father "I will put My trust in Him" and the

---

S. Lewis appear to part ways. Like Julian of Norwich (from whom he drew inspiration), Lewis rightly put emphasis on the freedom necessary to love. Unlike Julian and Barth, Lewis communicated a much more Origenist view of free will. Like Barth, Lewis did not hide his distaste for ideas which posed God as a monergist puppeteer, but as indicated in his commentary below, he possibly did not anticipate the way Barth is able to hold both of his (Lewis's) concerns together. See *Mere Christianity*, 52–53: "God created things that had free will. That means creatures can go wrong or right. Some people think they can imagine a creature which was free but had no possibility of going wrong, but I can't. If a thing is free to be good it's also free to be bad. And free will has made evil possible. Why, then, did God give them free will? Because free will, though it makes evil possible, is also the only thing that makes possible any love or goodness or joy worth having." By submitting that bad human use of freedom makes evil "possible," Lewis does not appear to have in view the pre-existence of Evil with a capital E, the nothingness that God separated from light in Gen 1:2, and of which all human evil is derived (and therefore causing human beings in the garden to make un-free choices).

one who says *to* the Father "here am I, and the children God has given me" (Heb 2:13).[14]

The consistency of the "on" (at one level, on-on-on) is the truth by which we are judged. In light of this dynamic consistency, there cannot be a rationale for the Fall (which is thus rendered to be by nature irrational), nor, by the same token, can there be a good reason for a soul terminating in hell (even more irrational).[15] For these things to happen irrationally can only mean that they fly in the face of the "on"—the fact that Christ is "all in all" even in the midst of wicked human choices.

If Origen's approach can be described as universalist, Barth's approach could be described as eschatological realism.[16] Because of his confidence in the "realistic content" of the gospel, Barth sees no need to reach for the tidy closure of universalism—where everyone inevitably comes around at the end of a circular journey. Just as we cannot explain the irrational, neither can we fathom the higher rationality of a God whose thoughts are above our best thoughts. If our theological system causes us to insinuate that God "has to do it this way, or everything unravels," then we have mistaken our theological capacities for the actual free activity of God. In this, we cannot hope for success.

In *Simul Sanctification* I elaborated at length on Barth's theological "actualism." In these volumes I have not used the word actualism, but I have described the actual, ongoing being-in-act of humanity in Christ. This is the derivative dynamic that allows us to say that what the Son of God Jesus Christ is doing for us in his true humanity, we are doing with him. Instead of being a wild theory, actualism is simply based on the reality of how things *are*.

It should be clear that between Origen's circular universalism and Barth's consistent actualism there is a massive difference in the understanding of human free will. This can be explained by considering the "off" in the middle of Origen's on-off-on narrative. Once "off" because of the fall, how does a person get back "on"? In Book One we discussed the grip of grace,

---

14. Jesus is quoting Isa 8:17–18.

15. "Even more irrational" because I imagine judgment day to be the unparalleled moment of clarity, therefore making false choices all the more "impossible" and absurd. We will return to this in the reading, "One Tree in the Garden."

16. See the outstanding article by Dalferth, "Karl Barth's Eschatological Realism," 14–45. Eschatological realism does everything a universalist would want without presuming upon God. The word "risk" is hard for universalists who want to nail it all down. But Barth's eschatological realism is not only a stronger realist position than universalism (because of its actualistic and not circular rationale), but it also gives human beings a real active role by changing the goal from salvation (first and foremost) to salvific participation in the defeat of Satan, the arch enemy.

and how consistent it is. If somehow we wriggled out of the grip when we "fell," or if God dropped us because of our disobedience, only to grasp us again when we come to faith, then the "grip of grace" is not much of a grip. We have to do something in order to get back into it. This conditional mentality sets the table perfectly for what is typically called freewill thinking about salvation. As soon as the "off" (red) displaces the "on" (green) all talk of an uninterrupted green determination (Barth's version of predestination) is lost. The continuous keynote between creation and redemption is severed. Instead, implicitly bequeathed to the human agent is the capacity to decide whether they want to freely choose to remain "off" or to become "on." Barth's favorite expression decrying this anthropocentric inflation of human agency is "Hercules at the crossroads."

Warring against Barth's actualism, the theological "off" described above is still at work in most soteriologies, including doctrines of universalism like Origen's.[17] This "off" traces over the artificial, time-worn lines that separate being and act, objective and subjective, justification and sanctification, de jure (in principal) from de facto (in fact), the *possibility* of Christ and the Spirit's fullness in our lives vs. the *actuality* of Christ and the Spirit's fullness, and static potential vs. active participation. To the extent we as human agents do any of the lifting or finishing or adding, to the degree any synergism is involved, we have become co-redeemers playing Hercules.

Conversely, Barth's actualism explodes all of the divisions, beseeching us to never let participation be "a second thing." In Barth's actualism, "living to God in Christ Jesus," we find the human dynamism that defies any notion of being "in Christ" as a static category. Repentance, belief, obedience, these things are required because of our creaturely determination. We have the opportunity to do them because in Christ we are already actually doing them, keeping perfect covenant with the Father. We are "disposed for participation in the salvation history which proceeds from this covenant" notes Barth. Without the opportunity of human repentance, he continues, what good would we be "to help determine universal history."[18]

Origen's circular thinking, along with its libertarian concept of free will, reemerged mightily through the sixteenth century Catholic theologian

---

17. For a thorough treatment on the universalism question, see my post on "Barth's Actualism vs. Universalism." Many universalists rightly decry both the synergistic (Arminian) and monergistic (Dortian Calvinist) articulations, but short of Barth's actualism they are forced to capitulate to one or the other, or a hybrid version of the two, at the end. Hence by not going far enough, they are forced to go too far, grasping onto language of inevitability or necessity to bridge the gap. The projection is a violation of both God's freedom and humanity's; it removes the integrity of human participants as co-belligerents with Christ on the day. This will be a theme in the coming pages.

18. *CD* III/4, 575–76.

Desiderius Erasmus's tract *On Free Will*. It was immediately confronted by Martin Luther's conception of double-predestination in *On Un-Free Will*, which, like Five-Point Calvinism in the next century,[19] put forth a stern dualism (not duality) when it came to election.[20] Against Luther's dualism (and Calvin who followed), Jacob Arminius and John Wesley would later turn back to the libertarian freedom of Erasmus (and thereby Origen) for inspiration.[21] These teachers spurned predestination as they knew it, preferring instead to emphasize God's foreknowledge. The Arminian persuasion of gospel articulation could at least claim something that the double-predestination reformers could not, namely that God loves everyone equally and that God the Son proved God's love by dying for all people on the cross.

Karl Barth refused to shortchange the love of God, but he also refused to follow suit with the Origen-Erasmus-Arminius-Wesley "free will" line

---

19. Not formulated by John Calvin himself (d. 1564), the expression of something resembling Five-Point Calvinism finds one of its earliest expressions in the Canons of the Synod of Dort from 1618–19.

20. In this type of double predestination, there are two types of people on two sides of God's ledger: those created to go to heaven as predestined, and those who were created to go to hell without a chance. Only for the first group could it be said that Christ died. Only the first group are predetermined to be the covenant people of God. See "The Liar's Religion" below for further assessment of this two-columned approach, and how Barth subverts the traditional monergist-synergist spectrum.

21. Origen's statement at the beginning of *First Principles* (4 [I.Preface]) is instructive: "This also is laid down in the Church's teaching, that every rational soul is possessed of free will and choice.... There follows from this the conviction that we are not subject to necessity, so as to be compelled by every means, even against our will, to do either good or evil. For if we are possessed of free will, some spiritual powers may very likely be able to urge us on to sin and others to assist us to salvation; we are not, however, compelled by necessity to act either rightly or wrongly, as is thought to be the case by those who say that human events are due to the course and motion of the stars." I hope the contrast of this with Barth's view of freedom is becoming clear. At first it may be difficult to distinguish Barth's position from theological monergism, the kind Origen fears above. At the same time, as we will cover in the upcoming reading "The Liar's Religion," the synergists following Origen inevitably fall into another type of dualism. For Barth it all depends on whether or not we can trust the God who designed human freedom exquisitely and expansively and yet in a particularly narrow way. Indeed, there is no such thing as coercion where human beings are irresistibly free (see Gal 5:22–23). See Barth on "the overruling love of the triune God" which shows a freedom that is absolute but not fatalistic (*CD* III/3, 118). For Erasmus's dependence on Origen, see Crouzel, *Origen*, 211. Crouzel cites A. Godin to buttress his assertion, *Erasme lecteur d'Origene*, Geneva, 1982, 469–89. Origen devotes a whole chapter of *First Principles* to free will [III.1]. Against the determinists of his day (Gnostics and astrological philosophers), Origen launches into a fascinating exegesis of Rom 9–11, using Paul elsewhere (Rom 2) and other Scripture to demonstrate that humans with free will are "responsible for our own destruction or salvation." [III.I.6]. Barth takes Erasmus to task regularly, but I have seen no evidence from Barth that he knew of Erasmus's reliance on Origen.

when it came to shortchanging the doctrine of predestination. If Barth disagreed with the free will position to choose between red and green, he also disagreed with the intractable dualism of Luther and Calvin's double predestination, which from all eternity, via God's choosing, locked people into either red *or* green. Following Barth, placemat anthropology makes an exclusive claim regarding what freedom is and how our true selves are created to operate in Christ, the one in whom all are elect.[22] We are free and green in the one who is the same yesterday, today and forever. He has included us all in his dynamic life and in his exquisite freedom from the very beginning—we are in Christ and in the one-directional freedom he provides for us from creation on. This creaturely truth is just as true in the tangled first heaven as it is in the clarity of the second heaven, and as it is in the fully revealed, unadulterated paradise of third heaven, "where righteousness dwells" (2 Pet 3:13).[23]

---

22. Election for all is unavoidably universalism from a 5-Point Calvinism or Dortian perspective.

23. Noteworthy is the convergence of Einstein's physics with the "yesterday, today, and forever" of God and the "on-on-on" of green humanity: "The difference between past, present and future is only a stubbornly persistent illusion." Quoted in Calaprice, *Ultimate Quotable Einstein*, 113.

88

Playing by the Book
Give Me Revelation![1]

Boast not against us, O our enemy! / Today we fall, but we shall rise again; / We grope today, tomorrow we shall see: / What is today that we should fear today? / A morrow cometh which shall sweep away / Thee and thy realm of change and death and pain.

—Christina Rosetti

He might have been a majestic, passive and beatific God on high. But He descends to the depths, and concerns Himself with nothingness, because in His goodness he does not will to cease to be concerned for His creature. He thus continues to act in relation to nothingness with the same holiness with which He acted as the Creator when He separated light from darkness. He continues to be the Adversary of this adversary because His love for the creature has no limit or end.

—Karl Barth

---

1. An acknowledgment of the song by the same title by the band Third Day.

It is unavoidable for all of us: we will never feel more exposed—or more understood—than on judgment day.[2] We will see that God doesn't fiddle with the knobs, seeking a lukewarm alternative somewhere between judgment and compassion; when he turns up the judgment, he doesn't turn down the compassion. Just as we do not stand before Christ solely in our pristine human form on the day, the one who knows all our secrets and checkered thoughts reveals in this moment that he also continues to share our conflicted plight in full solidarity with us. Scripture tells us that we appear before the "Son of Man,"[3] the one who enters fully into our humanity, the one described as "a man of suffering, and familiar with pain."[4] On the throne of judgment is "the suffering servant" Jesus Christ, still appearing as the "lamb who was slain" (Rev 13:8). As Jesus himself states in the gospels, this will be a very public event.[5]

John describes the scene later in Revelation, complete with the famous book of life: "And I saw the dead, great and small, standing before the throne, and books were opened. Another book was opened, which is the book of life. The dead were judged according to what they had done as recorded in the books" (Rev 20:12). John doubles down in the next verse: each person will be judged according to what they have done, and in the end, it comes down to whether or not a person's name is recorded in the "Lamb's book of life" (Rev 13:8).

At this point two questions need to be asked:

1. First, are we really judged based on the things we have done? Such an idea seems contrary to the economy of grace. Indeed, in theological terms we're used to pitting grace against "works." But from what we learned above, we also have to be careful not to leave "act" out of "being." Yes, there is a manner in which works are inadequate to get

---

2. The next four readings on the book of Revelation could cohere as a whole, longer, essay, but I broke them into smaller readings so as to make new material more digestible.

3. See Matt 16:13, 16, where Peter acknowledges the "Son of Man" is the "Son of God" (followed by references to the Son of Man at the judgment: Matt 24:30; 24:44; Luke 17:30; including "the man" who will judge the world, Acts 17:31). See also the opposite coupling in John 5:22, 27, where Jesus is described as "Son of God" and then "Son of Man" with the authority to judge. This passage emphasizes that the Father does not judge but has given all power to judge to the Son, the Son of Man who exists in solidarity with humanity.

4. Isa 53:3.

5. Matt 10:26; Mark 4:22; Luke 8:17; Luke 12:12. Nowhere more than in the second heaven will there be a time for us to feel something like what the woman caught in adultery felt, or what the leper felt, or Zacchaeus, or any of the biblical characters publicly encountered by Jesus.

us into God's good graces. However, because we have been careful to keep imperatives within the indicatives, we can say that God's grace actually *includes* all of the works that God requires. In Christ, we are those already doing good in keeping with immortality (see Rom 2:7).[6] We have acknowledged Barth's insight that participation is not a "second thing"; everyone is participating. In the dynamic movement of the vicarious humanity of Christ, we are doing what Christ our High Priest is doing. It follows that, in Christ, all humans are the good tree bearing nothing but good fruit.

All humans are also, in the flesh, the bad tree bearing nothing but bad fruit, following evil in all manner of self-seeking expressions; trees to be cut down and burned in the wrathful fire of God's love revealed at Calvary (see Rom 2:8). We are all two trees in one. Every human being has witnessed to Christ in certain actions, whether they have given credit or not, and every human being has rejected Christ, whether cognizant or not (see Rom 2:15). If in Christ the works are built-in, and if we are already "hearers and doers,"[7] then Paul's words about being judged by our works take on a much different tenor: "For it is not those who hear the law who are righteous in God's sight, but it is those who obey the law who will be declared righteous" (Rom 2:13).

Simply put, Rom 2:13 is a description of our true selves in Christ (green), where righteous works are included in participation with the righteous Savior. The judgment is against all of the works of the flesh, where our false selves (red), under the influence of the antichrist, will be exposed: "This will take place on the day when God judges people's secrets through Jesus Christ, as my gospel declares" (Rom 2:16). Paul says something similar at the end of Romans, "For we will all stand

---

6. Rom 2:7–11, interpreted the traditional way with its works-based emphasis, simply cannot be consistent with Paul's words about justification by grace. However, considering Barth's actualism, and by virtue of keeping being and act together, the works of the righteous *are included* in the indicative nature of the righteous humanity given to all human beings in Christ. Rom 1:19–20 describes well the Genesis 1 situation: "what may be known about God is plain to them, because God has made it plain to them. For since the creation of the world God's invisible qualities—his eternal power and divine nature—have been clearly seen, being understood from what has been made, so that people are without excuse." The problem is not that every creature is not implicated in the Genesis 1 indicative, or that the reality isn't happening, or that the green is not being revealed; the problem for post-fall humanity is the red, and that they do not have a preacher to share the Word as the interpretive key. Everyone knows God (Rom 1:21), and yet what God has plainly revealed is not plain to the Genesis 2 receiver because of the distortion of sin: "How can they hear without someone preaching to them?" (Rom 10:14).

7. CD I/2, 240. Barth's phrase is distilled from Rom 2:13 (see also Jas 1:22).

before God's judgment seat," where "each of us will give an account of ourselves to God" (Rom 14:10, 12). Which account will we give? Will it be that of the truth—our being and doing in Christ—or will it be that of the lie? The baseline of judgment is perfect righteousness and justice because we are already in Christ. We are not judged by his perfect justice and righteousness in order to gain entry to Christ, but because we already have our perfect being-in-act in him. This inevitably leads to the second question.

2. If Jesus Christ is the way, the truth, and the life of each person in being and in act, is everyone then in the book of life? We are immediately confronted with Rev 13:8 and 17:8, which both make plain that from the foundation of the world there are those "whose names have not been written in the Lamb's book of life." This seems to undermine our whole approach. It is clear the names that *are* written in the book of life are people belonging to the Lamb who was slain from the foundation of the world.[8] But who is not in that number? Whose names are *not* written in the book of life? Oddly, those *not* written in the book of life are constantly referred to in Revelation as the "inhabitants of the earth."[9] So we can start with the curiously illuminating fact that the phrase appears to be a comprehensive reference to *all* human beings, i.e., "all the inhabitants of the earth" (13:8).[10] When it comes to the Book of Life, then, this sounds like no one is "in" and everyone "out!" However, before resorting to such a pendulum swing, we can embrace John's phrase "inhabitants of the earth" when we remember that it identifies not God's good creatures directly, but the opposite image of God's good creatures. Every inhabitant is deceived by the beast (Rev 13:14). This goes along with John's framing in Revelation, founded on Satan's ploy of imitation, counterfeit, mirroring, mimicry, and the like. In sum, then, "inhabitants of the earth" designates all human beings, in this case solely defined by their flesh, or under the "red" mark of the devil. Indeed, all the references to the "inhabitants

---

8. Jesus's prayer to the Father in John 17:24 that "you loved me before the creation of the world" could point to Jesus's deity, or to his humanity as the first-born of all human creatures (before the fall), or to Christ as representing fallen human beings, or to all of these. We have already asserted that what the eternal God accomplishes in time counts for eternity. Jesus Christ's human death has in effect taken care of the mortal threat of Satan even before he creates human beings, establishing, if there was ever a doubt, the truth against the lie.

9. For example, Rev 3:10; 6:10; 8:13; 11:10; 13:8; 13:12; 13:14; 17:2; 17:8.

10. See also "the earth and its inhabitants" (13:12), and "inhabitants of the earth" (13:14).

of the earth" in Revelation are pejorative, describing subjugation to evil or sinful activity.[11] Like unconscious bias, the flesh (*sarx*) is not passive but antagonistic to the ways of the Spirit. Every person in their flesh is, in one sense, worshiping the beast (Rev 13:8). It should not surprise us, then, that the names of "the inhabitants of the earth" are not written in the Book of Life!

With these two aspects—the universality and the ungodliness—the force of the indictment against the inhabitants of the earth, the human race, seems to eliminate everyone from the Book of Life. At the same time, there are also comprehensive statements in the positive direction. Revelation 7 tells us that the servants of God number 144,000, the number of the twelve tribes of Israel times twelve. It seems apparent that the twelve tribes, like the twelve apostles, have a high-priestly function in Christ as a representative microcosm of the entire human race.[12] Just after this limited number is specified, John remarks that "there before me was a great multitude that no one could count, from every nation, tribe, people and language," worshiping the Lamb (7:9). Indeed, "every creature in heaven and on earth and under the earth" was singing praise to God (5:13). How do we reconcile "all the inhabitants of the earth" worshiping the devil, and "every creature in heaven and on earth" worshiping the Lamb? While the inhabitants of the earth are "marked"[13] with the satanic number 666 on their foreheads, the 144,000 are "sealed"[14] with the names of God, also on their foreheads.

These texts push us unavoidably to placemat anthropology. It seems apparent, based on who Jesus Christ is, that the true selves of every human—created and redeemed—are in the book. Those not in the book are the false selves of every person ever created. Everyone in their true self is there, everyone in their false self is simply *not*. They

---

11. Again, the mirroring theme in Revelation is so strong as to suggest that John is adopting a functional dualism to communicate what is really the duality of every person, i.e., for his theological purposes he is painting all the inhabitants of the earth as nothing but bad, or of the flesh. For example, Rev 6:10, "How long, Sovereign Lord, holy and true, until you judge the inhabitants of the earth"; Rev 8:13, "I heard an eagle that was flying in midair call out in a loud voice, 'Woe! Woe! Woe to the inhabitants of the earth"; Rev 13:8, "All the inhabitants of the earth will worship the beast"; Rev 13:14, "[the beast] deceived the inhabitants of the earth."

12. In Barth's words, Christ's apostles would be "a provisional representation of the sanctification of all humanity and human life as it has taken place in Him," *CD* IV/2, 620 (quoted in Book One).

13. Rev 13:16. We will discuss the apparent exception of Rev 20:4 and the martyrs.

14. Rev 7:3.

are not there, because there is no reality or truth that substantiates their existence. As Barth reminds us, John never says there are two columns in the book, one for those belonging to God, and one for those who do not.[15] "Not" is a negation. It has no meaning of its own, it is only parasitic to the positive. Again, there is an attempted mirroring of good by evil. If Revelation 1:8 reads of Jesus Christ, "who is, and who was, and who is to come," Revelation 17:8 reads of the beast, he "once was, now *is not*, and yet will come" (emphasis added). Again the mirrored version (17:8) is virtually indistinguishable to the reality (1:8), except for the key revelation in the middle of the chain. Jesus Christ *is*, Satan *is not*.[16]

---

15. *CD* II/2, 16.

16. While the phrases about God appear in different order (e.g., Rev 1:4; 1:8 ["is," "was," "is to come"]), only in the devil's phrases do we see the words "is not."

89

Test or War?

> [T]he creature can and will have a real part in the conflict with nothingness. It is certainly no mere spectator.
> —Karl Barth

> And it is not in the vacuum of creaturely self-sufficiency but under the wings of divine mercy that the fortitude thrives in which man is summoned and equipped to range himself with God, so that in his own place he opposes nothingness and thus has a part in the work and warfare of God.
> —Karl Barth

In the book of Revelation, chapters 12–13, John alludes to what we could call an evil counter-trinity: a red dragon (yes, the dragon is red—Rev 12:3), a beast from the sea (Rev 13:1) and a beast from the earth (Rev 13:11). In other places, John names the two beasts, "antichrist" (1 John 2:18; 2:22; 4:3; 2 John 1:7) and "false prophet" (cf. Rev 16:13; 19:20; 20:10). The antichrist has a fatal wound but was healed—mirroring Christ as far as possible, only to fall short of Christ's unique dying and rising. The third entity of the "unholy trinity" uses fire to force all the inhabitants of the earth to worship an "image" of the antichrist and breathes life into this counterfeit image (fire and breath being a mimicry, of course, of the work of the Spirit). John even gives words to the three evil spirits, which "came out of the mouth of the dragon, out of the mouth of the beast and out of the mouth of the false prophet" (Rev 16:13):[1] "Look, I come like a thief! Blessed is the one who stays awake and remains clothed, so as not to go naked and be shamefully exposed" (Rev 16:15). These voices mockingly invert the "naked and unashamed" description of Genesis 2:25, a description that points to humanity's perfection in Genesis 1.[2]

As comprehensive as the "triune" Satan's work is, it remains asymmetrical in relation to God's complete work. We noted above that all the inhabitants of the earth were marked with the number 666 on their foreheads. The number of the beast is 666 and, derivatively, so too is the number of "man" in the flesh (Rev 13:18, although most translations artificially insert an article, e.g., "*a* man").[3] The number 666 is short of the number of completeness: seven. This truth is echoed when, in Revelation 13:5, Satan is "given" forty-two months (that is, seven periods of six months, not seven months) by God to exercise his authority. There is a double asymmetry at play here on the primary and derivative levels: first, an asymmetry between God and Satan, and second, an asymmetry of humanity in the Spirit and humanity in the flesh.

While imitating the true God, Satan was allowed to deceive "every tribe, people, language and nation" (13:7) even though he was outmatched by the redemptive work of the Lamb and its similar, universal scope: "a great multitude that no one could count, from every nation, tribe, people and language" (7:9, also 5:9; see similar mirroring description between 11:18 and 13:16). While the drama of Revelation is highly symbolic and set in the eschatological age, it can also be seen as a metaphorical recasting of the temporal, contingent, or historical age of our current existence.

---

1. Again, note John's use of triple repetition to illustrate the evil trinity's mimicry. He could have easily said "out of the mouth" one time. John says here (Rev 16:13–14) that the spirits are mimicking the Exodus miracles in their actions, even if their words can't help but defy their actions, coming out as they do in the form of frogs!

2. Perhaps John's somewhat strange post-resurrection depiction of Simon Peter putting his clothes back on before jumping in the water to see Jesus (John 21:17) is related to the shame he had churning within before his cathartic moment with Jesus around the campfire. Paul's language of not wishing to be found naked should not be confused with John's positive representation of nakedness. We remember that Paul desires not to be found naked "in the wrong way," i.e., as a disembodied soul.

3. The number of the beast is the number of "man," not "a man." There would be no need to insert this article if the duality of humankind were to be embraced, as in placemat anthropology. When the duality is not embraced, for all humans to be marked with 666 poses a theologically intractable problem. It becomes easier to assign 666 to some humans, or to "a man."

PART SEVEN: IMMORTALS FALL

I mentioned earlier the idea that our present first-heaven-experience is really the ante-room to the veiled reality of human life with God. In a way that not even the contemporaries standing at Golgotha could have understood, it is inside the second heaven and not the first where the meaning of the cross is most fully and clearly revealed. This is where Jesus's words, "And I, when I am lifted up from the earth, will draw all people to myself" (John 12:32), will be most plain.

Far from the clarity of the second heaven, the first-heaven experience is marked by confusion. Even though all persons exist and are "found" from the foundation (and in the one foundation, Jesus Christ),[4] all persons are also "lost" in the web of deceit. This is placemat anthropology, the human duality of total green and total red in each person. To communicate the seriousness of evil and the severity of the contradiction—the mutual exclusion between righteousness and sin—John is content to speak of these as two different people groups (employing a functional dualism). He is building toward "the great tribulation" (Rev 7:14) where all are gathered, and Satan is allowed his "hour."[5]

In Revelation 17:8 he writes that the beast "will come up out of the Abyss and go to its destruction." At this point, all the inhabitants of the earth "will be astonished when they see the beast." John describes all human beings in their false selves, those "whose names have not been written in the book of life from the foundation of the world." Captivated by the flesh, these "inhabitants of the earth" will be "astonished" as flesh gives birth to flesh and the beast they have been worshiping becomes manifest. Other translations for "astonished" include "amazed," "marveled," "astounded," and "wondered after." These words mirror those used in John's gospel when referring to Jesus.[6]

On that day, Satan will do all that he can to prove that the lie is the reality. For those of us in the first heaven, he's already made quite a case. This effort seems to be what John refers to as "the hour of trial that is going to come on the whole world to test the inhabitants of the earth" (Rev 3:10). Satan is the "accuser";[7] he is the one who tests us, not God. From the foundation of the world, he has existed not only as parasitic and inferior, but also as defeated. Darkness opposes primal light just as the negation of Genesis

---

4. 1 Cor 3:11.

5. See Rev 17:12–14; 20:3; 20:7. See also Rev 17:12; 18:10; 18:17; 18:19.

6. See John 4:27; John 7:15. Cf. also Paul's description of worshippers of Christ marveling at him on the day (2 Thess 1:10).

7. Rev 12:10.

1:2 follows Genesis 1:1.[8] Part of Satan's self-deceit is that he thinks he can win the war that has always been lost. And yet, even in his death throes, he is strong. The hour of doom, when the antichrist is allowed to flaunt his woeful power,[9] is the moment of Jesus's own demise.[10] In Christ's demise is the antichrist's own destruction. This is the thunderous[11] revelation of the day, the second heaven.

What more can be said about this epic clash where Satan is allowed one hour to unleash warfare on Christ's army? The capture of the antichrist and the man of lawlessness (two-thirds of the evil trinity) is John's way of signifying the "already" dimension of what Christ has accomplished from the foundation of the world. It comports with Jesus's words about tying up the strong man (Matt 12:29; Mark 3:27). The dragon, meanwhile, is bound and locked into the Abyss for "1,000 years" (Rev 20:2). The fact that the strong man is "not yet" destroyed (i.e., his destruction is not yet fully manifest) is communicated by the dragon's reemergence from the abyss in Revelation 20 even while the other two "beasts" are already captured. The "hour" is the hour of the cross—but it is nuanced in its revelation. It is already accomplished, and not yet fully revealed.

If the "already" of evil's demise is signaled at the end of Revelation 19, the final revelation of evil's destruction is described in Revelation 20:10, when the "1,000 years" are over. In placemat terms, everything up to the hour of final revelation marks our first-heaven existence. There has never been a time of human existence where our salvation was not already accomplished, but it is in the second heaven that we see the full and final hour of judgment unfold. Here, amidst the "not yet" (the first heaven) we can live with a measure of clarity and confidence in the "already"; our death is behind us and now we can live as if we are already dead and die as if we are already alive. In other words, we can live in the boldness of the resurrection.

---

8. For more on the critical relationship between Gen 1:1 and Gen 1:2, see the reading "Newness" in Book One, and the section "Checkered Before 'the Fall'" in the introduction of this volume.

9. As cited above, see Rev 17:12–14; 20:3; 20:7. See also 19:19–21.

10. See John 12:23–33, especially v. 27: "Now my soul is troubled, and what shall I say? 'Father, save me from this hour? No, it was this very reason I came to this hour." Scripture tells us that the voice of Father's affirmation came following this testimony. Appropriate to the terrible glory of this hour, his voice sounded like thunder.

11. "Thunders," or peals of thunder, occur throughout Revelation and often signify God's judgment. Note particularly 11:19 and its probably intentional reflection of the gospel rendering of Christ's death: "Then God's temple in heaven was opened, and within his temple was seen the ark of his covenant. And there came flashes of lightning, rumblings, peals of thunder, an earthquake and a great hailstorm." See also Rev 16:17–18; Matt 27:45–52.

This seems to be the meaning of John's words in the first part of chapter 20, where he commends the martyrs for participating in the "already" of resurrection, "the first resurrection" (Rev 20:5).

He describes the early martyrs who went to their deaths *without* 666 marked on their foreheads (Rev 20:4). In our view, this signifies the certainty that believers carry with them into the judgment. Undeterred by the "not yet" they are without fear, living and moving with confidence *as if* they had already overcome. They live from the third heaven, where there is no sign of the beast. Revelation 20:6 resounds, "Blessed and holy are those who share in the first resurrection."[12] John explains that these first-heaven overcomers (including martyrs) already have enough second-heaven clarity in the Spirit and therefore have no need to wait for the full clarity of the judgment. Indeed, the greatest compliment Revelation gives to human beings in this world is that they are overcomers who rest in the Victor who has (John 16:33) and will overcome the world in the great tribulation at Calvary: "To the one who is victorious, I will give the right to eat from the tree of life, which is in the paradise of God" (Rev 2:7).[13]

The fact that the overcomers do not have a mark on their forehead in Revelation 20 does not mean that they avoid the judgment as if they are a different class of human. All the inhabitants of the earth are implicated, even the most confident and assured overcomer in the first heaven will still face the day, "the hour of trial that is going to come on the whole world to test the inhabitants of the earth" (Rev 3:10).[14] Remember, no one skips the judgment day. Nevertheless, the overcomers, those who know the judge best, are *those who most look forward to judgment*. Such a posture is synonymous with repentance.[15] By looking forward they are living backward, i.e., from the third heaven. With their big picture perspective, they are keen

---

12. This rings with the sound of Jesus's words to Thomas ("Blessed are those who have not seen and yet have believed," John 20:29). It honors those who have as much certainty as if they had touched Jesus's wounds like Thomas, the apostle who would himself be martyred. Also of note is that Rev 20:6 (along with Rev 2:11 and Rev 20:14) seem to point to the overcomer of the "first resurrection" as being one who is at once *most* zealous for the judgment of deliverance and *least* concerned about a "second death," the lake of fire.

13. The only other time Jesus uses this word "paradise" is with the repentant thief on the cross. It is fitting that this would be reserved for another human being who shares the physical space of Christ's overcoming victory (Luke 24:43). See "Coming Home" above.

14. The NIV translates the first part of this verse "I will keep you from the hour of trial" but the word "from" can also be translated "through," so it seems the better contextual sense of the verse is provided in the CEB, "I will keep you safe through."

15. Thanks to Cody Andersen for this insight.

to re-turn to the promised land of Genesis 1. These believers know that in their false selves they are condemned, but they know even more that in their true selves they are not condemned (and that there is thus one carefully defined sense in which they do not "come into judgment").[16]

Regarding this "test" that John speaks of we can say that it is no test in the way we think of test, as if the verdict is in doubt.[17] "A test," as Barth notes, "is an act of justified suspicion."[18] But God has no cause to fret. From God's side, it is finished. There is no wringing of hands. No return to the devil's domain of "bi-lateral freedom" (where "free choice" involves a choice with Christ *and* a choice against Christ). Here, no enticements are required. What his creatures know and have been equipped with in their freedom as children of God is enough.

---

16. It's because of P^2 (Pat's false self) that P^3 (Pat) is condemned and judged. As long as P^3 is also P^2, there is no avoiding this; everyone has a P^2. If you have sinned once it reveals you have a total red self that needs to be crucified with Christ. But it is also just as true that because of P^1 (Pat's true self), Pat (P^3) is not condemned or judged. See John 3:18, where both facets are put together: "Whoever believes in him is not condemned, but whoever does not believe stands condemned already." John 3:18a correlates with John 5:24, supporting a placemat understanding of judgment.

17. This test is not something with two legitimate results—pass or fail (although Satan would love to have the chance to open another rational column). As it is, Satan can only proceed to flaunt "as if" such a test is not already passed. See *CD* III/1, 264–66, for an illuminating discussion regarding the question of testing. The "test" spoken of here is that in Eden, although the following would seem also to apply at the eschatological hour of trial: "[Man] is not allotted a place midway between obedience and disobedience. His place is with and before the God who with his creation has chosen for him, deciding between good and evil, salvation and perdition, life and death. No other decision than that of obedience will correspond to this place; no other can be expected of him here; no other can be commensurate with his being; no other can be an act of the life given to him. In faithfulness to himself, and in continuance of the life given him, he can only be obedient. That he has the freedom to affirm this obedience has nothing to do with a temptation which overtakes him. . . . We must abandon the idea that in granting man the freedom to obey God put him on trial" (264); "What is implied by the tree of the knowledge of good and evil, and underlined by the prohibition, is simply that the given possibility of obedience is not the possibility of one choice as opposed to another, but of a free decision. . . . This certainly does not consist in his standing between good and evil and being able to choose between the two. But it does consist in the fact that the man who stands thus before the God who in his creation has determined him for good is not only subject to this divine decision but can respect it in the form of his own decision. This is the freedom which God gave him at this creation. It is in this and in no other way that He has determined him in His own decision for good. He expects and has made him capable of confirmation, of the obedience of his own free will and act" (265). Note that Barth (with the lower case "h" in "his") is not talking about God's own free will and act but humanity's. In other words, to respect God's freedom is for the human being to respect *their own* creaturely obedience and freedom.

18. *CD* III/1, 264. See whole discussion 264–66.

Without feeling the need to explain how the first human beings fell to Satan's tempting in Eden, God remains confident in his own work. Nevertheless, the cross tests *our* work.[19] In other words, how we interpret the test of the cross has everything to do with how the cross interprets *us*. Indeed, Christ's definitive passing of the test of death as our representative provides the clearest parsing of our true and false selves. We are brought through death into the freedom of who we truly are, and even while being shown this truth, the liar tempts us with his door to unfreedom. This is a test in the same way that, at a trial, the clear truth tests the jury.

The allusion to the door of unfreedom, one used by Barth, is representative of both borders of our placemat existence, that of Genesis 2–3 and that of the day of judgment. For that reason the door of unfreedom to which Satan beckons us is also the one which God has allowed to be opened to humanity: "God . . . had to give him the freedom which He has obviously given him, not to tempt or test him, *but to give him place for spontaneous obedience according to his creation.* He . . . had to be shown the possibility denied him for his salvation; that door had to be opened. In the freedom given him by God, man could not possibly will to make use of it."[20] Obviously, in Eden, when faced with the door that "man could not possibly will to make use of," man made the impossible, un-free, and disastrous choice to use it. The inherent venom of every un-free and lethal choice made by every human in history would need to be cumulatively absorbed until no sting was left. This entailed the worst human decision ever made and in which we are all implicated, the crucifying of the Son of God under Pontius Pilate.

Without trying to explain the incomprehensible possibility of choosing Satan's door at the beginning or at the end, Barth exalts in the opportunity we have as participants to freely affirm and spontaneously celebrate the victory over evil that the cross represents, even while aghast at our infatuation ("astonishment") with the beast. This celebration is part of our worship even now. What John describes as an "overcomer," then and now, is the overlapped, conflicted, person who shares the confidence of victory, the certainty that Christ has indeed "overcome the world."[21] Still, the astonishment of human beings in Satan's last stand, as with his Genesis 2–3 assault, proves that the lie can be compelling.[22] Even while overcomers experience

---

19. See 1 Cor 3:13.

20. *CD* III/1, 265, emphasis added.

21. John 16:33; see also 1 John 4:4, "The one who is in you is greater than the one who is in the world."

22. Not surprisingly, the only other time humans are "astonished" in Revelation appears to be in an allusion to the Garden of Eden, where they are also mesmerized by the physical seduction of the devil. Because Christ's death precedes creation in one

the exhilaration of clean, green robes, the torturous entanglement that persists in their experience all the way up to third heaven's gate shows the red tenacity of deceit (Rev 22:14–15).

If we have a greater chance than Adam and Eve to avoid the self-torment described, it is because we stand at the cross with a single, tree-of-life focus looking back at creation. At the judgment we are not stuck at a crossroads deluded by the double vision of two "free" options (good and evil). No longer looking through a mirror dimly, we have the opportunity to participate in the victory of the cross, passing Satan's final test and "showing" ourselves to be Jesus's disciples (John 15:8).

---

sense, the confrontation in the Garden is with an adversary already "hurled to earth" from the judgment of the second heaven. From there he "leads the whole world astray" (Rev 12:9). Satan knows his time is short (Rev 12:12). With the implied asymmetry, he is given authority for forty-two months (six multiplied by seven). He is allowed a mouth that utters blasphemy (Rev 13:5), and a parody that is tauntingly dangerous, even if it is just that, a parody: "Who is like the beast? Who can wage war against it?" (Rev 13:4; Cf. Ps 113:5; "Who is like the LORD our God, the One who sits enthroned on high?") John tells us that the "whole world was filled with wonder and followed the beast" (Rev 13:3). Of course, the Roman Imperial cult of John's time bears relative witness to the larger picture of the satanic source of all evil. Whether to Domitian or another example of great evil (Hitler), John's language about the beast and anti-Christ might be properly (derivationally) applied. What is disallowed in placemat terms is defining anyone as the anti-Christ in isolation from the total evil of every human under subjection to Evil with a capital E.

90

The Liar's Religion

O, wretched sin, what are you? You are nothing. For I saw that God is in everything; I did not see you. And when I saw that God has made everything, I did not see you. And when I saw that God is in everything, I did not see you. . . . And so I am certain that you [wretchedness] are nothing, and all those who . . . follow you and deliberately end in you, I am sure that they will be brought to nothing with you and eternally confounded.

—Julian of Norwich

The "book" spoken of by God in Exodus 32:32 has always, and quite rightly, been connected with the election of grace . . . it is described as the "book of life" in the New Testament (Phil 4:3; Rev 3:5; 17:8; 20:12, 15). One's name may not be in this book. It can be blotted out from it. And yet there are not two columns but only one.

—Karl Barth

WE DESCRIBED JOHN'S CONVICTION that Satan, or the trinity of evil, exists as a constricted negation. The serpent's lethal length is shorter than that of the One "who was, and is, and is to come." Interestingly, the serpent's prominence extends from the Garden of Genesis 2–3, where Adam and Eve

THE LIAR'S RELIGION

fall to his wiles, to the judgment of "the day." At these two bookends of his physical appearance—the border into the first heaven (from the original heaven of Genesis 1–2:4) and the border exiting the first heaven (the day of the second heaven)—he is *visibly* astonishing and compelling. In between these bookends, however, the invisible beast relies on his terribly visible destructive work.[1] This slinking serpent winds his way through human history as the one who "once was, now is not, and yet will come" (17:8), never attaining the same status as the one who *is*.

These similar borders of time before and after the first heaven with their manifestations of evil and judgment reveal the cross as the center of human history and the gateway to the third heaven. To grasp the distinctions between the three heavens, we chronologically ordered them like three plates of glass side-by-side. On that day of final manifestation, these glass plates slide suddenly together into one eternal moment of genuine time, and the serpent, caught in the seams of time, is sliced to pieces. In his assumption of sinful human flesh, the God-human Jesus Christ crushed the head of the serpent, and the curse itself is cursed.[2]

Until that day, even though his own work is already boundaried by God's work, Satan is the usurping prince of this world with his own spirit of disobedience. He continues to control human beings in the flesh. Revelation 13 describes "all the inhabitants of the earth" (what we have cited as John's designation for humans defined by the fall) as those made to worship the beast, deceived and coerced by him.[3] Evil controls us and we are in bondage to it. As John taught in his epistle, those who sin demonstrate themselves to be children of the devil.[4] Satan mimics the Lordship of Christ

---

1. If the cross is the center of human history, where the beast (albeit invisible) exerts his greatest destructive fury, the similarity of the two border scenarios are revelations of the cross in their own way. By border scenarios I mean the transition between the original heaven and the first heaven (at Gen 2:4) and the last throes of the serpent at the transition between the second heaven and third. We have established that God "stepped past" the abyss of evil (Gen 1:2) to create what is purely good in Gen 1, only to have the beast visibly emerge (at this first border) with a vengeance in Gen 2–3. The beast remains invisible in the first heaven, only to visibly reemerge (at this second border) from the abyss in the hour of trial. I see the first border, where the beast visibly emerges from the abyss preceding the traditional fall, reflected in Rev 11:7, and the last border, where Satan visibly reemerges from the abyss to go to his final destruction, reflected in Rev 17:8 and Rev 20:1. Again, Satan does not manifest physically in Scripture at the point where his venom is most biting (the cross), even though Mel Gibson's *The Passion of the Christ* demonstrated his presence throughout Christ's betrayal, trial, torture, and execution (e.g., Jesus memorably crushing the serpent's head in the garden scene).

2. Gen 3:15.

3. Rev 13:12; 13:14; 13:16.

4. Similarly, see Paul's testimony concerning his bondage to sin: "It is not I who do it [sin], but sin living in me" (Rom 7:17).

and the children of God under the Father's benevolent authority. Because Satan can only mimic the good, he foists a disobedience upon humanity that is forced, not free. He thereby contaminates our ability to grasp how human beings under the strongest authority, even as predestined, can be the most free. To meet this challenge we now turn to understand how, in Christ's non-coercive economy, God's predestining authority and human freedom are one.

Though the beast emerges in Revelation 11:7 and overcomes the inhabitants of the earth, the Lamb overcomes the beast in the warfare of Revelation 17:14. As cosmic as it is, this warfare applies to us as well. We are continually invited to participate because we are already participating. Against the truth of Christ and our true humanity, insisting on the lie is self-destructive. To resist the Spirit and to choose against Christ is to choose against one's real self, and therefore to choose against one's own true and free choosing. This refusal is purely irrational and defies explanation. It could only be as if one is simply *not* (in keeping with the nature of parasitic negation). This is what Julian meant by her comment directed at sin and wretchedness that "you are nothing, and all those who . . . follow you and deliberately end in you, I am sure that they will be brought to nothing with you,"[5] and what Barth meant when he said that there is no "death column" in the book of life.[6]

The fact that there is no "death column" may seem natural and consistent with what we have said from the beginning of Book One. But we must not underestimate how different this view is from the soteriologies, or salvation theologies, which have dominated the landscape of recent centuries. Rather than explaining evil, sin, and death as irrational and without explanation, some theologians have turned to where explanation *can* be found—a salvation template with two columns.

When theologies espouse humans to be ultimately saved by *God's decision* (God's sole decision) or by *human decision* (humans cooperating with God's initiative), the two column approaches of Calvinism and Arminianism seem to makes rational sense. For the Five-Point Calvinist, for example, the emphasis is on God's sovereign, "iron" will. God determined whom, from all eternity, would be in one column (saved) or the other (damned). One column is the life column, those for whom Christ died. The other is the

---

5. Julian, *Showings*, 166. See the more complete quotation cited in Book One, 340.

6. *CD* II/2, 16. Continuing from the quote at the top of this reading, Barth points to one column listing every created person's name, and yet, he notes, if Exod 32:32 is any indication, a name might perhaps be blotted out. In Exod 32:32 Moses pleads: "Please forgive their sin—but if not, blot me out of the book you have written." Paul says something similar in Rom 9:3.

death column, for those to whom Christ's atoning death was never meant to apply. Damnation, on this view, is not irrational. Instead, it is logical and appropriate in the eternal wisdom of God. The rationale is that God is merciful, having chosen a small contingent of humanity even though all deserve damnation. Only some human beings are in the good, elect column, because Christ died for them. On this view, grace functions as the exception to the rule of damnation.

As we hinted earlier, John Wesley vehemently disagreed with this kind of double-columned predestination. He once said that it "destroys all [God's] attributes at once. It overturns his justice, mercy, and truth. Yea, it represents the most Holy God as worse than the devil.... No Scripture can mean that God is not love, or that his mercy is not over all of His works."[7] In reaction to the double decree, Wesley rode the pendulum to the opposite side; he spurned two, fixed columns for two, unfixed columns. God knows (foreknowledge) which column we will join before we do so, but God does not determine who goes in either column. Instead, human beings stand at the crossroads of decision and (thanks to the notion of "prevenient grace") have the opportunity to choose between life or death, salvation or damnation, goodness or evil, inclusion or exclusion. Instead of the sovereign free-will of God, this puts human destiny in the "free" will of humans. Despite the notion of "prevenient grace," no one starts off in the good column. On Wesley's view, saving grace remains the exception to the rule.

If the approach of Five-Point Calvinism introduces a God who does not sacrificially love all human beings (God's love being commensurate with those for whom Christ died), then Wesley's Arminian alternative introduces a loving God who at bottom leaves the saving result up to us. Neither approach is satisfactory. If the "monergism" of Luther and Calvin (as inherited from Augustine) is dehumanizing in its determinism, the "synergism" along the lines of Origen, Erasmus, Arminius, and Wesley is overly humanistic (i.e., it provides too great a role for fallen human beings).[8]

In the teaching of Arminius and Wesley, "prevenient grace" only opens up the possibility that human beings can make the right decision in cooperation with God. The element of human cooperation, no matter how small, protects it from Calvinist monergism, but the result is that it becomes unavoidably synergistic (part God and part human) and therefore co-redemptive. It was the strict monergism of Martin Luther that so

---

7. Cited in Maddox, *Responsible Grace*, 39.

8. It should be noted that Augustine, Luther, and Calvin in their monergist teachings all preceded the codification of what became known as Five-Point Calvinism, leading to the question of whether Calvin himself was a Five-Point Calvinist! See J.B. Torrance, "Concept of Federal Theology," 15–39.

influenced Calvin. But Luther's monergism later morphed into something softer under the influence of Philip Melanchthon and the "Philipists," who carried on in Melanchthon's name by drafting the Lutheran Formulas of Concord (1577). Most Lutherans thus traded in the rigid, two-columned approach they had shared with Calvinists for a fluid two-column approach more like Arminianism.[9]

This book has promoted the view that grace is the rule, not the exception, and that there is only one column (with its negation) instead of two. The liar—the one who is *not*—does not get his own column. Providing this pretender with a theological column is only to give him a promotion. The negation would thus be given legitimate standing and substance.

This has been the devil's ploy from the beginning. By "spinning" the tree of the knowledge of good and evil without reference to the cross in the garden, the serpent conned the first human beings to buy into a two-columns approach. Most of us have operated with this conceptualization ever since. The devil promoted himself from a pure negation to something like a Manichaean darkness—an equal, oppositional force to the force of light in the world. Shifting the human perspective toward such a dualism gives Satan a much better chance to control the narrative. Indeed, without the interpretive key of the cross, the tree of the knowledge of good and evil takes on shades of what I call the "liar's religion."

Without calling it by name, we have warned against elements of the liar's religion throughout our book: Manichaeism has dualism, placemat anthropology (PA) has duality; Manichaeism has a tug of war, PA has Christ as Victor; Manichaeism has symmetry, PA has asymmetry; Manichaeism has parity, PA has priority; Manichaeism has evil as a necessity for good, PA has evil being parasitic to good; finally, Manichaeism interprets the tree of the knowledge of good and evil without Christ, PA interprets good and evil by reference to Christ on the tree.

A non-fixed, libertarian view of freedom minimizes human depravity and places human beings more generously at the midpoint where they could "freely" go either way. It was falsely understood that to be created in the image of God (in whom we have our *being*) means to be free like God is free (setting up a dangerous analogy of being).[10] In this view, human beings possess a bilateral freedom; they are free to go "left" or "right." As Barth saw it, there are two major problems to this: (1) Freedom is not an innate human

---

9. For a historical-theological summary on Protestant monergism and synergism, see my chapter "Hercules at the Crossroads."

10. See the Book One reading "Fulfilling the Law of Christ" where I outline the dangers of the *analogia entis*, the analogy of being.

property as it is in God, but gifted to human beings by grace alone,[11] and (2) God has gifted us with freedom that goes only in one direction, not "left" or "right." To say we are free as God is free leaves us to commit unfree acts and call them free. Blinded by the enemy, the first human beings fell prey to the devil's idea of free choice. They failed to act in concert with their free God-given determination. Blinded to God's grace, they lost sight of God's will and its singular direction—to go in the same direction that the Son of God goes. To go any other way is to go the way of the "anti-Christ."

---

11. *CD* III/2, 385–86. Thus, even though human beings are made in the very image of God, we should not assume the derivational "rules" about human freedom are the same as God's innate ones. This also explains why Barth found the "free-will" arguments attempting to explain the fall and hell so tiring. If we cannot even explain the fall, we should not try to explain how anyone could choose hell (i.e., refuse their innately free choice of heaven).

91

One Tree in the Garden

God did not say [to Adam and Eve] they were not to know good and evil, but that they . . . were intended to know evil in the way that Jesus Christ knew it, viz., by contrast with good. They did eat of the tree, consequently the human race knows good by contrast with evil. Adam knew evil positively and good negatively, and none of us knows the order God intended. . . . The fruit of the tree of the knowledge of good and evil gives the bias of insatiable curiosity on the bad line, and it is only by the readjustment through Jesus Christ that the bias on the other line enters in.

—Oswald Chambers

We began this volume with Barth's concept that all of the then is in the now, but not all of the now is in the then (thankfully!). All of Genesis 1 is in Genesis 2–3, even if not all of Genesis 2–3 is in Genesis 1. We recognized in the second saga how God the good and perfect Creator introduced us into the "garden" environment of Genesis 2 where there was all manner of evil. From the time we were placed in the garden of Genesis 2, everything was flipped around. In a fog of grey, forgetful of our lives in the distant land of Genesis 1, and offered only counterfeit directions by the enemy, "the creation was subjected to frustration" (Rom 8:20). Only with "eyes to see" could we glimpse the green of the gospel as the reverse side of our existence.

In the commandment of God which is "holy, righteous and good" (Rom 7:12), human beings are who they are in Christ, responding to the Father perfectly, doing what Christ their brother is doing. In Genesis 2, Satan has twisted the law of the Spirit of life to appear as the letter of the law. Under Satan's influence, this is the letter that kills.

"That we have the commandment," notes Barth, "is our true being."[1] However, the written code, the letter that kills—this is the "law" of Eden. The original commandment in the garden—the law of the Spirit of life—is still in the commandment, but it is now dimensionally obscured. It cannot be received reliably in its twisted, impure form. There in the first heaven, "what the law, weakened by the flesh, could not do, God did by sending his own Son in the likeness of sinful flesh" (Rom 8:3). Like signposts, these (the Torah, the Law and the prophets, the Holy Bible) could and would bear relative witness to the Word, but only in the perfect Word made flesh was the divine rescue and the divine plan possible.

Now, still in the postlapsarian first heaven of Genesis 2–3, we exist accompanied by the real law, the law of Christ, the law of the Spirit of life, the vicarious humanity of Christ, if we have ears to hear "the Gospel in the commandment."[2] Despite the challenge, by God's grace our "inner being" who "delights in God's law" (Rom 7:22) may obey from the heart (Rom 6:17) the inner essence of the commandment. This is deep calling to deep (Ps 42:7). Only in the Spirit can we have ears to hear despite the din of interference. Only by the Spirit of revelation can we acquire a semblance of vision through the grey fog for navigating the journey through the first heaven and into the second, walking by faith from the perspective of the third. Only by the Spirit can we interpret properly the tree of the knowledge of good and evil.[3]

There is an important distinction in the Garden of Eden between the tree of the knowledge of good and evil and the tree of life. Both trees are mentioned in Genesis 2:9 as in the center of the Garden. Reading from Revelation 22 (the very last chapter of the Bible) into the creation account, we can recognize the tree of life to be the first and central tree.[4]

---

1. *CD* I/2, 452.
2. *CD* I/2, 452–53.
3. This act of proper interpretation goes hand in hand with repentance, moving with the Spirit in the direction of grace and therefore against the flesh. In one sense repentance can't be a turning around, since in reality we are already going in the right direction (speaking of our being-in-act ontologically, in the law of the Spirit of life); but in another sense, if repentance corresponds with the reverse side of this worldly existence, it is by nature to turn around, or at least to flip around rightly!
4. Barth, I would contend, starts *Church Dogmatics* with the mindset of Rev 22 as

God gives the command not to eat of the tree, but, as Paul later alludes, "sin, seizing the opportunity afforded by the commandment, produced in me every kind of coveting." In what could be Adam's words as much as his own, Paul continues, "once I was alive apart from the law; but when the commandment came, sin sprang to life and I died" (Rom 7:8–9).[5] This law/commandment obviously alludes to the written code, the law that kills. We should not be surprised that, immediately upon the heels of God's command, Satan seized the moment by directing Adam and Eve's gaze to the tree of the knowledge of good and evil. Satan makes the second tree a priority because it presents an apparent balance, or symmetry, between good and evil. It is like the two columns (see "The Liar's Religion"). Insinuating that God hid knowledge from them, the serpent skews the picture, tilting it toward evil. He tries to flip the good column so that it is perceived as the *exception* to the rule. Even if he succeeds in establishing what merely appears as a sort of balance, however, he has achieved his goal. He established himself on par with the God and creator of all things.

Satan knows that the knowledge of good and evil does not come with built-in discernment between the two.[6] Human knowledge of good and evil is clouded by evil. In placemat terms, instead of green or red, Adam and Eve see grey, and the haziness of their checkered vision is apparent. The judgment required is something human beings were meant to exercise in revelatory dependence upon the Judge and the verdict of the cross. Satan, knowing we lack God's unique "power of distinction,"[7] succeeded in giving us something way above our pay grade. "It is poison," notes Barth, "for any being to stand in the place of God."[8] It is clear that once human beings disobey, for them to then eat from the tree of eternal life is to eternally

---

it reveals and relates to Gen 1. In his mind the whole content of what would have been Volume 5 is his guide, his North Star. The whole of the *Church Dogmatics* is therefore a kind of prolegomena to the day of revelation: the day of all days, all days of the day, all days in the day. Mark Edwards captures this sense in his recently published *Christ Is Time*.

5. Rom 5:12–19 tells us that even though different people sinned in different ways, Adam represented the disobedience of humanity just like Christ represented the obedience. We are all in solidarity with each representative.

6. See Barth's argument in *CD* III/1, 258–61, which is much along the same lines of Chambers at top of this reading. For example, p. 260: "Man is to know that his life originates and consists in the fact that God has affirmed and therefore denied, that He has chosen and therefore rejected, that He has willed one thing and therefore not willed another."

7. *CD* III/1, 258.

8. *CD* III/1, 262.

perpetuate this poisonous dualism (Gen 3:22).[9] Yet, if there was ever a threat of stamping eternity with this dualism, then God banishing humans from the Garden (Gen 3:24) returned the focus to stamping it out *for* eternity.

Just as we may struggle to understand why God allows Satan his "hour" to woo us in the end, we can only guess at why God allowed Satan to victimize the first humans (2 Cor 11:3). Still, it is at least worth imagining what it would have been like for Adam and Eve to start with the tree of life as the interpretive key for the other tree. This is the perspective we are given by reading the Bible from right to left. The tree of life in Revelation 22 points to Jesus Christ. It allows us to start with Jesus Christ, life himself, and to retrospectively recognize how he addressed evil in his death on the cross, even from the foundation of the world (Rev 13:8). From the outset this relegates evil to the inferior, subordinate, and defeated position, and the tree of the knowledge of good and evil therefore takes on a very different meaning.

Conversely, to start from the wrong direction and the wrong tree (the tree of the knowledge of good and evil), is to start with a dualism. The devil wants us to see evil as the parallel rival, not the parasitic problem. We then start with an overshadowing problem of sin and look for a solution to it, instead of seeing sin in light of the solution. When everything is flipped around, grace is then only an exception to the rule rather than the bedrock reality. Even if we start with the cross as breaking a log-jam, and thereby introduce a new life that emerges in the resurrection, Satan has us thinking on his terms. This is because, if the cross merely opens up the possibility that we can move from one column to the other (from death to life), it validates the column we "start" from, the death column, and the fundamental dualism that exists between the two.

Satan may know that he lost before he started, but his ability to twist and distort is astonishing. Beginning with Jesus Christ (human life) and him crucified (human death), however, Christ's resurrection (human life) connects the dots that reveal the end in the beginning and the beginning in the end, in spite of death.[10] We noted above that all of Genesis 1 is in Genesis 2–3, but not all of Genesis 2–3 is in Genesis 1. Similarly, the tree of life is in the tree of the knowledge of good and evil, even if the same cannot be said in reverse. Throughout this project we have engaged Barth's teaching on the

---

9. The first tree is a sign of grace and promise, meant to be rested under. The second tree was not meant to be grasped, but once it was, the grasping (restlessness) could not be allowed to contaminate the resting. See *CD* III/1, 256–57, for Barth's insights along these lines. Adam and Eve were "graciously withdrawn" (257) from the garden, a harbinger of final judgment (and deliverance) as the sword hanging over their exit indicates.

10. *CD* III/1, 281.

two Genesis sagas and how they relate to one another. The tree of life is not mentioned specifically in the first saga, but Barth locates it there theologically, matching the tree in Revelation 22. As the central tree, it is always the proper point of reference for the other, second tree, that of the knowledge of good and evil.[11] Not only does the resurrection witness to the fact that sin and death are the exception to the rule, it hearkens back to what we could call "the tree of reference," indicating that life has been the reality all along. There never was any symmetry between righteousness and sin, good and evil, life and death. The truth never needed to *be* established since it already was. The necessary aspect was the destruction of the lie, and the defeat of Satan at his own game.

Salvation is by subtraction. When looking from the devil's perspective we see two trees, and yet, when looking back from Revelation 22, we see only one. Where in Genesis two trees were described—"in the middle of the garden were the tree of life and the tree of the knowledge of good and evil" (Gen 2:9)—now, in the new Eden, only the tree of life stands. The one tree of life is still central, but in defiance of dualism it stands on *both* sides of the river that pours out from the throne of God. A singular tree—there is no need here for that other tree, the one that includes evil. And, despite what the devil told you, there was never a need to compare good and evil—as if they are apples to apples—in order to navigate through them. All we needed was Christ, who is our life.[12]

Revelation 22 has returned us to Genesis 1. Because human beings have been folded into the triune relationship, (and in the sense that we are in the Son, Jesus Christ, who loves the Father) we can say that God has loved every person from the beginning, and every person has loved God in return. That is the normal relationship of humanity in the Spirit. By giving us a peek at the end, God calls us back to the beginning: "You have forsaken the love you had at first. Consider how far you have fallen! Repent and do the things you did at first" (Rev 2:4–5).

---

11. *CD* III/1, 257–83. Notably, we could say there was a green tree (tree of life) and a grey tree (tree of good and evil), but red doesn't get its own tree.

12. See *CD* III/1, 283: "When the relationship is normal—and the act of creation as such produces a normal relationship—it [the grasping for fruit] does not even need to be prohibited. The purpose in the act of his creation is to live in absolute certainty, and therefore without any fear whatever of the threat of death and therefore without any hunger for life. The fear of death and the hunger for life do not correspond to his destiny. His real destiny is given him as he is given rest in the place whose centre is constituted by the tree of life, in the place in which the fear of death and the hunger for life are mutually excluded because he knows that he is protected from death and assured of life."

92

The Why Question

Christ put himself completely in your place. He was God and . . . he became the human being who of all, unconditionally all, has suffered the most. No human being was ever born or will or can ever be born who will suffer as he suffered. . . . Human sympathy usually shrinks back, prefers to remain, commiserating, on the safe beach; or if he ventures out does not want to go quite as far out as where the sufferer is—but what sympathy to go out further still!

—SOREN KIERKEGAARD

The real incarnation lay not in Christ's being made flesh for us, but in His being made sin. And the dereliction was the real descent into hell, the bottoming of salvation. Here beneath the depth of sin is the deeper depth of God. "If I make my bed in hell, Thou art there."

—P. T. FORSYTH

THE NEGATION OF A great and glorious God is great indeed, and in the same way, humanity's fall is the hardest and darkest imaginable. We must take both negations—the primary and derivative one—fully seriously. Our "post-fall" mortality, concurrent with our immortality, is acutely painful and deliriously confusing. In this life of the first heaven, our immortality doesn't exist without our mortality. Nor does our mortality exist without our immortality. These are not on parallel tracks, but integrated in the one person. They are inseparable but not mixed. In this world, then, P^3 is mortal and P^3 is also immortal. "Pat" lives even while Pat dies.

But if death is such an exception to the rule, why does God allow it? Why does he subject us to this worldly chaos which, in Hobbes's words, is solitary, nasty, brutish, and short? If all of the "then" is in the "now," then why the painfulness of the "now" at all? If the "already" has always been, if we are all in one sense in heaven, gloriously alive, then why the "not yet?" If we are all seated with Christ, then why are so many mistreated?

That Christ's perfect creation and redemption of the world seems so counterintuitive is partly due to the fact that the prevalence of evil seems to dwarf the presence of God. Theologically speaking, we can return to the idea of green as representing who Christ is, who we are, and what the universe is in its original and real form. Satan has no power to create, but his deception lies in his power to twist, contort, and confuse creation. He cannot destroy the green, but he can cloud our vision to such an extent that we no longer perceive it in the world around us.

Illustrating the perplexity of the human experience in the tension of the already-but-not-yet, Jesus himself asked the greatest Why question of all upon the cross. Hanging there on the tree, he cried out, "My God, My God, why have you forsaken me?" (Matt 27:46). There are three crucial aspects to this cry that we will address:

1) We first need to take this cry of Jesus at face value on the most obvious level. The crucified one is the person Jesus of Nazareth. If we do not remember that Jesus is a singular human being, a poor Palestinian Jew under the oppression of Roman colonial rule, then we go wrong. We dehistoricize the narrative and make it purely conceptual. I do think it is important that Jesus suffered as much as any singular human being has ever suffered. The cross, emphasizes James Cone, "was a public spectacle accompanied by torture and shame—one of the most humiliating and painful deaths ever devised by human beings."[1] We need to know that no one's suffering is outside of the agony of Christ's experience.[2]

2) If we do not remember that Jesus is God in the flesh, then God is outside of Jesus's suffering, looking on perhaps with a tear in his eye.

---

1. Cone, *Cross and the Lynching Tree*, 2–3.

2. It is probable that if Jesus had been simply beheaded and died instantly with all of his clothes on and without scourging and torture, etc., we would think of his suffering in more isolated terms and without the same scope of solidarity.

In this frightening case, God is not really experiencing the depths of human suffering. Such a God who is so distant from our fallen human experience cannot not be taken seriously and does not deserve our allegiance. I need to know that it is *God* who understands my existential and experiential pain, not just *Jesus*.

3) Jesus Christ is a singular human being, Jesus of Nazareth, and Jesus Christ is God. Putting the two together, we recognized the fact that Jesus of Nazareth in his singular humanity also contains all that makes up any and every human person. Only God can do this. We might imagine Christ's humanity as God's way of putting Adam's rib back in (see Gen 2:21), so that we may speak freely of the unfathomable human diversity of the very good creation (Gen 1:31) in the one Jesus Christ, the Second and Original Adam. As God, without favor to "maleness," Jesus can feel the whole spectrum of humanity's pain and suffering; his cry from the cross is as one human being, and as humanity. Both are important. It is as if God decided that if he was going to allow any person to experience forsakenness by God, he needed and wanted to walk through the same darkness. It is a mystery that we are unable to dissect, but I think he went even further than feeling everything that we feel. He addressed the source. He became sin, something more drastic than any one person's broken or sinful condition.

I think it important that Jesus's "cry of dereliction" from the cross is a quote from Psalm 22:1.[3] The implicit, big picture is already there, even if the Savior lost sight of it for a time during his execution. The first part of Psalm 22 prophetically portrays the crucifixion, but later in the Psalm, verse 24 sheds light on the bigger picture. Against any thought that the Father would turn his back on the Son in this moment of suffering, we read, "he has not despised or scorned the suffering of the afflicted one; he has not hidden his face from him." Sin is strong, but it cannot separate God from God. Evil is incomprehensibly deep, but it cannot break the incomprehensible bond of love and unity of the Holy Trinity.

Together, Psalms 22, 23, and 24 have been called a trilogy, and Jesus's cry from 22:1 a signal that Jesus himself is embarking upon the pathway

3. Much has been made of the fact that Jesus's cry from Ps 22:1 begins with an implicit statement of faith, "My God." George MacDonald writes, "He could not see, could not feel Him near; and yet it is '*My* God' that He cries. Thus the Will of Jesus, in the very moment when His faith seems about to yield, is finally triumphant. It has no *feeling* now to support it, no beatific vision to absorb it. It stands naked in His soul and tortured, as He stood naked and scourged before Pilate. Pure and simple and surrounded by fire, it declares for God" (quoted by C. S. Lewis in *George MacDonald*, 33 [emphasis original]).

portrayed by these three prophetic Psalms. If that is the case, then Psalm 22 most definitely describes the acute first-heaven hardships of Jesus, and Psalm 23 theologically interprets the Savior's Psalm 22 experience.[4] Even though I might feel like I am alone or abandoned during my trip through the dark times—the valley of the shadow of death—I can be assured that "Thou art with me." There is never a separation of Jesus from God, or of humanity from God. Indeed, God acts in love to assure us that nothing can separate us from the love of God in Jesus Christ (Rom 8:39). In the Spirit, the love of the Father for the Son and the love of the Son for the Father forms an inviolable Trinitarian unity, and we are all "knit in that knot" (Julian).

Paul's exclamatory verse from Romans 8 above receives its logic from the Trinitarian relationship in which we are enfolded, not the Aristotelian logic of non-contradiction. As Barth continually reminds us, God embraces the intrusive contradiction. He solves the contradiction by subjecting himself to it, even becoming it: "[God] makes His own the being of man in contradiction against Him . . . but in order to do away with it as He suffers it. He acts as Lord over this contradiction even as He subjects Himself to it."[5]

Without trying to answer the unanswerable, I have found that looking honestly at God the Son's cry from the cross, and his solidarity with the deepest pain of humanity, has profound pastoral implications. A couple of years ago, I asked a friend to read the essay toward the front of this book,

---

4. A quick search reveals the many titles given to this so-called trilogy of Psalms, but one point worth mentioning is that the synoptics all include Jesus's cry of dereliction, but John's gospel does not. So that, if Psalm 22 can be cast as the synoptic Psalm (and the one most indicative of the first heaven), Psalm 23 with its strong shepherd's theme can be cast along the lines of John's theological interpretation. In effect, John is reading Jesus's passion more from Psalm 24 (Jesus's) to Psalm 22, whereas the synoptics more from Psalm 22 to 24. We will perhaps never know why John, as an eyewitness, did not include Jesus's cry (unless he omitted it for the potential confusion it would cause!), but it seems clear that his emphasis was on Psalm 23:4 ("Even if I walk through the valley of the shadow of death I will fear no evil, for you art with me," ESV) and 22:24 ("He has not hidden his face from him"). Jesus's confidence in the faithful presence of the Father is seen in his remark to his disciples John 16:32 ("You will leave me all alone. Yet I am not alone, for my Father is with me"), and John 8:29 ("The one who sent me is with me; he has not left me alone").

5. *CD* IV/1, 185. On this same page in *CD* Barth warns against the "supreme blasphemy" of imagining that Jesus's cry of dereliction from the cross evidenced a contradiction in God himself, or a separation of Trinitarian persons. God can address the depths of human contradiction without being internally and schismatically contradicted in himself. In a way that echoes the sentiment of P. T. Forsyth at the top of this chapter, Barth here (185) declares, "The meaning of the incarnation is plainly revealed in the question of Jesus from the cross, 'My God, my God, why hast thou forsaken me?'" The full extent of *the Word became flesh* cannot be apprehended apart from *the Word became sin*.

"The Prevalence of Evil and the Presence of God," and to get his reflections on the biggest "why question" of all. This was his written reply:

> Jesus's cry of "why have you forsaken me" is still confusing to me. I think you're saying that Jesus knew he was going to rise, but in his cry he was speaking from the perspective of humanity. It's like in that moment he was in a way possessed by the burden of the sin, guilt, brokenness, hate, etc., experienced by humans every day, and thus he was voicing that perspective to show that he really did feel and understand us. In this way, *Jesus/God* wasn't really asking God/himself that question, but really it was a representation of humanity *in* Jesus that was asking God that question. But even if that assumption is correct, I still have a hard time with the silent answer to that question. I can find comfort in the fact that Jesus really did feel my pain and the pain of all humanity, but does God do a good enough job of answering Jesus'/humanity's cry? God answers the question of sin, through Jesus's resurrection, but he never answers the literal question Jesus poses on the cross, "*why* have you forsaken me." This is the part that your thesis cannot answer, and nobody can answer, and it's the question that seemingly holds power over everything. I think I get your point, but it still doesn't answer the ultimate question "why." In other words, why did the "saving" need to be done in the first place?

Here is my reply:

> I do NOT want the essay to come across as trying to explain evil, even with the cross, because evil is simply unexplainable and irrational. It's irrational because it has no root in God's good creation, so there is no rationale for it. Some things can be described but not explained. How could we ever explain something that has no rationale in God's created economy? (Like "Mama" always says, you can't fight irrationality with rationality!) So the main assertion I'm making is that God understands and would never allow something that he did not assume. But you're exactly right, God taking his own medicine helps, but it leads to more questions.
>
> People get caught up on the wrong, or at least derivative, "Why question"—i.e., why this or that in life? Again my attempt was not to answer the question but to draw both the holocaust and the cross into the mystery of the One who answers the question in himself, to reveal to us later. We will still have to be content with waiting for that revelation, I'm afraid. Can we

trust God's love the way the Son trusted the Father's love? Can we believe God is love in his inmost being? And that he is good?

I believe that each person has a true self, created in Christ (Eph 2:10), and that this true self is not static. In Christ everyone believes, everyone loves God. It's not that we don't have a true self, the problem is that it's covered over and dwarfed with the obscuring pain and brokenness of the world. If we believe, even just a little, during this life, it can only be a miracle. No one can talk another person into belief; we can ride the coattails of others only so far. With all the evidence to the contrary in this fallen broken world, it is certainly counterintuitive to adhere to such a truth claim, and cerebral types more than the rest will know that it is a miracle when it happens! When I say miracle I mean it's a revelation or manifestation of reality, an emergence or breakthrough into our experience. It's one that we taste and want to taste more, and this makes us want to gather with others who have "tasted and seen that the Lord is good." Then, even once we experience belief, it ebbs and flows. Doubt is part of faith, and in a backwards way proves it. We won't really and truly believe 100 percent or consistently until the fog clears.

Theodicy is the study of God and evil. Its focus is the why question, usually as it turns up in our everyday world and fallen existence. But what you have done, and what I plan to do in *The Goodness of Judgment*, is to move the theodicy discussion back to the very beginning—back to Genesis 1. Why didn't God solve this "evil thing" without us?!

The above interchange brought to mind another theological "Why" encounter that I had with Phil, a contractor who painted our house a few years ago.

I arrived home one day and Phil was pressure-washing our house before painting it. He saw my Bible and asked if I was a pastor. I said, "Well, I'm not really a 'pastor pastor,' but I am the director of a nonprofit ministry downtown." I did not know where Phil was coming from, so I didn't want to come on too strong at first. After telling him that we had bought a church and converted it into a community center for teenagers, I dropped a comment that I hoped would arouse curiosity: "Yeh, it's been great doing the new thing, even though I didn't see myself here a couple years ago: we actually got fired by another ministry organization that said we were too inclusive." My words hung in the air. Sure enough, Phil gave me a curious look and asked: "What do you mean by 'too inclusive.'"

"Well, Phil," I said, "I believe that every person belongs to God, that we are all his children because of what Jesus Christ has done for us. I believe when Jesus gave his life for you and me, for everyone, that he washed us clean and doesn't hold our sins against us. God the Father has redeemed his children, and that's the rhyme and reason of the universe. We don't have to live as his sons, but we are. He loves us so much and has done everything for all of us. My former organization would not tolerate me saying that to students."

Phil said, "Really? I thought that was what all Christians think?"

"No," I said, "there are some who think I was giving away too much—that those things I said about belonging to God, being his child, and being forgiven are not really true for us until we do something, until we respond in faith. But more and more I think people need to know they belong to God before anything else." Phil seemed to be leaning in.

"It's like this," I continued, "I believe Jesus is the Lord and Savior of us all. Without knowing anything at all about you, for instance, I can say, *Jesus is your leader*. I can say that because it is a fact whether you believe it or not. He simply *is* your leader, not because of what you've done but because of what he's done; he created you and redeemed you. That's the way God has set it up. If Christ is your leader, it's not too hard to see how pretending that he's not and acting like you are your own leader might not work very well!"

I couldn't tell if I had said too much. We were still standing in the same spot in the front yard and Phil looked down, shuffled his feet and continued. "Well, I grew up Catholic and a few years ago my wife and I started going to a Baptist church. We volunteered with the church to go help Hurricane Katrina victims, and then the bottom just fell out of our marriage. My wife got interested in another man on the trip. I couldn't believe it. I had tried to follow God and serve him, and then I ended up with a divorce, losing my wife and three kids. I haven't had much to do with God since."

I listened as Phil took some time to describe the details of the sad tale.

"I cannot imagine the pain you must have gone through with this," I said sadly. "This world can be brutal. I cannot tell you why s—t like this happens. If I was to give you any answers as to why, I'd be making them up. I don't know. But this is what I *do* know. You could be angry and resentful toward God for letting this happen—pointing your finger at him in blame. But in so doing you are actually attempting to keep at arm's length the only one who can really help you. And I don't know about you, but I know I need his help."

"Yeh, it sounds like you've been through some rough stuff too," Phil said.

"Well, yes, but losing a job is nothing like losing my wife and kids. I can't understand the depths of that kind of pain. And that brings me back to why I'm telling you to talk to God. It's ironic," I said, "but I believe when you start asking your Why questions to God you will discover how near he is to you."

"So Phil," I said, "can I challenge you to do something?" He nodded. "I think you should get in your car, or go home, or even while you're up on your ladder painting—just get somewhere where you can really have it out with God. I suggest you yell at him, scream and curse at him, ask him all your questions, ask him *Why*?! Tell him how unfair and unjust you feel it is that your marriage broke up when you were trying to follow him—let it all hang out. I believe He is with you and has never left you. You have a relationship with God because of what Christ has done, and for that to be real to you, you need to engage with him—don't worry about the words, just engage as honestly and openly as you can; talk to him, share your frustrations. I promise you won't offend him!

"In fact, my prayer for you is that the more raw you are with God, the more you will realize that he's not some divine being just watching over us, aloof in the clouds. No, you will realize that you are talking to a God who was stripped, beaten, and unjustly hung naked on a cross. A God who *does* understand. In fact, he carried *your* pain in his heart as he hung there, and he also carried your doubts on his lips. He even asked, 'Why God?' He knows your agony, Phil. That's the reason that asking or even screaming the why question peels the layers and reveals the intimate bond you have always had with him. He has been with you this whole time, he's carrying you through the valley and out the other side."

Phil the painter came back the next day and told me that he had done what I had suggested, getting it all off his chest with Jesus. After sharing about his meaningful encounter with the crucified and risen Christ, we stood in the front yard and joined together in a prayer of gratitude.

There are so many times when I simply have no answers, but somehow in the face of evil God continues to take care of his own reputation. Evil confounds us, but just as confounding, if not more confounding, are the times when belief emerges. People who have every reason not to believe, do.

93

Theodicy Revisited

Those who believe they believe in God but without passion in the heart, without anguish of mind, without uncertainty, without doubt, and even at times without despair, believe only in the idea of God, and not in God Himself.
—Madeleine L'Engle

The world, as it is, is not good enough to be true.
—William R. Inge

God has ways of validating himself, but that doesn't stop Satan from "[prowling] around like a roaring lion looking for someone to devour" (1 Pet 5:8). It seems that nothing gives Satan more pleasure than to obscure the goodness of God and humanity by wielding his number one instrument of confusion. The Why question cannot be answered. It can only be informed by the fact that the God who allows evil, pain, and death does not stay aloof from it. He in fact knows our personal pain better than we do. God in the flesh agonized with his own Why question, stepping into the painful mire of cosmic brokenness. But still, even if God does not cause evil, how can we live with a God who has the power to prevent, but still *allows* such things? Why so many exceptions to the rule? Why the pain? Why the trouble? Couldn't God have done it in a different way?

PART SEVEN: IMMORTALS FALL

Voltaire's riddle continues to have a stymieing effect. In statement form, it reasons thus: If God is all good, he couldn't be all powerful. And if God is all powerful, he couldn't be all good. You will find Voltaire's riddle repackaged in a variety of ways. I'll provide two examples.

I remember growing up and hearing the word "providential" used only for good things (e.g., "getting that pay raise was providential"), but rarely if ever for bad things (e.g., "it was providential that my dad died of a heart-attack at age 35"). Rob Neal's poem "Don't Ask God" is slightly dated, but he poignantly exposes the silly arbitrariness of our God-talk where, as theistic spin masters, we tend to co-opt God into a version of a rabbit's foot or good luck charm, implementing him into the narratives of our personal agenda:

"Don't Ask God" by Rob Neal[1]

Don't ask God for anything. No prayers, calls, or emails,
There is no help desk or 911, no prayer request line, or
Heavenly catalog to look through,
Hoping to find the item, the thing, the answer that
Will heal your wounds, balance your bottom line,
Calm your worries. . . .

Wait just a minute you say, what about
That touchdown I scored, that home run I hit,
My battle over cancer, the new promotion,
The miracle of my children, the jury who found me innocent. . . .

Didn't God play a part and answer my prayers?

The millions, perhaps billions of people who starved to death,
Were tortured, murdered, abused,
Died by tornado, earthquake, flood, disease,
Scream back with humanity and wonder
Why God favors home runs over eating, one person's miracle cure, over
Two hundred thousand dying in one tsunami. . . .

Could there be a greater cruelty than a God making such choices?
Your relationship with God is not so special after all,
It's not even personal or redeeming,
Or at least you should hope so.

If God plays favorites we're all doomed,
Like the draft lottery during Viet Nam,
The wheel just spins and lands on a number
Determining life or death,

---

1. Unpublished, used with permission.

THEODICY REVISITED

> Does God's roulette prayer wheel include
> Genocides and touchdowns, side by side?
>
> Don't bow your head in fervent prayer
> Seeking a magical hand to pick you, . . . you,
> Over the endless humans unable to wish for
> More than the next breath, the next drink,
> A morsel of food.
>
> Hear the Children around the globe screaming out
> The warnings most feared by humanity that
> Imminent death seems inescapable,
>
> The pasteurized certainty you'd have us believe,
> Prevents seeing into life's darkness, or the harrowing truth
> About your murderous intent to smoother and conquer,
> Everything in the way of your parochial beliefs,
> Dreamy hopes, and privileged life,
>
> Don't Ask God . . . instead, . . . look in the mirror,
> Through the light prism,
> Raw, naked, alone, . . . quietly now. . . .
> Watch. . . . Listen. . . . breathe. . . .
>
> Let your senses do their job,
> Their immaculate design brings in the Universe.
>
> Seek the divinity hidden in your darker shadows,
> Through the corridors of being alive,
> Touching the grace that surrounds all,
> Wanting your door to open. . . .

I quite like Neal's poem, because I think it does a masterful job deconstructing much unhelpful scaffolding that Christians have built around "Christian-ese" and their piously affected language.[2] While Neal's subject (for our purposes, Neal) deconstructs deftly, his reconstruction toward hopefulness comes up a bit short in my opinion. He gives up on the incarnate Lord, and throws us back on ourselves by encouraging us to seek our own divinity through the senses. But Neal comes so close! Note his usage of prism and mirror. The problem is that Neal, in trusting his senses to do their job of connecting us to "the universe," never quite sees through the mirror. What I mean is that he has not discovered, by revelation, the Lord Jesus speaking to him from the other side of the mirror—the Lord who *is* speaking and *from* whom, unbeknownst perhaps to Neal, Neal has derived

---

2. See also Bowler, *Everything Happens*. Without trying too hard to answer unanswerable questions, Bowler does a marvelous job deconstructing Christian faith without losing the hope of the gospel.

a vague sense of transcendence. As with any bottom up, natural theology approach, our self-reflection causes us to project our sensual ideas onto an often less than personal universal (in this case the transcendent). In Pascal's words, "Faith certainly tells us what the senses do not, but not the contrary of what they see; it is above, not against them."[3]

It is not impossible to stumble upon the transcendent in this way (from the bottom up), if only because the transcendent is already there in the immanent, and yet such sensual reliance means that discoveries are by nature fleeting and disjointed. When self-reflection includes too much reflection of self, the gaps are massive. There is no top-down coherence because the transcendence has no name. The perceived arbitrariness has shifted from God to the individual. Have I found what I'm looking for? How do I know? There is no salvation story, no metanarrative that includes every person. There is no possibility of a face-to-face encounter with the personal God revealed in Jesus Christ who understands and apprehends all of the dimensions of human existence that the poem so brilliantly lays out. Thrown about by the senselessness of life's absurdities there is no interpretive key, no anchor of constancy, no dependable love.

Instead, we can return to our placemat prism, and the fact that by God's revelation to us even while mired in Genesis 2–3, we can discover ourselves in Revelation 22 and Genesis 1. By finding Jesus Christ, the Creator, Son of God, firstborn creature, true human, false human, as the center of our existence, we find ourselves in him. And somehow, in the midst of the world Neal so graphically describes, faith, hope, and love spring up from the transcendent ground of a Savior God who came low and near to reveal to us the big picture: "Not only do we only know God through Jesus Christ, but we only know ourselves through Jesus Christ; we only know life and death through Jesus Christ. Apart from Jesus Christ we cannot know the meaning of our life or our death, of God or of ourselves."[4]

The second example of Voltairean repackaging is a viral rant by actor Stephen Fry, which has been watched on YouTube over 10 million times.[5] In this short clip Fry describes God as nothing but a monster for not exerting his omnipotence to stop the world's outrageous and senseless suffering. As I elaborate below, instead of reacting to his comments in God's defense, make an attempt to receive Fry's harangue as helpful. Seemingly unbeknownst

---

3. Pascal, *Pensees*, Fragment 185, 85.

4. Pascal, *Pensees*, Fragment 417, 148.

5. RTÉ One, "Stephen Fry on God." As of this book's release, Fry's segment had received over 150,000 thumbs up on YouTube.

THEODICY REVISITED

to him, Fry's critique illustrates that Satan can turn something completely around, baiting us to accuse God for the Accuser's own destructive path.

After watching the clip I found myself saying, "I wouldn't want to align with such a 'god' either—nor spend eternity with one." I also caught myself thinking that Fry's affable personality, much to his chagrin I'm sure, speaks of an affable creator! So, in one sense agreeing with Fry, we can say at least two things:

1. First, all of the things Fry says about "god" are accurate about Satan. God, on Fry's account, could only be a mean-minded, capricious monster who inflicts children with cancer, a selfish maniac who is to blame for all of the pain, injustice, and misery of the world. Fry is not describing the God I believe in who loves us more than he loves himself. However, there is one phrase Fry uses that I would *not* apply to Satan, that he "does not deserve our respect." Satan *does* deserve our respect. I believe there is a sense in which we must respect Satan in the same way that we respect a poisonous viper or an evil empire or a metastatic cancer. We must face the facts. Evil is strong, stronger than we can know or describe.

    Think about it. We are created perfect. No flaws. No chinks in our armor. Nothing incomplete or lacking. Nothing to be improved upon. Loved by God and loving God. And under Satan's guile we *still* make the wrong-headed and destructive choice. A choice of flesh and not Spirit; death not life.

    Evil is so strong that the true, loving God deemed it necessary to submit to it in order to destroy it (Rom 6:9). This is a common refrain in literary or screen sagas with Christ-characters: Aslan against the White Witch (*The Lion, the Witch, and the Wardrobe*), Harry Potter against Voldemort (*Harry Potter and the Deathly Hallows*), Neo against Mr. Smith (*The Matrix*). The main characters submitted to the strength of the evil magic in order to defeat it, because only they were aware of a deeper magic that "Satan" could not match. After all of his parasitic mirroring (Satan can't create, only corrupt) he had nothing left in the end. Christ's death drained all the evil power Satan had, and then Christ got up. The bottom line is this: what God did in Christ demonstrates not only how much he loves us, but how strong Satan/evil is. He is strong and brutal, monstrously so.

2. Next, Fry is right that the idea of kids being born with incurable cancer can't in any way be construed as good, and is in fact pure evil. Many of Fry's concerns are artfully articulated in Bart Ehrman's book

PART SEVEN: IMMORTALS FALL

God's Problem: How the Bible Fails to Answer Our Most Important Question—Why We Suffer. In fact, along with Fry, I recommend Ehrman's book, especially the last chapter, because here Ehrman rightly debunks all of the theories that theologians have used for centuries in attempts to grapple with the existence of evil. Even if he falls short of our final analysis, Ehrman opposes the right things:

- any congruency between good and evil
- that good needs a contrast to be good
- that the fall was necessarily accompanied by God's decision to grant human "free will"
- that redeeming means replacing
- that God somehow makes up for suffering by suffering himself
- the apocalyptic view when it claims that all will make sense later, etc.

Ehrman states that even if "God" were to reveal to him the secret behind all of the unjust carnage, it could never be enough. The damage has been done. There can be no overarching human metanarrative with a loving, all-powerful God; "this life is all there is."[6]

It is not surprising that Ehrman expresses a resonance with the character Ivan in Dostoevsky's *The Brothers Karamazov*. Ivan cannot reconcile all the good and all the evil in this world. He resorts to thinking of them as parallel lines, but he is deeply troubled that God would make allowance for the "line" of evil and the horrors of human suffering. Unlike Ehrman, Ivan has faint hopes in a "higher harmony," that somehow the parallel lines will meet in a way that reconciles the good and evil. On one hand Ivan acknowledges his tenuous hold to "childlike" trust in God, but on the other hand the many atrocities that he has witnessed war against his eyes of faith, taking him further afield from all hope. Ultimately Ivan, summarizes Ehrman, "takes his stand in the here and now,"[7] rejecting any chance of a higher harmony in a world where babies are thrown in the air to be caught on bayonets.

---

6. Ehrman, *God's Problem*, 276. Ehrman may reject our narrative as well, but his "drop the mic" conclusion fails to satisfy, and leaves much more to be considered. Even if Ehrman fails to read the Bible with our christological approach, however, this accomplished scholar does us a great favor with his exploding of biblicism. His tongue in cheek claim to be "biblical" by endorsing the lifestyle based on the book of Ecclesiastes (with its "Epicurean" slant) is a proper challenge to inerrantists.

7. Ehrman, *God's Problem*, 269. The discussion on Brothers Karamazov is 265–69.

Thankfully our faith does not rest blindly in the hope that Ivan's parallel lines will someday meet. God's economy in fact disallows it. Instead, the placemat claim is that these lines are starkly perpendicular, meeting in the cross of Jesus Christ. This is the way (different from an insufficient external view of God suffering) that God's suffering internally connects in solidarity with ours as part of a larger narrative of universal redemption. If our view is apocalyptic, it is not futuristic. It is a dimensional, actualistic construct not constricted by time and space, and interpreted by the green of grace.

Red is not green and cannot become green any more than a horizontal line is vertical, or can become vertical. God took all that he did not create, all of the horizontal, parasitic, twistedness of the red, and crucified it for the sake of all that is green, which is all that he did create and call good. The cross, then, provides a flat rejection of any "higher harmony" reconciling good and evil. Suffering will never "make sense." That is why to talk about our worldly existence based simply on being created good in Christ, without talking about brokenness, sin, disharmony, and all the effects of the fall, is to talk about humanity apart from Christ's cross, which is impossible. Just because I believe that God can bring good out of bad things doesn't mean that we should call bad things good. They are not. Brokenness and wholeness exist in the same space, but they are not the same thing.

Our theology of the cross therefore encourages us to be careful with "God created you exactly the way you are" rhetoric and Christian-ese. Of course, on one level the truth of these words is absolutely valid when speaking of who we are in our true, uncorrupted Genesis 1 selves, unaffected by the fall, our purely good (green) spiritual material bodies. To say those words (God created you exactly the way you are) in *an un-nuanced* fashion about a child born with cancer, or concerning a child with all kinds of problems stemming from the womb, however, is theologically imprecise.[8]

---

8. We have maintained in both volumes that there are good and wise reasons for less theologically precise statements, depending on the situation. Of course, I am always thinking about issues related to intellectual disabilities, or cognitive impairments. In Book One I stated that if I could go into my mother's womb and remove the anxiety gene, I believe I would be dealing with the fall's symptoms, not altering God's good and perfect creation. But with my grey vision I cannot make these statements about others, even if my friend Amy, who has Williams Syndrome (a disability caused by missing a part of chromosome 7) does not shy away from expressing her desire to be like "normal" people. I do perceive myself to be a candidate for his healing touch had I lived in Jesus's lifetime. I do *not* think Jesus would have said "you're perfect just the way you are" to any of us. However, the self-attested Messianic vision of Jesus in Luke 4 "to heal the blind," or his words in Matt 11:5 describing the same: "the blind receive sight, the lame walk, . . . the deaf hear," and the accompanying biblical accounts of Jesus's healings have historically been understandably troubling to those in the disabilities community. See Belcher, "Disability and the Terror of the Miracle Tradition," 162–81. Again, while

Here is the key. None of us can look in the mirror and say, "This is exactly the way I was created!" The accuracy we seek is inaccessible to us by sight or self-perception. Why? Because how we are created is different from how we are born. Don't get me wrong, the essence of Pat will always be Pat, and we will recognize each other in our spiritual bodies because that is *who we are* in a way more than our physical attributes or biological characteristics could ever define us in this perceptible realm. The continuity is there; the spiritual material body manifests through the biological body in a dimensional, not dualistic way. But just as important is the fact that our spiritual bodies precede our biological physiological bodies. (Some people call this a soul, but for me a soul is never without a body, as if it's just floating around). From the beginning of our gestation period, our created spiritual bodies (i.e., our material souls without problems) are always dimensionally present, and that is exactly why this problematic world hurts so much. We feel pain in the womb, and we feel pain outside of the womb.

In Book One we noted Gregory of Nazianzen's comment that Christ identified with us all the way to being a corpse. In one sense this is true: God died. In another sense, that is not all there is to say about God or about us. None of us is fundamentally identified with a corpse. In fact, I like to say that I'll never be more myself than when you see me laying in a coffin. Why? Because when you see "me," you don't really see me. I'm not there. This begs the question: "So . . . what is that part of me *now* (when I'm alive and kicking) that is not there *then* (in the coffin)?" This deductible exercise may help us to see that because of Jesus Christ, we are all so much more than our perceptible bodies. I'm not sure *why* we imagine that our beloved grandpa who dies at age 80 will look like an 80-year-old in heaven, or that a toddler whose life is cut short will look like a toddler. Is it because we want it that way? Or is it because Jesus was apparently the same age after the resurrection as he was at his death? If the 80-year-old is racked by illness and not really "himself" at age 80, maybe we'll move his heavenly age to 70 (tongue in cheek). It's all so arbitrary, and because of this, it is wise to loosen our grip on exactly what we will look like when we depart our perceptible bodies. If we don't insist that our bodies will look the same after our worldly

---

there is so much that we do not know about the nature of our birth bodies relative to those of our created bodies, the bottom line is that at the deepest level the beautiful wholeness of every person exists in every person. Without defining normality, or comparing types of brokenness, we can say that regardless of any forms of brokenness, every person exists as God's perfect and beloved child, created "very good." That is the reality. It's our placemat anthropology that uniquely allows us to hold simultaneously to both sides of any human situation, not pretending that everything is alright, while not proposing that we are in any way created wrong. In the discernment of the Spirit, we will find ourselves weeping with those who weep, and rejoicing with those who rejoice.

departure, it would be equally unwise to insist that we are only what we look like when we arrive in the delivery room. At death, Pat is Pat *minus* a lot of other stuff. At birth, Pat is Pat, *plus* a lot of other stuff.

What we have in the end is the clearest vision of who Jesus Christ is and who we have always been in him. That is why Barth encourages us with anticipation for the day: "It will be without the concealment that surrounds it. . . . It is the same revelation which we have had, but it is now without a veil."[9] The grey is gone and the green that has always been there appears greener, no longer obscured by the red. The Apostles John and Paul say as much:

> Dear friends, now we are children of God, and what we will be has not yet been made known. But we know that when Christ appears, we shall be like him, for we shall see him as he is. (1 John 3:2)

> The creation waits in eager expectation for the children of God to be revealed. . . . That the creation itself will be liberated from its bondage to decay and brought into the freedom and glory of the children of God. (Rom 8:19, 21)

> And the passage with which we began this volume: "For now we see as through a mirror dimly; then we shall see face to face. Now I know in part; then I shall know fully, even as I am fully known." (1 Cor 13:12)

For Bart Ehrman, the phrase "God's problem" is pejorative. Conversely, Karl Barth can embrace the fact that evil is fundamentally God's problem; it is "God's affair" in a way that smacks of good news. On this side, God has not answered the myriad subsidiary questions flowing from the big question: why has the Creator allowed evil to overtake his perfect creation? We can acknowledge at once the indescribable power of evil and the fact that, as the arch Adversary of *this* adversary, God in Christ has taken care of it. We can believe that the mystery of evil is wrapped up in the mysterious and glorious asymmetry of God crucified. Yet the incomprehensible resolution to an incomprehensible problem is one that we can only grasp in faith. If we could comprehend it, we would concoct all kinds of reasonable solutions that inevitably result in making Satan too strong or God too weak. By refusing to resort to a doctrine where redemption proves that creation was insufficient, or that its goodness was totally or even partially wrecked by evil, we have leaned hard into the mystery. There we find the ministry of Christ's cross for a hurting world.

9. *CD* II/1, 631.

94

The Human Mission?

Man as such, because he is the fellow of the man Jesus, is from the very first destined to share in the deliverance from evil effected in this one man, to participate in the conflict against the enemy of all creaturely being, to figure in the history of the victory over this enemy, to belong to the body of the Head in whom the triumph of the Creator has been achieved on behalf of the creature.

—Karl Barth

God does not contend with nothingness without allowing His creature a share in the contention, without summoning His creature to His side as His co-belligerent. Yet the contention remains his own. His is the cause at stake.

—Karl Barth

As He puts the cup of sorrow into our hand, He says, Can ye drink of the cup that I drink of? And shall we refuse or hold back from this fellowship with Jesus, in the sorrow which kills sin when it is received in the spirit of Jesus, in the filial spirit?

—Thomas Erskine

THE HUMAN MISSION?

THROUGHOUT THESE VOLUMES WE suggested that we have all been with Christ from "the beginning" (John 15:27), or from Genesis 1 onwards. In 1 John 2:24 we read, "See that what you have heard from *the beginning* remains in you. If it does, you also will remain in the Son and in the Father" (emphasis added). If we do not have a problem with the possibility that everyone who ever lived is together at the end, as the phrase "countless multitudes" of Revelation implies, then neither should we have a problem with the possibility of everyone who ever lived being together in the beginning.

In the following thought experiment, I take my cue from the book of Revelation and the cosmic battle so central to all of Scripture, the one that culminates in the day.[1] Imagine with me what it means to interpret Colossians 1:23 in a more direct, literal sense: "This is the gospel that you heard and that *has been proclaimed* to every creature under heaven" (emphasis added). Jesus Christ, vested with Trinitarian authority, might have called all created beings together in the Spirit and said this to them:

> OK friends, there is an enemy. He is the anti-Christ, pure evil. You may not know this yet, but he's stronger than you are, even though not as strong as I am. In effect, I've taken pains to make sure the war against evil has already been won. I wouldn't have created you otherwise, but part of your being created in me involves your participation in the whole process of victory.[2] Even if the outcome is not dependent on you, your role is a genuine one. You may have asked for less, but I wanted to share this pilgrimage with you. I wanted you with me.[3]

1. I have obviously taken a dimension that is "logically primary" and pulled the proverbial accordion out as far as possible to make room for a temporal narrative of the first-first heaven.

2. This narrative defers more than most to the drastic power of Satan. It relies on the theological concept of negation, and therefore the parasitic, "borrowed," power, which is power nonetheless. God "allows" evil, then, because it is conceptually attributable to what *is* on the one hand and what *is not* on the other. To have a good and powerful God is to have the negation. That's just the way it is. It follows that to have a good God create a good creature also involves a negation. As my friend says, "perhaps there was no other way for God to create us unless he allowed Satan to get his time with us too. And if that is the case, it can be understood. For it is better to be alive and subjected to temporary turmoil with eternal glory than to never have been alive at all. Some might say God would never submit himself to even a short-term loss, but we need look no further than Jesus's death to see the ultimate example of such loss. Is it bad theology to say God is OK with losing?" The cross is consistent with this rationale. God the Son, condescending to become human, died. He lost. Scripture even tells us that he allowed death to be his master (Rom 6:9). Of course, the cross is not the end of the story, but Jesus's death reminds us that even if Satan gets his "time" with us, including death, that "time" is never without Jesus.

3. See Matt 26:38–40. At the height of his trial in the Garden of Gethsemane, in the

Your participation in me involves the good and the bad. I have given you a personal and particular share in my glory and I have also given you a personal and particular share in my suffering. You enter the world under the authority of my name. If you suffer in my name, know that you are also glorified in my name. Listen to my Word: "Dear friends, do not be surprised at the fiery ordeal that has come on you to test you, as though something strange were happening to you. But rejoice inasmuch as you participate in the sufferings of Christ, so that you may be overjoyed when his glory is revealed. If you are insulted because of the name of Christ, you are blessed, for the Spirit of glory and of God rests on you" (1 Pet 4:12–14).[4]

Because of the way time works, even though the war has been won, the battles are not unimportant. The enemy remains strong. He doesn't think he has lost, and my creatures may at times forget my promise that we have won. The world you are entering may feel monotonous and mundane at times, you will miss the vibrant variety and joyous diversity that you have in this unadulterated sphere. As you enter the matrix of good and bad there will be confusion between what I have declared as false and true, old and new. In times of peril you will fret, but some will remember that I *have* delivered you and that therefore I *will* deliver you. The Spirit will accompany you, revealing exceptions that prove the rule, pointing to this reality. She will bring glad newness to the truth and is herself the deposit, or guarantee, that no matter what changes you face there, the transformational truth of who I am and who you are in me will remain. The enemy will have you doubting this. You may find

---

conflict of opposing determinations, Jesus tells his disciples, "My soul is overwhelmed with sorrow to the point of death. Stay here and keep watch with me" (Matt 26:38). When the disciples fall asleep, he asks (v. 40), "Couldn't you men keep watch with me for one hour?" We he rouses them the final time before his arrest, Jesus is more direct: "Behold, the hour has drawn near" (v. 45). We should take note of the use of "one hour" and its connections to our discussion of Revelation.

4. See also John 15:18–21. Following the idea that Jesus's words in John 14–17 are meant not only for the historical disciples in the upper room but also for all human beings as disciples, we can locate the calling of every human being in these words: "If the world hates you, keep in mind that it hated me first. If you belonged to the world, it would love you as its own. As it is, you do not belong to the world, but I have chosen you out of the world. That is why the world hates you" (15:18–19). It is noteworthy that Jesus tells his disciples essentially that what they do to me, they will do to you "because of my name," and that this framework stands for both bad, i.e., persecution "if they persecuted me, they will persecute you," and for good, i.e., "if they obeyed my teaching, they will obey yours also" (15:20). Any good that is done by anyone at any time, whether knowingly or not, is by the name of Christ in whom we all participate.

THE HUMAN MISSION?

yourselves perplexed and despairing, but continue to encourage and build one another up in love. In spite of what appear insurmountable odds, the gates of Hell will not prevail.

The halls of heaven reverberate with a chorus of call and response initiated by our king:

> "For I will be your God"
> "And we shall be your people"
> "I am the Lord your God"
> "My Lord and my God"[5]

Jesus continues:

> It's going to be costly. When you enter the world (i.e., the world of Gen 2), some of you will die in the womb. Others will die very young, others will die later. You will discover that I, too, have entered the world's historical timeline, and I also will suffer and die. Just as in my birth I represent every person's birth, in my death I will represent and gather everyone's death. Because I have already captured everyone's death in myself, your singular, earthly deaths will catch up to the representative reality of my own historical death.[6] Then, if not before, you will remember that you have always been, ever since creation, hidden with me in the heavenly realms. Because you have believed in me from the beginning, you will live, even though you die, and because of who I am you will never die. Your death will be a portal into the once familiar glory of your beginning, but your return to full clarity will be purposeful. Because you have shared my earthly pilgrimage into the fallen world, you will now stand before the

---

5. I can picture the enthusiasm building as this adoration of Jesus goes on and on, until the Lord's wave calms the innumerable crowd. Of course, we can think of many examples in real life and in movies where the prolific leader or entertainer whips the crowd into a frenzy, or maybe it's the pre-battle or pre-game speech to get the troops or the team hyped. Are these examples purely worldly machinations verging on the idolatrous, or do they bear witness to something positive deep within the created human psyche? Are our fandoms related to wanting to be a part of something bigger than ourselves? I remember when pandemonium broke out in the arena after my favorite team won a big game, and my pastor who was there said pejoratively, "now that is a worship service." Seeing only idolatry, he missed the connection between the celebration and the truth from which it was, however diminished, derived, once again sadly leaving the world's ecstasy with the ascendancy compared to the kingdom.

6. We will, in Paul's words, "fill up in my flesh what is still lacking in regard to Christ's afflictions" (Col 1:24), Christ having already taken all the specific sufferings of our pilgrimage with him in his own pilgrimage.

judgment seat fully clothed with your true self but also still simultaneously saddled with your false self.

Your opportunity for repentance in this moment is your invitation into a real—not feigned—participation in the victory over evil. This is what Holy Scripture refers to as "the day." But the back side of its genuineness is that it is also a risk of sorts.[7] Satan will marshal all the evidence that he can muster from the perceptible realm to try to get your allegiance at that fateful hour. He never fatigues against the impossible because he himself is impossible. In the final test, he will want to drag you down with him into the lake of fire.[8]

Like stupefied sleepwalkers, I realize that some of you will doubt me from the time of your embryonic origin in the world. Some of you will be heavily invested in the liar's scheme, not knowing any better about yourself or the world. But I will not leave you orphaned. I will make sure that each person has their "Doubting Thomas" moment with me. After seeing clearly, you will all have a chance to say with Thomas, "My Lord and my God," and declare your allegiance to God. I am confident that everyone who sees clearly will remember the truth and participate in the victory. Together, we will celebrate the final end of Satan and his angels. For those who participate, it's going to be a big party! My servant's words were never more true: "We share in his sufferings that we might also share in his glory." Now, who wants to join me?

Standing at the border of Genesis 2, there is only one real answer to this question: *we all want to join*.

Really? Yes, really. As beloved creatures, our deepest instinct and desire is to please God. As children of God in Christ, and within the context of trust and mutual love, our wills are one with Christ's. We will what Christ wills in freedom. In this primal sphere there is no extant evil to confuse us otherwise. Here, in the dimension logically primary to biological conception, there is no "natural descent, human decision or a husband's will" (John 1:13), but only the will of God. C. S. Lewis portrayed the original Adam thusly: "Paradisal man always chose to follow God's will. In following it he

---

7. It is a calculated risk, God knowing that Satan thinks more of himself and is deluded about his ability to persuade human beings to defect, even at the point of clarity. God could have avoided such risk by handling Satan without our participation, but if he is subjecting us to the warfare, he does not want us to miss out on the victory party.

8. We remember our exegesis of Rev 17:8 and how astonished human beings were at the potent fury of the beast, and how virtually indistinguishable the mirrored version is from the reality. The negation is so strong that the gospel asymmetry can only be seen by revelation.

also gratified his own desire.... The question 'Am I doing this for God's sake or only because I happen to like it?' did not then arise, since doing things for God's sake was what he chiefly 'happened to like.' His God-ward will rode his happiness like a well-managed horse."[9]

Some might view our Commander King's invitation as a forced, robotic choice—a contrived, "choiceless choice." Starting with a bad definition of freedom, we might be tempted to project our corrupt version of "free choice" into the equation. If the above narrative seems offensive to our fierce independence, we must ask ourselves: have I bought into the concept that no one—not even my purely good creator who made me, knows me, and loves me—is allowed to direct me or to predetermine my path without my permission?

Participation is purely free in and of itself. Instead of free choice, we are offered what Barth calls "the choice of a free decision." What if humans, created to be free, had been enthusiastic from the beginning about participating in Christ? What if this deepest reality is still true about all of us, and we have just forgotten? Nathan Hale's famous comment, "I only regret that I have one life, but to give for my country" pales in comparison to this dignifying call and response to be Christ's "co-belligerent" (Barth).[10]

---

9. Lewis, *Problem of Pain*, 98. Lewis properly speaks of this human obedience as derivative of the triune relations: "Now the proper good of the creature is to surrender itself to the Creator—to enact intellectually, volitionally, and emotionally, that relationship which is given in the mere fact of its being a creature. When it does so, it is good and happy. Lest we should think this is a hardship, this kind of good begins on a level far above the creature, for God Himself, as Son, from all eternity renders back to God as Father by filial obedience the being which the Father by paternal love eternally generates in the Son. This is the pattern which man was made to imitate—which paradisal man did imitate—and wherever the will conferred by the Creator is thus perfectly offered back in delighted and delighting obedience by the creature, there, most undoubtedly, is heaven, and there the Holy Ghost proceeds" (90–91). Unfortunately, while Lewis starts well, his version of the fall capitulates to the "free will" argument. From a placemat perspective, this is paradisal man falling off of his steed. Having lost the green continuity of true freedom and obedience, Lewis (in this same volume) describes fallen humanity in purely red terms: "[God] made all things good and for the sake of their goodness; that one of the good things He made, namely, the free will of rational creatures, by its very nature included the possibility of evil; and that creatures, availing themselves of this possibility, have become evil" (69). In this case, to the extent Lewis postures the human narrative as green-red-green, he is decidedly Origenist, not Athanasian.

10. See *CD* III/3, 355 for "co-belligerent." It is easy to go wrong with military metaphors, even if there are many of them in the Bible. If, as we argued earlier, the armor of God passage in Eph 6 emphasizes spiritual warfare and especially the discrimination by the sword of the Spirit between the true and false selves of every person as revealed in the second heaven, then co-opting biblical us–them language to fight the Crusades or to conflate "us" with Israel and Muslims with Israel's Old Testament foes (e.g., George Bush after 9/11) is a failure to "extinguish all the flaming arrows of the evil one" (to use

So there we are in the Genesis 1 realm, the original, unadulterated, heaven. We are met by the commanding officer who says, "Who's with me?" Thinking about it from a worldly perspective, you might doubt that every created human would sign up for this assignment. You might imagine them saying, "Can't you do this without us?" Yet in the realm before we enter this world, no one is upset that our commander did not give us a choice.

Jesus's words stirred us, we took up our King's charge thundering with confidence: "Yes, Lord we will stay alert and ready with you—Yes, Lord we will fight to the death for you."

Yet in spite of our intentions, and our resolve that to live is Christ and to die is gain, it is quickly evident that the prince of this world has used lethal gas to stoke confusion, making us fight against each other and against even ourselves. We have traded in the sword of the Spirit for the martial sword of this world, even as Jesus tells us to put our swords away. We are overcome with the fear of death, and we scatter.

Where Christ's pre-announced salvation plot is not detected, the pain and suffering of this perceptible realm seems meaningless. In the midst of our general confusion, some have caught a clearer glimpse of the plot in order to encourage the rest. Some in the group are already aware of the bigger, christological picture. They are those who will still grieve deeply the losses they've known in this life because the pain of such loss does not simply disappear. But they are encouraged, knowing that the pain of perceptible separation from their loved ones simply witnesses to the fact that they are never truly apart in the kingdom of God. Whether suffering or comforting, everything is held together in Christ (Col 1:17), "For just as we share abundantly in the sufferings of Christ, so also our comfort abounds through Christ" (2 Cor 1:5).

Whether or not we have knowledge of the big picture in Christ, the fact that loss hurts so badly points to something within telling us that this is not the way it is supposed to be. Satan wants to convince us that the perceptible realm is real, not the invisible realm. The wicked prosecutor piles up the evidence that we do not belong to a loving God. He is the deceiver and the father of lies. He wants to turn us to the lie. It was for this reason that the author of 2 Timothy prepared his hearers:

> So do not be ashamed of the testimony about our Lord. . . . Rather, join with me in suffering for the gospel, by the power of God. He has saved us and called us to a holy life—not because of anything we have done but because of his own purpose and grace. This grace was given us in Christ Jesus before the

---

another Eph 6 metaphor).

beginning of time, but it has now been revealed through the appearing of our Savior, Jesus Christ, who has destroyed death and has brought life and immortality to light through the gospel. (2 Tim 1:8–10)

From this perspective, our birth into this world is not a test that God gives us; it is a war. It is a war against Satan and evil. And it is a war that God has won in Christ. God is for us, not against us. In the truth of our created selves, we all know that God is love, we all believe in him and love him. Deep down, we know that God is good. As human beings, we are all on the same team. It is as though we are individual Allied paratroopers on D-Day, members of the beloved community of Genesis 1 dropped behind the lines of Genesis 2:4. Our goal as *individuals* is to find each other in our true selves as *persons* and to gather together in true community against the destructive forces that threaten to keep us divided.[11] This is the church as it is meant to be, a rediscovery and reemergence of personhood in the model of our original Trinitarian community. Against fleeting and often isolated visions of reality, and against the divide and conquer tactics of the enemy we insist on banding together: "And let us consider how we may spur one another on toward love and good deeds, not giving up meeting together, as some are in the habit of doing, but encouraging one another—and all the more as you see the day approaching" (Heb 10:24–25).

Even though God is not testing us, Satan will challenge us as long as he can. He wants us to validate his plentiful evidence, that is, that those who die young or who are born at a disadvantage, in oppressive circumstances or who suffer excruciatingly tragic lives, prove the indifference of God toward his creatures. Satan thinks he's gaining points, and to some degree he is. In our hour of trial, we may be tempted to agree with him, especially when the victims of tragic circumstances are those whom we describe as "innocents," those who have done "no wrong." But what if those who are most oppressed in this world, or who die in the womb, or who are victims of injustice, or who could be described in any way above, are really the "last who will be first?" What if the ones who were cut down early or who warred against the steepest odds are the ones who will be most honored for their participation? Are the ones who died on the beach in the D-Day invasion any less the victors than the ones who rode tanks into the enemy capital? Are they more?

---

11. I can't stress enough that implementing this analogy for anthropology means making the theological (ontological) adjustment that every human is part of the "Allies," and not that some are the good guys and some are the bad guys. The only "humans" these theological allies are fighting are the false humanities of every person under the influence of the enemy with a capital E.

Knowing that "human dignity transcends human calculation,"[12] should we not be crowning the world's marginalized with honor and the fullest integrity of heavenly citizenship right now, with greatest urgency?

James Cone presses us to remember that salvation is not primarily about a disconnected heaven. I quote: "Heaven cannot mean accepting injustice in the present because we know we have a home over yonder.... To believe in heaven is to refuse to accept hell on earth."[13] Instead of futuristic dismissal, using Jesus's dimensional language we pray for earth *as it is in heaven*. To ignore injustice and push it to the future is to follow Satan's lead of using time as an excuse. As we have seen, time is only a way to organize what is always *now*. To make good use of time is to "redeem the time," recognizing and calling out the green in the grey at all levels of human existence. "The oppressed," said Cone, "are the inhabitants of black ghettos, Amerindian reservations, Hispanic barrios, and other places where whiteness has created misery."[14] In *Your God Is Too White*, the authors make a similar indictment: "the policy of most white churches is not to speak out against the savage murder and beatings of black people by policemen; not to used their influence to change deplorable housing conditions; or not to use their influence to change the 'whiteness' of their local school curriculum."[15] *Both of the above quotes are from 1970.* Fifty-four years later, we have not redeemed the time.

All who have influence and privilege are complicit in contributing to the stifling oppression or crushing brutality that leave so many embittered in grey disillusionment. Who could blame the disenfranchised for losing the plot of the big picture? And yet, those out of touch with these challenges, those busy saving souls, are confounded when the Jesus of the cross, the Oppressed One, shows up with liberating force in poor communities in a way that puts espousers of disembodied salvation-speak to shame. The white bystander then stands to miss not only the Black Jesus as the "Oppressed One" but also as the "Resurrected One."[16]

We are all double agents of red and green. Of that there is no doubt. If people knew the truth of their green selves, they would know it in their neighbors too (can't have one without the other). Recognizing another dynamic at play in their lives and world, they would strive to be more aware of the red. But some, having completely forgotten their Genesis 1 selves, have

---

12. Cone, *Black Theology of Liberation*, 82.
13. Cone, *Black Theology of Liberation*, 149.
14. Cone, *Black Theology of Liberation*, 135.
15. Salley and Behm, *Your God Is Too White*, 111.
16. These terms are from Cone, e.g., *Black Theology of Liberation*, 120–26.

"lived in ignorance" (1 Pet 1:14). Languishing in the red, they are blind to it. More negatively, there are those of us who have been deceived and who actively turn against humanity, making destructive and self-destructive decisions, some glaring and some not so glaring.

All this will be exposed in the end when we are shown who Christ is and who we are, along with who we are not. Standing before the Lamb who was slain, will any still grasp for their false selves? It seems unlikely. But we tread carefully in view of the personal appearance of the risen Christ during "the forty days" (which we take to be a glimpse of the second heaven): "When they saw him, they worshiped him; but some doubted" (Matt 28:17). Will the holdouts have the final word? All we can say is that those we know who still harbor doubt have not yet had their full second-heaven experience. The day is not finished with them yet.

At the end of the forty days and before his ascension—in a harbinger of the second heaven—Jesus tells his band of followers that everything that has happened to him was long-ago predicted in "the Law of Moses, the Prophets, and the Psalms" (Luke 24:44) if they just had eyes to see it.

> Then he opened their minds so they could understand the Scriptures. He told them, "This is what is written: The Messiah will suffer and rise from the dead on the third day, and repentance and forgiveness of sins will be preached in his name to all nations, beginning at Jerusalem. You are witnesses of these things." (Luke 24:45–49)

Under the clarity of second heaven's judgment, and while living here in the first heaven, we are called as citizens of the third (and the original) heaven to be Christ's witnesses. Indeed, it is shocking that even when Jesus shows his disciples his hands and feet after his resurrection, some still doubted. Unlike Matthew's account, however, Luke's account provides a reason for this doubt: "he showed them his hands and feet. . . . They still did not believe it because of joy and amazement" (Luke 24:40–41). The reason boils down to one we may identify with: they did not believe it because it was too good to be true.

95

Double Agents and Situational Ethics

May not someone . . . take up the obviously abandoned cause of the state on his own responsibility for the salvation of the whole, and, since all other ways are barred, proceed at the risk of his own life to the elimination, i.e., the killing of this publicly dangerous person? Is this really murder, or is it an act of loyalty commanded "in the extreme," and therefore not murder? Might it not be that on occasion certain men not only may but must undertake it? . . . [Dietrich Bonhoeffer] did not give a negative answer to this question.

—Karl Barth

In the midst of the conflict, with our grey vision, what do we do about the fact that the line between right and wrong is incredibly blurred? Is it acceptable to kill someone like Hitler, even though he is really a brother and, in the truth of Christ, on the same team? Dietrich Bonhoeffer, a pacifist, was himself involved in the failed plan to assassinate Hitler in 1944. Situational ethics put us in these difficult positions where we wonder if doing what is "wrong" can actually be the right thing.[1] But how do we know for sure? Is it possible in certain cases for someone in the midst of this checkered existence to attain a clear-cut view—a second-heaven perspective on right and wrong brought forward in time? Can I get enough clarity in the Holy

---

1. Capital punishment is not in the same category with these kinds of situational judgments, and, in my mind, has no place in our justice system.

Spirit to confidently ascertain that another person is functionally inhuman in the spirit of the anti-Christ? This will always be a subjective decision, and not foolproof. This is the type of decision that Bonhoeffer was faced with. And, on the corporate scale, if there is such a thing as a just war, it would be similarly reasoned.[2]

Faced with such a situation myself, I hope my actions would come out of the desire to operate in a Christ-centered understanding of what "human" is, and in that moment declare the "un-humanity" of the person to be so strong as to require action. Take the example of a mass shooting: if a deranged man enters a school or bar and starts killing people, I might have to risk my life to kill him. But in so many of these situations, because of my own perspective being jaded by my sin, and no matter what my desire is to operate out of a Christ-centered approach, I *might* make the wrong

---

2. In an earlier reading we quoted Cone to the effect that a loving God without wrath does not plan to do much liberating. "Just war" is a slippery thing, but ideally it is a witness to the wrath side of God's love, whereby the evil manifest in persons of power most nearly threatens to be identical with the person or government in view. This is why in his 1970 *Black Theology of Liberation*, Cone can support the potential necessity to kill white persons in order to kill off whiteness. It is precisely because there is no us vs. them that an existential, even lethal, us vs. them is called for. With echoes of Malcolm X, Cone writes: "We will not accept a God who is on everybody's side . . . a view of God which does not represent God as being for oppressed blacks and thus against white oppressors. Living in a world of white oppressors, blacks have no time for a neutral God. The brutalities are too great and the pain too severe. . . . What we need is the divine love as expressed in black power, which is the power of blacks to destroy their oppressors, here and now, by any means at their disposal. Unless God is participating in this holy activity, we must reject God's love" (74). Admittedly, it is very difficult to hold on to love in employing wrath. The pendulum can swing from the wrong kind of love (sentimental hogwash) to "no love," or hate. Writes bell hooks in "Love as the Practice of Freedom": "Without love, our efforts to liberate ourselves and our world community from oppression and exploitation are doomed. As long as we refuse to address fully the place of love in struggles for liberation we will not be able to create a culture of conversion where there is a mass turning away from an ethic of domination. . . . I conclude that many of us are motivated to move against domination solely when we feel our self-interest directly threatened. Often, then, the longing is not for a collective transformation of society, and end to politics of domination, but rather simply for an end to what we feel is hurting us. This is why we desperately need an ethic of love to intervene in our self-centered longing for change (paras. 1–2). Wary of the black power movement as an expression of that love, hooks concludes: "When masses of black folks starting thinking solely in terms of 'us and them,' internalizing the value system of white supremacist capitalist patriarchy, blind spots developed, the capacity for empathy needed for the building of community was diminished" (para. 15). As hooks alludes, the question in just war is not just the beginning, of course, but whether resorting to existential warfare, which invariably kills "innocents" such as children, will get us to the fresh air of existential liberation that we seek. Obviously even at its very best it will only bear relative witness to the wrath of Christ's cross of love and to pure liberation.

judgment about whether this other sinful person really needed to be killed. This is not to mention that my chances of doing the right thing may be lessened by the spontaneity required by the occasion. If I am proved wrong after the fact, I have to live with it. The weight of such decisions is indescribable. We simply do the best that we can.

How many of these drastic situations (e.g., killing Hitler, going to war, the live gunman) might be avoided if we understood "placemat anthropology" in the first place—that all of us are pure children of God (green) and also corrupt (red) through and through. What if we understood that we are all on the same team? If the perpetrators of genocide had refused in the beginning to polarize people, if they had a theological and anthropological antidote against their "us-them" mentality, then would it have gone so far? Without mainstreaming our theological proposal, we will never know.

Many seem to have a sense that Emerson was right when he said, "There is a capacity for virtue in us, and there is a capacity of vice to make your blood creep."[3] Because of this unease, this dis-ease, we are used to devising scapegoats to help us deal with what we deem unacceptable about ourselves.[4] Instead of rejecting Isabel Wilkerson's admonition, we should pay heed: "Evil is not one person but can be easily activated in more people than we would like to believe when the right conditions congeal." It follows that we cannot "just wait until the bigots die away." Wilkerson continues, "It is much harder to look into the darkness in the hearts of ordinary people. . . . Because it means the enemy, the threat, is not one man, it is us, all of us, lurking in humanity itself."[5]

In 2018 the country song by Luke Bryan, "Most People Are Good," was released. As we have seen throughout, we often meet the indictment above with a "come on, people aren't that bad" reaction. If Bryan's sentiment is your experience, be thankful. Remember, however, that if we take subjective inventory and adhere to Bryan's sentiment without nuance, such a belief has no ability to prove the actual facts. The best definition of "common grace" points not to a diminishment of the abject evil in people but to a manifestion of what is deeper and truer about them (and to this latter more nuanced extent, Bryan is spot on). Common grace includes anything that defies the fall, anything that reveals total depravity to be less than the totality of our experience. In this connection I'm reminded of Jesus's comment "you who are evil give good gifts to your children" (Matt 7:11). We can be

---

3. For this quotation I give thanks to my Davidson mentor David Shi, "We Can't Ignore."

4. Wilkerson, *Caste*, 191. Wilkerson here cites Sylvia Brinton Perera to make her point.

5. Wilkerson, *Caste*, 267.

thankful that we never have to experience total depravity in its undiluted form, and it is not surprising that we might fail to recognize it since our experience of it is never outside the context of total righteousness. Until it rears its ugly head in undeniable ways, it may be difficult to discern the red through the grey haze.

Wariness about the universal presence of untold evil within us is an important part of our anthropological assessment and self-assessment. This wariness should always be accompanied by the awareness that people cannot face their darkest demons without the deeper and broader context of light. Just like we don't start with sin when it comes to gospel proclamation, we don't start with depravity when it comes to ethics.

Because Barth's Christ-centered anthropological perspective is directly connected to how persons are created (i.e., how they are reconciled and redeemed shows us something essential about how they are created), it should not surprise us that his ethics are concentrated in the last part-volume of his *Doctrine of Creation*.

We remember from our introduction how Barth calls us to a kind of "seeing through," since in this world we are always looking through a glass dimly (1 Cor 13:12). The gospel receiver "sees through the imperfections of being to its perfection. That this is not a direct vision, but a seeing through, makes it a struggle," notes Barth, but even if through a mirror dimly, "it can be and may be a true seeing."[6] With resurrection retrospection, the Spirit gives us a cruciform filter to envision the pure creaturely goodness of Genesis 1, "to see in the sign of that end the sign of the beginning."[7]

"Seeing through" the cross to Genesis 1, or retrospectively from redemption (the third heaven) to creation (the first-first, or original heaven) is a very simple principle, even if it's not an easy one. Barth's emphasis on our christologically informed guiding principle ("general ethics") leaves room for fluidity and discernment in the realm of specific situations ("special ethics"). He recognizes others may use his same guiding principle and make a different application.

Understanding this approach, we can implement Barth's general principle and use it to help us deepen our awareness of how do we see others in the world around us?

Are they whole or broken? Yes.

Are they God's friends or God's enemies? Yes

Are they created perfect just the way they are, or are they a fallen sinner? Yes

---

6. *CD* III/1, 380.

7. *CD* III/1, 281.

Are they lost or are they found? Yes
Are they a pre-fall or post-fall human? Yes
Are they living or dying? Yes
Are they innocent or guilty? Yes
Are they righteous or wicked? Yes
Are they sheep or goats? Yes
Are they a child of light or a child of darkness? Yes

The resounding answer to all these questions is *yes*. But no one is ever the *second* without also being the *first*.

Moving beyond the polarizing projections which beset us, we find refreshment in the reality of Jesus Christ, where there is no "us vs. them."[8]

∼

Where does all this go in the end? It might help to take a specific example of someone who is by all accounts one of the most vicious persons who ever lived, Joseph Stalin. In my imagination, I can actually see him in the second heaven being confronted by all the evil he has done and being "forced to deal." This will not be a quick interview. There will be no making light, no quick passage. As regards our baseball analogy, Stalin's time at second base may be longer than others, like the unrepentant thief on Calvary. In the context of God's wrathful love, and face-to-face with his victims, perhaps Stalin will grieve his wicked deeds. Perhaps he will be cut to the quick in seeing how Christ has taken his evil upon himself, absorbing it in order to destroy it. Perhaps he is revealed to be a humble, thankful, and worshipful human in the end. I could even imagine him saying, "Thank you for defeating me. I was not well, I wish you had killed me before I killed so many." In my imagination, I can see Stalin humbly receiving forgiveness from others and giving forgiveness to others.

Even with all that I have said before, I continue to return to the acknowledgment that this is a very delicate issue. Many victims cannot stomach the notion of being in proximity to their abusers or oppressors, regardless of measures to create a safe space. I am not sure I could imagine anything positive about such an interaction if my family had suffered under Stalin. The feeling of wanting someone who has hurt you or your loved ones to eternally suffer or "burn in hell" is something we can understand. Even though I have high hopes for what can happen in an atmosphere where there is no chance of re-victimization, I also know that this is something

---

8. The above two pages lean heavily on my essay "*Church Dogmatics* Volume III for Ordinary People" in Marty Folsom's important series *Karl Barth's Church Dogmatics for Everyone*.

that may not be experienced until we are directly and personally assured by the embodied presence of Jesus, the one most afflicted by grief, and a man of many sorrows.

So, is a bloodthirsty Stalin part of the overall victory? No—not until judgment day, at least. In one sense, Stalin's evil in this perceptible realm is the epitome of "man's inhumanity to man." We must try to stop him. Stalin is undeniably party to evil here, in the first heaven. The total wickedness that describes us all in a sense is especially manifest in him and his crimes. The second heaven is not a time to be "let off easy." What Stalin is being confronted with is heavy. I would not want to face it, but in the end we can hope for a cathartic victory. In this world Stalin is party to evil. In the second heaven he sees himself parted *from* evil by the cross. He must realize that he has been *crucified with Christ*, before he can know that his old self is not his true self. Once Stalin sees clearly what he has done and to whom, and to the extent that he recognizes and believes, there will be space for reconciliation with God and with his many victims (and, I dare say, with those who have wounded *him*). Again, rediscovering his true God and true self, and reconciled with his human neighbors, we can envision Stalin's life in the end to be as it was in the beginning in the Genesis 1 community of faith. That is victory, even if delayed.

By now it should go without saying that telling someone they are *created in Christ* is not all there is to the gospel. Even though that is our foundation as human beings—being created in Christ—we cannot know this until we discover our foundness, our redemption in Christ crucified. The enemy does not want us to know it. He lets us get so close, even to the point of knowing we are created in Christ; he knows that sin is strong enough to twist all talk about a human foundation in Christ into a humanistic foundation. This will cause us to think too highly of ourselves, as if we are founded in ourselves and can discover ourselves without the lens of the cross. It is only in the victorious knowledge that our Redeemer lives that we see through our foundness to our foundation.

Perhaps in his parasitic perspective, Satan really thought he had the victory at the cross. Satan, says L. E. Maxwell, "has photographed himself at Calvary."[9] In his own version of "it is finished," he poses with his vanquished prey. But because the parasite prince cannot create anything, the "terrible beauty" of the atonement is beyond him, and his characteristic mimicry boomerangs on itself. Evil implodes. The evil of crucifying Jesus defeats evil. Satan does not expect it, and Stalin does not know it until later. It is a perspective to which Stalin is blind until judgment day.

---

9. Maxwell, *Born Crucified*, 163.

The things that Stalin finds out later are things believers can cling to now. When people we know and love are "taken out" by evil here, in the first heaven, we can subsume it under the cross (put it under the interpretation of the cross). We gather to support and love one another, to grieve with and pray for one another, to serve and look out for each other. As the apostle says, we do not grieve as those without hope, but we cling to one another in view of the cross, the place where Jesus puts all the anguish of the world between two nails and says, "NO FURTHER." That is what church and fellowship is all about. The cross gives us a big-picture perspective, Jesus's solidarity with us in our suffering, our solidarity with him in his resurrection. Ostensibly taken out by evil, Jesus has taken care of the problem of evil *in his own person*. We continually draw comfort from Jesus's words in their past tense power, "In the world you will have tribulation. But take heart; I have overcome the world" (John 16:33, ESV). We can live as if we have already died and die as if we are already alive. Noted Cone, "death is beside the point when one knows that there is a depth to existence that transcends death . . . human beings do not have to live on the basis of mere physical existence."[10]

Most people are probably not thinking of the afterlife as a better life where all humans together, including once-enemies, might celebrate a cosmic victory. This is especially the case for soldiers with military experience. On the worldly level, soldiers engaged in warfare are thinking on a different plane than in my theological narrative. They are focused on what it means to live or die and to defeat their human enemy. They are probably not thinking on the level of doing battle with the bigger agenda to defeat Satan. They are one group of human beings wanting to send as many of their enemies as possible into the afterlife, if that is what is required for victory. They may not know, while here in the first heaven, that *Satan and the false selves of every human are the greater enemy than any one human being*, or that these things are a greater threat than any corporate purveyor of evil that opposes them at that time. That is why no matter whom we defeat in a war (because violence begets violence), there will always be more wars. Human leaders will continue to polarize and politicize "the other" instead of taking a placemat view.

Until the day, Jesus says, there will be "wars and rumors of wars," yet taken as a whole, Jesus's extended remark below illuminates our placemat hypothesis in a hopeful light. Like an Alzheimer's patient who acts out of character even though her love for her family burns somewhere underneath,

---

10. Cone, *Black Theology of Liberation*, 82.

our love has "grown cold." Yet still, in the gospel of salvation, there is the possibility that everyone may "endure" in the end:

> As Jesus was sitting on the Mount of Olives, the disciples came to him privately. "Tell us," they said, "when will this happen, and what will be the sign of your coming and of the end of the age?" Jesus answered: "Watch out that no one deceives you. For many will come in my name, claiming, "I am the Messiah," and will deceive many. You will hear of wars and rumors of wars, but see to it that you are not alarmed. Such things must happen, but the end is still to come. Nation will rise against nation, and kingdom against kingdom. There will be famines and earthquakes in various places. All these are the beginning of birth pains. "Then you will be handed over to be persecuted and put to death, and you will be hated by all nations because of me. At that time many will turn away from the faith and will betray and hate each other, and many false prophets will appear and deceive many people. Because of the increase of wickedness, the love of most will grow cold, but the one who stands firm to the end will be saved. And this gospel of the kingdom will be preached in the whole world as a testimony to all nations, and then the end will come. (Matt 24:3–14)

The green pastures of the Shepherd are the good and perfect will of God. Within his narrow paths of righteousness, creaturely freewill flourishes. This is revealed beautifully by the prophetic "I will" statements of Psalm 118, where the Psalmist points us to the final revelation and redemption of his "inmost being" who has always desired to do God's will. It is a "green" salvation that, seen from the end, is the sweetest salvation of all.

> I look in triumph on my enemie.s (v. 7)
> I will not die but live, and will proclaim what the LORD has done. (v. 17)
>   Open for me the gates of righteous;
> I will enter and give thanks to the LORD. (v. 19)
>   This is the gate of the LORD, through which the righteous
>   may enter.
> I will give you thanks, for you answered me; you have become my salvation. (v.21)
>   You are my God, and
> I will exalt you. (v. 28)[11]

---

11. I owe this insight to my pastor, the Rev. Dr. Louis Threatt.

Conclusion
Between Two Swords

Christian theology begins and ends with Jesus Christ. He is the point of departure for everything to be said about God, humankind, and the world.

—James Cone

On the last day . . . it will be in seeing [Jesus], as he is, that it will finally dawn on us what, in him, we have always been.

—Robert Capon

We have tried to set a new trajectory that evinces from Scripture a more coherent way to understand God and humanity. This was my goal, even if it meant reconfiguring (at least for the modern reader) themes such as creation, fall, righteousness, sin, atonement, and the eschaton as they speak to the gospel of Jesus Christ and him crucified.

Our view from this side of the mirror is as limited as trying to read the tapestry from the reverse side of upholstered strands and loose ends. There are always going to be gaps, like pieces missing from a puzzle. But thanks to God's self-revelation in Jesus of Nazareth, we have been given enough to apprehend in faith. We may rest in the God who has the complete picture. This gives us Julian of Norwich's confidence that any missing pieces to the puzzle are better than what we imagine. We remain hopeful that the end is good, and if it is not good, then it is not the end.

As with Karl Barth many years later, Julian recognized that Jesus Christ *is* humanity, even before the fall. In the person of Jesus Christ is "comprehended Adam, that is to say all men." To think of the first human beings making wrong decisions, even while united to Christ who is their life, this may seem strange. It may be a new idea. But if we take a step back, we realize that many today consider themselves dedicated Christians in union with Christ and yet make terribly ungodly decisions quite often. Sin happens now, just as it happened then.

Earlier we discussed Julian's image of our embedding in the womb as akin to our entering the fallen human state (an image she derived from her understanding of Christ's assumption of "our foul mortal flesh").[1] On Julian's view, this entry occurred without diminishment of the perfectly created good. This image has led our study in various ways. The key for our purposes is to separate creation (our spiritual-material bodies) from the biological, microscopic moment (the beginnings of our physical-material bodies). The biological process of human development is intrinsically flawed for all of us, and therefore cannot precede the fall. Only the spiritual (also material) body precedes the fall.

For practical purposes, the "fall" occurs at whatever is the biological starting point for each individual person. This is the equivalent of humanity being "formed" out of dust and placed in the garden (Gen 2:7–8). And, as with Genesis 1 and Genesis 2 and the one creation story, the spiritual body and the mortal body have a dimensional relationship in the one person, even in the womb. Quantifiable, physiological growth is meant to bear witness to non-quantifiable, spiritual growth, but the latter does not depend on the former. Regarding their spiritual bodies, each child is complete and whole by virtue of God's perfect creation, regardless of "complications" that may limit healthy growth in the womb. Because of this, it is my conviction that we will personally know the true and complete humanity of all children, regardless of the health of the pregnancy and the survival of the child.

Julian's theme of Christ representing true and false humanity corroborates our thesis, even if Christ's solidarity with fallen Adam in the womb of Mary is quite startling: "When Adam fell, God's Son fell.... God's Son could not be separated from Adam, for by Adam I understand all mankind. Adam fell from life to death, into the valley of this wretched world.... God's Son fell with Adam, into the valley of the womb of the maiden."[2] By speaking of Christ "falling" with Adam, the emphasis is on the lack of separation between Christ and Adam, not on Christ somehow reacting to the fall by himself falling, as if human sin dictated the terms.[3] To whatever degree

---

1. Julian, *Showings*, 278.
2. Julian, *Showings*, 274–75.
3. The church fathers following Origen saw Christ more explicitly in the account.

Christ fell in solidarity with humanity, such a measure was taken even before the fall, in the eternal halls of God, Christ being slain from "before the foundation of the world" (Rev 13:8, RSV). For Christ's incarnation to be described as pursuing fallen humanity into the womb of the Virgin does not show in Julian a concern to preserve the pristine condition of Mary's womb. By pointing to Christ's fallen condition in solidarity with fallen Adam, it reveals Julian's implicit rejection of the doctrine of the immaculate conception (that is, that Mary was conceived without the stain of original sin).[4] This is a theme for others to take up, but might it be one reason the Roman Catholic Church has not venerated Julian as a saint?

Human history—from fall to judgment—is what we have called (with Blake) the world of "joy and woe woven fine." Julian describes things similarly. She calls it a sphere of "well-being and woe," where Jesus is already our heaven. This is our world of placemat anthropology, what I have called the first heaven. This is where we are born, and where we die.

I began this book with a preface related to Barth's eulogy for his young son, and his exposition of 1 Corinthians 13:12. In between the Now (*now we see through a mirror dimly*) and the Then (*then we shall see face-to-face*) is what Barth called the "border." To the border or seam (or mirror) between the confusion of this world and the clarity of the next, I assigned a dimension of its own. The second heaven is an in-between or "otherworldly dimension" (Barth).[5] There we stand in the grey woven overlap of our true (green) and false (red) humanity, where the Oppressed One and Resurrected One (Cone) accompanies us. He is the compassionate one who never

---

With Ephesians, Christ is literally Adam, the bridegroom, with Eve representing all his beloved human creatures. Read this way, and to give integrity to the Gen 2–3 narrative, if Eve represents humanity and Adam represents Christ, then Eve's gift of the fruit to Adam could represent humanity's fall—an act to which Christ (as Adam) responded by entering into solidarity with humanity, willingly partaking of the curse. This "reactionary" narrative ignores the more theologically accurate one: Christ's taking on the fall and its effects from all eternity, logically prior to his creation of humanity. But then again, the nature of the Gen 2–3 account is not theologically prescriptive. It is descriptive, posturing everything as a historically sequential narrative. I have been told that the Franciscan and Dominican orders hold opposing views when it comes to prioritizing these narratives, the Dominicans holding to a more post-lapsarian, "reactionary" view (Gen 2–3), with the Franciscans refusing to describe Christ's coming as a "Plan B."

4. This controversial teaching of the Roman Catholic Church was not, in fact, made an official church teaching until the mid-nineteenth century, so it should come as no surprise that a medieval thinker like Julian would not be constrained by it.

5. See *CD* III/1, 413, where Barth speaks of "the two opposites of life" being "grounded in an eternal dimension." Barth's phrase "an eternal dimension" could also be translated "an otherworldly dimension." As cited in the preface, this is indeed how Barth foresees his own experience of the judgment, i.e., as standing before the Judge still *simul iustus et peccator* (simultaneously righteous and sinner).

stops carrying us and whose cross puts a full stop to the phrase "sin, death, and the devil." The judgment of the second heaven acts as a one-way filter intended to let immortality through but to say to mortality, "thou shalt not pass." While our first, second, and third environments are different, Jesus Christ remains the same. Barth assures us that in Christ "there is no distance between Now and Then, between here and there, however profoundly they are separated."[6]

After the bombing of the 16th Street Baptist Church in the fall of 1963, Dr. Martin Luther King was asked to deliver a eulogy for the four young girls killed in the blast (Carol McNair, Carole Robinson, Addie Collins, and Cynthia Wesley). I am drawn to King's words because of his perspective on time and eternity: "This afternoon we gather in the quiet of this sanctuary to pay our last tribute of respect to these beautiful children of God. They entered the stage of history just a few years ago, and in the brief years that they were privileged to act on this mortal stage, they played their parts exceedingly well. Now the curtain falls; they move through the exit; the drama of their earthly life comes to a close. They are now committed back to that eternity from which they came."[7] King's words resonate in many ways with the themes we explored in our study, including the idea of how we all "play our part" in the mission of human history. It is the theme about these girls going "back to the eternity from which they came" which I would most like to consider as we conclude.

Most people tend to think of eternity as future, an endless period of time. Then there are theological types who might speak of eternity in terms of looking back to the beginning of things, "from all eternity, God has. . ." (indeed, I have used such phrasing in this book). Speaking of God's relationship with humanity, we saw that Barth could agree with Origen that the end was like the beginning. God is "all in all" in both—at creation and at redemption/the eschaton. The more robust claim that we have made with Barth (and contrasted with Origen's position) is this: not only is the end like the beginning, but so is the middle. "Eternal life" (used by John more than everyone else combined) is like the kingdom of heaven. It is a hidden, present dimension, and it remains consistent all the way through human history, even during what Barth called "the fatal middle stretch between creation and consummation."[8] Throughout our study I have used a Pauline term—in

---

6. Barth in Busch, *Great Passion*, 13. Also quoted in preface.

7. King, "Eulogy for the Young Victims," para. 1.

8. *CD* III/2, 304. What Barth calls the "middle" is the time from Gen 2 to judgment day, our first and second heaven. And lest we fear Barth is backtracking, by "consummation" he does not mean the finishing of what has not been accomplished, but instead being the full, final, and clear revelation of what is already accomplished.

Christ—to describe where we humans are located, beginning, middle, and end. The "green" of placemat theology is the in-Christ dimension.

Following King's lead, one way to imagine how eternal life (or the kingdom, or being-in-Christ) is related to our chronological time might be to use the metaphor of a theater. From the audience, facing the stage, there is a left wing and a right wing. Picture yourself hidden from the audience behind the right wing. From your vantage point behind the right wing, in your mind's eye watch the actors walk across the stage starting from the other wing (i.e., left-to-right from the perspective of the audience). See the actors at first hidden from the audience, then coming into sight for the audience in the middle, and then leaving the stage and arriving in the wing where you stand, where they are hidden again from the audience's sight. Unlike the audience, *you saw the actors the whole time*. The audience sees the actors on stage as they transition from left to right. Yet from your perspective, not much has changed. That is because you are looking straight "down the line" of eternity, which is not a left-to-right line at all. Time, Barth reminds us, is shot through with eternity so that, *from where the audience sits, eternity looks like time, and from your vantage point in the wings, time looks like eternity*. That is what eternal life is all about; it is a consistent dimension that runs all the way through, and it follows that those of us on the stage are creatures of both time *and* eternity. To avoid a fatal theological pitfall, and to stay consistent with how God has revealed himself in time, we must constantly insist that eternity is in time, and not dualistically above or parallel to it. The eternal God reveals himself to us *in time*. Time is for us to live out the things that time cannot contain.

Hopefully the stage example provides a theological perspective that we often fail to apprehend in our sequential, time-space existence. From our "non-audience" vantage point(behind the wing to the audience's right), we perceived the true humanity of our metaphorical actors while they were still hidden from the audience in the opposite wing, yet to emerge. Their preexisting location is obviously not the first heaven represented by the central stage, but what we have called the *first*-first, or original heaven. It is the sphere of heaven that we recognized after establishing that there is more to humanity than what starts in the checkered womb.

Now, just as we placed a theological border between the second and third heaven (across which the actors leave the stage), we can retrospectively place another proper theological border. This border (across which the actors enter the stage) is between the original heaven of our creation (the first-first heaven, where we are only green) and the first heaven of the womb (where we are green interwoven with red). This marks the theological border of the Genesis 1 and the Genesis 2 account of creation. Humanity is not in an "on, off, on" circular journey; it is not green-red-green. Indeed, from where you stand in the wing, the green is consistent from beginning to end, despite the red. As we trace the green line from its origin and coming toward us, we also recognize that it includes *us*. We can see ourselves in Christ's story—chosen in him from "before the creation of the world" (Eph 1:3–6), and all the way up to now.

In Book Two we started our theological enterprise on the central stage of perceived human history.[9] Here all roads lead to the Roman cross when God the Son incarnate was executed. We know of no other starting point apart from the revelation of God's self in human history. We start our physiological and journey between the two borders of the "wing's edge," and in the midst of our cognitive dissonance; that is why we call it the first heaven. Without a theological lens to perceive differently, and being trapped in time and space, all human existence appears to be simply on the stage as seen by the audience. Maybe our first ultrasound picture at the obstetrician marks our perceptible beginning, and our last breath our perceptible end. In our worldly beginning, there is already some degree of problems going on, even at the microscopic level. Indeed, the first ultrasound takes place in world fallen, as Barth would say, from "tip to toe." With Barth, however, we also refused to consider this "fatal middle stretch" of the worldly stage as a "self-enclosed middle."[10] We have theologically traveled further back than the first ultrasound images to the first-first heaven, the theological location where there are human beings, but no human problems.

Taking things a step further in our illustration, now imagine being in the audience and visualizing *yourself* on the stage among the other actors. Try switching back and forth from that vantage point (in the audience) to the other, previous, vantage point (in the wing). From the wing you see yourself and others with a point of view "down the line," or from the end, and therefore from the beginning. From your point of view in the wing, the evil red on stage is already out-flanked, or sandwiched, even if from the limited purview of the audience it appears to rage with dominance. From the audience's perspective, Satan is a prince, but from the wing he is a pretender. Likewise, from the audience, some loved ones might seem already dead, but from the perspective of the wing, they are already (and always) alive. From the audience, all humans are grey. From the wing, they are shot through with green.

---

9. Whereas in Book Two we followed re-creation back to creation, in Book One we started with creation. We did not use *first*-first, or original heaven there because the three heavens template was not introduced until Book Two.

10. *CD* II/1, 623.

PART SEVEN: IMMORTALS FALL

As Dr. King points out, the girls killed in Birmingham returned to the same eternity whence they came. To the audience, the two wings of the stage, left (whence they came) and right—are not materially different. And, as magnificently displayed in the "Four Spirits" sculpture in front of the 16th St. Baptist Church, the girls leave our stage the same way they entered, as indefatigable, immortal, material souls—spiritual bodies. The border they cross in death is consistent with the first border they cross in their birth. The first border (Gen 2:4ff) is where the overlap of true and false humanity begins. The last border (the judgment) marks where the overlap ends. For whatever reason that God allowed the "fatal middle stretch," he also kept sin, evil, and falsehood between two unforgiving swords and the two gates that are really one—the sword at the edge of paradise going out (Gen 3:23) and the sword at the gate of judgment going in (Rev 1:16). Back through the gate, represented by two wings and two thresholds that are really one, the girls and all human beings are free to freshly gain what they could never lose.

Time is created, as are we. But the incarnate Son of God shares his own eternal, divine, time with us. In fact, as his creatures we cannot have one (time) without the other (eternity).[11] For us as creatures, time and eternity cannot be pulled apart.[12] Uniquely in his eternal Son, God has given us eternal life. As we asserted above, to be in Christ, to have eternal life, and to believe are all inseparable. The reason that believing is so emphasized in Scripture is that it is part and parcel of who we are as persons. It is that important. Every person believes, right now, irresistibly and yet non-coercively. All human beings love God. That is the thoroughness of our ongoing participation in the truth of the in-Christ dimension. But then there is the lie, and our false self that goes along with it. The anti-Christ dimension in all of us is unfathomably strong. In this book we warned against the us vs. them dualism that causes us to mislocate wickedness in the "other." Until we can reimagine creation as glorious, and what it means for all human beings

---

11. CD II/1, 612. If we do not "have time," notes Barth, we "do not have eternity either."

12. Temporal to us is one thing, temporal to God is another. Temporal to God relates to the creaturely humanity of Jesus Christ, the image of God in whom we are created. That is why Barth can talk about humanity not just in temporal terms but in terms of our existence with Christ in post-temporal and (by virtue of the post-temporal), pre-temporal terms. Without making us co-eternal with God, God the Son shares his post-temporal (and therefore pre-temporal) eternity with us. In other words, the grace of creation in Christ is God sharing himself with us, including God sharing his pre-temporality with us; something we simply cannot fathom without the revelation of post-temporal eternity. If there are elements of post-temporal eternity in the forty days after Easter, there's no reason to exclude pre-temporal elements of eternity in Genesis 1.

to be participants in Christ, we will never begin to interpret the depths of sin in the human heart. Meanwhile, the asymmetrical duality provided in placemat anthropology, as uniquely revealed in the life, death, and resurrection of Jesus Christ, leads us forward.

So, does everyone "go" to the third heaven? It is clear by now that this is the wrong question. Everyone is already there in a sense. It is being there and simultaneously not being there that is so painful. The best way we could describe such persons is that they are stuck in "the past." Having always been in the truth, they are still mired in the overlap of falsehood. Such a state is impossible to spatially conceive, because "surely" we cannot be in two places at the same time.[13] We remember that hell does not exist without heaven—we cannot be in hell without being in heaven, too. Still, we could imagine hell to be a supremely and increasingly painful straddling of dimensions. I offer my following reflection on this painful experience:

The Day of Peace

Are we there yet?
Yes
If you're justified you're glorified
Are we there yet?
Yes Seated with Christ
Are we there yet?
Yes
Hidden with Christ in God

Hell
The "not there" in the midst of the there
Straddling dimensions
Stretched thin
The torque of more revelation
Grace ever-increasing
Desperation for the stubborn

From always free
To nothing but free
Sweet release

---

13. To be in the unadulterated third heaven, but to also be stuck in the overlap of the second, conjures up the image of someone being severely stretched, scattered, and not at all gathered. A doctrine of sanctification that splits it from justification, meaning that it refuses to declare that we are home (in the third heaven) before we start, can contribute to the stress.

Heaven is happening. Every human being in one dimension is already loving God perfectly and is full of the Spirit. But hell is also happening, every human being hating God and neighbor, following the spirit of the anti-Christ. Our minds buckle at the thought that even two places (heaven and hell) can be—dimensionally considered—two dynamic things in one space happening concurrently. As unexplainable as it is, this overlap of heaven and hell is one we already feel in the first heaven, even if not as acutely as in the second heaven. Conversely, the third heaven is enjoyed by those who know salvation by subtraction. In crossing through the last veil, the synonymity of false and old has been finally realized, and hell's fury is forever forgotten.[14]

In the meantime, while everyone is *in* the third heaven, living *from* the third heaven is what we as existential believers are called to do in this world. Under the delivering judgment of the second heaven, we are empowered for the course here in the first heaven. Armed with the assurance of victory and confidence in the finished work of redemption, we are exhorted to walk together in freedom and "newness of life" (Rom 6:4, RSV) against the "oldness" of our false humanity. On this side of the veil the life of faith will be, in the midst of suffering, an existence laced with meaning and purpose by virtue of the incessant presence of the crucified and risen Christ and our true lives eternally hidden in his. We are "jars of clay," Scripture reminds us, fragile vessels carrying around the death of Christ in our deteriorating bodies, even while we also carry around the life of Christ, as if our spiritual bodies are animating the whole (2 Cor 4:10).[15]

If this is indeed not a test of God, but a war against evil, then we will embrace the thought of sharing "in [Christ's] sufferings, in order that we might also share in his glory" (Rom 8:17). We will grow up into Christ our Head (Eph 4:15), becoming more and more who we are in Christ, even while we continue to receive as faithful soldiers the hardships that are still

---

14. The heaven-hell theological relationship could be put like this: there is no such thing as hell without the concurrent dimension of heaven, but there *is* such thing as heaven without the dimension of hell.

15. See also 2 Cor 2:15–16 to see the dynamic aspects of these death and life aspects: "For we are to God the pleasing aroma of Christ among those who are perishing. To the one we are the aroma that brings death; to the other, an aroma that brings life." To the extent that we bear witness to the life aspect of our lives (and everyone's lives), we will be diametrically contrasted to the death aspect. See also Rom 8:10–11, which I paraphrase, "You have a mortal body that will someday die, but your spiritual body is already alive. In fact, because the Spirit who raised Jesus from the dead lives in you, that same Spirit who raised Christ is the one who animates even your mortal bodies now! In other words, the reason your mortal body has not collapsed already is because the Spirit in you not only fills your spiritual body but holds up your mortal body too!"

CONCLUSION

coming to us from the enemy. Over the span of our lives, short or long, we will suffer everything in our own respective bodies that Christ has carried for us in his own body to the cross (Col 1:24). If we can keep our heads from spinning, this means being cheered on from the wings by the great cloud of witnesses, which includes all the saints, even ourselves. "When Christ, who is your life, appears," says Paul, "then you will also appear with him in glory" (Col 3:4). From the fractured, dimly lit vantage point of the Now, seeing through the mirror to the Then involves not only seeing Christ clearly, but seeing our true self in him. Our false self will never feel more like an outlier. We marvel at the thought that when Christ comes to meet *us*, we are already with him. It is no wonder Robert Capon calls Colossians 3:4 "the most pregnant reference in all of Scripture."[16]

Despite my explaining the three heavens in a sequential manner, we must remember that these three heavens, with their consistency of divine and human truth, are simultaneous to one another (even if not completely concurrent).[17] Instead of three sheets of paper side by side on a table, it might instead help to imagine the three heavens as three transparencies stacked upon one another. Still, with our minds trapped in time and space, our grasp of the mystery will remain partial until that day when the other dimensions are unfurled before our eyes.[18] "'What no eye has seen, what no ear has heard, and what no mind has conceived'—the things God has prepared *for those who love him*" assures Paul (1 Cor 2:9). At this point, we can understand that last phrase ("those who love him") through the new lens of our placemat anthropology.

I began and ended this volume with reference to eulogies. Funerals are a place where the hopeful presence of God can be felt despite all that hell throws against it. It is a time, as Barth said, where we are brought to

---

16. Robert Capon, *Parables of Kingdom*, 114. This is Capon's translation of the second half of the verse: "When Christ, *your real life* appears, then you too will appear with him in glory" (emphasis added). See Capon's epigraph at top. See also the Message version for a similar take on the verse.

17. Even at this late stage it is worth clarifying that the asymmetry between good and evil is not lost in the simultaneous. The good is simultaneous to the evil, but it also came first and lasts longer. Thinking of these transparencies stacked on top of one another does not mean that sin, death, and evil are no longer "bracketed" by life and goodness. Evil is not a part of creation. It will ultimately be shown to be *apart from* creation.

18. If everything that we think is sequential is downloaded into the category "simultaneous," then, as time and space creatures, it would be natural for us to wonder whether judgment day has already happened. But "already happened" is "time-language," and from our limited perspective, it falls short in and of itself (when utilized without reference to the "not yet"). It is like asking what age we will be in paradise. The best answer is "yes."

the border, and where the veil often seems quite thin. Perhaps this thinness explains what can also be experienced as a "thick" or substantial presence of God, one capable of ministering hope even while bearing the weight of the most immense grief. Just as the Then and the Now cannot be separated in this world, no matter how distinct, we can affirm that nothing can separate us from the love of God: "neither death nor life, neither angels nor demons, neither the present nor the future, nor any powers, neither height nor depth, nor anything else in all creation, will be able to separate us from the love of God that is *in Christ Jesus* our Lord" (Rom 8:38–39, emphasis mine).

In Christ Jesus. We have come full circle from Book One, unpacking along the way a singular short verse with which we began, "We love because [God] first loved us" (1 John 4:19). Julian and others have distilled this truth of grace in its actuality: that God loves us *means* that we love God. The Father and the Son are inseparable in the Spirit, they love each other perfectly and extravagantly. You are created in this covenantal image of God. The truth of 1 John 4:19 is a Genesis 1 truth. You are in Christ. God loves you. You love God. That is how he made all of us, and that never changes. That is the claim on our lives. And that is the root of all love—that we are, from the beginning, persons in the person, sharing life with the Trinitarian persons, in the community that includes all human persons. This held true when our un-free, individualistic, choices threatened to destroy us. Freedom arrived anew in the person of the Son of God, who proved God's love by destroying in his own body all that needed destroying: "This is how we know what love is: Jesus Christ laid down his life for us" (1 John 3:16).

Epilogue
Dew Song

Graced to be your new creature
In your gospel song
Fresh upon heaven's dew
"I am in the Father, you're in me,
And yes, I am in you"

The Spirit's first cry—my being's own
Beneath sky of bluest blue
"As the Father has sent me," said ye
"So I am sending you"

Indeed You have trod before
This way, and therefore must go I
your armor not heavy I'm hidden in
Your will my heart's delight

Here I am Lord, send me
Through dimension's door
Armed with light into troubles ahead
That you have overcome before

World's bondage we all enter
Upon womb's conflicted walls
Always loved and free yet battle fierce
Amidst the enemy's calls

Some fall soon and some fall late
In face of our foe's power
So strong is he, he has us turned
'Gainst you and one another

Upon world's stage we falter

PART SEVEN: IMMORTALS FALL

Not sure of whose we are
To th'extent we fail, we've played the part
Intended by the Liar

To th'extent we're right it's by your grace
In Christ all credit due
Moments that Spirit of Truth reveal
Exceptions that prove the rule

We exit left battlefield behind
The Day sword's judgment falls
Before the door you meet us there
Our secrets you know all

How clear now our foolish ways
Our hands within the wounds
How clear now our righteousness
Alive from whence the tomb

Every knee bent before lambs throne
Acknowledging the name
Can it be "MY lord MY God"
One refuses to exclaim?

Now through the door we'll follow
When all is said and done
Leaving this world behind for home
Where heaven and earth are one

Gathered 'gain round the Lion/Lamb
All voices together sing
We know now best what below in part
That death has lost its sting
Temptations and sorrow left behind
Bells of deliverance ring
The serpent slain the victory won
All praises to our King

Epigraph Sources

Essay: "The Prevalence of Evil and the Presence of God: Keeping Depravity in its Proper Place"
Douglas Campbell, *Pauline Dogmatics*, 108.

Reading 56: First-Heaven Problems
Julian of Norwich, *Julian of Norwich: Showings*, 286.
Karl Barth, *Church Dogmatics* III/3, 348.
Dorothy Day, *The Duty of Delight: The Diaries of Dorothy Day*, 474.

Reading 57: "They Will All Know Me" (Because They Do)
T. F. Torrance, *Preaching Jesus Christ Today*, 28.
Von Balthasar, *Prayer*, 69–70.

Reading 58: The Rest of our Life
Hudson Taylor, *Spiritual Secret*, 179.

Reading 59: Gathered and Scattered
Willie James Jennings: *After Whiteness*, 135.

Reading 60: The Grace of Wrath
"Maya Angelou: What She Said Life Taught Her."
Howard Thurman, *The Growing Edge*, 18.

Reading 61: Children of Wrath?
Karl Barth, *Church Dogmatics* II/2, 270–71.
Ambrose, quoted from McKinnon and Oden, *Isaiah 1–39*, 95–96. Thanks to Tommy Grimm for this quote.

Reading 62: Vanier Exposed
Jean Vanier, *The Heart of L'Arche*, 66–67.

Reading 63: The Second-Heaven Intervention
Both quotes are from Jurgen Moltmann, *The Coming of God*, 255.

Reading 64: The Goodness of Judgment
Karl Barth, *Church Dogmatics* II/2, 741.
Karl Barth, *Church Dogmatics* III/4, 236–37.

Reading 65: The Big Picture
Luci Shaw, "But Not Forgotten," 47.
Richard Wright, quoted in Cone, *The Cross and the Lynching Tree*, xiii.

Reading 66: Deliverance Time!
George MacDonald, quoted in Lewis, *George MacDonald*, 95.

Reading 67: The Highest View of Scripture
Athanasius, quoted in Richard Bewes, *The Top 100 Questions*, 62.

Reading 68: Parting from the Red Sea Narrative
Christian Smith, *Bible Made Impossible*, 98.
Dietrich Bonhoeffer, *Christ the Center*, 73–74.

Reading 69: Merry Christmas, Malachi!
Karl Barth, *Heidelberg Catechism*, 45.
Karl Barth, *Church Dogmatics* IV/3.2, 922.

Reading 70: Repent and Believe
Willie James Jennings, *After Whiteness*, 153.

Reading 71: Standing Pat at the Gate
Hans Urs von Balthasar, *Prayer*, 232–33.

Reading 72: Damned and Delivered
Karl Barth, *Church Dogmatics* IV/3, 477.

Reading 73: Saved by the Blood?
Bethany Hanke Hoang and Kristen Deede Johnson, *Justice Calling*, 129.

EPIGRAPH SOURCES

Reading 74: Holiness or Wholeness?
David Benner, *Spirituality and the Awakening Self*, 33.

Reading 75: Seeing and Believing with Thomas
Thomas Erskine, quoted in Trevor Hart, *The Teaching Father*, 147.

Reading 76: Retributive vs. Restorative Justice
Martin Luther King Jr., "Montgomery Bus Boycott Speech," delivered on December 5, 1955.
Boesak, *Radical Reconciliation*, 108.
Volf, *Exclusion and Embrace*, 123.

Reading 77: Gender Bending?
C. S. Lewis, *Perelandra*, 200.

Reading 78: Coming Home
C.S. Lewis, *The Voyage of the Dawn Treader*, 115.

Reading 79: Reconciliation as Remembering Friends
Ray Anderson, *The Gospel According to Judas*, 14.

Reading 80: Nothing but Green
Clarence Jordan, "The Parables," talk given at Koinonia Farm, 1972. Transcribed from tape recording.
Julie Canlis, *A Theology of the Ordinary*, 56.

Reading 81: The Sword and the Spirit
Ben Myers, *The Apostles' Creed*, 94.

Reading 82: The Ship-Shape of the Atonement
G. K. Chesterton, *Everlasting Man*, 170.
Athanasius, *On the Incarnation*, 13.

Reading 83: Life in Spite of Death
Hans Urs von Balthasar, *Heart of the World*, 43.
Richard Wright, quoted in James Cone, *The Cross and the Lynching Tree*, 18.

Reading 84: Salvation by Subtraction
James Cone, *The Cross and the Lynching Tree*, 161–62.

Reading 85: Bringing Immortality to Light
W. E. B. Du Bois, *Du Bois on Religion*, 107.

Reading 86: The Power of Contrast (But Not the Need)
Evelyn Underhill, *The Spiritual Life*, 91–92.

Reading 87: Species of Origen?
Karl Barth, *Church Dogmatics* III/1, 281.

Reading 88: Playing by the Book: *Give Me Revelation!*
Christina Rosetti, *Complete Poems of Christina Rosetti*, no. 14, 144.
Karl Barth, *Church Dogmatics* III/3, 357.

Reading 89: Test or War?
Both quotes from Karl Barth, *Church Dogmatics* III/3, 359.

Reading 90: The Liar's Religion
Julian of Norwich, *Showings*, 166.
Karl Barth, *Church Dogmatics* II/2, 16.

Reading 91: One Tree in the Garden
Oswald Chambers, *Shadow of an Agony*, 71.

Reading 92: The Why Question
Soren Kierkegaard, *Without Authority*, 117. Thanks to Andrew Torrance for sharing this quotation with me.
P.T. Forsyth, *Positive Preaching and the Modern Mind*, 363. Thanks to Richard McIntosh for pointing me to this quote.

Reading 93: Theodicy Revisited
Madeleine L'Engle, *Walking on Water*, 32.
William Inge, *Personal Religion and the Life of Devotion*, 61.

Reading 94: The Human Mission?
Karl Barth, *Church Dogmatics* III/2, 146.
Karl Barth, *Church Dogmatics* III/3, 355.
Thomas Erskine, *Thomas Erskine of Linlathen*, 321.

Reading 95: Double Agents and Situational Ethics
Karl Barth, *Church Dogmatics* III/4, 449.

EPIGRAPH SOURCES

Conclusion: Between Two Swords
James Cone, *A Black Theology of Liberation*, 116.
Robert Capon, *Kingdom, Grace, and Judgment*, 41.

Bibliography

"Amnesia Victim Reunited With Fiancee." *KTRE News*, October 23, 2006. https://www.ktre.com/story/5576877/amnesia-victim-reunited-with-fiancee/.
Anderson, Ray S. *The Gospel According to Judas: Is There a Limit to God's Forgiveness?* Pasadena, CA: Fuller Seminary Press, 2000.
Associated Press. "Amnesia Sufferer Found in Denver Reunited With Washington Fiancee, Family." *Fox News*, October 24, 2006. https://www.foxnews.com/story/amnesia-sufferer-found-in-denver-reunited-with-washington-fiancee-family.
Athanasius. *The Life of Anthony and the Letter to Marcellinus*. Translated by Robert C. Gregg. Mahwah, NJ: Paulist, 1979.
―――. *On the Incarnation*. Edited and Translated by John Behr. Yonkers: St. Vladimir's Seminary Press, 2012.
Baillie, John. *A Diary of Readings*. New York: Oxford University Press, 1981.
Balthasar, Hans Urs von. *Heart of the World*. San Francisco: Ignatius, 1980.
―――. *Prayer*. Translated by Graham Harrison. San Francisco: Ignatius, 1986.
―――. *The Theology of Karl Barth*. Translated by Edward T. Oakes, SJ. San Francisco: Ignatius, 1992.
Barth, Karl. *Church Dogmatics*. Edited by Geoffrey W. Bromiley and Thomas F. Torrance. Translated by Geoffrey W. Bromiley. 4 vols. New York: T&T Clark, 1936–69.
―――. *Dogmatics in Outline*. Translated by G. T. Thomason. New York: Harper & Row, 1959.
―――. *The Epistle to the Romans*. Translated by Edwyn C. Hoskyns. 6th ed. New York: Oxford University Press, 1968.
―――. "An Exegetical Study of Matthew 28:16–20." *The Theology of Christian Mission*, edited by Gerald H. Anderson, 55–71. New York: McGraw-Hill, 1961.
―――. *The Humanity of God*. Translated by John N. Thomas and Thomas Wieser. Louisville: Westminster John Knox, 1996.
―――. *Learning Jesus Christ through the Heidelberg Catechism*. Translated by Shirley Guthrie. Grand Rapids, MI: Eerdmans, 1964.
Bauckham, Richard, and Trevor Hart. *Hope Against Hope: Christian Eschatology at the Turn of the Millennium*. Grand Rapids, MI: Eerdmans, 1999.
Beall, J. C. *The Contradictory Christ*. Oxford: Oxford University Press, 2021.
Belcher, Sharon V. "Disability and the Terror of the Miracle Tradition." In vol. 2 of *Miracles Revisited: New Testament Miracle Stories and Their Concepts of Reality*,

edited by Stefan Alkier and Annette Weissenrieder, 162–81. Berlin: Walter de Gruyter, 2013.

Benedict, Pope, XVI. *Great Christian Thinkers: From the Early Church through the Middle Ages*. Minneapolis: Fortress, 2011.

Benner, David. *Spirituality and the Awakening Self: The Sacred Journey of Transformation*. Ada, MI: Brazos, 2012.

Bewes, Richard. *The Top 100 Questions: Biblical Answers to Popular Questions Plus Explanations of 50 Difficult Bible Passages*. Ross-shire, UK: Christian Focus, 2002.

Blake, William. "Auguries of Innocence." In *Poets of the English Language*, edited by W. H. Auden and Holmes Pearson. New York: Viking, 1950. https://www.poetryfoundation.org/poems/43650/auguries-of- innocence.

Boesak, Allan. "Foreword." In *On Reading Karl Barth in South Africa*, Edited by Charles Villa-Vicencio, ix–xii. Grand Rapids, MI: Eerdmans, 1988.

———. *Radical Reconciliation: Beyond Political Pietism and Christian Quietism*. Ossining, NY: Orbis, 2012.

Bonhoeffer, Dietrich. *Christ the Center*. Translated by John Bowden. New York, NY: Harper & Row, 1966.

———. *The Cost of Discipleship*. New York: Touchstone, 1995.

———. *Life Together: The Classic Exploration of Christian Community*. New York: HarperOne, 1954.

———. *The Mystery of Easter*. Edited by Manfred Weber. New York: Crossroad, 1998.

Bowler, Kate. *Everything Happens for a Reason: And Other Lies I've Loved*. New York: Random House, 2019.

Brazier, P. H. "Karl Barth: Supersessionism and Israel, Yeshua and God's Election—A Dialectical Balance?" *The Evangelical Review of Theology and Politics* 3 (2015) A15–34, https://www.evangelicalreview.net/ph_brazier_review-article_on_barth-israel-jesus(free-sample).pdf.

Brettman, Stephanie Mar. *Theories of Justice: A Dialogue with Karol Wojtyla and Karl Barth*. Cambridge: James Clarke & Co., 2015.

Bruner, Frederick Dale. The Gospel of John: A Commentary. Grand Rapids, MI: Eerdmans, 2011.

Busch, Eberhard. *The Great Passion: An Introduction to Karl Barth's Theology*. Grand Rapids, MI: Eerdmans, 2004.

———. *Karl Barth: His Life from Letters and Autobiographical Texts*. Minneapolis: Fortress, 1977.

Bush, Michael D., ed. *This Incomplete One: Words Occasioned by the Death of a Young Person*. Grand Rapids: Eerdmans, 2006.

Byassee, Jason. *Surprised by Jesus Again*. Grand Rapids, MI: Eerdmans, 2019.

Calaprice, Alice, ed. *The Ultimate Quotable Einstein*. Princeton: Princeton University Press, 2010.

Calvin, John. *Institutes of the Christian Religion*. Edited by John T. McNeill. Translated by Ford Lewis Battles. 2 vols. Louisville, KY: Westminster John Knox, 1960.

Camhi, Leslie. "Peering Under the Skin of Monsters." *The New York Times*, March 17, 2002. https://www.nytimes.com/2002/03/17/arts/art-architecture-peering-under-the-skin-of-monsters.html.

Campbell, Douglas. *Framing Paul: An Epistolary Biography*. Grand Rapids: Eerdmans, 2014.

———. "Participation and Faith in Paul." *"In Christ" in Paul: Explorations in Paul's Theology of Union and Participation*, edited by Michael J. Thate, Kevin Vanhoozer, and Constantine R. Campbell, 37–60. Tubingen: Mohr Siebeck, 2014.

———. *Pauline Dogmatics: The Triumph of God's Love*. Grand Rapids, MI: Eerdmans, 2020.

Campbell, John McLeod. *The Nature of the Atonement*. Grand Rapids, MI: Eerdmans, 1996.

Canlis, Julie. *A Theology of the Ordinary*. Wenatchee, WA: GodSpeed, 2017.

Capon, Robert. *Parables of the Kingdom, Grace, and Judgment*. Grand Rapids, MI: Eerdmans, 2002.

Carr, Raymond. "Barth and Cone in Dialogue on Revelation and Freedom: An Analysis of James Cone's Critical Appropriation of 'Barthian' Theology." PhD diss., Graduate Theological Union, 2011.

———. "Merton and Barth in Dialogue on Faith and Understanding: A Hermeneutics of Freedom and Ambiguity." *The Merton Annual* 26 (2013) 181–94.

———. "Thelonious Monk, Icon of the Eschaton: Karl Barth, James Cone, and the 'Impossible-Possibility' of a Theology of Freedom." In *Karl Barth and Liberation Theology*, edited by Paul Dafydd Jones and Kaitlyn Dugan, 177–93. New York: Bloomsbury, 2022.

Carrega, Christina. "Brandon Bernard Executed After Supreme Court Denies Request for a Delay." *CNN*, December 11, 2020. https://edition.cnn.com/2020/12/10/politics/brandon-bernard-executed/index.html.

Carter, J. Kameron. *Race: A Theological Account*. Oxford: Oxford University Press, 2008.

Chambers, Oswald. *Shadow of an Agony*. London: Simpkin & Marshall, 1942.

Chesterton, G. K. *Everlasting Man*. n.p.: Bottom of the Hill, 2011.

Cohen, Andrew. "Timothy McVeigh and the Myth of Closure." *The Atlantic*, June 11, 2012. https://www.theatlantic.com/national/archive/2012/06/timothy-mcveigh-and-the-myth-of-closure/258256/.

Cohick, Lynn H. *The Letter to the Ephesians*. Grand Rapids: Eerdmans, 2020.

Colson, Chuck. "BreakPoint: The Eichmann in All of Us." BreakPoint, August 18, 2017. https://breakpoint.org/breakpoint-the-eichmann-in-all-of-us.

Cone, James. *A Black Theology of Liberation*. 40th Anniversary ed. Ossining, NY: Orbis, 2010.

———. *The Cross and the Lynching Tree*. Ossining, NY: Orbis, 2013.

Copeland, M. Shawn. "'Wading through Many Sorrows': Toward a Theology of Suffering in Womanist Perspective." In *A Troubling in My Soul: Womanist Perspectives on Evil and Suffering*, edited by Emilie Townes, 109–29. Maryknoll, NY: Orbis, 1993.

Crouzel, Henri. *Origen*. San Francisco: Harper & Row, 1989.

CultureContent, "Toni Morrison Takes White Supremacy to Task." YouTube, March 24, 2012, 2:43. https://www.youtube.com/watch?v=6S7zGgL6Suw.

Dalferth, Ingolf U. "Karl Barth's Eschatological Realism." In *Karl Barth: Centenary Essays*, edited by S. W. Sykes, 14–45. Cambridge: Cambridge University Press, 2009.

Davis, Fania E. *The Little Book of Race and Restorative Justice*. New York: Good Books, 2019.

Day, Dorothy. *The Duty of Delight: The Diaries of Dorothy Day*. New York: Random House, 2011.

BIBLIOGRAPHY

———. *Reckless Way of Love: Notes on Following Jesus*. Edited by Carolyn Kurtz. Walden, NY: Plough, 2017.

Edwards, Mark James. *Christ Is Time: The Gospel According to Karl Barth (and the Red Hot Chili Peppers)*. Eugene, OR: Cascade, 2022.

Ehrman, Bart. *God's Problem: How the Bible Fails to Answer Our Most Important Question—Why We Suffer*. New York: HarperOne, 2008.

Erskine, Thomas. *The Brazen Serpent*. Public Domain, 1879.

Ferencz, Ben. *Nuremburg Prosecutor and Peace Advocate*. Jefferson, NC: McFarland & Co., 2013.

Folsom, Marty. *Karl Barth's Church Dogmatics for Everyone*. Nashville: Zondervan Academic, 2025.

Forsee, Aylesa. *Albert Einstein: Theoretical Physicist*. New York: MacMillan, 1963.

Forsyth, P. T. *The Cruciality of the Cross*. Eugene, OR: Wipf & Stock, 1997.

———. *Positive Preaching and the Modern Mind*. Coromandel East, South Australia: New Creation, 1993. https://cruciality.files.wordpress.com/2007/07/positive-preaching-nc.pdf.

Francisco, Eric. "'Us' Jeremiah 11:11: How the Bible Verse Explains Jordan Peele's New Movie." *Inverse*, March 25, 2019. https://www.inverse.com/article/54328-us-jeremiah-11-11-spoilers-jordan-peele-ending.

Gilerman, Dana. "A Hitler Mask for 40 Koruna." *Haaretz*, September 13, 2001. https://www.haaretz.com/israel-news/culture/2001-09-13/ty-article/a-hitler-mask-for-40-koruna/0000017f-e84d-d62c-a1ff-fc7f93eb0000.

Givens, Tommy. *We the People: Israel and the Catholicity of Jesus*. Minneapolis: Fortress, 2014.

Gombis, Timothy. *The Drama of Ephesians*. Westmont, IL: InterVarsity, 2010.

Grace Communion International. "Jeff McSwain—Is It Possible to Preach an Unconditional Gospel Without Being a Universalist?" YouTube, December 13, 2013, 56:42. https://www.youtube.com/watch?v=Q9qwuoYfmvY.

Green, David B. "This Day in Jewish History Novelist Who Taught Israelis About the Holocaust." *Haaretz*, May 15, 2014. https://www.haaretz.com/jewish/2014-05-15/ty-article/.premium/novelist-who-taught-israelis-about-the-holocaust/0000017f-e84e-dc7e-adff-f8eff32b0000.

Grundmann, Christoffer H. "Christ as Physician: The Ancient Christus Medicus Trope and Christian Medical Mission as Imitation of Christ." *Christian Journal for Global Health* 5 (2018) 3–11. https://journal.cjgh.org/index.php/cjgh/article/download/236/545?inline=1.

Guite, Malcolm. "Poem XII, Jesus Dies on the Cross." In *Sounding the Seasons: Seventy Sonnets for the Christian Year*, by Malcolm Guite, 42. London: Canterbury, 2012.

Hallström, Lasse, dir. *Chocolat*. Produced by David Brown and Leslie Holleran. Los Angeles, CA, Miramax Films, 2000.

Hart, David Bentley. "The Spiritual Was More Substantial than the Material for the Ancients." *Church Life Journal: A Journal of the McGrath Institute for Church Life*, July 26, 2018. https://churchlifejournal.nd.edu/articles/the-spiritual-was-more-substantial-than-the-material-for-the-ancients/.

Hart, Drew. *Trouble I've Seen: Changing the Way the Church Views Racism*. Harrisonburg, VA: Herald, 2016.

Hart, Trevor. "The Capacity for Ambiguity: Revisiting the Barth-Brunner Debate." In *Regarding Karl Barth: Toward a Reading of His Theology*, by Trevor Hart, 139–72. Downers Grove, IL: IVP, 1999.

———. "Humanity in Christ and Christ in Humankind: Salvation as Participation in Our Substitute in the Theology of John Calvin." *Scottish Journal of Theology* 42 (1989) 67–84.

———. "Irenaeus, Recapitulation, and Physical Redemption." In *Christ in Our Place: The Humanity of God in Christ for the Reconciliation of the World*, edited by Trevor Hart and Daniel Thimell, 152–81. Milton Keynes, UK: Paternoster, 1989.

———. *The Teaching Father: An Introduction to Thomas Erskine of Linlathen*. Edinburgh, UK: Saint Andrew Press, 1993.

Hoang, Bethany Hanke, and Kristen Deede Johnson. *The Justice Calling: Where Passion Meets Perseverance*. Ada, MI: Brazos, 2016.

Hoard, Billie. "Bareface: C. S. Lewis and the Identity Claims of Transgender People." Medium, March 28, 2019. https://medium.com/@billhoard_34685/bareface-c-s-lewis-and-the-identity-claims-of-transgender-people-e53afad806a4.

hooks, bell. "Love as the Practice of Freedom." Unitarian Universality College of Social Justice, n.d. https://uucsj.org/wp-content/uploads/2016/05/bell-hooks-Love-as-the-Practice-of-Freedom.pdf.

Horowitz, Elliott S. *Reckless Rites: Purim and the Legacy of Jewish Violence*. Princeton: Princeton University Press, 2006.

Houtz, Wyatt. "Karl Barth on Demythologizing the Empty Tomb and Ascension." PostBarthian (blog), March 15, 2015. https://postbarthian.com/2015/03/15/karl-barth-demythologizing-empty-tomb-ascension/.

Jennings, Willie James. *After Whiteness: An Education in Belonging*. Grand Rapids, MI: Eerdmans, 2020.

———. *The Christian Imagination: Theology and the Origins of Race*. New Haven: Yale University Press, 2010.

Jenson, Robert. "Radicalising of the Communicatio: Jenson's Theology in Confessional Lutheran Perspective." In *The Promise of Robert Jenson's Theology: Constructive Engagements*, edited by Stephen John Wright and Chris E. W. Green, 131–40. Minneapolis: Fortress, 2017.

———. *Systematic Theology*. 2 vols. Oxford, UK: Oxford University Press, 2001.

Jordan, Clarence. "The Parables." Talk given at Koinonia Farm, 1972. Transcribed from tape recording by Jeff McSwain.

Julian. *Julian of Norwich: Showings*. Translated by Edmund Colledge, OSA, and James Walsh, SJ. Mahwah, NJ: Paulist, 1977.

Käsemann, Ernst. *Commentary on Romans*. Translated by Geoffrey W. Bromiley. Grand Rapids, MI: Eerdmans, 1994.

Kierkegaard, Soren. *Philosophical Fragments*. Edited and translated by Howard V. Hong and Edna H. Hong. Princeton: Princeton University Press, 1985.

———. *Without Authority*. Translated by Uden Myndighed. Princeton: Princeton University Press, 1997.

Kimmelman, Michael. "Evil, the Nazis and Shock Value." *The New York Times*, March 15, 2002. https://www.nytimes.com/2002/03/15/arts/art-review-evil-the-nazis-and-shock-value.html.

———. "Jewish Museum Show Looks Nazis in the Face and Creates a Fuss." *The New York Times*, January 29, 2002. https://www.nytimes.com/2002/01/29/arts/critic-

BIBLIOGRAPHY

s-notebook-jewish-museum-show-looks-nazis-in-the-face-and-creates-a-fuss.html.

King, Martin Luther, Jr. "Eulogy for the Young Victims of the 16th Street Baptist Church Bombing." Sixteenth Street Baptist Church, Birmingham, Alabama, September 18, 1963. Footnotes by Jemar Tisby (blog), September 13, 2023. https://jemartisby.substack.com/p/mlks-eulogy-after-the-16th-street.

———. "Montgomery Bus Boycott Speech." Delivered at Holt Street Baptist Church, Montgomery, Alabama, December 5, 1955. https://www.blackpast.org/african-american-history/1955-martin-luther-king-jr-montgomery-bus-boycott/.

Kruger, C. Baxter. *Jesus Christ and the Undoing of Adam*. Jackson, MS: Perichoresis, 2007.

———. "A Note on Union with Christ." *Clarion* (2017) n.p. https://www.clarion-journal.com/files/a-note-on-union-with-christ-edited.pdf.

Landström, Elsie. "Song to My Other Self." In *Our Many Selves*, by Elizabeth O'Connor, 35. New York: Harper & Row, 1971.

L'Engle, Madeleine. *Walking on Water: Reflections on Faith and Art*. New York: Random House, 2016.

Lewis, C. S., ed. *George MacDonald: An Anthology*. London: Geoffrey Bles, 1970.

———. *The Great Divorce*. New York: Macmillan, 1946.

———. *Mere Christianity*. New York: HarperCollins, 2001.

———. *Out of the Silent Planet*. New York: Macmillan, 1973.

———. *Perelandra*. New York: Macmillan, 1965.

———. *The Problem of Pain: Collected Letters of C. S. Lewis*. New York: HarperCollins, 2001.

———. *Reflections on the Psalms*. New York: HarperOne, 2017.

———. *Surprised by Joy*. London: Fount, 1998.

———. *The Weight of Glory*. New York: HarperCollins, 2001.

———. "The World's Last Night." In *Fern-seed and Elephants, and Other Essays on Christianity*, edited by Walter Hooper, 65–85. New York, NY: Collins, 1981.

Long, Charles H. "Legacy of Slavery: Unequal Exchange: A Colloquium on the Socio-Economic Legacy of Slavery." University of California, Santa Barbara, 2002.

Luther, Martin. *A Commentary on St. Paul's Epistle to the Galatians*. London: James Cundee, 1807.

MacDonald, George. *The Diary of an Old Soul*. Eastford, CT: Martino, 2015.

———. "Kingship." Unspoken Sermons, The Literature Network, n.d. https://www.online-literature.com/george-macdonald/unspoken-sermons/30/.

Maddox, Randy. *Responsible Grace: John Wesley's Practical Theology*. Nashville: Abingdon, 1994.

Maxwell, L. E. *Born Crucified*. Chicago: Moody, 2010.

"Maya Angelou: What She Said Life Taught Her." Inspired Angela (blog), May 28, 2014. https://inspiredangela.wordpress.com/2014/05/28/maya-angelou-what-she-said-life-taught-her/.

McKinnon, Steven A., and Thomas C. Oden, eds. *Isaiah 1–39*. Ancient Christian Commentary on Scripture 10. Downers Grove, IL: IVP, 2014.

McSwain, Jeff. "Barth's Actualism vs. Universalism: Ten Tenets to Rock Your Universe." Jeff McSwain (blog), n.d. https://www.jeffmcswain.org/barthsactualismvsuniversalism.

———. "Hercules at the Crossroads." In *Simul Sanctification: Barth's Hidden Vision for Human Transformation*, by Jeff McSwain, 98–119. Princeton Theological Monograph Series. Eugene, OR: Pickwick, 2018.

———. "Two Laws and the Gospel: Barth's *Simul* at the Heart of Romans." Jeff McSwain (blog), 2020. jeffmcswain.org/_files/ugd/062d55_4305e5e19250471f9ec1ffb53a4bbf08.pdf.

———. "The 'Yes' of Reality and the Meaning of Grace in Barth and Bonhoeffer." In *Movements of Grace: The Dynamic Christo-Realism of Barth, Bonhoeffer and the Torrances*, by Jeff McSwain, 69–106. Eugene, OR: Wipf & Stock, 2010.

Merton, Thomas. *New Seeds of Contemplation*. New York: New Directions, 2007.

Moltmann, Jurgen. *The Coming of God: Christian Eschatology*. Translated by Margaret Kohl. Minneapolis: Fortress, 1996.

Myers, Ben. *The Apostles' Creed: A Guide to the Ancient Catechism*. Bellingham, WA: Lexham, 2018.

Nagasawa, Mako. "God as Dialysis Machine: The Sacrificial Calendar as the Renewal of the Covenant and the Retelling of Moses' Mediation on Mount Sinai." The Anastasis Center for Christian Education and Ministry (blog), October 18, 2018. https://newhumanityinstitute.wordpress.com/2018/10/18/god-as-dialysis-machine-the-sacrificial-calendar-as-the-renewal-of-the-covenant-and-the-retelling-of-moses-mediation-on-mount-sinai/.

———. "Session Two: God Purifies Like a Dialysis Machine: The Jewish Sacrificial System and the Retelling of Moses' Ascent." The Anastasis Center, 2019 Conference Recordings. https://www.anastasiscenter.org/conference-2019.

Narvaez, Darcia F. "The Original Sin of Babies: Three Reasons Adults Are Tough-Minded with Babies." *Psychology Today*, Nov. 22, 2020. https://www.psychologytoday.com/us/blog/moral-landscapes/202011/the-original-sin-babies-0.

Nouwen, Henri. *Life of the Beloved*. New York: Crossroad, 2015.

———. *The Return of the Prodigal Son*. New York: Doubleday, 1992.

———. "Your Heart Is the Center of Your Being." Henri Nouwen Center, January 3, 2024. https://henrinouwen.org/meditations/your-heart-is-the-center-of-your-being/.

Parry, Robin. *Lamentations*. Grand Rapids, MI: Eerdmans, 2010.

Pascal, Blaise. *Pensees*. Translated by W. F. Trotter. Mineola, NY: Dover, 2003.

Peterson, Eugene. *A Long Obedience in the Same Direction*. Westmont, IL: InterVarsity, 2000.

Petersen, Robin. *On Reading Karl Barth in South Africa*. Edited by Charles Villa-Vicencio. Grand Rapids, MI: Eerdmans, 1988.

Phillips, J. B. *365 Meditations by J. B. Phillips for This Day*. Edited by Denis Duncan. Nashville: Word, 1975.

Pizzuto, Vincent. *Contemplating Christ: The Gospels and the Interior Life*. Collegeville, MN: Liturgical Press, 2018.

Placher, William C. *The Domestication of Transcendence: How Modern Thinking About God Went Wrong*. Louisville, KY: Westminster John Knox, 1996.

Pressman, Michael. "The Death of McVeigh: A Time to Reflect." *New York Times*, June 13, 2011. https://www.nytimes.com/2001/06/13/opinion/the-death-of-mcveigh-a-time-to-reflect.html.

Pronk, Neil. "Puritan Christianity: The Puritans at Home." *The Messenger* (Sept. 1997) 3–6.

Rosetti, Christina. *Complete Poems of Christina Rosetti*. Baton Rouge: Louisiana State University Press, 1986.

RTÉ One. "Stephen Fry on God | The Meaning of Life." YouTube, January 28, 2015, 2:24. https://m.youtube.com/watch?v=-suvkwNYSQ0.

Salley, Columbus, and Ronald Behm. *Your God Is Too White*. Downers Grove, IL: IVP, 1970.

Sayers, Dorothy L. *The Greatest Drama Ever Staged*. London: Hodder & Stoughton, 1938.

Selby, Holly. "Holocaust Show: Art or Affront?" *The Baltimore Sun*, March 17, 2002.

Shaw, Luci. "But Not Forgotten." *Sea Glass: New and Selected Poems*, by Luci Shaw, 47–48. Seattle: WordFarm, 2016.

———. "Winter Wheat." *Sea Glass: New and Selected Poems*, by Luci Shaw, 69. Seattle: WordFarm, 2016.

Shi, David. "We Can't Ignore the Menacing Evil that Lurks Within." *The Greenville News*, April 29, 2007.

Smith, Christian. *The Bible Made Impossible: Why Biblicism Is Not a Truly Evangelical Reading of Scripture*. Ada, MI: Brazos, 2011.

Spence Jones, Donald, HDM. *The Pulpit Commentary*. London: Wagnalls, 1907.

Stahl, Leslie. "What the Last Nuremberg Prosecutor Alive Wants the World to Know." *60 Minutes*, May 7, 2017. https://www.cbsnews.com/news/what-the-last-nuremberg-prosecutor-alive-wants-the-world-to-know/#article-entry.

Stanglin, Keith D. *The Letter and Spirit of Biblical Interpretation: From the Early Church to Modern Practice*. Grand Rapids: Baker Academic, 2018.

Stanley, Andy. *Irresistible: Reclaiming the New that Jesus Unleashed for the World*. Grand Rapids, MI: Zondervan, 2018.

Stewart, James S. *The Life and Teaching of Jesus Christ*. Nashville: Abingdon, 2000.

Swanson, Stevenson. "Jewish Museum's Holocaust Exhibit Igniting Outrage." *Chicago Tribune*, March 17, 2002.

Taylor, Howard, and Mrs. Howard Taylor. *Hudson Taylor's Spiritual Secret*. Chicago: Moody, 1989.

Taylor, Joan E. *What Did Jesus Look Like?* Edinburgh: T&T Clark, 2018.

Thomas, Ian W. *The Saving Life of Christ*. Grand Rapids: Zondervan, 1961.

Thurman, Howard. *The Growing Edge*. Richmond, IN: Friends United, 1956.

Tietz, Christiane. *Karl Barth: A Life in Conflict*. Translated by Victoria J. Barnett. Oxford: Oxford University Press, 2019.

Tilling, Chris. "Barth on Romans (Part 2)." OnScript, November 14, 2019. https://onscript.study/podcast/chris-tilling-barth-on-romans-part-2/.

Torrance, Alan. "The Theological Grounds for Advocating Forgiveness and Reconciliation in the Sociopolitical Realm." Centre for Contemporary Christianity in Ireland, 2006.

Torrance, Andrew. "Kierkegaard's Paradoxical Christology," in *Soren Kierkegaard: Theologian of the Gospel*, edited by Todd Speidell, Greg Marcar, and Andrew Torrance, 41–63. Eugene, OR: Wipf & Stock, 2021.

Torrance, James B. "The Concept of Federal Theology—Was Calvin a Federal Theologian?" *Calvinus Sacrae Scripturae Professor: Calvin as Confessor of Holy Scripture*, edited by Wilhelm H. Neuser, 15–39. Grand Rapids, MI: Eerdmans, 1994.

———. *Worship, Community, and the Triune God of Grace*. Carlisle, UK: Paternoster, 1996.
Torrance, Thomas F. *The Christian Doctrine of God: One Being, Three Persons*. Edinburgh: T&T Clark, 2001.
———. *The Mediation of Christ*. Rev. ed. Colorado Springs: Helmers & Howard, 1992.
———. "One Aspect of the Biblical Conception of Faith." *Expository Times* 68 (1956–57) 111–14.
———. *Preaching Jesus Christ Today: The Gospel and Scientific Thinking*. Grand Rapids, MI: Eerdmans, 1994.
———. *Space, Time and Resurrection*. Edinburgh: T&T Clark, 1976.
———. *Theology in Reconciliation: Essays towards Evangelical and Catholic Unity in East and West*. Eugene, OR: Wipf & Stock, 1996.
———. *The Trinitarian Faith: The Evangelical Theology of the Ancient Catholic Church*. Edinburgh: T&T Clark, 1995.
Tutu, Desmond. *No Future Without Forgiveness*. New York: Image, 2000.
Underhill, Evelyn. *The Spiritual Life: Four Broadcast Talks by Evelyn Underhill*. Eastford, CT: Martino, 2013.
Vanier, Jean. *The Heart of L'Arche: A Spirituality of Every Day*. Toronto, CA: Novalis, 1995.
Volf, Miroslav. *Exclusion and Embrace*. Nashville: Abingdon, 1996.
Webber, Christopher L., ed. *Love Came Down: Anglican Readings for Advent and Christmas*. Harrisburg, PA: Morehouse, 2002.
Weise, Elizabeth. "Epstein Accusers 'Angry as Hell.'" *USA Today*, August 12, 2019. https://go.gale.com/ps/i.do?id=GALE%7CA596270471&sid=sitemap&v=2.1&it=r&p=AONE&sw=w&userGroupName=anon~178a66fe&aty=open-web-entry.
Wiesenthal, Simon. *The Sunflower: On the Possibilities and Limits of Forgiveness*. New York: Schocken, 1997.
Wilkerson, Isabel. *Caste: The Origins of Our Discontents*. New York: Random House, 2020.
Williams, Rowan. "'Risen Indeed': The Resurrection in the Gospels." Lecture, February 28, 2008, at The Guildhall, Winchester.

Names Index

Abuelaish, Izzeldin, 1: 287
Ambrose, 2: 101
Ames, William, 1: 19
Angelou, Maya, 2: 94
Arad, Boaz, 2: 43
Andersen, Cody, 1: 244, 2: 284, 330
Anderson, Gary, 1: 316
Anderson, Lee, 1: 232, 276, 313
Anderson, Ray, 1: 208, 212, 332, 347, 372; 2: 244
Anselm, 2: 289
Aquinas, Thomas, xxvii
Arminius, Jacobus, 2: 318, 337
Athanasius, 1: xxix, 35, 60, 125, 133, 135, 147–48, 206, 230, 277, 343–44; 2: 74, 146, 161, 206
Aubrey, Allan, 1: 240, 246
Augustine, 1: 78, 122, 145, 183, 288, 289, 296; 2: 50, 128, 163, 337

Baldwin, James, 1: 385
Baillie, John, 1: 118, 174, 183, 277; 2: 238
Balthasar, Hans urs von, 2: 31, 58, 66, 71–74, 147, 173, 179, 278, 284, 301, 314
Barth, Karl, 1: xi–xx, xxv, xxvii–xxix, 10, 12, 24, 34, 50, 52, 72, 79, 80, 87, 91, 94, 95, 97, 101, 111, 116–17, 119, 120, 123–24, 126, 130, 135–36, 139, 141, 143–45, 147, 150, 156, 165, 177, 178, 200, 203, 214, 222–23, 227, 231, 233, 236, 245–46, 249, 260, 261–64, 267–69, 271, 275–78, 281, 283–85, 291, 311, 315, 327, 338–39, 343, 345–47, 360, 365–68, 371–73, 376–78; 2: x–xii, 2, 4, 6, 8–9, 17–18, 23, 27–28, 31–34, 37, 39, 46, 50, 55–57, 59, 60–63, 72, 92, 94, 98–99, 101–3, 105–6, 115, 117, 119, 124, 129, 133–36, 142, 144, 147, 149, 160, 163, 168, 181–84, 187, 189, 191, 208, 212, 218, 229, 231, 236, 246–47, 253–54, 257–58, 261–62, 265–66, 275–77, 282–85, 291, 292, 302–3, 305, 310–20, 322, 324, 325–26, 331–32, 334, 336, 338–44, 348, 361–62, 367, 372, 375–76, 380, 382, 383–84, 385–86, 389
Barth, Matthias, 2: x–xii
Basil, 1: 132, 133, 251
Bauckham, Richard, 2: 205
Beall, J. C., 2: 289
Begbie, Jeremy, 1: 7, 130
Bejski, Moshe, 2: 43
Belcher, Sharon, 2: 359
Bell, Rob, 1: 257
Benner, David, 2: 203, 208–11
Berry, Wendell, 1: 244
Bernard, Brandon, 2: 119–20
Blake, William, 1: xxiv; 2: 1
Boesak, Allan, 1: 240, 246; 2: 46, 220
Bonhoeffer, Dietrich, 1: xxix, 33, 87, 94, 100, 127, 171, 277, 280, 285, 312, 330; 2: 32, 57, 130–31, 148, 152, 167, 286, 372–73
Bowler, Kate, 2: 355

NAMES INDEX

Brazier, P. H., 1: 276, 345–46, 359; 2: 262
Brettmann, Stephanie Mar, 2: 246
Brock, Brian, 1: 243, 353–55
Brown, Charlene, 1: 245, 247
Bruner, F. Dale, 1: 149; 2: 261
Bunyan, John, 1: 174, 277; 2: 238
Burton, Nylah, 1: 388
Busch, Eberhard, 1: 233; 2: xii, 55, 291, 383
Byassee, Jason, 2: 149–50, 152, 276

Calaprice, Alice, 2: 117, 319
Calvin, John, 1: xxiv, xxix, 44, 66, 69, 70, 97, 138, 147; 2: 20, 50, 83, 174, 187, 188, 221, 274, 311, 318–19, 337–38
Camhi, Leslie, 2: 44
Campbell, Douglas, 1: 44, 105, 134, 260–61; 2: 23, 41, 108, 156
Campbell, John McCleod, 1: 64; 2: 177, 221, 224
Canlis, Julie, 1: 151; 2: 20, 252
Carroll, Suvya, 1: 232
Colson, Chuck, 2: 45
Capon, Robert, 1: 8; 2: 380, 389
Carlile, Brandi, 1: 314–15
Carr, Raymond, 2: x, 92, 284,
Carter, J. Kameron, 2: 51
Chambers, Oswald, 1: 43, 74; 2: 340, 342
Chesterton, G. K., 1: 317–18, 397; 2: 269
Chrysostom, 165
Coates, Ta-Nehisi, 356
Cohen, Andrew, 2: 226
Cohick, Lynn, 1: 50; 2: 23
Collins, Addie, 1: 58; 2: 383
Coltrane, John, 1: 256
Colyer, Elmer, 1: 19
Cone, James, 1: xxv, xxix, 81, 371, 385; 2: 90–92, 205–6, 280–86, 302, 346, 370, 373, 378, 380, 382
Copeland, M. Shawn, 2: 283
Crawford, Bob, 1: xxiv
Croasmun, Matthew, 1: 81
Crouzel, Henri, 2: 318
Curry, Michael, 1: 256

Dalferth, Ingolf U., 1: 283; 2: 316
Davis, Fania E., 2: 227
Day, Dorothy, 1: 129, 240; 2: 242–43, 246, 247
Dearborn, Kerry, 1: 399
Deddo, Gary, 1: xx, 227, 231, 323, 330, 350
DePue, Jonathan, 1: xx
DeStigter, Christopher, 1: 96
DeYoung, Paul, 1: 240, 246
Dinur, Yehiel, 2: 44–45
Dostoevsky, Fyodor, 1: 76; 2: 56, 358
Du Bois, W. E. B., 2: 297
Dueck, Ryan, 1: 344–45
Dugan, Kaitlyn, 1: xxvii
Dulles, Avery, 1: xxvii
Dwight, John Sullivan, 2: 256

Eastman, Susan, 1: 349
Eddy, Paul Rhodes, 1: 183
Edwards, Charles, 1: 5
Edwards, Jonathan, 2: 106
Edwards, Mark, 2: 342
Ehrman, Bart, 2: 357–58, 361
Eichmann, Adolf, 2: 44–45, 55
Einstein, Albert, 2: 60, 117, 319
Eldredge, John, 1: 114–15
Eliade, Mircea, 2: 280
Ellicott, Charles, 2: 34, 176, 178, 279, 288
Epstein, Jeffrey, 2: 226
Erasmus, Desiderius, 2: 318, 337
Erskine, Thomas, 1: xxvi, 99, 123, 147, 275, 299–300; 2: 170, 213, 222, 362
Evans, Darrell, 237

Fee, Gordon, 2: 150
Feld, Edward, 1: 195
Ferencz, Ben, 2: 56–57
Feuerbach, Ludwig, 1: 343
Folsom, Marty, 2: 376
Forsee, Aylesa, 2: 60
Forsyth, P. T., 1: 155, 157, 159, 164, 172, 295; 2: 97, 129–30, 185, 271–72, 345, 348
Francisco, Eric, 2: 144
Frush, Ben, 1: 409
Fry, Stephen, 2: 356–58

NAMES INDEX

Gilerman, Dana, **2:** 43
Givens, Tommy, **2:** 262
Godin, A., **2:** 318
Gombis, Timothy G., **2:** 195–96
Gorman, Michael, **1:** 230, 231
Green, Emma, **1:** xxi
Green, David B., **2:** 45
Gregory Nazianzen, **1:** 132–36, 350; **2:** 360
Gregory Nyssa, **1:** 37, 132–33
Grimm, Tommy, **2:** 393
Grundmann, Christoffer H., **2:** 126–27
Guite, Malcolm, **2:** 307

Hart, David Bentley, **1:** 15, 134
Hart, Drew, **2:** 293
Hart, Trevor, **1:** xxx, 44, 66, 71, 224, 225; **2:** 32, 85–86, 205, 222, 306
Hartgrove, Jonathan W., **1:** 402
Hazelton, Roger, **1:** 291
Helm, Angela, **1:** 386
Hertzberg, Arthur, **2:** 43
Hill, Wesley, **1:** 285
Hitler, Adolf, **1:** xxvii; **2:** 43–44, 55–56, 333, 372, 374
Hoang, Bethany Hanke, **1:** 113; **2:** 126, 192, 196, 251
Hoard, Billie, **2:** 232–33
Hoekema, Anthony, **1:** 50
hooks, bell, **2:** 373
Holmquist, Annie, **2:** 307
Holmquist, Quinn, **2:** 307
Houtz, Wyatt, **2:** 135
Hunter, Matthew, **1:** 37, 51
Hurtado, Larry, **1:** 202

Ignatius of Antioch, **2:** 127
Irenaeus, **1:** xxix, 71, 133, 135, 224–25, 230–31; **2:** 306

Jennings, Willie J., **1:** 22, 293–94, 296, 352, 358, 390, 394–96; **2:** 85, 89–90, 166, 249–50
Jenson, Robert, **2:** 257–59
Johnson, Junius, **1:** 8
Johnson, Kristen D., **1:** 113; **2:** 126, 192, 196, 251
Jones, Spence, **1:** 23

Jones, E. Stanley, **1:** 8, 241, 301, 336–37
Jordan, Clarence, **1:** 214; **2:** 252
Julian of Norwich, **1:** xxviii, xxix, 56–57, 61, 64, 82, 86, 124, 138, 139–41, 147, 177, 193, 219, 220, 266, 268–71, 315–16, 333–34, 340, 371, 373–74, 378; **2:** 4, 55, 58–59, 75, 98, 217, 240, 256–57, 265, 313–15, 334, 336, 348, 380–82, 390
Jung, Carl, **1:** 175

Käsemann, Ernst, **2:** 34
Kedmi, Roni, **1:** 29
Kendi, Ibram X., **1:** 161
Kettler, Christian, **1:** 227
Kierkegaard, Soren, **1:** 183; **2:** 279, 345
Kimmelman, Michael, **2:** 43–44
King, Martin Luther, 49, 78, 184, 237, 247, 299, 381; **2:** 220, 238, 383, 386
Kirschbaum, Charlotte von, **2:** x
Kleebat, Norman, **2:** 44
Kruger, C. Baxter, **1:** 30, 44, 129; **2:** 175, 222, 292

Landstrom, Elsie, **2:** 209
Laird, Martin, **1:** 297
L'Engle, Madeline, **2:** 353
Levinson, John, **1:** 359
Lewis, C. S., **1:** 29, 32, 85, 90, 167, 235, 341–43, 345–46, 357; **2:** 38, 65, 67, 85, 95, 136, 140–141, 145, 147–48, 177, 180, 191, 205, 219, 227-, 228, 231–32, 234–36, 264, 288, 310, 315, 347, 366–67
Little, Greg, **1:** 282
Long, Charles H., **2:** 91–93
Lowe, Edward, **1:** xxix, 122; **2:** 55, 91, 221
Lossky, Vladimir, **1:** 235–36, 276
Luther, Martin, **1:** xvi, xxix, 84, 97, 122, 144, 171, 305; **2:** 221, 257, 261, 318–19, 337–38, 383

NAMES INDEX

MacDonald, George, 1: 49, 255, 270–71, 359; 2: 30, 95, 130, 136, 138, 144–45, 227, 234, 347
MacMurray, John, 1: 13, 60
Maddox, Randy, 2: 337
Manning, Brennan, 1: 313
Manson, William, 2: 118
Mather, Cotton, 2: 95
Maxwell, L. E., 1: 216, 218, 219, 253; 2: 79, 290, 377
McInturf, Adam, 1: xxiv
McIntosh, Richard, 1: 396
McKenna, John, 1: 226–27, 258, 259, 307
McNair, Carol, 1: 58 2:383
McSwain, Jeff, 1: xi, xviii, xx, xxvi, 39, 40, 205; 2: 1, 11, 34, 94, 131, 160
McVeigh, Timothy, 2: 226–27
Meek, Sloan, 1: 232
Menachem, Reesma, 1: 80
Mengele, Josef, 1: 43–44
Merton, Thomas, 1: 234, 235, 241, 251, 313; 2: x, 25–27, 68, 127, 249–51
Migliore, Daniel, 1: 346
Milliner, Matthew, 2: 276
Mills, Dishon, 1: xxx
Milton, John, 1: 359
Moltmann, Jurgen, 2: 116, 118, 170
Morrison, Toni, 2: 283
Mozart, 1: 130
Mullins, Elizabeth, 1: 227
Murray, Pauli, 1: 21
Myers, Ben, 2: 263, 265

Nagasawa, Mako, 2: 224–25
Narvaez, Darcia F., 2: 95
Neal, Rob, 2: 354–56
Nee, Watchman, 1: 128, 219
Newton, John, 1: 332, 333
Niebuhr, Reinhold, 2: 57, 59, 280
Nouwen, Henri, 1: 24, 34, 35, 42, 46–48, 72, 191, 235, 238–39, 295, 368, 371–73; 2: 86, 175, 248
Nuth, Joan, 1: xx

O'Connor, Elizabeth, 1: 75–76, 248
Origen, 289, 360, 393; 2: 150, 311–19, 337, 381, 383

Palmer, Parker, 1: 82, 83
Parry, Robin, 2: 144
Pascal, Blaise, 1: 24, 266–69, 291; 2: 66–68, 356
Peele, Jordan, 1: 335; 2: 143–44, 264
Perera, Sylvia B., 2: 374
Peterson, Eugene, 1: 62, 107–8, 150, 213; 2: x, 239
Peterson, Robin, 2: 258
Phillips, J. B., 1: 6, 7, 45, 181, 320, 321–23; 2: 122
Piper, John, 1: 47–48
Pizzuto, Vincent, 2: 155
Placher, William, 2: 20
Plato, 1: 12–15; 2: 15, 22, 57
Pope Benedict XVI, 2: 312
Pope Pius XII, 1: xxvii
Pressman, Michael, 2: 226
Price, Charles W., 1: 121
Pronk, Cornelis, 2: 95

Randall, Ian, 1: 121
Rayburn, Jim, 1: 29
Rex, Linda, 1: xxx
Reid, Peter, 2: 82
Rillera, Andrew, 2: 258
Robinson, Carole, 1: 58; 2: 383
Rohr, Richard, 1: 42, 293
Rosenbaum, Joan, 2: 44
Rosensaft, Menachem, 2: 43
Ryle, John C, 1: 333

Sayers, Dorothy, 2: 42, 47
Scansen, Steve, 2: 151
Scott, Chuck, 1: 106
Selby, Holly, 2: 44
Selby, Thomas, 1: 143, 144
Shaw, Luci, 1: 208; 2: 132, 238–39
Shi, David, 1: 374
Sittser, David, 1: 1
Smith, Christian, 1: 20; 2: 152
Socrates, 2: 298
Solzhenitsyn, Alexander, 1: 386–87
Speidell, Todd, 1: xxvi, 229, 284
Stalin, Joseph, 2: 376–78
Stanglin, Keith D., 2: 206
Stanley, Andy, 2: 153
Stewart, James, 2: 14
Swanson, Stevenson, 2: 44

NAMES INDEX

Swinton, John, **1:** 5
Stott, John, **1:** 106–7, 121

Taylor, Ethan, **2:** 34
Taylor, Hudson, **2:** 64, 77–81, 83–84
Taylor, Joan, **2:** 46
Telford, Taylor, **1:** xxvii
Thein, Karel, **1:** 13
Thomas, Ian, **1:** 154, 222, 288; **2:** 82, 155–59
Threatt, Louis, **2:** 146, 379
Thurman, Howard, **1:** 59, 142; **2:** 95
Tietz, Christiane, **2:** x
Tilling, Chris, **1:** xviii, 9; **2:** 147
Tolstoy, Leo, **1:** 118–19
Townley, Jacob, **1:** 1
Torrance, Andrew, **1:** 147, 229–30, 239; **2:** 279, 396
Torrance, Alan, **1:** 34, 147, 221–22, 229, 230, 239, 256; **2:** 47, 75, 177, 208
Torrance, J. B., **1:** xx, xxix, 15, 19, 69, 117, 147, 173, 202, 226–30, 239, 323, 344, 351; **2:** 105, 177, 221, 222, 337
Torrance, T. F., **1:** xx, xxix, 19, 37–38, 133, 145, 147, 157, 171–73, 197, 199, 204, 226–28, 229–30, 239, 257, 284, 299, 344; **2:** 51, 66, 108, 118–19, 128, 163, 168, 206, 216, 312
Train, Daniel, **1:** 7

Turner, Nat, **2:** 91
Tutu, Desmond, **2:** 245–46
Twenge, Jean, **1:** 17

Underhill, Evelyn, 108; **2:** 305

Valys, Phillip, **1:** xxiv
Vanier, Jean, **1:** xxii, 182; **2:** 110–15
Vesey, Denmark, **2:** 91
Villa-Vicencio, Charles **2:** 258
Volf, Miroslav, **2:** 120, 220
Voltaire, **2:** 354

Watson, Lilla, **1:** 243
Webber, Christopher, **2:** 276
Webster, John, **1:** 284
Weise, Elizabeth, **1:** 226
Wesley, Cynthia, **1:** 58; **2:** 383
Wesley, John, **1:** 120, 305; **2:** 106, 318, 337
West, Cornel, **1:** xxi, 114
Whitefield, George, **1:** 106
Wiebe, Todd, **1:** xxx
Wiesenthal, Simon, **2:** 41–43, 47–48
Wilkerson, Isabel, **1:** 74–75, 119–21; **2:** 374
Williams, Rowan, **1:** 234–36, 276; **2:** 126
Wright, Richard, **1:** 81; **2:** 132, 278, 283

Zwick, Edward, 215

Scripture Index

Genesis

1	1: 82, 127, 133, 359, 360, 361, 362, 364, 365, 367, 368, 369, 370, 373,; 2: 3, 6, 7, 8, 15, 18, 19, 21, 39, 59, 65, 67, 69, 135, 170, 178, 211, 218, 222, 231, , 237, 240, 252, 255, 257, 259, 260, 262, 288, 298, 299, 300, 301, 302, 303, 306, 307, 308, 312, 313, 315, 322, 327, 331, 335, 340, 342, 343, 344, 350, 356, 359, 363, 368, 369, 370, 375, 377, 381, 384, 386, 390
1–2	2: 6, 18, 135, 255, 300, 307, 313, 381
1–3	1: 260
1:1	1: 360; 2: 18, 58, 328, 329
1:1–2:3	1: 360; 2: 6, 18, 335
1:2	1: 126, 367; 2: 8, 9, 19, 312, 315, 328, 329, 335
1:3	2: 21
1:26	1: 57
1:27	2: 230
1:28	2: 231
1:31	1: 60, 77; 2: 312, 347
2	1: 70, 361, 362, 364, 365, 367, 368, 369, 370, 374; 2: 6, 7, 8, 18, 21, 135, 170, 218, 255, 256, 298, 299, 300, 302, 303, 306, 307, 308, 313, 322, 340, 341, 365, 366, 381, 383, 384
2–3	1: 136, 360, 361; 2: 10, 18, 19, 24, 62, 65, 69, 231, 260, 300, 307, 332, 334, 335, 340, 382, 341, 343, 356
2:1	2: 302
2:4	1: 360, 362, 367, 369; 2: 6, 18, 260, 335, 369, 386
2:7	1: 359, 360, 370; 2: 300, 381
2:8	1: 360; 2: 7, 300, 381
2:9	1: 341, 344
2:21	2: 347
2:25	2: 327
3	2: 211
3:15	2: 335
3:19	1: 362
3:22	2: 343
3:23	2: 386
3:24	1: 361; 2: 6, 218, 260, 343
22:17	1: 68, 194
25	2: 157
25:25	2: 155
25:34	2: 157

Exodus

17	2: 157
17:6	2: 156
17:8	2: 156
21:24	1: 290
29:37	2: 225
32: 32	2: 334, 336
34	1: 330
34:6–7	1: 195

Leviticus

10:16–20	1: 225

Numbers

14:18	1: 195
24:20	2: 157

Deuteronomy

6:4–5	2: 72
10:16	1: 153
19:21	1: 290
25:17–18	2: 157
28:15	2: 102
30:6	1: 153
30:14	2: 261, 307
30:19–20	1: 242

1 Samuel

15:3	2: 98, 157
15:8–9	2: 158

2 Samuel

7:10	1: 21

1 Chronicles

17:9	1: 21

Nehemiah

9	1: 195
9:16–18	1: 195

Job

19:25	1: 22
19:25–26	1: 350

Psalms

1:1	1: 102
1:6	1: 102
1:1–3	1: 103
1:4	1: 104
1:4–6	1: 104
1:5	1: 104
5:4	1: 78
5:5	1: 103
5:12	1: 103
7:8	1: 102
7:9	1: 105
9:16	1: 104
10:1–2	2: 42
10:10–11	2: 42
14:1	1: 105
15:1–2	1: 104
17:13	1: 104
18:19	1: 58
22	1: 212; 2: 347–48
22:1–18	1: 105
22:1	2: 45, 347
22:19–31	1: 105
22:24	2: 347
23	2: 306, 347–348
23:4	2: 348
24	2: 347–348
25:6	1: 92
26:1–12	2: 207
28:9	2: 81
30:5	1: 237
32:11	2: 139
34:21	1: 104
36:9	2: 209
36:10	2: 139
37:9	1: 78
37:10	1: 104
37:28	1: 104
37:38	1: 104
37:40	1: 104
40:8	2: 215
42:7	2: 250, 341
51:5	1: 72; 2: 312
51:6	1: 166
51:10–12	2: 213, 248
58:3	2: 141
64:10	2: 139
68:2	1: 104
71:4	1: 101, 104
80	1: 149
80:16–18	2: 150
80:18	1: 149
82:4	1: 104
82:6	2: 301
84:7	1: 169
86:12–15	1: 195
92:12–14	1: 379

94:1–3	1: 42	40:25	2: 191
94:2	2: 48	40:29–31	2: 191
100:3	2: 30, 69	42:1	1: 195
101:8	1: 104	42:3	1: 321
103:8	1: 195	43:1–3	2: 154
103:12	2: 120	43:3–7	2: 154
104:35	1: 104	49	2: 169
113:5	2: 333	49:6	1: 195
118:7	2: 379	49:8	2: 168–69
118:17	2: 379	51:1	2: 117
118:19	2: 379	53:3	33, 211; 2: 45, 321
118:21	2: 379	53:6	2: 30, 70
118:22	1: 55	55:9	1: 133
118:28	2: 379	59:15–19	2: 195
119:105	2: 263	61:6	1: 195
119:119	1: 104; 2: 118	61:10	2: 223
126:6	1: 87		
130:3	2: 49, 162		
139:14	1: 72; 2: 312	## Jeremiah	
139:19	1: 104	1:5	1: 368
140:13	2: 138	4:22	1: 64
141:10	1: 104	11:11	2: 143–45
145:8–9	1: 195	13:24	2: 87
145:20	1: 104	17:9	1: 89
		31	2: 75
		31:3	1: 42
## Proverbs		31:32–33	2: 75
9:10	1: 321	31:33–34	2: 76
20:26–30	2: 88	31:33	2: 33
20:30	2: 88	32: 38	2: 74
21:10	1: 134		
25:4	2: 118	## Lamentations	
		3:22–23	1: 170
## Ecclesiastes		3:23	1: 92
12:14	2: 117		
		## Ezekial	
## Isaiah		11:19	2: 248
1:18	1: 335	13:5	2: 193
1:25–26	2: 118	22:18	2: 118
13:6	2: 193	36:26	2: 247–48
6:11–13	2: 151		
8:17–18	2: 316	## Joel	
25:8	2: 117	1:15	2: 193
28:16	1: 55	2:13	1: 195
30:18	1: 93	2:28–29	1: 338; 2: 63
40:3	2: 139		

Amos

9:9	2: 122

Jonah

4:2	1: 195

Habbakuk

2:4	1: 20

Zephaniah

1:14	2: 193
1:18	2: 162
3:17	1: 251

Zechariah

4:6	1: 384
12:10–14	2: 118
13:7	2: 251
13:9	2: 118

Malachi

1:2–3	2: 157
1:4	2: 157
3	2: 162
3:1	2: 160–61
3:2–3	2: 162
3:5	2: 161
3:18	2: 164
4:1	2: 162
4:1–3	2: 164
4:6	2: 165

Ecclesiasticus/Sirach

6:4	1: 134

Matthew

1:23	1: 33
3:8	2: 170, 215
5:20	1: 15
5:21–22, 27–28	1: 196
5:48	1: 305
6:12	1: 316
7:11	1: 78, 85; 2: 374
7:13–14	1: 43
7:13	2: 241
7:17–20	1: 94
7:19	1: 98
7:23	1: 315
7:24	2: 188
7:29	2: 277
8:23–25	1: 363
9:12	2: 172
10:16	1: 249
10:22	2: 190
10:26	2: 321
10:39	2: 287
11:10	2: 160
11:15	2: 359
11:29	2: 214
11:30	1: 253
12:29	2: 329
12:30	1: 122
12:31–32	2: 181
13:24–30	2: 169
13:39	1: 156
12:34–35	1: 78
13:47–51	2: 208
15:19	1: 389
16:13	2: 321
16:16	2: 321
16:24	1: 324
19:14	2: 237
19:24	2: 188
19:30	1: 396
20:16	1: 396; 2: 216
21:43	1: 55
24:3–14	2: 379
24:13	2: 194
24:30	2: 321
24:44	2: 321
24:51	2: 218
25:34	1: 156
25:41	2: 187
26:38–40	2: 363
26:38	2: 364
26:40	2: 364
26:45	2: 364
26:46	2: 176
26:50	2: 250
27:2	2: 262
27:28–30	1: 308

27:45-52	2: 329	14:42	2: 176
27:45	2: 190	15:29	2: 134
27:46	2: 346	15:34	2: 45
27:50	2: 164	15:39	2: 279
27:52	1: 363	16:14	2: 259
27:54	2: 279		
28:8-9	2: 259	## Luke	
28:17	2: 216, 259, 371	2:1	1: 29
		2:11	2: 301
## Mark		3:1-18	2: 105
1:2	2: 160	3:4-5	2: 139
1:9-11	1: 361	3:6	2: 139
1:12	361; 2: 87	3:17	2: 186
1:23	1: 152	4	2: 359
1:24	1: 245	4:18	2: 164
1:33	2: 87	5:31-32	2: 122
1:40-45	1: 38	5:31	2: 126, 172
1:41	1: 153	6:36	1: 35
2:2	2: 87	6:37	2: 126
2:5	1: 322, 323	6:41	2: 126
2:17	2: 122, 126, 172	7:11-17	2: 308
3:20	2: 87	7:13	2: 309
3:27	2: 329	7:27	2: 160
4:1	2: 87	7:47	2: 214
4:22	2: 321	7:50	1: 206
5:15	1: 84	8:4-8	2: 141
5:21	2: 87	8:5-7	2: 142
5:33-34	1: 206	8:12	2: 142
6:30	2: 87	8:13-14	2: 142
7:1	2: 87	8:17	1: 217; 2: 126, 321
7:21-23	1: 88	8:35	1: 84
7:35	2: 216	9	1: 209
8:1	2: 87	9:23	1: 324; 2: 286
8:22-25	2: 140	9:37-43	1: 209
8:34	1: 324	10:18	2: 121
9:14-32	1: 209	10:27	2: 72
9:22	1: 209	11:23	1: 54
9:24	1: 254; 2: 214, 247	12:2-3	2: 117
9:25	1: 209	12:2	1: 217; 2: 126
9:27-28	1: 210	12:4	2: 286
9:49-50	2: 88	12:12	2: 321
10:31	1: 396	12:46	2: 218-219
10:38	1: 153	12:50	1: 153; 2: 105
10:52	1: 206	13:30	1: 396
12: 30	2: 72	13:34	2: 89
14:21	2: 250	15	1: 46, 68, 215, 366; 2: 171
14:27	2: 251	15:1-10	1: 46
14:36	1: 40	15:11-32	1: 46

419

Luke (continued)

15:24, 32	1: 46
16	1: 320; 2: 171
17:21	2: 13, 58, 117
17:30	1: 321
18	1: 71
18:10–14	1: 67
18:19	2: 142
19	1: 68, 71
19:1–10	1: 38
19:9	1: 68, 69
19:10	1: 68
19:20	2: 170
20	2: 288
22:31–32	1: 325
22:53	2: 190
22:61–62	1: 325
23:34	1: 38; 2: 52, 167
23:43	2: 236
23:46	1: 211
24:1–8	1: 259
24:5	2: 135
24:13–49	2: 259
24:32	2: 268
24:37–42	2: 86
24:40–41	2: 216, 371
24:43	2: 330
24:44	2: 36, 371
24:45–49	2: 371
24:47	2: 175–76
24:49	1: 338

John

1:1–5	2: 146
1:1	1: 36; 2: 146
1:3	2: 308
1:4	2: 261
1:5	126; 2: 126
1:9	2: 261–62, 308
1:10	1: 29
1:12	1: 62, 162
1:13	2: 298, 366
1:14	1: 133, 195, 329, 347; 2: 134, 258, 275, 307
1:15	1: 126
1:16	1: 169
1:17	1: 20, 330
1:18	1: 30; 2: 153
1:29	1: 69
1:47	2: 154
2:19	2: 134
2:24	1: 181, 391
3:3	1: 62, 116, 165, 305; 2: 165, 298
3:6	1: 95
3:7	62
3:13	2: 19
3:16	1: 52; 2: 65, 153, 170
3:17–18	2: 179
3:18	2: 331
3:19–20	1: 65
3:36	2: 236
3:31	1: 15
3:36	2: 180, 236
4:21	1: 286
4:22	1: 21
4:24	2: 255, 307
4:27	2: 328
4:35	1: 291
4:42	1: 69
5:14	1: 91
5:17	1: 282; 2: 76
5:19	1: 154, 282; 2: 76, 268
5:22	2: 23, 321
5:24	2: 125, 236, 331
5:25–30	2: 125
5:27	2: 23, 321
5:29	2: 150
5:30	2: 268
5:39	2: 36, 149, 155
5:46	2: 36
6:47	2: 236
6:63	348; 2: 267
7:15	2: 328
7:16	2: 76
7:51	2: 176
8	1: 308
8:1–11	1: 38, 310
8:10–11	1: 309
8:11	1: 92
8:12	1: 310; 2: 261
8:4	1: 307
8:7	2: 126
8:12	1: 260
8:23	1: 15; 2: 301
8:28	1: 283; 2: 76

8:29	2: 348	14:17	1: 223; 2: 62–63
8:32	1: 223, 259	14:17–18	2: 205
8:34	1: 65, 244, 262, 310; 2: 111	14:19	2: 204, 288
8:36	1: 259	14:20	2: 63, 76, 205, 241
8:37	2: 171	14:23	2: 241
8:44	1: 216, 243, 244, 307; 2: 111	14:24	2: 76
8:47	1: 312	14:26	1: 223
8:51	2: 185	14:28	1: 285
8:58	1: 126, 308	14:29	1: 373
9	1: 298	14:30–31	2: 176
9:3	1: 92	14:30	2: 302
9:33	2: 76, 268	14:31	2: 76, 176
9:39	1: 161; 2: 162, 164	15:1–6	2: 150
10:7	2: 186	15:1	1: 148
10:9	2: 186–87	15:2–3	1: 151
10:10	1: 150; 2: 241	15:3	2: 260–61
10:14–15	1: 69	15:5	1: 154, 173, 205; 2: 76, 82, 268
10:16	2: 75	15:6	1: 148
10:17	2: 74	15:8	2: 128, 333
10:34	2: 301	15:12	2: 234
11:25–26	1: 371; 2: 151, 185, 288	15:13	1: 10; 2: 250
11:25	2: 279, 284	15:16	2: 176, 231
11:44	2: 241	15:17	2: 234
11:49–52	2: 162	15:18–21	2: 364
11:57	2: 176	15:18–19	2: 364
12:23–33	2: 329	15:19	2: 64, 170–71
12:27	2: 329	15:20	2: 364
12:32	1: 51, 55, 371; 2: 87, 161, 307, 328	15:22	2: 171
		15:24–25	1: 367
12:40	1: 332	15:24	2: 236
12:47	2: 162	15:27	1: 372; 2: 261, 363
12:48	2: 162	16:7–11	2: 216
12:49–50	1: 283; 2: 76	16:23	2: 176
13:1–17	1: 151	16:26	2: 176
13:10–11	1: 152	16:28	1: 194; 2: 87
13:19	1: 373	16:32	2: 348
13:23	2: 126	16:33	1: 69, 211, 340; 2: 65, 243, 330, 332, 378
13:31	1: 152		
13:34	2: 234	17	2: 262
14–17	2: 364	17:3	1: 55
14	2: 176	17:6	2: 261–62
14:6	51, 55; 2: 261	17:9	1: 91; 2: 170
14:7–9	1: 36	17:14	2: 261–62, 301
14:10	1: 283; 2: 75–76	17:16	2: 301
14:12	1: 285; 2: 75	17:19	1: 148
14:14	2: 176	17:18	1: 361
14:15	1: 305	17:24	2: 323
14:16	2: 63, 176	18	2: 176

John (continued)

18:6	2: 282
18:37	2: 177
19	1: 308; 2: 176
19:30	2: 224
20	2: 182
20:1–18	2: 259
20:17	1: 364; 2: 86
20:21–23	2: 242, 259
20:21	1: 370; 2: 301
20:23	2: 182
20:24–29	2: 166, 259
20:27	2: 216
20:29	2: 214, 330
21	2: 182
21:7	2: 259
21:9	2: 242
21:14–15	2: 217
21:15	2: 259
21:17	2: 327

Acts

1:8	2: 262
1:11	2: 134
2	1: 163; 2: 63, 89
2:17	1: 338; 2: 63
2:21	2: 194
2:38	2: 175–76
2:40	2: 139
3:14	1: 16, 97
4:12	2: 78
4:31	1: 163
5	1: 76
5:3	1: 163
7:55	1: 163
8:21	2: 139
9:11	2: 139
11:19	2: 89
13:9–11	2: 139
17:28	1: 229; 2: 161
17:31	2: 23, 167, 321
26:14	1: 241
26:20	2: 217

Romans

1:5	2: 70
1:9–10	2: 223
1:17	1: 20; 2: 223
1:18	2: 12, 69, 223
1:19–20	2: 322
1:20	2: 69, 170
1:21	1: 89; 2: 69–70, 76, 322
1:23	2: 70
1:24	2: 70
1:25	1: 18; 2: 69–70
1:26–27	2: 70
1:26	2: 70
1:28–32	2: 70
1:28	2: 70
2	2: 318
2:1	2: 126
2:4	1: 41, 323
2:7–11	2: 322
2:7	2: 322
2:8	2: 99, 322
2:13	2: 322
2:15	2: 322
2:16	1: 302; 2: 117, 322
3	1: 105; 2: 49, 275
3:4	1: 65
3:6	1: 349
3:9	1: 105, 317
3:10–12	1: 79, 317; 2: 70
3:21	1: 15
3:23	1: 105, 106, 317; 2: 49
3:23–24	1: 106; 2: 49, 82, 109
3:24	1: 106, 150; 2: 49, 212
4:5	2: 48, 164
4:25	2: 143, 198, 279, 303
5–8	2: 63
5	1: 97, 99, 165, 264; 2: 2, 109, 254, 256–57, 300–301
5:1	2: 223
5:2–5	2: 132
5:3	2: 281
5:5	1: 165; 2: 21
5:8	1: 40; 2: 198
5:9	2: 124–25
5:10	1: 10, 150; 2: 81, 250
5:12–19	2: 342
5:12	1: 30, 100, 106
5:15	1: 30, 100, 106; 2: 109
5:17	1: 165; 2: 109
5:18	1: 30, 31, 67, 100, 106, 229; 2: 48, 109, 125

5:19	1: 100; 2: 149	7:17	1: 11, 255, 314; 2: 335
5:20	1: 93, 127	7:18–19	1: 263
6	1: 31, 121, 260, 262, 264	7:19	2: 111
6–7	1: 121	7:20	1: 199, 255, 314
6:1–4	1: 117	7:22	1: 14, 166, 260, 349; 2: 215, 291, 300, 313, 341
6:3–4	2: 271		
6:4	1: 128, 170; 2: 276, 388	7:24–25	2: 185
6:5	1: 112; 2: 23, 199	7:24	1: 332
6:5–8	2: 48, 271,	7:25	1: 260; 2: 173
6:5–10	1: 117	8	1: 203, 262, 264; 2: 50, 313, 348
6:5–11	1: 116		
6:6	1: 146, 147, 218, 348; 2: 37, 144, 185, 271, 287, 289, 307	8:1	1: 100
		8:1–3	1: 100
6:8	1: 112, 199	8:2	1: 277, 327, 328; 2: 33, 34,
6:9	1: 365; 2: 143, 187, 266, 357, 363	8:3	1: 143, 151; 2: 341
		8:5	2: 63
6:10–11	1: 20, 218; 2: 109	8:5–11	1: 96
6:10	1: 193; 2: 187	8:6	2: 63
6:11	1: 23, 53, 394; 2: 137, 222, 290	8:7	1: 264; 2: 63, 313
		8:8	2: 63
6:11–13	1: 262	8:9	1: 166, 264; 2: 62
6:12	1: 369	8:10–11	2: 388
6:13	2: 128	8:10	1: 13, 123
6:14	1: 328	8:11	1: 4, 128, 165, 166, 350, 369; 2: 22, 63
6:16	1: 262		
6:17	1: 89, 93; 2: 300, 313, 341	8:12	2: 63
6:18	1: 121, 262	8:13	2: 107
6:19	2: 256	8:15	1: 40, 162
6:20	1: 262	8:15–16	1: 264
6:22	1: 121, 262; 2: 128	8:16–17	2: 237
6:23	1: 106; 2: 109, 197, 270	8:16	2: 237, 300
7	1: 119, 121, 199, 260, 264, 267, 314, 334; 2: 16, 50, 60, 184–85	8:17	1: 46, 366; 2: 388
		8:18	2: 133
7–8	1: 203	8:19	2: 17, 361
7:4	2: 34, 216	8:20	1: 365, 366; 2: 7, 70, 340
7:5	2: 216	8:21	1: 366; 2: 9, 361
7:6	1: 128, 262	8:23	1: 366
7:7–25	2: 60	8:26–27	2: 237
7:7	2: 34	8:26	1: 299
7:8–9	2: 342	8:27	1: 299
7:10–12	1: 327	8:29	1: 162; 2: 253
7:12	2: 34, 341	8:31–32	2: 195
7:14	1: 277	8:32	1: 150
7:14–20	1: 263	8:34	1: 299
7:14–23	2: 70	8:38–39	2: 390
7:14–25	2: 137	8:39	1: 145, 212; 2: 88, 348
7:15–20	1: 119	9	1: 47
7:15	2: 111	9–11	1: 195; 2: 86, 159, 318
7:16–17, 20	1: 264		

Romans (continued)

9:3	2: 336
9:13	1: 105; 2: 157
9:15	1: 105
9–11	1: 21, 105
10:8–9	1: 261
10:8	2: 240, 307
10:13	2: 194
10:14	2: 72, 322
11:32	1: 21, 105, 106, 195; 2: 7, 70, 86, 109, 159, 164
11:33	1: 70
11:36	2: 82
12:1–2	2: 174
12:1	2: 128
12:19	2: 168
12:20	2: 168
13:14	2: 304
14:10–12	2: 117
14:10	2: 126, 323
14:12	302; 2: 323
14:13	2: 126
16:16	2: 149
16:25	1: 8
16:26	2: 70

1 Corinthians

1:2	1: 151
1:8	2: 117, 193
1:10–16	1: 96
1:18–25	1: 145
1:18	2: 194, 289
1:23	1: 14, 144
1:30	1: 16, 17, 151, 158
2:2	1: 23; 2: 149
2:4–5	1: 63
2:6–7	1: 8
2:7	1: 25, 133
2:9	1: 357; 2: 389
2:14–16	2: 313
2:14	1: 96
2:15	1: 96
2:16	1: 18; 2: 173, 208
3:1, 3	1: 96
3:11–15	2: 117, 188
3:11	1: 55; 2: 328
3:12–13	2: 13
3:13	2: 332
3:16	1: 348; 2: 292
3:23	1: 96; 2: 58
4:3–5	2: 27, 117, 126
4:4–5	2: 30, 117
4:5	1: 302
4:18	2: 186
5:2	2: 186
5:5	2: 117
5:6–8	2: 178
5:9–13	2: 159
6:9–10	1: 196
6:11	1: 158
6:16	2: 292
6:19	1: 348; 2: 130
7:10	2: 229
7:12	2: 229
7:22	2: 128
7:25	2: 229
8:1	2: 186
8:6	1: 53
8:7	1: 53
10:4	2: 156
10:7	2: 64
10:13	1: 137
10:14	2: 64
11:7	2: 255
13	2: 252
13:10	2: 252
13:11	2: 237
13:12	1: 156; 2: ix, 17, 19, 220, 252, 361, 375, 382
14:20	1: 160
15	2: 256, 300–301
15:10	2: 13
15:19	2: 143, 279
15:21–22	1: 30
15:22	1: 8
15:42	2: 298
15:44	2: 298
15:45–47	1: 30
15:45–49	2: 300
15:50–54	2: ix
15:50	1: 134, 348, 356, 393; 2: 307
15:51	1: 356, 394
15:53–54	2: 302
15:55	2: 279
15:58	2: 190

16:13	2: 190	5:6–8	2: 237
16:20	2: 149	5:7	2: 17, 27, 228, 300
		5:8	1: 349
		5:10–11	2: 23
		5:10	1: 302; 2: 23, 38, 117

2 Corinthians

1:4	2: 117	5:11	2: 72
1:5	2: 167, 368	5:12	1: 166; 2: 300
1:8	2: 189	5:13	1: 84
1:10	1: 375; 2: 131	5:14	1: 146, 216; 2: 129, 163
1:12	2: 73, 179	5:14–15	1: 112, 116, 117, 128
1:18–20	2: 96	5:14–19	2: 48
1:20	2: 224	5:15	1: 8; 2: 87
1:24	2: 190	5:16	1: 240; 2: 27, 86–87
2:9	2: 176	5:17	1: 114, 119, 120, 126, 127; 2: 9, 247
2:14	1: 237; 2: 23, 128		
2:15–16	2: 388	5:19	1: 246, 302; 2: 169
2:15	2: 73, 194,	5:20	1: 302; 2: 169
2:17	2: 73, 179	5:21	1: 8, 144, 213; 2: 97
3	169; 2: 22, 34	6:1–2	2: 169
3:3	2: 23, 33	6:2	2: 168–69
3:4	2: 73	6:10	1: 237
3:6	2: 35, 36	6:17	2: 159
3:7–11	2: 35	7:12	2: 23
3:7	2: 34	8:9	2: 274
3:8	2: 35	10:5	1: 303
3:9	1: 15; 2: 36	10:6	1: 303
3:13	1: 169	11:3	2: 343
3:16	2: 21	11:6	2: 23
3:17	1: 170	12: 2	2: 19, 60, 117, 266
3:18	1: 169; 2: 20, 35, 274	13:12	2: 149
4	1: 362; 2: 22, 34		

Galatians

4:2	2: 72		
4:3–4	2: 21	1:4	2: 51, 193
4:4	1: 50, 193, 203; 2: 34, 211, 255	2:20	1: 102, 218, 255; 2: 34, 80, 98, 108, 127, 131, 144, 286–87
4:6	2: 21, 34	3:13	1: 98, 213
4:7	1: 348, 362; 2: 299	3:25	1: 328, 330
4:8	1: 93; 2: 133	3:27	2: 291
4:8–9	1: 237	3:28	1: 31
4:10	1: 379; 2: 22–23, 289, 388	4:6	1: 40
4:11	1: 13, 369; 2: 22	5:1	1: 253; 2: 190
4:12	2: 23, 35	5:16	2: 195
4:14	2: 23	5:19–21	1: 196
4:16	1: 13–15, 166, 168, 349; 2: 23, 300	5:22–23	1: 16; 2: 318
4:17	2: 132–33	5:25	2: 105
4:18	1: 212; 2: 17, 65	6:2	1: 286; 2: 33
5:1	1: 362; 2: 133–34, 237, 298	6:14	2: 178
5:4	2: 298		
5:5	2: 237, 299, 300		

Ephesians

1	1: 97, 193
1:1-4	2: 102
1:1	2: 275
1:3	1: 134, 160
1:3-6	1: 61, 62; 2: 385
1:3-10	1: 44
1:4	1: 17, 18, 47, 191; 2: 107
1:4-5	1: 162
1:4-6	1: 203
1:5	1: 46
1:5-6	1: 191
1:6	1: 46, 328; 2: 80, 275
1:7	1: 328
1:7-10	1: 62
1:9	1: 8
1:10	1: 21, 229, 371; 2: 87, 306
1:12	2: 131
1:13	1: 63
2:1-6	2: 240
2:1-3	2: 101, 106
2:1	1: 79
2:2	1: 124; 2: 7, 102, 106, 194
2:3	1: 216; 2: 103, 105, 109
2:4-7	2: 239
2:4-5	2: 103
2:4	1: 92
2:5	2: 107, 109, 194
2:6	1: 134, 155, 160; 2: 190
2:8	2: 107
2:10	1: 18, 44, 50, 61, 102, 127, 203; 2: 45, 107-8, 350, 2: 15
	2: 34
3:4	1: 8
3:14-15	1: 343
3:16	1: 166, 349
3:17-18	2: 10
3:18	1: 212
4:1	2: 190
4:15	1: 159; 2: 303, 388
4:18	1: 63
4:22-24	1: 217; 2: 304
4:24	2: 195
4:26	2: 99
4:30	1: 363, 374; 2: 12, 216
4:32	1: 316; 2: 181
5:6	2: 12
5:8-14	2: 216
5:16	2: 193
5:22-32	2: 231
5:27	2: 23, 308
6	2: 367-68
6:10-18	1: 255; 2: 193
6:11	2: 195
6:12	2: 194
6:13-14	2: 194
6:13	2: 136, 193
6:14	2: 190

Philippians

1	2: 190
1:6	1: 303; 2: 190, 193
1:9-11	2: 178
1:10	1: 14; 2: 117, 178, 190, 288
1:11	1: 16; 2: 142
1:21-23	2: 287
1:23	2: 239
1:27	2: 190
1:28	2: 190
2	1: 285; 2: 255-56
2:2	2: 313
2:5	2: 313
2:6-7	2: 255
2:7	1: 144; 2: 256
2:8	2: 255
2:12-13	2: 129, 133
2:15	2: 139
2:16	1: 14; 2: 117
2:25	1: 272
3:3-6	2: 307
3:6	1: 21
3:8-12	2: 287
3:9	1: 21
3:10	2: 167
3:12	1: 204; 2: 129
3:15	2: 288
3:18	2: 1, 178,
3:19	2: 178
4:3	2: 334
4:8	1: 375
4:9	1: 375

Colossians

1	1: 46

1:5	1: 292	3:4	1: 225, 277; 2: 78, 211, 389
1:10	1: 182	3:5–6	2: 12, 165
1:12–13	1: 141	3:5	2: 223, 286
1:13	2: 125	3:6	2: 224
1:14	1: 45	3:7	2: 103
1:15	1: 36, 38, 50, 133, 203; 2: 253, 255–56, 272, 274–75, 299	3:8	2: 223
1:16–17	2: 161, 253	3:9–10	1: 113; 2: 304
1:16	2: 45	3:10–11	2: 211
1:17	1: 229; 2: 45, 87, 368	3:12–17	1: 223, 292
1:18	2: 253, 308	3:13	1: 316; 2: 120, 181
1:19–20	2: 192	3:16	2: 211
1:21–22	2: 103	4:12	2: 288
1:21	2: 173		
1:22	1: 18, 25, 86, 150; 2: 23, 50, 197		

1 Thessalonians

1:3	2: 223
2: 13	2: 223
4:13	2: 309
5:2–3	2: 193
5:4	2: 196
5:11	1: 254, 380
5:17	1: 299; 2: 72, 223
5:26	2: 149

1:23–27	1: 123		
1:23	2: 363		
1:24	2: 167, 365, 389		
1:26	1: 133; 2: 33		
1:27	1: 8, 123; 2: 304		
1:28	1: 123; 2: 288,		
1:29	2: 13		
2:2	1: 8		
2:3	1: 70		
2:9	1: 36; 2: 258		

2 Thessalonians

1:8	1: 312
1:10	2: 328
2: 2–3	2: 190

2:9–10	1: 163
2:10	1: 16; 2: 78, 193, 288
2:11	1: 98, 154; 2: 271
2:11–13	1: 153
2:12	2: 108, 271
2:13	1: 79; 2: 271, 275
2:14	2: 34, 271
2:15	2: 128, 192, 285
2:17	1: 19
2:18–19	2: 97
2:18	1: 18; 2: 97
2:19	1: 170
2:20	2: 224
2:21	1: 252, 253
2:23	1: 252, 253
3	2: 223
3:1	1: 337, 338; 2: 165
3:1–2	1: 160; 2: 211
3:1–3	1: 44, 112, 253
3:1–4	1: 134
3:2	1: 337
3:3	1: 43; 2: 103, 211, 223–24, 286

1 Timothy

2: 4	1: 118
2: 5	1: 285; 2: 71
4:10	1: 41, 118; 2: 131, 154,
6:10	1: 54
6:12	2: 177
6:13	2: 176
6:14	2: 177

2 Timothy

1:8–10	2: 369
1:9	2: 194
1:10	2: 289
2	1: 324
2:12–13	1: 323
2:15	2: 149
2:22	1: 23

2 Timothy (continued)

3:13	1: 78
3:16	2: 153
4:1	2: 265

Titus

2:11–14	2: 14
2:11	1: 24, 330
2:13–14	1: 25
3:4–5	1: 41
3:5	1: 92, 116, 128; 2: 194

Philemon

1:2	1: 372

Hebrews

1	1: 285
1:3	1: 36; 2: 197–198
2: 9	1: 34, 229; 2: 97, 197,
2:11	1: 229
2:9–14	1: 147
2:9	2: 198
2:10–18	1: 105
2:11–18	2: 197
2:11	2: 45, 198
2:12–13	1: 229–30
2:13	2: 316
2:14–18	2: 45
2:14	2: 97, 224
3:1	1: 227
3:6	2: 177
3:14	2: 177
4:3	1: 157; 2: 290
4:12–14	2: 162
4:12	1: 217; 2: 265
4:15	1: 135
5:8	2: 282
5:13–14	290; 2: 265
7:27	2: 187
9:12	2: 187
9:26	1: 157
9:28	2: 134
10:10	2: 187
10:14	1: 25
10:19–21	2: 198
10:22	2: 198
10:23–24	2: 177
10:24–25	2: 369
10:26–27	2: 165
11	1: 196
11:1	2: 68
11:12	1: 194
12:1–2	1: 91; 2: 253
12:1	2: 2
12:2	1: 196; 2: 82, 108, 282
13:12–13	1: 361

James

1:17	1: 290
2: 17	2: 31
2: 19	1: 245
2: 24	2: 31
2: 26	2: 31
3:10–18	1: 179
3:17	1: 92
5:16	1: 254

1 Peter

1:1	2: 89
1:3–4	1: 112
1:3	2: 48, 104
1:6	1: xxiv
1:7	1: 133
1:14	2: 371
2:6–8	1: 55
3:4	1: 349
3:18	2: 86
3:19	2: 86
4:5	2: 265
4:6	2: 86
4:12–14	2: 364
4:13	2: 167
4:17	1: 312
5:8	1: 121; 2: 353
5:12	2: 190

2 Peter

1:3	1: 361
1:4	1: 230, 283
2:1	1: 54

2:15	2: 139	4:8	1: 193
3:1	2: 178, 313	4:16	1: 193
3:8	2: 121	4:17	2: 115, 198
3:9	1: xxix; 2: 188	4:18	1: 321; 2: 126
3:10	2: 193	4:19	1: 24; 2: 217, 390
3:11–13	2: 196	4:20	2: 246
3:11	2: 179	5:3	1: 301
3:13	2: 179, 319	5:11–12	2: 112–13
3:18	1: 303	5:11	2: 109, 170
		5:18	1: 311
		5:19	2: 65
		5:24	2: 125

1 John

1:5	1: 82, 126		
1:6	2: 115		

2 John

1:7	1: 151; 2: 78, 198	1:7	1: 14, 79, 348; 2: 326
1:8	1: 311; 2: 111	3:8–10	2: 112
1:9	1: 151		
2:1	1: 8, 97; 2: 112		

3 John

2:1–2	44		
2:2	145, 151; 2: 83, 112	11	2: 112
2:4	2: 111, 115		
2:10	2: 111		

Revelation

2:15–16	2: 64		
2:15	2: 64	1:4	2: 325
2:16	1: 254	1:7	2: 118, 167
2:18	1: 79; 2: 326	1:8	2: 194, 325
2:22	1: 79; 2: 326	1:9	1: 169
2:24	2: 363	1:16	2: 386
2:29	2: 112,	2:2	1: 78
3:1	2: 112	2:4–5	2: 344
3:2	2: 17, 361	2:7	2: 330
3:3	2: 165	2:11	2: 330
3:6–7	2: 111	3:5	2: 334
3:7	2: 112	3:10	2: 189–90, 323, 328, 330
3:8	1: 244, 311; 2: 111, 115	3:16	1: 178, 179
3:8–10	2: 111	5:6–14	2: 167
3:8–9	1: 179; 2: 149	6:4	1: 335
3:9	1: 260, 310, 311; 2: 111	6:10	2: 323–24
3:14	1: 113; 2: 112–113	7	2: 324
3:16	1: 52, 257; 2: 83, 126, 390	7:3	2: 324
3:19–21	1: 254	7:9	1: 356
3:20–22	1: 254	7:14	2: 328
4:2	1: 14, 348	7:15	2:134
4:3	1: 79, 122, 124; 2: 102, 113, 326	8:13	2: 323–24
4:4	2: 332	11:7	2: 335–36
4:5	2: 64	11:10	2: 323
4:7	2: 113	11:19	2: 329

Revelation *(continued)*

12:3	1: 335; 2: 326
12:9	2: 333
12:10	2: 328
12:12	2: 333
12–13	1: 79; 2: 326
13	2: 335
13:1	2: 326
13:3	2: 333
13:4	2: 333
13:5	2: 327, 333
13:8	1: 126, 308; 2: 321, 323–24, 343, 382
13:11	2: 326
13:12	2: 323, 335
13:14	2: 323–24, 335
13:16	2: 324, 335
13:18	2: 327
16:13–14	2: 327
16:13	1: 79; 2: 326–27
16:15	2: 327
16:17–19	2: 329
17:2	2: 323
17:8	2: 323, 325, 328, 335, 366
17:12–14	2: 328–29
17:12	2: 328
17:14	2: 336
18:10	2: 328
18:17	2: 328
18:19	2: 328
19	2: 329
19:13	2: 146
19:19–21	2: 329
19:20	1: 79; 2: 326
20	2: 329–330
20:1	2: 335
20:2	2: 329
20:3	2: 328–329
20:4	2: 324, 330
20:5	2: 330
20:6	2: 330
20:7	2: 328–29
20:10	1: 79; 2: 321, 326, 329
20:12	2: 321
20:14	2: 330
21:1	2: 58, 302
21:4	2: 117
21:5	2: 196
21:8	2: 187
22	1: 70; 2: 21, 237, 260, 303, 341, 343–44, 356
22:1–5	1: 34
22:5	2: 196
22:14–15	2: 333
22:15	2: 187
22:16	2: 142

www.ingramcontent.com/pod-product-compliance
Lightning Source LLC
Chambersburg PA
CBHW020604300426
44113CB00007B/504